BETWEEN ORDERS AND HERESY

Rethinking Medieval Religious Movements

Between Orders and Heresy

Rethinking Medieval Religious Movements

EDITED BY JENNIFER KOLPACOFF DEANE
AND ANNE E. LESTER

UNIVERSITY OF TORONTO PRESS
Toronto Buffalo London

© University of Toronto Press 2022
Toronto Buffalo London
utorontopress.com

ISBN 978-1-4875-0241-6 (cloth)
ISBN 978-1-4875-1529-4 (EPUB)
ISBN 978-1-4875-1528-7 (PDF)

___

Library and Archives Canada Cataloguing in Publication

Title: Between orders and heresy : rethinking medieval religious movements /
    edited by Jennifer Kolpacoff Deane and Anne E. Lester.
Names: Deane, Jennifer Kolpacoff, 1970– editor. | Lester, Anne Elisabeth,
    1974– editor.
Description: Includes bibliographical references and index.
Identifiers: Canadiana (print) 20210300841 | Canadiana (ebook) 20210300906 |
    ISBN 9781487502416 (cloth) | ISBN 9781487515294 (EPUB) |
    ISBN 9781487515287 (PDF)
Subjects: LCSH: Europe – Church history – 600–1500. | LCSH: Europe –
    Religious life and customs.
Classification: LCC BR270.B48 2022 | DDC 270.5–dc23

___

This book has been published with the help of a grant from the Federation for the Humanities and Social Sciences, through the Awards to Scholarly Publications Program, using funds provided by the Social Sciences and Humanities Research Council of Canada.

We wish to acknowledge the land on which the University of Toronto Press operates. This land is the traditional territory of the Wendat, the Anishnaabeg, the Haudenosaunee, the Métis, and the Mississaugas of the Credit First Nation.

University of Toronto Press acknowledges the financial support of the Government of Canada, the Canada Council for the Arts, and the Ontario Arts Council, an agency of the Government of Ontario, for its publishing activities.

*For our teachers and students,
who keep us eager learners, always*
and
In memory of Giles Constable (1929–2021),
magister semper, verbo et exemplo

Contents

List of Illustrations ix

Preface by John Van Engen xi

Acknowledgments xix

1 Introduction: Religion and Religious Worlds in Between 3
   JENNIFER KOLPACOFF DEANE AND ANNE E. LESTER

2 Herbert Grundmann, Confession and the "Religious Movements" 23
   LETHA BÖHRINGER

3 Francis of Assisi, the *Vita Apostolica*, and the Roman Church: Rethinking the Paradigms 45
   AMANDA POWER

4 Hypocrites! Critiques of Religious Movements and Criticism of the Church, 1050–1300 79
   SITA STECKEL

5 Crusading as a Religious Movement: Families, Community, and Lordship in a Vernacular Frame 127
   ANNE E. LESTER

6 Coming Together as an Apostolic Act: Confraternalism as an Umbrella for Medieval Religious Movements 170
   NESLIHAN ŞENOCAK

7 Reassessing the Links between "The Women's Religious Movement" and "The Origins of a Religious Literature in the Vernacular" in France   189
SEAN L. FIELD

8 "More Useful in the Salvation of Others": Beguines, *Religio*, and the *Cura Mulierum* at the Early Sorbonne   214
TANYA STABLER MILLER

9 Between Charity and Controversy: The Grey Sisters, Liminality, and the Religious Life   242
ALISON MORE

10 Women, Power, and Religious Dissent: Why Women Never Became Heresiarchs   263
JANINE LARMON PETERSON

11 Navigating Saintly Circles: Margherita Colonna and the Women's Religious Movement in Rome   288
LEZLIE KNOX

12 The "Clever Girls" of Prague: Beguines, Preachers, and Late Medieval Bohemian Religion   307
JANA GROLLOVÁ

Contributors   337

Bibliography   341

Index   393

Illustrations

5.1 Façade of St.-Adrien, Mailly-le-Château, Burgundy, ca. 1230   128
5.2 Detail, carved column, St.-Adrien, Mailly-le-Château, Burgundy, ca. 1230   128
5.3 Chansonnier, dit *Chansonnier Cangé*, fourth quarter of thirteenth century. Paris, BnF ms fr. 846, fol. 57v   145
5.4 Chansonnier, dit *Chansonnier Cangé*, fourth quarter of thirteenth century. Paris, BnF ms fr. 846, fol. 46v   146
5.5 Thibaut de Navarre, *Foire et Chant*, Paris, BnF ms fr. 12581, fol. 312r   147
5.6 Thibaut de Navarre, *Foire et Chant*, Paris, BnF ms fr. 12581, fol. 312v   148
8.1 Parish of St.-Eustache, Paris, France, ca. 1250   228

Preface

Study of the European Middle Ages has taken something of a religious turn over the last two generations or so. That statement may puzzle readers, especially those who think of this formative thousand years in the making and remaking of Europe's society, culture, and history as awash in religion, happily or unhappily, both driven and constrained by it. The realities of life in those centuries, however, and the varied roles religion did or did not play in their making have come under historical review ever since. That, in turn, has generated countless and ever-changing narratives with religion at the centre, or reduced to small roles, or cast mostly as trouble. So too, over the past generation or two in particular, we have continued to create new narratives or refurbish old ones, and in many of them religion plays a significant role for good or ill. Notions of religion too have been enlarged to include more than a hegemonic Christian religion and have uncovered far more diverse and invented forms of pursuing Christian identity or practice.

In this discourse the modern word "secular" often becomes religion's opposite. The word derives from a Latin term ("*saeculum*") that in the Middle Ages and beyond might refer to "an era in time" and to "this world," or to persons, properties, or things accounted of this world rather than divine, or it could simply designate a "layperson" as distinct from clergy or dedicated religious. Its varied uses, meanings, and implications are in fact even more diverse, spawning over the last two or three centuries a weighty interpretive literature in early modern and modern scholarship. In the late eighteenth century, the drivers of the French Revolution would angrily declare war on all that had until then, as they saw it, decimated any hope of a more satisfying and just life for all (or at least most) in the present world. Accordingly, they called for the wholesale demolition of "feudalism" and "Christianity" or "Christendom." With those terms, part inventions, part abstractions, they aimed comprehensively to name, define, and condemn all the social and religious structures that, as they saw it, had kept people mostly in bonds then. Over the thousand years increasingly now labeled the "Middle Ages," "feudalism" and "Christendom" had, they charged, deprived people of personal liberties in the social sphere and of religious liberty in the intellectual, sacred, and transcendent spheres. For such views of that period of European history there were, of course, precedents: the Renaissance dismissal of most foregoing "medieval" culture as dark or benighted and the Reformation's critique of that earlier millennium's religious beliefs and practices as shot through with superstition and falsehood. "Medieval" was, ironically in the context of this volume's theme, the "in between" that separated people from true religion (early Christianity) or enlightened culture and political order (the classical world). A little earlier, Edward Gibbon (1737–1794), in wonderful prose, had narrated the years between 200 and 1500 as the extended story of the long slow decay of the Roman Empire. Voltaire's amusing and biting characterization of it found mostly so much superstition and foolishness, at least when viewed from enlightened reason. These outlooks, well known of course, are rehearsed here because such definitions or redefinitions of the thousand years of European history we call the medieval era would have lasting effects on how its story was told – as would then too reverse efforts to idealize these "Middle Ages." These larger framing and interpretive structures, if themselves now dated, become an issue once again when, as in this volume, scholars try thoughtfully and inventively to consider how best we might approach or characterize history and religion in that thousand-year era.

The shock born of the French Revolution's upheaval and destruction released almost at once counter-energies in turn, varied and strong reactions we now label as Romantic and Restorationist (among other terms). For historians these would often work with and alongside impulses in nineteenth-century universities to bring scholarly learning (*Wissenschaft*) to bear on the whole realm of human knowledge, including especially our understanding and recounting of the past. Groups and societies set out now to recover texts and monuments and art from these "middle ages" – and often as well indeed its beliefs and practices. Efforts to sanitize, restore, glorify, and even emulate those "awful" Middle Ages now suddenly abounded and took all different forms. With respect to what we broadly call "religion," such enterprises powerfully shaped the forms religion would assume across Europe over the next century or more. This is especially true with respect to a shattered Roman Catholic church and papacy, which was now set upon "restoring" post-Revolution what it understood to be its "medieval" foundations, precedents, and heritage, thus, for instance, ultramontanist notions of papal authority, a Thomist vision of philosophy and theology, and so on through a long list. That endeavour turned out, against all odds, to be spectacularly successful, and would then importantly shape both the recovered materials and the narratives that historians of any or no religion now read or worked with. Such excavating and narrating of this presumed medieval past became thus both a religious and a scholarly enterprise, to which present-day scholars, however critical they may also be, are indebted. This transpired in varied forms, not only with respect to Roman Catholics but varied Protestant groups and sub-groups as well. Think of the Pre-Raphaelites in England, or the Prussian Protestant Bismarck referring angrily and dismissively to Canossa as he set about defining important matters of church and state for his reunited German nation.

This story has still more turns. In the mid-twentieth century, quite strikingly, digging into this medieval past to restore the present notably and ironically took something like an inverse direction. Scholars, not a few in religious orders, studied this medieval period in great depth and in innovative ways beneficial to all. Moreover, these same scholars and scholar-monks also began to draw upon the medieval teachings and precedents they uncovered to critique or rethink some of these present-day "restored" forms. Exemplary here were, for instance, Brian Tierney challenging notions of papal infallibility and Francis Oakley contesting papal monarchy (as did Tierney) precisely by way of medieval texts and precedents. Still other scholars saw now a far more complex range of philosophical and theological energies and outlooks at work in medieval universities than just Thomism. Jean Leclercq made monastic writings and outlooks accessible to any and all, not just the restored religious orders of the nineteenth century. Such a list could go on. This work, however, transformed the medieval field and also then the narratives regarding the nature of religion and religion's changing roles during that medieval millennium.

Before turning directly to the particular project of this volume and what inspired it, it is important to recognize as well that the post-Revolutionary vision of a new secular order also entered into the way in which historians studied and narrated that thousand years. Indeed, one could reasonably argue that in key respects medieval history first came fully into its own in the course of the nineteenth century. In that post-Revolutionary world, religion aside, the focus now turned to investigating that social world called "feudal," thus the structure of social relations. But it also took up urban and agricultural economies, markets, towns, trade, and now, of course, quite especially the nation itself and with it then national literatures as well as national spirits and styles. When historians dug into monastic or ecclesiastical sources, as they also certainly did, it was mostly to uncover records of their lands and rights and powers. All this and the political narratives that went with it came indeed largely to define the field of medieval history, also now in emerging textbooks. This held true as well, as we narrow in on our subject, for the early twentieth century, when Herbert Grundmann first went to university. Fine textbooks are still being written, and with new materials and insights, in this "secular" tradition, for instance, Christopher Wickham's *Medieval Europe* and various others.

Deep into the twentieth century both "secular" and "religious" historians lived and operated; but they were mostly in quite distinct academic departments and milieus with occasional cross-over although this was not very common. The break-down of these conceptual lines and their institutional frameworks – church or religious history mostly in seminaries, not history departments – is actually a comparatively recent phenomenon, and what would then follow from it, the eventual fracturing of deeper controlling narratives. While there are university historians who made such moves already in the early twentieth century, especially in England, more frequently it was "religious" – as medieval folks commonly titled monks and nuns and friars – who accelerated this move. Think of Giles Constable taught by the Benedictine Dom David Knowles, the many scholars inspired by the Dominican Marie Dominique Chenu, or especially all those now working in the afterglow of Jean Leclercq. One could go on with many more such examples. One can also trace out such a movement more concretely. Charles Homer Haskins, a defining figure in the American medieval community in the early twentieth century, wrote about secular institutions and intellectual history with learning culminating in the new university, with hardly a nod to religion even as he was treating many figures who were themselves "religious" (in the medieval sense of the term). Fifty years on from the publication of Haskins's *Renaissance of the Twelfth Century*, meant as a riposte to Renaissance historians, Giles Constable and Robert Benson organized a conference and produced a volume titled *Renaissance and Renewal in the Twelfth Century*. Here religion is everywhere present, beginning with its first two articles. Twenty years later Constable then produced a book he titled *The Reformation of the Twelfth Century*, this not meant as a riposte to Haskins but rather as an expansion of the twelfth-century story by anchoring it to the host of religious materials so many have now come to work on. So too Caroline Walker Bynum, supervised by Constable and beginning her academic career teaching in Harvard's Divinity School, took up largely neglected stories of such "in between" women, as these inspired and aspiring figures often were, and not only rendered their stories now matters of great interest but then intersected their interpretation very influentially into a then emerging feminist history. One could go on pointing towards such shifts, thus the crusades treated not only in terms of armies or commerce or European expansion but as a form of religion as well as a key factor in the sacralizing of war, and much else. At this present moment one might note that, if anything, medieval historians are somewhat more likely to write about religion or religiously inflected topics than about politics, commerce, law, agricultural economies, towns, and all the rest. Of course, it all belongs together in one complexly woven story – and that brings us to the contribution of this volume on forms of religion "in between." But to understand what that refers to and how it brought religion into the realm of history, one must turn to Herbert Grundmann's work on "religious movements" first published in German in 1935, with relatively little attention at first, and translated into English amidst increasing interest in 1995.

This volume of essays sprang first from reflections on the significant role played by Herbert Grundmann (1902–1970) in spurring historians on to think outside the lines, so to speak, when approaching the role and nature of medieval religion. His rethinking had begun in the later 1920s/early 1930s, a good century after the upheaval and realignments of the French Revolution, in a Germany still reeling in the aftermath of the First World War and a country still strongly defined by its Catholic and Protestant populations, but where too Jews were emerging as important medieval historians. Grundmann himself was from a not particularly religious Protestant (Lutheran) family, but became attracted to religious themes while in university at Leipzig in the 1920s, there under the influence of the innovative cultural historian Walter Goetz. Grundmann took an interest especially in spiritually driven and apocalyptic types, hence his dissertation on the great apocalyptic thinker Joachim of Fiore, not the kind of subject a respectable historian, religious or secular, would then normally have touched – as they did not then (also Grundmann) Hildegard of Bingen. In this volume's opening essay Letha Boehringer has nicely outlined what the archives and Grundmann's own papers reveal about his relationship to the church around the time he completed this path-breaking study of "religious movements." Politically, he found ways for better or worse to coexist with the new Nazi regime, as did many others, but did not join the party. Of more relevance here, he soon gave up any formal church membership, this notable in a country where at the time most of its Christian majority, whether Protestant or Catholic, routinely retained this formal bond to their baptism and cultural heritage whatever their level of practice or belief. As notably, I would add, he also did not join the "German national church" then being propagated by Hitler's Nazis as a religious vehicle of the party, nor too the "Confessing Church," a group of brave pastors and laypeople deeply critical of the regime, several of whom would then become martyrs for their stance. Grundmann himself, it seems clear, found established religious groups or institutions in his day wanting or at least not compelling, as indeed he would in the Middle Ages either Orders or "heresy" in itself, though he would over time refine and deepen his interest in the nature of medieval heresy.[1] In these personal moves one can almost envision a version of joining neither a religious order nor the radical dissenters, what he famously claimed were ultimately the only two options for the spiritually motivated in the Middle Ages, and neither finally satisfying.

What he found in his medieval sources and saw in his mind's eye, however, he presented first as an innovative and energetic movement (*Bewegung*) of religiously inspired people, and especially women. His term, not particularly apt or worked out, was inspired by or borrowed from the suffragist movements in his day. As for the source of what he found in his medieval sources, his vision of or response to a driving religiosity from within, we must look elsewhere. Fine a historian as Grundmann was, this openness to distinctive forms of interior religiosity had come from somewhere else, neither his historical training as such (though aided perhaps by Leipzig's turn to cultural history), nor any sustaining experience of his Protestant ecclesiastical birthright, or indeed from "Catholic" monastic life. Arno Borst, one of his most senior and respected students, claimed in his obituary (*Deutsches Archiv* 26 [1970], 328) that it sprang from Grundmann's experience of a Christian young people's group in his teen years. Such groups may well have sprung from or been part of "pietist" gatherings and expressions common in many Christian churches from the seventeenth into the early twentieth century. These were smaller and more intense gatherings or communities that fostered a religiosity grounded in deep interiority rather than formal liturgies or ecclesiastical structures. If this were so, what had once touched or formed him as an authentic or compelling experience of religion he looked to find in these medieval women, as he had earlier in Joachim of Fiore for his dissertation. He was not looking for or responding to religious structures in the first instance, nor had he found them truly to work, though the sophisticated historian in him recognized their practical role in sustaining such groups, and he adroitly credited Pope Innocent III with realizing this too in his approving some "unusual" or "marginal" groups. It was something from within that opened up medieval religious life for him in refreshing new ways.

One of Grundmann's Catholic students, Kaspar Elm, would subsequently turn to the institutional or legal dimensions of such distinct or free religious groups not inside formal orders and yet not necessarily found heretical. A selection of his essays is available now in English thanks to James Mixson.[2] Elm argued for a medieval church open to and more adaptable in the face of religious enthusiasm, open therefore too to theoretical and legal spaces for at least some independent religious seekers and practitioners. For such cases Elm invented the now widely used term "semi-religious," these persons viewed or represented thus more or less as "religious" too, at least in their form of living something like them, and potentially acceptable, thus "semi." Elizabeth Makowski explored these same legal materials from a more critical perspective, especially as it touched women, as in effect still challenging their full legitimacy or by being defined as "quasi-religious" made subject potentially to intervention or other constrictive consequences.[3] The present writer explored this same issue in the context of the Netherlandish Devotio Moderna movement with a stance somewhere in the middle. Such groups and persons decidedly presented a challenge for church leaders and could face serious push-back, often in legal form. Yet both lay and religious authorities also sought variously to devise forms that would address rather than merely crush such religious initiatives.[4] This is a position something like what one finds in another volume much cited in these essays, *Labels and Libels*.[5] Indeed some "in between" groups would settle into a mostly accepted status, for instance, the beguines, while others faced periodic trouble, sometimes from local authorities, more often from ecclesiastical prelates and parish priests.

In this volume of essays note is taken regularly of the shortcomings in Grundmann's rather rigid view of medieval religious orders as such. The same holds to a lesser degree for his handling of medieval heresy, a matter that he would, however, later explore with great nuance. For all the import of Grundmann's vision of "religious movements," ones deeply involving women too, his account of the larger practice of religion ultimately gets reduced to a hopeless binary: for the truly religiously moved or inspired, life either in orders or in heresy. This incidentally leaves out the whole question of the religiosity in the thousands of parishes across medieval Christendom.

Hence, then, the import of this volume. Undertaken in important ways still in the spirit of Grundmann's initial endeavour, these essays explore instead the various spaces and possibilities "in between" orders or heresy. In fact, such "in between" expressions of an independent aspiring religiosity were numerous in the higher and later Middle Ages. They were also as variable in their notions of the interior life as they were in their expressions of the external life and structure. This volume opens up the reality of a complex external environment on the ground and a whole variety of differing forms. We should remember too that for many or most of these people, especially among the poorer but some of the wealthier too, in actual practice the first point of tension would have been with their family and local parish church, where obligations and allegiance were expected. Along with wide varieties of religious inspiration, expression, and practice, this involved too just as crucially matters of class and gender and not a few legal squabbles. The approach of this volume opens our vision to a far more diverse and alive "in between," sometimes troubled, but one in which people, both clerical and lay, sought workable solutions, whether or not it worked out. This is precisely the messiness of such religious life lived "in between" – and of course also the interest. Here were all different figures seeking to realize a religious life for themselves in a space they entered into or themselves constructed, distinct from orders or open dissent but often lived too in whole or in part outside their parish. Religious life lived "in between" grew out of their own spiritual aspirations and inclinations. If the characterization of Herbert Grundmann above has a measure of accuracy, the intentions and shape of these "in between" groups may not fit the way he came finally and formally to order his innovative "religious movements," as caught in an impossible binary between orders and dissent. But it may actually come closer to the spirit of the man himself.

John Van Engen

NOTES

1 For a translation now of his key essays on heresy, see Jennifer Kolpacoff Deane, ed. Steven Rowan, trans. *Herbert Grundmann (1902–70): Essays on Heresy, Inquisition, and Literacy* (Woodbridge: York Medieval Press 2019).
2 *Religious Life between Jerusalem, the Desert, and the World: Selected Essays by Kaspar Elm.* Translated by James D. Mixson (Leiden: Brill, 2016).
3 Elizabeth Makowski, *A Pernicious Sort of Woman: Quasi-religious Women and Canon Lawyers in the Later Middle Ages* (Washington, DC: Catholic University of America Press, 2005).
4 John Van Engen, "Friar Johannes Nyder on Laypeople Living as Religious in the World," in *Vita Religiosa im Mittelalter: Festschrift für Kaspar Elm zum 70. Geburtstag*, Franz J. Felten, Nikolas Jaspert, and Stephanie Haarländer (Berlin: Duncker and Humbolt, 1999), pp. 583–615. See also ibid., *Sisters and Brothers of the Common Life: Devotio Moderna and the World of the Later Middle Ages* (Philadelphia: University of Pennsylvania Press, 2008), chapters 3 and 6.
5 Letha Böhringer, Jennifer Kolpacoff Deane, Hildo van Engen, eds., *Labels and Libel: Naming Beguines in Northern Medieval Europe* (Turnhout: Brepols, 2014).

Acknowledgments

This volume began, as so many collaborations do, with a series of conversations between the editors. We realized that we had each come to read and to understand Herbert Grundmann's work, especially his monumental book, *Religious Movements in the Middle Ages*, in different ways and from quite different perspectives: Jennifer through the lens of heresy and the German scene; and Anne through the 'women's religious movement' in the context of France and Flanders. The different national traditions and the scholarly trajectories our readings encompassed – heresy and order; Germany and France – came together in yet more fascinating ways within the Anglophone scholarship after 1995, once the English translation of Grundmann's work garnered wider readership. We also noted the new directions the field had taken, scaffolded, as it were, on Grundmann's scholarly shoulders, and thus encompassing histories of religious movements in new, exciting, and unbounded ways. It seemed to us a good moment to broaden our conversation to include a host of other voices and perspectives. Thus in 2015, for the eightieth anniversary of the Grundmann's book (and the twentieth anniversary of the English translation), we put together seven sessions at the International Medieval Congress at Leeds to take up the question of Grundmann's legacy. This volume is a product of those conversations, of the robust and lively presentations and exchanges that followed, and the dogged work of the contributors in the years afterwards.

We would like to thank all those who took part in the sessions at Leeds: John Arnold, Michael Bailey, Peter Biller, Letha Böhringer, Louisa Burnham, Sean L. Field, Jörg Feuchter, Ian Forrest, Koen Goudriaan, Fiona Griffiths, Julie Hotchin, Lezlie Knox, Robert Lerner, Tanya Stabler Miller, James Mixson, Sara Moens, R.I. Moore, Anneke Mulder-Bakker, Stefanie Neidhardt, Amanda Power, Mark Pegg, Marcela Perett, Andrew Roach, Neslihan Şenocak, Daniel Stracke, and

Shelley Amiste Wolbrink; and the engaged and often impassioned audience who attended and offered comments, questions, and reflections on Grundmann and his work. For many of us present, these remain some of the most memorable Leeds sessions because they sparked such intense engagements with the past in the present. We also thank Axel Müller and Steven Vanderputtern, who organized the thematic strand that year on the topic of "Reform and Renewal" and who had confidence in our vision; and we thank the full staff of the Leeds Conference for their support in facilitating and promoting the sessions.

We also thank the many people who encouraged us along the way in conversations behind the scenes, in email exchanges, and in on-going correspondence as well as in reflections and recommendations: Brenda Bolton, Scott Bruce, Caroline Walker Bynum, Giles Constable, Cecilia Gaposchkin, Patrick Geary, Jacques Dalarun, Jereon Deploige, William Chester Jordan, Conrad Leyser, Henrietta Leyser, David Mengel, Maureen Miller, Kenneth Mills, and Jean-Claude Schmitt. We are especially grateful to John Arnold, Peter Biller, and John Van Engen, who were instrumental in helping us conceptualize the shape, trajectory, and place of a volume like this in our field. Finally, we thank to the two outside readers, whose comments and suggestions strengthened the volume in numerous ways and helped us sharpened its claims.

We have benefited from the support of our institutions, and we recognize the Center for Medieval and Early Modern Studies and the Center for the Humanities and the Arts at the University of Colorado Boulder for support in sponsoring the Leeds sessions and a follow-up conference in the fall of 2016 on "Religion and the Master Narrative." We thank the University of Minnesota and University of Minnesota Morris for financial support, especially the Grant in Aid of Research, the Imagine Fund, and the Faculty Research Enhancement Funds. And Johns Hopkins University for support towards publication. We are grateful to have worked with Suzanne Rancourt and the immensely patient and wonderful production team at University of Toronto Press. Sharon Park improved the whole through her careful copy-editing before the manuscript as we went to press. We also thank Laurence Bond and Pelia Werth for their work constructing the Index. Bringing this project to completion during a pandemic presented unique challenges and we are grateful to everyone for their perseverance and commitment to the project throughout.

From the start, our families have listened patiently as this project evolved, as we became friends and collaborators, and as Grundmann and his legacy came to play a large role in our intellectual lives. Thank you Brad, Lucy, and Tess; and Scott, Mira, and Vivienne for your support along this journey. It is our hope that this volume will inspire yet more conversations and collaborations to come.

BETWEEN ORDERS AND HERESY

Rethinking Medieval Religious Movements

1 Introduction: Religion and Religious Worlds in Between

JENNIFER KOLPACOFF DEANE AND ANNE E. LESTER

As part of his religious conversion and throughout his time as the leader of a religious movement, Saint Francis (d. 1226) took to singing and praying in French. Not his native tongue, French was, for Francis, the language of commerce, movement, travel, and exchange, and it became a meaningful medium through which to praise God when singing alone or asking merchants or devout women for aid and alms.[1] Although he certainly spoke a local dialect of Italian and knew some Latin – having even written briefly in that learned language – Francis's use of French throughout his life as a mode of devotional communication signals the multiplicity of available options and spiritual vocabularies present and at work in the world during the high and later Middle Ages. Praying in French, much like begging for alms and preaching in the vernacular, was part of his search for a simultaneously reverent and inclusive spiritual model for a religious life that reached beyond the confines of a cloistered world.

Until recently, however, few scholars recognized Francis's use of "religious French" as a unique vehicle of its own, obscured as it was by the rigid distinction that occluded the space between religious Latinate literature and vernacular secular texts. Indeed, traditional binary historiographical models that pit one category against a presumed opposite – not only Latin/vernacular but also clerical/lay, regular/irregular, male/female, and orthodox/unorthodox – have simplified such complexities. The multifaceted and interlocking origins of many religious impulses that were later reformed or recognized as formal "orders" has further been overlooked by the practice of writing "orders' histories" – that is, by a historiographical tradition written first by members of a specific order for the order itself.[2] This tendency had the effect of siloing overlapping or interconnected impulses and ideas that often cut across and among various orders. A related interest in cultivating foundation narratives crafted around a charismatic "founder" further obscured the interconnected role of women, the poor, and the marginalized in the origins and trajectories of religious impulses and then orders as they developed over time. Because scholarship on medieval religion has so long favoured the richly documented narratives of ecclesiastical institutions, it absorbed many of their prejudices and certainties.[3] To be sure, such simplified, polarized models reflect more about nineteenth- and twentieth-century historiographical interpretations than they do about medieval practice. Yet, a tendency remains to treat counterexamples (including beguines, tertiaries, lay associations, hermits, and so on) as exceptions to the categorical rule. It is difficult to look for or within archival collections for those at the margins of institutional histories, or for those moved aside in favour of an ordered and orthodox path. As historians of women, the poor, or non-traditional subjects know well, such work requires new lines of questioning and new methodologies. The present collection asks that we shift the analytical gaze to consider anew the "troublesome" middling, hybrid, protean, blended, and complex realities that persisted "in between" the sharply drawn lines of ecclesiastical institutions and schemes for ordering and excluding.[4]

Among categorical binaries, none has more profoundly shaped twentieth- and twenty-first-century historical narratives of medieval Christian religion than that of "orders" and "heresy." The long-held presumption of the solidity of monastic practices and the correspondingly crisp, sequential model of "ordered" institutional development – for example, from Cluniac to Cistercian to the Friars – is more reflective of a desire to construct a grand narrative arc of regulated progression than it is of developments and experiences of the religious life as it was lived.[5] Moreover, over the course of the nineteenth and twentieth centuries, research tools and edited collections often shaped by nationalist and confessional agendas that emerged in those periods have exacerbated this approach and made it more difficult to look at developments and influences across orders simultaneously rather than over time. More recently, scholars have demonstrated how a deeply rooted tendency to evaluate piety through the framework of hierarchical institutions (especially the inquisitorial process) has flattened the ranging, multidimensional, and creative varieties of late medieval belief and behaviour into a confrontational dynamic of heresy and persecution.[6] What has been lost in the process is an understanding of the "multiple worlds" which John Van Engen identified as a feature of the diverse, dynamic, and vibrant socio-spiritual networks that spread across and transformed high and late medieval Europe.

It is ironic that a calcified model of orders and heresy gained privileged footing in modern historical scholarship largely through the work of a scholar who decried its utility, the German medievalist Herbert Grundmann (1902–1970), one of the most innovative thinkers of his day. Even as a young man Grundmann had identified and begun to excavate the problem of inquisitorial sources as historical evidence. A disinclination to adopt inherited frameworks unquestioned was, and remains, a hallmark of his work, as is his attention to variety, tension, contradictions, and change within medieval religious and intellectual thought.[7] Most notably for later historiography, he discerned behind all late medieval religious expression a shared family tree: spiritual movements of all sorts, he argued, whether labelled orthodox or heretical, arose in response to certain historical conditions and could be analysed in an organic relationship to one another (rather than as distinct histories unto themselves). As James Mixon recently noted, Grundmann was "one of the few scholars of his generation open to taking religion seriously as a subject of inquiry. [Moreover] he was convinced of the power of religious movements as a force in cultural history, one that cut across institutional boundaries, and across the borders between church and society."[8] The very first line of his masterwork *Religiöse Bewegungen im Mittelalter* (*Religious Movements in the Middle Ages*), published in 1935, staked the bold and paradigmatic claim, as rendered in the English translation sixty years later, that "[a]ll religious movements of the Middle Ages achieved realization either in religious orders or in heretical sects."[9] Yet it was, as many of the essays here make clear, his broader convictions about the more protean nature of religion in history, as a subject of historical inquiry, that continued to galvanize new research and ways of thinking.

Herein lies the fascination of Grundmann's thesis and method. Memorable in its simplicity and utility, the metaphor of late medieval bifurcation was so frequently referenced and quoted that it took on a life of its own in the historiography. By contrast, the "between" and far more elaborate aspects of his argument have remained harder to grasp and thus to apply and to reference. Grundmann, of course, never denied the existence of a dynamic realm complicating or resisting the model he laid out; it was in the very subtitle of his book.[10] But the claim that medieval religious movements culminated either in orders or heresy became a historiographical polestar. Nevertheless, the topic of historians' perspectives on such vibrant middle ground still preoccupied him decades later, as he articulated with force and conviction in a 1965 essay only five years before his death: "The historian, with all respect and understanding for the office, cannot permit this way of seeing – the form of questioning and judging, which only had to decide between orthodoxy and heresy – to intrude if he wishes to understand the intellectual and religious life of that time in its variety of views, in its tensions and contradictions, and hence in its symptoms and causes of change."[11] During the intervening eighty years since the first publication of Grundmann's text, a vast corpus of scholarship has emerged that reaffirms some aspects of his narrative and that challenges others. Moreover, many new sources have come to light or received scholarly attention in ways that complicate and destabilize Grundmann's thesis. Recent scholarship, especially among American and European scholars, has emphasized archival research that privileges local and variant histories, histories from below and from the micro-context, and that seek out the experiences of women as much as men. These methodological approaches have opened a perspective on the past to which Grundmann simply did not have access, even if he was aware of what such local research might have yielded.[12]

In the last several decades, under the influence of anthropology, sociology, and cultural history, scholars have returned to the archives in search of ideas and behaviours rather than the history of an order or the thread of an inquisitorial process.[13] In turn, new groups and communities have come to the fore. Building on Grundmann's thesis, whether consciously or not, recent monographs, collections of essays, conference panels, and research centres have focused on the origins of movements. Scholars have traced the roots of these movements from their inception, often around a charismatic leader or gathering of likeminded men and women to their eventual "reform" or acceptance of a rule and "evolution" into a new religious order.[14] It is commonplace in the scholarship that popes, bishops, abbots, confessors, and secular leaders often sought to graft the spontaneous piety of laymen and laywomen onto established monastic structures, thereby anchoring untethered religious impulses to formal religious orders and institutions. Correspondingly, ideas and movements outside the structures of authority risked classification as dissent and could become suspect of heresy. Despite seeing new groups and movements, the question of how to narrate a history of devout men and women who do not fit within the established historical categories of an order or a heresy has yet to be resolved, let alone questioned with much consistent force. Even simply naming such individuals or communities is a daunting task – the sources are often contradictory and imprecise, making finding such people or groups within historical records the first challenge – rendering narrative coherence in the absence of a fixed vocabulary doubly so. In the face of these historiographical challenges, we have undertaken this project with the conviction that such research is necessary and will lead to new insights and methodologies for understanding the dynamics of religion in the past.

Not surprisingly, as many of the essays here make clear, the wealth of evidence emerging from the archives or from new readings of source collections has served to reframe the contours and extent of formal ecclesiastical power and its reforming goals and ends. In some respects, local histories complicate, if not diminish, the reach of the papacy into the everyday lives of individuals in the medieval world, making the work of priests, canons, legates, and representatives all that much more important for understanding the dynamic links Grundmann laid out. It is time to build on this work and to develop a new narrative: to look again, through the lens of the many new sources that have come to light in the intervening decades, and to re-conceptualize the landscape of religious movements in the Middle Ages, addressing all that could and did occur in the space between orders and heresy.

In the past two decades, religious movements that found expression in forms outside of, or deliberately eschewing, institutional definition have been the focus of especially vibrant research. The essays gathered here likewise re-evaluate some of the major themes, categories, and constructs relating to the shape and role of religious movements in the Middle Ages. Together they illuminate the diverse social and religious ecosystem that, upon closer examination, flourished in realms traditionally mapped along the borders of, or *in between*, orders and heresy. While we challenge the interpretive value of that binary for use by modern scholars, the conceptual framework of order and heresy was a powerful and authentically medieval mechanism that cannot simply be excised from consideration. It was, so to speak, in the very air medieval people breathed and a historical force in its own right, its influence discernible across the many contexts and vantage points addressed in the following essays. Order and heresy gave medieval lay and religious people models and exemplars as well as positions and claims to push against and to reject. Historians would be short-sighted to dismiss the historical paradigm altogether even if, as this volume argues, it is in need of revision and reframing. Indeed, many people – much like Francis singing of the spirit in French – chose a path, at least initially, that sat outside, beyond, and between the hierarchically defined poles of "heresy" and "order." The challenge we take up here is to uncover, analyse, and align those "in between" histories with some of the dominant narratives that are familiar to students and also to suggest new ways forward. The "in between" that emerges in these essays is a discursive middle ground, a space of invention, critique, ambivalence, and, as originally imagined, of movement and reinterpretation. Looking closely at this middle space invites new subjects to inhabit the centre of the narrative crafted, for example, around the parish rather than the papacy, the penitent rather than the preacher, or the poet-singer rather than the theologian.

Charting New Ground

The idea for this volume emerged from the editors' shared research agendas and our common observation that more work was needed to explain the emergence of religious movements during the high Middle Ages and to account for how these impulses changed over time. Both of us believed that the time had come for a scholarly re-evaluation of the term and the conceptualization of "religious movements" as first proposed and elaborated by Grundmann. We were especially interested in how his concept emerged within its historiographical moment, in Germany during the 1920s and 1930s, and how his ideas were received, interpreted, taught, and later applied across different national and methodological contexts.

To that end, we organized a strand of sessions convened in the summer of 2015 at the International Congress on Medieval Studies at Leeds University, United Kingdom. That year marked the eightieth anniversary of the first publication of *Religiöse Bewegungen im Mittelalter* (1935), and the twentieth anniversary of its translation into English as *Religious Movements of the Middle Ages*, published by the University of Notre of Dame Press in 1995. The response was overwhelming. The sessions, seven in total, brought together dozens of scholars working in the United States, the United Kingdom, Australia, Germany, and the Netherlands and asked them to assess the impact of Grundmann's arguments and to chart where new work on religious movements is headed. As noted by many in attendance, Grundmann approached the study of religion and spirituality through a distinctly sociological lens and offered connections and interpretations that were startlingly different from the vantage point of scholars who had studied one specific order or individual, often within a distinct religious or monastic tradition.

Our focus in this volume is thus on the motives, interactions, behaviours, and relationships shaping medieval religious worlds that – like Saint Francis's devotional expression in French – have not been part of the dominant historiographical or narrative focus thus far. By foregrounding the dynamic, creative, and highly diverse later medieval socioreligious landscapes flourishing within the interstices of ecclesiastical structures, our aim is twofold: to bring to light avenues of religious experience on the part of women, peasants, townspeople, and marginalized groups that have not been foregrounded and to analyse how those experiences shaped and reshaped definitions of order and heresy in turn. As John Van Engen has noted, "the working of medieval parishes, especially in the later Middle Ages – priests in charge of the chancel, laypeople of the nave, wardens of assigned accounts and tasks, patrons or guilds or confraternities contributing altars and stained-glass windows, people finding places of belonging at the baptismal font, church porch, churchyard, and so on – all suggests more interactive forms of ownership and responsibility, at least for some classes of people, than we sometimes credit."[15] To develop a "ground up" rather than "spire down" perspective of high and later medieval religious culture requires new questions, new source evidence, and new interpretive frameworks.

Each of the eleven essays included here individually re-evaluates major themes, categories, and constructs relating to the role of religious movements in the Middle Ages, including, for example, the implementation of apostolic ideals, the contours of communities, the dynamics of pastoral relationships, and networks of lay and religious participation. They are organized both to echo chronological historical developments and to challenge some deeply embedded historiographical presumptions and tools – particularly that of conceptual rigidity regarding historical labels, institutional power, and individual charisma. Although each chapter slices across the historiographical grain in different ways, variously extending, critiquing, or otherwise engaging with Grundmann's theses and legacy, the first four essays take up Grundmann's work, contemporary context, and paradigms explicitly. The seven essays that follow offer more specific readings and reconstructions of the worlds "in between" and analyse religion as it was lived, practiced, and written about in specific locales in the later medieval world, ranging from Paris to Prague and from Utrecht to Umbria. In this way, the volume offers new ways of approaching medieval religious belief and activity beyond the binary of orders and heresies and charts new directions for future work.

The Essays

The volume opens with **Letha Böhringer**'s consideration of Herbert Grundmann and his individual position vis-à-vis the religious and political impulses of his day. One of the few historians to have studied Grundmann's personal papers and other archival documentation, Böhringer explores Grundmann's membership and departure from the Protestant church, traces the evidence delineating his relationship to

National Socialism, and considers the impact of both of these forces on his intellectual arguments laid out in *Religious Movements* (written between 1926 and 1934). As she quotes him saying, his intention was "most of all to position the activities of the church, the orders and the heretics which had been often investigated separately into the larger picture of the religious, spiritual and social movement; from thence, details can be really understood and many events can only be explained in this way." Her chapter offers a historical and historiographical framework through which to engage Grundmann and his ideas as a product of their particular moment of conception. The remaining ten essays pick up this theme, addressing an array of contexts and issues that follow the legacy of his conceptualization – whether affirming, challenging, or extending Grundmann's perspective – and together contribute a fuller and more holistic view of late medieval religious life.

Amanda Power considers the apostolic model from the distinct vantage point of Franciscan historiography, drawing our attention to the contradictions and problems in historical representations of Saint Francis of Assisi. Tracing the many parallels between Franciscan historiography and hagiography, she critiques the pervasive tendency to regard Francis as exceptional and thus "outside" the historical paradigms of medieval religious movements. Even Grundmann, who generally tried to subordinate the influence of charismatic individuals to the broader sociological and spiritual impulses of the day, could not avoid adopting a special view of Francis and his embodiment of the *vita apostolica*. "The result is that where the various explanatory paradigms of Franciscan historiography meet Grundmann's 'movement,'" Power argues, "we find a peculiar unstated consensus that the historical facts of Francis's life and thought are difficult to establish but certainly constitute an especially authentic form of Christianity." Power analyses the distorting historiographical consequences of that tendency across a wide range of associated figures, paradigms, and concepts embedded in Franciscan narratives.

Next, **Sita Steckel** examines the medieval mode of critique, criticism, and accusations of hypocrisy in the religious life. By the later Middle Ages, critique had become a fundamental part of reform practices and vernacular satire that laid bare the gaps between normative customs and lived practice. As Steckel argues, unlike polemical debates held publicly at the University of Paris, allegory served "to express criticism of a particular religious group, but its protean, ubiquitous and somewhat mischievous nature ... enforced reflection on the broader problem of discerning 'genuine' religiosity." Exploring the complex and powerful workings of hypocrisy both as a charge levelled and as "seeming" religion – that is, the potential for true religion in unexpected and humbled quarters – allows Steckel to analyse the deep anxieties medieval men and women harboured about concepts like sanctity, religious truth, and proof. Indeed, Steckel shows the ways that "hypocrisy as a 'boundary' category [functioned], with a dynamic performative ability to challenge and to destabilize established ways of understanding religion."

The capaciousness of religious movements is a point of departure for **Anne E. Lester**'s chapter, which addresses the place of the crusades and crusading in relation to Grundmann's formulation. Although Grundmann hardly mentioned crusading in his own research, Lester sets the development of his theses within the context of other scholars working in the early decades of the twentieth century, namely Carl Erdmann and Paul Alphandéry, who were interested in the creation and evolution of religious ideology and collective belief through the development of crusading as a concept and a practice. Offering a different barometer for measuring the crusades as a religious movement, Lester looks closely at how the crusades were experienced and conceptualized for women and men during the thirteenth century under the pressures of repeated failed campaigns, compounded fiscal pressures, and the prolonged regency of female kin when male crusaders died or never returned from the east. In this context, a new register of "vernacular crusading" emerged, one that was dialogic, ambivalent, and expressed through an idiom of vernacular literature and material objects and endowments rather than the Latinate chronicle record or papal bull. Seen from below and using the documentary sources associated with Mahaut of Courtenay, countess of Nevers, Auxerre, and Tonnerre, Lester argues that crusading could find a compatible place within Grundmann's framework, as an "in-between" expression of the religious life.

Neslihan Şenocak takes up the theme of religious activity outside of ecclesiastical institutions and challenges Grundmann's binary emphasis on poverty and preaching by pointing to the powerful historical role of medieval confraternities. Reflecting on the definitive features of confraternal corporations as an inspirational point of origin, a kinship model, and a salvific purpose, she argues that the confraternal model was the most sweeping and ubiquitous religious movement of the central and later Middle Ages. Contrasting directly with the traditional historiographical emphasis on preaching and poverty, confraternal organizations and other booming collaborative spiritual modes represented a growing certainty that "acting as a community offers a surer path to salvation than acting alone." In other words, the twin ideals of poverty and preaching alone are not sufficient for attaining, or even understanding, medieval apostolic ideals.

Next, **Sean L. Field** addresses Grundmann's famous thesis about the role of women in developing vernacular religious literature in Germany in collaboration with mendicants, calling for a broader and wider comparative analysis of women's writing from the church's "unsettled margins." Focusing on the French scene in particular, Field examines the writings and contexts of Marguerite of Oingt, Marguerite Porete, Agnes of Harcourt, and Felipa of Porcelet. Like their sisters in German-speaking lands, their "religious communities organized themselves into lasting, regulated forms of life without clerical Latin training, but with the need for contemplation and theological study and a capacity for absorbing and imparting the treasures of Latinate theological and religious education." Although the influence of mendicants on women's writing in French remains palpable, Field argues that "Grundmann's focus on the mendicant orders must be widened to embrace other contexts in which women wrote." The model, therefore, needs to be more elastic to accurately represent the range of medieval laywomen's influence on vernacular religious writing.

Similarly interested in revealing historiographically neglected spaces of gendered religious influence and exchange during these centuries, **Tanya Stabler Miller** focuses her essay on the world view of Robert of Sorbon (secular cleric and founder of the Sorbonne, which would later become part of the University of Paris) and his perspective on lay religious women, or beguines. In contrast to Grundmann's representation of such women as failed nuns who "did not find reception into the new orders" and were thus "subject to the temptation of heretical obsession," Robert offered a much different view. By elevating "beguine" status as something both laudable and accessible, he challenged the exclusivity of orders by ascribing monastic ideals to lay religious women and to secular clergy. Miller argues that Robert "advanced and created a permanent space for reforming circles of secular clerics 'between' the categories so crucial to Grundmann's framework" – circles in which he considered women "more inclined to good than men" and whose "public visibility was both virtuous and necessary." The deep appreciation for lay religious women as part of the college's core mission to preach and to serve is a potent example of later medieval enthusiasm for the religious life *outside* of rules and walls.

The flexible and historically enduring nature of that enthusiasm, as well of the institutional and historiographical challenges that come with trying to reconstruct it in the archives, forms the basis of **Alison More**'s essay on the "Grey Sisters" of northern Europe. Although they are typically referred to as Franciscan tertiaries, or belonging to the Franciscan third order, More argues that "closer inspection of these women and the context from which they emerged shows that the term 'grey' describes more than the indeterminate colour of their habits … they not only stood between the religious and secular spheres, but their complex origins also place them between order and, if not heresy, at least controversial heterodoxy." Emphasizing the struggle of medieval clergy as well as modern scholars to label and categorize such women, More notes that the historical complexities make it methodologically challenging to reconstruct a fuller image of such groups "betwixt" canonical categories. Moreover, communities such as the Grey Sisters "frequently changed name, patronage, activities and even order affiliation with no apparent pattern or obvious reasons for doing so"; it thus requires careful attention to the source records to reconstruct their medieval past and modern legacies.

Janine Larmon Peterson's essay similarly takes up this tension around historical and historiographical terminology but shifts our attention to the gendered political dimensions of the categories of "heretic" and "heresiarch" in the later Middle Ages. Observing that female figures such as Maifreda da Pirovano, a relapsed heretic found guilty of preaching and teaching doctrinal error and executed in 1300, met the canon law criteria for "heresiarch," Peterson poses the question of why they appear in the historical – and thus historiographical – record merely as "heretics." The absence of women labelled as heresiarchs, she argues, cannot be explained simply with reference to a dismissive medieval misogyny in which women were deemed "as gullible and duplicitous, [and] too intellectually and emotionally weak to attract followers." Rather, she points to a fundamental disjuncture between two simultaneously operating sets of labels: on the one hand, the traditional definitions used by canon lawyers to identify "heretics" and "heresiarchs"; and on the other, a potent and specifically *territorial-political* understanding of the same terms introduced by papal and inquisitorial powers in the late thirteenth and early fourteenth centuries. Among the many historiographical consequences of this gap between theory and practice is that women's roles in later medieval religious movements are underestimated – across public and private realms alike.

Lezlie Knox's essay also engages with Grundmann's idea of a "women's religious movement" to consider questions of definitions, religious space beyond ecclesiastical institutions, and the relationship between political and spiritual authority in the thirteenth and fourteenth centuries. Analysing the life, death, and textual *vitae* of a pious young Roman noblewoman named Margherita Colonna (d. 1280), Knox traces how her family attempted to secure her canonization as the saintly founder of an informal religious community and why that attempt was ultimately unsuccessful. Surveying the topographic sweep of Rome's lay religious communities in the thirteenth and fourteenth centuries, she argues that a historiographical overemphasis on Franciscan influence has hidden the range and diversity of lives such as Margherita's. According to Knox, one of Grundmann's most important contributions is the reminder to look beyond the neatly regularized image of communities represented in normative documents, to seek the "organic and flexible arrangements that existed in practice."

In the volume's final essay, **Jana Grollová** picks up and extends the theme of bonds between preachers, beguines, and familial religious cultures, pulling our attention east to Prague – a region whose histories, due to linguistic barriers and historiographical divisions, are rarely included in studies of medieval European religious cultures. Charting the proliferation of small, independent, local networks of beguines and beguine houses across the city, Grollová explores their meaning in the dynamic historical context of fourteenth- and fifteenth-century Bohemia. By applying the insights of recent Western scholarship to Czech sources (material typically treated separately in the historiographical silos of Hussite revolution and reform), she reveals how these women cultivated familial and religious networks grounded in preaching, parish centres, and the burgeoning world of vernacular translation of religious works. Such volumes, created for and in conversation with beguines, also shaped growing and divisive ideas of dissent and heresy in the context of Jan Hus's innovations and amid the *Utraquist* controversy. Through this, women of late medieval Prague (whether married, widows, or "virgins") developed powerful connections with enthusiastic preachers to play a vital and resolutely "vernacular" role markedly distinct from the elevated register of imperial politics and papal condemnation.

Our aim in this volume is twofold: first, to show how and in what ways Grundmann's thesis and paradigms are still present, vital, and operative in new work dedicated to religious movements and, second, to suggest how scholars have surpassed those frameworks, opening new perspectives and delineating new terrain to explore. Readers will encounter multiple threads of Grundmann's ideas and interpretations woven through each essay. To this end, and in the hope of exposing the interconnected weave of Grundmann's ideas and our own thinking, we have chosen to present the essays within the volume in sequential chapters rather than dividing or classifying each contribution into separate subsections. This choice not only reflects and reinforces the interlocking nature of Grundmann's ideas but also demonstrates how the essays themselves share many of these themes in common. It will become apparent to any reader that where the thread of one idea is put down, another is taken up. Our goal in this sense is to embrace and to lay bare the messiness of complexity rather than to pare down and package it into neat categories, for to do so would be to lose singular stories and experiences in favour of smoothing the narrative arc.

Together the essays make clear that it is time to expand the methodological possibilities for future research in religious history. Grundmann's work was instrumental in laying out several paths forward on many fronts which opened new ways of thinking about the dynamics of reform, vernacularity, preaching, women's roles, poverty, and community, to name but a few. We hope that this volume, by drawing on his example, will continue to do the same. Indeed, in the past fifty years – from the time of the second edition of *Religious Movements* (1965) through its translation into Italian (1980) and then English (1995) – newer methodological approaches have intersected in fruitful ways with Grundmann's initial thesis and ideas. Feminist scholarship and gender history, committed as they are to discovering new voices and analysing dynamics of power behind and within archival records, have vastly enriched our picture of where women were, what they were doing, and what their thoughts, ideals, and ambitions were with respect to the religious life. Likewise, work on marginal groups – the poor, the sick, the disabled, lepers, children – has shifted how we see and understand the apostolic movement's embrace of humility and poverty as a political, social, and religious statement and practice.

Within the context of power and communication in medieval Europe, Francis's embrace of visible poverty and his ability to shift communicative registers – praying, singing, begging in French – speaks to how attuned medieval people were to signs and symbols of critique and change in the process of reform and re-envisioning a better world in their midst. Reading Grundmann's ideas after the linguistic turn and its prolonged destabilizing effects on history as a discipline, we can now see textual registers and the influence of vernacular and cultural production in an entirely new manner. This is not to say that one needs to theorize such textual readings at all times, but it is to recognize that texts, even short, staccato texts – letters, prayers, inquisition registers, charters for gifts of meagre size – communicate on multiple registers and frame a cultural understanding of religion as practice that reverberated in ways Grundmann had only begun to consider. Relatedly, new projects have theorized and challenged older conceptions of traditional periodization and temporal frameworks structuring "renaissance" and "reform" and have turned to the complex and vibrant period of the late fourteenth and fifteenth centuries. These projects have also taken up Grundmann's tacit charge to find and to follow spaces where ideas germinated in networks and in conversation rather than the single corpus of one or two learned masters. Thinking theoretically – about networks, cultural production, and fields or frameworks – is very much in line with the shaping force of Grundmann's insights as a kind of sociology of religion.

In bringing together this selection of scholarship, we are aware that the present volume is not exhaustive. Missing, as readers will no doubt notice, are essays reflecting on the dynamics of religious movements and those spaces between heresy and order in the Iberian context, North Africa, and the Levant. In part, this reflects Grundmann's own scope (or limitations) and the era in which he worked, which did not extend geographically or conceptually into or across the Mediterranean or Iberian world or beyond the Christian tradition. Likewise, for Grundmann, vernacularity was conceptualized in relation to Latin and the hierarchical structures of the Roman Church in contrast to the multilingual, dynamic, and interconfessional worlds south of the Pyrenees and the Alps and east of the Adriatic. Similarly, vernacular literature in the Iberian or North African context, where Judeo-Arabic was used, or where macaronic texts were more common, where political decisions were drawn up in two or more languages with different but equivalent valences, could raise entirely different interpretative questions with respect to religious ideas, currents, and movements. In this sense, we offer this volume not as a definitive statement of new work but as a compass pointing towards new territories and trajectories. In the Mediterranean, Iberian, and Levant contexts, Grundmann's conception of religious movements might take on a very different guise if applied to the military orders, hospital orders, or orders charged with the ransom of captives and safe passage where an interfaith mercenary logic prevailed, or in relation to different constructions of heresy, apostasy, and conversion.

Finally, recent work on religious difference, conversion, and the perception and construction of an "other" – whether Jewish, Muslim, heretical, or of lesser status, like "little women (*mulierculae*)" – has enriched our understanding of the diversity of the medieval world, the movement of ideas and people, and the ways religious history interacts with and shapes our writing about the past and our ability to see and understand complex experiences on their own terms. Indeed, following the meaning, application, and trajectory of conceptualizations such as religious ideology, idiom, and conversion – as a status, a process, or an imperial ambition – could complicate and extend Grundmann's framework in myriad ways. Much remains to be done – to be uncovered, puzzled, positioned, and framed – and in doing so it should be possible to see yet more depth to the spaces that flourished *between* orders and heresy.

To think more broadly about Grundmann's work in the context of medieval religion and religions also allows us to see the framing of his arguments more clearly. Grundmann's interests in legal statutes and orders, vernacularity, and his use of papal documents – that is, general rather than local archival sources – informed a set of questions that led to specific outcomes focused on evolution and an achieved end. But other framings existed behind these sorts of texts. As the authors here show, an openness to practice and community, to the cultivation of confraternities and deliberately ill-defined associations that resisted being legislated, also persisted alongside orders, monastic codifications, and papal decrees. This openness means that affiliation did not always go under one set of naming practices or one form of regulated association but could be and remained flexible and oral, rather than codified. Similarly, the vernacular was never only a binary practice, however much nineteenth-century scholars and nascent academic departments hoped to divide French and Italian from German and Slavic, or from Latin and Greek. Medieval people spoke, sang, prayed, and interacted in many different languages and registers, many of which were never written down. As several of the essays here suggest, language offers and offered the possibility of fluidity and of recovering interactions among different classes, genders, and groups of people who lived and spoke in dialects and in the *between* linguistic modes of everyday life and devotion.

Finally, the essays here all turn to local worlds rather than papal registers or theological treatises for their interpretations and thus demonstrate again the complex layers of the religious life as lived in parishes, on street corners, in small chapels and domestic spaces. This sort of granularity was something in which Grundmann was certainly interested but which was hard to capture during the time he wrote and worked. Having excavated the space between decrees, statues, and canon law, we can now work further and closer to the ground to see what living a life of and in religion entailed and to envision other categories and paradigms from which to generate narratives of experience and belief. We may also, as some of the essays here suggest, alter the language we use. "Religion" or "religious experience" may not do all that scholars want it to do by way of describing the intersections of beliefs, practices, habits, inheritances, hopes, and feelings that mediated how one lived their life in relation to concepts of the divine or the spirit and its force in the world.[16] Likewise, what we mean by "vernacular" or "heresy," or concepts and terms like "magic" and "spiritual" or "spirituality," might very usefully be investigated and revised.[17] One cannot craft a narrative without language, but our terminology too can hamper how a new narrative takes form.

This volume offers a new approach to the paradigm Grundmann laid out and that took on a life of its own in the decades that followed. As we suggest, although the narrative arc of orders and heresy had great appeal, it was limited and limiting. Nevertheless, finding other narratives or strategies that encompass the complexity and messiness of religion in history in all its variety is no easy task. We have begun the process here as a collaboration by drawing on the expertise of a series of scholars each working in a particular locale. One way to imagine something other than a binary is, perhaps, to look more closely at the forms in nature, that is, to envision the fractal patterns made by experiences, habits, and behaviours as they echo, replicate, and ripple across time, into other languages, rituals, and beliefs. Rather than seeking after an "achieved realization" we may, as the essays here suggest, come to understand more of religion in the past by looking at its manifestations and articulations *before* they were fixed into a canonical or theological definition. Religion may be better understood and narrated as a series of modes or lines of thought and behaviours that could be traced, retraced, and linked. Although, at the time, there were few examples for how to narrate or even uncover such things, this ambition lies, as noted above, within the very subtitle of Grundmann's seminal work: *The Historical Links* Between *Heresy, the Mendicant Orders, and the Women's Religious Movement in the Twelfth and Thirteenth Century, with the Historical Foundations of German Mysticism*. The links mentioned here were not made explicit in *Religious Movements*, and this was a clear shortcoming of the book. But the fact that Grundmann suggested they were there, at least at the outset, is perhaps his most important enduring contribution.

By opening and responding to a foundational study like Herbert Grundmann's *Religious Movements* in the ways the authors here have done, our hope is to continue to build upon, critique, and shift his ideas in ways that he might have appreciated and that would have resonated with "religious" thinking from the period he studied so closely. Indeed, to modernize a set of ideas, to translate them into a vernacular setting, and to add to, critique, and enhance is very much a medieval way to study the past and to bring about reform, as Grundmann made clear. Moreover, to linger in the spaces Grundmann's paradigm cracked open – between the columns of church portals, alongside roadways, in ports, hostels, hospices, or even ruins, in those spaces of change and flux, where the complexity and multilingual "messiness" of religion was activated – may be, as Francis and others like him well understood, the very best place to encounter something like the divine at work in the world. This, after all, was surely what Francis was up to, in the cultural idiom of sung French, as he gathered listeners around him before he came to kneel barefoot in front of the pope with fragments of the Gospels in hand.

NOTES

1 For a discussion of the role of French in Francis's conversion and religious life, see Augustine Thompson, *Francis of Assisi: A New Biography* (Ithaca: Cornell, 2012), 8, and for begging alms in French, 21. His use of French is also noted by André Vauchez, *François d'Assisi: Entre histoire et mémoire* (Paris: Fayard, 2009); in English as *Francis of Assisi: The Life and Afterlife of a Medieval Saint*, trans. Michael F. Cusato (New Haven, CT: Yale University Press, 2012), 21–2, 76.

2 On this tradition, see John Van Engen, "The Christian Middle Ages as an Historiographical Problem," *The American Historical Review* 91 (1986): 519–52. For a new approach to writing monastic history that embraces the recognition that there existed simultaneously a plurality of approaches and ideals to the religious life and "many different attempts to realize them," see Steven Vanderputten, *Medieval Monasticisms: Forms and Expressions of the Monastic Life in the Latin West*, Oldenbourg Grundriss der Geschichte, vol. 47 (Berlin: de Gruyter, 2020). Vanderputten thus argues for the use of the plural "monasticisms" to acknowledge this new interpretation, 1–5.

3 On this tendency for writing about medieval religion, see Christine Caldwell Ames, "Medieval Religious, Religions, Religion," *History Compass* 10 (2012): 334–52.

4 Such habits of thought inhere in systems of knowledge creation in part as a legacy of Cartesian and Enlightenment forms of ordering common to growing state bureaucracies and religious orders alike. See Michel Foucault, *Les Mots et les choses* (Paris: Gallimard, 1966); in English: *The Order of Things: An Archaeology of the Human Sciences* (New York: Vintage, 1970, reprinted 1994); and *L'Archéologie du Savoir* (Paris: Gallimard, 1969); in English: *The Archaeology of Knowledge and the Discourse on Language*, trans. A.M. Sheridan Smith (New York: Vintage, 1982).

5 The Cistercian order provides the archetypical example of this phenomenon. See Constance Hoffman Berman, *The Cistercian Evolution: The Invention of a Religious Order in Twelfth Century Europe* (University of Pennsylvania Press, 2000); Janet Burton and Julie Kerr, *The Cistercians in the Middle Ages* (Woodbridge: Suffolk: Boydell, 2011); and Elizabeth Freeman, *Narratives of a New Order: Cistercian Historical Writing in England, 1150–1220* (Turnhout: Brepols, 2002). For comment on the grand narrative, see also Anne E. Lester, *Creating Cistercian Nuns: The Women's Religious Movement and Its Reform in Thirteenth-Century Champagne* (Ithaca: Cornell University Press, 2011).

6 Ever since Robert Lerner's *Heresy of the Free Spirit in the Later Middles Ages* (Notre Dame, IN: University of Notre Dame Press, 1972) picked up and extended Grundmann's source-critical approach to inquisitorial sources and historiographical interpretations, scholarship on medieval religious cultures and heresy exploded. In particular, concern for how inquisitors' categories and thought processes have shaped (or distorted) modern historians' interpretation of the historical record has become a central methodological question. The bibliography on heresy and inquisition is vast, as are responses to the challenge of gleaning historical insight from polemical sources; as a starting point, see R. I. Moore, *The War on Heresy* (Boston: Belknap Press, reprinted 2014); Christine Caldwell Ames, *Righteous Persecution: Inquisition, Dominicans, and Christianity in the Middle Ages* (Philadelphia: University of Pennsylvania Press, 2008); Mark Gregory Pegg, *The Corruption of Angels: The Great Inquisition of 1245–1246* (Princeton, NJ: Princeton University Press, 2001); and the series of recent volumes in the *Heresy and Inquisition* series (Woodbridge: York Medieval Press) edited by John Arnold, Peter Biller, and Lucy Sackville.

7 Jennifer Kolpacoff Deane, ed., *Herbert Grundmann (1902–1970): Essays on Heresy, Literacy, and Inquisition*, trans. Steven Rowan (Woodbridge: York Medieval Press, 2019).

8 James D. Mixson, ed. and trans., *Religious Life between Jerusalem, the Desert, and the World: Selected Essays by Kaspar Elm*, Studies in the History of Christian Traditions, vol. 180 (Leiden: Brill, 2016), 10. For a further assessment of the role of religion in the study of history, see the essay by Anne E. Lester in this volume.

9 Herbert Grundmann, *Religious Movements in the Middle Ages: The Historical Links Between Heresy, the Mendicant Orders, and the Women's Religious Movement in the Twelfth and Thirteenth Century, with the Historical Foundations of German Mysticism*, trans. Steven Rowan (Notre Dame, IN: University of Notre Dame Press, 1995), 1.

10 Although often elided, save for in a first note, the subtitle too lays bare what he was most interested in over the long term, that is, the

Historical Links Between *Heresy, the Mendicant Orders, and the Women's Religious Movement in the Twelfth and Thirteenth Century, with the Historical Foundations of German Mysticism.*

11 Originally published as "Ketzerverhöre des Spätmittelalters als quellenkritische Probleme," *Deutsches Archiv für Erforschung des Mittelalters* 21 (1965): 519–75. English translation in Deane, ed., "Heresy Interrogations in the Late Middle Ages as a Source-Critical Problem," 126–79.

12 The work of his student, Kaspar Elm, as one example, is a strong indication of what Grundmann understood as the potential for such research. To suggest this is not to diminish the singular contribution of Elm himself but to underline the ways their scholarship and that of scholars trained by Elm has continued in this vein in very positive ways. See the comments in Mixson, ed., *Religious Life between Jerusalem, the Desert, and the World*, 1–27. Moreover, two major research initiatives within Germany have taken up Grundmann's approach, albeit with a slightly different framing: AGFEM [Arbeitskreis geistliche Frauen im europäischen Mittelalter] (https://agfem.wordpress.com/), which brings together scholars from myriad disciplines to study religious women and their orders and congregations in a social historical context, and the Research Center for Comparative History of Religious Orders (FOVOG-Dresden) (https://tu-dresden.de/dcpc/fovog#intro), directed by Gert Melville, which has for nearly three decades taken a comparative approach to the study of monastic orders and has published over eighty volumes in the series *Vita regularis*. In the United States, Van Engen and his students have led the way in pursuing research on those "in between" orders and heresy, between *regula* and *saeculum*, stretching across Europe during the high Middle Ages. Van Engen addressed this "in-betweenness" and what Elm called "semi-religious" status in many of his articles, but see especially: John Van Engen, "Friar Johannes Nyder on Laypeople Living as Religious in the World," in *Vita Religiosa im Mittelalter: Festschrift für Kaspar Elm zum 70. Geburtstag*, ed. Franz J. Felten, Nikolas Jaspert, and Stephanie Haarländer (Berlin: Duncker and Humblot, 1999), 583–615; and Van Engen, *Sisters and Brothers of the Common Life: The* Devotio Moderna *and the World of the Later Middle Ages* (Philadelphia: University of Pennsylvania Press, 2008).

13 Ames, "Medieval Religious, Religions, Religion," makes this point well but, curiously, makes no mention there of Grundmann and his thesis. On these trends in relation to more traditional, institutional-driven narratives, see also the comments offered by Caroline Walker Bynum, "More Popes than Piety? Approaches to Religion in the *New Cambridge Medieval History*," *The Catholic Historical Review* 93 (2006): 268–72.

14 For example, see the new appraisals of Saint Francis referenced above, note 1. Other examples include Jacques Dalarun, *L'impossible sainteté: La vie*

retrouvée de Robert d'Abrissel (v. 1045–1116) fondateur de Fontevraud, (Paris: Cerf, 1985, reprinted 2007) and Dalarun, *François d'Assisi en questions* (Paris: CNRS, 2016).

15 Van Engen, "Recovering the Multiple Worlds of the Medieval Church: Thoughtful Lives, Inspired Critics, and Changing Narratives," *The Catholic Historical Review* 104 (2018): 589–613, at 592.

16 For discussions of the limits of religion and religious history, see, for example: Ames, "Medieval Religious, Religions, Religion"; Van Engen, "Friar Johannes Nyder on Laypeople Living as Religious in the World"; Van Engen, "Professing Religion: From Liturgy to Law," *Viator* 29 (1998): 323–43; Jean-Claude Schmitt, "Une histoire religieuse du Moyen Age est-elle possible? (Jalons pour une anthropologie du christianisme médiéval)," in *Il mestiere di storico del Medioevo*, ed. Fernando Lepori and Francesco Santi (Spoleto: Centro italiano di studi sull'alto Medioevo, 1994), 73–83; Caroline Walker Bynum, *Fragmentation and Redemption: Essays on Gender and the Human Body in Medieval Religion* (New York: Zone, 1994); and Peter Biller, "Words and the Medieval Notion of Religion," *Journal of Ecclesiastical History* 36 (1985): 351–69.

17 See the discussions of such terms in Michael D. Bailey, "Was Magic a Religious Movement?" in *The Sacred and the Sinister: Studies in Medieval Religion and Magic*, ed. David J. Collins (University Park: Pennsylvania State University Press, 2019), 143–62; Giles Constable, *The Reformation of the Twelfth Century* (Cambridge: Cambridge University Press, 1996), esp. 1–43; this is also addressed in *Labels and Libels: Naming Beguines in Northern Medieval Europe*, ed. Letha Böhringer, Jennifer Kolpacoff Deane, and Hugo van Engen (Turnhout: Brepols, 2014).

2 Herbert Grundmann, Confession, and the "Religious Movements"

LETHA BÖHRINGER

In the introductory statement to his seminal study *Religious Movements in the Middle Ages,* Herbert Grundmann claims: "All religious movements of the Middle Ages achieved realization either in religious orders or in heretical sects."[1] According to him, heresy and orthodoxy are basically two sides of the same coin and, to some extent, defined by the eye of the beholder. In the introduction to the 1995 English translation, Robert Lerner credits this concept as revolutionary: "The greatest synthetic daring of Grundmann's book was to emphasize the common point of departure of groups that ultimately became located on either side of papally defined orthodoxy."[2] This all-encompassing and non-ideological way to regard all things religious was uncommon for German research in 1935, when Grundmann's book first went into print. At that time, scholarly lines were distinctly drawn between Catholics and Protestants, mapping out different ways to characterize the medieval church, the papacy, religious orders, and – most controversially – those groups labelled "heretical."

Mutual distrust still burdened relationships between the denominations during the early and middle decades of the twentieth century. Chancellor Otto von Bismarck's *Kulturkampf* against the influence of the Catholic Church in the 1870s was by no means forgotten. The Catholic population of the *Kaiserreich's* biggest state, Prussia, fought the traumatic experience of being considered second-class citizens, and they grappled with bias on many sides – namely, that Catholics were an inferior breed lacking education and proper patriotism and were prone to vice of all kinds.[3] A tendency to remain among one's own was facilitated by the fact that most areas of Germany were inhabited by either Catholics or Protestants – a situation rooted in the Peace of Augsburg (*Augsburger Religionsfrieden*) of 1555, which essentially granted the many territorial princes of the Holy Roman Empire the right to determine their subjects' confession. Towns and cities were more diverse, especially since the nineteenth century, but even so, Catholics and Protestants had their own newspapers, schools, clubs, and spaces for social gatherings. At universities, membership of the Burschenschaften (fraternities along political lines aiming to establish lifelong "old boy networks") was neatly divided between Catholics and Protestants. Entering government service, one's career would, to some degree, depend on whether one lived in Catholic Bavaria or in Protestant Prussia. In academia, journals and learned societies had either a Catholic or a Protestant base and editorial board. The *Monumenta Germaniae Historica* (MGH), for example, was a Prussian-run institution from 1871 to 1945, with a predominantly Protestant Zentraldirektorium and rank and file. In 1876, during the *Kulturkampf*, Catholics founded the *Görres-Gesellschaft zur Pflege der katholischen Wissenschaften* as the most important network for Catholic scholars to stand their ground. It exists to this day.

It is no wonder that sobriety and impartiality in medieval history, especially in the history of religion, did not flourish in Germany – and it goes without saying that Jewish scholars had a hard time finding a place.[4] There was always a tinge of partiality: Catholics were prone to "defend" the medieval church, even in its uglier aspects, while Protestants preferred to side with the outcasts and the oppressed, labelling them "proto-reformers." Both parties, of course, claimed to reveal "the truth," not only about the course of history but also about their own set of beliefs. Grundmann himself muses about this in an unprinted notice in his papers:

> If one applies at the outset to the history of heresy the categories of a "proper" middle ages and an opposition against this medieval way of life, one cannot achieve more than the Protestant historians of heresy who found proto-reformation everywhere they could not find modified Catholicism. And there's little difference with Catholic historians either, to whom all heresies were just that – heresies, errors derived from ill perception or from moral deficiency. With Preger and Denifle as their most worthy representatives, this confessionally-biased history on both sides has produced a lot of useful work, unearthed a great deal of source material and established some critical distinctions. But the question of intellectual history was for them pared down to the desire to find testimony bearing witness to their confession. For us, that is not enough. We want to know what kind of intellectual problems were raised in heretical movements, what kind of religious and philosophical themes excited individuals as well as whole circles, exciting them to the extent that they dared to oppose the all-supporting and overarching cultural structure of the Catholic Church.[5]

Grundmann's own approach thus offers a whole new perspective. His book is, indeed, a milestone in the research on orthodoxy, religious deviance, and the negotiation of consent. But what was Grundmann's own stance regarding religion? As Arno Borst (1925–2007), who was one of his students, stated in his teacher's obituary,[6] Grundmann left the Protestant church early in the 1930s;[7] what, then, was his frame of mind when he researched and penned his extraordinary contribution? And what was his attitude towards the Nazi seizure of power? Based on his papers at the University of Leipzig's archives, the following analysis sets forth some initial observations for further discussion.

Herbert Grundmann's conduct has been under scrutiny for the past two decades, and his relationship to the National Socialist (NS) regime is still a subject of debate. Only recently, have twentieth-century German historians in general and medievalists in particular been accused of having supported the Nazis and their belligerent and murderous ambitions. For a long time (a narrative I heard myself in the 1970s), the "bad boys" among historians who fell for Nazism lock, stock, and barrel were scholars of ancient history with their adulation of Führer figures and protohistoric archaeologists with their obsession with heroic "Germanentum."[8] Medievalists, however, were considered largely distant from the regime, with only a few regrettable exceptions, such as Theodor Mayer (1883–1972),[9] who was ostracized after the war. So when the *Historikertag* (the biennial congress of Germany's two professional associations of historians) of 1998 in Berlin unveiled unpleasant truths about iconic figures of German post-war research – to name just a few, Theodor Schieder (1908–84), Werner Conze (1910–86), and Grundmann's close friend Hermann Heimpel (1901–88) – tempers flared and voices were raised.[10] Many participants found it hard to digest that their venerated teachers had published items that are despicable to read today and had worked within groups supporting Nazism. One particularly appalling case is that of Karl Bosl (1908–93), who enjoyed a successful career at Würzburg and Munich after the war while claiming that he took part in active resistance against the Nazis. The image of Bosl the "resistant" was an utter fraud; he had joined the Nazi Party (NSDAP) in May 1933, and a closer look revealed many instances when he catered to the regime quite willingly.[11] As with all professions and layers of German society during the Third Reich, in general there was less black-and-white with fervent adherence and active resistance but many shades of grey. After the war, supporters, opportunists, and opponents were more or less forced to work together by necessity to eke out a living and to reorganize German society – a society in much denial until a new generation in the 1960s started to ask piercing questions.[12]

In her 2005 book, Anne Christine Nagel demonstrated how smoothly medievalists handled the transition from Nazism to the young Federal Republic and revealed more unpleasant truths about party membership and related matters.[13] Even earlier, in 2004, Nagel published an article which shed some light on the conduct of Grundmann, who had always claimed distance from the regime, as he never was a member of the Nazi Party. Nagel consulted Grundmann's papers in Leipzig and gathered evidence that he was, in fact, not so distant.[14] His unprinted radio addresses of the 1930s, his wartime speeches, his contribution to a notorious handbook of medieval history (1941),[15] and his presentation in front of SS cadets (1943)[16] testify to at least a certain degree of ingratiation, opportunism, and practical accommodation, if not identification with, National Socialism. It should be noted, however, that the documents Nagel and others cite, which express approval of Hitler, the Nazi Party, and their politics date after the Nazi seizure of power – well after *Religious Movements* was outlined, phrased, and presented as a Habilitationsschrift to the University of Leipzig in July 1933.

To date, however, no complete biographies have been written about Herbert Grundmann. The obituary essays written by his friend Hermann Heimpel and his pupil Arno Borst are major sources for his life story, as is the biographical sketch in English by Robert Lerner.[17] Grundmann was born in 1902 in a small town in Saxony. He grew up in Chemnitz, then an industrial city of some 300,000 inhabitants, and his father owned a small textile business which later failed during the Great Depression. When he entered the University of Leipzig in 1921, he first studied economics but soon thereafter focused on history. In 1926, he finished his dissertation on the unique theologian Joachim of Fiore. Grundmann's *Doktorvater* was Walter Goetz (1867–1958), a follower of Friedrich Naumann (1860–1919) and an unorthodox figure in German academia because of his liberal ideals and political activity with left-wing liberals.[18] Goetz, who had succeeded Karl Lamprecht (1856–1915) as director of the *Institut für Kultur- und Universalgeschichte* of Leipzig, provided scholarships for gifted students so they could pursue an academic career. Supported by such funds, Grundmann travelled to Italy and France and started to prepare his *Habilitationsschrift* on *Religious Movements*, which was submitted in 1933 and adapted as a book that was published in 1935. For several years, he found modest employment in the service of the *Historische Kommission of the Bayerische Akademie der Wissenschaften*, editing the acts of the Diet of Augsburg of 1530, and as a *Privatdozent* at Leipzig University.

In 1939, Grundmann attained his first university chair position at the University of Königsberg in East Prussia. When the Red Army approached the easternmost German border in 1944, he secured himself another *Lehrstuhl* in Münster in Westphalia and had his family leave Königsberg. He himself served within the Reichswehr for some years without seeing battle but actively fought the Red Army early in 1945. After a few weeks, he was injured and was transported behind the lines – the injury resulted in a stiff left wrist, but in his letters Grundmann never complained. He knew this had saved his life – his whole platoon perished. After the war, Grundmann was soon cleared by the so-called Denazification (*Entnazifizierung*) process,[19] and able to continue his career. His reputation was already well established, and he quickly became a medievalist of great influence, a member of learned societies in Germany and abroad (the Academies of Munich, Göttingen, and Leipzig and the National Academies of Paris, Rome, Brussels, and Vienna) and head editor of eminent book series and journals (such as the ubiquitous manual *Gebhardt. Handbuch der deutschen Geschichte* and the journals *Deutsches Archiv für Erforschung des Mittelalters* and *Archiv für Kulturgeschichte*). When he became president of the MGH in 1958, he left Münster for Munich; in 1970, he died there at the age of sixty-eight. At some point during the 1990s, his widow, Annelies Grundmann (1906–2009), gave his papers to the University of Leipzig. They are easily accessible due to a useful inventory and the fact that Grundmann always used a typewriter – he kept carbon copies of his own letters and elaborate manuscripts of his lectures. Annelies Grundmann, a historian herself, pre-sorted the material and added useful comments and dates.

Within these papers, there is revealing correspondence on the matter of Grundmann's lack of affiliation with a church. Soon after the war, his *Doktorvater* Walter Goetz expressed deep discomfort with Grundmann's religious status, fearing that it might be an impediment to his career.[20] In the general atmosphere of those days, the Catholic and Protestant churches appeared as unblemished pillars of society with moral standards. People who had given up membership during the Nazi regime were regarded with disgust.[21] Yet Germans knew that membership of the NSDAP could have been sought for very different reasons, such as fear, duress, or opportunism. Many civil servants (teachers, professors, administrators) joined the party to keep their jobs or get tenure,[22] whereas, by way of contrast, some death camp guards never did.[23] Membership alone was thus not necessarily a sign of strong Nazi convictions.[24] To give up church membership,[25] however, was considered an entirely different matter – as a sign of personal adherence to Nazi ideology in general, and in particular to racism, antisemitism, anti-Christian propaganda, and even a crude neo-pagan and (pseudo-) Germanic set of beliefs and rituals, including solstice celebrations.[26]

Grundmann's response to Goetz, a densely typed six-page letter in 1945, reveals how much he felt unfairly chastised. The tone of this letter shows that he was deeply hurt. He explains that he left the Protestant church in October 1934 – just eighteen months into the Third Reich. Grundmann defends himself indignantly, as he would for the rest of his life, saying that he was never a party member; yet, as he complains to Goetz, people "let me blatantly sense and hear since my return [from his time as a British POW] that I have this other 'blemish' as if it was just as bad."[27] Then he justifies himself in great length. He reminds Goetz of the quarrels within the Protestant church after the Nazi seizure of power when the ministers and the brethren were divided among the pro-regime movement of the German Christians (*Deutsche Christen*) and the opposing Confessing Church (*Bekennende Kirche*). In Saxony, Grundmann recalls, this quarrel became particularly intense and even ugly. Pressured to take sides, he explains that while the *Deutsche Christen* were not an option, neither could he join the *Bekennende Kirche*:

> I found the representatives of the Confessing Church thoroughly consequent, sincere and awe-inspiring in their faith; but through their decisiveness I realized even more clearly that I do not share their set of beliefs, in short: I cannot in all honesty, without hypocrisy, "accept as true" and subscribe to the Athanasian creed and the *Confessio Augustana* [the Lutheran articles of faith in 1530]. I had and have too much insight and respect for true faith to pretend to share it, against my conviction, simply in order not to give offence. This is why I left the church in October 1934, from a need for honesty and clarity.[28]

Grundmann continues in a more apologetic tone. He gives room to the consideration that he might have been rash in his decision but can still – after due consideration – find no reason to revoke it and re-enter the church. He elaborates that he cannot see the point of formalized church religion and feels that the churches have lost their authority and, consequently, their impact on the German people. Grundmann acted on his convictions; he never resumed church membership, although the absence of a creed was frowned upon in post-war Germany well into the 1970s and even later in some circles.

Does Grundmann's reasoning from 1945 hold true for the situation in 1933 and 1934? His respect for the *Bekennende Kirche*, which birthed opponents like Martin Niemöller (1892–1984) and martyrs like Dietrich Bonhoeffer (1906–1945), could be a post factum statement. As a matter of fact, he and many other members of German universities signed a manifesto welcoming the new regime in November 1933 ("Commitment of the Professors at German Universities and Institutes of Higher Education to Adolf Hitler and the National Socialist State").[29] Was his decision to leave the church a further sign of sympathy towards the Nazi seizure of power? Hardly so. The Nazis took a hostile stance towards the churches only after 1935, but in 1933 and 1934, the party and regime reached out to the churches, and their biggest success was the *Reichskonkordat* between the Holy See and the German Reich. Signed in July 1933, it soothed the worries of the Catholic population; henceforth, there was very little open opposition.[30] Protestant support of National Socialism began even earlier:[31] The German Christian Faith Movement (*Glaubensbewegung Deutsche Christen*) started to gather in 1930, mainly by younger radical ministers who demanded a unified German church to replace the 28 *Landeskirchen*. At the Prussian elections for the numerous bodies of church governance in November 1932, the *Deutsche Christen* already secured a third of the vote, and they soon triumphed in Germany. The ministers preached varying degrees of adherence to Nazi ideology, racism, and anti-Semitism, but a bridge was crossed when a Prussian synod of September 1933 embraced an *Arierparagraph* that based access to church positions as a minister or administrator on "Aryan" descent, thus placing lineage and "race" before baptism. As a reaction to this blatant breach of the Christian faith, opposing ministers founded the Emergency Covenant of Pastors (*Pfarrernotbund*), culminating in the "Declaration of Barmen," which led to the formation of the Confessing Church in 1934. But in 1933 and 1934, a huge wave of pro-Nazi enthusiasm swept the majority of Protestant congregations; services were held to express gratitude for the nation's salvation and its great *Führer*, and anniversaries and celebrations of all kinds (mass baptism, mass weddings, etc.) sported Nazi uniforms, a sea of flags at the altars, Nazi songs, and matching sermons. While Protestant churches had seen a significant decline in membership during the 1920s,[32] now people came back in droves.[33]

Therefore, when Grundmann left the *Landeskirche* of Saxony in 1934, he acted counter to the general trend. Strong Nazi convictions at that time would have resulted in church attendance. But his disdain for the *Deutsche Christen* is quite palpable in his 1945 letter, and he felt that they were simply beneath him. Still, his assertion that he respected the Confessing Church too much to join without proper conviction must be taken with a grain of salt. Grundmann remembers correctly that the *Kirchenkampf* was particularly ugly in Saxony, but this conflict within the Protestant church evolved only after he had already left.[34] There were only five attendants from Saxony at the synod of Barmen in May 1934, and at this time there were hardly any Saxon congregations with an affiliation to the *Pfarrernotbund*.[35] Did Grundmann even know anything about them? At this time, he did not have an actual choice between the two groups. Be that as it may, it is still possible that he thought he had to take sides and, in that situation, decided to quit altogether. This version of events, as laid out in the letter to Goetz, was repeated by Grundmann in his denazification questionnaire of 1947. In the latter, he provided the exact date for leaving the church: 26 October 1934.[36]

A scholarly feud was taking place in the backdrop, although it is uncertain as to what extent it influenced Grundmann's frame of mind and, eventually, his decision to leave the church. Although the timeline of events during the early part of 1934 remains obscure, it was eventually in the course of 1935 that Grundmann clashed with a powerful figure in Protestant academia. Erich Seeberg (1888–1945) was a minister from a Baltic dynasty of pastors and a professor of church history at the University of Berlin; in 1933, he was dean of the Theology Department.[37] Like Grundmann, Seeberg was interested in mysticism and speculative theology. A few years earlier, in 1928, he had reviewed Grundmann's thesis in a complaisant manner.[38] Seeberg applied a "völkisch" approach to the famous mystic Meister Eckhart, whom he saw as a paragon of the German character. In 1934, he published a small treatise in which he pointed out that Eckhart's German sermons, not his Latin works, formed the key to his ideas.[39] However, Seeberg's views were not well received; among the negative reactions was Grundmann's rather scathing review in 1935.[40] He accused Seeberg of poor scholarship, defective reconstruction of Latin texts, and an insufficient, even mistaken, grasp of the Meister's main principles of thought. According to Grundmann, only Eckhart's Latin works grant full access to his meaning and philosophy.[41]

The controversy was fuelled by two competing enterprises for editing Meister Eckhart's works.[42] Seeberg, very well-connected and a member of the Nazi Party since May 1933, headed a commission instituted by the Notgemeinschaft der deutschen Wissenschaft, which planned to publish Meister Eckhart's collected works. But there was already another editor: Raymond Klibansky (1905–2005), a Heidelberg *Privatdozent* of philosophy commissioned by the *Heidelberger Akademie der Wissenschaften*. Klibansky had already fallen out with a collaborator of Seeberg's on the issue of access to a manuscript from the library of Nicolas of Cusa. As Klibansky, who was Jewish, lost his job and emigrated after the Nazi seizure of power, Seeberg felt that he could control the editions of Meister Eckhart. However, Klibansky's first fascicle of Meister Eckhart's *Opera omnia* came out with the Felix Meiner Press at

Leipzig in 1934. Seeberg reacted immediately and published a review in September of that year.[43]

The idea of two competing Eckhart editions apparently instigated quite a stir. At some point in 1934, there were at least two conversations between the head of the press, Felix Meiner, and Grundmann on the matter. Both did not look upon Seeberg's enterprise with a friendly eye. Ernst Benz (1907–1978), a young *Privatdozent* of Protestant theology and a pupil of Seeberg's, seems to have been involved either in person or via letters to Grundmann. Benz reported some pieces of those conversations to his teacher. Seeberg – aggressively defending his project – wrote an angry letter to Professor Wolfgang Schadewaldt (1900–74, at the time a classicist at the University of Leipzig), outright denouncing Meiner as a liar and schemer. A copy of that letter, dated 1 December 1934, is in the Grundmann papers (according to Grundmann, it was handed to him by Hermann Heimpel).[44] Another letter in Grundmann's papers reveals that Seeberg's networks laboured intensively to suppress any criticism. The Reich Bureau for the Promotion of German Literatures (*Reichsstelle zur Förderung des deutschen Schrifttums*) wrote to the Meiner Press on 10 December 1934, explaining that the Seeberg edition was supported by "Party and State" and that any criticism would be considered hostile to both. The *Reichsstelle* threatened: "We formally warn you against uttering such statements."[45] Apparently, Felix Meiner forwarded this letter to Grundmann, who mentioned the threats in a letter to Ernst Benz a few days later.[46]

Grundmann was still inclined to mitigate the situation and wrote a diplomatic letter to Seeberg in January 1935 defending Felix Meiner and claiming that there had simply been some misunderstanding. But he did stand his ground criticizing the two competing editions openly; he conceded, however, that he would not oppose the edition of the Emergency Community (*Notgemeinschaft*). Seeberg answered in a conciliatory manner, now blaming Klibansky for spreading rumours, and added "Aktenmaterial" (documentary evidence of some sort) to his letter. In February 1935, Grundmann sent these papers back with a rather frosty repetition of his assessment that two editions were unnecessary and unfortunate. Push came to shove when his review of Seeberg's Meister Eckhart essay appeared in the fall of that year. The two scholars had a falling out; one last letter from Seeberg to Grundmann, dated 21 November 1935, made it very clear that the Berlin professor considered Grundmann simply incompetent and incapable of following his way of thinking.[47]

Although most of the controversy surfaced when Grundmann had already left the church, it is possible that the actions and opinions of Seeberg, a minister and theologian, already revolted him at an earlier time, perhaps even influencing his decision. It should be duly noted that in this conflict, a nameless and untenured junior scholar stood up against a very powerful figure in academia. Seeberg's biographers observed that he "held a thousand strings in his hand"[48] as a "Strippenzieher"[49] (that is, a "string-puller," a negative term for a manipulating and scheming power broker working in the background) who had the power to harm Grundmann and did not hesitate to do so.

In 1936, Seeberg had his pupil and employee Ernst Reffke (1912–?) publish a negative review of Grundmann's *Religious Movements* in the *Zeitschrift für Kirchengeschichte*.[50] Seeberg was one of the main editors of that journal – and it should be remembered that in the German academic tradition, these editors accepted papers and distributed reviews usually without consulting peer reviewers. The following year, Seeberg dropped the mask of scholarly composure entirely and published a venomous article moving against all his critics. He described at length the quarrel concerning the Cusanus manuscript, pouring hatred and anti-Semitic contempt against Klibansky, and then turned viciously against the critics of his Eckhart paper. He claimed that Grundmann and another scholar in Leipzig (the Protestant theologian Heinrich Bornkamm, 1901–77, hence a colleague of Seeberg) "chatter along in a high-handed manner without any understanding of Meister Eckhart," and asked rhetorically "whether such products of essentially reactionary research producing shelf-warmers are still recommendations for positions or promotions."[51] The "shelf-warmer" is, of course, Grundmann's book on *Religious Movements*, and Seeberg made it very clear that he saw no reason to give this author a university position.

Seeberg's article was truly a torrent of hatred, and when it came out in May 1937, Grundmann decided to apply for membership in the NSDAP. He had received quite a few mixed or negative reviews of his book in Germany (by contrast, reviews abroad were rather enthusiastic) and faced an uncertain future while still living on the modest income of his editorial job at the *Historische Kommission* of the Bavarian Academy of Science.[52] He also had to support his parents (i.e., his father and his stepmother), and planned to marry in August 1937. He made a request for financial support to the National Socialist Association of University Lecturers (*Nationalsozialistischer Dozentenbund*) in September 1937. Thus, the date of his application for Nazi Party membership is revealing: According to his own declaration, he applied in July 1937.[53] This application – for reasons hitherto unknown[54] – did not result in party membership, and after the war, Grundmann could rightfully claim that he was never a member of the Nazi Party. After two more years, he finally became a professor of medieval history at the University of Königsberg in East Prussia in 1939.

To sum up, Grundmann's departure from the Protestant church in October 1934 was due to personal convictions rather than political opportunism. Even before, Grundmann was not attracted to organized forms of religion or church institutions. He decided to act on his frame of mind and lay open that he preferred to view religion from the "outside," not as an opponent of religious ideas or sentiments but as an observer not bound by loyalties or confession. In this particular period after the Nazi seizure of power, he acted counter to the political mainstream and made potent enemies because he did not tolerate shallow scholarship in his special field of research. Alexander Patschovsky characterizes him as "the authentic free spirit," and thus describes his teacher's religious frame of mind in a nutshell.[55] Grundmann was no atheist, but he kept his convictions to himself and remained fiercely independent regarding his own religion.[56]

As mentioned above, Grundmann hailed Hitler's rise to power at the end of 1933, but his motives are unknown – perhaps general dislike of the Weimar democracy, relief about the end of political turmoil and the end of the communist threat, or even some attraction to Nazi politics. At that time, intense persecution of union activists, socialists, and communists was underway, and the organized boycott against Jewish shops and enterprises indicated what the Nazis were capable of doing. Grundmann did not seem impressed. On the other hand, he was not a Nazi activist. This is even confirmed by a Nazi organization. When the above-mentioned NS-*Dozentenbund* granted financial aid to Grundmann – obviously after some intense political inquiry – the file compiled on him remarks critically that he only recently became a political supporter and had been "totally indifferent" earlier, "even after 1933."[57]

Yet this does not necessarily indicate that he was distant from the regime in general. For example, there is a distinct ambiguity in his manner of writing: although he rebuked Seeberg's distorted characterization of Meister Eckhart, he used a *völkisch* vocabulary himself in articles of 1935 to point to the specific German traits of the Meister.[58] There is no doubt that over the course of time, he warmed up to the regime considerably and supported the war effort. He hailed Hitler as a man of action; the underlying Nazi ideology, in his words, was weird enough, and he gave room to the possibility that the Nazis would eventually fail, but for the time being, he evidently thought that they were the better option.[59]

What does this reveal about the man who researched and wrote *Religious Movements*? Grundmann worked on this manuscript between

1926 and 1934,[60] and there is no sign that he aligned with Nazism during this period.[61] In a letter he wrote to Willy Andreas (1884–1967, one of his employers at the *Historische Kommission*) in 1934, he outlined his project: "I intended most of all to position the activities of the church, the orders and the heretics which had been often investigated separately into the larger picture of the religious, spiritual and social movement; from thence, details can be really understood and many events can only be explained in this way."[62] This approach is characteristic of Grundmann, who did not believe in dividing up history into sections that are treated neatly apart from each other: political, economic, social, urban, and religious history; the history of individual orders; the history of sects and cults; and so forth. According to him, dissecting history only offers bits and pieces, but putting the mosaic together reveals the whole picture. This goes back to the school of Karl Lamprecht, as Robert Lerner points out in his preface to the translation of *Religious Movements*.[63] Grundmann saw the medieval church mainly as a social body spreading and forking into several branches of orders and sects. He was fundamentally undogmatic about that; his disinterest in creed let him analyse what he found with unbiased curiosity, open-mindedness, and sound judgment.

As for the book itself, it was not much of a success, indeed a shelf-warmer, as Seeberg had spitefully commented. Grundmann blamed its lacklustre appeal on the political situation; in the preface to the reprinted edition from 1961, he observed: "Those times did not favour its theme, at least not in Germany, and the times were also hostile to its marketing abroad."[64] In so saying, Grundmann implied that his research did not appeal to Nazi Germany, which is true considering the Nazi Seeberg, but there was definitely some interest in German mysticism and other topics of the book. However, the second statement about marketing the book hits the mark. The Leipzig papers reveal that Grundmann had difficulty finding a press: It was a thick manuscript, and Germany was still recovering from the Depression. He finally found an editor but had to contribute from his own savings to finance the publication. It seems that the rather expensive book did not sell well, as few scholars and even libraries in Germany and abroad were in a position to afford it. The bulk of the printed edition burned in the warehouse of the press during the bombing of Berlin in the Second World War, and as demand for it grew steadily after the war, Grundmann launched a reprint in 1961 with the addition of a new summary article.

The majority of German historians never commented on their behaviour during the years of Nazi rule and kept strict silence, as did Grundmann.[65] Yet there is a discernible break in scholarly topics and approaches in his publications before 1935 and after 1945. This "brokenness in oeuvre and conduct" has been observed for most of his colleagues as well.[66] Karl Ferdinand Werner shrewdly noted as early as 1967 that the academic establishment deemed itself far and above the perfidy of the SS and the Nazi Party while actually being their allies in one way or another, if they so desired.[67] In pursuing ambition and positions of power, a whole generation failed to accept responsibility for the outcome. Further studies of the Grundmann papers will have to deal with this issue.

NOTES

My special thanks to Jennifer Deane for correcting the English of this article. All translations from German sources and publications are mine.

1 Herbert Grundmann, *Religious Movements in the Middle Ages* (Notre Dame: University of Notre Dame Press, 1995), 1.
2 Robert Lerner, "Introduction to the Translation," in Grundmann, *Religious Movements*, ix–xxix, quote xviii.
3 Michael B. Gross, *The War against Catholicism: Liberalism and the Anti-Catholic Imagination in Nineteenth-Century Germany* (Ann Arbor: University of Michigan Press, 2004); Manuel Borutta, *Antikatholizismus: Deutschland und Italien im Zeitalter der europäischen Kulturkämpfe* (Göttingen: Vandenhoeck and Ruprecht, 2011).
4 Rebekka Habermas, "Piety, Power, and Powerlessness: Religion and Religious Groups in Germany, 1870–1945," in *The Oxford Handbook of Modern German History*, ed. Helmut Walser Smith (Oxford: Oxford University Press, 2011), 453–80; Habermas remarks that "only those Jews who entered into a symbiosis with the Protestant German majority culture" (459) via baptism could expect to be accepted; see Horst Fuhrmann, *"Sind eben alles Menschen gewesen": Gelehrtenleben im 19. und 20. Jahrhundert* (Munich: Beck, 1996), 100–15, with revealing life stories. http://141.84.81.24/cgi-bin/digilib.pl?ident=088502&dir=0&img=0&tit=Fuhrmann.
5 Universitätsarchiv Leipzig (henceforth: UAL), Nachlass Grundmann 28 fol. 92v–93r: "Geht man von vorn herein mit den Kategorien eines eigentlichen Mittelalters und einer Opposition gegen diese mittelalterliche Lebensform an die Ketzergeschichte heran, so wird man wenig weiter gelangen als die protestantischen Kirchenhistoriker, die überall Vorreformation fanden, wo sie nicht modifizierten Katholizismus feststellen konnten. Und der Unterschied von katholischen Historikern ist dann nicht sehr groß, für die alle Häresien – eben Häresien sind, Irrtümer aus Verblendung oder aus sittlichem Manko. Diese konfessionell befangene

Geschichtsschreibung beider Parteien – Preger und Denifle als ihre verdientesten Repräsentanten – hat sehr viel nutzbare Arbeit geleistet, sehr viele Quellen gehoben und manche Unterscheidungen festgelegt. Aber die geistesgeschichtliche Frage engte sich ihnen immer ein zu dem Wunsche, Wahrheitszeugen ihrer Confession zu finden. Das genügt uns nicht. Wir wollen wissen, welche geistigen Probleme in den Ketzerbewegungen akut wurden, welche religiösen und philosophischen Motive immer wieder Einzelne und ganze Kreise erregt haben, so erregt, daß sie gegen das alles tragende und alles überwölbende Kulturgefüge der katholischen Kirche zu treten wagten." The text is laced with abbreviations, which are written out in the above excerpt, but does not contain many corrections. Maybe it was a concept for a paper that was never finalized. The Leipzig inventory suggests a date around 1930. The two eminent scholars mentioned are the Protestant minister and professor of theology Wilhelm Preger (1827–96) and Father Heinrich Denifle, a Dominican (1844–1905).

6 Arno Borst, "Herbert Grundmann (1902–1970)," *Deutsches Archiv für Erforschung des Mittelalters* 26 (1970): 327–53; reprint: Herbert Grundmann, *Ausgewählte Aufsätze 1*, MGH Schriften 25, 1 (Stuttgart: Anton Hiersemann, 1976), 1–25. Translation: *Herbert Grundmann (1902–1970): Essays on Heresy, Inquisition and Literacy*, ed. Jennifer Kolpacoff Deane (York: York Medieval Press, 2019), 221–49. (Woodbridge: York Medieval Press, 2019).

7 Lerner, "Introduction," 251n36 recalls a conversation with Grundmann's son Thomas, who erroneously dates Grundmann's leaving the church "sometime in the 1920s."

8 Volker Losemann, "Classics in the Second World War," in *Nazi Germany and the Humanities: How German Academics Embraced Nazism*, ed. Wolfgang Bialas and Anson Rabinbach (London: Oneworld, 2007), 306–40; Achim Leube and Morten Hegewisch, eds., *Prähistorie und Nationalsozialismus. Die mittel- und osteuropäische Ur- und Frühgeschichtsforschung in den Jahren 1933–45*, Studien zur Wissenschafts- und Universalgeschichte 2 (Heidelberg: Synchron, 2002); Uta Halle, "Archäologie, Germanen und Wikinger im Nationalsozialismus," in *Germanenideologie: Einer völkischen Weltanschauung auf der Spur*, ed. Martin Langebach (Bonn: Bundeszentrale für politische Bildung 2020), 102–38.

9 Anne Christine Nagel, *Im Schatten des Dritten Reichs. Mittelalterforschung in der Bundesrepublik Deutschland 1945–1970*, Formen der Erinnerung 24 (Göttingen: Vandenhoeck and Ruprecht, 2005), 159 sqq. http://digi20.digitale-sammlungen.de/de/fs1/object/display/bsb00046270_00001.html.

10 Winfried Schulze and Otto Gerhard Oexle, eds., *Deutsche Historiker im Nationalsozialismus* (Frankfurt am Main: Fischer, 1999) with an enlightening introduction: Winfried Schulze, Gerd Helm, and Thomas Ott, "Deutsche Historiker im Nationalsozialismus. Beobachtungen und

Überlegungen zu einer Debatte," 11–48; and with the controversial papers of Götz Aly, "Theodor Schieder, Werner Conze oder Die Vorstufen der physischen Vernichtung," 163–82, and of Wolfgang J. Mommsen, "Vom 'Volkstumskampf' zur nationalsozialistischen Vernichtungspolitik in Osteuropa. Zur Rolle der deutschen Historiker unter dem Nationalsozialismus," 183–214; Wolfgang J. Mommsen, "'Gestürzte Denkmäler'? Die 'Fälle' Aubin, Conze, Erdmann und Schieder," in *Historische Debatten und Kontroversen im 19. und 20. Jahrhundert*, ed. Jürgen Elvert and Susanne Krauß (Stuttgart: Steiner, 2003), 96–109.

11 Benjamin Z. Kedar and Peter Herde, *A Bavarian Historian Reinvents Himself: Karl Bosl and the Third Reich* (Jerusalem: Hebrew University Magnes Press, 2011).

12 Philipp Gassert and Alan E. Steinweis, eds., *Coping with the Nazi Past: West German Debates on Nazism and Generational Conflict, 1955–1975*, Studies in German History 2 (New York and Oxford: Berghahn, 2006); one of the first scholars to question the stance of German medievalists was Karl Ferdinand Werner, *Das NS-Geschichtsbild und die deutsche Geschichtswissenschaft* (Stuttgart: Kohlhammer, 1967).

13 Nagel, *Im Schatten*; see the extensive review of Peter Herde, full of personal observations, "Mittelalterforschung in der Bundesrepublik Deutschland 1945–1970," in *Bausteine zur deutschen und italienischen Geschichte. Festschrift zum 70. Geburtstag von Horst Enzensberger*, ed. Maria Stuiber and Michele Spadaccini (Bamberg: University of Bamberg Press, 2014), 175–218. https://opus4.kobv.de/opus4-bamberg/frontdoor/index/index/docId/25030.

14 Anne Christine Nagel, "'Mit dem Herzen, dem Willen und dem Verstand dabei': Herbert Grundmann und der Nationalsozialismus," in *Nationalsozialismus in den Kulturwissenschaften 1: Fächer – Milieus – Karrieren*, Veröffentlichungen des Max-Planck-Instituts für Geschichte 200, ed. Hartmut Lehmann and Otto Gerhard Oexle (Göttingen: Vandenhoeck and Ruprecht, 2004), 593–618; Nagel, *Im Schatten*, 214 and following.

15 Herbert Grundmann, "Das hohe Mittelalter und die deutsche Kaiserzeit," in *Die Neue Propyläen-Weltgeschichte 2: Der Aufstieg des Germanentums und die Welt des Mittelalters*, ed. Willy Andreas (Berlin: Propyläen, 1940), 173–350; summarized by Nagel, "Mit dem Herzen," 608–12; critical analysis by Stephanie Kluge, "Kontinuität oder Wandel? Zur Bewertung hochmittelalterlicher Königsherrschaft durch die frühe bundesrepublikanische Mediävistik," *Frühmittelalterliche Studien* 48 (2014): 39–120, at 63–7.

16 Herbert Grundmann, "Reich und Kaisertum im Mittelalter," in *Germanische Gemeinsamkeit. Vorträge gehalten an der SS-Junkerschule Tölz*, Germanien und Europa 1, ed. Der Reichsführer-SS and SS-Hauptamt

(Posen: Feldmüller, [1944]), 73–92; this publication does not figure in the list of Hilda Lietzmann, "Bibliographie Herbert Grundmann," *Deutsches Archiv für Erforschung des Mittelalters* 26 (1970): 354–65; reprint: Herbert Grundmann, *Ausgewählte Aufsätze 1*, 26–37. Summaries and quotes from this paper: Karen Schönwälder, *Historiker und Politik. Geschichtswissenschaft im Nationalsozialismus*, Historische Studien 9 (Frankfurt and New York: Campus, 1992), 226 and following; Nagel, *Im Schatten*, 75–9.

17 See note 6 for Borst and note 2 for Lerner; Hermann Heimpel, "Herbert Grundmann," *Historische Zeitschrift* 210 (1970): 781–6.

18 Short autobiography by Walter Goetz, "Aus dem Leben eines deutschen Historikers," in Goetz, *Historiker in meiner Zeit. Gesammelte Aufsätze* (Cologne and Graz: Böhlau, 1957), 1–87; on his political activities, see Ulf Morgenstern, "Politische Publizistik Leipziger Ordinarien in der Weimarer Republik," in *Sachsens Landesuniversität in Monarchie, Republik und Diktatur*, Beiträge zur Leipziger Universitäts- und Wissenschaftsgeschichte A 3, ed. Ulrich von Hehl (Leipzig: Evangelische Verlangsanstalt, 2005), 221–37.

19 Winfried Schulze, *Deutsche Geschichtswissenschaft nach 1945*, HZ Beihefte 10 (Munich: Oldenbourg, 1989), 121 and following on the procedure of denazification. For the results concerning medievalists, see Nagel, *Im Schatten*, 26 and following. For the larger picture, see James F. Tent, *Mission on the Rhine: Reeducation and Denazification in American-Occupied Germany* (Chicago: University of Chicago Press, 1982); Frederick Taylor, *Exorcising Hitler: The Occupation and Denazification of Germany* (New York: Bloomsbury, 2011).

20 Indeed, Grundmann's non-affiliated religious status led to some intrigue during the lengthy process of his election as president of the MGH in the 1950s, as traced by Peter Herde, "Die Auseinandersetzungen über die Wahl Herbert Grundmanns zum Präsidenten der Monumenta Germaniae Historica (1957–1959)," *Zeitschrift für bayerische Landesgeschichte* 77 (2014): 69–135, at 103.

21 This is the downside of the triumphant attitude of many representatives of the churches as well as their flocks immediately after the war – self-criticism set in much later; see Karen Riechert, "Der Umgang der katholischen Kirche mit historischer und juristischer Schuld anlässlich der Nürnberger Kriegsverbrecherprozesse," in *Siegerin in Trümmern. Die Rolle der katholischen Kirche in der deutschen Nachkriegsgesellschaft*, ed. Joachim Köhler and Damian van Melis (Stuttgart, Berlin, and Cologne: Kohlhammer, 1998), 18–41; Martin Greschat, "Zwischen Aufbruch und Beharrung. Die evangelische Kirche nach dem Zweiten Weltkrieg," in *Die Zeit nach 1945 als Thema kirchlicher Zeitgeschichte*, ed. Victor Conzemius, Martin Greschat, and Hermann Kocher (Göttingen: Vandenhoeck and Ruprecht, 1988), 99–126; on the ongoing controversy, see Mark Edward

Ruff, *The Battle for the Catholic Past in Germany, 1945–1980* (Cambridge: Cambridge University Press, 2017).

22 This argument was introduced as early as 23 August 1945, by the German Bischop's Conference of Fulda; see Konrad Repgen, "Die Erfahrung des Dritten Reiches und das Selbstverständnis der deutschen Katholiken nach 1945," in Victor Conzemius et al., *Die Zeit nach 1945*, 127–79, pastoral letter 161 and following.

23 As observed by Mark Edward Ruff, "Katholische Kirche und Entnazifizierung," in *Die katholische Kirche im Dritten Reich. Eine Einführung*, ed. Ruff and Christoph Kösters (Freiburg, Herder, 2011), 142–53, at 145.

24 Peter Rassow (1889–1961), a liberal like Walter Goetz and not a friend of the regime, relates to Siegfried A. Kaehler (1885–1963) his experiences with the American occupying forces in a letter from 31 May 1945. Rassow felt the duty to explain to the Americans that "party membership is not at all an adequate criterion for Nazi spirit" ("Da war es die erste Aufgabe, ihnen klar zu machen, daß etwa die Zugehörigkeit zur Partei gar kein hinreichendes Kennzeichen für Nazi-Geist ist"). The whole letter is in print: Schulze, *Deutsche Geschichtswissenschaft*, 66–74, quote at 65 and following. In the process of denazification, formal party membership was, consequently, deemed insufficient evidence to induce punishment; see ibid., 129 and Herde, "Mittelalterforschung," 183 and following.

25 Church membership dropped in significant numbers between 1937 and 1941; see Sven Granzow, Bettina Müller-Sidibé, and Andrea Simml, "Gottvertrauen und Führerglaube," in *Skepsis und Führervertrauen im Nationalsozialismus*, ed. Götz Aly (Frankfurt am Main: Fischer, 2006), 38–58; at the end of the war in May 1945, however, 95 per cent of the German population – including many party members – still belonged to either the Catholic or the Protestant church; see Armin Nolzen, "Nationalsozialismus und Christentum. Konfessionsgeschichtliche Befunde zur NSDAP," in *Zerstrittene "Volksgemeinschaft." Glaube, Konfession und Religion im Nationalsozialismus*, ed. Nolzen and Manfred Gailus (Göttingen: Vandenhoeck and Ruprecht, 2011), 151–79.

26 Klaus Vondung, *Magie und Manipulation: Ideologischer Kult und politische Religion des Nationalsozialismus* (Göttingen: Vandenhoeck and Ruprecht, 1971), 104 and following with many examples of such celebrations and their lack of appeal to the general population; Michael H. Kater, *Das "Ahnenerbe" der SS 1935–1945: Ein Beitrag zur Kulturpolitik des Dritten Reiches*, Studien zur Zeitgeschichte 6, 4th ed. (Munich: Oldenbourg, 2006). https://www.degruyter.com/viewbooktoc/product/228710?null.

27 UAL, Nachlass Grundmann 138, fol. 50–52, quote fol. 50v: "zumal ich nicht durch Parteizugehörigkeit usw. politisch belastet bin. Aber man läßt

es mich allerdings seit meiner Rückkehr unverhohlen spüren und hören, daß ich diesen anderen 'Schönheitsfehler' habe, als sei das kaum weniger schlimm."

28 Ibid.: "Die Vertreter der Bekenntniskirche dagegen fand ich in ihrer Glaubenshaltung durchaus konsequent, aufrichtig und aller Achtung wert; nur wurde mir durch ihre Entschiedenheit umso deutlicher bewußt, daß ich ihren Glauben nicht teilen, kurz gesagt: das Athanasianum und die Confessio Augustana nicht ehrlich 'für wahr halten' und also nicht mit gutem Gewissen, ohne zu heucheln, unterschreiben kann. Ich hatte und habe zu viel Sinn und Ehrfurcht für echten Glauben, um gegen meine Überzeugung, nur um keinen Anstoß zu erregen, so zu tun, als ob ich ihn teilte. Deshalb, aus dem Bedürfnis nach Ehrlichkeit und Klarheit, bin ich im Oktober 1934 aus der Kirche ausgetreten." Grundmann repeats this reasoning in the questionnaire of his denazification of 1947: "am 26. X. 34 ausgetreten, weil ich bei der Spaltung der evang. Kirche in 'Deutsche Christen' und 'Bekenntniskirche' keinem von beiden aus ehrlicher Überzeugung zugehören konnte." (Landesarchiv Nordrhein-Westfalen, Abt. Rheinland, NW 1039-G 357, fol. 1v, p.2).

29 "Bekenntnis der Professoren an den deutschen Universitäten und Hochschulen zu Adolf Hitler und dem nationalsozialistischen Staat" (Dresden: Limpert, presumably 1934). https://archive.org/details /bekenntnisderprooonatiuoft; the manifesto was printed together with translations into several languages; Grundmann's name: p. 135. As he was not yet an employee of the University of Leipzig, he figures among "Einzelne Wissenschaftler"; Anselm Faust, "Professoren für die NSDAP. Zum politischen Verhalten der Hochschullehrer 1932/33," in *Erziehung und Schulung im Dritten Reich 2: Hochschule, Erwachsenenbildung*, Veröffentlichungen der Historischen Kommission der Deutschen Gesellschaft für Erziehungswissenschaft 4,2, ed. Manfred Heinemann (Stuttgart: Klett-Cotta, 1980), 31–49.

30 Habermas, "Piety, Power," 468–70.

31 Manfred Gailus, "Die kirchliche Machtergreifung der 'Glaubensbewegung Deutsche Christen' im Jahr 1933," in *Täter und Komplizen in Theologie und Kirchen 1933–1945*, ed. Gailus (Göttingen: Wallstein, 2015), 62–80.

32 Habermas, "Piety, Power," 463; Manfred Gailus, "Zur Einführung," in *Täter und Komplizen*, 15–31, at 15: In 1933-4, for the first time since 1918, there were more entries than exits.

33 Kyle Jantzen, *Faith and Fatherland: Parish Politics in Hitler's Germany* (Minneapolis: Fortress, 2008), 50: "Saxon Lutherans flocked to their churches" with significant numbers of re-entries. Jantzen traces the development by comparing the histories of three congregations, one of which is in Pirna near Dresden in Saxony.

34 Martin Onnasch, *Um kirchliche Macht und geistliche Vollmacht. Ein Beitrag zur Geschichte des Kirchenkampfes in der Kirchenprovinz Sachsen 1932–1945*, Greifswalder theologische Forschungen 20 (Frankfurt/Main: Lang, 2010), 294–7 on the fight between several church governances in Saxony.
35 Ibid., 91.
36 See note 28.
37 Stephan Bitter, "Umdeutung des Christentums. Der baltische Theologe Erich Seeberg im Nationalsozialismus," in *Deutschbalten, Weimarer Republik und Drittes Reich* 1, 2nd ed., ed. Michael Garleff (Cologne, Weimar, Vienna: Böhlau, 2008), 267–96; Manfred Gailus, "Der Berliner Kirchenhistoriker Erich Seeberg als nationalsozialistischer Theologiepolitiker," in *Täter und Komplizen*, 216–43.
38 *Theologische Literaturzeitung* 53 (1928): 585 and following.
39 Erich Seeberg, *Meister Eckhart*, Philosophie und Geschichte 50 (Tübingen: Mohr, 1934), 9 on "the soul of the Meister speaking in his German writings" ("so kann man wohl fragen, … ob nicht grade die Seele des Meisters in den deutschen Schriften spricht"). It should be remembered that this was not a purely scholarly discussion; in 1930, Alfred Rosenberg's infamous "Der Mythus des 20. Jahrhunderts" had come out in which Meister Eckhart figures among the witnesses to the superior Aryan race.
40 Thomas Kaufmann, "'Anpassung' als historiographisches Konzept und als theologiepolitisches Programm. Der Kirchenhistoriker Erich Seeberg in der Zeit der Weimarer Republik und des 'Dritten Reiches,'" in *Evangelische Kirchenhistoriker im 'Dritten Reich,'* Veröffentlichungen der Wissenschaftlichen Gesellschaft für Theologie 21, ed. Kaufmann and Harry Oelke (Gütersloh: Kaiser, 2002), 122–272, 197 and following.
41 *Historische Zeitschrift* 152 (1935): 572–80; Grundmann warns of a "distorted picture not in accord with the true figure of Eckhart or, in short, with his texts," 573 ("verzeichnetes Bild …, das mit der wahren Gestalt Eckharts oder, schlichter gesagt: mit den Texten nicht in Einklang zu bringen ist"); his conclusion on 579: Eckharts "real frame of mind" ("eigentliche Lehrmeinung") should be mainly derived from his Latin works ("die lateinischen Schriften werden dabei die wichtigsten Dienste leisten müssen").
42 See Kaufmann, "Anpassung," 194–7 on the controversy and 195n379 on Seeberg's intrigues against the Meiner press.
43 Erich Seeberg, review of: Magistri Eckardi Opera Latina auspiciis instituti sanctae Sabinae in Urbe ad codicum fidem edita. Fasc. 1: Super oratione dominica, edidit R. Klibansky, Leipzig: Meiner, 1934, *Deutsche Literaturzeitung* 55 (1938): 1777–81; this issue of the journal (Heft 38) came out on 23 September 1934. On the surface, the review is polite and benevolent ("wohlgelungen," "well done"), but Seeberg accuses Klibansky

of showing off with a far too extensive commentary ("Methode des Luxus," both quotes: 1780), a barely disguised anti-Semitic slander.
44 UAL, Nachlass Grundmann 98, 3 fol. 87, a copy of the original letter.
45 UAL, Nachlass Grundmann 98, 3 fol. 16: "Wir müssen das umsomehr bedauern, als die Eckart-Ausgabe der Notgemeinschaft von Partei und Staat unterstützt und unter dem Gesichtspunkt eines wahrhaft volksbildenden Werkes bearbeitet wird. Wir machen Sie also darauf aufmerksam, dass eine Einstellung gegen diese Eckart-Ausgabe der Notgemeinschaft gleichzeitig als Kritik an Partei und Staat aufzufassen ist und wir Sie in aller Form vor derartigen Äußerungen Ihrerseits warnen! Heil Hitler."
46 A letter dating from 22 December 1934, UAL, Nachlass Grundmann 98, 1 fol. 48 and 49.
47 Exchange of letters between Grundmann and Seeberg in 1935: UAL, Nachlass Grundmann 98, 3 fol. 90–9.
48 Bitter, "Umdeutung," 267: "Seeberg hatte in Berlin ... tausend Fäden in der Hand."
49 Gailus, "Zur Einführung," 29.
50 *Zeitschrift für Kirchengeschichte* 55 (1936): 699–701.
51 Erich Seeberg, "Die verlorene Handschrift. Zur Geschichte der Meister Eckhart-Ausgabe," *Nationalsozialistische Monatshefte* 8 (1937): 386–97 (Heft 86 from May 1937), 395: "Aber dagegen will ich mich mit aller Energie wehren, daß in Deutschland Kritiker auftreten, die von Eckhart und seinen Deutern sehr hochmütig daherreden, ohne irgend etwas von ihm zu verstehen.... Herr Grundmann und Herr Bornkamm – beide in Leipzig – reden in ebenso anmaßender wie abgestandener Weise über Eckhart und hüllen sich je nach dem in den Mantel des 'objektiven' Priesters der Wissenschaft oder der Religion.... Sind eigentlich derartige Erzeugnisse einer nun einmal wirklich der Substanz nach reaktionären Wissenschaft, die sich mit dem Hervorbringen von Ladenhütern erschöpft, noch immer Empfehlungen für Berufungen oder Beförderungen?"
52 I am currently preparing an article on the genesis of the *Religious Movements* and the reception of the book, which will appear in the journal *Mitteilungen des Instituts für Österreichische Geschichtsforschung*.
53 Universitätsarchiv Münster, Best. 10 (Kurator) Nr. 2310: Grundmann's personal file comprising the file of Königsberg, which was forwarded to Münster. The file contains a list of 28 June 1939, with Grundmann's signature, specifying membership of the party and its branches. He states that a Leipzig Ortsgruppe of the party supported his application of party membership dating from 25 July 1937, but that the execution was delayed without his fault.

54 Several search requests to the Bundesarchiv at Berlin Lichterfelde and to the Staatsarchive of Leipzig and Dresden gave no results; moreover, a great deal of file evidence was destroyed during the war; see note 57.
55 Alexander Patschovsky, "'Studi su Gioacchino da Fiore' di Herbert Grundmann," *Florensia* 3–4 (1989–90): 113–19, a lecture given at the presentation of the Italian translation of Grundmann's dissertation. Patschovsky states that Grundmann opened a new page of Joachim's contribution and that from this page "diviene visibile l'unica forma di orientamento normativo della propria esistenza che sia possibile all'uomo moderno senza vincoli confessionali o religiosi: appunto la forma storica. Questa era la situazione personale di Grundmann che si misconosce in modo abbastanza radicale, se in uno come lui – l'autentico spirito libero che pensa in maniere secolare – si ritiene de poterla ricondurre a residui di protestantesimo" (119).
56 Peter Herde relates personal information from the Grundmann family: Far from being atheists, the parents had the children brought up with religious instruction; all three were baptized at their own request, probably as adolescents before their confirmation. Annelies Grundmann was a Protestant church member most of her life but gave up formal membership in an advanced age, Herde, "Auseinandersetzungen," 71n9. Herde considers it highly unlikely that Grundmann left the church for political reasons and assumes that his motivation was based on his personal religion; see also Herde, "Mittelalterforschung," 206.
57 Johannes Piepenbrink, "Das Seminar für Mittlere Geschichte des Historischen Instituts 1933–1945," in *Sachsens Landesuniversität*, 363–83, quote 374: "erst seit kurzem sich politisch betätigt, früher, auch nach 1933 noch vollkommen indifferent." The document is: Bundesarchiv Berlin Lichterfelde (former Document Center) R 9361 VI, 957; the quote is from a handwritten note, image 279 of the microfilm. On images 304 and 305, there is a letter from the "Hauptstelle" at Munich (no date, but apparently early in 1938) to one of the Dozentenbund's officials at Leipzig, asking to observe Grundmann's political development very closely ("Ich bitte Sie den Bewerber weiterhin scharf im Auge zu behalten, um seine politische Weiterentwicklung verfolgen zu können") because of his too liberal stance ("auf liberalistischem Boden stand"); the letter is partially damaged. The Dozentenbund's obvious distrust might have been a reason why Grundmann was not accepted into the Nazi Party.
58 Herbert Grundmann, "Meister Eckhart," in *Die Großen Deutschen* 1, ed. Willy Andreas and Wilhelm von Scholz (Berlin: Propyläen, 1935), 230–45, reprint in *Ausgewählte Aufsätze*, 278–94: Eckhart's impact "in die Tiefe seiner deutschen Volksgemeinschaft" (287) because of their shared

"Glaube aus der Tiefe und Eigenart deutschen Wesens" (289). The style of this paper, directed to a broader, non-scholarly audience, can only be described as bordering on cheesy; by way of contrast, Grundmann's paper of the same year, 1935, published a year later in "Dante und Meister Eckhart," *Deutsches Dante-Jahrbuch* 18 (1936): 166–88, reprint in *Ausgewählte Aufsätze*, 295–312, is much more sober, with an emphasis on the Christian and orthodox roots of the Meister and a clear dismissal of "Germanic" origins of his thought (308): "Sicherlich schießt man heute manchmal weit über das Ziel hinaus, wenn man in Eckharts Denken gar zu handgreiflich nach den Spuren eines arteigenen deutschen oder gar eines vorchristlich-germanischen Glaubens sucht, die nun einmal in seinem christlich-katholischen Bewußtsein nicht zu finden sind."

59 UAL Nachlass Grundmann 98, 2 fol. 134–7, letter to Johannes Kühn (1887–1973) from 15 March 1934, one of Grundmann's teachers at Leipzig; a short quote in Piepenbrink, "Das Seminar," 375.

60 Borst, "Grundmann," 5: mentions nine years of work on the book; this would cover the years 1926 to 1934, from the initial ideas and outlines to the preparation of the manuscript for print.

61 Nagel, "Mit dem Herzen," 595 observes that, on first sight, the book reveals no contiguousness to National Socialism ("auf den ersten Blick keine Nähe zum Nationalsozialismus"); she does not mention a dissenting second look.

62 UAL Nachlass Grundmann 98, 1 fol. 4r: "Es kam mir dabei hauptsächlich darauf an, die im Einzelnen so oft untersuchten Vorgänge der Kirchen-, Ordens- und Ketzergeschichte endlich einmal in den großen Zusammenhang der religiösen, geistigen und sozialen Bewegung hineinzustellen, aus dem das Einzelne erst voll verständlich und auch viele Tatbestände erst ganz aufgehellt werden."

63 Lerner, "Introduction," xvi.

64 Grundmann, *Religious Movements*, xxvii.

65 In his denazification questionnaire, Grundmann did not, as he was requested, list in detail his publications of the Nazi period but claimed that they were "purely scientific" and "absolutely not political in nature" ("nur rein wissenschaftliche (underlined), ganz unpolitische (underlined) Veröffentlichungen, Vorlesungen, Vorträge": Landesarchiv Nordrhein-Westfalen, Abt. Rheinland, NW 1039-G 357, fol. 5v/p. 10).

66 Schulze et al., "Deutsche Historiker," 25: "Gebrochenheit im Werk und Verhalten der Zeitzeugen."

67 Werner, *NS-Geschichtsbild*, 73: "Hier sehe ich die große Mitschuld der deutschen Patrioten, die sich weit erhaben dünken über die Niedertracht von SS und Partei, deren Verbündete sie doch – und nicht mehr nur in einem äußerlichen Sinne – waren, wenn sie solches wollten."

3 Francis of Assisi, the *Vita Apostolica*, and the Roman Church: Rethinking the Paradigms[1]

AMANDA POWER

One of the most iconic images of the medieval period is Giotto's painting of Saint Francis of Assisi and the birds.[2] The saint stands with a companion, bending forward against a wide golden sky to preach to rows of enraptured birds. One hand is held out in blessing – the gesture at once gentle and assured. More birds are arriving all the time; many different species are represented. With all the charm of this odd, tender scene, Francis is the embodiment of idealized Christian rationality, for in this place and time, and perhaps all places and times, his is a profoundly rational act. It disrupts complacency, unsettles expectation, and provokes disturbing recognitions of truth. Through the rupture it opens, apostolic power pours again into quotidian reality, bringing healing and the promise of eternal peace to a broken world.[3]

Much of the scholarship on the history of the religious life associated with Francis has been driven by fascination with the disharmony between this luminous figure and the messy human business of developing the Order of Friars Minor, securing its right to exist and defining the terms of its existence in the sprawling, competitive, legalistic, materialistic societies of the medieval Latin West. The conventional tale of this order's history is told in the tragic mode.[4] It is one of charisma institutionalized, holy inspiration tamed, harsh poverty softened into laxity, humility dissolved into pride of intellect, unity of purpose fractured, and a grieving saint fleeing from betrayals by his own followers with prophecies of disaster in his mouth. And yet, so the story goes, through his flight and subsequent stigmata, Francis retained in himself the fierce purity of the apostle, so intensely bound into Christ that the wounds inflicted by man on God blossomed in his human flesh. It was this quality with which he imbued the Roman Church through his vow of absolute obedience to the pope and his order by the example of his life.[5]

This is an old and enduring narrative in which the explanatory paradigms associated with hagiography, devotional historiography, confessional agendas, interpretative battles within the Roman Church, fascination with exceptional individuals, romantic medievalism, and even sociological theory – notably Max Weber's analysis of charisma's role in institution-building – are now layered intractably together. All these paradigms position the person credited with the founding of a religious life as the embodiment of its "inspiration," its "charisma," and the key to determining the nature of its origins and emerging character. Their continuing interpretative influence presents a significant difficulty for academic historians because they start at what is, from our perspective, the wrong end. They begin with the unstable nexus – Saint Francis of Assisi – of multiple ideas that have been crafted and negotiated over the centuries by skilled propagandists, including, of course, Francis himself. For well over a century, critical work within these paradigms has focused on disputing over which elements of this richly imagined construct might be treated as reliable evidence of historical events and personalities, and the criteria by which such judgments might be reached – a debate seen in the field as so significant that it is known as *"the* Franciscan question."[6] The wider historical context has been relevant to this discussion chiefly as it may support or elaborate an interpretation of Francis's life and legacy. As we will see, these paradigms have been consciously resistant to the implications of Herbert Grundmann's early contextual work on the multiple "religious movements" of the period, among which he included those of women. Aside from Dominic, comparisons with the narrative arcs around other founding or prominent men and women, whether subsequently deemed orthodox or heterodox, have rarely been undertaken within this literature.[7] This makes Francis appear exceptional and obscures the ways in which he and his followers drew on both contemporary and long-standing strategies for creating holy authority.

All this is made more problematic by the tendency of the explanatory paradigms to link Francis in one way or another to Jesus Christ and thereby to the heart of Christian authenticity.[8] Similarly, they take the view that Francis, more than any other human since the original apostles, practiced the *vita apostolica* – a set of behaviours imagined as life lived in the potent liminal region between mutable human time and God's unchanging eternity. Many who write about Francis also regard him as a saint in the Roman Catholic sense: possessing, therefore, absolute qualities of holiness beyond human critique, continuing consciousness, and contemporary intercessory powers. These connections imbue him with a spiritual, moral, or ethical significance that transcends place and time and frequently permits him to slip from the category of history into the far more analytically elusive field of "religion."[9] The preoccupation with the difficulty of recovering "the historical Francis" from the array of surviving texts seems, perversely, to have legitimized this slippage rather than raising the alarm against it. Uncertainty about the detail seems to facilitate interpretations based on the explanatory paradigms. Even Grundmann, who consciously sought to evade confessional pitfalls, relied on hagiographies of Francis for his reconstruction of papal handling of the early community, a tendency that has persisted in the literature.[10] His "religious movements" were largely undifferentiated in their essentials: He was content to accept that they emerged in pursuit of "Christian" ideals and therefore looked much the same wherever they appeared. It was their very uniformity that made them a "movement."[11] The result is that where the various explanatory paradigms of Franciscan historiography meet Grundmann's "movement," we find a peculiar unstated consensus that the historical facts of Francis's life and thought are difficult to establish but certainly constitute an especially authentic form of Christianity. This doctrinally correct but intellectually indefensible position has tended to find its way into studies of many kinds when a brief account of the origins of the "Franciscan" orders and the *vita apostolica* is required, including in studies of later developments in the orders' histories.[12] When this happens, historians are, often unwittingly, producing "emic" histories: histories in which the analytic categories are the product of the world view and agendas of the institution that is being studied, rather than derived from "etic" independent methodologies and questions.[13] The implications of this unnoticed and unremarked situation for our general understanding of medieval religion and society are extremely serious and will be drawn out in what follows.

Have these same tendencies operated among specialists working on the early decades of the orders? A great deal of work has focused on the orders' internal histories that goes beyond these paradigms in a variety of directions. There are now studies in a number of languages that examine, among other matters, discrete aspects of institutions, organization, economies, and structures; communities and convents rather than individuals; and the growth and diverse experiences of different provinces. Many of these have been explored through comparisons with other religious orders and in relation to aspects of wider society, particularly Italian urban environments and local economies, the Capetian dynasty, and Latin interactions with non-Christian populations. New studies offer the opportunity to make comparisons with currents in spirituality across the regions subject to the Roman Church, including individuals and groups that resisted categorization and institutionalization – in contrast to Francis's ambition to achieve ecclesiastical approval and the privileges that came with it.[14] There are also extensive literatures on topics such as learning and the universities or the practicalities of preaching and pastoral care.

All this material, especially cumulatively, offers a much richer picture of complexities and practical functioning than the Francis-centred framework. However, since it generally tends to accept, at least implicitly, the notion of some degree of original inspiration that was personified in Francis and distinct from quotidian practice, it has not overtly disrupted the underlying assumptions already outlined. However, it is suggestive. We can see, for example, that the friars had an almost ubiquitous presence in the political activities of the Latin West – secular and ecclesiastical – from within a decade of the confirmation of their rule. Women were ahead of the friars in developing performative spiritual practices in urban environments, and they might have had greater freedom to retain the informal and improvisational qualities described in Franciscan hagiographic literature.[15] Most of the men and women associated with the orders were members of social elites and in various ways supported strategies for enhancing and extending the authority of those groups in society – for when moral authority is based on *renouncing* wealth, it is effectively placed beyond the reach of those with no wealth to renounce. They wielded considerable individual and collective power; their impact was felt in the courts, churches, and cities of the Latin West and was carried outwards into Eurasia and northern Africa, where friars frequently represented the Latin West in its official dealings and fragile lines of communication brought their ideas as far as China and India. They would subsequently play significant roles in the colonization of the Americas.[16]

The conflicted and contested nature of the internal and public discourses surrounding the "apostolic" way of life of these groups has been regarded as evidence of the difficulties of institutionalizing "inspiration" or "charisma" – which often really means holiness, even "goodness." These are – without Weber's methodological subtlety – treated as objectively benign, recognizable, and permanent categories, rather than the contextually dependent, often normative in their essentials, and sometimes repressive subjectivities that they are.[17] Yet, if we draw on studies that look beyond these discussions and reflect on the extraordinary influence exercised by these men and women across diverse regions and different social strata, the possibility of a different interpretation emerges: that of a strategic fluidity and adaptability; a repurposing of that self-consciously fierce ethical engagement that had long served to provide the religious with many kinds of legitimization within their pursuit of cultural hegemony.[18] This kind of power – the power of the *vita apostolica* – was not the violent coercive aspect of church and state power but the supple, quiet power that ran through, beyond, around, and sometimes against more explicit operations.[19] It enriched and productively complicated these operations, with its apparent interpretative independence, critique, and creativity. There were few tangible measures of any particular instance of its success – the repentant, excitable crowds of one day were the sinners of the next – but this mercurial quality was much of its point. Faith, as envisioned in this place and time, was not intended to be static or comfortable. It was meant to be unstable, an arena in which the refractory soul continuously struggled to subdue itself to obedience to authority in this life and the next.[20] By these means – by the performative exposure of the difficulties of individual and collective striving after salvation – popular investment in the governing ideologies and rationalities of the Latin West was deepened.

Examining the *vita apostolica* and the activities of "Franciscan" men and women in this light also requires conversations that "internal" histories of the orders have often eschewed. Scholars have tended to focus on life, individuals, texts, ideas, and internal processes, disputes, and conflicts, usually based on material generated with only limited attention to wider contexts and consequences. This approach has enabled evasion of engagement with studies of the involvement of these groups with multiple forms of persecution, including torture and judicial murder, especially of heterodox thinkers and Jews; the promotion of attacks on Muslims and others through crusade preaching; the dissemination of misogynistic ideas and practices in universities, public preaching, and other contexts; the intensification of disciplinary surveillance of the population; and the suppression and "re-education" of dissenters.[21] Further, given the importance of the figure of Francis to the Westernized ecological imagination during the current times, when radically altering this imagination is essential to our collective future, there must be a fresh examination of the attitudes towards planetary life associated with him and their contemporary use by those intent on promoting the same anthropocentric cosmologies and discredited ontologies.[22] Through these complicating analyses, we can begin to discern the outlines of an unsettlingly different type of "religious movement" and begin to ask what it was doing, for whom, to what ends, and with what immediate and longer-term consequences for society.

To be able to develop such inquiries as fully as they require, it is essential to scrutinize critically the paradigms and agendas that have silently shaped and continue to inform the scholarship on which medieval historians draw to write about the orders associated with the figure of Francis and the wider religious impulses to which they may belong. We can trouble, reconceive, or even reject the consciously transhistorical and transcultural constructions of "religious movements" and the *vita apostolica* – constructions designed over the centuries, as we will see, to retain ideological command of the past and unwittingly reproduced by academic historians.[23] The notion of the *vita apostolica* has been particularly important for connecting the orders and the movement, solidifying their standing as virtuous groups innately connected to early Christianity and positioning them in relation to the Roman Church. The implications of a reappraisal of these ideas are, therefore, far-reaching for our understanding of the contours of life and power in this period and beyond. It should be emphasized that this essay is not intended to be a bibliographical or historiographical survey or to provide additional comment on well-known difficulties in the field of Franciscan studies. An extensive literature already serves these ends. Instead, it seeks to stimulate critical reflection on the specific issue of the framing and paradigmatic assumptions in the study of the Franciscan orders, medieval institutions, and the purposes and patterns of behaviour and thought that we call "religious."

The Problem of the People

While Francis speaks to the birds in Giotto's image, his *socius* stands behind him, identically clad in the habit of the Minors but upright, watchful, witnessing the whole scene, as the saint is intent on the birds. This other friar has no halo about his head, and the story is very plainly not about him, even if it is unfolding for his salvation and for all creation – and therefore requires his witness to be meaningful. Much of the founder-centred scholarship has taken broadly this view of those understood as Francis's first companions and subsequent followers. It tends to resist the possibility suggested by David Flood that Francis and the brothers worked out the early form of their life through collective discussion of their experiences and that they were common authors of their Rule and other texts usually attributed solely to Francis.[24] If those roles are denied to them, they appear to be of little concern to this line of research except as they testify to and amplify the founder's ideas.[25]

Instead, interest has focused on those involved in the official processes of interpreting and implementing ideas considered to have originated with Francis. These were predominantly the ministers and theologians of the male order, together with high-ranking clergy, particularly the order's cardinal-protectors. Despite the prominence in the historical record of these men, it is the perceived character of their relationship with Francis's legacy that has determined their narrative or analytic function in the histories of their order.[26] The scholarship places later innovations that seem "Franciscan" as originating with Francis.[27] Indications that members of the orders were choosing, or being directed by various forces, to develop different ways to envisage their lives and work are often considered as evidence of their failure to be "Franciscan," of an order going in a direction not sanctioned by its founder, rather than pursued as important lines of inquiry in their own right.[28]

Proximity to Francis has been an important criterion for significance. Where direct personal connections with Francis are harder to see, or do not exist, as in the case of most of the groups of women later subsumed into a single "Franciscan" order, aspects of their life and history unconnected with Francis are simply omitted from mainstream narratives, apparently leaving little to say.[29] When the women are discussed at all, beyond the recent and often discrete field devoted to Clare of Assisi and her sisters, or scattered studies of particular houses, it is chiefly in the negative terms of their limitations and difference, their inability to be fully "Franciscan," and the burden they imposed on the male order.[30] The variety of their experience is flattened out in a peculiar language of gender essentialism.[31] Grundmann's demonstration that women across the Latin West had been experimenting with similar ideas to those of Francis before he adopted them seems not to be part of the story.[32] Similarly, there is a strong geographical bias in these kinds of studies. In comparison to Italy, little attention has been given to the distinctive histories of provinces beyond the Alps, in central and eastern Europe, the eastern Mediterranean, or elsewhere.[33]

It seems, then, that it has often been unclear how – and perhaps why – scholars might study the diverse, mobile, connected, inventive communities of men and women who pursued a multitude of purposes and ambitions throughout the fabric of Latin societies and far beyond.[34] Yet these are, one would think, people who must be studied both on their own terms and in a wide range of contexts, if historians are not to risk badly misunderstanding the character and dynamics of many aspects of the period.

Perhaps the greatest challenge faced when this is attempted is the terminology for describing the women and men of the orders now associated with Francis.[35] All the available words are the products of normative processes of definition. These processes have themselves created emotional, pragmatic, and institutional loyalties to particular terms. "Franciscan" ties the identities of the modern orders together but also confines them within programmatic interpretations that have little to do with the medieval past. These interpretations are designed in part to elude the weight of history by perpetually relocating the order's meaning in its founding myths.[36] The term was not used in the thirteenth century. Applied anachronistically, as is common practice, it obscures the crucial questions of the forms in which, or even the extent to which, Francis mattered, either to those who entered "his" orders or to the rest of society. Early papal documents do not necessarily mention him when promoting the orders externally, nor do all the early external accounts of the new orders; the early forms of life for San Damiano do not refer to him, and we have extensive writings from members of the order about their concerns and objectives in which he is never mentioned at all.[37]

The label is particularly problematic in the case of the women.[38] Even Clare in her letters to Agnes of Prague focused on her love for the figures of Christ and Mary, not Francis.[39] There is a similar set of difficulties in using variants of Clare's name, such as "Poor Clares" or "Clarissans," to describe the women. The "Order of Friars Minor" reflects an earlier nomenclature, a commitment knowingly chosen by those who entered that order after its official establishment, but is no help for integrating women. For them, almost any definition gives the victory to individuals and processes that operated in spite of the women's own preferences.[40] Referring to women variously as the "second order" and "tertiaries" is largely anachronistic, while both endorsing the gendered hierarchies that were at that time being more intensively formulated by clerics and monks and entrenching all the problems of an authenticity that diminishes as it becomes more remote from Francis.[41] A letter of 1216, written by Jacques de Vitry, described "many people of both sexes" whom he encountered in the surrounding region during a visit to the papal curia. He reported that they were called "lesser brothers and lesser sisters."[42] A number of historians have used this as evidence of the character of the early formation of the orders, and it certainly presents an attractive solution to the terminological problem. However, among other objections, we do not know of whom he was speaking.[43] There is, in short, no satisfactory solution. We are without a collective noun that places all these people on equal terms and allows for interpretations less determined by a founding figure. Historians working on them are forced into using a language that was designed to do precisely what it still does: imposes meanings, categories, and hierarchies on them while making alternative interpretations difficult to contemplate and harder to discuss.[44]

The Problem of the Paradigms

The next problem is the restrictive nature of the paradigms that appear to offer ways to escape the focus on Francis of Assisi and "his" legacy. The most influential remains that proposed by Grundmann. He explicitly situated his work as an attempt to move beyond the existing confessional approaches to religious history, with their "limits and weaknesses [that have] weighty consequences for comprehending historical development as a whole," and their neglect of women's experiences.[45] Within a few decades of its 1935 publication, his book had become, as Van Engen put it, "the foundation for the historical study of medieval religious life," and has for a long time served as at least the basis for an answer to the problem of how to go beyond Francis as the prime mover in Franciscan history.[46] Grundmann attempted to subordinate the role of charismatic individuals to the wider impulses of "religious movements" that sprang up throughout Christian lands in the late eleventh and twelfth centuries. In his view, these movements were dedicated to the pursuit of an identifiable set of practices and aspirations that together comprised the *vita apostolica*, the apostolic life.[47] He conceived these movements as pressing on the ecclesiastical hierarchy from outside and as having an uncertain relationship with existing orthodoxies. In this reading, the papal curia distrusted the various movements since their way of life constituted criticism of the hierarchical church. The consequence was that many of those that could not readily be transformed into stable religious houses were condemned as heretical, but Pope Innocent III tried implementing a new policy following his 1198 election. He focused on including these movements in the church by encouraging them to become religious orders obedient to the papacy, obedience being the principal measure of orthodoxy. Thus, although Francis's ideas had much in common with twelfth-century "movements," including elements that had earlier been treated as heretical, his own order emerged within the protective context of Innocent's new policy and became, probably, its greatest success.

While some historians of the Franciscan orders found Grundmann's work broadly persuasive, its rejection by others has created the rather misleading impression that his thesis *was* a distinctively different paradigm. The idea that Francis belonged to a world of similar "movements" struggled for traction in works devoted to his order, most likely because it ran against an array of interests invested in emphasizing his exceptionalism. In this context, there has perhaps been an instinctive dislike for the feasible inference that Francis's orthodoxy was produced by Innocent's strategy rather than by the authenticity of his endeavour, or indeed that heresy and orthodoxy might be subjective categories deployed strategically to test and secure what really mattered: obedience.[48] However, what was missed in this response, and what made it possible for many historians of the order to include aspects of

Grundmann's thesis as background, was that his essentialized notion of the *vita apostolica* underwrote theirs.

This was observed by David Flood, who objected to Grundmann's model on the grounds that the lives of the early brethren had little to do with what he saw as the "cultural model" of the *vita apostolica*. Flood's view was that theirs was a distinctive, localized response to the values dominating civic society in Assisi and its environs. Grundmann's conception was too remote from social and economic realities – and in this respect, Flood thought, no great departure from mainstream Franciscan historiography.[49] Flood considered that describing Francis as another person pursuing the *vita apostolica* "satisfies the need to see Francis as a saint rather than a radical. [It made him] good rather than critical."[50] Nonetheless, while most of these responses to Grundmann within this field aimed to restore the focus to Francis and the little group in Assisi, in practice the dialogue itself had broadened the contextual thinking around Francis, and much work on the order continues to use Grundmann and the various studies that have explored and built on his thesis.[51]

The interpretative framework in which *vita apostolica* "movements" constituted the most dynamic element in the religious life of the period received support in the 1950s from Marie-Dominique Chenu's account of the twelfth century as a time of "evangelical awakening."[52] Chenu imagined a spontaneous, widespread return to the gospel and the primitive, apostolic life of the church by the laity and some religious. It initially bypassed ecclesiastical institutions and conventions, but then – precisely through the process of confrontation with society that had been demanded by Christ but eschewed by monks – flooded the sterile, monasticized, propertied, worldly church with the authentic vigour of a true, evangelical Christianity. The result was a "vibrant church and a revitalized theology."[53] Chenu's was lauded as "the leading interpretation of medieval intellectual history to have appeared since World War II."[54] Often interwoven with Grundmann's interpretation, it continues to shape modern views of medieval religious life. For some historians, it may have been Chenu's construction of events that made Grundmann's paradigm more palatable, removing its ambiguities by positioning Francis's gospel rule, and its acceptance by Innocent III, as a culmination of the "evangelical" processes that Grundmann had identified.[55] Yet it cannot be stated strongly enough that these combined paradigms are not really alternatives to each other when it comes to the Franciscans. Here, despite their different confessional provenances, they supplement each other within broadly the same world view.[56] Whether the emphasis is on the Christian inspiration of a saintly founder or movements that appear objectively to have captured the authentic qualities of the first apostles, such that the historian can describe them straightforwardly as pursuing the *vita apostolica*, matters relatively little. Both rely on early accounts of Francis to categorize the orders as "apostolic" and are compatible with the modern Catholic, and more generally Christian, social imaginary.

The Problem of Subjectivity

This brings us to the third problem. While historians have been aware for some decades of the effects of the heavy bias in extant sources towards male, clerical, and monastic perspectives, there has been almost no parallel awareness of the effects of the dominance of their modern counterparts in the field of medieval religious history.[57] In the case of Franciscan history, the field has been – and, to a considerable extent, continues to be – populated by scholars with a broadly shared ideological commitment. Many have been members of the modern Franciscan orders interested in Francis and the origins of their order for institutional, theological, and devotional purposes. Others have been professional historians working within the academic framework of the universities, but many of them have been members of religious orders or lay Catholics. Some superb historical scholarship, especially editorial work, has emanated from the first group, but most of it – and there is a great deal of it[58] – does not advance wider historical inquiry very far and confines itself to a narrow and increasingly dated set of methods, sources, and questions.[59] The convictions of the second, considerably more diverse, group appear at times to have limited the types of questions that have been asked, instilled a sometimes surprising confidence in the witness of hagiographical sources and, unsurprisingly, taken for granted that Francis and those who properly followed his "authentic" and "apostolic" inspiration were objectively benign forces in society and history. Set against the many studies exploring the violence, misogyny, anti-Semitism, repression, and persecution that deeply marked the activities and conscious aims of the *ecclesia dei* of this period – in all of which the friars were implicated – the enclosed garden of Franciscan studies, suffused with the great capacity of humanity to love its gods, is a curious place.

The field is also well defended. When historians challenge the field's assumptions too strongly, there can be a disquieting uniformity of hostile response or neglect.[60] Where the peculiarities of Franciscan historiography are discussed, the distinction between pious and professional scholarship tends to be obfuscated by the fallacy that being a member of a modern religious order pursuing its contemporary agendas in contemporary conditions gives a person a privileged insight into the distant past that should be sought out by professional historians.[61] In short, there can be few other areas of historical study in which a powerful organization, which has by design profoundly affected society over centuries and has a long history of obfuscation and concealment of its actions, is left so free to tell its story in its own way.[62] There is, of course, no reason why scholars should not pursue research in accordance with their own subjectivities – indeed, how can it be avoided? – or even institutional and ideological objectives, but significant weaknesses emerge when, for decades on end, most people working in a field share roughly similar subjectivities and institutional and ideological objectives.[63]

Shaping the Past for a Catholic Future: Chenu and Vatican II

The question that must now be asked is: What have been the results of this situation for historical understanding? If we return to Chenu and note that he was not a historian but a Dominican theologian who thought the details of the past ultimately mattered only as they enabled one to discern "the signs of the times" – "the hidden force within the event, which was its soul and transmuted it thereafter into a permanent symbol" – it must give pause for thought.[64] His was not a private confessional loyalty purportedly held apart from his scholarly output. Instead, his purpose throughout his life was to work towards what he conceived of as a renewal of the Catholic Church. He and other theologians called for a *ressourcement*, a return to what they considered to be the sources of their faith, and a *recentrement*, a refocusing on Christ.[65] In Chenu's view, Christian history was vital because it was the sphere in which God made himself intelligible for each generation, in a living, developing faith, and its study would enable theologians to engage with contemporary culture.[66] In these activities, he was embattled and for a time silenced by ecclesiastical authorities, but he exercised an important influence on the thinking of Vatican II, particularly on the constitution *Gaudium et Spes* – on the church in the modern world.[67] He understood *évangélisme* as apostolic action, based in gospel literalism, that was wholly immersed in the world and its sufferings, which meant listening to the world and understanding it, rather than merely instructing it.[68] The directives of Vatican II, as we will see, shaped Franciscan studies for many decades afterwards.

One of the main strategies in Chenu's scholarly output was to find in the twelfth century the changes that he thought could and should happen in the twentieth, discovering in medieval sources the dynamics he perceived to be at work in the Roman Church of his own day. These dynamics included: an ecclesiastical hierarchy marked by repressive and sterile authoritarianism, a radical evangelical awakening inspired by a return to the Gospels and driven by engagement between laity and elements within the church, and the flooding of the former by the latter to produce a reinvigorated *ecclesia dei*. A thread of danger ran through this process: the risk that the laity "would grossly abuse their evangelical liberty ... would claim that the right to teach derived from that liberty." During the medieval period, this disturbing possibility had been carefully contained within the articulation of renewed relations by the revitalized church. The risk was in any case worth taking in both periods, given that the characteristics of the *vita apostolica* operated "more spontaneously and sooner among laymen than among clerics, who were bound within an institutional framework."[69] Every aspect of the parallel was intended to show that renewal not only had to take the particular form of *ressourcement* but that it always *had* taken that form: that this was how the Holy Spirit worked. It also assumed that the only significant radical critiques of ecclesiastical institutions were directed at their renewal – the rest delegitimized as mere heresy or presumption. History thus became an extremely powerful tool in the hands of Catholic theologians pressing for change.[70] Chenu and Etienne Gilson wrote prefaces for *La théologie au douzième siècle* that went to some lengths to justify Chenu's rejection of "positivist" scholarly method in favour of "an interior comprehension of events and of texts *beyond what even the authors of these saw or said at the time*" (my italics).[71]

Reviewers of the French edition, which appeared nearly two years before the first announcement of Vatican II in January 1959, were aware of Chenu's commitments but did not consider that they impaired the scholarly value of his work.[72] Indeed, some believed Chenu's perspective "a particular advantage of the book."[73] Few reviewers of the 1968 English translation mentioned the matter at all, at most thinking that it was "immensely relevant in the post-Vatican II era."[74] The effect of all this approbation was to transform Chenu's openly ideological writings quietly and quickly into a serious interpretative framework for academic historians of all confessions and none.[75] This has had significant consequences. In combination with Grundmann, this framework has flattened out and simplified the study of anything that could conceivably be categorized as a "religious" or "evangelical" movement, awakening, or way of life. Their perceived characteristics and aspirations are defined by the model, rather than by the evidence and the language used at the time.[76] Everything that happened across the landscapes of Europe is pulled into a relationship with the medieval papacy. The grit and grain of ordinary restless thoughts are purified away until all local meaning is lost in a universalizing and transhistorical abstraction that tells us little about the medieval past. Within the same Roman Catholic imaginary of "movements," "heresy" is still treated by many historians as a definite social phenomenon rather than a subjective, political, and punitive label.[77]

Chenu's paradigm has also influenced studies of the institutional church of the later medieval period. If reform movements with consistent characteristics were to be imagined as the engines of spiritual renewal throughout history, they required a powerful institution perennially in need of *the same kind of* reform.[78] When Chenu located a *ressourcement* in the twelfth century, it had to be accompanied by a complementary import to make any sense: namely, the ultramontane Roman Church of the nineteenth and early twentieth centuries as it appeared to aspiring reformers writing in the shadow of an antagonistic magisterium. Their church did not seem to them to be historically contingent. Instead, they saw as perpetual qualities its tendency towards highly centralized organization, hierarchy, and dogma, a tight grasp on the Catholic faithful and a carefully crafted image of institutional continuity, built on the rock of Peter and guided by God.[79] Thus, they presented the vitality of medieval religious life as partially laic and external to its institutions, which were depicted as defensive, static, and already resolutely clerical. Medievalists should seriously consider the influence of this paradigm on the wider discipline – specifically whether the uneven, contested, improvisational, and diverse manifestations of medieval ecclesiastical authority are too often given anachronistic form in modern historical writing, shaped by the monolithic features of a much later church.

Arguing with Francis

As far as histories of twelfth- and thirteenth-century religious life are concerned, Chenu and Grundmann, along with Weber, remain among the most recognizable and frequently cited purveyors of these paradigms. This is despite the fact that the paradigms were, of course, not new ideas. Certainly they had roots that reached tenuously down to the ideologies written into the medieval source material.[80] However, they drew their real strength from a peculiar common ground created within the vigorous *Kulturkampf* of the later nineteenth century: namely, that Francis of Assisi embodied the most authentic Christian practice.[81] Each of the men was interested in the period of creative tension that they envisaged arising from the interaction between an institution and revitalizing forces. Their intellectual formation had occurred in the wake of highly charged debates, which had explored this dynamic through arguments around the nature of Catholicism and its relations with the politics of modernity, especially in questions of social justice and ecology. Socialists had begun to present Jesus as having fought for equality and fraternity and Christianity as a movement that could be completed in socialist revolution.[82] More broadly – and sometimes in opposition to socialist thought – Christianity was being conceived as foundational to liberalism, with freedom of conscience as its central value.[83] Notably, Ernest Renan, in his bestselling 1863 *Vie de Jésus*, treated Jesus as a historical figure, albeit one who was as close to perfection as is humanly possible.[84] He connected Jesus and Francis and considered the "le grand mouvement ombrien" to most resemble "le mouvement galiléen."[85] In 1884, he wrote that Francis was, perhaps, "the only perfect Christian since Christ … his only desire was to practice evangelical morality, to realize the primitive ideal of Christian perfection." Renan placed Francis in "an extraordinary movement of religious reform" and suggested that in other circumstances he might have been regarded as a heretic.[86]

Scholars with a range of confessional loyalties were increasingly interested in aspects of medieval religious life that could be fitted into a narrative of mounting protest and reform, culminating in the Reformation.[87] In these various contexts, Francis was envisaged as standing outside the institutional church, seeking to purify it, and at times as one whose spiritual aspirations were in opposition to it. He came to represent for a wide and diverse audience a Christian morality opposed to capitalism, industrialization, and exploitation of the natural world.[88] These various trends culminated in the *Vie de S. François d'Assise*, published by Renan's student Paul Sabatier in 1893 and placed on the Index of Forbidden Books by the Vatican the following year. In this influential and enormously popular reading, Francis "longed for a true awakening of the church in the name of the evangelical ideal which he had regained," but his movement towards an authentic lay Christianity had been appropriated and corrupted by the Roman Church. This capacity of that church to render the radical "witnesses of liberty against authority" indistinguishable from their antithesis, the clergy, Sabatier considered to be "one of the bitterest ironies in history."[89] He later suggested that the contemporary form of the medieval movement was the "experience of increased religious life which is the essential characteristic of the Modernist movement." It had "awakened" lay consciences and given them "a clear vision of a renewed Catholicism."[90]

In reaction to such ideas, nineteenth-century contemporaries began to deploy Francis once again in papal rhetoric as an example of obedience. In his 1882 encyclical *Auspicato concessum*, Leo XIII urged the faithful to "revive" the memory of Francis. Leo, too, drew a parallel between the twelfth and nineteenth centuries, suggesting that widespread imitation of Francis would be a remedy for evils of the present by restoring obedience and the proper sense of social hierarchy that was being unsettled by socialists. The possibility of the Franciscan orders coming to a different conclusion by reading Francis's own writings in this context was discouraged.[91] Both Leo and his successor Pius X bound all members of religious orders to adhere to their constitutions and rules, and specifically not to the "sources."[92] All Catholics with teaching or research roles were required in 1909 to take the "Oath against Modernism," swearing to accept the "unerring teaching authority of the Church" and the view that it was not "permissible for a historian to hold things that contradict the faith of the believer."[93] It is notable that when the brothers at Quaracchi began publishing Franciscan sources in 1885, they focused on official chronicles, materials concerning later periods, and collections of constitutions.[94] Reflection on the example of an order's founder was nonetheless encouraged as a source of inspiration.[95] In 1926, Pius XI instructed Catholics that Francis had been "sent by Divine Providence for the reformation not only of the turbulent age in which he lived but of Christian society of all times ... there has never been anyone in whom the image of Jesus Christ and the evangelical manner of life shone forth more lifelike and strikingly than in St. Francis."[96]

The idea that reform was a continuous and recognizable practice throughout ecclesiastical history – together with ongoing disputes over whether evangelical movements operated inside or outside the church, and whether they were marked by radicalism or obedience – played out in the proceedings and interpretations of the Second Vatican Council (1962–5). The figure of Francis was, yet again, important. In the week before the Council, John XXIII went on pilgrimage to Assisi, following his radio broadcast appeal for "a church of the poor" the month before. These gestures were viewed as a way of carving out space for a "progressive" agenda in the face of resistance from the Roman Curia.[97] Vatican II had many implications for what came next among Catholic medievalists. The most obviously important was its directive that the modern religious orders renew their lives according to "the founder's spirit and special aims."[98] This required the intensification of the focus on the earliest sources that had been stimulated by Sabatier, and it imbued the "Franciscan question" with considerable urgency.[99] Many of the influential studies and new critical editions of the early materials for the orders' history were products of this endeavour, or were purposed to serve it. Some declared this in their prefaces and advertising materials, and a number of them carried certification from ecclesiastical authorities that they were "correct in faith and morals."[100] Some of these works are foundational for academic scholars, who may not have noticed their provenance and purpose or have heard of Vatican II. In the long run, the requirement to return to the sources caused great difficulty for those who attempted it.[101] Despite the enormous energy invested in the endeavour, the extant historical material – extraordinarily rich for many lines of inquiry – appears incapable of delivering institutional or academic certainty on the specific questions of either the founder's spirit or special aims. It can only facilitate the expression of personal feelings on the subject framed around citations from early texts.[102] Much of the writing on Francis and the early orders, even at times by professional medievalists, is little more than this.

A second factor has been subtler in its operation on the historiography. This is the Council's view of nature and purpose of the religious life and the different directions in which its pronouncements were developed by theologians and other commentators. Broadly speaking, the religious life was positioned in Council documents within the church but not within the hierarchical structures. It was presented as detachment from the world but of profound importance to the world, as it was a manifestation in the world of the transformative power of God and thus a force for renewal and teaching.[103] In the decades immediately afterwards, some theologians interpreted the religious life as a vital act of radical witnessing and abandonment of the self to God and to fraternal community, carried out in a world given over to materialism and secularism. When Franciscans read their sources in the light of this interpretation, they found in Francis the same radical retreat into a life of gospel-directed poverty and submission that was itself a powerful call for humanity to return to God.[104] Once again, the hegemonic agendas of the Roman Church were introducing confusions into historical study. Editions of the early Franciscan sources explicitly aimed to provide tools "for those working to insert the evangelical message into our times."[105] Many people seemed genuinely to think that attempting to return to primitive Christianity was inherently socially progressive.[106] Yet as long as Francis continued to be positioned as the person in history who most embodied the *vita apostolica*, even the notion of primitive Christianity would be misleading. His form of life had been of its time, place, and political circumstances – a highly located subjectivity – and had a remote relationship with the biblical texts describing the activities of the early apostles in the Roman province of Judea. A major consequence of all this seems to be that a rather closed dialectic within Franciscan thought interpreted Francis's life in the light of the Vatican II characterization and, in turn, the Vatican II characterization in the light of Francis's life.

What Next for the Study of the "Franciscan" Orders?

Given the enormous influence of these paradigms and their ramifications for the history of religious life in this period, it is important to set out this complicated and little-known background in some detail. We can now say that the underlying narratives of the Franciscan orders, accepted and repeated by most people working in this area, have very often been the products of competing agendas around modern Roman Catholicism and approaches to *ressourcement*. Grundmann's work aimed to liberate the field from these influences and open it up for academic study. Unfortunately, he did not sufficiently challenge some of the core assumptions, which meant that aspects of his interpretation could be built into the programmatic writing of the theologians who shaped post–Vatican II ideas about the religious life. Those parts that were ignored by the theologians – particularly Grundmann's revolutionary work on women's movements, as well as his sense of the proximity of heresy and orthodoxy – remained marginal to the study of the orders. The history of both women's spirituality and of heresy in this period have grown into distinct, dynamic fields embedded in the evolving methodologies, historiographies, and conceptual questions of the wider historical discipline. Both areas are marked by careful attention to language and labels and to the workings of power through this language. Little of this has, by and large, informed the Francis-centred histories, which continue to be stymied by global enthusiasm for the saint. It may be time for Grundmann's proposal to come full circle. The sorts of questions that have been asked about those accused of heresy, and that are now at last being asked about women who have conventionally been treated within imposed ecclesiastical categories, could be provocatively extended to the men.

How should we go about this? As indicated above, there is a great deal of material relating to different aspects of the orders' history to build upon, and more are appearing all the time. The growing body of literature exploring the regional ecclesiastical and monastic worlds of the Middle Ages could help provide a sharper contextual assessment of the roles, mechanisms, and influence of the papacy. For these reasons, it seems plausible that the basis for a variety of revisionist accounts already exists. In constructing these, it will be vital to undo the work that Grundmann's paradigm has done – ultimately in alliance with Chenu and others – to place the ferment of those days into a model of "authentic" apostolicity adjudicated as orthodox or heretical by the papal curia. Such critical reappraisal should be informed by a greater awareness that when historians use the labels "orthodox," "apostolic," and, of course, "heresy," as if these were objective or stable categories, an "emic" Roman Catholic history is being produced because the historian's analytical tools are concepts generated by the institution to justify and defend its actions. The same thing happens when historians write of "God," rather than "their god": as if the notions of god found in this temporally, spatially, and culturally specific body of Latin and European vernacular texts comprised a universal entity.[107] The anachronistic adjective "Franciscan," when applied to groups or individuals across time and space, similarly serves to delimit possibilities by making Francis the stable, perennial referent for identity. All these labels blunt the keen sense of specificity, immediacy, locality, and variety that historians must have if they are to detect diversity rather than finding uniformity.

With all this in mind, it is particularly important that questions around the practical functioning of power, including the dynamics of production of "Christian" cultural hegemonies and the ways in which these shaped social inequalities, be reintroduced to the study of these men and women. At the least, there should be much greater precision in our handling of familiar labels, transhistorical paradigms, and "virtuous" categories. We might do better to treat them as emic constructs, as we would treat any other kind of located, programmatic, ideological writing by members of a governing elite. For example, it is striking that although intense scrutiny has been given to the construction of heresy in our sources, there has been no parallel critical investigation of the construction of *apostolic* spirituality. Instead, it stands as a stable referent and a self-evidently virtuous category. Mark Pegg, in examining the consequences of inquisitorial activity for the ordinary population, concluded that the inquisitors, "through demanding that a particular style of truth be understood ... forever changed the way in which men and women thought about themselves."[108] We need to now ask: did the church's more approving labels have the same disquieting transformational power? As Christine Caldwell Ames pointed out in relation to the study of the inquisition, there remains a reluctance to associate the darker, persecutory aspects of religious belief and behaviour with religion itself.[109] Ian Forrest has explored the ways in which apparently benign practices such as "trust" and "faith" shaped social inequalities when only some kinds of people – generally higher status men – were viewed by ecclesiastical authorities as trustworthy allies in governing local populations and were able to entrench power over their neighbours and to shape church policy and judgments.[110] Along similar lines, scholars should consider the notion that the *vita apostolica*, which does not seem persecutory in the slightest, might serve as a tool of power, a justification for domination of human and non-human life, and a mechanism for tightening social and gender hierarchies, justifying harsh treatment of Jews and others, silencing dissent, and protecting certain forms of privilege.

We must think harder about what it meant for the population when groups or individuals claimed, were described by religious authorities in documents with the force of law, and were accepted by at least some of the laity, including powerful ruling dynasties, to be living after the example of the apostles.[111] The methods of coercion used by the inquisition were not subtle, but the methods of apostolic spirituality *were*. This was the fierce love and self-sacrifice of Christ's disciples, the possibility of miraculous happenings, the afterglow of Pentecostal fire, and the Word of God spreading through the peoples. This was not the threat of hell but the promise of heaven. This was not persecution; it was inclusion. Dominique Iogna-Prat considered something akin to this in his *Ordonner et exclure*, in which the great monastery of Cluny becomes in his imagination the whole Christian church and fills the world, flooding the secular sphere with the sacred; bringing the laity into its own monastic, otherworldly spaces; and subjecting it to the disciplines of the monastic life.[112] The price of inclusion was obedience and submission to ecclesiastical and secular authority, however unjustly wielded. It required the acceptance by women and lower-ranking laymen in particular, together with marginalized groups, such as Jews, of a wealth of both open and concealed exclusions. Above all, it required that everyone living in the entangled regions of western Eurasia accept the truths witnessed by apostolicity as their society's truths, with all the vast impoverishment of thought and imagination that such repressions must bring. Regardless of how far it actually succeeded at the time – another important question that tends to be obscured by the emic potencies of the category – this was undoubtedly the nature of the project so often celebrated in secondary literature as "authentically Christian," just as it was the intention and hope of the Vatican II reformers whose accounts have been so foundational to modern scholarly understanding of medieval religious life.

If we return to Giotto's image and think again about its meaning in this context, perhaps Francis stands more darkly against the golden sky, and his identically clad, deferential, mutely witnessing companion seems to foreshadow the fate of the gathered birds. For the birds now seem to be on the brink of losing their individuality and their capacity for independent thought, as they perch at his feet. In these terrifying times, we should pause to consider that the fate of our world might have been very different if Francis had, instead, been depicted as listening to the diverse voices of the birds.

NOTES

1 I would like to thank Kirsty Day for her insightful comments on this piece, and the convenors of the Oxford Medieval Seminar and St. Andrew's Intellectual History Seminar for giving me the opportunity to present successive versions. This essay is dedicated to the memory of David Luscombe, whose kindness, intellectual generosity, and unfailing scholarly support has meant a great deal to me, and will be much missed.
2 Described here is the version in the right-hand corner of the predella panel from "St. Francis receiving the stigmata," made for the church of San Francesco in Pisa and currently held in the Louvre. See Julian Gardner, *Giotto and His Publics: Three Paradigms of Patronage* (Cambridge, MA: Harvard University Press, 2011), esp. 30–6.
3 On the ideas communicated through various depictions of the scene, see Rosalind B. Brooke, *The Image of St. Francis: Responses to Sainthood in the Thirteenth Century* (Cambridge: Cambridge University Press, 2006), esp. 171, 182–3, 192–8, 326; Chiara Frugoni, *Francesco e l'invenzione delle stimmate: una storia per parole e immagini fino a Bonaventura e Giotto* (Torino: Einaudi, 1993), 233–55; and on Francis's gestures more generally, see Raoul Manselli, "Il gesto come predicazione per san Francesco d'Assisi," *Collectanea Franciscana* 51 (1981), 5–16.
4 This tendency marks the early hagiographies but took its most influential form in Paul Sabatier, *Vie de s. François d'Assise* (Paris: Fischbacher, 1894). That "Francis" is mutable is often noted. See esp. Jacques Dalarun, *François d'Assise en questions* (Paris: CNRS editions, 2016); André Vauchez, *Francis of Assisi: The Life and Afterlife of a Medieval Saint*, trans. Michael F. Cusato (New Haven, CT: Yale University Press, 2013); Patricia Appelbaum, *St. Francis of America: How a Thirteenth-Century Friar Became America's Most Popular Saint* (Chapel Hill: University of North Carolina Press, 2015).
5 As Flood notes, the emphasis on Francis's "purity" by the institutional church and its agents "removes him from the contests of history and turns him wholly towards God. As a result, Francis's Christian life exemplifies the church's teachings … [Francis] has become a useful pastoral symbol." David Flood, *Francis of Assisi and the Franciscan Movement* (Quezon City:

FIA Contact Publications, 1989), 149 and 147–67 for the full argument. On the formal significance of his canonization, see Roberto Paciocco, "Una conscienza tra scelta di vita e fama di santità. Francesco d'Assisi frater e sanctus," *Hagiographica* 1 (1994), 207–26; Giovanni Miccoli, *Francesco d'Assisi: realtà e memoria di un'esperienza cristiana* (Torino: Einaudi, 1991), 82–3.

6 See Jacques Dalarun, *The Misadventure of Francis of Assisi*, trans. Edward Hagman (New York: Franciscan Institute, 2002).

7 For example, as Grundmann pointed out, the wealthy Marie d'Oignies pursued an "apostolic" life by renouncing marriage and property, helping lepers, and converting others to the religious life, "as Francis would later do." Herbert Grundmann, *Religious Movements in the Middle Ages*, trans. S. Rowan (Notre Dame: University of Notre Dame Press, 1995), 83. A very different but equally productive comparison could be the self-fashioning and subsequent hagiographic crafting of the figure of Bernard of Clairvaux. See Adriaan H. Bredero, *Bernard of Clairvaux: Between Cult and History*, trans. Reinder Bruinsma (Edinburgh: T&T Clark, 1996).

8 Even Weber considered Francis to have lived by "the absolute ethic of the Gospels" and therefore, like Christ, to be "not from this world." Christopher Adair-Toteff, *Max Weber's Sociology of Religion* (Tübingen: Mohr Siebeck, 2016), 91, and see also 40, 71; and Christopher Adair-Toteff, "Max Weber's charismatic prophets," *History of the Human Sciences* 27, no. 1 (2014): 3–20. On the problem in, principally, Italian historiography, see Raimondo Michetti, "Francesco d'Assisi e l'essenza del cristianesimo (a proposito di alcune biografie storiche e di alcuni studi contemporanei)," in *Francesco d'Assisi fra storia, letteratura e iconografia*, ed. Franca Ela Consolino (Soveria Mannelli: Rubbettino, 1996), 37–67.

9 On the implications of scholarship that treats "religion" as "sui generis, unique, and sociohistorically autonomous," see Russell T. McCutcheon, *Manufacturing Religion: The Discourse on Sui Generis Religion and the Politics of Nostalgia* (New York: Oxford University Press, 1997), quotation at 3.

10 Most recently: Steven Vanderputten, *Medieval Monasticisms: Forms and Experiences of the Monastic Life in the Latin West* (München: De Gruyter Oldenbourg, 2020), 118–22.

11 *Religious Movements*, see esp. 1–5, 55–66, 86–8.

12 Gert Melville, *The World of Medieval Monasticism: Its History and Forms of Life*, trans. J.D. Mixson (Kalamazoo, MI: Cistercian Publications, 2016), 162; André Vauchez, *The Laity in the Middle Ages*, trans. Daniel E. Bornstein (Notre Dame, 1983), 34.

13 The terms are borrowed from cultural anthropology (for definitions, see Alan Barnard, "Emic and Etic," in *Routledge Encyclopaedia of Social and Cultural Anthropology*, 2nd ed., ed. Alan Barnard and Jonathan Spencer (London: Routledge, 2010). Although it cannot be discussed here, the

problematic nature of the distinction is also worth noting, given that "etic" Western scientific methodology also has its roots in Roman Catholic notions of universal truth.

14 As Constance H. Berman observes: "The most successful of such hermit monks and nuns were, of course, those for whom no record survives." In Constance H. Berman, *The White Nuns: Cistercian Abbeys for Women in Medieval France* (Philadelphia: University of Pennsylvania Press, 2018), 5.

15 On the variety of female activities and the narratives produced to label and constrain their behaviour and legacies, see Alison More, *Fictive Orders and Feminine Religious Identities, 1200–1600* (Oxford University Press, 2018); Letha Böhringer, Jennifer Kolpacoff Deane, and Hildo van Engen, eds., *Labels and Libels: Naming Beguines in Northern Medieval Europe* (Turnholt: Brepols, 2014). For a longer history of some of these qualities in female religious life, see Steven Vanderputten, *Dark Age Nunneries: The Ambiguous Identity of Female Monasticism, 800–1050* (Cornell University Press, 2018).

16 For reflections on the ambivalences within the Franciscan role in European colonialism, see Julia McClure, *The Franciscan Invention of the New World* (Basingstoke: Palgrave Macmillan, 2016).

17 On the use of "ideal types," see Max Weber, "Objectivity in Social Science and Social Policy," in his *The Methodology of the Social Sciences*, ed. and trans. E.A. Shils and H.A. Finch (New York: Free Press, 1949), 50–112.

18 "Cultural hegemony" is conceived here in the Gramscian sense as a dialectic between consent and coercion, a dialectic which appears to operate through majority consent. See Peter D. Thomas, *The Gramscian Moment: Philosophy, Hegemony and Marxism* (Leiden: Brill, 2009), esp. 161–5.

19 Much study of the power of the medieval church has focused on precisely the coercive aspect, stimulated by studies such as R. I. Moore, *The Formation of a Persecuting Society: Power and Deviance in Western Europe, 950–1250* (Oxford: Blackwell, 1987); James B. Given, *Inquisition and Medieval Society: Power, Discipline, and Resistance in Languedoc* (Ithaca: Cornell University Press, 2001). For further comment, see John H. Arnold, "AHR Reappraisal: Persecution and Power in Medieval Europe," *The American Historical Review* 123, no. 1 (2018): 165–74. This line of inquiry and its implications have been completely ignored by most historians of the Franciscan order.

20 These are the power relations identified by Michel Foucault as the site of the creation of the self-disciplining, self-regulating subject.

21 See *Frati minori e inquisizione: atti del XXXIII Convegno internazionale* (Spoleto: Fondazione Centro italiano di studi sull'alto Medioevo, 2006), but for continuing concern that Franciscan inquisition is insufficiently studied, see Marina Benedetti, "Frati Minori e inquisizione. Alcuni casi nell'Italia medievale," *Dossiê Temático: "Franciscanos e franciscanismos: origens e*

difusão," *Territórios & Fronteiras* 9, no. 1 (2016): 84–96. For the other issues, see Christoph T. Maier, *Preaching the Crusades: Mendicant Friars and the Cross in the Thirteenth Century* (Cambridge: Cambridge University Press, 1994); Geraldine Heng, *The Invention of Race in the European Middle Ages* (Cambridge: Cambridge University Press, 2018); Amanda Power, "The Uncertainties of Reformers: Collective Anxieties and Strategic Discourses," in *Thirteenth Century England XVI*, ed. Andrew Spencer and Carl Watkins (London: Boydell and Brewer, 2017), 1–19.

22 The 2015 papal encyclical *Laudato si'*, intended for wide consumption, drew on Francis's well-known canticle. For some of the many critiques, see the essays by Sharon A. Bong, Ivone Gebara, and others in Grace Ji-Sun Kim and Hilda Koster, eds., *Planetary Solidarity: Global Women's Voices on Christian Doctrine and Climate Justice* (Minneapolis: Fortress Press, 2017); Bronislaw Szerszynski, "Praise Be to You, Earth-Beings," *Environmental Humanities* 8, no. 2 (2016): 291–7; Will Jenkins, "The Mysterious Silence of Mother Earth in *Laudato Si'*," *Journal of Religious Ethics* 46, no. 3 (2018): 441–62. On the limitation of Westernized ecologies, see Prasenjit Duara, *The Crisis of Global Modernity: Asian Traditions and a Sustainable Future* (Cambridge: Cambridge University Press, 2015).

23 I borrow the "transhistorical and transcultural" from Talal Asad, *Genealogies of Religion: Discipline and Reasons of Power in Christianity and Islam* (Baltimore: Johns Hopkins University Press, 1993), 28–9. As this essay will discuss, there is an internal politics that insists on the feasibility of continuous "authentic" renewal within a religious order that holds the order in a kind of ahistorical moral stasis, immune from the passage of time and without responsibility for its actions in the world (see this volume, 56–8).

24 This was the thesis explored in David Flood, *Frère François et le mouvement franciscain* (Paris: Éditions ouvrières, 1983) and substantially reworked in his *Francis of Assisi and the Franciscan Movement*. See Flood's critique of "the impossible disengagement of Francis from his brothers [that] characterizes Italian scholarship on the early Franciscan years" in Flood, "Read it at Chapter: Francis of Assisi and the *Scritti*," *Franciscan Studies*, 60 (2002), 341–57, quotation at 341. It was widely disputed: e.g., Jacques Dalarun, *Francis of Assisi and Power*, trans. A. Bartol (New York: Bonaventure Institute, 2007), comment on Flood at 192–3.

25 See Rosalind Brooke, *Scripta Leonis, Rufini et Angeli sociorum S. Francisci* (Oxford: Clarendon Press, 1970), 9–25.

26 On the "the shadow history of the Minorite order" produced by these priorities, see Kevin L. Hughes, "Bonaventure's defence of mendicancy," in *A Companion to Bonaventure*, ed. J. Hammond et al. (Leiden: Brill, 2013), 509–41, quotation at 510.

27 Neslihan Şenocak, "The Making of Franciscan Poverty," *Revue Mabillon*, n.s. 24 (2013), 5–26.
28 Amanda Power, *Roger Bacon and the Defence of Christendom* (Cambridge: Cambridge University Press, 2012), esp. 13–15.
29 To take some studies that cover the period to the sixteenth century: In Heribert Holzapfel, *Handbuch der Geschichte des Franziskanerordens* (Freiburg: Herdersche Verlagshandlung, 1909), just 21 pages of 688 concerned women; John Moorman gave them 34 pages of 592 in *A History of the Franciscan Order from its Origins to the year 1517* (Oxford University Press, 1968); Grado Giovanni Merlo, *Nel nome di san Francesco: Storia dei frati Minori e del francescanesimo sino agli inizi del XVI secolo* (Padua: Editrici Francescane, 2012), devoted 29 pages of 438 to women. These counts refer to dedicated chapters and do not include *passim* references.
30 Kirsty Day, "Hagiography as Institutional Biography: Medieval and Modern Uses of the Thirteenth-Century *Vitae* of Clare of Assisi," in *Writing the Lives of People and Things, AD 500–1700: A Multi-disciplinary Future for Biography*, ed. Robert F. W. Smith and Gemma L. Watson (Farnham: Ashgate, 2016), 261–80; Albrecht Diem, "The Gender of the Religious: Wo/Men and the Invention of Monasticism," in *The Oxford Handbook of Women and Gender in Medieval Europe*, ed. Judith M. Bennett and Ruth M. Karras (Oxford University Press, 2013). See the editors' introduction to Gert Melville and Anne Müller, eds., *Female "vita religiosa" Between Late Antiquity and the High Middle Ages: Structures, Developments and Spatial Contexts* (Berlin: LIT Verlag, 2011). For examples, see Moorman, *History*, 206, 214–16, 408; Merlo, *Nel nome*, 118.
31 On this phenomenon, see Catherine M. Mooney, "*Imitatio Christi* or *Imitatio Mariae*? Clare of Assisi and Her Interpreters," in *Gendered Voices: Medieval Saints and Their Interpreters*, ed. Catherine M. Mooney (Philadelphia: University of Pennsylvania Press, 1999), 52–77, esp. 52–3.
32 See Letha Böhringer in this volume.
33 Most individual provinces are covered in one or more monographs, many now dated. Recently, new collections of essays on individual provinces have been appearing, largely within their respective national historiographies. Nonetheless, a narrative history that examines the spread and regional variations of the order across the Latin West without prioritizing Italy and possibly Paris, and includes the women on anything approaching equal terms, does not exist.
34 See Emma Furniss, "The Franciscan Order in Late-Medieval and Early-Modern Western Europe: A Historiographical Survey," *Monastic Research Bulletin* 12 (2006), 1–10.
35 Kirsty Day, *Constructing Dynastic Franciscan Identities in Bohemia and the Polish Duchies* (unpublished doctoral diss., University of Leeds, August 2015), esp. 16–24.

36 On the last point, see Guiseppe Buffon, *Sulle trace di una storia omessa: Storiografia moderna e contemporanea dell'Ordine francescano* (Grottaferrata: Frati Editori di Quaracchi, 2011). For a systematic account of the process of creating normative interpretations, see Achim Wesjohann, *Mendikantische Gründungserzählungen im 13. und 14. Jahrhundert: Mythen als Element institutioneller Eigengeschichtsschreibung der mittelalterlichen Franziskaner, Dominikaner und Augustiner-Eremiten* (Berlin: LIT Verlag, 2012), part II.

37 For early documents for both orders that omit reference to Francis, see Giovanni Sbaraglia, ed., *Bullarium Franciscanum sive Romanorum Pontificum* (Rome, 1780, repr. ed. Porziuncola, 1983), noting esp. docs. 1, 3–5, 17, 23; together with Marie-France Becket et al., ed. and trans., *Claire d'Assise: Écrits* (Paris: Cerf, 1985), 200. For other examples, see Amanda Power, "The Problem of Obedience among the English Friars," in *Rules and Observance: Devising Forms of Communal Life*, ed. Mirko Breitenstein et al. (Berlin: LIT Verlag, 2014), 129–67.

38 On the difficulties in relation to the case of Beguines, see Böhringer, Deane, and van Engen, eds., *Labels*.

39 Becket et al., *Écrits*, 82–118, mentioned once at 106.

40 See Catherine Mooney, *Clare of Assisi and the Thirteenth-Century Church: Religious Women, Rules, and Resistance* (Philadelphia: University of Pennsylvania Press, 2016) and Bert Roest, *Order and Disorder: The Poor Clares Between Foundation and Reform* (Leiden: Brill, 2013), who uses the phrase "Damianites/Poor Clares and Minoresses" for the people under discussion.

41 See Roest, *Order*, 1, on the "neat but mythical concept of 'three orders' within one Franciscan order family"; Alison More, "Institutionalizing Penitential Life in Later Medieval and Early Modern Europe: Third Orders, Rules, and Canonical Legitimacy," *Church History* 83, no. 2 (2014): 297–323; More, *Fictive Orders*, esp. 41–50.

42 "multi enim utriusque sexus"; "Fratres Minores et Sorores Minores," *Lettres de Jacques de Vitry, 1160/1170–1240*, ed. R. B. C. Huygens (Leiden: Brill, 1960), 75.

43 On these points, see Catherine Mooney, "The 'Lesser Sisters' in Jacques de Vitry's 1216 Letter," *Franciscan Studies* 69, no. 1 (2011): 1–29.

44 Attentive readers will notice that the present essay is no more successful than others in producing a consistent, coherent, and clear alternative vocabulary.

45 Grundmann, *Religious Movements in the Middle Ages*, quotation at 2.

46 John Van Engen, "The Christian Middle Ages as an Historiographical Problem," *The American Historical Review* 91, no. 3 (1986): 519–52, at 523. Grundmann's work underpinned attempts to "decentre" Francis as recently as Donald S. Prudlo, ed., *The Origin, Development, and Refinement of Medieval Religious Mendicancies* (Leiden: Brill, 2011).

47 For an early general survey of the notion, see Ernest W. McDonnell, "The *Vita Apostolica*: Diversity or Dissent?" *Church History* 24, no. 1 (1955): 15–31.
48 On Francis's obedience, see: Thadée Matura, "L'Eglise dans les écrits de François d'Assise," and Andrea Boni, "L'obbedienza ecclesiale di S. Francesco al papa e ai vescovi," in *Antonianum* 57 (1982), 94–112 and 113–55, respectively.
49 David Flood, "The Grundmann Approach to Early Franciscan History," *Franziskanische Studien* 59 (1977), 311–19, 317.
50 Flood, *Francis*, 74–5.
51 See, for example, Giovanni Grado Merlo, *Tra eremo e città: studi su Francesco d'Assisi e sul francescanesimo medievale* (Assisi: Edizioni Porziuncola, 1991), which took seriously the relationship between Francis's ideas and the context sketched by Grundmann, but also strongly asserted Francis's exceptionalism and agency. Recent re-interpretative work continues to use Grundmann's model as a base: e.g., Giacomo Todeschini, *Franciscan Wealth: From Voluntary Poverty to Market Society*, trans. Donatella Melucci (New York: Saint Bonaventure University, 2009), esp. 28–40 [no direct acknowledgment]; Giorgio Agamben, *The Highest Poverty: Monastic Rules and Form-of-Life*, trans. Adam Kotsko (Stanford University Press, 2013), 91–2.
52 See especially Marie-Dominique Chenu, "Moines, Clercs, Laïcs. Au carrefour de la vie évangélique" and "Le réveil évangélique," in *La théologie au douzième siècle* (Paris: Vrin, 1957), parts of which were translated by Lester K. Little under the significantly different title of *Nature, Man and Society in the Twelfth Century* (Chicago: University of Chicago Press, 1968). Grundmann drew on Chenu's interpretation when he added the substantial "Neue Beiträge zur Geschichte der religiösen bewegungen" to the 1961 edition of *Religiöse Bewegungen*. Given the publication history of the latter, Anglophone scholars, in particular, probably first encountered the two works at much the same time.
53 Quotations at Chenu, *Nature*, 269.
54 John W. Baldwin's review in *The American Historical Review* 76, no. 5 (1971): 1526.
55 Chenu, *Nature*, 239. For example, in explaining the *vita apostolica* at the outset of *Clare of Assisi*, Mooney sounds as if she is using Grundmann, but heretics are not mentioned, and she only cites Chenu (although later uses Grundmann on a particular point). Vauchez, in *Francis*, gives a long account of Francis's "religious context" that seems heavily based on Grundmann but does not cite him at all (33–56), while Chenu's characterization is quoted in the main text (38).
56 One reviewer of Lester K. Little's *Religious Poverty* praised it for being "a synthetic exercise, piecing together the ideas and approaches of Chenu,

Duby, Le Goff and Grundmann." *Catholic Historical Review* 66, no. 4 (1980): 610.
57 Grundmann discussed the problem but with the expectation that his own work would break with it. See Grundmann, *Religious Movements*, 1–4. John Van Engen noted: "Narratives born of confessional polemics have largely given way, though they still influence our interpretive structures in surprising ways," but did not pursue the matter of commitments to Christianity that did not take overtly polemical forms. John Van Engen, "The Future of Medieval Church History," *Church History* 71, no. 3 (2002): 492–522, at 492.
58 "al punto da essere incontrollabili di un singolo studioso," wrote Grado Merlo nearly thirty years ago, noting the 1,188 titles collected in the Capuchin *Bibliographia Franciscana* for 1981–5 alone. Grado Merlo, "La storiografia francescana dal dopoguerra ad oggi," *Studi Storici* 32, no. 2 (1991): 287–307, at 306.
59 See recent pleas for a broadening of scholarly activity and interpretative priorities: respectively, Bert Roest, "Franciscan Studies and the Repercussions of the Digital Revolution: A Proposal," *Franciscan Studies* 74 (2016), 375–84; Buffon, *Sulle trace*; Francesco Victor Sánchez Gil, "La importancia de *Archivum Franciscanum Historicum* para la historiografía Franciscana moderna balance de un centenario (1908–2007)," *Archivum Franciscanum Historicum* 101, nos. 3–4 (2008): 453–89, esp. 482–3.
60 For example, Bert Roest complained of "the apparent lack of impact" of his earlier demonstration that a Franciscan school system was emerging from 1220 onwards, even in works that cited his study. Bert Roest, "The Franciscan School System: Re-assessing the Early Evidence (ca. 1220–1260)," in *Franciscan Organisation in the Mendicant Context: Formal and Informal Structures of the Friars' Lives and Ministry in the Middle Ages*, ed. Michael Robson and Jens Röhrkasten (Berlin: LIT Verlag, 2010), 269–96, 254. See Neslihan Şenocak, *The Poor and the Perfect: The Rise of Learning in the Franciscan Order, 1209–1310* (Ithaca: Cornell University Press, 2012), 24. Despite the agreement among reviewers that provocative questions had been asked in Kenneth Baxter Wolf, *The Poverty of Riches: St. Francis of Assisi Reconsidered* (Oxford: Oxford University Press, 2003), engagement with these questions is largely absent from subsequent studies. Bizarrely, given a historiography that seems to do little else, Wolf is criticized for introducing contemporary concerns into his analysis of Francis. Daniel J. Schultz, "Histories of the Present: Interpreting the Poverty of St. Francis," in *World of St. Francis of Assisi: Essays in Honor of William R. Cook*, ed. Bradley Franco and Beth Mulvaney (Leiden: Brill, 2015), 176–92. A comparable phenomenon can be observed in the responses to Jeremy Cohen, *The Friars and the Jews: The Evolution of Medieval Anti-Judaism*

(Ithaca: Cornell University Press, 1982). In this case, although reviewers tended to agree on its shortcomings, its thesis has been a fundamental point of reference for scholars of medieval anti-Semitism (e.g., Rebecca Rist, *Popes and Jews, 1095–1291* [Oxford: Oxford University Press, 2016], esp. 1–6) but not of the friars.

61 See Giovanni Miccoli's claim that any professional historian "che sia degno di questo nome" – worthy of the name – would want to engage with those who purport to be living lives very similar to those the historian studied. "Prefazione" to Merlo, *Nel nome*, xv; and similar, if more nuanced, implications in Dalarun, *François*, esp. 7–9; Merlo, "La storiografia," 291–2, although he concludes by hoping that if the two groups must remain distinct, they can at least exist symbiotically (307). For a useful illustration of the slippery ground occupied by historians who want to find abstract "Christian" experiences in historical "reality," see André Vauchez, "François d'Assise rendu à l'histoire: l'œuvre de Giovanni Miccoli," *Etudes franciscaines*, n.s. 1 (2008), fasc 1–2, 7–19. In a similar spirit, the new series of *Etudes franciscaines* wants to meet academic standards but also to remain accessible: "une façon franciscaine d'exprimer la dimension fraternelle et solidaire d'une quête intellectuelle et spirituelle attentive à l'échange de dons qui la nourrit."

62 For a useful parallel, see Carol Symes's discussion of how ecclesiastical elites appropriated, silenced, and repackaged participant views on the events of 1095–9, crafting a view that has remained dominant until the present day. Carol Symes, "Popular Literacies and the First Historians of the First Crusade," *Past & Present* 235, no. 1 (2017): 37–67. On long-term patterns of concealment, see Dyan Elliott, *The Corrupter of Boys: Sodomy, Scandal, and the Medieval Clergy* (Philadelphia: University of Pennsylvania Press, 2020).

63 See the observations in Merlo, "La storiografia," 296–7.

64 "Il ne s'agit donc pas tant d'établir avec érudition le détail du fait passé, mais de discerner dans ce fait la puissance secrète qui en, fut l'âme et le transmute désormais en symbole permanent dans la suite des temps" in Marie-Dominique Chenu, "Les signes des temps," *Nouvelle revue théologique* 87, no. 1 (1965): 29–39, at 32. For an earlier statement, see Marie-Dominique Chenu, *Une école de théologie: le Saulchoir* (Paris: Les éditiones du cerf, 1985), ch. 5. Fergus Kerr notes: "Chenu was no more interested than [other Catholic theologians] in historical scholarship for its own sake." See Fergus Kerr, *Twentieth-century Catholic Theologians: From Neoscholasticism to Nuptial Mysticism* (Oxford: Blackwell, 2007), 22. See also Gerd-Rainer Horn, *Western European Liberation Theology: The First Wave (1924–1959)* (Oxford: Oxford University Press, 2008), esp. 103–10.

65 Gabriel Flynn, *Yves Congar's Vision of the Church in a World of Unbelief* (Aldershot: Ashgate, 2004), 28–36; Gerd-Rainer Horn, *The Spirit of Vatican*

II: *Western European Progressive Catholicism in the Long Sixties* (Oxford: Oxford University Press, 2015), esp. 25–31. For more detail, see Gabriel Flynn and Paul D. Murray, eds., *Ressourcement: A Movement for Renewal in Twentieth-Century Catholic Theology* (Oxford: Oxford University Press, 2011).

66 Grant Kaplan, "The Renewal of Ecclesiastical Studies: Chenu, Tübingen, and Theological Method in *Optatam Totius*," *Theological Studies* 77, no. 3 (2016): 567–92; Thomas F. O'Meara and Paul Philibert, *Scanning the Signs of the Times: French Dominicans in the Twentieth Century* (Adelaide: ATF Press, 2013), 23–4.

67 On early agenda-setting, see André Duval, "Le message du monde," in *Vatican II commence: approches francophones*, ed. É. Fouilloux (Leuven: Bibliotheek van de Faculteit der Godgeleerdheid, 1993), 105–18.

68 For the connections between Chenu's thought and the contents and implications of the constitution, see Christophe F. Potworowski, *Contemplation and Incarnation: The Theology of Marie-Dominique Chenu* (Montreal and Kingston: McGill-Queen's Press, 2001), 25–32, 143–54, ch. 5.

69 Chenu, *Nature*, 219–30, quotations at 219. Grundmann was his main reference.

70 John W. O'Malley, *What Happened at Vatican II?* (Cambridge, MA: Harvard University Press, 2010), 77–8.

71 Chenu, "Introduction," *Nature*, xviii–xix. On Chenu's view of history, see Potworowski, *Contemplation*, esp. ch. 3.

72 E.g., Gabriel Le Bras in *Archives de sociologie des religions* 4 (1957), 177–9; René Roques notes: "le P. Chenu n'a pas cru devoir cacher ses sympathies ni taire ses jugements," in *Revue de l'histoire des religions* 156, no. 2 (1959): 212–22, at 221.

73 "Vielmehr zielt die Absicht des Verfassers auf deren geistigen Untergrund, auf das geistige 'Klima' … und das macht einen besonderen Vorzug des Buches aus," Wolfhart Pannenberg, in *Theologische Literaturzeitung* 86 (1961), 355–60, 356.

74 John R. Sommerfeldt, *The Catholic Historical Review* 57, no. 3 (1971): 480–2, at 481.

75 Van Engen notes that despite his purpose being internal reform, the effect of his work "not altogether unintended" was "to draw many others" into the study of his themes. Van Engen, "Christian Middle Ages," 525. This strategy was not unique to Chenu. For example, David Knowles believed that, as a Catholic holding a distinguished Cambridge chair, "it was right to appeal to as wide an audience as possible, not with apologetics, but with history in which Christianity was taken for granted as true" and that this possibility for "penetration and real influence" made scholarship "a real apostolate," a view, he added, that was shared by Pius XI. Alberic

Stacpoole, "The Making of a Monastic Historian – II," *Ampleforth Journal* 58, no. 2 (1975): 19–38, 19.
76 For a critical discussion of this, see Robyn Parker, *Creating the "Hermit-Preachers": Narrative, Textual Construction, and Community in Twelfth- and Thirteenth-Century Northern France* (unpublished doctoral diss., University of Sheffield, 2014).
77 See R.I. Moore, *The War on Heresy* (London: Profile Books, 2012).
78 This may account for why crusades were not at this point considered a "religious movement." See Anne Lester's essay in this volume.
79 Whether the reformers were correct in their perceptions even of the Roman Church of their own day is another matter. Through its battles with rival groups, it was rapidly transforming itself into a new and potent force in European society and politics. See Christopher M. Clark and Kaiser Wolfram, eds., *Culture Wars: Secular-Catholic Conflict in Nineteenth-Century Europe* (Cambridge: Cambridge University Press, 2003); Margaret Anderson, "The Limits of Secularization: On the Problem of the Catholic Revival in Nineteenth-Century Germany," *Historical Journal* 38 (1995): 647–70.
80 See the influential Gerhart B. Ladner, *The Idea of Reform: Its Impact on Christian Thought and Action in the Age of the Fathers* (Cambridge, MA: Harvard University Press, 1959), which referred readers to Grundmann and Chenu for "the later stages of the *vita communis et apostolica*" (402). See Philippe Buc, *The Dangers of Ritual: Between Early Medieval Texts and Social Scientific Theory* (Princeton: Princeton University Press, 2001), on analytical frameworks that have their origins in the ideas of the very texts they study.
81 On this period, see Clark and Wolfram, eds., *Culture Wars*.
82 E.g., Edward Berenson, *Populist Religion and Left-wing Politics in France, 1830–1852* (Princeton: Princeton University Press, 1984), esp. 36–76; Louise D'Arcens, *Comic Medievalism: Laughing at the Middle Ages* (Woodbridge: Boydell, 2014), 68–87, esp. 79ff.
83 Robert D. Priest, "The 'Great Doctrine of Transcendent Disdain': History, Politics and the Self in Renan's Life of Jesus," *History of European Ideas* 40, no. 6 (2014): 761–76, at 770–1, 775.
84 Alan Pitt, "The Cultural Impact of Science in France: Ernest Renan and the *Vie de Jésus*," *Historial Journal* 43, no. 1 (2000): 79–101; Nathalie Richard, *La Vie de Jésus de Renan, la fabrique d'un best-seller* (Rennes: Presses universitaires de Rennes, 2015).
85 Ernest Renan, *Vie*, 2nd ed. (Paris: Michel Lévy, 1863), 183. He included the Poor of Lyons, Beghards, Humiliates, and others in this movement.
86 Ernest Renan, "Francis of Assisi," in *New Studies of Religious History* (New York: Scribner and Welford, 1887), 305–29, at 315–16.
87 This was in contrast to earlier Protestant polemics. Heimann, "Secularisation," 406.

88 See Appelbaum, "St. Francis," 793, 797–800. He remains so: e.g., Pope Francis's 2015 controversial encyclical *Laudato Si'*. See Xue Jiao Zhang, "How St. Francis Influenced Pope Francis' *Laudato Si'*," *Cross Currents* 66, no. 1 (2016): 42–56.

89 Paul Sabatier, *Life*, xvii, xii–xv. Much has been said of Sabatier's influence, including two dedicated volumes: *Paul Sabatier e gli studi francescani: atti del XXX Convegno internazionale* (Spoleto: Fondazione Centro italiano di studi sull'alto Medioevo, 2003); *La "questione francescana" dal Sabatier ad oggi: atti del I Convegno internazionale* (Assisi, 1974). His work and his scholarly idealism are still valued for the intellectual and methodological stimulus they provided (see here the several ironies in Pacifico Sella, "Genesi di un periodico scientifico: l'*Archivum Franciscanum Historicum*," *AFH* 101, nos. 3–4 (2008): 343–62), but its central argument cast a long shadow. For example, a recent study begins with Sabatier's assessment of Francis and ends vigorously with the assertion that Francis's faith was: "non una fede qualunque in un Dio qualunque, ma la fede nel Dio di Gesù Cristo trasmessa e custodita dalla Chiesa romana." Felice Accrocca, *Francesco e la Santa Chiesa Romana: La scelta del Vangelo e la codificazione difficile di un ideale* (Assisi, Cittadella Editrice, 2015), 151.

90 Paul Sabatier, *Modernism: The Jowett Lectures, 1908* (New York: Charles Scribner's Sons, 1908), quotations at 32–3, 175. For the papal position on the modernists, see Pius X's 1907 encyclical *Pascendi Domini Gregis*.

91 As they did later, for example, Giuseppe Buffon, "Le début du renouveau conciliaire France dans le milieu Franciscain (1943–1979)," *Revue d'Histoire Ecclésiastique* 105, no. 3 (2010): 689–732.

92 For example, in Leo XIII's bull of 1900 *Conditae a Christo* and the 1917 Code of Canon Law. See Gaston Courtois, *The States of Perfection According to the Teaching of the Church: Papal Documents from Leo XIII to Pius XII*, trans. John A. O'Flynn (Dublin: M.H. Gill and Son, 1961), 49.

93 Pius X, "The Oath Against Modernism," Papal Encyclicals Online, last modified 20 February 2020, http://www.papalencyclicals.net/Pius10/p10moath.htm.

94 On source publication, see Seton, "Rediscovery," 250–6; Charles-Olivier Carbonell, "De Ernest Renan à Paul Sabatier: naissance d'une historiographie scientifique de saint François en France (1864–1893)," in *L'immagine di Francesco nella storiografia dall'Umanesimo all'Ottocento* (Assisi: Università di Perugia, 1983), 225–49.

95 "Letter to the superiors general of orders and religious institutes" (1901); Pius XI, "Unigenitus dei filius," 19 March 1924, in Coutois, *States of Perfection* (*Acta Sancta Sedis*. Rome, 1865–1908), 17, 22, 58.

96 Pius XI, "Rite Expitatis," Papal Encyclicals Online, last modified 20 February 2020, http://www.papalencyclicals.net/pius11/p11ritex.htm.

Similar concerns had been expressed five years earlier by Benedict XV in *Sacra Propediem*.
97 Peter Hebblethwaite, *John XXIII: Pope of the Council* (rev. ed. London: Harper Collins, 1994), 425–6, 371.
98 Norman Tanner, ed., *Decrees of the Ecumenical Councils*, 2 vols. (London: Sheed and Ward, 1990), 2:939–40. The Franciscans in particular engaged in an intensive program of study to establish what, precisely, had been their founder's "spirit and special aims."
99 A point not discussed in Dalarun, *Misadventure of Francis of Assisi*, 30–41.
100 Influential examples include: Cajetan Esser, *Origins of the Franciscan Order*, trans. Aedan Daly (Chicago: Franciscan Herald Press, 1970); Lawrence C. Landini, *The Causes of the Clericalization of the Order of Friars Minor 1209–1260 in the Light of Early Franciscan Sources* (Chicago: Pontificia Universitas Gregoriana, 1967); David Flood and Thadée Matura, *The Birth of a Movement: A Study of the First Rule of St. Francis*, trans. Paul Schawrtz and Paul Lachance (Chicago: Franciscan Herald Press, 1971). Cajetan Esser's edition of the early sources, *Opuscula sancti patris Francisci Assisiensis* (Grottaferrata: Collegii S. Bonaventurae Ad Claras Aquas, 1978) was similarly published "cum permissu superiorum." Indeed, Paolazzi's 2009 new critical edition updating Esser was actively commissioned by the ministers of his order. Carlo Paolazzi, "Novità nel testo critico degli *Scripta* di Francesco d'Assisi, in rapporto all'edizione Esser," *Archivum Franciscanum Historicum* 102, nos. 3–4 (2009): 353–90, at 353.
101 Mary Finbarr Coffey, "The Complexities and Difficulties of a Return *ad fontes*," in *A Future Full of Hope?*, ed. Gemma Simmonds (Blackroom: The Columba Press, 2012), 38–51. For some of historiographical developments in these decades, see Merlo, "La storiografia"; Dalarun, *Misadventure*, 36–50.
102 Hence, Jacques Le Goff, *Saint Francis of Assisi*, trans. Christine Rhone (London: Routledge, 2004) presents "the true Saint Francis, or – perhaps better … – *my* Saint Francis" (xi); and André Vauchez's struggles throughout his *Francis* to reconcile his recognition of his own subjectivity as a historian with his conviction that great truths are embodied in his subject.
103 "Lumen gentium," VI, 44.
104 For example, Leonardo Boff, *Saint Francis: A Model for Human Liberation*, trans. John W. Diercksmeir (London: SCM Press, 1985); for analysis, see Giovanni Iammarrone, "The Renewal of Franciscan Religious Life since Vatican II," trans. Edwards Hagman, *Greyfriars Review* 9, no. 3 (1995): 331–55.
105 "a quanti operano per un inserimento del messaggio evangelico nel nostro tempo," *Fonti francescane* (Padua-Assisi, 1977), 7.

106 Ian Linden, *Global Catholicism: Diversity and Change since Vatican II* (London: Hurst, 2009), 26.
107 On the entrenched problem of a Eurocentric, papal-focused view of medieval Christianity, see Dorothea Weltecke, "Space, Entanglement and Decentralisation: On How to Narrate the Transcultural History of Christianity (550 to 1350 CE)," in *Locating Religions: Contact, Diversity, and Translocality*, ed. Reinhold Glei and Nikolas Jaspert (Leiden: Brill, 2017), 315–44.
108 Mark Gregory Pegg, *The Corruption of Angels: The Great Inquisition of 1245– 1246* (Princeton: Princeton University Press, 2001), 129.
109 Christine Caldwell Ames, "Does Inquisition Belong to Religious History?" *The American Historical Review* 110, no. 1 (2005): 11–37.
110 Ian Forrest, *Trustworthy Men: How Inequality and Faith Made the Medieval Church* (Princeton: Princeton University Press, 2018).
111 On the complexities of resistance to the idea, see Guy Geltner, *The Making of Medieval Antifraternalism: Polemic, Violence, Deviance, and Remembrance* (Oxford: Oxford University Press, 2012).
112 Dominique Iogna-Prat, *Ordonner et exclure. Cluny et la société chrétienne face à l'hérésie, au judaïsme et à l'islam (1000–1150)*, 2nd ed. (Paris: GF Flammarion, 2004), and William Chester Jordan, *Men at the Center: Redemptive Governance under Louis IX* (Budapest: Central European University Press, 2012).

4 Hypocrites! Critiques of Religious Movements and Criticism of the Church, 1050–1300

SITA STECKEL

A discussion of criticisms of medieval religious movements, a theme that is contained but not elaborated in Herbert Grundmann's seminal work, finds a congenial starting point in the medieval poem *Roman de la Rose*.[1] One of the most popular literary works of the later Middle Ages, this poem by Guillaume de Lorris (d. after 1240) began as a courtly allegory of love. But its continuation, by the cleric Jean de Meun (d. after 1280), changed in tone. Whereas Guillaume de Lorris had set up a chivalrous story of the main protagonist, *Amant*, falling in love with the Rose and attempting to gain her favour, Jean de Meun turned the contemplation of love into a satirical critique of society. The latter treated courtly love with cynicism and the eventual conquest of the Rose as a drastically sexual one.

One allegorical character that appears during *Amant*'s long quest is *Faus Semblant*, False Seeming, presented as the child of Fraud and Hypocrisy.[2] In his long introductory speech, *Faus Semblant* explains his own "protean" nature: He can change his appearance and gender at will and has many dwelling places. Defending his own perpetual and thus reliable falsity, he extols the uses and high potential of hypocrisy for anyone striving for worldly goods.[3] Unsurprisingly, he quickly becomes an important ally in *Amant*'s battle for the Rose.

Both in the poem and in its modern interpretation, there is little doubt about the targets of this satirical barb. Though *Faus Semblant* himself admits that hypocrisy may be found both in the world and in the cloister, he believes that it finds a particular home in the cloister, especially among false monks, a bad sort of the religious who hide an evil nature under their cowls.[4] He therefore appears as a *Jacobin* or *Cordelier*, a Dominican or Franciscan, and is usually depicted accordingly in illustrations of the *Roman*.[5] *Faus Semblant* is thus mainly a device to criticize the habited religious, particularly the mendicant friars. Scholarship has long tied this critique to the notorious quarrels between the mendicant friars and the secular clergy, which had flared up at the University of Paris and elsewhere during the mid-thirteenth century, sparking a series of polemics between the mendicant friars and their critics.[6] An episode of renewed conflict revolving around the papal bull *Ad fructus uberes* (1281) forms the immediate backdrop to Jean de Meun's work.

Yet the charge of widespread hypocrisy in the *Roman de la Rose* is ultimately broader than this context indicates, extending to the church as a whole. In spite of his diverting literary style, Jean de Meun leaves little doubt that his characters view the church as declining, a diagnosis expressed through recurring eschatological references.[7] *Faus Semblant* acknowledges freely that he is a harbinger of the Antichrist. The pale face of his companion *Astinence Contrainte*, Forced Abstinence – a shady beguine whose attractive unholiness rivals that of *Faus Semblant* – is linked to the fourth horse and rider of the Apocalypse, the pale horse, carrying death (Rev. 6:6).[8] This alarming biblical image had long been closely associated with the last age of the world, expected to be an age of hypocrisy.[9] *Faus Semblant* and *Astinence Contrainte* in fact set this eschatological scenario in motion, conceiving the Antichrist in their illicit union.[10]

While these elements of criticism directed at the church were not new in the *Roman*, their crystallization in the allegorical character of *Faus Semblant* throws their function and impact into unusually sharp relief. Unlike the more overt polemics at the University of Paris, the allegory not only served to express criticism of a particular religious group (a strategy that Kathryn Kerby-Fulton has called "ordo prophecy").[11] The variable, ubiquitous, and somewhat mischievous nature of *Faus Semblant* also prompts reflection on the broader problem of discerning "genuine" religiosity.[12] As a religious vice, hypocrisy may find its dwelling place anywhere, even (or perhaps particularly) in the cloister. After a short speech on the presence of bad apples across all religious orders and houses, *Faus Semblant* enlarges on a closely related problem – as he argues, genuine religiosity may also be found under the worldly clothes of laypeople. His argument thus suddenly encroaches on the hierarchy of lay and clerical estates – and, as it happens, on the hierarchy of genders, as *Faus Semblant* points to holy women, non-ordained but nevertheless often saintly, as proof of his argument.[13]

In making these connections, the literary device of *Faus Semblant* shows that arguments which are easily explained and classed as "religious polemics," with known targets and contexts, may nevertheless tie deeply into a broader problematization of religious institutions and their underlying cultural hierarchies. The search for a "genuine" religiosity – a protean, and therefore dynamic and at times destructive, idea – calls into question the very distinction between formalized religious observance and everyday piety, jeopardizing in turn the distinction between laypeople and the religious estates as well as the power relations predicated upon such differences. The allegory of *Faus Semblant* thus reflects a society in which religion was felt to become unmoored from the hierarchies and symbolic distinctions nominally delimiting and defining it. Hypocrisy as a "boundary" category, with a dynamic performative ability to challenge and to destabilize established ways of understanding religion, makes this issue tangible.[14]

This characteristic of hypocrisy invites further historical investigation and makes the concept highly intriguing and relevant for an innovative history of medieval religion. The impulse to pursue its destabilizing effect is further galvanized by the state of research: While substantial studies of hypocrisy and criticisms of religiosities exist, much of the scholarship remains disparate and fragmentary and therefore invites attempts to connect it into a new whole.

This aim leads us deeply into the territory first charted by Herbert Grundmann: As a preliminary search for *hypocrisia* and related terms in extant digitized texts shows, the concept is intertwined closely with the trajectory of Grundmann's *Religious Movements*. Before the controversies between the mendicant friars and the secular clergy at the University of Paris caused the concept of hypocrisy to "go viral," as Nicholas Watson puts it, there were notable conjunctions that largely coincide with the movements described by Grundmann.[15] Of course, the term "hypocrisy" was already developed and differentiated markedly during the formative period of Christianity in Late Antiquity and recurs across the medieval centuries in didactic and exegetical texts. But it was also deployed in polemical texts and text passages with regularity, with increasing use of the term during the twelfth and thirteenth centuries.[16] The term appears in the polemics of eleventh-century church reformers in the so-called Investiture Contest and more frequently in the two areas highlighted by Grundmann, religious orders and heresy. It is highly visible in the battle against heresy, which intensified from the eleventh century onwards. But it also formed a key term in debates surrounding the emergence of new religious orders – both the twelfth-century monastic and canonical orders, such as the Cistercians or Premonstratensians, and the thirteenth-century controversies between the new mendicant orders and the secular clergy.

Postulating a new trajectory of "religious history" rather than "church history," Grundmann envisioned these movements as a set of recurring and related religious innovations.[17] As he saw it, a new religious engagement of the laity led to contests and emulations of forms of the apostolic life, resulting in repeated conjunctures of institutional or counter-institutional religious renewal, eventually influencing and shaping new lifeforms for the clergy, religious orders, and lay movements. One possible hypothesis is that charges of religious hypocrisy simply form a "dark side" of the religious energy of these recurring religious innovations. It appears highly plausible that new forms of religiosity would typically find critics. This is indeed a view expressed, for example, in Giles Constable's magisterial treatment of the *Reformation of the Twelfth Century*, where he remarks that "even the greatest reformers ran into criticism."[18]

But Constable's appraisal is also representative of a deep rift within the extant historiography: The different traditions of research which have so far dealt with criticisms of particular religious movements, and with hypocrisy in particular, ascribe very different causes, qualities, and impacts to such criticisms. Once we cross a historiographical watershed around 1250, interpretations tend to flow towards a "Renaissance" or "Reformation" narrative, which connects and contrasts late medieval and early modern cultures. In this setting, criticisms of religious elites as hypocritical – and criticisms of the church more generally – are largely understood as part of a broader current of "anti-clericalism." Anti-clerical discourse is seen as an important and significant factor in late medieval society, ultimately resulting from the "crisis" or even "decay" of late medieval ecclesiastical institutions, afflicted by problems which eventually caused the Reformation but also enabled and intensified a growing emancipation of the late medieval laity.[19] Critical evaluations of the friars like those suggested by the *Roman de la Rose* have been understood as a sub-type of anti-clericalism in this context. That this perspective on "anti-fraternalism" (as it is typically labelled) implies a highly teleological viewpoint has only very recently been problematized.[20]

In contrast, criticisms of religious orders dating to the long twelfth century, occurring before this historiographical watershed, have only attracted fragmented attention. Though criticisms and polemics of the religious renewal of the period were acknowledged, a dominant historiographical narrative portrayed the period as one of consolidation and centralization of the papal church. Critiques below this level thus appeared as a mere side issue, a by-product of successful reform, as illustrated by Constable's verdict and brief treatment of polemics against monks and nuns.[21] This means that twelfth-century criticisms of the religious life were taken much less seriously, and viewed as much less transformative, than later medieval critiques.

Grundmann's perspective, which suggests a more sustained, drawn-out transformation spanning from the eleventh to the fourteenth centuries, might offer a more integrated view on these phenomena. If we take his arguments seriously, it seems less natural to treat closely related phenomena on either side of the 1250 "watershed" moment so differently – especially as we already know of close intellectual links between late thirteenth-century criticisms of the church and earlier texts. While treating the high Middle Ages as a period of "renewal" and the later Middle Ages as one of "decay" appears legitimate in specific, circumscribed contexts, a deeper conceptual separation of these periods is more problematic. Such a separation mainly depends on separate narratives and frameworks of "church history," which were by and large shaped by older Christian, confessional identities, either emphasizing high medieval renewal (originally a Catholic proposal) or the Reformation (the Protestant counter-proposal) as the foundations of modernity.[22] More recent research has repeatedly suggested that a focus on religious history or the "history of religious culture" needs to replace these inherited forms of church history – and this shift implies new forms of periodization and a problematization of the ways we model and frame religious change.[23]

Within this historiographical context, the extant criticisms of medieval monks and nuns, clerics, friars, or beguines have so far been studied separately from each other, within the largely inward-looking research areas of church reform, heresy, clerical culture, monastic orders, mendicant orders, or female religiosity, which all include some form of the 1250 historiographical "watershed."[24] This fragmentation has recently been flagged as a genuine issue for medieval studies, and for the study of medieval religion in particular.[25] Intriguingly, Grundmann himself already deplored similar issues and sought to overcome them by considering different forms and institutions of medieval religious life together, observing their interplay and drawing conclusions about their long-term dynamics from the high to the later Middle Ages.[26] Of course, both the demarcations between current research fields and the reasons for their separation are rather different today than they were in 1935, when Grundmann described a research landscape largely organized along confessional identities. There are, moreover, many pioneering studies that cross established boundaries today – or address the spaces "in between" them, as emphasized in the editors' introduction to this volume. But overall, current structural pressures towards specialization – primarily, the existence of dedicated subfields dealing with only one aspect of medieval religion, as well as the growing pressure on scholars to publish as many short works as possible within these subfields, rather than attempting experimental work or new syntheses – appear to have created a new version of the fragmentation encountered by Grundmann.[27]

Current research may therefore derive important insights from adapted and updated versions of Grundmann's "connected" thinking and from his observations on long-term dynamics. Rather than focusing on the conceptual history of hypocrisy in a specific context, the present chapter will attempt to engage with these underlying issues, reapplying some of Grundmann's strategies to the ground originally staked out in *Religious Movements*. As it aims to sketch larger dynamics of religious history, the present chapter will neither present a detailed overview of various criticisms of different religious movements during the high Middle Ages, nor offer any sort of exhaustive discussion of the conceptual and semantic history of hypocrisy. Both themes would demand much more room and a significant amount of in-depth preparatory research. Yet the specific issue of hypocrisy offers a valuable thread to revisit Grundmann's vision of the inner dynamics of Latin Christianity: What do the charges of religious hypocrisy made against different religious movements imply, and are they somehow all connected to each other? What sort of trajectory can be constructed if we de-centre the well-known stories of late medieval anti-clericalism and anti-fraternalism and straddle the "watershed" between the high and late Middle Ages? This chapter attempts to formulate explorative answers to some of these questions by discussing charges of hypocrisy in some of the religious movements highlighted by Grundmann.

The path charted is largely an attempt to show the gradual entanglement of different forms and themes of criticism. A section devoted to rhetorical forms and connotations of the term "hypocrisy" first discusses the disparate and broad spectrum of possible uses during the eleventh and earlier twelfth centuries. To this aim, it explores how superficially similar but thematically distinct charges of hypocrisy were deployed in the battles over church reform and against heresy. The next section narrows the focus to a third institutional context, which developed accusations of hypocrisy as a high-frequency polemical argument, namely the various criticisms surrounding the new monastic orders of the twelfth century. This section attempts to tease out particular functions and underlying social anxieties of the charge of "false" religiousness against monks, which gradually acquired distinct themes and forms. The following section engages with the closely related phenomenon of criticisms of thirteenth-century mendicant orders and compares criticisms of the friars with the earlier texts, gauging how this particular strand of discourse developed new themes and accents. A conclusion draws the findings together, reflecting on the ways we might reimagine or expand the trajectories originally laid out by Grundmann.

False Religion: Rhetoric against Hypocrisy in the Battles Concerning Church Reform and Heresy

Of the elements making up the *Roman de la Rose*'s diagnosis of religion – an unmasking of hypocritical false religiosity, the association of such hypocrisy with eschatological meaning, and the idea that it had spread within the church and especially among different types of religious – at least the first two go far back, forming part of the intellectual heritage of late antique Christianity.[28] To simplify for the sake of clarity and leave aside exegetical texts, this section highlights discussions of hypocrisy that occurred in two main contexts during the early and high Middle Ages, one that is more didactic and the other more polemical.[29]

The didactic tradition, largely based on patristic texts, discussed hypocrisy primarily as individual vice. In this context, hypocrisy was not only conceived as adhering to a "double standard," as various ancient texts suggested, but hinged on the religious implications of a discrepancy between *intus* and *foris*.[30] Specifically, the fathers warned that an outwardly faultless religious practice of Christians – and especially of those engaged in the *vita religiosa* – might nevertheless be marred by a false inward motivation. Possible "false" motivations ranged from everyday human weakness, such as a religious vanity which wanted to outshine others in the community to hidden worldliness and secular calculation, or even more outrageous instances of deceit and machinations hiding under a pious façade, which might then be ascribed to demonic or devilish influence.[31]

Forms of polemical usage typically built on the latter, "escalated" view of hypocrisy and therefore used the rather harsh rhetoric and dramatic metaphors of the biblical texts mentioning hypocrisy. These either associated hypocrisy with the "false prophets" announced for the end times (e.g., 1 Tim. 4:1–2 and 2 Tim. 3:1–7), who were envisaged as the "wolves in sheep's clothing" (Matt. 24:11 and 7:15), or with the Pharisees, accused of being like "whited sepulchres, which look beautiful on the outside but on the inside are full of the bones of the dead and everything unclean" (Matt. 23:27). Accusations of this nature aimed to discredit an opponent's claim to religious authority, and at times accused opponents of having devilish intentions, especially when the events were viewed in an eschatological framework linking them to the Antichrist and the last age of the world.[32]

During the earlier and high Middle Ages, there were, as it appears, no clear-cut approaches to discussing hypocrisy at first. Even a didactic text for monks might have used, for example, the more dramatic biblical metaphors usually reserved for polemics to make its point. In the early twelfth century, Abbot Bernard of Clairvaux (d. 1153) thus melded biblical metaphors with a didactic intention in his *Sentences*, addressed mainly to his fellow monks. He presented hypocrisy as the third of four vices actively separating the soul from God: worldly levity, immoderate sadness, vain hypocrisy, and tumid arrogance.[33] Gathering relevant biblical passages, he warned against hypocrisy as a vice that turned people into "pretend Christians, who do not want to be but desire to be seen as, who outwardly pretend to an appearance of saintliness, but are wolves under their sheep's clothing. Their whitewash is that of whited sepulchres, hiding the decay of dead bones."[34]

More explicitly polemical charges of hypocrisy abounded during the later eleventh and early twelfth century, as the large-scale tangle of controversies and civil wars that we call church reform and the Investiture Contest generated important new forms of public debate about religion.[35] Intriguingly, however, it seems that the polemics of the church reform period typically did not engage with the concept of hypocrisy in a coherent or systematic manner. Rather, they reflected the considerable scope and variety of rhetorical strategies within the quarrels, and the period up to c. 1120 appeared as one of experimentation. Reformers like Bernard of Clairvaux, or his predecessor Cardinal Humbert of Silva Candida (d. 1061), often used charges of hypocrisy as freestanding invectives, typically as one item in longer lists of pejorative labels and criticisms addressed to reform-resistant clergy.[36] But the overall thrust of the increasingly elaborate "rhetoric of reform," developed by the Gregorian party during the later eleventh and early twelfth century, stood in tension with extant conceptualizations of religious hypocrisy.[37] The scathing criticisms of reformers concerned the visible worldliness and secular entanglements of the church, not the outward holiness of religious individuals motivated by the wrong inner disposition. As Bernard of Clairvaux wrote, echoing earlier polemicists, the "provosts, deans, archdeans, bishops and archbishops" with their active political careers and trappings of nobility exhibited "whorish splendor, a behavior worthy of mimes and royal pomp," where "gold was on the reins, on the thrones, on the spurs – in fact, the spurs glittered more than the altars."[38] Bernard castigated this as hypocrisy, as the prelates' claim to religious authority stood in direct contrast to their irreligious life. But this was not the typical form of religious hypocrisy. The prelates' vice was not hidden, but openly displayed, as Bernard admitted in a telling addendum: "Woe to this generation, who should beware the leaven of the Pharisee – if this should still be called hypocrisy, as it cannot hide in its abundance and does not care to hide in its impudence!"[39]

Bernard's addendum illustrates the underlying rhetorical constructions of religious identity and alterity. Overall, his polemic referenced a basic distinction of Christianity from worldliness, which can be mapped onto the distinction between sacred and profane. This construction, which defined Christianity as one with "religion" in a modern sense, was absolutely pervasive within the emerging rhetoric of reform.[40] The concept of religious hypocrisy, on the other hand, relied on a different metaphorical game and an additional element in the construction of the boundary of religion: Hypocrisy complicates the distinction between religion and irreligion by adding a distinction of inner/outer, rhetorically unmasking a hidden irreligious agenda under a treacherous "semblance of piety" (e.g., *species pietatis*, 2 Tim. 3:5).[41] It thus postulates a basic distinction of "true" versus "false religiosity," which is ultimately at odds with a distinction of "religiosity" versus "worldliness" and therefore runs counter to the typical thrust of reform rhetoric.

Given this conceptualization, we should rather expect to find charges of hypocrisy from the opponents of Gregorian reform and among the supporters of King Henry IV, who found themselves confronted by opponents laying a supercharged claim to religious authority. The concept was indeed prominent on that side of the conflict but, typically for the period, had no clear-cut definitions, metaphors, or invectives connected to it as yet. A common denominator of accusations can be teased out of a range of different accusations: The Gregorian reforming side was typically portrayed as pretending to strive for Christ but actually going against and beyond his commandments to further their own worldly power.[42]

Altogether, the charges of hypocrisy set up demarcations of religious alterity, providing boundary markers which could be used to construct religious difference from within the church, accusing Christian opponents of being "no true Christians." This form of difference neither extended to the charge of worldliness nor to an alterity conceived as alien and monstrous, which might be applied to distanced cultural "others," such as pagans and Jews. The problem with hypocrites was that they appeared just like Christians – even like virtuous Christians, appearing better than most.

That apparent Christians might not really be Christian, and might be devious rather than pious, was also the resounding message of the most dramatic polemical rhetoric that instrumentalized the eschatological scenario of the end of days, prophesied in the Bible to "distinguish the false from the true."[43] This framework, which largely goes back to New Testament polemics, could be used to give polemical rhetoric a sense of increased urgency, polarization, and drama; it derived from the recognition that the world was engaged in an end battle between good and evil, Christ and Antichrist, and that good Christians must act *now* to fight all representatives of the enemy.[44]

While this eschatological framework for religious polemics was far from new during the twelfth century, it is intriguing to note where and how it was typically used. From the early Middle Ages onwards, the biblical warnings against false prophets and hypocritical "wolves in sheep's clothing" had mostly been applied to heretics. In particular, the Pauline warnings against false prophets and false preachers threatening Christendom during the end times (1 Tim. 4:1–2; 2 Tim. 3:1–7, etc.) had always offered themselves up for polemical use against dissenters. This rhetoric therefore appeared repeatedly during the early medieval period and became familiar once heterodoxy established itself as a concern after c. 1000. Like the early Christians engaging with competing sects, the clergy of the period indeed found themselves confronted with ascetic religious *virtuosi* who tempted the believers away from them.[45] Bishops like Gerard I of Cambrai (d. 1051) thus warned their clerics to stay vigilant, citing the warnings of the Apostle Paul (at the synod of Arras in 1025): "Keep to this as an inviolate sign of your faith, and remember that the apostle Paul prophesied that *'in the last days, some will renounce the faith by paying attention to deceitful spirits and teachings of demons, through the hypocrisy of liars whose consciences are seared with a hot iron. They forbid marriage and demand abstinence from foods, which God created to be received with thanksgiving by those who believe'* (1 Tim. 4:1–2)."[46] Almost a century later, around 1116, Bishop Hildebert of Le Mans (d. 1133) made the same connection, linking a seeming holiness to a false and even diabolical message when referring to the wandering preacher Henry of Lausanne (d. c. 1148). He denounced Henry as a "pseudo-prophet" and a "Devil's snare and arms-bearer of the Antichrist," who "simulated religion in his habit and education in his words."[47]

The battles over church reform also led to instances of crossover and conceptual borrowing of such motifs and gave rise to a marked phase of experimentation with eschatological scenarios in the decades after 1100.[48] Older exegeses targeting heretics or other enemies were repeatedly adapted to fit the conflicts of the high medieval church. Commenting on the ongoing struggles over papal jurisdiction during the early twelfth century, the *Historia Mediolanensis* of Landulf of St Paul (d. after 1136–7), a Milanese cleric with ties to France first complained about wandering, hypocritical "pseudo-prophets" troubling the Italian cities.

But in the next breath, Landulf also accused papal officials in Milan of meddling in the Milanese church and doing the work of the Antichrist.[49]

The fluidity of such ascriptions and interpretations becomes clear from the polemical writings of Bernard of Clairvaux, who came to reflect on hypocrisy in several, apparently largely unconnected instances. Bernard's attack on secular-minded prelates, as described above, not only upbraided the clerics for their decadence, opulence, and worldly behaviour. He also suggested that such worldly prelates held their offices because they were "servants of the Antichrist," whose connivance had led to their installation in high offices.[50] Making a similar argument in one of his *Parables*, Bernard adapted older exegesis concerning the end times – in particular, he used the image of the four horsemen of the Apocalypse in Revelation 6:1–8, in which the white, red, and black horses preceded the fourth, pale horse carrying death. In his *Parable VI*, Bernard updated extant explanations which connected the four horsemen to the different ages of the church and the threats characterizing them. Traditionally, the first white horse signified the peace of Christ, while the red, black, and pale horses signified the threats to this peace by tyrants, heretics, and hypocrites – with "tyrants" and "heretics" typically identified with the Roman emperors and powerful heresies of Late Antiquity, such as Nestorianism, while the hypocrites were viewed as a scourge of the end times. As Bernard argued, however, sacrificing the heretics of Late Antiquity, the third rider on the black horse, stood for the hypocrisy of the bad prelates of his day, while the rider on the pale horse signified the coming of the Antichrist.[51]

This interpretation diverged significantly from several early and high medieval ones, which connected the issue of hypocrisy only to the rider on the pale horse and thus to the last age of the church.[52] This more emphatically apocalyptic interpretation soon eclipsed Bernard's suggestion, once the immediate battles of the Investiture Contest were over and heresy regained centre stage. In particular, the appearance of various forms of heresy labelled as "Catharism," which developed powerful followings in the Rhineland and in Southern France, prompted a conjuncture of anti-heretical rhetoric charged with eschatological overtones.[53]

In the polemical fight against this enemy, heresy naturally returned to the status of the last and worst threat to the church, and the heretics of the day were associated with the hypocrites of the last age.[54] Bernard appears to have fallen in line with this interpretation of dangers associated with the "pale horse" and the last age of the church, largely at the prompting of German ecclesiastics. In a letter that solicited Bernard's help in 1143, the Premonstratensian prior Everwin of Steinfeld (d. 1152) had identified current heresies with the threats of the last ages, arguing that sermons were needed to combat a particular group of "heretics who shall appear toward the end of the world, of whom, speaking through the Apostle [Paul], *'the Spirit manifestly saith that in the last times some shall depart from the faith, giving heed to spirits of error and doctrines of devils, speaking lies in hypocrisy,'*" and so on.[55] Though Everwin did not discuss whether the end times were actually at hand, heeding patristic warnings in this respect, he managed to create an atmosphere of dramatic urgency by stating that it felt as if this were the case – as many other rhetoricians would do after him. Everwin implored Bernard of Clairvaux to "stand forth against the new heretics who everywhere in almost all churches boil up from the pit of hell as though already their prince were about to be loosed and the day of the Lord were at hand."[56]

Bernard of Clairvaux quietly discarded his own earlier interpretation and took up Everwin's line of argument. But he added his own considerable rhetorical verve to the eschatological scenario, combining it with several biblical passages discussing heresy and hypocrisy in his further sermons against heretics. Given Bernard's huge popularity and his sermons' wide circulation, these texts did much to consolidate an image of heretics as devilish hypocrites, while also cementing the association of hypocrisy with the last days. In his *Sermo* 66, Bernard not only identified the heretics of his day with the "lying hypocrites" of the last age mentioned in the Pauline prophecies.[57] He also combined several alarmist biblical images:

> These are the ones who come in sheep's clothing, in order to denude the sheep and despoil the rams. And does it not seem to you that both things have been attained, when the people have been robbed of their faith, and the priests of their people? Who are these robbers? They are sheep according to their bearing, but foxes according to their deceit and wolves according to their deeds and cruelty. These are the ones who want to be seen as good without being good, and to avoid being seen as bad though they want to be bad.... For malice always harms less when it is out in the open, and a good man is not deceived except through the simulation of good.... With them, it is not about cultivating the virtues, but about colouring the vices with a leaden colour simulating them. And to this superstitious impiety, then they apply the name of religion.[58]

As the last lines especially suggest, this amounts to an aggressive polemical reinterpretation of the older didactic concepts of hypocrisy: Bernard had earlier argued that "vain hypocrisy" was a fairly widespread human attitude of applying double standards, shared by monks and the religious, which had the potential to draw their souls away from God. In the cited passage, he reinterpreted hypocrisy as a strategic device of devilish enemies of Christ, who were already removed from God and now engaged in hypocritical deceit to hide this fact from their hapless victims.

Sources from Germany bear out that this demonized image of heretics – seen as only outwardly pious, but in reality harbingers and agents of the Antichrist – was taken up and spread. The image was used in the sermons addressed to the Cathar heretics by the Benedictine abbot Ekbert of Schönau (d. 1184), who participated in the interrogation and burning of heretics at Cologne in 1162.[59] Remarkably, there was a close association of allegorical personifications of hypocrisy and heresy, appearing as the handmaidens of the Antichrist, in the *Ludus de Antichristo*, a Latin play dating to the 1150s and addressing courtly and clerical audiences.[60] This association also appears in a well-known, influential letter-sermon of Hildegard of Bingen (d. 1179), addressed to the clergy of Cologne, which showcases a mechanism of polemical rhetoric to which we will return below.[61] Hildegard not only warned against outwardly pious ascetics who hid their status as disciples of the devil under a guise of religiosity, aiming at the "Cathars" in Cologne. In the same breath, she also upbraided the clergy for their moral laxity. She thus combined the two rhetorical constructions of religious alterity discussed above, that of "worldliness" and of "false religiosity," into a new whole. As Hildegard argued in a scenario which diagnosed a "world turned upside down," the clergy was worldly and lax instead of saintly – and this deficiency created a space into which devilish hypocrites (such as the Cathars) could creep. Equipped with a seeming religiosity and chastity, which was the opposite of their devilish inner nature, they offered the outward trappings of religiosity that the people craved. The two strands of polemical rhetoric we have seen separately in Bernard of Clairvaux's writings, the "rhetoric of reform" and the warnings against "false religiosity," were thus neatly combined.

While Hildegard had a fairly clear opinion of which threat was the greater one – her interpretation of the last days clearly framed the lax prelates as the main issue afflicting the church – her interweaving of two different constructions of religious alterity is revealing in this context.[62] Her text not only proved to have a long afterlife in further intra-Christian controversies, especially from the thirteenth century onwards, as we shall see below.[63] Much like Bernard of Clairvaux's interpretative manoeuvring, her innovative polemic also illustrates how a polemical discourse on the state of the church, born during the great conflicts of the eleventh-century church reform, became interlaced with new elements and fragments of interpretation from other contexts, gathered up in episodes of controversy like the dramatic confrontations with Catharism in Cologne. While the motif of hypocrisy represented only one thread in this process of conceptual transfer and entanglement, its applicability to any sort of "false" religiosity made it particularly useful for linking different strands of discourse.

False Superiority: Charges of Hypocrisy against and between New Religious Orders

This entanglement of different polemical traditions featuring hypocrisy also appears in texts debating the emergence of new religious orders. As Grundmann noted and more recent studies confirm, the perception of new religious communities was mostly positive but could be ambivalent and outright hostile at certain moments. New types of strict ascetic practices, represented by various charismatic founders, could attract either praise or suspicion.[64] Polemical engagements with such new communities were therefore many and varied.[65] Just before the middle of the twelfth century, the ongoing multiplication of new religious forms became so notable as to cause dismay so that the growing diversity of religious orders, described as (nimia) *diversitas religionum*, emerged as an additional strand of debate.[66]

A first glance at the relevant materials suggests that polemical charges of hypocrisy are different and somewhat more "tame" in this context. Most debates about the reform of monasticism were, of course, conducted within the channels of ecclesiastical conflict resolution, namely at synods or within treatises and letter-treatises circulating in ecclesiastical networks. In such texts, partly formalized modes of argument and admonition prevailed, with safeguards meant to avoid escalation.[67] Intra-ecclesiastical debates therefore retained many elements of solution-oriented "discussion," rather than "dispute"-like rhetoric intent on legitimizing the forceful exclusion of religious opponents.[68]

However, the exchanges between representatives of the old and new forms of religious life were not free of disparaging rhetoric. The well-known letter-treatises exchanged from the mid-1120s onwards between Abbot Peter the Venerable of Cluny (d. 1156) and Bernard of Clairvaux as a representative of Cîteaux are resounding examples. Though both authors knew that general conventions and monastic humility discouraged open criticism of fellow monks and fellow Christians, and even cultivated a somewhat stilted formal *amicitia*, they still veered towards invective with regularity.[69] Bernard of Clairvaux, for example, penned lengthy protestations that he did not wish to engage in *detractio*, and he had never done so.[70] Yet in his first text concerning the matter, the letter *Ad Robertum*, he called a Cluniac prior a wolf in sheep's clothing and left little doubt that a move from Clairvaux to Cluny implied a "desertion" of the true monastic calling.[71] In his later *Apologia*, Bernard defended the Cistercian austerity of clothing so enthusiastically that he ended up insinuating, rather imaginatively, that Cluniac monks regularly spent time visiting cloth markets, intent on finding the best fabrics, visiting all the shops, fingering the materials, and choosing the finest qualities at high prices.[72]

Abbot Peter of Cluny, unsurprisingly, defended Cluniac customs by calling out the Cistercian criticisms as arrogance and hypocrisy. In his long letter 28 to Bernard of Clairvaux, written in 1127, he used hypocrisy as a central conceptual lever to derail the Cistercians' claim to superiority. Instead of arguing for the superiority of Cluny, Peter set out to defend the principle of diversity, of adaptation to local context, and of abbatial sovereignty, enshrined in the *Rule of St Benedict*.[73] This was an implicit rebuttal of the Cistercians' attempt to enforce the *Rule* to the letter, which was (in the style of the anti-Gregorian rhetoric discussed above) indirectly unmasked as hypocritical because it went beyond genuinely Benedictine concerns. Peter also aimed to teach a lesson on monastic humility. In the opening lines of his treatise, he vehemently upbraided the Cistercians for arrogance, describing them as hypocrites: "Woe! a new type of Pharisees has returned to the world, who keep themselves separate from the others and hold themselves superior!... You constitute yourselves as saintly, as singular, as the only true monks in the world ... and for this reason, you pretend to wear a habit of unusual colour, so that you among all the monks of the world show yourself brilliant among the black ones to distinguish yourselves."[74]

This was only the first of a series of criticisms against the Cistercians pertaining to their white (i.e., undyed) habits.[75] But Peter's attack also pinpointed a central issue of this intra-monastic debate with great precision: Diversity was a well-established characteristic of the monastic life and – as Giles Constable observed – could be defended and legitimized as a diversity of circumstance, purpose, or historically grown *consuetudines*.[76] Yet, the Cistercians were not only calling themselves different – they were insinuating that they were *better*, that there was a hierarchy between them and other religious communities. This was an idea that Peter energetically refuted, in particular by labelling such attempts to rise above others as hypocrisy.

Other monastic perspectives on this issue confirm that hierarchy was the central issue around which accusations of hypocrisy among different monastic observances revolved – the charge was that of a "false religious superiority" rather than of "false religiosity." For example, in a long, pointedly balanced evaluation of the Cistercians, the Benedictine chronicler Ordericus Vitalis (d. c. 1142), writing before 1141, enumerated various examples of their superior asceticism. But he then added a mildly formulated and yet stinging verdict: "Mixed with the good ones, there are also hypocrites. They are clothed with gleaming white or varied coverings, and thus fool men and make a great spectacle for the people. Many wish to attain the image of a servant of God rather than the virtue. With their multitude, they cause observers to feel contempt; given the limits of unreliable human perceptions, they make proponents of the approved monastic life look rather despicable."[77] As this short remark highlights, Orderic was upset that the Cistercians generated interest in themselves by their innovations and by wearing gleaming white habits, which seemed to signal superiority over traditional monasticism and swayed "unreliable human perceptions" in their favour.

Monastic authors like Orderic Vitalis made this point implicitly, but it was soon made more openly by outsiders, particularly clerics, who entered the debate from the 1130s onwards. The Cistercians often drew the ire of clerics who clashed with them over privileges, especially the monks' sweeping freedoms from paying tithes for the vast lands gifted to them during the course of the twelfth century.[78] But many observers were also disquieted by the agrarian innovations and fairly radical social experiments taking place in the early Cistercian order. One critical voice which has rarely been discussed in the mainstream of historical research is that of Paganus Bolotinus, an otherwise unknown canon of Chartres, who authored a poetical invective about the religious novelties of his day before 1138. He railed particularly about "white-habited new monks" – without, however, naming the Cistercians directly.[79] This poem, which was known to Orderic Vitalis in Normandy and was thus probably one of the typical, semi-public "circular" poems moving among the ecclesiastical and scholastic networks of the twelfth century,[80] strikes a powerful note. It not only vehemently criticizes the new monks, but also situates this criticism in an eschatological framework.

The criticisms uttered by Paganus mostly faulted the new order of white monks for its economic activities, in which the monks tended to do rather well for themselves. Their successes opened them up to criticism of duplicity, where hypocrisy was understood as divergence between outer humility and inner greed. As Paganus wrote:

Having no order, this execrable order, going clothed in lambskin, wants to be viewed as religious. But it does not testify to its religion in deeds. Barns, storehouses, and coffers are filled, heaping goods are multiplying, but these gains do not sate. No plenty gained in daily quest can temper the thirst they have in their immoderate breasts. And they are called poor, who have more than abundance! So, I hold true what is witnessed: a greedy heart never softens. It damns the greedy as it keeps wanting. It speaks sweetly even as it is bitter: a wolfish heart in a lamb's clothing.[81]

These statements bring us back to the polemics discussed above: While Paganus's further passages charged the new monks with arrogating a false position of superiority to themselves, this paragraph visibly returned to harsher accusations, namely the charge that the new monks put on the semblance of a "false religion" while secretly pursuing secular motives. Perhaps because of this impression, Paganus also arrived at an overall diagnosis of his time, which used the eschatological framework of the four horsemen of the Apocalypse. Discussing the ages of the church, which to him culminated in an age of hypocrisy, he wrote: "Let us not doubt that the end of days is near, as we see so many monsters of new religiousness rise. They signify the time of the pseudo-prophets…. At last, the pale horse appears: this is the time of the hypocrites, whom death justly leads to the death of their souls…. This evil root was born from the Pharisees, and their seed fills the earth now a hundredfold: … As minds have darkened in modern times, the noble estate of religion is all decayed."[82] We can thus observe a third polemical adaptation of the older eschatological framework: After Bernard of Clairvaux and others identified the worldly clergy as the hypocrites prophesied for the end times, and just a few years before the motif was revised for the Cathar heretics in the early 1140s, the new monastic orders also attained the doubtful honour of being cast as the hypocrites presaging the last days.

This makes Paganus's text remarkable. He was not completely isolated in labelling the new monks "pseudo-prophets," as the anonymous Latin sermon *Adtendite a falsis prophetis*, ascribed to Peter Abelard, also used this motif during this period.[83] But it did not elaborate on the eschatological element, which was also markedly absent or toned down in later critiques – even in the overall harshest criticisms of the Cistercians, those emerging from the Welsh-English circles around Walter Map (d. 1210) and Gerald of Wales (d. 1223) during the later twelfth century.[84] While Walter Map in particular appears to have baited Cistercian monks frequently in public meetings at court and in episcopal palaces, and attacked them on various fronts in his writings, he tended to cast them as worldly and grasping rather than as demonic.[85] Although Walter did label the Cistercians as hypocrites, wolves in sheep's clothing, and even pseudo-prophets, and allegedly also compared them with Jews, he refrained from associating them with the end times in any detail.[86] One further extant poem titled *Discipulus episcopi Golie de grisis monachis*, which is unfortunately anonymous but probably belongs to the context of late twelfth-century England, also contains an identification of the Cistercians with pseudo-prophets and "servants of Satan."[87] However, this poem also lacks explicit references to the last days.

Several factors may have contributed to this low profile of eschatological motifs. Eschatological framing and demonization were aggressive rhetorical mechanisms "of last resort," so that even daring satirists like Walter Map may have hesitated to use them against orthodox Christians (which may explain the anonymity of the *Adtendite de falsis prophetis* and *De grisis monachis*). Moreover, the increase in rhetorical links between hypocrisy and heresy from the 1140s onwards may have made the violence of this argument even more apparent. On the other hand, most of the twelfth-century polemics and poetical invectives authored by non-monks charged the Cistercians with worldliness and greed rather than hypocrisy, drawing the focus away from the marked false holiness of the hypocrites presaging the last days, and more towards a classical "rhetoric of reform" incriminating their growing worldliness.[88]

Nevertheless, Paganus's text (which pre-dates the 1140s link between hypocrisy and heresy) unmistakably identifies the new monks with the hypocrites presaging the last days. Thus, one of the broad eschatological criticisms of the church uttered in the *Roman de la Rose*, or at least a prefiguration of its overall eschatological pessimism concerning religious orders, was already shifting into place before the mid-twelfth century.

Looking forward to the argument of the *Roman de la Rose*, moreover, Paganus's poetical complaint foreshadows later, more generalized critiques of the state of the religious life. The fact that Paganus addressed bad monks and hermits generally rather than a particular group may have been largely due to caution, taking some polemical sting out of the criticisms.[89] It also set a significant shift of perspective in motion: Paganus not only underlined the number of "monstrous" new religious observances – "tot monstra religionum" – giving us one of the first complaints about the growing *diversitas religionum*, he also explicitly deplored the decay of the "noble order of monks" ("nobilis ordo religionis degenerauit"), referring to the monastic estate overall, not just particular new or old orders.[90] Reform discourses had, of course, long produced laments that the monastic life was decayed or decaying. But these diagnoses had typically been connected to accusations of growing worldliness. Paganus, in contrast, now expressed the idea that monasticism was in crisis because of its inner conflicts.

In the following decades, this diagnosis of an overall crisis of monasticism due to its inner controversies was reflected in a handful of texts, which typically discuss hypocrisy on a more abstract level and contemplate its consequences. One of them is John of Salisbury's *Policraticus*, written around 1156–9 and largely dedicated to the moral philosophy of government.[91] This text contains one chapter (l. vii, c. 21) specifically dedicated to the vice of hypocrisy, understood as concealing worldly ambition under a false pretext of religion, and uses this theme to analyse the debates surrounding monasticism.

In this passage, John of Salisbury criticizes hypocrisy by way of a quasi-personification. In a conceptualization echoed notably by *Faus Semblant* in the *Roman de la Rose*, he describes how ambition itself may take on the guise of a religious life and hide, just like a wolf in sheep's clothing, among various monastic observances, such as the Carthusians, Cistercians, Cluniacs, Templars, or Hospitallers.[92] John then describes both the typical behaviour of such hypocrites and the impact they have, from a markedly clerical standpoint: The hypocrites "censure the people" and "accuse clerics," they criticize others, and "if some blemish has attached itself to the Church while it wanders the earth [they] expose it for public inspection, in order that they may be seen to be immune themselves from all blemishes."[93] They use their special privileges to disturb the established order of the church, secure the favour of princes, enter unasked into pastoral care, and "readily exonerate the powerful and the more wealthy upon receipt of favours and payment."[94] Yet they abhor criticism: "If you reproach them, you are called an enemy of religion and an opponent of the truth."[95]

In John of Salisbury's long disquisition, the verdict that monasticism as a whole is in crisis is more specific than in Paganus Bolotinus's brief assertion. John mentions monasticism as a whole only in passing, as *religio* or the *professiones*, but he explicitly diagnoses that the different orders, and by extension all monks, suffer from the polemics exchanged between and about them.[96] Carefully distinguishing hypocritical monks from "truly religious men," he argues that the hypocrisy of some individuals will nevertheless damage the orders as a whole. As he explains, "[W]hen these men disdain the Church, none are so disturbed with utter propriety as those truly religious men upon whom all of these injuries will back up. The people are roused to anger, but the religious orders are more justly stirred up against the disgrace of these hypocrites. For this blemish is said to have been caused not by the hypocrite but by the Cistercians or the Cluniacs or others in whose apparel these jugglers and ventriloquists dress and whose lives they falsify."[97] With this argument, he not only foreshadows the hide-and-seek of *Faus Semblant* in the *Roman de la Rose*; he paints a picture of widespread controversy and mutual criticisms and recriminations, causing damage to the reputation of monasticism (and of the clergy) as a whole. Though couched in religious language, this keen diagnosis of contemporary dynamics makes its point without recourse to the pale horse of the Apocalypse suddenly plunging the world into hypocrisy.

The Premonstratensian canon Anselm of Havelberg (d. 1158) offered another, slightly earlier explanation for the ongoing multiplication of religious orders by approaching the problem with a complementary perspective. In his *Anticimenon*, written during the 1140s, he formulated one of the most spirited defences of the diversity of twelfth-century religious life. Anselm of Havelberg specifically defended the new orders against charges of hypocrisy.[98] He also took up the issue of criticism and disharmony among religious orders, discussing the overall effects of the debates and shining a particular light on the consequences of the religious orders' multiplication and variability for observers. As he explained:

> Many people are amazed and sceptical at this, to the point of finding such variety scandalous and declaring it scandalous to others.... "Why does God's church present so many new things? Why do so many orders arise in her? Who could count the orders of clerics? Who is not astonished at the many kinds of monks? Who is not even scandalized by the number of them, disgusted by the great variety and disagreement among the many forms of religious life? Who can, still further, fail to scorn the Christian religious life when it is subjected to so much variety, and changed by so many new practices, disrupted by so many new laws and customs…?" As these people say, a practice at one moment advocated for the sake of the kingdom of heaven is thereafter forbidden by the same people who instituted it or by others, again for the sake of the kingdom of heaven, or a practice now banned as sacrilege is soon declared holy and salubrious.[99]

While John of Salisbury had emphasized that criticisms sparked by one hypocrite could damage a whole monastic order and its reputation as a result of the quarrels, Anselm of Havelberg emphasized the relativism imputed to aspects of religious life. If some people considered particular religious practices as sacred, as undertaken "for the sake of the kingdom of heaven," while others did not and preferred different practices instead, the sacrality of these observances themselves was necessarily called into doubt. This forced observers to judge the inward disposition of actors rather than their outward practice but questioned the relationship between *intus et foris* at the same time.

This dynamic, which might be described in sociological terms as a "relativization" of religious authority, caused inadvertently by the growing plurality of diverging religiosities, is also described in a second, perhaps even more insightful, literary text.[100] The *Speculum stultorum*, authored by the English Benedictine Nigel de Longchamps in the 1180s, is a sharp satire of the state of the church in the form of a long, poetical beast epic that echoes Anselm of Havelberg's observation in a compelling literary adaptation.[101] Nigel addressed his text to "foolish" monks who continued to strive for worldly gain even in the cloister. Like John of Salisbury, he used personification to demonstrate the consequences of stupidity and worldly ambition hidden under hypocrisy: His text follows the adventures of Burnellus the Ass, a redoubtable hero who embarks on various (futile) endeavours to better his social standing. After various disastrous episodes, Burnellus decides to enter the religious life. However, confronted with the specific and widely diverging characteristics of the many extant orders (which Nigel debated in a long passage with visible enthusiasm), he has considerable difficulty choosing an order. Following his own foolish logic, Burnellus therefore decides to found a new and better order, combining the "best points" of the older ones. Given that his rationale is a hypocritical one, however, Burnellus actually wants to combine the orders' most permissive rules: He wants to ride like a Templar, drink like a Cluniac, eat meat like a canon, and take a wife like a cleric (an interesting addition, turning the secular clergy into one of many *religiones*), but forego frequent masses like the Carthusians, go without annoying underwear like the Cistercians, and dispense with any restricting belts like the nuns.[102]

This caricature of the practical consequences of monastic hypocrisy elaborates on the relativization-by-diversity concept described by Anselm of Havelberg. If no practice is really sacrosanct, as each order has its strict points and its laxities, the monastic life is taken into the realm of complete arbitrariness, and hypocrites like Burnellus will always find a way of defending their lifestyle. While the *Speculum* clearly bases its overall diagnosis on the debates concerning different forms of the *vita religiosa*, the addition of clerics as one "order" among many enlarges the scope of the critique to encompass not only the monastic world but also the church as a whole. In the *Speculum*, which set a pattern for early estates satire, all estates of the church have their weak points, and all of them offer openings for hypocrites.[103] This is already fairly close to the diagnosis of the *Roman de la Rose*.

False Brothers within the Church: Charges of Hypocrisy against the Mendicants

Comparisons between the forms of polemical rhetoric accusing various opponents of hypocrisy thus far reveal different discursive traditions that used the same rhetorical elements and images. However, polemicists expressed themselves with considerable nuance so that distinct strands and patterns of rhetoric, such as the propagandistic anti-heretical sermons and the letter-treatises of competing monastic leaders, remained visibly different in spite of occasional transfers and borrowings. The next episodes of intra-Christian disputes, the escalating controversies surrounding the new mendicant orders, can be described as catalysts for a significant broadening of the critical discourses discussed so far. More importantly, they witnessed significant conceptual and textual entanglement between different strands of polemical rhetoric.

During the debates at the University of Paris, which escalated from the 1250s onwards, the rhetoric used against the mendicants began to employ highly aggressive terminology, namely the language previously reserved largely for heretics as the "false religious." This transfer of anti-heretical polemics into the new discourse of anti-fraternalism has been recognized in specific research contexts, but it deserves closer attention. Grundmann, and others in his wake, tended to interpret this borrowing as an indicator of the similarity between the new fraternal orders and new heterodox movements.[104] As Grundmann argued, the lifestyles of the two were closely related, and their divergence in status was largely forced upon them by the shifting official demarcations of orthodoxy.[105] Various scholars have also pointed to the well-known anecdote that the early Italian Franciscans coming to Germany were asked whether they were *heretici* and, not understanding the question, mistakenly answered with "yes" so that they were chased from town.[106] For Grundmann, this parallelism between orthodox and heretical religious movements is an important, and even essential, point in situating religious "movements" across and between the heterodox/orthodox divide. However, given the frequency with which established communities viewed religious newcomers with suspicion, and given the particular charges levied against them, such reactions may also be understood as evidence of an accumulation of critical perceptions and negative rhetoric concerning different religious lifestyles.

This is borne out by developments. Grundmann himself noted how the arrival of the Dominicans and Franciscans in Cologne during the 1220s led to conflicts that prompted a rediscovery and deployment of Hildegard of Bingen's polemical letter from the 1160s, as briefly discussed above.[107] But this apparent rediscovery was not spontaneous, nor solely prompted by the apparent similarity between mendicants and heretics, as Grundmann suggested. As the Cistercian Caesarius of Heisterbach (d. c. 1240) noted, the clergy of Cologne had consciously brought an alarmist interpretation of Hildegard's text to their bishop's attention. In a situation of escalated conflict, they apparently dropped the caution that had held back most earlier authors from associating cloistered religious with the age of hypocrisy and the end of days. By insinuating that Hildegard's warnings against hypocritical harbingers of the Antichrist might actually apply to the friars, the clergy of Cologne now added considerable urgency to their legal complaints against the new religious communities, which were quickly becoming their rivals.[108] When the bishop did not show himself unduly alarmed by their warning, the local clergy even took recourse to the typical medium for influencing popular opinion. They proceeded to pay Henry of Avranches (d. c. 1260), a professional poet, to write a more elaborate, poetical version of Hildegard's letter, grandly titled *Prophetia Hyldegardis de falsis fratribus*, and put this into circulation.[109] The poem, or more generally the knowledge of Hildegard's prophecy warning against false and hypocritical new religious orders, sparked a number of additional hostile evaluations of the early mendicant orders during the 1240s and 1250s.[110] While there is no reason to doubt Grundmann's overall argument, we should probably emphasize much more strongly the controversies surrounding the religious innovations of the twelfth century and how they formed an important background for the evaluation of the next wave of newcomers during the thirteenth century.

During the quarrels at the University of Paris, older polemical stereotypes against heretics were then revived and applied to the friars on a much broader scope. The university actually went through its own controversy concerning the role of the friars in the corporation and took up clerical concerns about the friars' role in pastoral care.[111] But the eschatological elements of polemics were greatly amplified for further specific reasons as well. During the 1240s and 1250s, Joachite Franciscans were cultivating their own versions of eschatological, prophetic literature, predicting the rise of a new elite of "spiritual men" and the decay of the established church.[112] This rhetoric was extremely alarming for clerical audiences and could be instrumentalized against the Franciscans. A more traditional view of the last age, employing the established

Pauline warnings against hypocrites and Hildegard's prophecy (and a quickly tailored pseudo-Hildegardian forgery), was therefore developed as "counter-eschatology" to discredit the Franciscans.[113] This traditional vision of the last days also had the advantage of providing the clerical party with their own version of the dramatic, colourful rhetoric of an imminent final battle.

More importantly in our context, the theme of hypocrisy suddenly moved to the centre stage of the controversy due to political circumstances. When a party supporting the rights of the secular clergy, led by canonist and theologian William of Saint-Amour (d. 1272), engaged with the Dominicans and Franciscans at Paris over their rights within the university, the papacy came down very firmly on the side of the mendicants.[114] The university masters failed to be intimidated by this decision and continued to protest, utilizing the legitimate authority of the *studium* and the wealth of older polemical material gathered at their fingertips. Alexander IV therefore decreed measures curtailing further debate on the topic.[115] But rather than silencing the clerical side's protest, this restriction of the legal forum seems to have encouraged a small group around William of Saint-Amour to translate most of their pre-existing legal arguments and complaints into the language of eschatological theology. While they could not directly attack the friars anymore, William, as a master of theology, could and did attack anonymous "dangerous hypocrites" in writings which concerned biblical warnings about the last age. He eventually poured the circulating legal complaints into the new format of an eschatological treatise, *On the dangers of the last days*.[116]

In his treatise, addressed to the French prelates, William gathered several different strands of arguments from theological sources and tied them together in an argumentation which no longer used hypocrisy as one polemical charge but as its central dominating topic. While William remained careful not to state directly that the last days were at hand, he asserted quite forcefully that the church was already under threat from false prophets and hypocrites, as prophesied by Paul for the times "nearing" the last days. He then identified the prophesied hypocritical actors further, naming "false preachers" and "false apostles," who were entering pastoral care against the will of the clergy. His words indicated the mendicants in all but name.[117]

In contrast with the brief, roughly sketched warning from Paganus Bolotinus against new monks over a hundred years earlier, William of Saint-Amour's polemical argument was substantial and backed by many theological authorities. As Penn Szittya has remarked, it tied entire traditions of biblical interpretations concerning the Pharisees, the false prophets and the *antichristi*, and harbingers of the Antichrist neatly together.[118] Moreover, William added a more openly propagandistic part to his treatise, ending it with over forty "signs" (*signa*) of "true" and "false apostles," which contained coded reproaches against the mendicants (in the style of "true apostles do not deceive men into giving them their temporal goods," "true apostles do not go to preach to those who have other apostles").[119] He also penned sermons that adapted some of the most incendiary arguments for preaching in public places, and he preached in Paris and Mâcon himself.[120]

Many scholars, particularly those who first studied William's antifraternal rhetoric in the 1970s and 1980s, viewed this extreme rhetoric as rather unusual. There has even been debate over whether William of Saint-Amour really "meant" his identification of the friars with the harbingers of the Antichrist, or whether it was some sort of parody.[121] Against the background of twelfth-century rhetoric against heretics and new religious orders, it is even more notable how William completely collapsed the earlier careful distinctions, which had kept charges of hypocrisy against monks largely tied to their arrogance and claims to superiority, while heretics were painted as deceitful harbingers of the Antichrist whose pretended religiosity put them far beyond the pale of true Christianity. William now wrote out what twelfth-century authors only hinted at: He applied some of the worst anti-heretical propaganda to groups that must be considered the rising pastoral and intellectual elite of the day and that enjoyed the unrestrained approval and protection of the papacy. In transferring various concepts from anti-heretical polemic to his anti-fraternal writing, William constructed another new boundary of "genuine religiosity" within the church, playing the clergy as successors of the "true apostles" against the "pseudo apostles" of the mendicant orders. Danger was no longer threatening principally from outside the church, or in the future, but from within the church itself.

Read closely, however, William of Saint-Amour's rhetoric was no straightforward demonization of the friars and must be understood in its communicative context. Using established polemical techniques, William drew upon well-known accusations and suggested possible comparisons, especially to heretics, as Hildegard had done. Her letter to the clergy of Cologne juxtaposed the pious, saintly, and chaste heretics with the sinful, worldly, and lazy clerics losing their parishioners, showing a "world turned upside down." In a slightly different technique, more suggestive than decisive, William of Saint-Amour juxtaposed the friars, who were expressly sent to preach to the people and to combat heretics, with all the problems usually associated with heretics. The dangerous hypocrites he warned against preached without the assent of the bishops and thus "without being sent" (*non missi*). Like the false preachers who were warned against by Paul, the friars "penetrated the homes" and "seduced the weak women."[122] But beneath the cover of polemical eschatology, these arguments largely appealed to canon law. In particular, William used rhetorical images that had become closely associated with the legal battles against heresy in papal decretals, especially the late twelfth-century cornerstones of legal persecution of heresy and illegitimate preaching, such as *Ad abolendam* (1184), *Vergentis in senium* (1199), and *Cum ex iniuncto* (1199). All of these warned of heretics as "ravening wolves" and "Satan disguised as an angel of light."[123] He thus urgently reminded his audience, especially clerics and prelates aware of the legislative frame of pastoral care, that twelfth-century popes had outlawed any preaching outside of diocesan structures, as this undermined the authority of bishops and clerics. As William hammered home in a series of implicit comparisons, the wide-ranging preaching rights given to friars in this present moment might pose the same threat.[124]

The effects of this argument, and the more openly persuasive elements of his treatise, which clearly appealed to broader audiences, gave an immense boost to the theme of hypocrisy, as well as to pessimistic perceptions of the state of the church. But unlike Hildegard of Bingen or Anselm of Havelberg, who laid blame on particular social groups (the lax clergy for Hildegard, the hypocritical laypeople for Anselm), William of Saint-Amour gave no clear identification of the eschatological *personae* in question.[125] Like Paganus Bolotinus, he instead opened the horizon towards a generalized perception of hypocrisy within the church. His warnings against widespread hypocrisy and false religiosity remained pointedly diffuse and undirected, raising suggestions and possibilities rather than clear accusations. But this very quality appears to have made his polemic effective and thus dangerous: William's treatise sought to mobilize readers and listeners, inviting them to question, to compare, and to reason for themselves whether the current situation was dangerous and where the dangers might lie. This was particularly visible in his many "signs" of false apostles, which offered readers and listeners an education in discerning true and false religiosity (and thus hypocrisy) for themselves.[126] The debate stirred up by this sort of mobilization provided the immediate backdrop for generalized criticisms of the sort contained in the *Roman de la Rose*.

A last set of threads not only runs between the polemics of the university quarrels and the more fundamental criticism of religious authority in the *Roman de la Rose* but also links back to earlier twelfth-century strands of discourse. In particular, there is a clear succession of vernacular polemical or satirical poems adapting and transforming the other strand of debate observed above – the critical evaluation of the multitude and diversity of new religious orders (*diversitas religionum*), traced here from the invective poetry of Paganus Bolotinus to the *Speculum stultorum*. As seen in these two examples, this debate had already prompted a relativization regarding the authority of religious life and led to pessimistic visions of the church as a whole. From the late twelfth to the mid-thirteenth century, poets translated these criticisms into the vernacular, enabling new audiences to participate and contributing to a "normalization" of aggressive criticism of religious actors as hypocrites.[127] This emergence of new vernacular traditions constitutes a final Grundmannian theme, making the potential lay interest in ongoing debates about different religious movements at least indirectly visible.[128]

One notable text continuing the tradition discussed above is an early instance of Old French estates satire, the so-called *Bible* ("Book") of Guiot de Provins (d. c. 1206). He was a professional poet who entered monasticism late in life and, wearing the habit of a Cluniac, wrote a scathing critique of both secular and religious estates of society in his later years, between c. 1194 and 1206.[129] His *Bible* is not only remarkable for offering an absolutely merciless verdict on the church of his day, castigating the upper ranks of the church (the pope, cardinals, bishops, and priests) in the vernacular for straying from the straight path and being motivated largely by greed. Guiot also discussed various religious orders (Cluniacs, Cistercians, Carthusians, Templars, Hospitallers, Grandmontensians, Premonstratensians, Austin Canons) and lay observances in a vivid and intriguingly personal manner. As a Cluniac monk, he painted a particularly bleak picture of the debates engulfing the competing monastic orders of his day, particularly Cistercians and Cluniacs, and – citing much detail from his own experience – castigated both his own order and that of the Cistercians for their internal strife and institutional decay. As Guiot puts it, again prefiguring the allegorical strategies of the *Roman de la Rose*, the three "ladies" gracing the monasteries in the past – Charity, Truth, and Justice – had now been replaced with repugnant, stinking old crones: Treason, Hypocrisy, and Simony ruled the monastic world.[130] In addition to an insistence on hypocrisy among the Cistercians, which clearly echoes earlier accusations against them, Guiot de Provins exemplified the mechanism of relativization already highlighted by Anselm of Havelberg and the *Speculum stultorum*, now in a highly accessible manner.[131] Based on a rich tapestry of detail and alleged eyewitness accounts, Guiot proceeded to discuss many good points of the various orders. However, he always found something to complain about as well, leaving no doubt that there was no perfect choice. This was also markedly true of his own choice of the Cluniac observance, to which he did not seem completely reconciled.

While the topic of hypocrisy itself was not necessarily always prominent in these types of texts, the accompanying sense of dissatisfaction with the religious orders of the day was well established by the early thirteenth century and was increasingly extended into estates satire, including among clerics and laypeople.[132] The particular topic of hypocrisy among religious orders also remained visible during the thirteenth century. For example, a vernacular song excerpted, translated, and reworked the relevant passages of the *Speculum stultorum*, melding them into a light-hearted, satirical song about a new "Order of perfect ease" (*Ordre de Bel-Eyse*) made up of all the lax elements of the older orders.[133] While we cannot date this text with any certainty beyond its manuscript, written during the reign of Edward II (d. 1327), the song tacks points of criticism of the Minorites and Preachers onto the list contained in the *Speculum stultorum*, illustrating that criticisms of the friars could be absorbed seamlessly into older patterns of critique of religious orders.

From the 1250s and the period of conflict at the University of Paris onwards, however, we encounter better-documented vernacular strands of polemic. In a stroke of luck, the party supporting the clerical side, who had great difficulties facing down the ascetic, well-educated, and well-supported mendicant friars, managed to attract the poet Rutebeuf (d. c. 1285) to their cause during the 1250s.[134] He wrote several highly incendiary polemical *Dits* for the secular party, breaking down their biblical argumentations about hypocrisy and related vices and translating them into more popular, easily understandable metaphors and images. Rutebeuf repeatedly incriminated the falsity and machinations of the friars, contesting their claims to religious authority, and in turn sacralized the position of William of Saint-Amour, whom he characterized as a persecuted, martyr-like figure. While redrawing the boundaries of true religion in this way, Rutebeuf's polemical *Dits* also coined several of the allegories which went on to populate the *Roman de la Rose* and later literary texts, such as the allegories of *Faus Semblant* and *Astinence Contrainte*.[135] Unlike William of Saint-Amour's polemics, which were hampered by papal restrictions, Rutebeuf's openly partisan poems called the friars by name.

Rutebeuf also wrote copious poems addressing the situation of the church as a whole and typically diagnosed its state as dire – often personifying it as *Ecclesia*, who uttered emotionally charged complaints reminiscent of devotional Marian laments.[136] In addition, Rutebeuf directed strong words at the religious orders. In a sort of localized version of the arguments of the *Speculum stultorum*, Guiot's *Bible*, and the *Ordre de Bel-Eyse*, Rutebeuf's *Ordres de Paris* linked widespread complaints against monastic houses to particular local establishments, suggesting that the religious orders of Paris participated in the ongoing decay.[137]

The *Roman de la Rose*'s central element of critique – the idea that hypocrisy or decay had spread fully within the church and especially among different types of religious – was thus far from new during the 1280s but also far from merely echoing the secular-mendicant quarrels of the university. Rather, the *Roman*'s critique combined and reinforced negative evaluations of the church which had been present in Latin and vernacular literature from the last decades of the twelfth century onwards. What was new in the *Roman* and other thirteenth-century texts was mainly the way in which these texts – in parallel to William of Saint-Amour's suggestive Latin invitations to discern between true and false – encouraged non-Latinate audiences to enter the fray. Ultimately, such texts enabled audiences to form new "communities of interpretation," consisting of interested laypeople with or without the guidance of Latinate experts favouring a specific side of the conflict.[138] The mix of persuasive strategies offered by poets such as Guiot de Provins or Rutebeuf – arguments, pithy biblical quotations, and allegorical or symbolic figures like the "fox disguised in a habit" – enabled both interested laypeople and non-Latinate religious to participate in a comparative critical discourse in which they were invited to view, compare, debate, and eventually judge the diverging forms of religious life (described as multiple *religiones* or *status*) for themselves. Just like the Latin and vernacular repertoires of argument making up this new critical or "evaluative" discourse, the accompanying attitude of active, participatory observation must be viewed as a highly significant product of the polemics and controversies triggered by new religious movements, given shape by their long-term interplay: If hypocrisy was all-pervasive, as it was already diagnosed around 1280, discernment and careful choice had to be its logical consequences.[139]

Conclusion: Internal Pluralization of Christianity as a Long-Term Perspective

This chapter cautiously claims that revisiting the innovative trajectory of Grundmann's *Religious Movements* opens up potential opportunities to transform our perspective on the religious dynamics of the high and late Middle Ages. As the "red thread" of hypocrisy shows, for example, the religious movements of the high Middle Ages not only sparked religious renewal, but indeed also a "dark side" of religious polemics. Slowly and gradually, the recurring conflicts surrounding heresies and church reform, new monastic orders, mendicant orders, and lay movements contributed to the rise of a new religious "other": the holier-than-thou hypocrite who was infiltrating all estates and orders of the church. While other stereotypes embodying religious difference were understood to be visibly different from the religious elite – for example, the worldly, decadent prelate or the alien or monstrous Pagan, Jew, and Saracen – the polemical construct of the "hypocrite" was the negative version or "evil twin" of the genuinely religious, ascetic figure of the reformer.

In the framework of Herbert Grundmann's legacy, this stereotype was clearly neither a product of the heterodox challenge to the church nor of the rise of new religious orders, nor simply of the university quarrels between the mendicant friars and the secular clergy. Instead, it emerged in a process of gradual entanglement and transfer between different strands of discourse, in which "hypocrisy" accumulated new meanings and nuances. The study of hypocrisy indeed opens a window onto an ongoing multi-centric debate within the Latin church – or, rather, a series of debates and more practical engagements which all negotiated the concept of "genuine" religiosity. So far, this process has typically only been appreciated in partial aspects. Its full dimensions and inner connections become visible once we stop treating the study of heresy, particular mendicant or monastic orders, clerical culture, lay religiosity, vernacular literatures, or religious polemics as separate research fields.[140]

Connecting extant but artificially separated religious histories can thus offer a new and different understanding of particular phenomena, as well as of long-term transformations. The focus on hypocrisy could, with some more effort, probably yield an alternate "genealogy" of medieval anti-clericalisms: As discussed above, criticism of the church, particularly lay criticism, has typically been understood as a phenomenon of the late Middle Ages. In most research, it is still explained with reference to the grand narratives underlying the historiographical "watershed" around 1250: We assume that there was an emancipation of the laity from the church based on education (the "Renaissance" narrative) and that there was a new interest in religious reform among the laity because of the obvious "decay" of the late medieval church (the "Reformation" narrative). The focus on religious movements pursued here does not, of course, invalidate these much-discussed observations altogether. But the trajectory and chronology indicated by the conceptual development of religious hypocrisy strongly underline different causal dimensions.

Most importantly, the concept of hypocrisy, with its marked problematization of discernment and verification of authenticity, illustrates beautifully that a driving issue generating the renegotiations of religion during the long twelfth and thirteenth centuries was the ongoing process of internal pluralization within the church (supported, we may assume, by the intensifying external pluralization prompted by interreligious encounters).[141] Religious elites were no longer only battling to defend the religious program of Christianity against worldliness and dilution which might be understood as "decay." They competed over similar versions of this program, which had repercussions for the concept of religion itself. The pluralization of religious elites now established a new emphasis on "genuine" Christianity and introduced various forms of intrareligious difference.[142]

Together with ongoing practical innovation and everyday conflict, the ensuing repeated controversies over religious authenticity and hypocrisy – which addressed heresy and new religious orders but also lay movements and non-Christian faiths, which have not been treated here – all generated polemical texts designed to mobilize and instruct new, partly lay, audiences. In a process we might call the "formation of a polemical society," targeted attacks on individual groups and competing traditions converged into a clamour of mutual recriminations among clerics, monks, nuns, mendicants, and heterodox reformers from the high Middle Ages onwards. Texts meant to engage and persuade soon invited laypeople to enter this fray and take sides.[143] This, in turn, led to the stabilization of a fairly coherent "evaluative vocabulary" concerning Christian religiosity, made up of biblical metaphors, literary images, and spoken and written arguments, available in Latin and European vernaculars.

The chronology of this transformation calls any "Renaissance" narrative strongly into doubt, as it undermines the straightforward causal link between the growth of the laity's education and literacy and the emergence of anti-clericalism. Rather, one could turn the argument around, asking whether it was not the growing diversity of religious "options" from the thirteenth century onwards that forced laypeople to make new choices and to acquire the forms of religious education necessary to inform these decisions.[144] Especially in poetry and literary texts from the late twelfth and thirteenth centuries, such processes of evaluation and choice were actually modelled in detail, with both strongly partisan attitudes and more distanced, "impartial," and "observing" positions on offer.

Studying this new repertoire of texts on religion also indicates that causal links between anti-clericalism and late medieval "decay" are far from easy to postulate: While the ecclesiastical institutions of the fourteenth and fifteenth centuries certainly had their share of dysfunction, and therefore became anchor points for renewed reform discourses, the sizable body of religious critiques from the twelfth and thirteenth centuries underscores that it was largely a situation of institutional *renewal* and institutionalized *diversity* that generated and popularized diagnoses of decay. The emergence of generalized *Kirchenkritik* can indeed be largely tied to transformations of the twelfth and thirteenth centuries. Separate critiques of the clergy on one side and the *diversitas religionum* on the other merged into criticisms of all "religious estates" and "all the church," which quickly attained Europe-wide distribution. On this foundation, which was largely established by the end of the thirteenth century, later "anti-clericalisms" then set new accents. In the perspective taken here, these later forms of religious critique, up to and including the Protestant Reformation, often appear strongly characterized by local reform movements. While they might address some issues – such as the hierarchy of lay and clerical – on a more fundamental level, they also partly narrowed, rather than broadened, the scope of criticisms, such as introducing a focus on the clergy.[145] The conjunctures of "hypocrisy" studied in this chapter suggest that we might well abandon a static concept of "anti-clericalism" and aim to reconstruct a long-term, cross-disciplinary genealogy of historical "criticisms of religiosity" instead.[146]

Looking towards this and other future endeavours, one may reflect on the use and impact of such perspectives. Revisiting the chronology and framing of Grundmann's work may, ultimately, not have the effect of revolutionizing the way medievalists see the Middle Ages. Many of the sources used here are well known, and many of the observations made on long-term developments are, if not established, at least not very surprising. However, a new approach to the *longue durée* of religious history may very well have the potential to revolutionize the way medievalists present our period to scholars specializing in other epochs and disciplines. Within the sociology of religion and even within parts of modern history, the medieval centuries too often remain reduced to an "age of faith," dominated by a monolithic church which only became dynamized with the Renaissance.[147] Even more importantly, the ongoing dialogue between scholars focusing on Christianity and on other religious traditions – Jewish, Islamic, and Pagan, as well as Buddhist or Taoist – remains dependent on our advances in a connected history of religious cultures and is strongly hampered by remaining vestiges of older "church history" trajectories. In these contexts, a revised

Grundmannian model of interrelated religious cultures can bring out the fact that the medieval Latin Church witnessed many innovations, such as new religious movements, which can be compared across cultures and periods in the context of an emerging history of religious plurality and diversity.[148] Similarly, the conceptual entanglement relating intra-Christian polemics and reforms to controversies about heresy (and, only occasionally visible here, other religions, such as Judaism) clearly only forms one strand of a broader, transculturally connected history of religions and their critics. Tracing the concept of hypocrisy further would, for example, invariably lead us to interreligious encounter, such as the polemical comparisons linking Cistercians to Jews, or the fact that charges of hypocrisy were also made against Jews and Muslims – by Christians but also within their own respective traditions. Taking up the particular legacy inherent in Grundmann's insistence on the long term, and renewing his vision of an integrated, connected perspective on different forms of religiosity, may thus be an important step towards formulating new overarching narratives concerning religion in history. We need not follow every step Grundmann took on this path, of course, but it may make sense to retrace his territory and push its boundaries further outward.

NOTES

1 I would like to express my gratitude to the editors for their kind invitation to contribute to this publication, even though I missed the original IMC sessions, and for their ensuing patience and support. The present chapter develops topics which I am currently exploring in a broader monographic study but also draws heavily on collaborative work and discussions within the research network "New Religious Histories," which has evolved in successive IMC sessions at Leeds in 2014–18 and the 2018 conference at St Catherine's College, Oxford, co-organized by Amanda Power, Emilia Jamroziak, and myself. For the original impulse to research hypocrisy, I am indebted to a paper by Nicholas Watson, "Whited Sepulchres: Towards a History of Hypocrisy, 1100–1400" (2010), kindly sent to me by Professor Watson in 2010. Thanks also to Pia Döring (Münster), whose own work on hypocrisy has given me many ideas; she is preparing a volume which will appear as Pia C. Döring, ed., *Verstellungskünste. Religiöse und politische Hypokrisie in Literatur und bildender Kunst* (forthcoming in 2022).
    On the *Roman de la Rose*, see the contributions in Christine McWebb, *Debating the "Roman de La Rose": A Critical Anthology* (New York: Routledge, 2007); Alastair J. Minnis, *Magister Amoris: The Roman de La Rose and Vernacular Hermeneutics* (Oxford: Oxford University Press, 2001);

Sylvia Huot, *The Romance of the Rose and Its Medieval Readers: Interpretation, Reception, Manuscript Transmission*, Cambridge Studies in Medieval Literature 16 (Cambridge: Cambridge University Press, 1993).

2 On *Faus Semblant*, see particularly Richard K. Emmerson and Ronald B. Herzman, "The Apocalyptic Age of Hypocrisy: Faus Semblant and Amant in the Roman de La Rose," *Speculum* 62, no. 3 (1987): 612–34; Guy Geltner, "'Faux Semblants': Antifraternalism Reconsidered in Jean de Meun and Chaucer," *Studies in Philology* 101 (2004): 357–80; Jonathan Morton, *The Roman de la Rose in Its Philosophical Context. Art, Nature, and Ethics* (Oxford: Oxford University Press, 2018).

3 The whole speech fills *Roman de la Rose*, ll. 11.006–980. I use the translation in Guillaume de Lorris and Jean de Meun, *The Romance of the Rose*, trans. Charles Dahlberg (Princeton: Princeton University Press, 1971). For critical editions and manuscripts, see https://www.arlima.net/il/jean_de_meun.html#ros.

4 See *Roman de la Rose*, trans. Dahlberg, ll. 11.023–4.

5 Timothy L. Stinson, "Illumination and Interpretation: The Depiction and Reception of Faus Semblant in Roman de La Rose Manuscripts," *Speculum* 87, no. 2 (2012): 469–98.

6 For a brief overview, see Guy Geltner, *The Making of Medieval Antifraternalism: Polemic, Violence, Deviance, and Remembrance* (Oxford: Oxford University Press, 2012), esp. 4–45; Andrew Traver, "The Forging of an Intellectual Defense of Mendicancy in the Medieval University," in *The Origin, Development, and Refinement of Medieval Religious Mendicancies*, Brill's Companions to the Christian Tradition 24, ed. Donald Prudlo (Leiden: Brill, 2011), 157–96.

7 See Emmerson and Herzman, "Apocalyptic Age," passim.

8 *Roman de la Rose*, trans. Dahlberg, ll. 12.065–74.

9 See the references below at note 52.

10 *Roman de la Rose*, trans. Dahlberg, ll. 14.709–16; see Emmerson and Herzman, "Apocalyptic Age," 619–23.

11 Kathryn Kerby-Fulton, *Reformist Apocalypticism and Piers Plowman*, Cambridge Studies in Medieval Literature 7 (Cambridge: Cambridge University Press, 1990), at 133–5.

12 On this potential of hypocrisy, see Watson, "Whited Sepulchres"; generally Kerby-Fulton, *Reformist Apocalypticism*, 133; and e.g., Dyan Elliott, "Seeing Double: John Gerson, the Discernment of Spirits, and Joan of Arc," *The American Historical Review* 107, no. 1 (2002): 26–54.

13 *Roman de la Rose*, trans. Dahlberg, ll. 11.092–122.

14 On concepts and renegotiations of "religion" during the medieval period, see, generally, (with a problematization of terminology) Dorothea Weltecke, "Über Religion vor der 'Religion': Konzeptionen

vor der Entstehung des neuzeitlichen Begriffs," in *Religion als Prozess: Kulturwissenschaftliche Wege der Religionsforschung*, ed. Thomas G. Kirsch, Rudolf Schlögl, and Dorothea Weltecke (Paderborn: Ferdinand Schöningh, 2015), 13–34; Christina Brauner and Sita Steckel, "Wie die Heiden – wie die Papisten. Religiöse Polemik und Vergleiche vom Hochmittelalter bis zur Konfessionalisierung," in *Juden, Christen und Muslime im Zeitalter der Reformation/Jews, Christians and Muslims in the Reformation Era*, Schriften des Vereins für Reformationsgeschichte 219, ed. Matthias Pohlig (Gütersloh: Gütersloher Verlagshaus, 2020), 41–91. On historical dynamics of religion in medieval Europe, see, generally, Christine Caldwell Ames, "Medieval Religious, Religions, Religion," *History Compass* 10, no. 4 (2012): 334–52; Christine Caldwell Ames, "Does Inquisition Belong to Religious History?," *The American Historical Review* 110, no. 1 (2005): 11–37; Barbara Newman, *Medieval Crossover: Reading the Secular against the Sacred* (Notre Dame: University of Notre Dame Press, 2013); taking up these and other impulses, my approach is that of charting the boundaries of historical forms of the "religious field," see Sita Steckel, "Historicizing the Religious Field: Adapting Theories of the Religious Field for the Study of Medieval and Early Modern Europe," *Church History and Religious Culture* 99, nos. 3–4 (2019): 331–70, esp. 342–7.

15 See Watson, "Whited Sepulchres," 5.
16 This and the following statement is based on my own preliminary analysis of the results from a semantic search in the Library of Latin Texts databases, Series A and B (issued by Brepols Publishers) that I hope to publish in the future. As a preliminary and rough statistic, I simply offer the occurrence of terms beginning with hypocri* in this corpus. While this table needs be correlated to the varying number of words per century available in the corpus and does not indicate how many texts belong to exegetical, didactic, or polemical genres, it gives a rough idea of increasing use in the twelfth and thirteenth centuries.

century	5th	6th	7th	8th	9th	10th	11th	12th	13th
occurrence	266	263	95	75	213	13	21	513	959

17 Herbert Grundmann, *Religious Movements in the Middle Ages* (Notre Dame, Indiana: University of Notre Dame Press, 1995). On Grundmann's life and work, I have consulted Robert Lerner's "Introduction to the Translation," in Grundmann, *Religious Movements*, ix–xxv; Arno Borst, "Herbert Grundmann," *Deutsches Archiv für Erforschung des Mittelalters* 26 (1970): 327–53; Anne Christine Nagel, "'Mit dem Herzen, dem Willen und dem Verstand dabei': Herbert Grundmann und der Nationalsozialismus," in *Nationalsozialismus in den Kulturwissenschaften*, vol. 1, *Fächer, Milieus,*

Karrieren, ed. Hartmut Lehmann and Otto Gerhard Oexle (Göttingen: Vandenhoeck & Ruprecht, 2004), 593–618; Martina Wehrli-Johns, "Voraussetzungen und Perspektiven mittelalterlicher Laienfrömmigkeit seit Innozenz III. Eine Auseinandersetzung mit Herbert Grundmanns 'Religiösen Bewegungen,'" *Mitteilungen des Instituts für Österreichische Geschichtsforschung* 104 (1996): 286–309; Stephanie Kluge, "Kontinuität oder Wandel? Zur Bewertung hochmittelalterlicher Königsherrschaft durch die frühe bundesrepublikanische Mediävistik," *Frühmittelalterliche Studien* 48 (2014): 39–120, at 101–2.

18 Giles Constable, *The Reformation of the Twelfth Century* (Cambridge: Cambridge University Press, 1998), 31. For recent reappraisals of historical religious movements, see, e.g., Michael Driedger and Johannes C. Wolfart, "Reframing the History of New Religious Movements," *Nova Religio: The Journal of Alternative and Emergent Religions* 21, no. 4 (2018): 5–12 and Andreas Pietsch and Sita Steckel, "New Religious Movements before Modernity? Considerations from a Historical Perspective," *Nova Religio*, 13–37.

19 See, e.g., contributions in Peter A. Dykema and Heiko A. Oberman, eds., *Anticlericalism in Late Medieval and Early Modern Europe*, Studies in Medieval and Reformation Thought 51 (Leiden: Brill, 1993); Hans-Jürgen Goertz, *Antiklerikalismus und Reformation. Sozialgeschichtliche Untersuchungen* (Göttingen: Vandenhoeck & Ruprecht, 1995); and the problematization in Klaus Schreiner, "Gab es im Mittelalter und in der Frühen Neuzeit Antiklerikalismus?" *Zeitschrift für Historische Forschung* 21, no. 4 (1994): 513–21. On the role of the laity in late medieval and early modern religious culture, see the overview in Sabrina Corbellini and Sita Steckel, "The Religious Field during the Long Fifteenth Century: Framing Religious Change beyond Traditional Paradigms," *Church History and Religious Culture* 99 (2019): 303–29, esp. 321–9.

20 See Penn R. Szittya, *The Antifraternal Tradition in Medieval Literature* (Princeton: Princeton University Press, 1986), and for a critical approach, Geltner, *The Making of Medieval Antifraternalism*.

21 See Constable, *Reformation*, at 31–5 and 131–4. The only comprehensive monograph is Giovanni Lunardi, *L'ideale monastico nelle polemiche del secolo XII sulla vita religiosa* (Noci: Pontificium Athenaeum Anselmianum, 1970).

22 See Amanda Power's contribution in this volume.

23 On the shift from "church history" to a "history of religious culture," see Ames, "Medieval Religious," 334–5. For a discussion of periodization and narratives, see Alexandra Walsham, "Migrations of the Holy: Explaining Religious Change in Medieval and Early Modern Europe," *Journal of Medieval and Early Modern Studies* 44, no. 2 (2014): 241–80; Fred van Lieburg, "In saecula saeculorum. Long-term Perspectives on Religious

History," *Church History and Religious Culture* 98, nos. 3–4 (2018): 319–43; Corbellini and Steckel, "The Religious Field," 312–21. The argument against the combined narratives of "high medieval renewal" plus "late medieval decay and early modern reform" is also made in the new handbook by Alison I. Beach and Isabelle Cochelin, eds., *Cambridge History of Western Monasticism*, 2 vols. (Cambridge: Cambridge University Press: 2020).

24 The only field of research which cuts across all these topics, and has indeed found many connections between them, is the study of medieval eschatological thought. See especially Kerby-Fulton, *Reformist Apocalypticism*, and generally Bernard McGinn, *Visions of the End: Apocalyptic Traditions in the Middle Ages* (New York: Columbia University Press, 1979); Wolfram Brandes, Felicitas Schmieder, and Rebekka Voss, eds., *Peoples of the Apocalypse: Eschatological Beliefs and Political Scenarios*, Millennium-Studien/Millennium Studies 63 (Berlin/Boston: De Gruyter, 2016).

25 See the forthcoming publication documenting the 2018 Oxford conference of the "New Religious Histories" network (above, note 1) and the literature in note 27.

26 Grundmann, *Religious Movements*, 3–4.

27 A publication on this issue based on the 2018 Oxford conference (see note 1) is in preparation. For history in general, see the trenchant analysis by Jo Guldi and David Armitage, *The History Manifesto* (Cambridge: Cambridge University Press, 2014); a discussion of the results of this fragmentation for research on medieval and early modern religion is offered by Walsham, "Migrations of the Holy," esp. 257–9; Corbellini and Steckel, "The Religious Field," esp. 304–21.

28 See Albin Lesky, "Hypokrites," in *Studi in Onore di Ugo Enrico Paoli*, Pubblicazioni della Università degli studi di Firenze – Facoltà di lettere e filosofia, ser. 4, 1 (Firenze: F. le Monnier, 1955), 469–76; Frederic Amory, "Whited Sepulchres: The Semantic History of the Hypocrisy to the High Middle Ages," *Recherches de Théologie Ancienne et Médiévale* 53 (1986): 5–39; Delphine Carron, "Intus Nero Foris Cato. Une sémiologie de l'hypocrisie," in *Intus et foris: Une catégorie de la pensée médiévale?*, ed. Manuel Guay, Marie-Pascale Halary, and Patrick Moran (Paris: Presses de l'Université Paris-Sorbonne, 2013), 171–83; see also the forthcoming volume by Döring, ed., *Verstellungskünste*.

29 The definition of polemic underlying this chapter is a broad one, encompassing all sorts of texts attacking the position of an opponent. See, generally, Sita Steckel, "Verging on the Polemical. Towards an Interdisciplinary Approach to Medieval Religious Polemic," *Medieval Worlds* 7 (2018): 2–60, at 11–12.

30 See Amory, "Whited Sepulchres"; Carron, "Intus Nero Foris Cato."
31 See esp. the discussion of Gregory the Great's views in Amory, "Whited Sepulchres," 25–30.
32 See below and generally Amory, "Whited Sepulchres," 34–8; Michael A. Ryan, "Antichrist in the Middle Ages: Plus ça change . . .," *History Compass* 7, no. 6 (2009): 1581–92.
33 Bernardus Claraevallensis, "*Sententiae* III, no. 109," in *Opera Omnia*, vol. 3, ed. J. Leclercq and H. Rochais (Rome, Editiones Cistercienses, 1963), 182–3.
34 Bernhard, *Sententiae* III, No. 109, 18: "ficti christiani, qui non appetunt esse quod videri desiderant, qui exterius praetendunt speciem sanctitatis, sub pelle ovina lupi rapaces. Hi sunt paries dealbatus, sepulcra plena ossibus tantum mortuorum" (translation S.S.).
35 See Leidulf Melve, *Inventing the Public Sphere: The Public Debate During the Investiture Contest (c. 1030–1122)*, Brill's Studies in Intellectual History 154 (Leiden: Brill, 2007); Ian S. Robinson, *Authority and Resistance in the Investiture Contest: The Polemical Literature of the Late Eleventh Century* (Manchester: Manchester University Press, 1978).
36 See, e.g., *Humberti Cardinalis Adversus Simoniacos Libri Tres*, MGH LDL 1, ed. Friedrich Thaner (Hanover: Hahn'sche Buchhandlung, 1895), 95–253, at l. II, c. 46, 195: "In quibus nihil nisi intractabilis ira et vana pompa hypocrisisque et insidiae, hebitudo quoque atque sterilis et proterva verbositas procreantur."
37 On this "rhetoric of reform," see Constable, *Reformation*, 125–66 (quote at 125). See also Robinson, *Authority*.
38 Bernardus Claraevallensis, "*Sermo 33*," in *Opera Omnia*, vol. 1, ed. J. Leclerq and H. Rochais (Rome: Editiones Cistercienses, 1957), 244: "Inde is, quem quotidie vides, meretricius nitor, histrionicus habitus, regius apparatus. Inde aurum in frenis, in sellis, in calcaribus: plus calcaria fulgent quam altaria…. Pro huiusmodi volunt esse et sunt ecclesiarum praepositi, decani, archidiaconi, episcopi, archiepiscopi."
39 Ibid., 243–4: "Vae generationi huic a fermento pharisaeorum, quod est hypocrisis, si tamen hypocrisis debet dici quae iam latere prae abundantia non valet, et prae impudentia non quaerit!"
40 While the conceptual boundaries of Christianity and of religion (e.g. *lex, religio, cultus*) often coincided in these controversies, they also frequently diverged during the medieval period. See the literature in note 14 above. On reform rhetoric in this context, see Constable, *Reformation*, esp. 135–7.
41 See Amory, "Whited Sepulchres," esp. 9–12; Carron, "Intus Nero Foris Cato."
42 Sigebert of Gembloux's *Apologia* for married priests thus likened the Gregorians to Pharisees because they were attempting to enforce a particular norm not covered by biblical precepts. The *Tractatus*

de Investitura Episcoporum found the new claim to papal authority hypocritical. The *Liber de unitate ecclesiae conservanda* compared them to Pharisees because of their uncharitable divisiveness. See Sigebert of Gembloux, "Apologia," in *MGH Libelli De Lite 2*, ed. E. Sackur (Hannover: Hahnsche Buchhandlung, 1892), 436–48, at 440; "Tractatus de Investitura Episcoporum," in *MGH LDL 2*, ed. E. Bernheim, 495–504, at 502; Walram of Naumburg, "Liber de unitate ecclesiae conservanda," in *Scriptores rerum germanicarum in usum scolarum*, ed. W. Schwenkenbecher (Hanover: Hahnsche Buchhandlung, 1883), 173–284, at 225.

43 Kerby-Fulton, *Reformist Apocalypticism*, 133 (about apocalyptic thought in general).

44 On these functions, see, e.g., Charles B. Strozier and Katharine Boyd, "The Apocalyptic," in *The Fundamentalist Mindset: Psychological Perspectives on Religion, Violence, and History*, ed. Charles B. Strozier et. al. (New York: Oxford University Press, 2010), 29–37.

45 See, e.g., Amory, "Whited Sepulchres," 9–12; Ian J. Elmer, "Pillars, Hypocrites and False Brothers. Paul's Polemic against Jerusalem in Galatians," in *Polemik in der frühchristlichen Literatur: Texte und Kontexte*, Beihefte zur Zeitschrift für die neutestamentliche Wissenschaft und die Kunde der älteren Kirche 170, ed. Oda Wischmeyer and Lorenzo Scornaienchi (Berlin: De Gruyter, 2011), 123–53.

46 Gerard of Florennes, "Acta Synodi Atrebatensis," in *Patrologia Latina*, ed. J.P. Migne (Paris: Migne, 1853), 142: cols. 1271–1312, at col. 1311 (highlighting of the biblical citation by S.S.): "Hoc tantum servate fidei vestrae intemeratum signaculum, recolentes hoc quod Paulus apostolus praedixerat, quia 'in novissimus diebus discedent quidam a fide, attendentes spiritibus erroris et doctrinis demoniorum in hypocrisi loquentium, et cauteriatam habentium conscientiam suam; prohibentium nubere, abstinere a cibis, quos Deus creavit ad percipiendum cum gratiarum actione fidelibus.'" Bible passages are translated according to the New Revised Standard Version here and in the following. On the context of this passage, see Walter L. Wakefield and Austin P. Evans, *Heresies of the High Middle Ages. Selected Sources Translated and Annotated*, Records of Western Civilization (New York: Columbia University Press, 1991), at 82.

47 Hildebert of Le Mans, "Hildeberti Cenomannensis Epistolae," in *Patrologia Latina*, vol. 171, ed. J.P. Migne (Paris: Migne, 1854), cols. 151–311, at. col. 242: "[S]ecuti quemdam pseudoprophetam, quem qui secuti sunt, persecuti sunt semetipsos. Henricus is erat, magnus diaboli laqueus et celebris armiger Antichristi. Huic et habitu religionem et verbis litteraturam simulanti tandiu praescripti fratres adhaeserunt, donec eis et turpitudo in vita et error innotuit in doctrina." On Henry, see the

comprehensive discussion by Kai Hering, "Reform, Häresie und Schisma im frühen 12. Jahrhundert. Der Wanderprediger Heinrich, gen. von Lausanne und sein historisches Umfeld," *Cistercienser Chronik* 122/23 (2016/15): 427–56; 93–119; 477–507.

48 See McGinn, *Visions of the End*, 88–143; Hans-Joachim Schmidt, "Sinngebung von Vergangenheit und Zukunft – Vorstellungen zum Antichrist im hohen Mittelalter," in *Der Antichrist. Historische und systematische Zugänge*, Studien zur christlichen Religions- und Kulturgeschichte 14, ed. Mariano Delgado and Volker Leppin (Stuttgart: Kohlhammer, 2011), 137–71.

49 L.C. Bethmann and W. Wattenbach, eds., *Landulfi (iunioris) Historia Mediolanensis*, MGH SS 8 (Hanover: Hahnsche Buchhandlung, 1848), 32–100, at 36 (Epistola Ystoriografi): "[tribulationes] e quibus tota fere Italia pseudoprophetis per detestabilem ypocrisim circumcurrentibus maculata est.... Igitur quamplurimi qui ordinis ecclesiastici falsis praedicationibus esse videbantur, actibus vero misere hypocrisim sedule insistentes, ut lupi rapaces sese sub ovina pelle tegentes, dimissis plebibus ac ruptis canonibus, et alii multi misterio Romani edocti, honoris sanctae Ambrosianae ecclesiae lividi, quasi tirampni nullam ordini Ambrosiano reverentiam impendentes, urbem Mediolanensium fascinatis laicis ac zizaniis superseminatis Antichristi facetiis incubuerunt."

50 Bernardus Claraevallensis, "*Sermo 44*," in *Opera Omnia*, vol. 2, ed. J. Leclercq and H. Rochais (Rome: Editiones Cistercienses, 1970), 244: "Ministri Christi sunt, et serviunt Antichristo.... Neque enim haec merito cedunt, sed negotio illi quod perambulabat in tenebris."

51 Bernardus Claraevallensis, "*Parabola VI*," in *Opera Omnia*, vol. 6.2, ed. J. Leclercq and H. Rochais (Rome: Editiones Cistercienses, 1970), 287–8: "Mutato paululum ordine, primum enim tempus fuit persecutionis; equus albus in ecclesia tempus est pacis, rufus persecutionis, niger hypocrisis, pallidus Antichristi."

52 See Amory, "Whited Sepulchres," 9–12 and, e.g., Richardus de Sancto Victore, "*In Apocalypsin Johannis*," in *Patrologia Latina*, vol. 196, ed. J.P. Migne (Paris: Garnier, 1880), cols. 683–886, here l. ii, c. vii, col. 767.

53 See esp. Uwe Brunn, *Des contestataires aux "Cathares": Discours de réforme et propagande antihérétique dans les pays du Rhin et de la Meuse avant l'Inquisition* (Paris: Institut d'études augustiniennes, 2006); Beverly Mayne Kienzle, *Cistercians, Heresy, and Crusade in Occitania, 1145–1229: Preaching in the Lord's Vineyard* (Rochester: York Medieval Press/Boydell Press, 2001); Lucy J. Sackville, *Heresy and Heretics in the Thirteenth Century: The Textual Representations*, Heresy and Inquisition in the Middle Ages 1 (York: York Medieval Press, 2011), 13–40.

54 This and other rhetorical mechanisms are set out briefly in Beverly Mayne Kienzle, "Preaching as Touchstone of Orthodoxy and Dissidence in the Middle Ages," *Medieval Sermon Studies* 43 (1999): 19–54.
55 Quoting the translation of Wakefield and Evans, *Heresies of the High Middle Ages*, 127–8 (biblical quotation highlighted by S.S.). For the context, see briefly ibid., 126–7.
56 Ibid., 128.
57 See Bernardus Claraevallensis, "*Sermo 66*," in *Opera Omnia*, 2:179.
58 Ibid., 178: "Non sufficit haereticos esse, nisi et hypocritae sint, ut sit supra modum peccans peccatum. Hi sunt qui veniunt in vestimentis ovium, ad nudandas oves et spoliandos arietes. Annon tibi utraque res impleta videtur, ubi et fide plebes, et plebibus sacerdotes depraedati inveniuntur? Quinam isti praedones? Hi oves sunt habitu, astu vulpes, actu et crudelitate lupi. Hi sunt qui boni videri, non esse, mali non videri, sed esse volunt.... Etenim minus semper malitia palam nocuit, nec umquam bonus nisi boni simulatione deceptus est.... Neque enim est apud eos virtutes colere, sed vitia colorare quodam quasi virtutum minio. Denique superstitionis impietatem nomine religionis intitulant."
59 See Eckbertus Abbas Schonaugiensis, "*Sermones*," in *Patrologia Latina*, vol. 195, ed. J.P. Migne (Paris: Migne, 1855), cols. 11–102, esp. *Sermo* v, col. 26–7.
60 See Gisela Vollmann-Profe, ed., *Ludus de Antichristo*, Litterae – Göppinger Beiträge zur Textgeschichte 82, vol. 2, *Edition und Übersetzung* (Lauterburg: Kümmerle, 1981), 18.
61 Hildegardis Bingensis, *Epistolarivm. Pars prima, I-XC*, ed. Lieven van Acker, CCCM 91 (Turnhout: Brepols, 1991). Ep. xvR, 34–47.
62 See, e.g., Richard K. Emmerson, "The Representation of Antichrist in Hildegard of Bingen's Scivias: Image, Word, Commentary, and Visionary Experience," *Gesta* 41, no. 2 (2002): 95–110; Andra Alexiu, "Magistra Magistrorum: Hildegard of Bingen as a Polemicist against False Teaching," *Medieval Worlds* 7 (2018), 170–89.
63 See Kathryn Kerby-Fulton, "Hildegard of Bingen and Anti-Mendicant Propaganda," *Traditio* 43 (1987): 386–99; Kathryn Kerby-Fulton, Magda Hayton, and Kenna Olsen, "Pseudo-Hildegardian Prophecy and Antimendicant Propaganda in Late Medieval England: An Edition of the Most Popular Insular Text of 'Insurgent Gentes,'" in *Prophecy, Apocalypse and the Day of Doom: Proceedings of the 2000 Harlaxton Symposium*, Harlaxton Medieval Studies 12, ed. Nigel J. Morgan (Donington: Shaun Tyas, 2004), 160–94.
64 See Gert Melville, "*Duo novae conversationis ordines*. Zur Wahrnehmung der frühen Mendikanten vor dem Problem institutioneller Neuartigkeit im mittelalterlichen Religiosentum," in *Die Bettelorden im Aufbau. Beiträge*

zu Institutionalisierungsprozessen im mittelalterlichen Religiosentum, Vita Regularis. Ordnungen und Deutungen religiosen Lebens im Mittelalter 11, ed. Gert Melville and Jörg Oberste (Münster: LIT, 1999), 1–23; Miriam Czock, "Zwischen Heiligkeit und Häresie. Rhetorik und Verwendung von Bildern in Briefen zu Tanchelm, Heinrich und an Robert von Arbrissel," in Sakralität und Devianz: Konstruktionen – Normen – Praxis, Beiträge zur Hagiographie 16, ed. Klaus Herbers and Larissa Düchting (Stuttgart: Franz Steiner Verlag, 2015), 253–74.

65 Besides the controversy between Cluny and Cîteaux – on which see Adriaan H. Bredero, *Cluny et Cîteaux au douzième siècle: l'histoire d'une controverse monastique* (Amsterdam: APA-Holland University Press, 1985) – see the debates mentioned by Constable, *Reformation*, 31–5 and 131–4.

66 See esp. Giles Constable, "The Diversity of Religious Life and Acceptance of Social Pluralism in the Twelfth Century," in Constable, *Culture and Spirituality in Medieval Europe*, Variorum Collected Studies Series 541 (Aldershot: Variorum, 1996), 29–47; Ernest W. McDonnell, "The 'Vita Apostolica': Diversity or Dissent," *Church History* 24, no. 1 (1955): 15–31; Micheline Fontette, "Religionum Diversitatem et la Suppression des Ordres Mendiants," in *1274. Année charnière mutations et continuités. Lyon–Paris 30 septembre–5 octobre 1974*, Colloques internationaux de Centre national de la recherche scientifique 558 (Lyon: Éditions du CNRS, 1977), 223–9.

67 See, e.g., Sita Steckel, *Kulturen des Lehrens im Früh- und Hochmittelalter: Autorität, Wissenskonzepte und Netzwerke von Gelehrten*, Norm und Struktur 39 (Cologne: Böhlau, 2011), 1023–4.

68 See Marcelo Dascal, "On the Uses of Argumentative Reason in Religious Polemics," in *Religious Polemics in Context. Papers presented to the second international Conference of the Leiden Institute for the Study of Religions (LISOR), held at Leiden, 27–28 April 2000*, Studies in Theology and Religion 11, ed. Theo L. Hettema and Arie van der Kooij (Assen: Van Gorcum, 2004), 3–20, at 5–6.

69 On *amicitia* in this context, see Julian Haseldine, "Friendship and Rivalry: The Role of Amicitia in Twelfth-Century Monastic Relations," *Journal of Ecclesiastical History* 44, no. 3 (1993): 390–414, and Haseldine, "Friendship, Intimacy and Corporate Networking in the Twelfth Century: The Politics of Friendship in the Letters of Peter the Venerable," *English Historical Review* 76, no. 519 (2011): 251–80. On the controversy, see Bredero, *Cluny and Cîteaux*; Gillian R. Knight, *The Correspondence between Peter the Venerable and Bernard of Clairvaux: A Semantic and Structural Analysis*, Church, Faith, and Culture in the Medieval West (Aldershot: Ashgate, 2002).

70 See Bernardus Claraevallensis, "*Apologia*," in *Opera Omnia*, 3:31, 108.

71 Bernardus Claraevallensis, "*Epistolae*," in *Opera Omnia*, vol. 7, ed. Leclerq and Rochais (Rome, Editiones Cistercienses, 1974), no. 1, 4.

72 Bernardus Claraevallensis, "*Apologia*," s 3: c. 26, 102.
73 See Giles Constable, ed., *The Letters of Peter the Venerable* (Cambridge, MA: Harvard University Press, 1967), 1: ep. 28, 52–101.
74 *The Letters of Peter the Venerable*, esp. 28, 57: "O o pharisaeorum nouum genus rursus mundo redditum, qui se a ceteros diuidentes, omnibus praeferentes.... At uos sancti, uos singulares, uos in universo orbe uere monachi ... uos inter omnes constituitis, unde et habitum insoliti coloris praetenditis, et ad distinctionem cunctorum totius fere mundi monachorum, inter nigros uos candidos ostentatis."
75 On monastic dress and the debate surrounding it, see the overview in Alejandra Concha Sahli, "The Meaning of the Habit: Religious Orders, Dress and Identity, 1215–1650" (unpublished PhD diss., University College London, 2017), at 19, 33–52.
76 Constable, "The Diversity of the Religious Life."
77 Marjorie Chibnall, ed., *The Ecclesiastical History of Orderic Vitalis*, Oxford Medieval Texts, vol. 4, *Books VII and VIII* (Oxford: Clarendon Press, 2004), l. viii, c. 26, 327: "Mixti bonis hipochritae procedunt, candidis seu uariis indumentis amicti homines illudunt, et populus ingens spectaculum efficiunt. Veris Dei cultoribus scemate non uirtute assimilari plerique gestiunt, suique multitudine intuentibus fastidium ingerunt, et probatos coenobitas quantum ad fallaces hominum obtutus attinet despicabiliores faciunt."
78 See Giles Constable, *Monastic Tithes: From Their Origins to the Twelfth Century*. Cambridge Studies in Medieval Life and Thought N.S. 10 (Cambridge: Cambridge University Press, 1964), 220–306.
79 See Jean Leclercq, "Le poème de Payen Bolotin contre les faux ermites," *Revue Bénédictine* 68, nos. 1–2 (1958): 52–86.
80 On various forms of this poetry, see, e.g., Peter Dronke, *The Medieval Poet and his World* (Rome: Edizione di Storia e Letteratura, 1984), 145–358; Petra Aigner, "Poetry and Networking in High Medieval France (ca. 1100): Baudri de Bourgueil and His Scholarly Contacts," in *Networks of Learning. Perspectives on Scholars in Byzantine East and Latin West, c. 1000–1200*, Byzantinistische Studien und Texte 6, ed. Sita Steckel, Niels Gaul, and Michael Grünbart (Münster: LIT, 2014), 33–56; Jennifer A. Jahner, "Verse Diplomacy and the English Interdict," in *Thirteenth Century England* XV: *Authority and Resistance in the Age of Magna Carta*, ed. Janet Burton, Phillipp Schofield, and Björn Weiler (Woodbridge: Boydell Press, 2015): 99–114; Marian Weiß, *Mittellateinische Goliardendichtung und ihr historischer Kontext: Komik im Kosmos der Kathedralschulen Nordfrankreichs* (unpublished PhD diss., Justus-Liebig-Universität Gießen, 2018).
81 Leclercq, "Le poème," 77: "Ordinis expers, ordo nefandus, pellibus agni / Cum sit amictus, uult reputari religiosus, / Nec tamen actis

religionem testificatur. / Horrea, penus, archa replentur; res cumulatae / Multiplicantur; multiplicatis nec saturantur, / Nullaque prorsus cotidiani copia questus / Immoderatos pectoris eius temperat estus. / Plus et habundans, pauper habetur. Iam puto uerum / Quod perhibetur: pectus auarum non miseretur. / Dampnat auaros, cum sit auarus. Dulcia fatur / Cum sit amarus: corde lupinus, uestibus agnus" (translation here and below S.S.).

82 Ibid., 78, in context: "Iam quia finis temporis instet, ne dubitemus, / Cum tot oriri religionum monstra uidemus." Ibid., 81: "Temporis huius pseudoprophete significantur. / Primus equorum uenerat albus, sacra nouorum / Tempore primo milia signans Christicolarum. /Post rufus exit, tempora signans martiriorum. / Post niger exit, tempora signans scismaticorum. / Vltimus exit pallidus: hic est hypocritarum, / Iusta suarum quos male ducit mors animarum…. / Hec mala radix ex Phariseis orta uidetur, / Germine cuius centuplicato terra repletur…. / Ipsa moderno tempore mentes dum uiciauit / Nobilis ordo religionis degenerauit."

83 See L. J. Engels, "Adtendite a falsis prophetis (Ms. Colmar 128, ff. 152v-153v). Un texte de Pierre Abélard contre les Cisterciens retrouvé?" in *Corona gratiarum. Miscellanea historica, patristica et liturgica Eligius Dekkers OSB*, Instrumenta Patristica et Mediaevalia 11 (Brepols Publishers: Turnhout, 1975), 2:195–228.

84 See Margaret Sinex, "Echoic Irony in Walter Map's Satire against the Cistercians," *Comparative Literature* 54, no. 4 (2002): 275–90; Brian Golding, "Gerald of Wales and the Cistercians," *Reading Medieval Studies* 21 (1995): 5–30; Joseph Charles Castora, *The "Speculum Ecclesiae" of Giraldus Cambrensis and the Cistercians of Southern England and Wales*, 3 vols. (PhD diss., New York University, 1990); Lewis Thorpe, "Walter Map and Gerald of Wales," *Medium Ævum* 47, no. 1 (1978): 6–21.

85 See the remarks of the editors in Walter Map, *De Nugis Curialium – Courtiers' Trifles*, ed. M. R. James, Christopher Nugent Lawrence Brooke, and R. A. B. Mynors, *Oxford Medieval Texts* (Oxford/New York: Clarendon Press, 1983), xxiv, xxxi, xlv–xlviii; and my forthcoming article, Sita Steckel, "Rhetorische Spaltungen. Zur Dynamik von Invektivität im Inneren des hoch- und spätmittelalterlichen lateinischen Christentums," *Saeculum* 70, no. 1 (2020): 39–74.

86 See esp. Walter Map, *De Nugis curialium*, dis. i., c. 25, 86–8. Walter's views on Jews are reported by Gerald of Wales, see Thorpe, "Walter Map and Gerald of Wales," 12.

87 Daniel N. Bell, "*De grisis monachis*: A Goliardic invective against the Cistercians in London, B.L. Cotton Vespasian A.XIX," *Studia Monastica* 41 (1999): 243–59.

88 See note 37.
89 Leclercq, "Le poème," esp. 77–8.
90 Ibid., 81, v. 194. On contemporary use of *ordo*, see Gert Melville, "Zur Semantik von *ordo* im Religiosentum der ersten Hälfte des 12. Jahrhunderts," in *Studien zum Prämonstratenserorden*, Veröffentlichungen des Max-Planck-Instituts für Geschichte 25, ed. Irene Crusius and Helmut Flachenecker (Göttingen: Vandenhoeck & Ruprecht, 2003), 201–24.
91 John of Salisbury, Policraticus, *Of the Frivolities of Courtiers and the Footprints of Philosophers*, trans. Cary J. Nederman, Cambridge Texts in the History of Political Thought (Cambridge: Cambridge University Press, 1990).
92 John of Salisbury, *Policraticus*, 168.
93 Ibid., 168 and 170.
94 Ibid., 170.
95 Ibid., 171.
96 E.g. ibid., 172.
97 Ibid., 174.
98 Anselm of Havelberg, *Anticimenon: On the Unity of the Faith and the Controversies with the Greeks*, trans. Ambrose Criste and Carol Neel, Cistercian Studies Series 232 (Collegeville: Cistercian Publications, 2010), l. 1, c. 1, 47. On hypocrisy, see ibid., l. 1, c. 10, 66–8; on Anselm's overall argument, see Markus Schürer, "Innovation und Variabilität als Instrumente göttlicher Pädagogik: Anselm von Havelberg und seine Position in den Diskursen um die Legitimät religiöser Lebensformen," *Mittellateinisches Jahrbuch: internationale Zeitschrift für Mediävistik* 42, no. 3 (2007): 373–96.
99 Anselm of Havelberg, *Anticimenon*, l. 1, c. 1, 47.
100 To use terminology inspired by sociological approaches, especially Peter L. Berger, *The Many Altars of Modernity: Toward a Paradigm for Religion in a Pluralist Age* (Boston: De Gruyter, 2014).
101 Nigel de Longchamps, *Speculum stultorum*, ed. John H. Mozley and Robert R. Raymo, University of California English Studies 18 (Berkeley, CA: University of California Press, 1960).
102 Ibid., 76–86.
103 On estates satire, see Jill Mann, *Chaucer and Medieval Estates Satire: The Literature of Social Classes and the General Prologue to the Canterbury Tales* (Cambridge: Cambridge University Press, 1973).
104 See, e.g., Michel-Marie Dufeil, *Guillaume de Saint-Amour et la polémique universitaire parisienne, 1250–1259* (Paris: A. et J. Picard, 1972), 29, and notably Grundmann, *Religious Movements*, 67.
105 Grundmann, *Religious Movements*, 65–7.

106 See Grundmann, *Religious Movements*, 66, referring, e.g., to Michele Faloci-Pulignani, "Legenda trium sociorum ex Cod. Fulginatensi," *Miscellanea francescana di storia, di lettere, di arti* 7 (1898), 81–107, at § 62, 103.
107 See notes 61–3 above.
108 Caesarius of Heisterbach, "Vita Engelberti," in *Die Wundergeschichten. Einleitung, Exempla und Auszüge aus den Predigten des Caesarius von Heisterbach*, Publikationen der Gesellschaft für Rheinische Geschichtskunde 1, vol. 3, ed. Alfons Hilka (Bonn: Hanstein, 1933–7), c. 7, 245–6.
109 Konrad Bund, "Die Prophetin, ein Dichter und die Niederlassung der Bettelorden in Köln," *Mittellateinisches Jahrbuch* 23 (1991, 1988): 171–260; see also Magda Hayton, "Prophets, Prophecy, and Cistercians: A Study of the Most Popular Version of the Hildegardian Pentachronon," *Journal of Medieval Latin* 29 (2019): 123–62.
110 See, e.g., Sita Steckel, "Narratives of Resistance: Arguments against the Mendicants in the Works of Matthew Paris and William of Saint-Amour," in *Thirteenth Century England XV. Authority and Resistance in the Age of Magna Charta*, ed. Janet Burton, Phillipp Schofield, and Björn Weiler (Woodbridge: Boydell Press, 2015), 157–77, at 165.
111 See Andrew G. Traver, "Rewriting History? The Parisian Secular Masters' Apologia of 1254," *History of Universities* 15 (1999): 9–45; Jacques Verger, "*Coacta ac periculosa societas*. La difficile intégration des réguliers à l'Université de Paris au XIIIe siècle," in *Vivre en société au Moyen Âge: Occident chrétien VIe–XVe siècle*, Le temps de l'histoire, ed. Claude Carozzi, Daniel Le Blévec, and Huguette Taviani-Carozzi (Aix-en-Provence, 2008), 261–80.
112 See Marjorie Reeves, *The Influence of Prophecy in the Later Middle Ages: A Study in Joachimism* (Oxford: Oxford University Press, 1969), 145–228.
113 See Kerby-Fulton, "Hildegard of Bingen and Anti-Mendicant Propaganda," 394; Kerby-Fulton, Hayton, and Olsen, "Pseudo-Hildegardian Prophecy."
114 After initial concessions; on the developments and documents of this controversy, see with references to the literature by Traver, "The Forging"; Andrew Traver, ed., *The Opuscula of William of Saint-Amour: The Minor Works of 1255–1256*, Beiträge zur Geschichte der Philosophie und Theologie des Mittelalters N.F. 63 (Münster: Aschendorff, 2003).
115 See, e.g., *Chartularium Universitatis Parisiensis* I, Nos. 259, 261–2 and 264, at 298–302.
116 See William of Saint-Amour, *De periculis novissimorum temporum*, ed. and trans. Guy Geltner, Dallas Medieval Texts and Translations 8 (Paris/Leuven/Dudley: Peeters, 2008). On the context, see briefly Traver, "The Forging," 162–6.

117 William of Saint-Amour, *De periculis*, ed. Guy Geltner, esp. 50–1, 58–9.
118 See the overview of the argument in Szittya, *The Antifraternal Tradition*, 31–60.
119 William of Saint-Amour, *De periculis*, 122–3, 128–9.
120 Traver, "The Forging," 166; *The Opuscula of William of Saint-Amour*, 53–74.
121 See the overview in William of Saint-Amour, *De periculis*, 14–15.
122 See, e.g., William of Saint-Amour, *De periculis*, 50/1, 66/7.
123 See *Corpus juris canonici, 2: Decretalium collections*, ed. Aemilius Ludwig Richter and Aemilius Friedberg (Leipzig: Tauchnitz, 1879; reprint Graz: Akademische Druck-und Verlagsanstalt, 1959), col. 780 (*Ad Abolendam*, 1184), col. 782 (*Vergentis in Senium*, 1199), col. 786 (*Quum ex iniuncto*, 1199).
124 William of Saint-Amour, *De periculis*, esp. 45–77; 107–11.
125 This distinguishes him from the "ordo prophecy" concept described in Kerby-Fulton, *Reformist Apocalypticism*, 133–4.
126 E.g., in his treatise, William of Saint-Amour, *De periculis*, 113–39 and in his sermon *Qui amat periculum*, in *The Opuscula of William of Saint-Amour*, 173–7. For this strategy in later texts, see Fiona Somerset, "'Mark Him Wel for He Is on of Þo': Training the 'Lewed' Gaze to Discern Hypocrisy," *ELH* 68, no. 2 (2001): 315–34.
127 On this idea, see Steckel, "Rhetorische Spaltungen," and the theoretical considerations in Dagmar Ellerbrock et al., "Invektivität – Perspektiven eines neuen Forschungsprogramms in den Kultur- und Sozialwissenschaften," *Kulturwissenschaftliche Zeitschrift* 2, no. 1 (2017): 2–24.
128 See Grundmann, *Religious Movements*, 187–201.
129 See John Orr, ed., *Les œuvres de Guiot de Provins, poète lyrique et satirique*, Publications de l'Université de Manchester. Série française 1 (Manchester: Manchester University Press, 1915). On Guiot, see M. Tietz, "Guiot de Provins," in *Lexikon des Mittelalters* (Munich/Zurich: Metzler, 1989), 4: col. 1787.
130 See *Les œuvres de Guiot de Provins*, ed. Orr, vv. 1145–55, 45–6.
131 Ibid., vv. 1207ff., 47.
132 See the list in Mann, *Chaucer and medieval estates satire*, 203–6.
133 See *Le Ordre de Bel-Eyse*, in *The Political Songs of England, from the Reign of John to that of Edward II*, ed. Thomas Wright (London: Camden Society, 1839), 137–48.
134 See Jean Dufournet, *Rutebeuf et les frères mendiants: Poèmes satiriques* (Paris: H. Champion, 1991); Tiberius Denkinger, "Die Bettelorden in der französischen didaktischen Literatur des 13. Jahrhunderts, besonders bei Rutebeuf und im Roman de la Rose," *Franziskanische Studien* 2 (1915): 63–109, 286–313.
135 See Dufournet, *Rutebeuf et les frères mendiants*, 53; see the Old French in Edmond Faral and Julia Bastin, eds., *Œuvres complètes de Rutebeuf* (Paris: Éditions A. et J. Picard, 1959), 1:261–2.

136 See, e.g., Dufournet, *Rutebeuf et les frères mendiants*, 51–2 ("La Complainte de Guillaume de Saint-Amour").
137 See Dufournet, *Rutebeuf et les frères mendiants*, 103–6 ("Chanson des Ordres").
138 On communities of interpretation, the importance of the vernacular in related contexts, and parallel episodes in the fifteenth century, see the overview in Corbellini and Steckel, "The Religious Field," 322–4.
139 On the issue of choice, see the literature in note 144.
140 For the latter, particularly fragmented, field, see the discussion in Steckel, "Verging on the Polemical"; also Steckel, "*Une querelle des theologiens*? 'Polemics' in the Historiography of the Secular-Mendicant Controversy," in *Les régimes de polémicité au Moyen Âge*, ed. Bénédicte Sère (Rennes: Presses universitaires de Rennes, 2019), 83–97.
141 On this aspect, which could not be discussed here, see briefly Ames, "Medieval Religious," 337–9.
142 See the literature in note 14, particularly Weltecke, "Über Religion," and Brauner and Steckel, "Wie die Heiden," for further thoughts on the relationship of intra- and interreligious differences.
143 On this observation, see briefly Lerner, "Introduction to the Translation," xxi.
144 For the idea of religious "options," see John Van Engen, "Multiple Options: The World of the Fifteenth-Century Church," *Church History* 77, no. 2 (2008): 257–84, and the contributions in the forthcoming volume by Matthias Pohlig and Sita Steckel, eds., *Über Religion entscheiden. Religiöse Optionen und Alternativen im mittelalterlichen und frühneuzeitlichen Christentum / Choosing my Religion: Religious Options and Alternatives in Late Medieval and Early Modern Christianity* (forthcoming in 2021).
145 This view contrasts directly with the argument made by Wendy Scase, *Piers Plowman and the New Anticlericalism*, Cambridge Studies in Medieval Literature 4 (Cambridge: Cambridge University Press, 1989), esp. x, though this is largely a question of perspective.
146 The concept has indeed been criticized as anachronistic for the medieval period (see Schreiner, "Gab es im Mittelalter"), though the definition proposed in Dykema and Oberman, eds., *Anticlericalism*, x, is an inherently dynamic one.
147 See Ames, "Medieval Religious," 3345.
148 See esp. Driedger and Wolfart, "Reframing the History"; Pietsch and Steckel, "New Religious Movements" (as note 19).

5 Crusading as a Religious Movement: Families, Community, and Lordship in a Vernacular Frame

ANNE E. LESTER

In the town of Mailly-le-Château in central Burgundy, thirty kilometres south of Auxerre, the parish church of St.-Adrien commands the central square. Today the *mairie*'s office faces the church's austere façade. Like many churches of the region, St.-Adrien dates to the early thirteenth century.[1] Its central doorway is a pointed Gothic arch that holds a delicate trilobe entrance carried on slim respond pillars between two tall and sturdy buttresses. A curtain wall shores up the full façade cut by two lancet windows on either side of the door. The right side of the church has an additional rounded staircase, giving access to a small bell tower with a squat conical roof. As if to balance the tower, a hefty flying buttress stands to the left, securing in place the topmost clerestory arcade which carries two more high lancet windows. Between the west façade buttresses at the upper level of the clerestory is an open gallery supported by five freestanding columns. The base of each column features the figures of four men and in the centre one woman (fig. 5.1). The four men's bodies twist and contort, labouring under sacks of grain and bundles hoisted over their shoulders. They move in space, walking, carrying, and shifting, animated with legs bare and visible through short trousers, the common dress of labouring free peasants and serfs. The woman at the centre, by contrast, stands tall and faces outward, her right hand placed firmly on her hip in "a gesture of power and authority."[2] Her left hand has been partly broken, but it still secures the cords of her long cloak of nobility and a large cross, similar to other sculpted crusader crosses (fig. 5.2).

St.-Adrien and Mailly-le-Château were part of the familial domains of the counts of Auxerre and Nevers, and the façade sculpture was possibly commissioned in the 1220s or 1230s to depict Mahaut (in English, Mathilda) of Courtenay (b. 1188–d. 1257), countess of Nevers, Auxerre,

128 Anne E. Lester

Figure 5.1. Façade of St.-Adrien, Mailly-le-Château, Burgundy, ca. 1230. Centre, Mahaut of Nevers; serfs and labourers on side columns.

Figure 5.2. Detail, Mahaut of Nevers, St.-Adrien, Mailly-le-Château.

and Tonnerre.³ Her sculpted relief is similar to the image that graced her personal seal: forward facing, with long hair and wimple in a pose of unambiguous leadership.⁴ On the façade, she is remembered both as crusader and beneficent lord, commemorated for the liberties and franchises she offered to the burghers and serfs of her domains in 1229 and again in the decades that followed. The façade sculpture depicts the entwined commitments of crusading, financial obligation and aristocratic charitable patronage that characterized female lordship in ways that reshaped social relationships in the first half of the thirteenth century.

As her sculpted image suggests, Mahaut's life offers a useful case study for understanding the place of crusading in relation to the religious movements animating the thirteenth century that were the focus of Herbert Grundmann's work. Although we know almost nothing of Mahaut's participation, with her husband Hervé of Donzy, in the Fifth Crusade (1217–21), her religious commitments more broadly suggest a picture of what I will call "vernacular crusading" – that is, the intertwined ways that crusade devotion was made manifest in the west through patronage, through grants of personal and corporate franchise, and through a concern with practices of religious reform and lordship more broadly.⁵ Like many of her female contemporaries, Mahaut hailed from a crusader family that supported the movement over generations, taking part to different degrees but in a manner often overlooked or understudied because it was rarely recorded in the chronicle tradition.⁶ To this end, this chapter takes up three central questions: How did crusading interact with the religious movements to which Grundmann drew attention? Why does crusading as a religious movement play no role in Grundmann's argument? And how did vernacular culture shape the lay experience of crusading and inform a practice of "vernacular crusading" at home in the west?⁷

The experiences and decisions of Countess Mahaut provide a touchstone and a narrative through-line to explore these questions.⁸ Mahaut's intertwined crusade and lordship commitments afford an opportunity to consider the ideas and practices linking grants of franchise, aristocratic identity, and crusade ambitions. Mahaut's actions suggest other ways of seeing religious movements at work in the world. Although she never joined a religious order or supported heretics, she was part of numerous overlapping religious impulses, which guided her decisions and tempered their effects. That Mahaut may have appeared saint-like on the façade of a parish church should provoke scholars to consider how and why crusading and charitable female lordship (moving beyond the male chivalric ideal) were connected, and how we might reframe different historiographies that have too long remained separated.

※

From our contemporary vantage point, which has witnessed a veritable efflorescence of scholarship on the crusades, crusading, and crusader culture, it is curious indeed that Herbert Grundmann's monumental study of religious movements has virtually nothing to say about the crusades or how crusading coincided with the history of religious movements he set out to analyse. Although other related themes appear within his published essays and in *Religious Movements*, Grundmann never pursued the deeper resonances between crusading and reform, the growth of the papacy as tied to crusade campaigns, crusading and the preaching missions undertaken by the friars and Francis himself, or the clear connections between crusading and the women's religious movement as articulated in the hagiographical accounts of women like Marie d'Oignies and Elizabeth of Hungary.[9] By contrast, Grundmann's interests in themes of eschatology and mysticism led him to Joachim of Fiore, a figure who loomed large in thirteenth-century prophetic and eschatological writing connecting the end of days with the successes and failures in the Holy Land. Yet even in his treatment of Joachim, he made no attempt to address crusading.[10] Likewise, despite his attention to the "social aspects of the religious movement," to the role of preaching in the movements' origins, the pursuit of the *vita apostolica* as informed by a commitment to poverty and the allure of the *vita communis*, and the potential Eastern influence behind the rise of heresy in the west, no mention is made of crusading, pilgrimage, the Holy Land, or crusade preaching. For Grundmann, writing first in the 1920s and 1930s and revisiting and revising his work throughout the later 1960s, the crusades and crusade spirituality had no role to play within his conception of the origins of the religious movements and their final evolution as either heretical sects or formal orders. Indeed, for him, the two themes occupied two very different historiographical traditions.

By contrast, several scholars working at the time, most notably Carl Erdmann (1898–1945) and Paul Alphandéry (1875–1932), did pursue the connection between the religious impulses of the laity and the reforming interests of the institutional church in the practice of crusading. Carl Erdmann's study *The Origin of the Idea of the Crusade*, published in 1935 – the same year as Grundmann's first edition of *Religious*

Movements – traced the formation of the concept of holy war and its practice in the west in relation to Jerusalem as a final aim, looking especially at the period before 1095, that is, before the advent of the First Crusade.[11] He was particularly interested in the evolution of the concept of holy war and its acceptance among "the masses," looking to the role of liturgy, art, banners, and symbols as a means of expression. Erdmann was also attentive to what we might now call channels of communication between the papacy – as the point of origin for a set of theological concepts anchored to religious texts – and the Christian laity who received such ideas. Indeed, Erdmann and Grundmann shared a fascination with the connections between the papal leadership and the laity and the capacity for one to influence the other. Both men also shared contemporary experiences in academic circles, working for the *Monumenta Germaniae Historica*, and serving in the German army during the Second World War despite their disapproval of National Socialism. Grundmann held a desk job in 1944 and was then stationed with an anti-tank unit in East Prussia until February 1945, when he was wounded and soon after taken prisoner by the British.[12] Erdmann served as an interpreter with the German army in the Balkans, where he died following an illness in 1945.[13] Both of their books had a lasting impact and shaped religious history and crusade scholarship, but they are rarely treated together.

Paul Alphandéry also wrote in a similar contemporary moment, although the trajectory of his work and its reception was somewhat different. Alphandéry was drawn to the Crusades through an interest in the intersection of emotions, religious impulses, and social conditions. In a series of course lectures offered at the École des Hautes Études (section Sciences Religieuse) during the 1920s and 1930s, he traced what motivated collective action and collective movements; pilgrimage, prophecy, and visionary literature; the role of the poor and the rhetoric of poverty; as well as the conjunction of popular preaching and heresy.[14] For Alphandéry the Crusades were the culminating product of collective action and ideas yoked to Holy Land pilgrimage and channelled through the efforts of preachers, such as Fulk of Neuilly (d. 1201), and the directives of the papacy.[15] Yet, it was not the papal documents that interested him but, rather, the reception and reshaping of ideas and thoughts, a form of "collective psychology" that constituted the mental and emotional context for the movement. Alphandéry was a close reader of Freud and was compelled by the idea of a shared consciousness reflective of the collective mentality behind religious sentiment that could motivate a communal spirit.[16] Where Erdmann sought to understand the origins, precursors, and motives for the First

Crusade, Alphandéry demonstrated the continuity of a collective will over the course of the twelfth and thirteenth centuries as it moved – as he conceived of it – from a primarily noble pursuit to one involving the lower classes and even the poor. He found resonances in the preaching, papal letters, and directions of the crusade campaigns that seemed to express, in his words, a "*collective d'ame,*" a collective soul and spirit.[17] But Alphandéry was also attentive to the social conditions of those who took part in each crusade expedition. He examined preaching and how ideas circulated as well as how crusade expeditions were funded and supported through prayers, alms, and ideas of liberty and peace.[18] In this way, his approach to the Crusades as a collective movement mirrors Grundmann's sense of the conjoined development of ideas and social shifts, barely perceptible in the moment but profound in their cumulative effects. Likewise, both men eschewed the blatantly materialist interpretations present in much of the contemporary scholarship, which viewed the Crusades as a financial and colonial undertaking and interpreted the interest in the *vita apostolica* in similar economic terms as a rejection of accumulated wealth and mercantile influence.[19]

Yet unlike Erdmann and Grundmann, the reception and acceptance of Alphandéry's ideas never gained the same momentum. In the spring of 1932, Alphandéry died suddenly, leaving behind a mass of lecture notes and a series of unfinished projects relating to prophesy and mysticism as well as the Crusades. It fell to his favoured student, Alphonse Dupront, who had recently completed a thesis on the Crusades, to compile and edit Alphandéry's lectures. The results were published in two volumes, the first focused on the First Crusade (1954), and the second covered the expeditions of the thirteenth and fourteenth centuries (1959).[20] Yet, by that point interest in the Crusades had shifted. The resonances of crusading as a "collective will" or spirit, which were strongly felt in the decades following the First World War, were no longer interpreted in the same manner following the Second World War and the horrors of Nazism, when the idea of a common animating spirit or will among the people found little appeal or reception. During the latter period, colonial and military interpretations of crusade expeditions again took centre stage. As a result, scholars have not considered Grundmann's and Alphandéry's work together or examined how their attention to social forces shaped interpretations of religious history and in turn produced a conceptualization of the crusade movement very much in line with the other movements of reform and the apostolic life that Grundmann elaborated so clearly.[21]

The separation of crusade studies from the study of religion and religious life grew further entrenched, as John Van Engen has observed, through the development of disciplinary subfields and the trajectory of social and political history as a discipline separate from the study of religion.[22] As a consequence, the study of the Crusades took shape under the umbrella of political, legal, and diplomatic history. Scholars of the Crusades traced the canonical definitions and papal articulation of its ideals, analysed and edited the diplomatic correspondence of its leaders, charted the military and political consequences of fundraising and bureaucratic growth for royal and princely interests, and followed the material motives and colonial ambitions fuelling the crusader states in the east.[23] Only at the close of the twentieth century, as the study of religion moved more clearly into the domain of anthropology and history, did crusader religion and crusade spirituality, and especially the religious motives for crusading, garner renewed study. Giles Constable led the way by studying crusader charters as a monastic historian would, for religious intentions and spiritual language.[24] Indeed, Constable's insight – that crusaders were present often in monastic charters and that such legal texts could be used as a way to gauge the spiritual sense of the movement – has come to redefine the field in significant ways. By the late 1980s, Jonathan Riley-Smith also turned to the close analysis of crusader charters to account for motivations, spiritual leanings, and a rhetoric of religious intension that allowed him to draw out a picture of crusading that encompassed a world far greater than a warrior's chivalric cohort.[25] His students– among them Christoph Maier, Penny Cole, Jonathan Phillips, Marcus Bull, Caroline Smith, Rebecca Risk, William Purkis, Nicholas Paul, and Jochen Schenk – have reshaped the field of crusader studies, taking the Crusades as manifestations of religious impulses and ambitions affecting and reflecting ideals and beliefs within society as a whole.[26] We are now well situated to bring the historiographical threads of religious movements and crusading back together. Indeed, my point here is not to critique Grundmann for neglecting the Crusades but to address two questions more precisely: How can crusading as an ongoing process that shaped medieval Europe be brought into conversation with Grundmann's conceptualization of religious movements and their evolution, especially during the twelfth and thirteenth centuries? And how might Grundmann's precocious focus on the role of women and vernacularity help us to rethink crusading as a religious movement with broader effects?

Just before their departure for Damietta in September 1218, Mahaut of Nevers and Hervé of Donzy (1173–1222) drew up a joint testament. This document and a charter confirmed upon their return are all we know of Mahaut's participation in the Fifth Crusade.[27] Prior to this, Hervé had taken part briefly in the early campaigns of the Albigensian Crusade (1209–29) and fought at the siege of Carcassonne (August 1209), but he returned north soon after concluding his required forty days of service. In 1213 or 1214 he took the cross for a second time, taking his vow before Cardinal Robert Courson, papal legate and crusade preacher. In August 1216, Hervé is mentioned by name in Pope Honorius's letter to departing crusades, instructing them to put aside funds for at least eight sergeants to accompany them east.[28] The couple's testament, written en route from Genoa, detailed bequests made for their commemoration, established anniversary Masses for their souls should they not return, and made provision for their burial at the Cistercian Abbey of Pontigny.[29] In addition to donations for the monasteries of Quincy, Regny, Rougement, Bourras, Bardelles, La Charité, Jully, Parthenon, L'Épeau, Bellary, and Pontmorigny and the churches of St-Étienne of Bourges, St-Aignan, and Châteauneuf, they released several knights who had mortgaged their lands to the count and countess, and they left endowments for chapels at Druye, St-Hilaire, Decize, and Cosne. As charitable alms, they set aside thousands of pounds, half of which were to be distributed to peasants in the countryside who had suffered injustices, 500 pounds were to be given out among the count and countess's servants, and 200 pounds were given to two ladies (*damoiselle*), who accompanied the countess to the east, to aid in their marriages once there (presumably in Syria, Egypt, or Greece). What remained was to be distributed to the poor in alms.[30] Mahaut and Hervé charged the bishops of Nevers and Auxerre with executing these final wishes.

While much is standard about such a departure testament, the attention to the poor, the staggering amount set aside for alms and charity – in addition to the costs of crusading – and the attention to restorative, even redemptive, justice is revealing.[31] So too is the unusual clause setting aside funds to provide for two aristocratic women whom the countess was to escort to the east to be married and for whom they provided funds for doweries. Here we catch a glimpse of women's roles in the crusade movement. In the case of Mahaut, she took part as a vowed crusader who made provisions for her own spiritual legacy and who oversaw those of others. It is helpful to recall that Mahaut would have been thirty years old at the time, and Hervé forty-five. They travelled east as seasoned lords, well-versed in the obligations and risks of crusading. As Elizabeth Siberry has shown, Mahaut and Hervé hailed from crusader families, stretching back to participation in the First Crusade in 1095.[32] But Mahaut's interest seems also to have been with an eye to settlement in the east. Her father, Peter of Courtenay (who retained title only to the county of Auxerre after Mahaut's marriage), was offered the throne of the Latin Empire in Constantinople and left for the east in 1216, only to die there in prison between 1218 and 1219.[33] She may have felt that settling in the east was a part of the crusade mission and thus supported the cause materially as well as spiritually. We cannot know if the two *damoiselle* took crusade vows themselves. Most revealing is the fact that by 1218 crusading had taken on dimensions much broader than simply campaigning in the east or participating in warfare. Crusading came to be associated with charity, redemption, penitence, prayer, and lordly continuity that required women's participation.

Together the count and countess spent less than a year on campaign. Arriving in Damietta, Hervé played a prominent role in the second siege of the city.[34] By August 1219, once Peter of Courtenay's death was made known, Hervé and Mahaut returned to the west to settle affairs and consolidate the lordships of Nevers, Tonnerre, and Auxerre.[35] Before he departed, Hervé extended loans to several of the knights in his entourage, borrowing from Genoese citizens to support those who stayed in the east.[36] Two telling charters from 1219 locate the count and countess back in the west: The first consisted of a grant to the inhabitants of Donzy and the monks of l'Epeau for the use of firewood, and the second involved the future marriage of their daughter, Agnès, with the king's consent. Both transactions concern the restoration of peace and order in the counties, and in the first specifically Mahaut is described as Hervé's companion and wife (*socia et uxor nostra comitissa*).[37]

Hervé died in 1222 in his castle at St-Aignan and was buried, as he instructed in his testament, not far from Auxerre in the Abbey of Pontigny, in the chapel of Thomas Becket.[38] In the years that followed, Mahaut honoured his memory through numerous endowments in his name, and after the death of her daughter Agnès in 1226, she added bequests in Agnès's name as well.[39] In 1223, as she began to rule on her own, Mahaut initiated a series of franchise grants to towns throughout her domains at Ligny (1223) and Tonnerre (1224), where the canons of Notre-Dame de Tonnerre and the townspeople expressed their gratitude by promising to celebrate a Mass of the Holy Spirit in her honour during her lifetime, and a Mass for the dead after her death.[40] In April 1226, following the death of her daughter and her son-in-law, Guy of Châtillon, count of St.-Pol, Mahaut gave a chapel and some land outside of Auxerre to found a new community of nuns at Celles, which would become the Cistercian nunnery of Les Isles, in the memory of her "dearest daughter (*karissime filie Agnetis*)," her son-in-law, and her husband Hervé.[41] In the same year she married Guy IV, count of Forez.[42]

That September, while in residence at Montbrison, they enfranchised the serfs of Montbrison and La Marche in return for annual payments of 5 s. from each hearth – that is, establishing a sort of a hearth tax. In 1227 they offered partial franchises and communal status to the towns of Châteauneuf (sur-Allier) (1227) and Corbigny (1228).[43]

At the same time, the count and countess remained attentive to the religious needs of their domains. In 1230 they granted the Grandmontine monks at Bellary a new set of domains, where they could find greater solitude as their order prescribed, because their previous location was too close to woods used by butchers to keep pigs, shepherds keeping the animals, and charcoal makers, whose fumes and smoke disturbed the monks' solitude.[44] In the same year, Guy of Forez founded a house of penitent women dedicated to Mary Magdalene and under the rule of St. Augustine in or near his castle at Montbrison, just outside the town. He provided the community with revenues from grain and money in cash payments and reserved the right of patronage. If the community were not established in a fixed place, or if it came to have fewer than four women, the gifts for the foundation would return to the count and his heirs.[45] Finally, in 1230, Mahaut granted all women of servile condition throughout her lands the ability to marry a free person and to become free of the condition that constrained their mobility. In other words, she freed such women from hereditary servile status.[46]

Grants of franchise continued into the 1230s. In 1229 Guy and Mahaut granted the privileges of a commune to the inhabitants of Mailly-le-Château, near Auxerre, with which this essay began.[47] In July 1231 they reconfirmed the franchise of the burghers of Nevers, guaranteeing rights given to them by Mahaut's father, Peter of Courtenay, in 1194. A similar grant was extended to the burghers of Auxerre in 1194.[48] In July 1233 the pair granted the burghers of Vermanton the franchise of a commune according to the customs of Lorris.[49] From the end of the twelfth century through the middle of the thirteenth, grants of franchise cascaded across the counties of Nevers, Auxerre, Tonnerre, Champagne, St.-Pol, and Chartres and the lordships of Picardy and the Ile-de-France. Indeed, such grants of communal and personal liberty in exchange for annual payments became commonplace. The monies gained by the comital and lordly families offering such freedoms were used to fund other aristocratic pursuits, namely castle building and fortification, crusading, and religious endowments.[50] Franchise, that is, the grant of liberty or freedom from a specific set of constraints, had a charitable connotation, not simply an economic end. It was a form of good and charitable lordship. Without radically restructuring power relations in the region, grants of franchise offered lords a way to capitalize on aristocratic grants of liberty yet still collect funds without coercion or abuse of their power. It allowed crusading lords to profit on the perception of a charitable practice, not unlike grants to monastic houses in return for subsidies or one-time payments.

During this time, Mahaut's patronage of religious women continued apace as well. In 1235 she founded the Cistercian convent of Le Réconfort in the diocese of Autun, near her castle of Monceaux and not far from Nevers and Auxerre. The foundation had modest beginnings, but it would be where Mahaut eventually chose to be buried.[51] In the same year, Guy IV of Forez took the cross to crusade with Count Thibaut IV of Champagne, on what would become known as the Barons' Crusade (1239–41). Guy encumbered numerous debts in the process and endowed the countess with not only the regency of the county during his absence but also the financial responsibility for repaying a sum of 16,000 *lbs.* to fund his portion of the expedition.[52] Guy campaigned briefly in the east. In 1240 he was taken captive with Amaury of Montfort, and after eighteen months they were freed. During his return journey, in the summer of 1241, Guy fell ill in the small town of Castellaneta in the province of Apulia, not far from Brindisi. There, on his deathbed, he composed his testament dated to 10 August 1241.[53] Only three months before this, Mahaut oversaw the establishment of the Dominicans in Auxerre, founded inside the city walls in a house given over to the friars by Amice the widow of Gautier of Joigny and their son. At the end of the charter, Mahaut noted that she was acting with the full administrative power of the count while he was across the sea (*nobili viro Guidone marito nostro in transmarinis partibus existente, et nobis in ejus absentia totius comitatus administrationem gerente*).[54] The religious impulses, ideas, and commitments behind domestic lordship and crusading were part of the same framework that came to define the crusade movement as it was brought to fruition in the Holy Land while also carried out – through franchise, patronage, and charity – in the west. Although historians have long studied these activities separately, thinking through the workings of religious movements shows how they were intimately and personally entwined, allowing us to see the "links" between and behind such phenomena.

Collective Commitments of Crusade Families

As Elizabeth Siberry has shown, Mahaut was part of a powerful line of crusaders binding the family of the counts of Nevers to the eastern Mediterranean and the ideals of crusader salvation and self-sacrifice. Indeed, Mahaut's forebearers participated in the First, Second,

Third, and Fourth Crusade campaigns. She and her husband took part in the Fifth, and her second husband on the Barons' Crusade in 1239. Her children and grandchildren too would marry men who continued the tradition, joining the French king, Louis IX, on his first expedition in 1248 and travelling on an independent crusade in 1266.[55] Although the sources are rarely explicit about the influence women exerted in motivating their fathers, husbands, brothers, sons, and nephews to take the crusade vow, Mahaut's example suggests she was a lynchpin for such repeated decisions.

It is now clear that women played a forceful role in cultivating the conditions for a continued, multigenerational commitment to crusading as a religious practice, and we might even say religious movement.[56] As the sources that detail crusade preparation make clear, crusading relied upon fostering ongoing connections to local religious houses, supporting new spiritual initiatives in preaching and penance, and upholding a broader sense of Christian peace, charity, and devotion. Riley-Smith's studies of the narrative and charter evidence for families of first crusaders "suggest that [families] must have been predisposed in some way to respond to the earliest calls to crusade."[57] Moreover, because they had to finance expeditions themselves, "they were exceptionally dependent on family support and this gave the kindred influence at a crucial stage in the development of crusading and no doubt reinforced a collective commitment to it."[58]

With rare exception, chroniclers did not elaborate on such commitments because they did not seem integral to the deeds accomplished in the east. Rarely do such anterior religious preparations appear in sermons urging men and women to take the vow and take up arms, and rarely are religious orientations the concern of popes and reformers outside of generalized encyclicals and letters condemning usury. Riley-Smith and others formed their conclusions from the aggregation of thousands of charters, which demonstrated that participation in expeditions to the east was dependent upon a broader religious awareness and engagement that supported new religious houses, the practice of local charity towards the poor, the support and spreading out of small parish churches and local chaplaincies, and gifts to hospitals, *domus-Dei*, and leper houses, all with an eye to a broader salvific effect. In a study of the charter evidence from the lords of Boves, Olivier Leblanc came to similar conclusions. In the absence of narrative references, Leblanc traced the multigenerational commitments of Picard knightly families to the crusade endeavour. Using the Boves family as a case study, he argued that it was the women of the Boves line who determined the family's favourable response to crusading. As he notes, "as with the practice of donations to religious communities, the instigation to take the cross clearly passed through marriage to sisters and daughters."[59] More recently, Theodore Evergates and Randall Pippenger have made a similar case for the influential role of women in the context of Champagne.[60] It was women and those who remained at home who oversaw the implementation of what I call a vernacular crusade culture and who cultivated devotion to its ideals.

For all the specificity of Riley-Smith's account of the First Crusaders' motivations, his articulation of the religious endeavour was left in vague terms. The Crusade was successful, indeed gained its sense of coherence and execution, due to the interpretation and action of "clusters of crusaders ... found in kin groups ... which bred a collective commitment" manifest in the twelfth century in crusading and settlement in the east.[61] Here we are back to the language of Alphandéry, of a collective will, or a *"collective d'ame,"* a soul and spirit. This language resonates with Grundmann's interpretations of religious movements. The dynamics and details of the "kin groups," as Riley-Smith suggested, provides the context for the cultivation of such a collective commitment. Noble households, extended "families" in the broadest medieval sense that were inclusive of their retinues, chaplains, tutors, servants, and indeed kin, became both the incubator and the storehouse for such ideas and interpretations.[62] Much of the interpretative work of crusading was done not through papal correspondence or preaching channels that would find expression in ecclesiastical texts but, rather, through vernacular stories, poems, songs, and oral histories tied to gifts of objects that became crusader heirlooms freighted with personal and ritual associations. Crusader experiences of travel, loss, separation, and death in the east and on campaign framed and reframed theological directives, prohibitions, and incentives, such as the papal protection of a crusader's property and penitential indulgences that cleansed the stain of sin. As Grundmann well understood, this work was done in a vernacular register that more effectively captured oral traditions and opened them to a wider – especially female – audience in the form of vernacular prose histories and poetry. Again, the counts of Nevers and their extended family offer a useful case study in that they cultivated both traditions.

Vernacular Crusade Frame

Vernacular can mean many things. It is a register of language and expression, as well as a way of thinking and communicating – an "idiom," to use Marisa Galvez's word. Fundamentally, the vernacular reached beyond and outside clerical Latinate culture to encompass a set of ideas, images, and materials used to perform and communicate personal, familial, and sacred conceptions of authority and experience. As Grundmann described, the vernacular afforded a different range of expression for religious ideas and sentiments fundamental to the religious movements he identified. In the vernacular, Grundmann asserted, "language was given new tasks to perform, opening new possibilities which permanently marked its vocabulary and forms of expression, immensely enriching them."[63] Grundmann's crucial insight was not only to identify this connection, but also to "ask what the particular circumstances [were] which generated a religious literature in the vernacular, and what influenced the character of this writing?"[64] In the German context, Grundmann identified the rise of the women's religious movement and the concomitant need for mendicant preachers to communicate with women as the setting in which "their sermons developed into a pious literature in the vernacular."[65] This form of religious prose literature emerged "where the relationships corresponding to it grew into a solid system, [that is,] where religious communities of laity or women organized themselves into lasting, regulated forms of life without clerical Latin training, but with the need for contemplation and theological training and a capacity for absorbing and imparting the treasures of Latinate theological and religious education."[66] Female religious communities, especially those overseen by Dominican and Franciscan confessors, offered one such context in which a pious, engaged, religious discourse took root.

Building on Grundmann's insight, it is clear that the thirteenth-century noble household fostered a similar spiritual context, especially in the age of crusading.[67] There, Latinate clerics, canons, and female kin performed the translation work – both of language and of idiom, that is, of meaning and of *sense* – and the intellectual work taken up by a growing cadre of aristocratic poets and *chansonnier*. Indeed, although expressive of a different set of religious ideas from the German mysticism on which Grundmann focused, the corpus of crusader literature and so-called crusader songs functioned in a similar capacity and employed the vernacular to generate a new religious literature. Until recently, however, such crusader songs and histories were read almost exclusively by historians of the Crusades or French literature rather than historians of religious life or religious movements more broadly.[68]

It is now clear that the vernacular crusade prose and poetic corpus – in both the composition and compilation of texts – was constituent of, rather than marginal to, the development of a crusade ideology and the experience of crusading.[69] Recent scholarly work has also made clear that it was the context of the aristocratic household, and its extended form as a mobile crusader household, that generated the production, patronage, and audience for such texts, a corpus that Grundmann might also recognize as a "religious literature in the vernacular."[70] Vernacular crusade composition synthesized complex theological ideas and images and translated them into the vernacular idiom. Verse proved especially useful for capturing the doleful sacrifices that the crusader and his lady made when one undertook a journey that led to a prolonged separation and perhaps death. Images of self-sacrifice; the separation of body from heart or soul; attention to remaining and replacement objects, like a ring or a chemise; and a clear articulation of taking up the cross all echo and interpret theological ideas and images about Christ's role in the world and Christlike sacrifice. It should be no surprise, then, that the imagery of crusader songs shared leitmotifs of separation from one's lover, longing for union, and the wounded self that appear in vernacular mystical treatises written for and especially by religious women.[71]

Thinking through the lens of crusading as a religious movement – one dependent on and shaped by women as much as men, as argued above – it becomes clear that vernacular crusade compositions in both prose and poetry crafted a discourse that simultaneously fostered a heightened sense of devotion and offered a space of critique. The latter could, on the one hand, be seen as critical of crusading, even resistant, and on the other as reform minded. In a recent study of crusade lyric and romance, Marisa Galvez identifies what she calls "a courtly crusade idiom whose movement … can [be] tracked through various constellations of genres, manuscripts, and objects related to being a *crucesignatus*."[72] As Galvez demonstrates, the concept of an *idiom* is useful, especially when dealing with sources that do not directly address the roles of women or were not produced by the clerical elite in service of the papacy, or those charged with formulating a clear "crusade ideology."[73] Crusade songs and vernacular texts produced after the Fall of Jerusalem in 1187, moreover, mark the emergence of a "crusade idiom" in that they "gave voice to an ethical unsettledness and equivocation." As Galvez defines it, "the [crusade] idiom speaks resistance and ambivalence through literature and art."[74] As a medium of translation patronized by women as often as men, vernacular crusade compositions as well as material aspects of crusading opened a space where both ideals – religious and chivalrous, spiritually minded and materially driven – could be present at the same time. For Galvez, "the idiom [as a discursive space] maintains both … and keeps adapting these competing ideals according to changing historical and social conditions."[75]

We can thus begin to imagine a context of crusade recruitment and participation during the lifetime of Mahaut of Nevers that could simultaneously embrace and amplify Innocent III's notion of crusading as "an instrument for the moral transformation of society," in which the crusader and penitent laymen and -women could each "campaign" in their own arenas as part of a unified crusade movement.[76] But we can also see the ways that a vernacular crusade idiom afforded the space to conceptualize separation as a source of critical ambiguity, if not resistance, one mired in the material realities of campaigns that had to be financed, debts that had to be repaid, and a spiritual authority that could be widely interpreted and commented upon. Rather than framing only doctrine and its reception through a preached sermon, vernacular crusade literature translated and reframed such ideas for and within the crusader household.

Between 1187 and 1270 a new repertoire of crusader verse emerged that directly participated in and further transformed the crusade idiom, as Galvez has outlined. Begun in the period of disillusionment and shock occasioned by the loss of the relic of the True Cross following the Battle of Hattin (4 July 1187) and then the loss of the city of Jerusalem (2 October 1187), a new corpus of crusader songs was composed, reflecting upon and informing changes in the crusade movement.[77] Known as *chansons de départie*, or songs of departure, these new verse compositions drew attention to the affective anxiety of leave-taking and the separation of body and heart, of lover and beloved, that crusading came to entail.[78] From the 1190s onwards, these feelings were heightened as crusading functioned less as a brief absence and more as a final destination as more crusaders died in the east or spent prolonged periods of time in Muslim captivity. In turn, a focus on sacrifice – self-sacrifice and penance, one shared by those who remained at home – emerged as a prominent theme within verse compositions.

Such images resonate through many of the songs composed and collected in the early thirteenth century. Writing between 1190 and 1202, Guy IV, Châtelain de Coucy, sung of the separation of the heart from the body as a profound sacrifice. Lost in a memory of his lover, he laments, "When I call to mind her simple courtesy and the sweet words with which she is accustomed to speak to me, how can my heart remain within my body? If it does not part from there it is assuredly most wretched" (*Et quant recort sa simple courtoisie et les dols mos ke suet a moi parler, coment me puet li cuers el cors durer? quant ne s'em part, certes molt est mauvais*).[79] Echoing such an idea and writing (most likely) during the Third Crusade, Conon de Béthune describes the crusader, "Sighing for [his lady] as [he] set out for Syria" (*Por li m'en vois sospirant en Surie*), noting that "I am not leaving her at all! If my body goes off to serve our Lord, my heart remains entirely in her service" (*Ja ne m'en part je mie! Se li cors va servir Nostre Signor, li cuers remaint del tot en sa baillie*).⁸⁰ Another contemporary, Hugh de Berzé, complained in verse composed during his journey east in June 1202 as part of the Fourth Crusade, that "had I known as well, when I decided on this parting, that it would have tormented me so, I should have left my soul in your [his lady's] service and gone to thank God for ever allowing me to aspire to your love" (*Se je seüsse autretant a l'enprendre que li congiés me tormentaist ensi, je laissasse m'ame en vostre merci, s'alaisse a Deu graces et mercis randre de ceu que ainz soffristes a nul jor que je fusse beans a vostre amour*). As the song closes, he says, "I marvel how a man's heart can hold out when he bids his lady farewell at the moment of his departure; instead, he should send it to her in France from Lombardy" (*Merveille moi coment puet cuers durer ki prent congié a sa dame a l'aler; mais mandast li de Lombardie en France*).⁸¹ The slippage between lady, lover, and God, between heart, soul, and body, each of which rules and is ruled by different obligations and orientations, produces an effect of pronounced ambiguity and ambivalence, if not critique. The vernacular idiom here addresses what could not be said in Latin or uttered from a cleric's mouth. It also speaks to and sometimes even voices (ventriloquizing, perhaps) the lady's perspective on the loss of her lover, articulating again and again that the crusade sacrifice was always a doubled suffering of loss, of heart, of self. As Linda Paterson and others have noted, these themes only redouble in later compositions as the thirteenth century progressed.

Vernacular lyric carried a personal and emotive charge and offered a space where poet and audience could address feelings of ambivalence and critique, if not resistance, to crusading. While it would have been much harder, and potentially heretical or suspect, to speak against papally mandated expeditions to the east and to southern France in Latin, vernacular verse offered a discursive register with greater latitude and, importantly for our purposes, with an audience and patronage network of women. While poetic depictions of the lamenting, loving, or mournful wife, lover, or mother certainly functioned as normative tropes in their own right (not all women mourned the absence of a husband or son), prescribing ideas of femininity as much as masculinity, they simultaneously offered a comment on the disruptive effects of repeated crusade losses and prolonged absence. Separation and the severing of body from self or heart were themes that had a political and social force, pointing out the personal and material losses encumbered through the crusade movement's relentless renewal. Tokens and gifts – shirts, rings, endowments, even the songs themselves – were bestowed within the songs in an attempt to elide distances and to make the personal authority and charisma of a lover or a kinsman felt and enduring. Vernacular verse compositions could critique, comment upon, and reshape ideas of crusading that lay at the heart of its articulation and practice. What may once have been a triumphant experience of pilgrimage and penance had become a penitential undertaking rooted in sacrifice, loss, and separation. Crusading came to resonate with a set of religious images and concepts much more closely aligned with the contemporary thirteenth-century practices of the *imitatio Christi* and the kinds of mystical discourse emerging in the vernacular among women connected to the Cistercian and later Dominican orders and among beguines. These practices longed for a mystical union, or reunion, with the Godhead, which was often predicated on or triggered by interactions with the material manifestation of Christ in the form of the host at the Mass or other relics associated with the Passion.[82]

Crusade songs were composed in a wide array of vernacular languages, including German, Italian, Occitan, Catalan, Picard, and various dialects of French. They remained a fluid and self-referential medium in which echoes of songs could be incorporated into newer compositions and songs themselves might be embedded within narrative Romance texts, put into the mouths of protagonists before a climactic moment of departure or separation.[83] Among the northern French *trouvères*, however, between 1170 and 1250, a distinguished cohort of composers flourished. Most of them came from aristocratic, if not noble, families and took part in the crusade expeditions that form the context for their verse. Conon de Béthune, Guiot de Dijon, the Châtelain (Houn) d'Arras, Châtelain de Coucy, Houn d'Oisy, and Thibaut of Champagne are the most well-known. Their compositions circulated within aristocratic households and would eventually be copied together when formal bound presentation volumes of *chansonniers* were created.[84] These poets and the milieu they inhabited shaped the ongoing discourse and practice of crusading from the courtly setting outwards. Moreover, they did so in open dialogic form, making transparent the conversations, exchanges, laments, and critiques that lay behind crusading whether in moments of departure; in the weariness of longing; when facing death and captivity; or simply remembering familiar spaces of garden, castle, and chamber (fig. 5.3). Indeed, as Galvez notes, the verse compositions "affirm the male crusader's sacrifice, [but] they [also] represent a complex female voice and in many cases a popular perspective on crusade departure. They change the paradigm of remembering: for the lady, the act of remembering is an ongoing exchange between two people who remain apart."[85] As such, the vernacular also performs a "refusal of lamentation" to embrace "dialogic and disruptive songs that recover different voices."[86] This

Figure 5.3. Chansonnier, dit *Chansonnier Cangé*, fourth quarter of thirteenth century. Paris, BnF ms fr. 846, fol. 57v. Illuminated initial detail of a lady with staff and her lover on a palfrey pictured in gold within the initial letter inhabiting visually separate spaces.

strategy presents an experiential contrast to that generated by the papal chancery, which was often relentless in its ambitions, single-mindedness, and penchant for abstract categorization.

The pliable nature of the vernacular message was likewise reflected in its material medium. Most poems and verse were performed, received, and transported orally and then, with the aid of parchment, written down first as pieces of texts (*envoi*) or small songbooks. When songs were sent to recipients they travelled, no doubt, like other texts on single parchment sheets or in rolls, like administrative account records and lists (fig. 5.4).[87] The process of gathering single songs into fair-copied presentation volumes for multiple users must be imagined and patched together. Although only a small handful of crusader songbooks or *chansonnier* are still extant, where it is possible to trace manuscript provenance or follow references to patronage and commissions for such compilations, it is clear that women played a major role as patrons and collectors, charged with cultivating the memory and ethos of crusading as a religious act.[88]

The flexible use and meaning of texts are underlined further when it is possible to analyse them in their manuscript-archival context. As

Figure 5.4. Chansonnier, dit *Chansonnier Cangé*, fourth quarter of thirteenth century. Paris, BnF ms fr. 846, fol. 46v. Illuminated initial of singer or poet with a *rotulus* or *libellus*.

Galvez has shown, drawing on the work of Daniel O'Sullivan, the placement of verse within manuscript compendia further shaped the context and reception of vernacular crusading within a nexus of lordly, aristocratic concerns that encompassed administrative burdens and the pull of religious vows and spiritual ideals. For example, in BnF français 12581, dated in a colophon to 1288, Thibaut of Champagne's lyrics are copied just following or, as Galvez argues, "adjacent to" a list of the Champagne fairs. The lyrics record the dates the fairs were convened throughout the annual cycle, and then the rents owed by merchants and venders, presumably as revenue to be collected in the name of the count (figs. 5.5–5.6).[89] This short administrative record embedded within a literary and commemorative context functioned on multiple levels, situating the verse within the economic and social workings of Champagne as an ongoing administrative capital and offering an orientation within the literary world of the text to the events outside of it and their respective values. Viewed from outside or beyond the page, as a

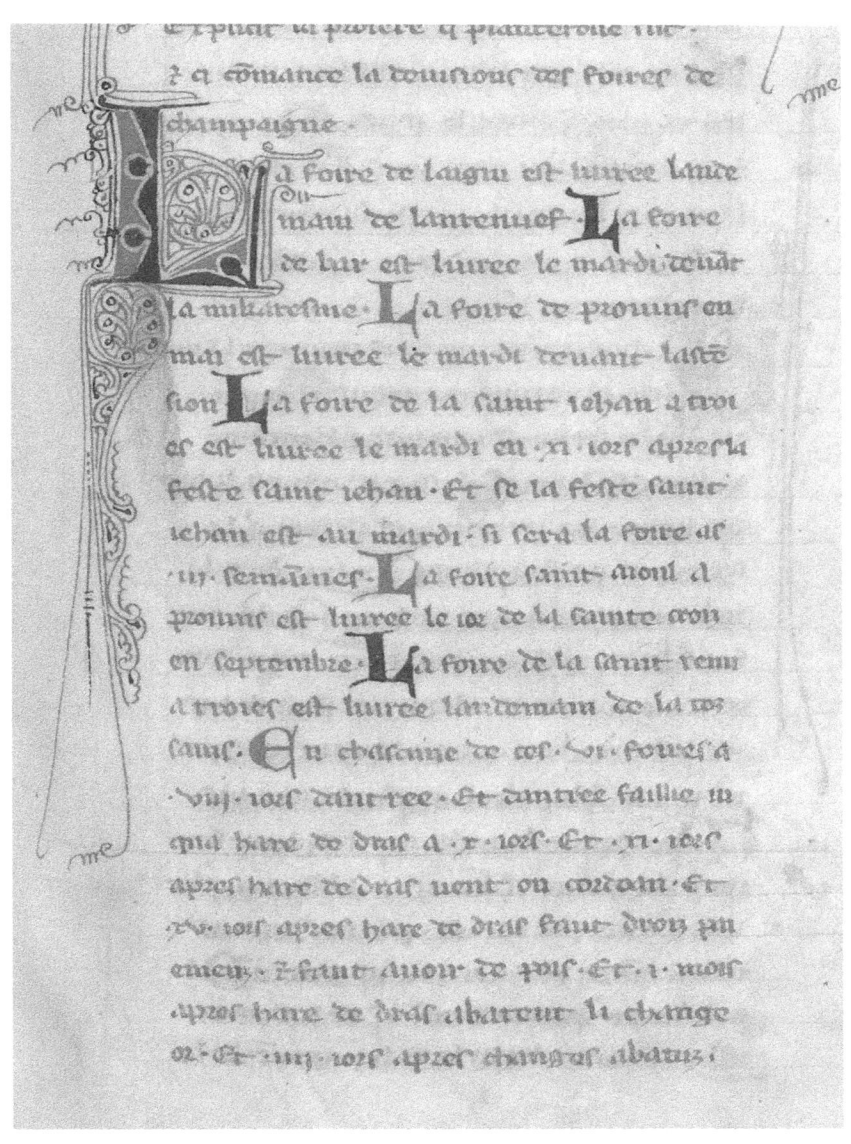

Figure 5.5. Thibaut de Navarre, *Foire et Chant*, Paris, BnF ms fr. 12581, fol. 312r. Showing the lists of fairs and the "maison des draps" and the corresponding rent payments.

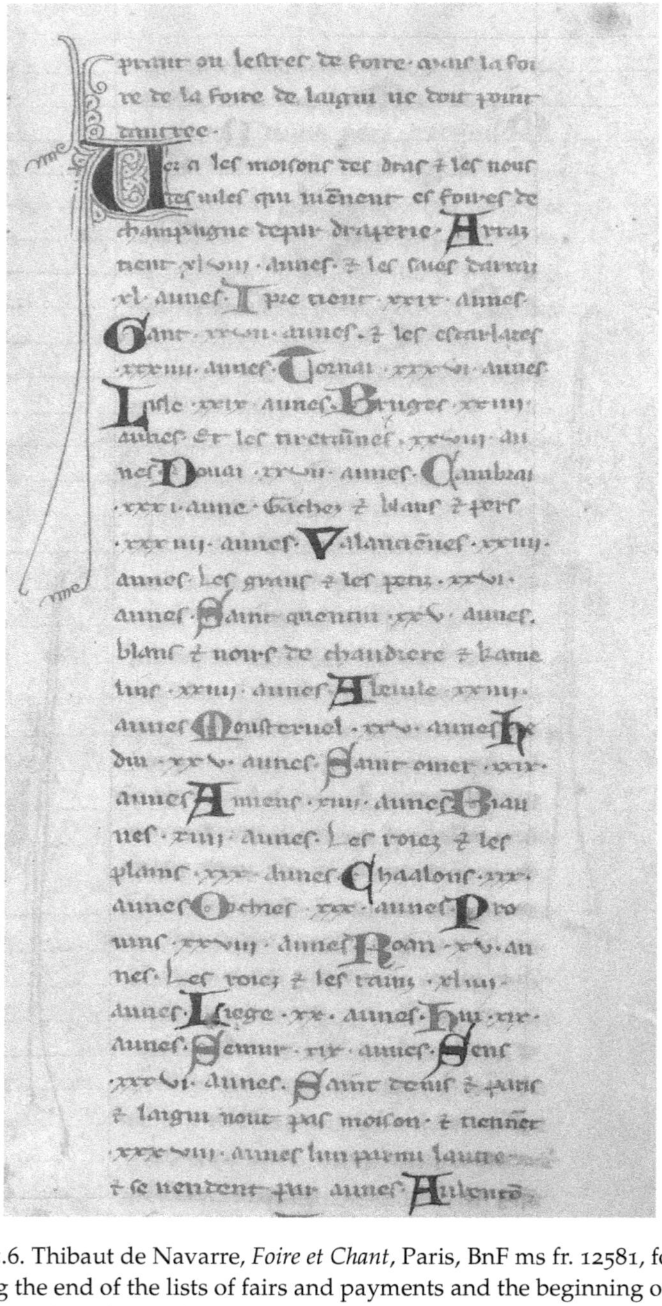

Figure 5.6. Thibaut de Navarre, *Foire et Chant*, Paris, BnF ms fr. 12581, fol. 312v. Showing the end of the lists of fairs and payments and the beginning of the chanson attributed to Thibaut.

whole manuscript, these adjacent texts may also have functioned as a more totalizing administrative tool, representing the needs of a regent at home who was charged with overseeing income received within the calendar year and administering the production of a vernacular crusade idiom tied to Thibaut's own memory preserved through the continued performance of his songs.[90] In a similar manner, vernacular crusading asks that we consider crusading beyond and outside the expeditions themselves, to encompass the debts, burdens, worries, and memories left at home, often in the hands of mothers and wives who ably administered and shaped the legacy and meaning of crusading.

The poetic collections find parallels in newly produced vernacular prose compilations, especially prose histories, which have been called pseudo-histories, and historical romance texts, such as the Pseudo-Turpin *Chronicle*, the *Life of William Marshall*, the *Grail Cycle*, and Jakemés's *Roman du Castelain de Couci et de la dame de Fayel*.[91] It is beyond the scope of this essay to offer any substantive engagement with the content of these narratives and their religious commentary. It is clear, however, that prose texts also adhered to the patronage patterns outlined above and were collected, copied, and commissioned initially for families of crusaders and female kin especially, who used these texts to frame a vernacular crusade idiom. Families like the counts of Nesle and the counts of St.-Pol commissioned vernacular histories that were passed down as individual manuscripts or within compilations through successive generations, moving with heirs as they married or remarried and even travelling with them to the east and back again.[92] The movement of such collections within and beyond households informed how ideas of crusading circulated as part of a broader religious movement, framing how crusaders and their kin interacted with pious ideals and practices over the course of the thirteenth century. As images of self-sacrifice, distance, and longing, penitential separation and techniques of a self-reflective confessional mode were scripted into these narratives. They shaped and were shaped by the enactment of such religious ideals and rituals in the world: in departures and *tournées*; in financial transactions and fundraising campaigns; and in acts of lordship pronounced through patronage practices, franchise, monastic donations, and testamentary largess that provided mechanisms of care and mercy long after death. The vernacular texts were also witness to the ways that "political autonomy and crusade piety [were] intimately intertwined."[93] Indeed, the patronage of vernacular texts – many of which were critical of royal and clerical authority – and the practice of personal pious endowments served to preserve the political autonomy of lords such as Thibaut of Champagne, Jean II of Nesle, and Mahaut of Nevers.

There can be little doubt that crusade songs and vernacular histories circulated within the court of Nevers, Auxerre, and Tonnerre and would have been known to Mahaut. Familial connections to the first patrons of some of these texts bear this out. Mahaut's mother, Agnès of Nevers, had married Peter of Courtenay, who was himself closely tied to the counts of Flanders and then to the Latin Empire of Constantinople. Some of the earliest vernacular histories were produced for and in connection with the court of Flanders, specifically during the reign of Countesses Jeanne and Marguerite of Flanders.[94] Mahaut herself may have heard crusader songs performed during her time on the Fifth Crusade, and while her second husband, Guy of Forez, campaigned with Thibaut IV of Champagne on the Baron's Crusade in 1239. They may even have heard the count perform some of his own songs. Similarly, the earliest vernacular translation of the *Chronique* of Pseudo-Turpin was commissioned by Yolande of Hainaut and Hugh IV of St.-Pol c. 1202. The St.-Pol, like the counts of Nevers, also fostered a long crusader lineage. Mahaut's daughter Agnès married Guy III of Châtillon, count of St.-Pol, in 1221. Although both died young (in the same year, 1226), they might have emerged as significant patrons of vernacular literature in their own right.[95]

To return to Mahaut once more, the archival record, including a series of testamentary bequests, makes clear that the practice and ideals – the very idiom – of vernacular crusading persisted in traceable patterns among the counts of Nevers, visible in particular in endowments and alms-giving and through testamentary bequests of objects. As Guy of Forez, Mahaut's second husband, lay dying on 10 August 1241, at Castellnata, outside of Brindisi, he drew up his final testament, bequeathing the precious objects he had with him to his closest kin and companions. Guy's gifts reveal the force of things in shaping memories and religious practice within the context of crusading. This was crusading not in its triumphant guise but in its doleful losses, suggesting the ways that spirit persisted beyond the body, carried by objects. As he distributed these goods, Guy was surrounded by his chaplain, brother William, and a Franciscan friar, his cleric, and his household knights. In their company he gave the German emperor "a diamond of great value and a belt of silver gilt. To the countess of Nevers, [his] wife, two from among my most opulent pieces of gold cloth among many others and an [emerald] which [he noted] I always wear on my hand and a small ruby which I had from John *Papinum*. And to [his] son Guy, my sapphire which hangs from my collar ... and my good ruby and cameo which I wear on my finger ... to my lady Agnès, his wife, three and ... two...."[96] To [his] son Reynald a better emerald and the True

Cross which the master of the knights Templar gave to me."[97] Guy also allotted payments to his knights and household, one presumes, for the remainder of their time away. In his last days he thought carefully and deliberately about who would cherish objects that had been part of his person – worn on the collar, on the hand, near the heart – objects that held memories of him that would move with them even in his absence. Such thoughtful gifts likewise carried forward a vernacular crusade piety and practice of their own.

Countess Mahaut continued to rule Nevers, Auxerre, and Tonnerre for sixteen years after Guy's death. During this time, she supported a wide array of religious institutions and individuals throughout her domains, confirming donations and endowing masses for herself and her husband and children at Fontenay, Saint-Germain in Auxerre, Saint-Loup de Noe, Lézinnes, the chapter of Sens, and with the monks of Reigny.[98] She was an early and avid supporter of the Franciscans, creating endowments of lands and rights to sustain their new house in Auxerre, and she oversaw the construction of a chapel with a portable altar where they could pray.[99] She continued to support the Dominican house in Auxerre that she had helped found in 1241 through confirmations of additional donations and in support of students and teachers (*tutorum et pupilli*) who came under the Dominicans' care.[100] In 1253, she gave the land (*platem*) that had been the site of the Jewish cemetery in Auxerre to the new foundation of Les Écoliers, also known as the *Bons-Énfants*, or poor scholars, so they could build their own house.[101] And she continued to oversee and confirm donations made to the Cistercian nuns of Les Isles.[102] In the summer of 1257, in what must have been one of her final acts, she established yet another anniversary for herself, this time at the church of St-Germain in Auxerre, funded from the annual rents of the market of Auxerre.[103] Just before her death in 1257, she drew up a final testament. In a forceful statement of her independent mind, she assigned annual rents to a list of over forty religious houses from across her domains and beyond, giving to monks and nuns and the cathedrals of Nevers and Auxerre, as well as to well over a dozen hospitals, *domus-Dei*, and leper houses. She made provisions for the poor and stipulated that the executors of her will were personally to distribute such gifts by hand. Finally, she elected to be buried at the Cistercian abbey of Le Réconfort (*Consolationis B. Marie*).[104] Although she made no mention of discrete objects like the ring or gold cloth she had received from Count Guy, her testament bears witness to what it meant to support and live within the religious movements of her day.

That Mahaut's example played a role in shaping the practice of vernacular crusading is suggested in the testamentary dispositions made by her successors. In 1248, when her grandson, Gaucher of St.-Pol, lord of Donzy (d. 1249), prepared to depart with Louis IX on crusade, he too drew up a will. Gaucher made elaborate provisions for the poor within his domains, not only asking that funds be set aside but also instructing the executors of his will to personally distribute alms to the poor each year with their own hands. One presumes these were repeated acts performed both to care for those in need and as an echo of Gaucher's penitential mindset on crusade, a vernacular – that is, an everyday and commemorative – iteration of the crusade ideal.[105] In the next generation, Mahaut's great granddaughter (Mahaut II) married Eudes of Burgundy, who held the title Count of Nevers. In 1265, he too took the cross and campaigned in the east. Eudes died in Acre on 7 August 1266, and in the days and months that followed, his executors drew up a long final account-inventory, covering five rolls (*rotuli*) of parchment.[106] In addition to the detailed payments made to his knights, sergeants, pages, and his household in the fullest sense, the document records the objects Eudes had with him in the east, including: jewellery; plate; precious cloth; armour; furniture in his chamber, pantry, kitchen, and stables; clothes and the furnishings of two chapels; a reliquary of the True Cross; and numerous vestments. Also listed were books, including a missal, a breviary, two *romans* described as *le Roman des Loherains* and the *Roman de la terre d'Outremer*, and a *chansonnier*, which may have included a collection of crusader songs.[107] Many of the objects not sold to cover his debts were given to the hospital in Acre and to other poor houses of religion (*fu départie au povres hopitauz d'Acre, et au povres maisons de religion*).[108] Eudes's support of the poor, his possession of vernacular prose and poetic literature, and his crusade ambitions echo that of Mahaut. As Jonathan Riley-Smith noted, Eudes "had a reputation for sanctity and [his] tomb in Acre was to be the scene of healing miracles after his death."[109] Here crusade success came to be measured less in the stark terms of ideology and the orthodox terrain of Christian violence against a Muslim other but through the practice of religious lordship and charitable values that were passed through families, often through the female line. These were spoken beliefs and practices that found no record in Latin and on parchment but must be collected and reconstructed from traced actions, gifts, and in the case of Mahaut and Eudes, the popular recognition of a kind of almost sanctity.

Mahaut's practice of lordship, her enduring religious patronage, *and* her repeated involvement with crusading (as both as vowed crusader and regent wife) together were emblematic of the imbricated nature of religious movements by the middle of the thirteenth century. Taking a crusade vow was yoked to grants of franchise and to support of the poor, financial and penitential acts alike. These forms of practiced piety, what I have called vernacular crusading, were part of a religious idiom, a discourse, that brought the urgency of the Holy Land into the west in quotidian and sometimes challenging ways. Through testamentary gifts, vernacular poetics, grants of franchise, and gifts to the poor as enduring forms of lordly care, it is possible to discern an idiom of action that is different from the ideology of order and heresy determined by ecclesiastical decree. Tracing this vernacular manifestation of the crusade movement is to follow a set of ideas that, in Galvez's words, "refuses to be easily appropriated by successive ideological movements, especially those that depend on fantasies that create a collective identity through the exclusion of and violence against others."[110] It is also to see the strong force of families, of women, and of the vernacular register in shaping religious movements that lie beyond the stark paradigm of Grundmann's master narrative, in the spaces and sources between orders and heresy. These were the linking sentiments and practices – like Mahaut sculpted *between* the serfs of Mailly-le-Château, or Guy of Forez caught penitent and dying *between* Syria and France – that formed the substance of religion as it moved in the world.

Appendix: Lineage of Mahaut of Nevers and Associated Crusade Campaigns

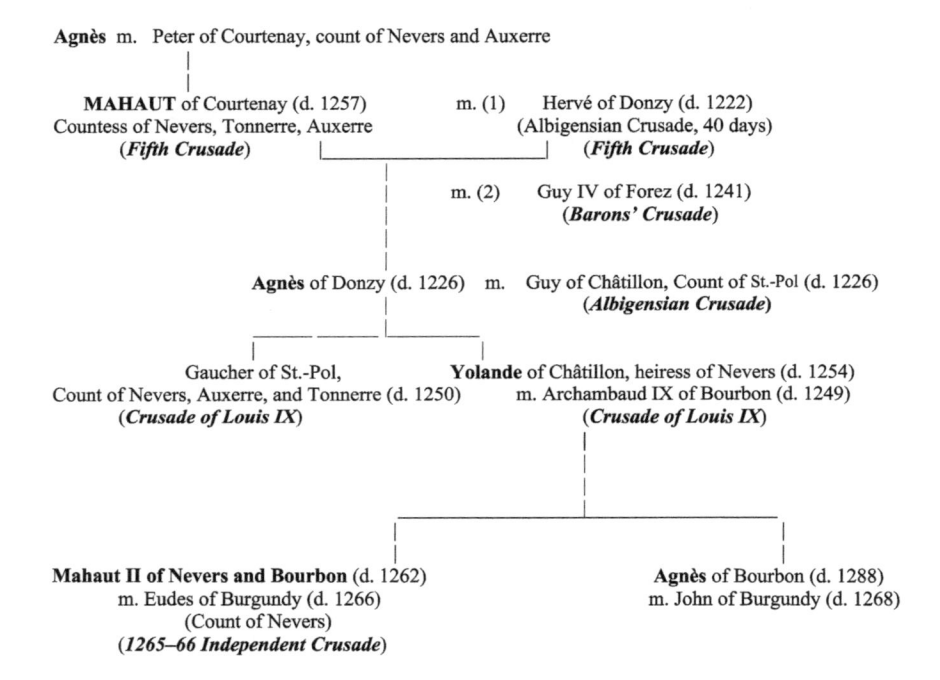

Agnès m. Peter of Courtenay, count of Nevers and Auxerre
|
MAHAUT of Courtenay (d. 1257) m. (1) Hervé of Donzy (d. 1222)
Countess of Nevers, Tonnerre, Auxerre   (Albigensian Crusade, 40 days)
(*Fifth Crusade*)   (*Fifth Crusade*)

m. (2) Guy IV of Forez (d. 1241)
(*Barons' Crusade*)

Agnès of Donzy (d. 1226) m. Guy of Châtillon, Count of St.-Pol (d. 1226)
(*Albigensian Crusade*)

Gaucher of St.-Pol,   **Yolande** of Châtillon, heiress of Nevers (d. 1254)
Count of Nevers, Auxerre, and Tonnerre (d. 1250)   m. Archambaud IX of Bourbon (d. 1249)
(*Crusade of Louis IX*)   (*Crusade of Louis IX*)

Mahaut II of Nevers and Bourbon (d. 1262)   **Agnès** of Bourbon (d. 1288)
m. Eudes of Burgundy (d. 1266)   m. John of Burgundy (d. 1268)
(Count of Nevers)
(*1265–66 Independent Crusade*)

NOTES

I thank the participants of the Hopkins European Seminar and the Beyond the Elite Workshop convened at the Hebrew University of Jerusalem under the direction of Elisheva Baumgarten for their extremely valuable questions and comments. Thanks also to Scott Bruce, Cecilia Gaposchkin, Nicholas Paul, Randall Pippenger, and Theodore Evergates for their comments and close reading. Any errors that remain are mine alone.

1 St.-Adrien shares many characteristics with the region's gothic churches, including the cathedral of Nevers and abbey churches built for the Cistercian order during the early thirteenth century. The simple forms with cut-in doorways and arched windows echo the style of La-Cour-Notre-Dame de Michéry, not far from Auxerre. On this, see Anne E. Lester and William Chester Jordan, "La Cour Notre-Dame de Michéry: A Response to Constance Berman," *Journal of Medieval History* (1999): 43–54. See also Monica Bloch, "A Message Carved in Stone: The Triforium sculpture of Nevers Cathedral," in *Pictoral Languages and their Meanings:* Liber Amicorum *in Honor of Nurith Kenaan-Kadar*, ed. Christine B. Verzar and Gil Fishhof (Tel Aviv: Tel Aviv University Press, 2006), 63–9.

2 For the identification of this figure with Mahaut of Courtenay, see Nurith Kenaan-Kader, "Pictorial and Sculptural Commemoration of Returning or Departing Crusaders," in *The Crusades and Visual Culture*, ed. Elizabeth Lapina et al. (Burlington, VT: Ashgate, 2015), 91–104, at 98. By contrast, Willibald Sauerländer has argued that such a precise attribution is not possible and reflects rather a nineteenth-century interest in identifying figural sculpture with specific individuals, as Maximilien Quantin suggested. See the comments in Willibald Sauerländer, *Von Sens bis Strassburg: Ein Beitrag zur kunstgeschichtlichen Stellung der Strassburger Querhausskulpturen* (Berlin: W. de Gruyter, 1966), 113–16, in reference to Maximillen Quantin, *Répertoire archéologique de dèpartement de l'Yonne* (Paris: Imprimerie Impériale, 1868), 36. I thank Orsolya Mednyanszky for discussion of this matter. For my part, while it is certainly true that a precise identification is not possible, it is feasible that the sculpted figure would have evoked Mahaut, just as the iconography of her seal would do the same. If there is ambiguity in identification, I suspect that was also intended; as such, this image aligns with my broader point concerning vernacular crusading and the exercise of female lordship.

3 For Mahaut and the county of Nevers, see René de Lespinasse, *Le Nivernais et les comtes de Nevers*, 3 vols. (Paris: H. Champion, 1909–14), vol. 2 [Hereafter: Lespinasse, *Le Nivernais*, all citations are to vol. 2.]. See also, Constance Brittan Bouchard, "Three Counties, One Lineage,

and Eight Heiresses: Nevers, Auxerre, and Tonnerre, Eleventh to the Thirteenth Centuries," *Medieval Prosopography* 31 (2016): 25–46; and Patrick Corbet, "Entre Aliénor d'Aquitaine et Blanche de Castille. Les princesses au pouvoir dans la France de l'Est," in *Mächtige Frauen? Königinnen und Fürstinnen im europäischen Mittelalter (11.-14. Jahrhundert)*, Vorträge und Forschungen 81, ed. Claudia Zey, Sophie Caflisch and Philippe Goridis (Ostfildern: Jan Thorbecke, 2015), 225–47; and Constance H. Berman, "Archives from Houses of Cistercian Nuns and Their Evidence for Powerful Thirteenth-Century Secular Women," *Medieval Feminist Forum: A Journal of Gender and Sexuality* 51 (2016): 132–44.

4 For her seal, see the image reproduced in Maximilien Quantin, *Recueil de pièces pour faire suite au cartulaire générale de l'Yonne* (Auxerre: Siège de la société; Paris: Durand and Pédone-Lauriel, 1873), 200. See also: http://www.sigilla.org/moulage/bourgogne-117-9246.

5 Mahaut and Hervé were married in October 1199. Despite her status as major baron from central France, Mahaut and Hervé of Donzy are barely mentioned in James Powell's classic study of the Fifth Crusade, *Anatomy of a Crusade: 1213–1221* (Philadelphia: University of Pennsylvania, 1986). Nor does she appear in more-recent studies of the expedition which tend to focus on papal rhetoric. See, for example, E.J. Mylod et al., eds., *The Fifth Crusade in Context: The Crusading Movement in the Early Thirteenth Century* (Abingdon: Routledge, 2017). Jessalynn Bird's article on preaching and reform does address the appeal of the crusade's rhetoric for women; see Bird, "Crusade and Reform: The Sermons of Bibliothèque Nationale, MS nouv. acq. lat. 999," 92–113.

Yet, as is clear in the case of Mahaut and numerous other women, crusading as a set of religious, financial, and political commitments had a profound impact on their lives and practice of lordship. See, for example, Theodore Evergates, *Marie of France: Countess of Champagne, 1145–1198* (Philadelphia: University of Pennsylvania Press, 2019). As Evergates shows, crusade campaigns punctuated her life and shaped her role as regent of the county and the administrative strategies she set in place to uphold that authority.

6 See Elizabeth Siberry, "The Crusading Counts of Nevers," *Nottingham Medieval Studies* 34 (1990): 64–70.

7 For a treatment of the specific crusade idiom that developed at this time, especially after 1187 and the fall of Jerusalem, see Marisa Galvez, *The Subject of the Crusade: Lyric, Romance, and Materials, 1150–1500* (Chicago: University of Chicago Press, 2019); and below. I take vernacular here to be both a shared register of communication beyond and outside of clerical Latinate culture and a cultural idiom of ideas, images, and materials used to perform and communicate personal, familial, and sacred conceptions of

authority and experience. I thank Nick Paul for his comments on this topic and for the following references: On a related set of ideas, see Nicholas L. Paul, "Possession: Sacred Crusading Treasure in the Material Vernacular," *Material Religion* 14 (2018): 520–32. Further, on concepts of the vernacular, see Jocelyn Wogan-Browne et al., eds., *The Idea of the Vernacular: An Anthology of Middle English Literary Theory, 1280–1520* (Exeter: University of Exeter Press, 1999), and Jason Baird Jackson, ed., *Material Vernaculars: Objects, Images, and Their Social Worlds* (Bloomington: Indiana University Press, 2016), 1–11.

8 A fuller treatment of Mahaut is needed and warranted from the sources. For a brief discussion of her biography, see Constance Brittan Bouchard, *Sword, Miter, and Cloister: Nobility and the Church in Burgundy, 980–1198* (Ithaca: Cornell University Press, 1987), 340–51; and Bouchard, "Three Counties, One Lineage, and Eight Heiresses." The fullest treatment of Mahaut and her husbands remains: Lespinasse, *Le Nivernais*, vol. 2, *Maisons de Donzy, de Bourbon, de Flandre (1200–1384)*.

9 For the role of women, and specifically women as targets of preaching campaigns, see Christoph T. Maier, "The Roles of Women in the Crusade Movement: A Survey," *Journal of Medieval History* 30 (2004): 61–82; and Anne E. Lester, "A Shared Imitation: Cistercian Convents and Crusader Families in Thirteenth-Century Champagne," *Journal of Medieval History* 35 (2009): 353–70.

10 Joachim plays virtually no role in *Religious Movements*. He was rather the focus of Grundmann's first study, which began as his PhD dissertation: *Studien über Joachim von Floris*, Beiträge zur Kulturgeschichte des Mittlealters und der Renaissance 32 (PhD diss., Leipzig, 1926) (Leipzig and Berlin, 1927; reprinted in 1966; translated into Italian in 1989). He would continue to return to Joachim throughout his career, see also: idem, "Kleine Beiträge über Joachim von Fiore," *Zeitschrift für Kirchengeschichte*, n.s. 11, 48 (1929): 137–65; "Dante und Joachim von Fiore: Zu Paradiso X–XII," *Deutsches Dante-Jahrbuch* n.s. 5, 14 (1932): 210–56; *Neue Forschungen über Joachim von Fiore*, Münstersche Forschungen 1 (Marburg: Simons, 1950; translated into Italian in 1997); "Federico II e Gioacchino da Fiore," *VII Centenario della morte di Federico II Imperatore e Re di Sicilia (10–18 dicembre 1950). Atti del Convegno Internazionale di Studi Federiciani* (Palermo: Renna, 1952), 82–9; "Zur Biographie Joachims von Fiore und Rainers von Ponza," *Deutsches Archiv für Erforschung des Mittlelalters* 16 (1960; translated into Italian in 1997), 437–546; "Lex et Sacramentum bei Joachim von Fiore," in *Lex und Sacramentum im Mittelalter*, Miscellanea Mediaevalia 6, ed. Paul Wilpert (Berlin: De Gruyter, 1969), 31–48. By contrast, newer works have situated Joachim in direct relation with crusade ideology; see, for example, Robert E.

Lerner, "Joachim of Fiore as a Link between St. Bernard and Innocent III on the Figural Significance of Melchisedech," *Mediaeval Studies* 42 (1980): 417–26; Michael F. Cusato, "An Unexplored Influence on the '*Epistola ad fideles*' of Francis of Assisi: The '*Epsitola universis Christi fidelibus*' of Joachim of Fiore," *Franciscan Studies* 61 (2003): 253–78; and Brett E. Whalen, "Joachim of Fiore and the Division of Christendom," *Viator* 34 (2003): 89–108; Whalen, "Joachim of Fiore, Apocalyptic Conversion, and the 'Persecuting Society,'" *History Compass* 8 (2010): 682–91: https://doi.org/10.1111/j.1478-0542.2010.00700.x.

11 First published as Carl Erdmann, *Die Entstehung des Kreuzzugsgedankens*, Forschungen zur Kirchen- und Geistesgeschichte, vol. 6 (Stuttgart: Kohlhammer Verlag, 1935; reprinted in 1965 and again in 1974); In English: *The Origin of the Idea of Crusade*, trans. Marshall W. Baldwin and Walter Goffart (Princeton: Princeton University Press, 1977). Erdamnn's intentions are very clearly laid out in the author's preface, xxxiii–xxxvi, of the English translation.

12 See Robert Lerner, "Introduction to the Translation," in Grundmann, *Religious Movements in the Middle Ages: The Historical Links between Heresy, the Mendicant Orders, and the Women's Religious Movement in the Twelfth and Thirteenth Century, with the Historical Foundations of German Mysticism*, trans. S. Rowan (Notre Dame: University of Notre Dame Press, 1995), xi. And Böhringer in this volume, 26–7.

13 See the "Translator's Note" at the front of Erdmann, *The Origin of the Idea*, x. Much has been written about Erdmann's contribution to crusade historiography; see, for example, T.S.R. Boase, "Recent Developments in Crusading Historiography," *History* 22 (1937): 110–25; John Gilchrist, "The Erdmann Thesis and the Canon Law, 1083–1141," in Peter W. Edbury, ed., *Crusade and Settlement: Papers Read at the First Conference of the Society for the Study of the Crusades and the Latin East presented to R.C. Smail* (Cardiff: University College Cardiff Press, 1985), 27–45; John France, "Holy War and Holy Men: Erdmann and the Lives of the Saints," in *The Experience of Crusading*, 2 vols., ed. Marcus Bull et al. (Cambridge: Cambridge University Press, 2003), 1: 193–208; Christopher Tyerman, "Erdmann, Runciman and the End of Tradition?" in *The Debate on the Crusades*, ed. Tyerman (Manchester: University of Manchester Press, 2011), 182–215.

14 These lectures were gathered and partly reworked by his student, Alphonse Dupront, after Alphandéry's untimely death on 25 May 1932. They subsequently appeared in two volumes: Paul Alphandéry and Alphonse Dupront, *La Chrétienté et l'idée de Croisade: 1. Les premières croisades* (Pairs: A. Michel, 1954); and *2. Recommencements nécessaires (XII–XIII siècles)* (Pairs: A. Michel, 1959). They were subsequently reprinted under the same title in the series Bibliothéque de l'Évolution de l'Humanité in 1995 with a new postface by Michel Balard, which sets the

work in context and discusses its reception. For a sense of Alphandéry's contributions both as a teacher and a scholar, see the remembrances offered by Sylvain Lévi, François Proché, and Charles Picard in the *Revue de l'histoire des religions* 105 (1932): 139–48; and A. Koyré, "Les travaux de Paul Alphandéry," *Revue de l'histoire des religions* 105 (1932): 149–57, which also lists the courses Alphandéry offered at the École from 1901–32. See also Laurent Morelle, "Le prophétisme médiéval latin dans l'oeuvre de Paul Alphandéry: À propos d'archives récemment mises au jour," *Mélanges de l'École française de Rome, Moyen Age* 102 (1990): 513–32.

15 See Alphandéry and Dupront, *La Chrétienté et l'idée de Croisade*, especially the fourth and fifth part of the new edition, which turns to "Les forces de continuité" (209–24) and addresses developments over time, after the First and Third Crusades, traditional end points for many studies. There is an entire chapter addressed to the preparation for the Fourth Crusade and the preaching of Fulk of Neuilly, 265–97.

16 See Michel Balard, "Postface," in Alphandéry and Dupront, *La Chrétienté et l'idée de Croisade*, 573–85. This approach was not without critique, as Balard notes. See also the review of the second volume by Jean Richard in *Revue belge de philologie et d'histoire* 38 (1960): 500–4. For the broader context and reception of Alphandéry's ideas within Dupront's work and his reading of Freud, see Dominique Iogna-Prat, "Alphonse Dupront ou la poétisation de l'Histoire," *Revue Historique* 300, no. 4 (608) (1998): 887–910, on Freud, 892. Before his death, Alphandéry published a study titled "Quelques documents médiévaux relatifs à des états psychasthétiques," in the *Journal de psychologie normale et pathologique* 25 (1929): 763–87.

17 Like Erdmann, Alphandéry noted the power of signs and symbols to unify. The cross taken up and sewn onto garments, banners, and staffs, as well as supernatural signs like stars, comets, etc., together were part of a complex of religious perceptions and practices. Together, "ils ne sont plus le symbole individual, mais le présage d'une immense action commune, la cause surnaturelle d'un mouvement collectif." Alphandéry and Dupront, *La Chrétienté et l'idée de Croisade*, 63; this idea, however, is threaded throughout the study; see also 160–221, 339–442. Indeed, where Erdmann focuses solely on the first expedition, Alphandéry and Dupront carried forward these ideas and observations over time wherein the miraculous and eschatological thinking becomes a recurrent theme.

18 The authors are especially good at piecing together preparations for the Fourth and Fifth Crusades. See Alphandéry and Dupront, *La Chrétienté et l'idée de Croisade*, 264–422.

19 See Balard, "Postface," 578–87; and Lerner, "Introduction," xvii–xviii.

20 See Balard, "Postface," 573–85; and Iogna-Prat, "Alphonse Dupront ou la poétisation de l'Histoire."

21 Scholars interested in the broader shaping of ideas connecting the laity and crusading and who have been strongly influenced by Erdmann and Alphandéry include: E. O. Blake, "The Formation of the 'Crusade Idea,'" *Journal of Ecclesiastical History* 21 (1970): 11–31; and Marcus Bull, "The Roots of Lay Enthusiasm for the First Crusade," *History* 78 (1993): 353–72. For a broader overview of historiographies on the Crusades, see Michel Balard, "L'historiographie des croisades au XXe siècle (France, Allemagne et Italie)," *Revue Historique* 302 (2000): 973–99; and Giles Constable, "The Historiography of the Crusades," in *The Crusades from the Perspective of Byzantium and the Muslim World*, ed. Angeliki E. Laiou and Roy Parviz Mottahedeh (Washington, DC: Dumbarton Oaks, 2001), 1–22.

22 John Van Engen, "The Christian Middle Ages as an Historiographical Problem," *The American Historical Review* 91 (1986): 519–52. Indeed, what falls within "religious history" is still a hotly contested and changing question. On this, see Christian Caldwell Ames, "Medieval Religious, Religions, Religion," *History Compass* 10 (2012): 334–52. https://doi.org/10.1111/j.1478-0542.2012.00836.x.

23 On the broad historiographical trends in crusader studies, see Constable, "The Historiography of the Crusades," on the Wisconsin school, for example.

24 Constable brought the study of charters, which has previously been the domain of monastic and economic historians, into the purview of crusade historians. See, foremost, his early article: Giles Constable, "The Second Crusade as Seen by Contemporaries," *Traditio* 9 (1953): 213–79, at 257, where he observed quite succinctly, "Many of the more popular ideas [about the crusade] are illustrated in the charters issues by crusaders … [to] be found in local cartularies and collections." This observation maps nicely on to the interests of scholars like Grundmann and Alphandéry, even as they rarely turned to collections of such documents, as traditionally "diplomatics" was pursued separately from "religious history" and adhered to quite different methodological conventions. In this vein, Constable published three more field-defining articles, including: "Medieval Charters as a Source for the History of the Crusaders," in *Crusade and Settlement*, ed. Edbury, 73–89; and "The Financing of the Crusades," in *Outremer: Studies in the History of the Crusading Kingdom of Jerusalem Presented to Joshua Prawer*, ed. Benjamin Kedar, Hans Eberhard Mayer, Raymond C. Smail (Jerusalem: Yad Izhak Ben-Zvi, 1982), 64–88; reprinted in Giles Constable, *Crusaders and Crusading in the Twelfth Century* (Farnham: Ashgate, 2008), essays 10, 3, and 4, respectively.

25 This work culminated in Jonathan Riley-Smith, *The First Crusaders, 1095–1131* (Cambridge: Cambridge University Press, 1997).

26 See: Penny J. Cole, *Preaching the Crusades to the Holy Land, 1095–1270* (Cambridge, MA: The Medieval Academy of America, 1991); Christoph T. Maier, *Preaching the Crusades: Mendicant Friars and the Cross in the Thirteenth Century* (New York: Cambridge University Press, 1994); Christoph T. Maier, *Crusade Propaganda and Ideology: Model Sermons for the Preaching of the Cross* (Cambridge: Cambridge University Press, 2000); Jonathan Phillips, *Defenders of the Holy Land: Relations between the Latin East and the West, 1119–1187* (Oxford: Clarendon Press, 1996); Marcus Bull, *Knightly Piety and the Lay Response to the First Crusade: The Limousin and Gascony, c.970–1130* (Oxford: Clarendon Press, 1998); Caroline Smith, *Crusading in the Age of Joinville* (Aldershot: Ashgate, 2006); William Purkis, *Crusading Spirituality in the Holy Land* (Woodbridge: Boydell, 2008); Rebecca Rist, *The Papacy and Crusading in Europe, 1198–1245* (London: Continuum, 2009); Nicholas L. Paul, *To Follow in Their Footsteps: The Crusades and Family Memory in the High Middle Ages* (Ithaca: Cornell University Press, 2012); and Jochen Schenk, *Templar Families: Landowning Families and the Order of the Temple in France, c. 1120–1307* (Cambridge: Cambridge University Press, 2012).

27 See Lespinasse, *Le Nivernais*, 86–96. The two were married in 1200 and had two children: William who died early, between 1207 and 1214; and Agnès, who married Guy of Châtillon, the count of St.-Pol, both of whom died in 1226, leaving two young children, Yolande and Gaucher. For this succession, see Bouchard, "Three Counties," 35–6; and Siberry, "Crusading Counts," 68.

28 Lespinasse, *Le Nivernais*, 89; See Powell, *Anatomy of a Crusade*, 33–50; *Regesta Honorii Papae III*, ed. Petrus Pressutti, 2 vols. (Hildesheim: G. Olms, reprinted 1978), 1: 4, no. 14.

29 "Actum apud Januam super mare anno domini MCC octavo decimo, mense septembri," in Edmond Martène and Ursin Durand, *Thesaurus novus anecdotorum*, 5 vols. (Pairs: Sumptibus F. Delaulne, 1717), 1: 867–9; Extract in Quantin, *Recueil*, 95 no. 215 (Sept. 1218).

30 "De alia medietate sic ordinavimus, ut duabus domicillis quae nobiscum pro Deo et pro nobis transfertaverunt ducentae librae conferantur pro illis maritandis." Martène, *Thesaurus*, 1: 868.

31 On redemptive justice in the crusade context, see William Chester Jordan, "*Etiam Reges*, Even Kings," *Speculum* 90 (2015): 613–34; and Anne E. Lester, "From Captivity to Liberation: The Ideology and Practice of Franchise in Crusading France," *Anglo-Norman Studies: Proceedings of the Battle Conference 2017* 40 (2018): 147–63.

32 Siberry, "Crusading Counts," on Mahaut, see throughout; for Hervé, 67n21.

33 For the context in the east, see Filip Van Tricht, *The Latin* Renovatio *of Byzantium: The Empire of Constantinople (1204–1228)* (Leiden: Brill, 2011);

and Van Tricht, "Robert of Courtenay (1221–1227): An Idiot on the Throne of Constantinople?" *Speculum* 88 (2013): 996–1034.
34 Lespinasse, *Le Nivernais*, 93; Powell, *Anatomy of a Crusade*, 115, 117–18, 144, 229.
35 Both Robert of Auxerre, and the Chronicle of Tour note under the year 1219: "Eodem anno, mense Augusto, Herveus comes Niverensis a partibus rediit transmarinis *cum uxore sua*." See L'Espinasse, *Le Nivernais*, 93n4.
36 Lespinasse, *Le Nivernais*, 94.
37 Lespinasse, *Le Nivernais*, 96–7. The acts are calendared in Abbé de Marolles, *Inventaire des titres de Nevers* (Nevers: Paulin Fay, 1873), col. 270; and Maximilien Quantin, *Cartulaire générale de l'Yonne*, 2 vols. (Auxerre: Perriquet, 1854–60), 2: no. 236.
38 Lespinasse, *Le Nivernais*, 108.
39 Lespinasse, *Le Nivernais*, 118; After the death of her daughter, Agnès, she was also remembered in Mahaut's donations; see 127–8; Quantin, *Recueil*, 156, nos. 338 and 339. Guy of Châtillon died in August 1226, while campaigning outside of Avignon with Louis VIII as the Albigensian Crusade came to a close. The king died in November of the same year, leaving the regency to Blanche of Castile. In the same year, Mahaut and Guy of Forez founded a chapel at Entrains, fulfilling one of Hervé of Donzy's last wishes to construct a chapel there and set it under the jurisdiction of the bishop of Auxerre. See Lespinasse, *Le Nivernais*, 135–6.
40 Quantin, *Recueil*, 137, nos. 313; and 140, 318.
41 "pro remedio anime karissime filie Agnetis quondam uxoris comitis S. Pauli, et pro remedio anime karissimi Domini et mariti nostril Hervei quondam comitis Nivernensis." Abbé Jean Lebeuf, et al., *Mémoires concernant l'histoire civile et ecclésiastique d'Auxerre et de son ancient diocese* (nouv. ed.), 4 vols. (Auxerre: Perriquet, 1848–55), 4: 92–3, no. 155 (April 1226); and 94, no. 160 (1229); see also Marie-Élisabeth Henneau, "Les Isles," in *Les Cisterciens dans l'Yonne*, ed. Terryl Kinder (Pontigny: Les Amis de Pontigny, 1999), 163–72.
42 On the counts of Forez, see Edouard Perroy, *Les familles nobles du Forez au XIIIe siècle* (Saint-Étienne: Centre d'Études Foréziennes, 1976–7).
43 Lespinasse, *Le Nivernais*, 133 and 140. Marolles, *Les titres*, col. 510 and 515.
44 Lespinasse, *Le Nivernais*, 145–6.
45 Jean Louis Alphonse Huillard-Breholles and A. Lecoy de la Marche, *Titres de la maison ducale de Bourbon*, 2 vols. (Paris: H. Plon, 1867–74), 1:32, nos. 146 and 147 (1230).
46 Lespinasse, *Le Nivernais*, 146.
47 Lespinasse, *Le Nivernais*, 153.
48 Lespinasse, *Le Nivernais*, 152–3.
49 Quantin, *Recueil*, 192–3, no. 425 (July 1233).

50 See Lester, "From Captivity to Liberation."
51 Virtually nothing has been written about Le Réconfort, which was converted into a male priory of the order in 1460. See *GC* 4: col. 101; Terryl Kinder, ed., *Les Cisterciens dans l'Yonne* (Pontigny: Les amies de Pontigny, 1999), 165 and 182; Lespinasse, *Le Nivernais*, 167, 172.
52 Lespinasse, *Le Nivernais*, 175–6; and Quantin, *Recueil*, 204–5, no. 451.
53 Huillard-Breholles, *Titres de la maison ducale de Bourbon*, 1: 46–7 no. 221 (10 Aug. 1241); and Lespinasse, *Le Nivernais*, 179–80. See below.
54 Lebeuf, *Memoires d'Auxerre*, 101–2, no. 173 (May 1241).
55 Siberry, "Crusading Counts"; see also Philippe Murat, "La croisade en Nivernais: transfert de propriété et lute d'influence," in *Le concile de Clermont de 1095 et l'appel à la croisade. Actes du Colloque Universitaire International de Clermont-Ferrand (23–25 juin 1995)*, Publications de l'École française de Rome 236, ed. Valéry Giscard d'Estaing (Rome: École Français de Rome, 1997), 295–312.
56 See especially Riley-Smith, *First Crusaders*; Paul, *To Follow in their Footsteps*; Schenk, *Templar Families*. For all three authors the roles of women and families are integral to their arguments throughout.
57 Riley-Smith, *First Crusaders*, 187.
58 Riley-Smith, *First Crusaders*, 187.
59 "Au XIIe siècle, les femmes du lignage … ont sans doute determine la famille à répondre favorablement à la croisade. À l'instar de la pratique des donations aux communautés religieuses, l'incitation à prendre la croix passe manifestement par le marriage des soeurs et des filles." In Olivier Leblanc, "Picardie, croisades et sires de Boves," in *Questions d'histoire orient et occident du IXe au XVe siècle (Actes du colloque d'Amiens 8,9, et 10, octobre 1998 organisé par le CAHMER)*, ed. Georges Jehel (Paris: Éditions du temps, 2000), 29–55, at 46.
60 See Theodore Evergates, "Aristocratic Women in the County of Champagne," in *Aristocratic Women in Medieval France*, ed. Evergates (Philadelphia: University of Pennsylvania Press, 1999), 73–110; and Evergates, *Marie of France: Countess of Champagne, 1145–1198* (Philadelphia: University of Pennsylvania Press, 2019); and Randall Pippenger, "Crusading as a Family: A Study of the County of Champagne, 1179–1226" (PhD diss., Princeton University, 2018).
61 Riley-Smith, *First Crusaders*, 189–90.
62 For the extent of such families, see Jonathan Riley-Smith, "Towards and Understanding of the Crusade as an Institution," in *Urbs Capta: The Fourth Crusade and Its Consequences/La IVe Croisade et ses consequences*, Réalités byzantines 10, ed. Angeliki Laiou (Paris: Lethielleux, 2005), 71–88; and Alphonse-Martial Chazaud, ed., "Inventaire et comptes de la succession d'Eudes, Comte de Nevers (Acre 1266)," *Mémoires de la Société nationale des*

antiquaries de France 32 (1870): 164–206, which lists all the men in Eudes's pay and service.

63 Grundmann, *Religious Movements*, 187.

64 Grundmann, *Religious Movements*, 187.

65 Grundmann, *Religious Movements*, 192. There were certainly long-standing connections between religious women, both those who professed as nuns in formal communities and those who remained in the world and established religious orders, especially among Augustinian canons and the Cistercians. Numerous mirrors and spiritual guides, like the *Speculum Virginum*, written in Latin, make these connections clear. What was new in the mid- to late thirteenth century was the translation of such ideas and practices into a vernacular idiom.

66 Grundmann, *Religious Movements*, 195.

67 That this occurred also among noble households, especially around the royal court of France and the schools of northern Europe, has been established by scholars such as: Tracy Chapman Hamilton, "Queenship and Kinship in the French *Bible Moralisée*: The Example of Blanche of Castile and Vienna ÖBN 2554," in *Capetian Women*, ed. Kathleen Nolan (New York: Palgrave, 2003), 177–208, at 182–3; Claire M. Waters, *Translating* Clergie: *Status, Education, and Salvation in Thirteenth-Century Vernacular Texts* (Philadelphia: University of Pennsylvania Press, 2016); Aden Kumler, *Translating Truth: Ambitious Images and Religious Knowledge in Late Medieval France and England* (New Haven, CT: Yale University Press, 2011); Richard W. Kaeuper, *Holy Warriors: The Religious Ideology of Chivalry* (Philadelphia: University of Pennsylvania Press, 2014); and Martin Aurell, *The Lettered Knight: Knowledge and Aristocratic Behavior in the Twelfth and Thirteenth Centuries* (Budapest: Central European University Press, 2017).

68 This historiographical separation is further entrenched by the fact that vernacular texts tend to be the purview of French scholars working in French departments who analysed the corpus of linguistic variants and who separated the poems of the northern *trouvères* from those of the southern *troubadours*. More recently, the songbooks of the *trouvères* have emerged as a focus of study on the part of musicologists. See, for example, the work of Emma Dillon on "The Romance of Song: The Early Trouvères and Their Reception, 1150–1350," a project funded by the Leverhulme Trust. Many of these texts and their linguistic and manuscript traditions are available digitally in the pioneering project "Troubadours, *Trouèvers* and the Crusades," put together by Linda Paterson and housed at the University of Warwick: https://warwick.ac.uk/fac/arts/modern languages/research/french/crusades/. See also Linda Paterson, with Luca Barbieri, Ruth Harvey, and Anna Radaelli, *Singing the Crusades:*

French and Occitan Lyric Responses to the Crusading Movement, 1127–1336 (Cambridge: D.S. Brewer, 2018).

69 See, for example: D.A. Trotter, *Medieval French Literature and the Crusades, 1100–1300* (Geneva: Librairie Droz, 1988); Stephen G. Nichols, "Urgent Voices: The Vengeance of Images in Medieval Poetry," in *France and the Holy Land: Frankish Culture at the End of the Crusades*, ed. Daniel H. Weiss and Lisa Mahoney (Baltimore and London: The Johns Hopkins University Press, 2004), 22–42; and Galvez, *The Subject of the Crusades*.

70 Grundmann expanded on his ideas about women's roles in the advent of German vernacular literature in an additional essay: Herbert Grundmann, "Die Frauen und die Literatur im Mittelalter. Ein Beitrag zur Frage nach Entstehung des Schriftums in der Volkssprache," *Archiv für Kulturgeschichte* 26 (1935; printed 1936): 129–61, reprinted in the collection *Ausgewählte Ausfätze* (1978) and translated into English (2019) as "Women and Literature in the Middle Ages: A Contribution on the Origins of Vernacular Writing," in *Herbert Grundmann (1902–1970)*, ed. Jennifer Kolpacoff Deane (Woodbridge: York Medieval Press 2019), 30–55.

71 On such shared images, see Barbara Newman, *From Virile Woman to WomanChrist: Studies in Medieval Religion and Literature* (Philadelphia: University of Pennsylvania Press, 1995), and quite incisively, Stephen G. Nichols, "Urgent Voices."

72 Galvez, *The Subject of Crusade*, 2.

73 Galvez goes further and sets the concept of "idiom" as she develops it in her study in contrast to "ideology": one generated within a broader social context, the other emerging from and in response to a set of ideas and beliefs cultivated by those in power – in this case, the papacy and ecclesiastical hierarchy charged with formulating and conveying the definition and privileges of the crusader. Galvez, *The Subject of Crusade*, 3–5.

74 Galvez, *The Subject of Crusade*, 6.

75 Galvez, *The Subject of Crusade*, 11.

76 On the translation of papal concepts and preaching propaganda into a vernacular register, see Galvez, *The Subject of Crusade*, 10–11, 90–1; here Galvez is citing Powell, *Anatomy of a Crusade*, 56–7; see also Nichols, "Urgent Voices."

77 See Jaye Puckett, "'Reconmenciez novele estoire': The Troubadours and the Rhetoric of the Later Crusades," *MLN* 116 (2001): 844–89; Paterson, et al., *Singing the Crusades*, 253–7, summarizing the changes charted in the volume as a whole.

78 Paterson, et al., *Singing the Crusades*, 7–13; on rituals of departure, see William Chester Jordan, "The Rituals of War: Departure for Crusade in Thirteenth-Century France," in *The Book of Kings: Art, War, and the*

Morgan Library's Medieval Picture Bible, ed. William Noel and Daniel Weiss (London: The Walters Art Museum, 2002), 98–105.

79 I use the editions and translations provided by Paterson et al. on the Warwick site. For the lyric, see Châtelian de Coucy, *A vous amant, plus k'a nul'autre gent* (RS 679, lns. 21–4), https://warwick.ac.uk/fac/arts/modernlanguages/research/french/crusades/texts/of/rs679/#page2. See also Jean Longnon, *Les Compagnons de Villehardouin: Recherches sur les croisés de la quatrième croisade* (Geneva: Librairie Droz, 1978), 118. He died at sea en route to Syria in 1203. He would become the protagonist of the late thirteenth-century romance based loosely on his life and context, known as the *Roman du Châtelain de Coucy et de la Dame de Fayel*. See Galvez, *Subject of Crusade*, 87–113; and for the broader context, see Richard Leson, "Heraldry and Identity in the Psalter-Hours of Jean of Flanders (Manchester, John Rylands Library, MS. Lat. 117)," *Studies in Iconography* 32 (2011): 155–98.

80 Conon de Béthune, *Ahï!, Amors, com dure departie* (RS 1125, lns. 9, 6–8), https://warwick.ac.uk/fac/arts/modernlanguages/research/french/crusades/texts/of/rs1125/#page1; Longnon, *Les Compagnons*, 146–9.

81 Hugues de Berzé, *S'onques nuns hons por dure departie* (RS 1126, lns. 17–22, 49–51), https://warwick.ac.uk/fac/arts/modernlanguages/research/french/crusades/texts/of/rs1126/#page1; Longnon, *Les Compagnons*, 213–14.

82 On the close and imitative qualities of these religious experiences, see Lester, "A Shared Imitation," and Galvez, *The Subject of Crusade*, 90–1. On the Passion relics, see Cynthia Hahn, *Passion Relics and the Medieval Imagination: Art, Architecture and Society* (Berkeley: University of California Press, 2020).

83 Galvez, *The Subject of Crusade*, esp. 87–113.

84 See Paterson, et al., *Singing the Crusades*, and the website: https://warwick.ac.uk/fac/arts/modernlanguages/research/french/crusades/, which links to some of the fair-copy manuscripts. Also see Galvez, *The Subject of Crusade*, 153–206.

85 Galvez, *The Subject of Crusade*, 113.

86 Galvez, *The Subject of Crusade*, 113.

87 See Marisa Galvez, *Songbook: How Lyrics Became Poetry in Medieval Europe* (Chicago: University of Chicago Press, 2012). Single charters and letters patent were the most common way for crusaders to send directives, messages, donations, and requests for loans, and to detail administrative decisions from the east. Cartularies retain a handful of incoming records of this sort. *Rotuli* were also common forms of transmitting lists and account records that were typically intended to be copied into bound volumes. Two examples include the relic list sent by Robert of Clari after 1205, on which see Anne E. Lester, "Translation and Appropriation: Greek Relics

in the Latin West in the Aftermath of the Fourth Crusade," *Translating Christianity: Studies in Church History* 53 (Cambridge: Cambridge University Press, 2017), 88–117; and the final account-inventory of Eudes of Nevers discussed below. See also Carol Symes, "Popular Literacies and the First Historians of the First Crusade," *Past and Present* 235 (2017): 37–67. Galvez addresses this process for the songs and administrative *roles* of Thibaut of Champagne; see Galvez, *The Subject of Crusade*, 164–77.

88 Much more work is needed on the manuscript tradition and with the still extant *chansonniers*. Emma Dillon is undertaking some of this as noted above, note 68. See Caroline Smith, *Crusading in the Age of Joinville*.

89 See the "Songs of Thibaut de Champagne," in BnF fr. 12581, fol. 312r–v. Galvez, *The Subject of Crusade*, 164–77; Daniel O'Sullivan, "Thibaut de Champagne and Lyric Authoritas in ms Paris, BnF fr. 12615," *Textual Cultures* 8 (2013): 31–49.

90 Thibaut appears to have produced himself, or overseen the production of, an "early authoritative compilation" of his verse as a sort of personal songbook, or *libellus*, which was then disseminated or taken up for copying. This is affirmed by the fact that in most examples of his verse the songs appear in "almost exactly the same order," suggesting the desire to adhere to an original production rather than random sampling. Galvez, *The Subject of Crusade*, 166–7, esp. nn17–22.

91 On the vernacular prose tradition, see Gabrielle M. Spiegel, *Romancing the Past: The Rise of Vernacular Prose Historiography in Thirteenth-Century France* (Berkeley: University of California Press, 1993). Other studies of such prose texts include Lynn Tarte Ramey, "Jean Bodel's Jeu de Saint Nicolas: A Call for non-Violent Crusade," *French Forum* 27 (2002): 1–12; Kathy Krause, "Genealogy and Codicology: The Manuscript Contexts of the *Fille du comte de Pontieu*," *Romance Philology* 59 (2006): 323–42; and Nicholas L. Paul, "In Search of the Marshal's Lost Crusade: The Persistence of Memory, the Problems of History and the Painful Birth of Crusading Romance," *Journal of Medieval History* 40 (2015): 292–310.

92 Jean II, lord of Nesle, castellan of Bruges, is mentioned in the colophon of Brussels ms. 11145, as the patron of a copy of the *Perlesvaus* dated to the second half of the thirteenth century. He took part in the Fourth Crusade and was closely involved with affairs in Flanders and in the Latin Empire. See Galvez, *The Subject of Crusade*, 115–52. On the patronage of the counts of St.-Pol, see Richard Rouse and Mary Rouse, "French Literature and the Counts of Saint-Pol, ca. 1178–1377," *Viator* 41 (2010): 101–40, reprinted in R. Rouse and M. Rouse, *Bound Fast with Letters: Medieval Writers, Readers and Texts* (Notre Dame, IN: University of Notre Dame Press, 2013), 308–56. As the Rouses show, the crusader and religious vernacular patronage of the counts extended long into the fourteenth century, as did the crusader

objects they passed within the family. See also Sean L. Field, "Maire of Saint-Pol and her Books," *English Historical Review* 513 (2010): 255–78.
93 Galvez, *The Subject of Crusade*, 144.
94 Mary D. Stanger, "Literary Patronage at the Medieval Court of Flanders," *French Studies* 11 (1957): 214–29; Olivier Collet, "Littérature, histoire, pouvoir et mécénat: La cour de Flandre au XIIIe siècle," *Médiévales* 19 (2000): 87–110; and Nicolas Dessaux, ed., *Jeanne de Constantinople Comtesse de Flandre et de Hainaut* (Paris: Somogy, 2009).
95 Rouse and Rouse, "French Literature and the Counts of Saint-Pol," 308–17.
96 The text is corrupted here and illegible. Guy's son, also named Guy, inherited the count of Forez and after his father's death negotiated the division of Guy senior's lordship and moveable wealth with his stepmother, Mahaut. See Quantin, *Recueil*, 221, no. 484 (March 1242/3).
97 "presentibus fratre Guillelmo de Vichiaco capellano meo et fratre Guillelmo de ... socio ejusdem ordinis fratrum Minorum, Stephano clerico meo, domino Hugone de Cicunum milite, Berterando camerario meo, Renaldo Pantinum magistro serviente meo. In primo legavi domino imperatori Alamannie unum diamantum quem multum diligebam et unum cinctorium argenti deaurati. Comitisse Nivernensi uxori mee duos de ditioribus pannis meis deauratis et duos meletinos et duos zendatos et unum ... [sma]raldinum quem semper gerebam in manu mea et parvum rubinum quem habui de Johanne Papinum. Guidoni filio meo saphirum meum qui pendebat ad collum ... et meum bonum rubinum et lu cameum quem gerebam in digito meo, lapidem asininum et meum bonum ensem. Domicelle Ailis uxori ejus tres ... et duos covelidas (?). Renaldo filio meo clerico smaraldinum meliorem et veram crucem quam magister militie Templi dedit mihi." In Huillard-Breholles, *Titres de la maison ducale de Bourbon*, 1:46–7, no. 221 (10 Aug. 1241). The document itself is of interest, as it was written on cotton paper, which at this time was used in the kingdom of Naples, though not in the north. It was also written in an Italian script, therefore dictated while in Italy, one presumes in vernacular French, but transcribed in Latin.
98 See Quantin, *Recueil*, 224, no. 490 (Sept. 1243); for attests to a crusade departure donation to the Templars of Saulce, 249, no. 525 (Aug. 1248); for the nuns of Lézinnes, 256, no. 540 (Oct. 1251); for rents to the chapter of Sens to found an anniversary Mass, 258, no. 545 (Dec. 1252); for lands and rents to the Cistercian abbey of Reigny for an anniversary Mass, 273, no. 570 (26 June 1257 and 21 July 1257).
99 "nos concessimus Fratibus-Minoribus de Altissiodoro, locum illum qui dictur *Lafertez* et de *Brahanay*, situm in justicia nostra ... its quod dicti fratres poterunt in eodem loco construere oritorium, et in eodem oratorio cum altaribus portalibus celebrare." Quantin, *Recueil*, 227–8, no. 494

(4 Nov. 1243). In 1252 she supplemented this foundation with additional confirmations; see Lebeuf, *Mémoires d'Auxerre*, 105, no. 181 (April 1252).

100 Lebeuf, *Mémoires d'Auxerre*, 102, no. 173 (Oct. 1245).

101 "Scolaribus morantibus apud Autissiodorum, quo Boni-Pueri nuncupantur, plateam sitam Autissiodori, prope domum Fratrum-Predicatorum in qua fuit aliquando cimeterium Judeorum." Lebeuf, *Mémoires d'Auxerre*, 106, no. 183 (July 1253).

102 Lebeuf, *Mémoires d'Auxerre*, 106, no. 184 (1254).

103 Lebeuf, *Mémoires d'Auxerre*, 110, no. 190 (17 July 1257).

104 Lebeuf, *Mémoires d'Auxerre*, 110–11, no. 191 (1257).

105 The original parchment document is in the Archives départementales de la Nièvre, series H, fonds Saint-Martin de Nevers (July 1248). It has been edited by H. de Flamare, "La Charte de départ pour la Terre-Sainte de Gaucher de Châtillon, baron de Donzy," *Bulletin de la Société Nivernaise* 13 (1886–9): 174–82. See also Jordan, "The Rituals of War," 102.

106 Chazaud, "Inventaire et comptes de la succession d'Eudes, Comte de Nevers," where he discusses the nature of the text. The original is Paris, Archives nationales de France, carton J, 821, no. 1. I am editing this text with Laura K. Morreale, *Crusading and the Material Outremer: The Account-Inventory of Eudes of Nevers, Acre 1266: An Edition, Translation and Commentary* (in preparation). See: https://materialoutremer.lauramorreale.com/.

107 "Li dui grant romanz et li Chançoners por xxxi bezants. Ce fu li romanz des Loheranz et li romanz de la terre d'outre mer, et li Chançoners." Chazaud, "Inventaire et comptes de la succession d'Eudes, Comte de Nevers," 188. For the contents of the *chansonnier*, see Jonathan Riley-Smith, "The Crown of France and Acre, 1254–1291," in *France and the Holy Land*, ed. Weiss and Mahoney, 45–62, at 51.

108 Chazaud, "Inventaire et comptes de la succession d'Eudes, Comte de Nevers," 195.

109 Riley-Smith, "The Crown of France and Acre," 51.

110 Galvez, *The Subject of Crusade*, 253.

6 Coming Together as an Apostolic Act: Confraternalism as an Umbrella for Medieval Religious Movements

NESLIHAN ŞENOCAK

Collective rather than private worship was the norm in religious life and devotion during the Middle Ages. Taking "associative religiosity" as its starting point, this essay argues that confraternalism was the dominant form of religious associations in the Middle Ages, exhibiting itself not only in local religious confraternities and in the orders of friars but also in wider movements such as the Order of Penance. Confraternal associationism was conceived as an essential feature of apostolic life by these religious communities. This complicates the dominant narrative of Herbert Grundmann, who placed the twin pillars of apostolic life on poverty and preaching.

Grundmann's work *Religious Movements* pioneered the quest to bring the popular and learned traditions closer by pointing out the commonalities between them. He was one of the first historians to challenge the imprint of medieval clerical notions of orthodoxy on modern scholarly understanding of medieval religiosity. In the face of a historiography that presented a polarized and mutually exclusive division of the medieval religious landscape into the religious orders and institutional church on one side and lay communities and religious women on the other, Grundmann pushed for fluidity in the boundaries of orthodoxy. He did this by marking the common elements between the papally sanctioned mendicants, heretics, and the women's movement. For Grundmann, the nexus of this commonality was the desire to live the apostolic life. After having spoken of the eleventh-century French heretics who, when interrogated, claimed to live the apostolic life, and of Robert Arbrissel taking up itinerant preaching in pauper's clothing, Grundmann laid out his claim:

> There was obviously a common motivation behind these contemporary episodes: the model of the apostles had become an ideal, expressing itself

in a demand for evangelical itinerant preaching and voluntary Christian poverty. For the time being, however, no unified religious movement arose from these themes. In some cases, they led to novel forms of monasteries or orders following a brief transitional stage of apostolic itinerant preaching; in other cases, when tied with heretical ideas in open opposition to the hierarchical Church and persecuted by it until its demise, they would come to conjure up the great heretical challenge to the twelfth-century Church. These two developments can only be studied separately, but their common motivations have to be kept in mind in order to understand the course and destiny of the movement for religious poverty, in which the two strands eventually reconverged into a single force after developing separately throughout the twelfth century.[1]

Grundmann's identification of itinerant preaching and voluntary poverty as the twin pillars of apostolic life led to the labelling of popular religious movements as "apostolic" movements. Other studies written during the 1940s and 1950s, now mostly forgotten, reinforced the connection between poverty and preaching on one side and apostleship on the other.[2]

This focus on preaching and poverty no doubt allowed the historians of medieval religion to understand the medieval religious on their own terms rather than through the lens of a Protestant anti-clericalism that saw the Church as a community of power-hungry and greedy individuals. This revisionist work of the recent decades tends to focus on the towering figures, such as Norbert of Xanten, Rupert of Deutz, Peter Damian, or Francis of Assisi, but it can certainly profit from the incorporation of lesser-known religious confraternities. It is, however, important to avoid a circularity of argument. The focus on preaching and poverty as the distinctive features of apostolic life emerged from intellectual and orthodox texts that bore the seal of a respected medieval churchman, which then in turn became the litmus test to identify non-clerical religious movements as apostolic. If the historian's starting point were not the writings of towering papally sanctioned figures but, rather, for example, the rule or statutes of much lesser-known religious confraternities, the identifying elements of *vita apostolica* can be and indeed are different.

The sources and studies concerning medieval religious life that have become available since the 1960s reveal that a wide variety of movements and communities claimed affinity with the apostolic life, even when itinerant preaching and voluntary poverty were absent in their religious framework. Therefore, it might be more appropriate to see "apostolicity" or "apostleship" as a *topos* that was used to argue for the perfection of a chosen religious form of life, rather than as an inherent and identifiable feature of a few select religious movements. That is to say, it is not expedient for historians to call a religious movement "apostolic" by looking at whether it is engaged in itinerant preaching or whether it embraces poverty. Rather, it should be recognized that a wide variety of religious movements chose to identify their way of life as apostolic or likened themselves to the apostolic community. Indeed, "apostolicism" is a mode of building up religious authority that was pervasive throughout all medieval religious communities and institutions – the best example being the popes regarding themselves as the heir of the Apostles and claiming authority through apostolic succession.[3]

As Jean Leclercq observed, monks and canons regular identified their lives with the *vita apostolica*.[4] From the eleventh century onwards, the emergence of canons regular and newly reformed monasteries, such as Cîteaux, Camaldoli, Vallombrosa, etc., gave rise to a polemical literature in which each claimed their way of life (*forma vivendi*) as the proper apostolic one. To offer a brief example: The author of an anonymous twelfth-century work titled "Dialogue between a Cluniac and a Cistercian" responds to the Cluniac monk's assertion that the life and the habit are penitential, and the tonsure of monks does not signify the clerical but rather the penitential life; his reply is that the life of monks is apostolic, their habit is angelic, and their tonsure is a sign of perfection and clerical status.[5] Grundmann largely ignored this literature in the first edition of *Religious Movements*, but for the 1955 edition, he added a new section. Admitting that monks, too, considered their way of life as apostolic, Grundmann held fast to the point that itinerant preaching and a new interest in poverty were the marks of the new *vita apostolica* observed in the religious orders of the twelfth century, and the lay movements shared these characteristics.[6]

One can choose, the way Grundmann did, to speak of a "new" *vita apostolica* akin to the mendicant way of life that evolved from an "old" model followed by the monks. An equally rational alternative for the historian is to avoid assigning a fixed meaning to the term and admit that it is an umbrella concept, which could be – and in fact was – adopted to inspire and justify a diversity of devotional lives, activities, and communities. The most significant and basic aspect of the *vita apostolica*, and the one that is unquestionably common in all the different movements that claimed to have followed it, was the tendency to form associations, or what we might call an "associative religiosity." Used here as an analytical concept, associative religiosity is an essential feature of medieval religious forms of devotion, in that it presupposes that the ideal form of devotion is carried out not privately but within a community of believers. It takes its cue from the Apostles, who were not lone hermits but a group, a small community centred around Christ, acting and living together. Even though they dispersed throughout the known world as individuals, in the Christian cosmology they are not conceived as individuals in their own right but as a community or, more particularly, a fraternity. This is further reinforced by literary texts like the "Acts of the Apostles," which provided the associative form of community a metaphysical plane of existence.

The key point here is that for the medieval laity of the twelfth century and beyond, confraternal associative religiosity, rather than a privately observed religiosity, was understood to be the quintessential aspect of *vita apostolica*. This existed alongside the Grundmannian aspects of poverty and preaching, which are certainly associated with *vita apostolica*, albeit less uniformly diffused. In other words, the most common and diffused aspect of the medieval *vita apostolica* was not poverty or itinerant preaching but the coming together with other faithful believers to pray and worship. Below I will present the essential features of this confraternal associative religiosity, its relation to the *vita apostolica*, and how the newly emerging religious movements, such as the Order of Penance, alongside mendicants, organized themselves in this particular mode.

Confraternalism as a Model of Apostolic Community

Roughly forty years ago, Pierre Michaud-Quantin published a book titled *Universitas* in which he investigated the corporate nature of a wide variety of medieval institutions.[7] Essentially a legal historian, Michaud-Quantin examined numerous medieval associative institutions from the lens of the corporation as a Roman legal and social institution, ranging from social and political examples, such as guilds, communes, and courts, to religious institutions, such as religious orders, cathedral chapters, and confraternities. The important merit of this book was in the first place to draw attention to the highly collective and associative nature of medieval society. He argued that the medieval society was not a society made of individuals but, rather, made of smaller societies, a *universitas universitarum*. Michaud-Quantin also underlined elements common to all of these diverse institutions, such as a collective will, democratic voting, right to representation, lawmaking and statutory regulations, and oath-taking. Building upon his conclusions, I argue that the devotional religious institutions of the Middle Ages – be it religious orders, single monasteries, cathedral chapters, or religious confraternities – should be distinguished from the social, political, and economic ones and set aside as a particular kind of corporation. The framework upon which the religious communities are founded is best termed confraternalism.

What are the features of a confraternal corporation that distinguish it from other types of *universitas*? The first distinguishing feature is its source of inspiration. If the courts, city communes, and guilds were based on Roman corporations, confraternal associations were based on the model of the apostolic community. The second distinguishing feature is its end. A confraternal corporation existed to save souls, both of its own members and of others. This feature also distinguished it from other medieval corporations, which had "earthly" goals, such as efficient and just administration, governance (in the case of courts and communes), or collective economic regulation (merchant guilds) as their ends. Thirdly, a confraternal religious community mimicked the kinship ties between brothers and sisters: members regarded one another on equal social footing and addressed one another as "brother" and "sister," even when they came from different social classes. There were divisions of labour and various offices to help with the administration of affairs, but at least in theory there was the understanding that the offices were there to serve the community, not to dominate others.

The numerous religious orders, collegiate churches, cathedrals, and monasteries are all well-known examples of this tendency to associate and fraternalize. Perhaps lesser known are the religious confraternities of three types: lay, clerical, and mixed. Involving thousands of people in the entire countryside and cities of Europe, the confraternal movement dwarfs the much better studied religious movements, such as the Waldensians, Humiliati, mendicants, and even the Crusades in terms of the sheer number of people involved. Confraternities were ubiquitous in every corner of Europe and attracted men and women from all ranks of society.[8] They have, however, not been studied in conjunction with other religious communities, such as the religious orders or collegiate churches, as part of the same phenomenon. Without discounting their structural differences and devotional forms, all these institutions, however, were clearly part of the same associative religiosity, which the original apostolic community inspired.

The historiography of the local religious confraternities of the Middle Ages, which sprang up in thousands of villages and cities of Europe, does not match the long and well-established historiography of the religious orders and monasteries. The confraternities have been largely missing in the grand narratives of popular religion, as they were missing also in Grundmann's seminal work. Yet the reason for this discrepancy has more to do with the production and maintenance of records in the

Middle Ages, and of the respective "paper trails," than with the importance and ubiquity of medieval confraternities as devotional institutions. There are several reasons why the religious orders had more and better-maintained records than many of the early confraternities: The presence of literate men among the members facilitated record-keeping (record-keeping becomes a regular feature of the confraternities only after the thirteenth century). A fixed physical space, such as a monastery or friary, allowed for the preservation of documents produced, i.e., archives (whereas most confraternities met in a church at regular intervals). The institutional recognition, fiscal stability, and continuity led to the accumulation of records until their transfer to the state and ecclesiastical archives in the modern period, which made their study attractive to historians (this also became the case with confraternities after the fourteenth century). Lastly, medieval intellectuals or well-educated men and women wrote their reflections on religious and ecclesiastical matters, thus making themselves and their communities a focus for scholarly interest in subsequent ages (think of Rupert of Deutz, Peter Damian, Thomas Aquinas, etc.). These are the most pertinent reasons why monasteries and religious orders occupy a larger part of the medieval religious historiography in comparison with confraternities. It is no coincidence that most of the existing studies of confraternities are from the late thirteenth century, after emerging literacy and some permanency in institutional framework allowed for record-keeping. Still, overwhelmingly, most modern studies concern Italian urban confraternities of the fifteenth century and beyond, where the field is reasonably well developed.[9] One important reason for this scholarly focus on late medieval and early Renaissance confraternities in Italy is their investment in art patronage, which made them a nexus especially for art historians.

Centuries before the French Revolution popularized *fraternité* as one of the foundational creeds of the people's liberation movement, confraternalism took root within European society. It was so ubiquitous that its most celebrated scholar, Gilles Meersseman, himself a Belgian Dominican, titled his book *Ordo Fraternitatis* to make the point that the medieval men and women who were members of the religious confraternities formed a third order, neither clergy (*ordo clericorum*) as such nor completely lay (*ordo laicorum*) with respect to the various religious activities they pursued. Confraternities appear in various texts from the eighth century onwards; already in the ninth century, Regino, the Benedictine abbot of Prüm (882–899), wrote that the bishops should inquire about the confraternities active in their diocese during their visitations.[10] These early confraternities were essentially religious organizations that sometimes included both clergy and laity. Each confraternity had its statutes, its own organizational structure (e.g., a leader, elders), and most importantly, a series of religious activities outlined in its statutes. The members met at regular intervals for a common Mass and meal as well as public confession. They prayed for each other's souls and for the souls of dead members. Quite interestingly, confraternities were both a rural and an urban phenomenon. Even a small village parish boasted confraternities.[11]

"Where two or three come together in my name, there I am in the midst of them": The Confraternity as an Apostolic Institution

Evidence from the records between the tenth and the thirteenth centuries indicate that confraternities modelled themselves after the apostolic community and had a clear sense that a communal nature of worship registered a sacrality by inviting Christ's presence. The following section addresses the evidence from confraternity statutes and liturgy – one from Paris and a few others from Italy.

The Parisian Confraternity of Twelve Apostles

One of the notable efforts of eleventh-century church reformers was their push for the secular clergy to live communally, giving way to the phenomenon of canon regulars and strengthening and encouraging the collegiate structures. Long before the Gregorian reform, however, the secular clergy felt the need and desire to form a devotional community that went beyond the immediate clerical community of a cathedral or church. Interestingly, some of these confraternities of clergy emerged within existing communities. For example, the clergy of a cathedral chapter might have still opted to form or belong to a confraternity that was distinct from the chapter in its religious purpose and its activities. The clerical confraternity imitated the apostolic community, as its members looked up to the Apostles as original pastors, and its work aimed at saving the souls of the clergy itself. Such clerical confraternities, therefore, followed a form of *vita apostolica* that was different from that of monks.

When reading Meersseman's opus magnum on the medieval confraternities, the evidence reveals a clear pattern: The earliest non-monastic confraternities that we know of began as distinctly clerical confraternities. Some of them seem to have admitted lay people over time to become mixed confraternities, whereas others kept their strictly clerical membership for posterity.[12] In general, even though they were very common in places like Italy, clerical confraternities are among the least-studied topics within the vast scholarship of medieval confraternities.[13] In certain cities, such as Verona, the entirety of urban priests and the priests of the contado would come together in respective confraternities known as *clerus intrinsecus* and *clerus extrinsecus*.[14]

One of the earliest known clerical confraternities is the Confraternity of Twelve Apostles (*fraternitas duodecim apostolorum*), established by the clergy of the Parisian cathedral chapter.[15] Evidence for its existence appears in two distinct manuscripts: a Vatican manuscript that contains the ninth-century sacramentary of the Paris cathedral with additions made until the eleventh century; and a (possibly) ninth-century Bern manuscript originating in Fleury.[16] The Paris manuscript contains the names of the twelve clerics of the confraternity, eight priests, two deacons, one cleric, and one cleric as *aba*, possibly indicating his position as head of the confraternity. These names were recorded in an early eleventh-century hand, according to the analysis of Meersseman.[17]

The Bern manuscript contains a homiletic address to the congregation presumably done at the beginning of confraternity meetings. According to Meersseman's analysis, this homily is in large part based on a well-known hymn, *Congregavit nos* (also known as *Ubi Caritas*), which was traditionally sung during the Maundy Thursday celebrations, mixed with citations from Gregory I. Emphasizing the importance of coming together to unite with Christ, the chant reinforces the notion that Christ will *only* be present when his disciples come together in unity to worship him. Meersseman published the full text of this homily, rendering the lines from the original hymn *Congregavit nos* in italics.[18]

"All who gather in this congregation, listen and understand. Here follows the homily or chant of the confraternity.

> *The love of Christ made us brothers come together.*
> *Let us rejoice and be pleased in him.*
> As his subjects in turn, we serve in fear of Christ.
> ....
> *For as the love binds also those who are absent*
> *So the discord can unbind those who are present*
> *Let us all feel one undividedly*
> *Lest we who came together will get divided.*
> Since the Lord says to his disciples (John 13:35) "They will recognize you to be my disciples, if you have love for one another."
> *Now that we have become one by coming together*
> *Let us make sure that we love with our whole mind*

> *The conflicts shall cease, the quarrels shall cease.*
> *So, our Christ will indeed be among us.*
> As the blessed Gregory said "Where brothers unified glorify God, there God blesses them." God bestows upon us, beloved brothers, a great reassurance when he says in the Gospels, "Where two or three come together in my name, there I am in the midst of them" (Matt. 18:20).[19]

In the homiletic address cited above, it becomes clear that the clergy of this confraternity modelled themselves after the Apostles and believed that collective worship rather than individual and private worship would be more pleasing to God and more conducive to receiving God's blessings. The emphasis falls again and again on the critical words of *congregare in unum*, "coming together as one." At the heart of this effort to become a confraternity lies the conviction that this is what God wants, as Matthew 18:20 attests.

Certainly, worshipping God as a community was nothing new by the ninth century. It was preceded by monasteries or by structures such as minsters and baptismal churches (*pieve*), where the clergy lived together. However, considering the fact that the Confraternity of Twelve Apostles grew out of a cathedral chapter, where members of the community already conducted the liturgy together, the question inevitably arises: Why did the canons think it necessary to start a confraternity? One can only suggest a hypothetical answer: that the services conducted in the cathedral were obligations of the office of each priest, but the confraternity was for worship and prayer that each priest voluntarily wanted to do with a view to save his own soul. The clergy might have thought they had a higher chance of saving their souls if they prayed to God together, in unison.

The Bern manuscript contains the statutes of this confraternity, which had a special devotion to St. Peter because of his status as the head of the apostles.[20] On the feasts of St. Peter and of all other Apostles, the members were to congregate to chant. But the general sense of the statutes was to create an apostolic community among the clergy where there was no discord, no vanity, no gossip, no dishonesty, and no envy.[21] The brothers were to help and to pray for each other when one of them became sick. They were again expected to be present at the burial of a member and to pray for them with others.

Lay Confraternities of Italy

It is not surprising that a devotional trend that emerged among the clergy would soon be adopted by the laity. If this new form of worship is understood to be privileged in pleasing God, as it was supported by passages from the Gospel and attracted respected religious individuals in society, it would soon be imitated or followed by others who would want to take advantage of its spiritual value. In a recent study on five twelfth-century rural confraternities in Italy, I have argued that the religious confraternities were essentially pastoral organizations, existing to secure the salvation of the souls of its members.[22] Below, I will use some of the evidence from that study to demonstrate the apostolic claims made by these confraternities.

What these Italian confraternities have in common with each other and with the ninth-century Parisian confraternity discussed above is their references to the same biblical verses in Matthew 18:20. Even though they were drawn up in different parts of Italy, the statutes of three twelfth-century confraternities – Imola, Pescia, and Montefusco – explain the rationale behind their congregation in those verses, "When two or three gather in my name, I am in the midst of them." The act of coming together to pray rendered the confraternity a sacred institution through the presence of Christ.[23] In the twelfth-century statutes of the confraternity of Santa Maria of Montefusco, the perception of apostolicity is clearly stated: "We come together just as the twelve apostles came together in one, and we have death before our eyes and keep vigil daily, so that when the Lord's order comes, it will find us unanimously vigilant."[24]

The two features Grundmann saw as the defining features of the twelfth-century apostolic life – itinerant preaching and voluntary poverty – were completely missing in these confraternities. Preaching took place at the congregation meetings in the Pescia and Montefusco confraternities, but this was a far cry from the itinerant preaching with a view to conversion. Rather, the surviving sermons were aimed at strengthening confraternal ties and encouraging members to fulfil their responsibilities. The following is from a sermon preached at the Pescia confraternity:

> Therefore, let us pray among ourselves so that we can merit access to the celestial reign. Let us send among us the Holy Gatherer who may bring us together where the apostle brings together, and where no one falls and where the shepherds are gatherers because the good pastor brings together, and the bad one disperses. He brings together just as the Lord says: "I am the good shepherd; the good shepherd gives his soul for his sheep."[25]

Moreover, there was no particular emphasis on voluntary poverty in the confraternities. One of their most striking aspects is that people from all ranks of society could be admitted to membership. Just as the Apostles represent a mixed group of men from different social and professional strata, so too did the membership of confraternities mimic the apostolic community; lay members could be rich, poor, noble, non-noble, male, or female, and the clergy could represent diverse ranks, from archpriest down to clergy in minor orders. Each member had to pay a fee to be admitted – but in the Pescia confraternity, poor people who could not pay the entrance fee were to be shown mercy and still accepted into the confraternity.[26] Thus, preaching and poverty were not the key confraternal practices but, rather, prayer, regular gatherings to celebrate the Mass, and sharing a common meal were in adherence to Acts of the Apostles 2:42: "They devoted themselves to the apostles' teaching and to fellowship, to the breaking of bread and to prayer."

Instead of focusing on poverty, the statutes and sermons ordered caution against assuming hierarchies within the fraternity based on one's social position. The confraternity as a religious institution operated on the Christian premise that everyone is equal before God. The statutes of Montefusco stress that, "No brother should presume to pronounce words of hatred or sit at the head of the table or presume to be superior, but should consider all his equals; there is no greater falsity or danger or detraction than the jealousy among the brothers, for it cannot please God."[27] The instruction given here is very much akin to the statute of the Parisian confraternity that also prohibits vanity and discord among the brothers. The same idea of equality is prominent also in a sermon preached to the Pescia fraternity, which was based on Bruno of Segni's commentary on Psalm 132:

> "You are all brothers and should not call anyone on earth father, for one is your father who is in heaven. This is what we say every day. 'Our father who is in heaven.' And rich and poor, noble and non-noble, God and servant, emperor and beggar, all say by one voice 'our father who is in heaven.' So, they appear to be children of one father and as such, brothers."[28]

The confraternalism here distinguishes itself from the secular world order by preventing anyone to rise above others through a position of authority. Those who are elected as leaders are still equal to the rest. Perhaps here we should be reminded of the fact that Francis of Assisi, whose movement was much closer to a lay confraternity than a religious order at least initially, chose to call the administrators of the order "ministers" to indicate their status as servants to the rest of the community, rather than calling them authority- and hierarchy-infused names, such as master or prior.

Confraternalism in Voluntary Penance: A Case in Point

By the twelfth century, confraternalism had become a common and ubiquitous phenomenon. This is most clearly exemplified in the transformation of the Order of Penance. The Order of Penance (*ordo poenitentiarum*) comes across as an umbrella term for those who voluntarily converted to a life of penance without joining a religious order or monastery. These penitents were distinguished from the involuntary penitents (*poenitentia coactitia*), such as those who committed a crime and were forced to do penance as a form of punishment. In the works of the early church fathers, the term *poenitentia* was used interchangeably with *metanoia*, which designated conversion (*conversio*) from a life of sin to a life lived closer to God, i.e., turning towards God.[29] As indicated by the term "*ordo poenitentiarum*," a life of turning away from sin towards God, is as much a particular form of life as that of monks or clergy.

Before the twelfth century, the penitents appear in the sources as individuals living in their homes and not as communities of penitents bound together by a common space or a set of statutes. Yet, in the twelfth century we encounter the first confraternities of penitents.[30] This was acknowledged by Meersseman, and in the same study he criticizes Grundmann for completely ignoring the studies on, and the historical originality of, the first penitent confraternities. He derides Grundmann for likening the penitential groups to the Humiliati and for suggesting that the married penitents were isolating themselves to live under the direction of monks and priests.[31] Did Grundmann discount the existence and autonomous nature of the penitential confraternities because it did not fit his idea of *vita apostolica* based on the twin notions of poverty and preaching? We cannot know, but Meersseman's meticulous study of the rise of penitential confraternities leaves no doubt that these associations of penitents were distinct from other twelfth-century religious movements of Waldensians and Humiliati.[32]

According to Meersseman, there was a visible increase in the number of penitential confraternities around 1215, which is incidentally also the date of the Fourth Lateran Council. The earliest known set of statutes (*propositum*) of a penitential confraternity appears to have been written by someone well-versed in canon law around 1215.[33] The model described is a mixed confraternity of men and women, and it is worth noting that the first items of these statutes are concerned with the members' clothing. There is a strong emphasis on the modesty of clothing and on distinguishing the members from the rest of the population (*seculares*), i.e., those who have not converted to the life of penance. All members are required to wear undyed clothes; their mantles should be closed, not open in the way that *seculares* wear them;[34] they are not supposed to dance or attend any lewd parties or spectacles;[35] and they are to pray at all seven canonical hours, to confess three times a year, and to take the communion at Christmas, Easter, and Pentecost. For a confraternity of the "converted," who dedicated their lives to penance, confession and communion only three times a year seems rather infrequent, but this gives us a valuable context for understanding what a radical change Lateran IV introduced with its injunction that all people should confess and take the communion at least once a year. Several statutes of the confraternity have provisions for fasting. Members are not supposed to own or carry with them any weapons that can inflict mortal wounds (*arma mortalia*). Each member contributes one *denarius* to the treasurer, who then distributes the collected money to the poor and sick members of the confraternity, then among other poor and as offerings to the church where they gathered. Once a month they are supposed to meet in a church selected by their ministers and hear the Divine Office (*audient divina*).

Contrary to Grundmann's thesis, which suggested that preaching was an essential element of all religious movements in this period, the members of this confraternity had little interest in giving or hearing sermons. One of the most interesting items in this respect is that whenever possible they made provisions to have a religious man educated in the Gospels but did not expect him to preach. Rather, he was sought out to give counsel and comfort the members to persevere in their penance and the works of piety.[36] Yet another interesting item is that the members were not allowed to leave the confraternity, unless they entered a religious order. This attests to the recognition of the Order of Penance as a proper religious *ordo* since, according to a decretal established by Innocent III in 1206, one could only leave a religious order to enter another one that is stricter, not to one that is less strict.[37] It was possible, on the other hand, for a member to be ejected from the confraternity, if they exhibited incorrigible behaviour. There is no clause in the statutes admonishing any degree of poverty. Rather, the core of the confraternity is penance exhibited through frequent praying and fasting.

It is common in the Franciscan historiography to associate the origins of the Order of Penance with the Franciscan Third Order.[38] This is mostly due to the fact that Francis wrote two letters addressed to lay penitents, one dating from the period of 1209–15 and the other from 1221, which was also the year in which Pope Gregory IX's chancellery penned the *Memoriale Propositi*, a *forma vita* for penitent laymen and laywomen.[39] However, as Meersseman has already demonstrated, the *Memoriale* has much more in common with the statutes of the unknown confraternity discussed above than with Francis's letters.[40] The Order of Penance is then something like a devotional franchise, realizing itself in hundreds of penitential confraternities throughout Christendom. Furthermore, the publication of *Memoriale* for penitential confraternities and associations attests to the fact that the latter were numerous enough and novel enough before 1221 to warrant the attention of the papacy and the effort to offer some form of regulation. However, our knowledge about them during this early period is limited only to the cases where the statutes of a penitential confraternity survived.

Conclusion

The most sweeping, ubiquitous, and diverse movement of the Middle Ages from the tenth century onwards was the confraternal movement. It engulfed people from across all social divisions: the rich and poor, men and women, noble and peasant, clergy and laity. Two aspects of this movement appear to be pivotal: the belief that community worship was more sacred than individual worship and a strong normative effort to create an egalitarian brother-sisterhood, with members standing as equals before God no matter what their station in secular life. The late fourteenth-century movement of the *Devotio Moderna*, Sisters and Brothers of the Common Life, had its origins in this type of medieval confraternalism.[41]

The confraternal movement thus does not fit the broad picture of the *vita apostolica* as presented by prevailing historiographical approaches. Emphasis did not rest on preaching or voluntary poverty but, rather, on communal prayer, celebration of the Mass and communal meals at regular intervals, mutual support in sickness and at burial, and the creation of an ethically vigilant apostolic community. In the thirteenth century, the confraternity became another facet of religious existence. Various religious undercurrents, such as the voluntary penitential movement, were absorbed into the confraternal movement, later giving way to penitential confraternities and thereafter the *Disciplinati*. In fact, after the thirteenth century, the specialization of confraternities in particular forms of devotion increased exponentially: the *Laudesi* confraternities, for example, bent on singing Lauds for Christ and Mary; the flagellating *Disciplinati*; confraternities dedicated to the care of orphans, prostitutes, the homeless, prisoners, and pilgrims; military confraternities, etc. At the heart of this apparent diversity, however, rests the common assumption that associative piety, or the coming together with other devout Christians for collective worship, offered a surer path to salvation than any solo endeavours to live the *vita apostolica*.

NOTES

1 Herbert Grundmann, *Religious Movements in the Middle Ages: The Historical Links Between Heresy, the Mendicant Orders, and the Women's*

Religious Movement in the Twelfth and Thirteenth Century, with the Historical Foundations of German Mysticism (Notre Dame, IN: University of Notre Dame Press, 1995), 9.

2 In his 1941 book, *Francis of Assisi: Apostle of Poverty*, Ray Petry wrote: "I have tried to set forth from the sources the all-encompassing demands which the ideal of poverty made upon one who felt himself called to be Christ's special apostle of renunciation. Not what his ideal became in later hands but what it meant in his own apostleship is the main theme of this book." R.C. Petry, *Francis of Assisi: Apostle of Poverty* (Durham: Duke University Press, 1941), vii; or "The concept vita apostolica embraced three basic principles: imitation of the primitive church, poor, simple, and penitential, with interests and activities restricted to the spiritual domain; a passionate love for souls at home and far afield; and evangelical poverty in common, either predicated on mendicancy or mitigated by the work of one's own hands." E. McDonnell, "The *Vita Apostolica*: Diversity or Dissent," *Church History* 24 (1955): 15–31, at 15.

3 On the development of apostolicism as a discursive trend employed by the papacy, see George E. Demacopoulos, *The Invention of Peter: Apostolic Discourse and Papal Authority in Late Antiquity* (Philadelphia: University of Pennsylvania Press, 2013).

4 Jean Leclercq, *La vie parfaite: points de vue sur l'essence de l'etat religieux* (Paris: Éditions Brepols, 1948).

5 F. Martene and D. Durand, eds., *Dialogus inter cluniacensem et cistercensem, testo in Thesaurus novus anecdotorum tomus quintus* (Lutetiae Parisiorum 1717), 1644.

6 This section comes after the appendix in the 1955 edition and is titled "New Contributions to the History of Religious Movements in the Middle Ages."

7 Pierre Michaud-Quantin, *Universitas. Expression du mouvement communautaire dans le Moyen Âge latin* (Paris: Vrin, 1970).

8 Some of the major publications on the medieval confraternities are: *Le movement confraternal au Moyen Âge: France, Italie, Suisse: Table Ronde: Papers* (École Française de Rome, 1987); Gilles Meersseman and G. P. Pacini, *Ordo fraternitatis: confraternite e pietà dei laici nel Medioevo*, 3 vols. (Rome: Herder editrice e libreria, 1977). Most recently, Marina Gazzini has been the most prolific scholar of lay medieval confraternities in Italy. Her online bibliography that covers the whole of Europe is the best bibliography on this subject available at present; see "Confraternite religiose laiche," Reti Medievali, last modified September 2007, http://rm.univr.it/repertorio/confrater.html. For France, see Catherine Vincent, *Les confréries médiévales dans le Royaume de France: XIII–XVe siècle*, Bibliothèque Albin Michel Histoire (Paris: A. Michel, 1994), and Catherine Vincent, *Des charités bien*

ordonnées: les confréries normandes de la fin du XIIIe siècle au début du XVIe siècle (Paris: Ecole normale supérieure, 1988). For England, see the most recent Gervase Rosser, *The Art of Solidarity in the Middle Ages: Guilds in England, 1250–1550* (Oxford: Oxford University Press, 2015); For Spain, see J. Sánchez, ed., *CXIX Reglas de Hermandades y Cofradía andaluzas. Siglos XIV, XV y XVI* (Huelva: Universidad de Huelva, 2002). A recent contribution covering Europe is Monika Escher-Apsner, ed., *Mittelalterliche Bruderschaften in europäischen Städten: Funktionen, Formen, Akteure / Medieval Confraternities in European Towns: Functions, Forms, Protagonists* (Frankfurt/Main: Peter Lang, 2009).

9 See, for example, the historiographical paper of Konrad Eisenbichler, "Italian Scholarship on Pre-Modern Confraternities in Italy," *Renaissance Quarterly* 50 (1997): 567–80, which is an excellent concise survey, even if slightly outdated now, of the scholarship on predominantly Renaissance confraternities in Italy. Among important books covering Renaissance confraternities in the English language are Konrad Eisenbichler, *Crossing the Boundaries: Christian Piety and the Arts in Italian Medieval and Renaissance Confraternities* (Kalamazoo: Medieval Institute Publications, 1991); John Henderson, *Piety and Charity in Late Medieval Florence* (Chicago: University of Chicago Press, 1997); Nicholas Terpstra, *Lay Confraternities and Civic Religion in Renaissance Bologna* (Cambridge: Cambridge University Press, 1995); Christopher F. Black, *Italian Confraternities in the Sixteenth Century* (Cambridge: Cambridge University Press, 1989). Renaissance confraternities in Italy have attracted a disproportionately greater interest from scholars since many of them were patrons of art and thus their records have often been examined by historians of art and music as well as historians interested in Italian Renaissance in general. For more detailed discussion, see my "Twelfth-Century Italian Confraternities as Institutions of Pastoral Care," *Journal of Medieval History* 42 (2016): 202–25.

10 Regino de Prüm, *De ecclesiasticis disciplinis et religione christiana*, Lib. II, Cap. V, "Percunctandum de confratriis et fraternitatum societatibus qualiter in paroechia agantur." *Patrologiae Cursus Completus. Series Latina*, ed. J.P. Migne. 221 vols (Paris: Migne, 1844–1864) [Hereafter PL], vol. 132, col. 287A.

11 For a list of around eighty confraternities from the Charles M. de La Roncière, *Religion paysanne et religion urbaine en Toscane (C. 1280–C. 1450)* (Aldershot: Variorum, 1994).

12 Meersseman, *Ordo fraternitatis*, 1: 150.

13 Antonio Rigon stands out as the most prolific scholar of exclusively clerical confraternities. See his *Clero e città. "Fratalea cappellanorum", parroci, cura d'anime in Padova dal XII al XV secolo* (Padova: Istituto per la storia ecclesiastica padovana, 1988); Bianca Betto, *Le nove congregazioni*

del clero di Venezia (sec. XI–XV). Ricerche storiche, matricole e documenti vari (Padova: Editrice Antenore, 1984); Tommaso Carpegna Falconieri, "Le congregazioni del clero secolare a Roma e la loro documentazione (secoli X–XVI)," in *Realtà archivistiche a confronto*, 23–30. Most recently, Rocca Giancarlo published a list of all recorded clerical confraternities in "Per un primo censimento delle associazioni sacerdotali in Italia dal medioevo a oggi," *Rivista di storia della Chiesa in Italia* 64 (2010): 397–517. Several articles in this collection also deal with medieval clerical confraternities: Gilberto Zacchi, ed., *Realtà archivistiche a confronto: le associazioni dei parroci. Atti del Convegno di Ravenna (24 settembre 2010)* (Modena: Mucchi Editore, 2011).

14 Maureen C. Miller, *The Formation of a Medieval Church: Ecclesiastical Change in Verona, 950–1150* (Ithaca: Cornell University Press, 1993), 58–9.
15 Meerrseman, *Ordo fraternitatis*, 1: 150–69.
16 These are Vat. Ottob. Lat. 313 and Bern, Burgerbibliothek, AA 90 no. 11. Concerning the description and dating of the manuscripts, see Meerseman, 1: 150–1 and 155. Meersseman argues convincingly that the two confraternities mentioned in these two different manuscripts are the same one. See ibid., 167.
17 Ibid., 152.
18 I cite here the parts that emphasize the importance of coming together, marking in italics the lines from the *Congregavit nos*.
19 For the full text of the homily, see Meersseman, *Ordo fraternitatis*, 1:156–7.
20 Ibid., 161–5.
21 Ibid., 162, Statute no. 5: "Nulla sit inter vos fratres discordia, nulla superbia, nulla ira, nulla ebrietas, nulla invidia, nulla falsitas"
22 Şenocak, "Twelfth-Century Italian Confraternities."
23 For a fuller discussion of the statutes of these confraternities, see Şenocak, "Twelfth-Century Italian Confraternities," 213–15.
24 "Congregemus nos sicut duodecim apostolic congregate sunt in unum, et mortem ante oculos nostros habeamus et cotidie vigilemus, ut cum venerit eius mandatum unanimiter vigilantes nos inveniat." Giovanni Vitolo, *Istituzioni ecclesiastiche e vita religiosa dei laici nel Mezzogiorno medievale: il codice della Confraternita di S. Maria di Montefusco (sec. XII)* (Roma: Herder, 1982), 112.
25 "Ergo (23v) oremus inter nos, fratres, ut ad celestia regna mereamur accedere. Mittamus inter nos sanctum congregatorem qui nos congreget ubi congregat apostolus, ubi vero nemo corruit et ubi sunt pastores congregatores, quia bonus pastor congregat, malus autem dispergit. Congregat sicut Dominus dicit: 'ego sum pastor bonus; bonus pastor animam suam dat pro ovibus suis.'" Vitolo, *Istituzioni*, 107.
26 "Hoc quoque si aliquis paupertate coactus adimplere non potuerit, voto prius adimpleto, prepositi misereantur ei secundum quod miserendum cognoverit." Lucca, Bib. Cap. 530, fol. 50r.

27 "Unusquisque frater non presumat ad verba odii aut discumbat in primo loco aut maiorem esse, sed omnes coequales; et non est fortior falsitas aut periculum aut detractio, quam si est inter fratres invidia, quia Deo piacere non potest." Vitolo, *Istituzioni*, 111.

28 "Et alibi. Omnes vos fratres estis, et patrem nolite vocare vobis super terram unus est pater voster qui in celis est. Ipse est autem cui cotidie dicimus. 'Pater noster qui est in celis.' Et dives et pauper, nobilis et ignobilis, dominus et servus, imperator et mendicus, omnes una voce dicunt 'pater noster qui est in celis' ut se unius patris filios et se fratres esse ostendant." Lucca, Bib Cap., fol. 11r. For the full text of the commentary, see PL, vol. 164, col. 1188A.

29 See, in particular, Aloys Herman Dirksen, *The New Testament Concept of Metanoia* (Washington, DC: The Catholic University of America, 1932), 32–59.

30 Meersseman, "Disciplinati e Penitenti del Duecento," in *Il movimento dei Disciplinati nel settimo centenario dal suo inizio (Perugia, 1260): convegno internazionale: Perugia, 25–28 settembre 1960* (Spoleto: Arti grafiche Panetto & Petrelli, 1962), 44. "Fatta astrazione per qualche rara associazione di Penitenti rurali comunitari nel sec. XII; essi non si ragruppavano in comunità religiose e non si curavano nemmeno di formare una confraternita; del resto in nessuna città erano così numerosi da poter costiure una associazione vera e propria."

31 See ibid., n2, for a discussion of Grundmann's complete disregard of penitential confraternities vis-à-vis Meersseman's meticulous study.

32 His first study published in 1954 was "Pénitents ruraux communautaires en Italie au XIIe," co-written with E. Adda and published in *Revue d'histoire ecclésiastique* 49 (1954): 343–90. In 1961 he published *Dossier de l'ordre de la pénitence au xiiie siècle* (Fribourg: Éditions Universitaires, 1961). His three-volume opus magnum *Ordo fraternitatis* (see note 8 above) followed in 1977.

33 The statutes of this confraternity were published by Meersseman in his *Dossier*, 88–90.

34 "de panno humili sine colore induantur" (n1) ... "Chlamydes habeant integras, non apertas, ut portant seculares." Ibid., 88n2.

35 "Ad convivia honesta vel ad spectacular vel coreas non vadant." Ibid., 88n5.

36 "Et tunc, si commode possit, habeant unum virum religiosum in dei verbo instructum, qui eos moneat et confortet ad penitentie perseverentiam et opera pietatis facienda." Ibid., n21

37 F. Donald Logan, *Runaway Religious in Medieval England, c. 1240–1540* (Cambridge: Cambridge University Press, 2002), 43.

38 Alison More, "Institutionalizing Penitential Life in Later Medieval and Early Modern Europe: Third Orders, Rules, and Canonical Legitimacy," *Church History* 83 (2014): 296–322, at 301. The most recent study on the

connection between the Order of Penance and the Franciscans is Ethan L. Yee, "The Burden of Forgiveness: Franciscans' Impact on Penitential Practices in the Thirteenth Century," (PhD diss., Columbia University, 2019).

39 Armstrong, Regis J., J.A. Wayne Hellmann, and William J. Short, eds., *Francis of Assisi: Early Documents*, 3 vols. (New York: New City Press, 1999), 1: 41–5 and 46–52.

40 For a critical edition of the *Memoriale*, see Meersseman, *Dossier*, 92–112.

41 On the *Devotio Moderna*, see John H. Van Engen, *Sisters and Brothers of the Common Life: The* Devotio Moderna *and the World of the Later Middle Ages* (Philadelphia: University of Pennsylvania Press, 2008).

7 Reassessing the Links between "The Women's Religious Movement" and "The Origins of a Religious Literature in the Vernacular" in France[1]

SEAN L. FIELD

The concluding chapter of Herbert Grundmann's 1935 *Religious Movements in the Middle Ages* begins with the bold assertion that "Together with the religious movement of the thirteenth century, there arose a religious literature in the vernacular." Rejecting meaningless formulations such as "a newly awakened religious feeling sought expression in the mother tongue," Grundmann sought instead a precise explanation for "the particular circumstances which generated a religious literature in the vernacular." He was not looking for evidence of vernacular preaching by Latinate churchmen, since translation on the fly had always been necessary when addressing the laity. Nor was he interested in churchmen composing vernacular religious verse, since "poetry is a literature of presentation, not reading." Rather, Grundmann wanted to identify the circumstances that produced a religious prose literature written in the vernacular, which was to be read directly by its intended audience.[2]

Grundmann's general argument was that this literature could only arise "when a new stratum formed between laity and clergy, one which, like the clergy, wanted to read and even write religious works, sermons, prayers, and not least the Holy Scripture, but like the 'laity' could neither read nor write in Latin." That is, a religious prose literature in the vernacular could only develop where "religious communities organized themselves into lasting, regulated forms of life without clerical Latin training, but with the need for contemplation and theological training and a capacity for absorbing and imparting the treasures of Latinate theological and religious education."[3] What was this new "stratum"? Who were these new "religious communities"? Grundmann's answer, essentially, was "women" and "women's communities."[4] He was not thinking of the nuns and abbesses of the traditional Benedictine world but, rather, those communities whose institutional status had been shaped by the new "women's religious movement"; in other words, beguines and members of the early, amorphous communities that eventually came into the orbits of the new mendicant orders. Grundmann argued that it was only when male mendicants "came into contact with the women's religious movement that their sermons developed into a pious literature in the vernacular."[5] Most specifically, male mendicants at first translated for the women, putting a vernacular religious literature into their hands as readers; then the women themselves began to write, employing their vernacular literacy in a search for self-expression and mutual edification. This was the crucial shift, from women as consumers to producers of vernacular religious literature.

Grundmann proceeded in the rest of his chapter to develop this argument for Germany, focusing on "women's religious communities attaching themselves to the Dominican Order,"[6] and on the process by which this dynamic sparked the literature and language of "German mysticism." He showed that as institutional relations between the male and female Dominicans solidified in the second half of the thirteenth century, supplying vernacular religious literature to their sisters became part of the male Dominicans' charge. As German Dominicans preached to and translated for religious women, the women themselves then began to write their own vernacular religious literature, perhaps best exemplified by Mechthild of Magdeburg's masterwork of mysticism, *The Flowing Light of the Godhead*.[7]

What about the course of events outside Germany? Grundmann offered a long footnote, suggesting that similar developments probably took place in France (and Italy), to the extent that mendicant relations with the women's religious movement followed more or less similar patterns there.[8] But since few specifics were then known about those relations for France, he could not properly treat the French scene. Grundmann did note, however, that for the north of France the earliest example of extant vernacular religious prose to emerge from the "women's religious movement" was Agnes of Harcourt's *Life of Isabelle of France* (now dated to c. 1283),[9] while the earliest example "of any importance" for Provence was the *Life of Douceline of Digne* by (almost certainly) Felipa of Porcelet (c. 1297).[10] Both of these texts were composed in Franciscan circles. Thus, the evidence strongly suggested that women whose communities had joined together with the mendicant movement were indeed the first to produce a female-authored religious prose literature in northern and southern French vernaculars.

By contrast, the writings of the Carthusian prioress Marguerite of Oingt, including her Franco-Provencal *Mirror* (by 1294) and *Life of Beatrice of Ornacieux* (1303–10), were obscure until their modern edition of 1965, and thus went unmentioned by Grundmann.[11] Although

Grundmann was well aware of the historical existence of the "heretic" Marguerite Porete, burned at the stake in Paris in 1310, he was not able to consider her place in the history of vernacular religious literature because at the time of his writing, the late thirteenth-century *Mirror of Simple Souls* had not yet been reconnected to her name.[12]

These four authors created the earliest extant works of vernacular religious prose literature by women in the regions that make up modern France.[13] This paper analyses them as a group, in light of recent scholarship, to assess the extent to which Grundmann's model can explain how, when, and why women began writing vernacular religious prose in France.[14] Specifically, did these works arise from sustained relationships between male mendicants and the women's religious movement? If so, did male mendicants first provide translations that then sparked a process that allowed the women themselves to begin writing in the vernacular? And were these authors driven by a desire to express spiritual themes analogous to those found in the "German Mysticism" of Mechthild of Magdeburg and Meister Eckhart?

In answering these questions, this essay makes three arguments. First, to account for all four of our early authors, Grundmann's focus on the mendicant orders must be widened to embrace other contexts in which women wrote from the unsettled margins of ecclesiastical institutions. Second, most of our authors focused on issues of institutional legitimacy more than on mystical themes. Finally, recent discoveries concerning Agnes of Harcourt's writing process show that parts of Grundmann's model apply particularly well in this case. When writing the *Life of Isabelle of France*, Agnes of Harcourt indeed drew on recently translated vernacular texts made available by mendicant friars.

Beyond the Mendicants: Women Writing in Other Contexts

When these four female authors are considered together, they form a more heterogeneous group than Grundmann might have predicted.[15] Specifically, the two women he did not list – the two Marguerites, Porete and of Oingt – complicate his picture by moving outside mendicant circles. Marguerite Porete and her book offer one kind of challenge.[16] Writing sometime between roughly 1285 and 1305, Marguerite was several times labelled a *beguina* in the documents generated by her inquisitorial process,[17] and recently unearthed evidence confirms she was once part of the beguinage of Sainte-Élisabeth in Valenciennes.[18] Thus she is rightly considered one of the great "beguine mystics," along with contemporaries such as Mechthild of Magdeburg and Hadewijch.[19] Thematically, the *Flowing Light of the Godhead* and the *Mirror of*

Simple Souls share a number of similarities, and both reflect the tendency towards "Free Spirit" impulses that Grundmann noted as characteristic of the women's religious movement.[20] In that sense, Marguerite appears as a satisfying French analogue to German developments.

However, Mechthild emerged from a mix of beguine, Cistercian, and Dominican influences (a perfect fit for Grundmann's argument), while these kinds of relationships are only hinted at for Marguerite. It does seem likely that Marguerite had some kind of tie to Franciscan circles, since the first recommender of her book was a local Franciscan and echoes of Franciscan discourse have been detected in her text.[21] And she was demonstrably in contact with other male ecclesiastics, such as the secular master of theology Godfrey of Fontaines and the Cistercians of Villers, as she searched for authorities who would offer support for her work.[22] Still, concrete evidence for sustained personal or institutional relationships with male mendicants is lacking in her case.[23]

The other Marguerite, of Oingt (c. 1240–1310), was from the region of Lyon. She became prioress of the Carthusian nunnery of Poleteins by 1288 and wrote a Latin *Page of Meditations* before her Franco-Provençal *Mirror* and *Life of Beatrice*. She seems to have enjoyed a supportive relationship with an identifiable male ecclesiastic, the prior Hugh of Amplepuis, who brought a text of her visions for approval to the Carthusian General Chapter in 1294.[24] Thematically, her brief *Mirror* is Christ-focused in a way that is quite removed from the apophatic ideas of the *Mirror of Simple Souls*, though it does contain the daring statement that for God's saints, "it seems to every one of them that he is a little god, because they will be His sons and heirs."[25]

Marguerite of Oingt's example thus challenges two aspects of Grundmann's argument. First, her position as an author writing outside mendicant circles indicates that Grundmann's framework should be widened to include contexts in which women's communities occupied the uneasy margins of the orders that had emerged from the eleventh and twelfth centuries.[26] The essential point of Grundmann's analysis, after all, concerned sustained institutional contact between churchmen and women in newly emerging communities. Although the Carthusians were an older order, the female branch was still very much in the midst of finding a solid place for itself in the thirteenth century.[27] Second, Marguerite of Oingt is the only one of these four women to have written an extant text in Latin, so her decision to move to the vernacular for her later writings must have depended as much on her intended audience (presumably her fellow nuns) as on her level of Latinity.[28] In this sense, Marguerite of Oingt seems to occupy the place Grundmann had envisioned for a male mendicant (providing her own Latin text that then sparked her own vernacular writing) as well as the place he envisioned for women.

Thus, considering Marguerite Porete and Marguerite of Oingt as part of the earliest group of women to write French religious prose suggests some of the limits of Grundmann's model. Sustained contact with male mendicants was not necessarily the unique catalyst for the emergence of this literature. Women could begin writing either without any obvious spur from male churchmen (in the case of Marguerite Porete) or in a non-mendicant ecclesiastical context (Marguerite of Oingt). Furthermore, since some women were perfectly capable of writing religious literature in Latin but chose the vernacular anyway, that choice cannot be entirely explained by imagining the women's religious movement as a "stratum" uniquely placed between the clergy and the laity.[29]

Beyond Mysticism: The Primacy of Institutional Issues

Agnes of Harcourt's *Life of Isabelle of France*, Felipa of Porcelet's *Life of Douceline of Digne*, and Marguerite of Oingt's *Life of Beatrice of Ornacieux* are strongly linked by their focus on institutional issues.[30] Whereas Grundmann's analysis of German women emphasized their authorial desire to express impulses towards mysticism, each of these three French authors was an abbess or prioress primarily interested in using her portrayal of a charismatic female figure to address issues of institutional legitimacy. The texts of Agnes of Harcourt and Felipa of Porcelet emerged from strikingly similar institutional dynamics. Both women succeeded the charismatic founders of their communities, which existed on the edges of the Franciscan mainstream, and both wrote to explain who the revered founder had been, how the community had come into existence, and why its very specific version of female Franciscan identity was legitimate.[31]

It was this institutional imperative – the need to establish their communities' legitimacy within a Franciscan context – that more than anything drove these authors to take up their quills.

Isabelle of France (1225–1270), sister of King Louis IX, had founded the female Franciscan house of Longchamp just west of Paris. A first version of the rule she helped write was approved in 1259, the first nuns entered in 1260, and a revised version of her rule, granting her the coveted title of *Sorores minores* (Sisters minor), was approved in 1263.[32] Isabelle never became a nun at Longchamp herself but lived on the abbey grounds as a royal lay patron. Her biographer, Agnes of Harcourt, came from a Norman noble family close to the Capetians and served two terms as abbess; the first (c. 1264–75) covered the years just before and after Isabelle's death, and the second (1281–7) included the period in which the *Life of Isabelle* was composed.[33] By the 1280s, Agnes needed to explain why the *Sorores minores* existed at all (in distinction to the dominant Order of St. Clare, founded by Pope Urban IV in 1263), what Isabelle's battles had been, and how she had secured the cooperation of powerful male figures, such as Pope Alexander IV and the Minister General Bonaventure, in establishing her house and order. Notably, Agnes's Isabelle is not in any way a mystic or visionary but, rather, a saintly patron whose hagiographic representation shelters and legitimates the sisters of Longchamp.

Felipa of Porcelet (d. c. 1316) came from the same elite level of upper nobility as did Agnes of Harcourt, and her family also enjoyed close ties to the Capetians.[34] Although (unlike Agnes) Felipa had been a wife and mother, in her widowhood she joined Douceline of Digne's fledgling group of Franciscan-inspired beguines. After Douceline's death in 1274, Felipa stepped into her leadership role as the prioress of the beguine "Order" of Roubaud, made up of the two communities Douceline had founded in Hyères and Marseille. These communities followed a rule that Douceline had solicited from and probably helped to compose with her brother, the Franciscan theologian Hugh of Digne (d. c. 1255).[35] Yet, Douceline's creation of a unique beguine/Franciscan institutional setting in Provence had only dubious ecclesiastical standing.[36] In addition to her brother, Douceline's main advisors had been John of Parma, removed from his position as Franciscan Minister General in 1257, and Jaucelin, Provincial Minister for Provence from 1262 to 1272, who acted as her confessor.[37] Thus, Felipa had an even trickier task than Agnes, since neither her order nor her rule had ever received formal papal approval. Moreover, Felipa was attempting to show that a rule and a female Franciscan identity developed with Franciscan leaders who leaned towards the radical "Spiritual" wing of the order (including a now-discredited former Minister General) could provide a legitimate, enduring institutional setting for these communities. Hence, in her *Life of Douceline*, a string of visions by Douceline and other beguines repeatedly serve to demonstrate that God and St. Francis recognize Roubaud's legitimacy.[38] Douceline herself was without any doubt a visionary and mystic, but Felipa – the actual author of the vernacular prose life – was interested in the content of visions by and about Douceline primarily insofar as they validated the institutional identity she was struggling to preserve.

Marguerite of Oingt's relationship to the subject of her biography, Beatrice of Ornacieux, was slightly different but still raised some of the same institutional issues.[39] Beatrice came from a noble family of the

Dauphiné. She became a Carthusian nun at Parménie and was selected to act as first prioress of the new community of Eymeux in 1303. But the community struggled to survive, and Beatrice died that same year. Thus, Beatrice was not the founder of Marguerite's own community; rather, both served as prioresses in the Carthusian Order. Yet, Marguerite was a leader of her own community, just as Agnes and Felipa had been, and she sought to portray Beatrice as a legitimating model for women of her order, both in her charity and humility and in her role as founder of a new (if short-lived) house. Like Douceline, Beatrice experienced visions, and Marguerite was somewhat more interested in relating their spiritual (often Eucharistic) content than Felipa had been for her subject.[40] But as Felipa had done for Douceline, Marguerite also worked to demonstrate Beatrice's status as a figure of religious authority and as a charitable figure in relation to her sisters.[41]

Hence, these three *Lives* indicate that Grundmann underestimated the role of institutional imperatives in motivating the earliest female authors of French religious literature. Whereas for Germany he could move immediately from the emergence of a female-authored vernacular religious literature to the language of mysticism, in France one has to bypass the central texts to get to Marguerite Porete and the *Mirror of Simple Souls* (and to a lesser extent, Marguerite of Oingt's *Mirror*) before one can find a counterpart to a figure such as Mechthild of Magdeburg. In fact, the earliest examples of women's vernacular religious literature in France focus on exactly the kind of battles Grundmann was one of the first to fully explicate – that is, questions about what it meant, institutionally, for a female community to adopt a Franciscan model, to become part of the Franciscan Order on the women's own terms, or indeed to struggle along on the difficult fringes of the not particularly welcoming Carthusian Order.[42] When Isabelle of France founded Longchamp, there was not yet an "Order of St. Clare," or any other house of female Franciscans in the area of Paris. Thus, when Agnes of Harcourt wrote about Isabelle from the perspective of the 1280s, her task was to legitimate her own status as abbess of a house of *Sorores minores* (not Clarisses), and to convince readers that the foundress's saintly life authorized this branch of the Franciscan family.

When Douceline of Digne founded Roubaud, her preference for a semi-religious life combining the "beguine" name with an imitation of St. Francis was a daring novelty in Provence. When Felipa of Porcelet wrote about Douceline in the 1290s, she too had to legitimate her own role as prioress of Roubaud and explain why these Franciscan-inspired beguines should be seen as holy rather than dangerous, as suspicion of both beguines and Spiritual Franciscans increased during this time.

When Beatrice of Ornacieux helped found the new Carthusian community of Eymeux, the very idea that Carthusian women had a legitimate role in expanding and solidifying their order remained in question. When Marguerite of Oingt wrote about Beatrice a few years later, it was the legitimacy of this project itself that she sought to defend. Although today Marguerite Porete is far better known than Agnes of Harcourt, Felipa of Porcelet, or Marguerite of Oingt, the *Mirror of Simple Souls* proves to be the outlier within the first generation of women's vernacular religious literature in France.

New Evidence for the Sources and Composition of Agnes of Harcourt's *Life of Isabelle of France*

The foregoing analysis has argued that Grundmann's model should be expanded to include non-mendicant settings and to stress institutional as much as spiritual motivations. At the same time, several recent discoveries concerning the earliest of our texts, Agnes of Harcourt's *Life of Isabelle of France*, indicate that his model of friars supplying vernacular religious literature to women who then begin to write themselves retains considerable explanatory force.

What inspired Agnes of Harcourt to write, and where might she have located specific models for how to construct a hagiographic text? The first work associated with Agnes's name is actually the "Letter on Louis IX and Longchamp."[43] Dated December 1282, this brief French narrative was evidently intended to influence the canonization hearings for Louis IX that were taking place at just that moment at Saint-Denis.[44] The call for witnesses to Louis's sanctity and miracles elicited this response from Agnes and other senior nuns at Longchamp who had encountered the king in his role as patron of the abbey.

Writing about Louis IX's relationship to Longchamp probably caused Agnes to envision a more extensive text on Isabelle, the true founder of the community. Moreover, Agnes relates in her preface that Charles of Anjou, youngest brother of Isabelle and Louis, had directly asked her to write such a life (a request that must have been made in 1283). Charles himself was a strong promoter of the broader idea of Capetian sanctity; thus, it was in some sense the enthusiasm generated by the canonization process for Louis IX that provided the specific impulse to write about Louis's sister.[45] There is no doubt about Agnes's familiarity with religious writings, since she owned a book containing "lives of the holy fathers" (*"vie des saincts peres"*) and another "large book of sermons" (*"1 grant [livre] de sarmons"*), according to Longchamp's inventory of 1305.[46] It is not clear from that inventory whether these (no longer extant) books were in French or Latin, or exactly which "holy fathers" were included in their pages, but evidently Agnes was a literate woman with some kind of hagiographic texts at hand. Recent scholarship, however, has now given us two new and precise indications of the vernacular saints' lives that were directly available to her in writing the *Life of Isabelle*.

The first of these discoveries concerns the earliest French version of the *Legenda* of Clare of Assisi. Following Clare's death on 11 August 1253, a canonization process was opened in October 1253, testimony was gathered from the nuns of San Damiano and townspeople of Assisi in November 1253, and she was quickly canonized on 15 August 1255. A trail of new discoveries that leads from Clare to Agnes of Harcourt begins with Marco Guida's recent demonstration that the author of Clare's *Legenda* was none other than Thomas of Celano, best known as the author of several *vitae* of Francis of Assisi.[47] This new precision about the authorship of Clare's Latin *legenda* in turn provides the backdrop for exciting work by Martine Pagan on this text's earliest French translation. In an article published in 2014, Pagan inventoried fourteen extant manuscripts of three "families" of French translations.[48] Of these three families, the "long" version is clearly the earliest and exists in eight manuscripts. In turn, out of those eight manuscripts, Pagan identified Bibliothèque nationale de France (BnF) ms. fr. 2096 and Archives nationales (AN) LL 1601 as closest to the original translation. In concluding this first article, Pagan promised a new edition of the text that would be based on BnF ms. fr. 2096 – a logical choice since existing descriptions listed the date of this manuscript as late thirteenth century, whereas AN LL 1601 was thought to date from the first quarter of the fourteenth century.

However, by the time Martine Pagan published her follow-up article with the promised edition later in 2014, she realized that the AN manuscript was more important than it had initially seemed.[49] Working with Patricia Stirnemann, Pagan now dated BnF ms. fr. 2096 to between 1275 and 1280 but revised the date of AN LL 1601's creation to between 1280 and 1285. Both manuscripts were copied in the region of Paris and in fact depend on a common, now lost, model. Furthermore, Pagan now showed that these two manuscripts were actually created in tandem, by a single person or team, since a process of linked, nearly simultaneous correction tied them together. This process of correction took place in relation to the Latin original, almost certainly as an extended part of the process of translation itself.[50]

It is thus of great interest to note that AN LL 1601 was without any doubt created at Longchamp.[51] Based on Pagan's new evidence of interdependent creation and correction, it follows that the other early manuscript, BnF ms. fr. 2096, was produced there as well. In other words, Pagan's meticulous examination of the manuscripts has revealed a previously unsuspected fact: The first French translation of Thomas of Celano's *Vita* of St. Clare was done at Longchamp. Based on the newly precise dating of the two relevant manuscripts, this process of translation must have taken place before 1280.[52]

Once the French *Life of Clare* had been localized to Longchamp, Pagan proceeded to compare it with Agnes of Harcourt's *Life of Isabelle*. She recognized "an inflection, a phrasing, a tonality which leaves the two texts seeming extremely close." Among passages that show notable parallels, at least one very clear example of textual dependence was identified, and a brief but conclusive analysis revealed that the *Life of Clare* must have functioned as an intermediary between the Latin *Legenda* and the *Life of Isabelle* (see Appendix A). It thus seems evident that Agnes knew the French *Life of Clare* before writing her *Life of Isabelle* (a fact already implicit in Pagan's dating of the former to before 1280). As Pagan cautiously hypothesized, these indications pointed to Agnes of Harcourt as a central figure in producing the translation itself: "At this point in our study, nothing forbids the idea that this abbess of Longchamp could have sponsored (and why not have translated herself?) the *Legend of Clare* before composing the *Life of Isabelle*."

Thus, Grundmann's model applies here with great accuracy; the friar Thomas of Celano wrote the Latin *Legenda* of Clare, the saint central to papal attempts to shape the direction of female Franciscan institutional identity, and it would almost certainly have been a friar who put this legend into the hands of the nuns of Longchamp – if not in translation, then to be translated. The Franciscan masters of theology at the University of Paris were all (according to Agnes of Harcourt) at times in Isabelle's quarters at the royal palace on the Ile-de-la-Cité as they consulted on Longchamp's new rule in the years immediately after 1255;[53] among these Franciscan masters, men such as Guibert of Tournai (who authored one of the first important sermons on Clare known from Paris)[54] and Eudes of Rosny were particularly close to Isabelle as advisors or confessors. In the 1270s, after the death of Isabelle, it is possible that an illustrious friar such as these two, or one of the less well-known friars resident at Longchamp, had a hand in the translation, perhaps at the urging of Agnes of Harcourt. It is also possible that Agnes and her sisters produced the translation with only tacit approval from the friars. In any case, the translation was produced exactly at the intersection between Franciscans and the first female Franciscan community in the vicinity of Paris. With that "spark" having been lit, Agnes and her community then wrote their French "Letter on Louis IX and Longchamp" in

1282 (which makes specific mention of Clare as a model, in words put in the mouth of the saintly King Louis) and the *Life of Isabelle* shortly thereafter.

A second discovery goes even further in showing Agnes of Harcourt's use of recently produced vernacular models. In addition to Clare of Assisi, the other great female saint of the early thirteenth century was Elizabeth of Hungary, who died in 1231 and was quickly canonized in 1235. Latin hagiographic writings about Elizabeth mushroomed before and after her canonization, most importantly a *Libellus* in which the recollections of four of her early followers were given a prologue and conclusion and worked into something more like a traditional *vita*.[55] As Elizabeth's posthumous fame spread across Europe, she attracted intense devotion in France, in particular around the Capetian court. Joinville famously reported an example of such devotion expressed by Blanche of Castile (mother of Isabelle of France and Louis IX) at a public celebration in 1241.[56] Vincent of Beauvais included a brief biography of Elizabeth in his *Speculum historiale*, written and revised several times between 1244 and 1254;[57] an anonymous French Franciscan composed a lengthier Latin *Vita* of Elizabeth between approximately 1250 and 1280;[58] and a rhyming poem was composed by Rutebeuf for Isabelle, the daughter of Louis IX (hence the niece of Isabelle of France), between 1255 and 1270.[59] Each of these texts was largely based on the earlier *Libellus*.

If Rutebeuf's French poem is the best-known early vernacular version of Elizabeth's life, it was not the only one; at least three other French lives were written in verse by the early fourteenth century, and three more in prose.[60] It is one of the latter that concerns us here. In a 2009 article, the Hungarian scholar Levente Seláf demonstrated that the prefatory section of Agnes of Harcourt's *Life* was in very large measure taken from the earliest of these French prose lives of Elizabeth.[61] This anonymous text bears a prologue beginning, "*Bonne chose est penser lire et escrire et souvent recorder les saintes conversations des amis nostre seigneur*," and an incipit for the body of the main text, "*Madame sainte Elizabeth fut estraite de reaul lignie quar ele fut fille au roi Andrieu de Hongrie.*"[62] The core of the text is at least partly based on the Latin *Libellus*. We must await Seláf's forthcoming critical edition and study for a full understanding of the work's genesis.[63]

Several points, however, are already clear. First, Seláf's interpretation is accurate beyond any doubt; this *Life of Elizabeth* preceded the *Life of Isabelle*, and Agnes used it directly, adapting it only lightly to her needs (see Appendix B, which amplifies Seláf's demonstration). Second, the prologue to the French prose *Life of Elizabeth* did draw a few passages from the prologue to the older Latin *Libellus*, but for the most part it was newly composed (see again Appendix B). Third, the newly composed parts (which are the vast majority) of this prologue to the French prose *Life of Elizabeth* clearly reveal the hand of a male cleric. Not only is the lengthy prologue subdivided into a characteristically scholastic ten-point structure outlining why attention to saints' lives is beneficial, but it is also followed by a new six-fold division. Furthermore, in the latter section, biblical and patristic quotations are given in Latin and then translated into French. In other words, this *Life* must have been written (and in small measure partly translated from the earlier Latin *Libellus*) by a cleric, rather than by the nuns of Longchamp or another female community (once again, see Appendix B). Third, as Jacques Dalarun has recently pointed out, Longchamp's inventories of 1325 and 1339 record a book that must be a French *Life* of Elizabeth of Hungary, and so the odds seem very high that this is the same volume upon which Agnes was able to draw.[64]

Finally, Agnes of Harcourt seems to have added this preface to her work at a concluding (not initial) stage of the composition, as demonstrated by a seventeenth-century description of the autograph copy of the *Life of Isabelle* that was preserved at Longchamp up to the Revolution.[65] In this case the pre-existing *Life of Elizabeth* allowed Agnes and the nuns of Longchamp to present their new work with the confidence of an accepted, more polished prefatory flourish that established the new *Life*'s literary merit. In sum, the vernacular work was created by a male cleric, and Agnes of Harcourt and the nuns of Longchamp had it at their disposal by 1283.[66] Whether or not the original author/translator was a Franciscan, it was very likely through Franciscan channels that the work came to be known at Longchamp. It then exercised enough influence to provide a direct model for passages in the *Life of Isabelle* by around 1283.

Agnes of Harcourt was able to use at least two earlier examples of vernacular hagiography when she composed her *Life of Isabelle*. These were, not coincidentally, lives of the two most famous female saints of the first half of the thirteenth century, the Franciscan-influenced Elizabeth of Hungary and the quintessential Franciscan woman Clare of Assisi. Both lives had been written in Latin, and both were translated into French versions before 1280. On some level, Franciscan friars almost certainly had a hand in making both texts available at Longchamp before 1283. Most importantly, both vernacular texts then played a direct role in shaping the very first (extant) work of female-authored vernacular religious prose in French, Agnes of Harcourt's *Life of Isabelle*. The *Life of Clare* seems to have been at the back of Agnes's mind as she wrote, informing her presentation and her language, if only rarely providing text directly. By contrast, the *Life of Elizabeth* was used much more explicitly, but as a "finishing touch" rather than a piece of fundamental scaffolding.

On this level, Grundmann's predictions about what future research would find in France seem to have been substantially borne out: Friars wrote Latin texts and at least helped to get them into vernacular form and into the hands of this Franciscan abbess; out of that moment emerged the earliest extant vernacular religious writings by a woman in the north of France, the "Letter on Louis IX and Longchamp" and the *Life of Isabelle de France*. At the same time, Agnes of Harcourt is revealed as an extraordinarily creative author (and possible translator). She worked with the "cutting edge" vernacular hagiography of her day to inform and enrich her own authorial production, taking little bits from her models but building on them to create something entirely new.[67]

Conclusion

This essay has argued that some elements of Grundmann's model need to be modified to fit the French context. While several of the earliest examples of women writing French religious literature do clearly emerge from the interaction between Franciscans and nascent women's communities (Agnes of Harcourt, Felipa of Porcelet), several others do not (Marguerite of Oingt, Marguerite Porete). While Marguerite Porete's *Mirror of Simple Souls* (and, to a lesser extent, Marguerite of Oingt's *Mirror*) exemplify some of the same kinds of mystical language found in the writings of German authors, such as Mechthild of Magdeburg, the *Lives* of Isabelle of France, Douceline of Digne, and Beatrice of Ornacieux focus more on issues of institutional identity and legitimacy. And yet, new discoveries about the very first of these texts, Agnes of Harcourt's *Life of Isabelle*, reinforce certain aspects of Grundmann's model concerning the powerful influence of friars' interactions with women's communities as the spark that could ignite women's desire and confidence to write. We should surely not try to stretch Grundmann's insights beyond the point where they can be useful. In this case, however, the more evidence that emerges, the more it seems that Grundmann's vision of the "origins of a vernacular religious literature" retains a measure of explanatory force.

Appendix A

The chart below details several parallels between the French *Life of Clare* and Agnes of Harcourt's *Life of Isabelle*. The first column also provides the original Latin from Thomas of Celano's *Legenda*. The third example is particularly clear in showing that the French *Life of Clare* stands as an intermediary between the Latin *Legenda* and the *Life of Isabelle*.

This table was developed in partnership with Jacques Dalarun and Martine Pagan. It is a pleasure to acknowledge their collaboration and to thank them for permission to print this comparison.

Celano's *Legenda*[68]	*Life of Clare*[69]	*Life of Isabelle*[70]
vocem audivit dicentem sibi (p. 94) [See Acts 9:4]	[2] Et tantost oi une voiz qi li dist	[line 346] elle oy devant matines une voix qui li dit ... et tantost
Denique suis eam nobiliter maritare volentibus (p. 96)	[4] Et quant si ami la voudrent hautement marier	[line 48] Elle fu juree de ses amis.
Porro in ieiuniis tantus erat rigor abstinentiae suae, ut de viatico tenui, quod sumebat, vix corporaliter viveret, nisi eam virtus alia sustentaret (p. 132)	[18] ele menjioit si tres petit que nul cors n'en vesquist se la vertu de Dieu ne la soustenist.	[line 119] ele maigoit si tres petit que nul cors humain n'en peut estre soutenus se la grace de Dieu ne le feist.
unius remedii salutarem sumit effectum (p. 212)	[51] et tantost ele fu garie	[line 481] et tantost ele fu guerie
quos vulgari sermone scrofulas vocant (p. 224)	[59] d'une maladie qu'en apele escroeles	[line 333] une maladie ... que l'en apele l'orguelleux.
	[60] pucele ... delivree	[miracle 35] pucele ... delivree

Appendix B

This appendix first gives short excerpts from the opening sections of the prologue to the earliest French prose life of Elizabeth of Hungary to illustrate its use of scholastic scaffolding and biblical quotations given first in Latin and then translated into French. It then gives a comparison, in parallel columns, between passages from the prologue to the Latin *Libellus de dictis quatuor ancillarum s. Elisabeth confectus*, the French prose *Life of Elizabeth*, and Agnes of Harcourt's *Life of Isabelle*. Credit for first demonstrating the dependence of the *Life of Isabelle* on the *Life of Elizabeth* belongs to Levente Seláf, who is currently preparing a critical edition of the French prose *Life of Elizabeth*. I thank him for his advice and generosity in discussing his findings with me before their publication.

Life of Elizabeth, **Opening Section of the Prologue, BnF ms. fr. 13496, fol. 155rb:**

Bone chose est penser, lire, et escrire, et sovent recorder les vies et les saintes conversacions des amis notre seingnour et des amies et les miracles et // (fol. 155va) les vertuz que Deux oevra en els et par euls et els devotement et devotemant honorer. Quar ice nous profite en x. choses. La premiere chose si est que ce vaut a notre foi essaucier et confermer. La seconde si est que ce vaut a la confusion des hereses et des autres anemies notre seignour, et nommeemant dou deaiible qui est vaincuz par les bones oevres que li saint et les saintes hont fait en terre. La tierce chose si est....

(Fol. 156ra) En cele gloire ou les sainz et les saintes sont, hont il encores autres .vi. chouses, des queles la premerainne est soverainne sapience, quar il lisent et voient cleremant ou livre de vie....

(Fol. 156rb) La sisiesme chose si est acomplissemant de touz lour desirriers, quar chascuns ne voudroit havoir autre chose que il ha, ne plus, ne autre manière. Et ce dist David li prophetes, *Satiabor cum apparuerit gloria tua* [Psalms, 16 :15]. C'est a dire, Sire Deux ie serai saoulez en votre grant gloire et raempliz ne iusqu'a lors li miens cuers ne puet estre saoulez....

Libellus, Prologue[71]	***Life of Elizabeth*** **(BnF ms. 13496, fols. 156vb–157v):**	***Life of Isabelle*** **(from *Writings of Agnes of Harcourt*):**
Prima continet statum infantie et pueritie usque ad annos nubiles. Secunda statum matrimonii. Tercia statum soluti matrimonii post mortem mariti usque ad religiosi habitus assumptionem. Quarta extunc usque ad mortem ipsius. Ultimo annexa sunt miracula, que post mortem dominus ad tumbam eius pro ipsa operatus et ex infinitis quaedam circiter CL per testes idoneos sollempniter et sufficienter probata, que in Romana curia examinata sunt et approbata.	Pour ices .x. profiz que nos havons dit par-dessus, havons proposemant de descrivre la vie sainte Elisabeth selonc ce que Deux nous donra sa grace a l'onour de Deu et de cele beneuree sainte et a l'edification de sainte eglise. Premieremant dirons qui ele fust et de quel gent estraite. Apres dirons de s'enfance et de sa conversation qu'ele mena avant qu'ele fut mariee. Apres de la vie qu'ele mena en mariage. Apres de la vie qu'ele mena en voveté iusques alores qu'ele entra en religion. Apres de sa vie qu'ele mena en religion et de son trespassemant de ceste mortel vie a vie pardurable. Apres commant ele fut canonizee, et escripte et nombree ou nombre des sainz par l'auctorite l'apostole et de sainte eglise. En la fin dirons aucuns des miracles qui sont granz et mervoilloux tant en i ha que apoinnes les porroit l'on nombrer.	Nous avons propose d'escrire la vie de nostre saincte et benoite dame et mere madame Yzabeau de France ... selonc ce que Diex nous donrra sa grace, a l'onneur de Nostre Seigneur Jesu Crist et de ceste benoite saincte et a l'edification de sainte eglise. Et premierement nous dirons qui ell fu et de quex gens estraite, et apres dirons de s'enfance et de sa conversation, quelle vie elle mena.

Nostra enim Elysabeth vitiorum exstirpatrix, virtutum fuit plantatrix, scola morum, exemplum penitentie, speculum innocentie, que singula beviter prosequamur....	Madame sainte Elizabeth fut estraite de reaul lignié quar ele fut fille au roi Andrieu de Hongrie.... Encores fust elle si noble de lignaige encore fut el plus haute et plus noble de mors. Icele soule est veraie noblesce qui est aornemant de l'ame par bonte et par sainte vie. Et après elle fut fille et espouse et especiaul amie notre seingnour Iesu Crist. Touz ses desirriers, toute s'entention, touz ses labours si fu pechie destruire et planter vertu en soi et en autrui. Ele fu mirouiers d'innocence, exemples de peneance, rose de pacience, lis de chastee, fontainne de misericorde. Ele fut escole de toutes bones mors, quar ele fut escoliere especiaul de l'escole Jesu Crist, qui dist a ses disciples, Aprenez de moi, quar ie suis douz et debonaires, et humbles de cuer. Iceste licon especiaulmant retint ma dame sainte Elizabeth empres notre Dame. Quar en toutes ses œuvres n'apert fors humilitez, douceurs, et debonairetez, selonc ce que Salemonz enseignge, Tant comme tu est plus granz huumlie toi en toutes tes œuvres et en tes chouses.	Nostre saincte mere et dame madame Ysabeau fut estraicte de royal ligniee, et fut fille du tres noble roy Loys de France.... Et ja soit ce qu'elle fust si noble de lignage, encore fut elle plus haute et plus noble de mœurs. Elle savoit bien que icelle seule est la vraye noblece qui est ornement de l'ame par bonte de l'ame et par saincte vie.... Elle fut fille et espouse et especial amie de Nostre Seigneur Jesu Crist, et touz ses desiriers et tout s'entention et tous ses labours si furent de destruire pechiez et de planter vertus en soy, et en autrui. Elle fu mirouir d'innocence, exemplaire de penance, rose de patience, lis de chastee, fontaine de misericorde. Elle fu escolle de toutes bonnes mœurs, quar elle fut escolie especial de l'escole de Nostre Seigneur Jesu Crist, qui dist a ses disciples, Apprenez de moi que je sui doux et deboenneres et humbles de quer. Cette lecon retint bien especialement notre benoite et sainte et noble dame et mere madame Issabel, quar en toutes ses heuvres n'apparoit fors humilite de quer et debonnerete, selon ce que Salemon ensenge, Tant comme tu es plus grans, humilie toi en tes heuvres et en toutes choses.

NOTES

1. I thank Jennifer Kolpacoff Deane and Anne Lester for their helpful criticisms, and Jacques Dalarun and Martine Pagan for their generous collaboration.
2. Herbert Grundmann, *Religious Movements in the Middle Ages: The Historical Links between Heresy, the Mendicant Orders, and the Women's Religious Movement in the Twelfth and Thirteenth Century, with the Historical Foundations of German Mysticism*, trans. Steven Rowan, with an introduction by Robert E. Lerner (Notre Dame, IN: University of Notre Dame Press, 1995), 187. For recent French attention to Grundmann and the study of medieval women, see Piroska Nagy, "Avant-propos," *Memini: Travaux et documents* 24 (2018), special issue *Modèles de sainteté féminine, de Claire d'Assise à Isabelle de France: l'intertextualité à l'ouvrage*, https://journals.openedition.org/memini/1070; and Sylvie Duval, "Pour une relecture de la vie religieuse féminine chrétienne en Occident à la fin du Moyen Age," *Mélanges de l'École française de Rome* 128, no. 2 (2016), special issue *Le genre, une nouvelle approche du fait religieux*, https://mefrim.revues.org/2579.
3. Grundmann, *Religious Movements*, 195.
4. Grundmann addressed closely related issues in essays of 1935 and 1958, translated as "Women and Literature in the Middle Ages: A Contribution on the Origins of Vernacular Writing," and "*Litteratus—Illiteratus*: The Transformation of an Educational Standard From Antiquity to the Middle Ages," in *Herbert Grundmann: Essays on Heresy, Inquisition, and Literacy*, ed. Jennifer Kolpacoff Deane, trans. Steven Rowan (Woodbridge: York Medieval Press, 2019), 30–55, 56–125.
5. Grundmann, *Religious Movements*, 192.
6. Grundmann, *Religious Movements*, 195.
7. Mechthild of Magdeburg, *The Flowing Light of the Godhead*, trans. Frank Tobin (New York: Paulist Press, 1998).
8. Grundmann, *Religious Movements*, 393n44.
9. Grundmann cited the eighteenth-century Latin translation in the *Acta sanctorum*, though the French was available in Du Cange's edition of 1668 (on which the *Acta sanctorum* translation was based). For modern edition and English translation, see Sean L. Field, *The Writings of Agnes of Harcourt: The Life of Isabelle of France and the Letter on Louis IX and Longchamp* (Notre Dame, IN: University of Notre Dame Press, 2003); for a new French translation by Anne-Françoise Lerquin-Labie that incorporates the latest scholarship, see Jacques Dalarun, Sean L. Field, Jean-Baptiste Lebigue, and Anne-Françoise Leurquin-Labie, *Isabelle de France, sœur de Saint Louis. Une princesse mineure* (Paris: Éditions franciscaines, 2014), 272–313.

10 Grundmann cited the editions by Albanès (1879) and Gout (1927), still the editions of record today. An English translation is now available in Kathleen Garay and Madeleine Jeay, trans., *The Life of Saint Douceline, a Beguine of Provence* (Cambridge: D.S. Brewer, 2001).

11 Antonin Duraffour, Pierre Gardette, and Paulette Durdilly, eds., *Les œuvres de Marguerite d'Oingt* (Paris: Société d'Édition Les Belles Lettres, 1965). It is true that Grundmann could have consulted E. Philippon, *Œuvres de Marguerite d'Oyngt, prieure de Poleteins* (Lyon: N. Scheuring, 1877), and that his footnote was evidently not intended to be exhaustive. For English translation, see *The Writings of Margaret of Oingt: Medieval Prioress and Mystic*, trans. Renate Blumenfeld-Kosinski (Newburyport, MA: Focus, 1990).

12 Romana Guarnieri made her famous announcement in 1946, but at that time no copy of the French (Picard) *Mirror of Simples Souls* was yet known; Guarnieri's provisional edition appeared only in 1961, and a more widely available printing in 1965. Although Grundmann had access to the 1961 edition, it came too late to impact the second edition of *Religious Movements* published in that same year (his additions to the first edition of 1935 had largely been written by 1955). Grundmann did address Marguerite and the *Mirror* more fully in a 1965 essay, translated as "Heresy Interrogations in the Late Middle Ages as a Source-Critical Problem," in *Grundmann: Essays on Heresy, Inquisition, and Literacy*, 126–79. The standard edition of the *Mirror* is now Romana Guarnieri and Paul Verdeyen, *Marguerite Porete, Le mirouer des simples ames/Margaretae Porete Specvlvm simplicivm animarum*, CCCM 69 (Turnhout: Brepols, 1986) [but see important corrections in Geneviève Hasenohr, "Retour sur les caractères linguistiques du manuscrit de Chantilly et de ses ancêtres," in *Marguerite Porete et le Miroir des simples âmes: Perspectives historiques, philosophiques et littéraires*, ed. Sean L. Field, Robert E. Lerner, and Sylvain Piron (Paris: Vrin, 2013), 103–26]; for an English translation, see *Margaret Porete, The Mirror of Simple Souls*, trans. and intro. Edmund Colledge, J.C. Marler, and Judith Grant (Notre Dame, IN: University of Notre Dame Press, 1999).

13 Surely other works have not survived; Grundmann in fact postulated the loss of a whole generation of early efforts at vernacular religious writings by women in beguine circles in the Low Countries, specifically noting (in Grundmann, *Religious Movements*, 392n41) that a lost life of Julianne of Mont-Cornillon (d. 1258) written by Eva of Saint-Martin must have been in Walloon.

14 "France" is obviously a problematic term for the thirteenth century, when the boundaries of the French kingdom were quite different from those of the modern country. Similarly, "French" is imprecise in a linguistic landscape that included not only the north–south divide but also regional

dialects. Nevertheless, to avoid constant qualifiers, I refer to "France" for regions within the boundaries of the modern country; and I refer to literature in both langue d'oil (including Picard) and langue d'oc as "French."

15 A fine overview that includes all of these authors is Renate Blumenfeld-Kosinski, "Holy Women in France: A Survey," in *Medieval Holy Women in the Christian Tradition, c. 1100–c. 1500*, ed. Alastair Minnis and Rosalynn Voaden (Turnhout: Brepols, 2010), 241–65.

16 On Marguerite's authorship of the *Mirror*, see Sean L. Field, Robert E. Lerner, and Sylvain Piron, "A Return to the Evidence for Marguerite Porete's Authorship of the *Mirror of Simple Souls*," 43 (2017): 153–73. A wider range of issues can be surveyed in two essay collections: Field, Lerner, and Piron, eds., *Marguerite Porete et le* Miroir des simples âmes; and Wendy Terry and Robert Stauffer, eds., *A Companion to Marguerite Porete and the* Mirror of Simple Souls (Leiden: Brill, 2017).

17 Sean L. Field, *The Beguine, the Angel, and the Inquisitor: The Inquisitorial Trials of Marguerite Porete and Guiard of Cressonessart* (Notre Dame, IN: University of Notre Dame Press, 2012).

18 Jörg Voigt, "Margarete Porete als Vertreterin eines freigeistig-häretischen Beginentums? Das Verhältnis zwischen den Bischöfen von Cambrai und den Beginen nach dem Häresieprozess gegen Margarete Porete († 1310)," *Meister Eckhart Jahrbuch* ("Meister Eckhart und die Freiheit") 12 (2018): 31–54, at 49. Huanan Lu also noticed the archival document in question, independently of Voigt, and more fully analyses its importance. See Huanan Lu, "Le béguinage Ste-Élisabeth à Valenciennes (XIIIe-XIVe siècles)" (PhD diss., École des Hautes Études en Sciences Sociales, 2021), and her forthcoming article in *Revue du Nord*.

19 For instance, Bernard McGinn, *The Flowering of Mysticism: Men and Women in the New Mysticism – 1200–1350* (New York: Crossroad, 1998), chap. 5.

20 Grundmann, *Religious Movements*, chap. 7; Grundmann, "Heresy Interrogations."

21 John Van Engen, "Marguerite (Porete) of Hainaut and the Medieval Low Countries," in Field, Lerner, and Piron, eds., *Marguerite Porete et le* Miroir des simples âmes, 25–68, at 29; Sylvain Piron, "Marguerite, entre les béguines et les maîtres," in ibid., 69–101, at 95.

22 Sean L. Field, "The Master and Marguerite: Godfrey of Fontaines' Praise of the *Mirror of Simple Souls*," *Journal of Medieval History* 35 (2009): 136–49; important perspective added by Sylvain Piron, "Marguerite in Champagne," *Journal of Medieval Religious Cultures* 43 (2017): 135–56.

23 For indirect scholastic influences on Marguerite, see Piron, "Marguerite, entre les béguines et les maîtres." And for Marguerite's connections with the Puys (poetic competitions) at Valenciennes, see Barbara Newman,

Medieval Crossover: Reading the Secular against the Sacred (Notre Dame, IN: University of Notre Dame Press, 2013), 113–22.
24 Blumenfeld-Kosinski, trans., *Writings of Margaret of Oingt*, 15.
25 Blumenfeld-Kosinski, trans., *Writings of Margaret of Oingt*, 47.
26 For example, Anne E. Lester has shown that the "women's religious movement" also found expression in Cistercian forms in Champagne, blurring the line Grundmann had drawn between Cistercian and mendicant patterns. See Anne E. Lester, *Creating Cistercian Nuns: The Women's Religious Movement and Its Reform in Thirteenth-Century Champagne* (Ithaca: Cornell University Press, 2011).
27 Blumenfeld-Kosinski, trans., *Writings of Margaret of Oingt*, 2–6; Frans Hendrickx, "L'histoire infortune des moniales chartreuses du Dauphiné et du Sud de la France et leur vie religieuse," *Analecta cartusiana* 55 (1982): 167–80.
28 See remarks in Marie-Pascale Halary, "Quand l'unique change de langue: Littérature spirituelle et 'langue courtoise' chez Marguerite d'Oingt," in *L'Unique change de scène. Écritures spirituelles et discours amoureux (XIIe–XVIIe siècle)*, ed. Véronique Ferrer, Barbara Marczuk and Jean-René Valette (Paris: Classiques Garnier, 2016), 137–54, esp. 152–3.
29 However, in *"Litteratus-Illiteratus"* Grundmann made the wider point that across the Middle Ages elite women were more likely to be literate in Latin than were elite laymen.
30 I have made this point from a different perspective in "Agnes of Harcourt, Felipa of Porcelet, and Marguerite of Oingt: Women Writing about Women at the End of the Thirteenth Century," *Church History* 76 (2007): 298–329.
31 On Felipa, see also Madeleine Jeay, "La Vie de sainte Douceline par Felipa Porcelet: les mobiles d'une hagiographe du XIIIe siècle," in *Dix ans de recherche sur les femmes écrivains de l'ancien régime: Influences et confluences. Mélanges offerts à Hannah Fournier*, ed. Guy Poirier (Québec: Les Presses de l'Université de Laval, 2008), 17–36.
32 On Isabelle, see William Chester Jordan, "Isabelle of France and Religious Devotion at the Court of Louis IX," in *Capetian Women*, ed. Kathleen Nolan (New York: Palgrave, 2003), 209–23; Field, *Isabelle of France: Capetian Sanctity and Franciscan Identity in the Thirteenth Century* (Notre Dame, IN: University of Notre Dame Press, 2006); Anne-Hélène Allirot, *Filles de roy de France: Princesses royales, mémoire de saint Louis et conscience dynastique (de 1270 à la fin du XIVe siècle)* (Turnhout: Brepols, 2010), chap. 8; Field, *The Rules of Isabelle of France: An English Translation with Introductory Study* (St Bonaventure, NY: Franciscan Institute Publications, 2014); Dalarun et al., *Une princesse mineure*; and Field, *Courting Sanctity: Holy Women and the Capetians* (Ithaca: Cornell University Press, 2019), chap. 1.

33 Sean L. Field, "Agnes of Harcourt as Intellectual: New Evidence for the Composition and Circulation of the *Vie d'Isabelle de France*," in *Women Intellectuals and Leaders of the Middle Ages*, ed. Kathryn Kerby-Fulton, Katie Ann-Marie Bugyis, and John Van Engen (Cambridge: D.S. Brewer, 2020), 79–95.

34 Martin Aurell, *Une famille de la noblesse provençale au moyen âge: les Porcelet* (Avignon: Archives du Sud, 1986).

35 See chapter 3, where Douceline "wanted to write a rule" and "wanted to have the advice of the holy father [Hugh] in the writing of it." Garay and Jeay, *The Life of Saint Douceline*, 32.

36 On Douceline, see the bibliography in Field, "Women Writing About Women," 307n29; and in Sean L. Field, "On Being a Beguine in France, c. 1300," in *Labels and Libels: Naming Beguines in Northern Medieval Europe*, ed. Letha Böhringer, Jennifer Kolpacoff Deane, and Hildo van Engen (Turnout: Brepols, 2014), 117–33, at 124n23; as well as Sergi Sancho Fibla, "Li vida de Doucelina de Dinha, de Felipa Porcelleta. Imaginería, práticas devocionales y legitimacion de la vida beguina en el Mediterráneo," in *Voces de mujeres en la Edad Media: Entre Realidad y Ficción*, ed. Esther Corral Díaz (Berlin: De Gruyter, 2019), 296–308; Field, *Courting Sanctity*, chap. 2; and idem, "Douceline of Digne and Isabelle of France: Forming Female Franciscan Identities in Thirteenth-Century France," in *Franciscan Women: Female Identities and Religious Culture. Medieval and Beyond*, ed. Lezlie Knox and David B. Couturier (St Bonaventure, NY: Franciscan Institute Publications, 2020), 83–98.

37 On Jaucelin, see Pierre Peano, "Ministres provinciaux de Provence et Spirituels," *Cahiers de Fanjeaux* 10 (1975): 41–65, at 44. Stories he related to Felipa are incorporated into chapter 10 of the *Life of Douceline*. John of Parma also makes his strongest appearance in the same chapter.

38 See, for example, visions in chapter 14. This point is treated further in Field, "Douceline of Digne and Isabelle of France." See also Sancho Fibla, "Li vida de Doucelina de Dinha, de Felipa Porcelleta."

39 In addition to bibliography in Field, "Women Writing About Women," n36 and n39, see Nathalie Nabert, "Le vie de Béatrice d'Ornacieux par Marguerite d'Oingt, une biographie à l'ombre de la croix?" in *L'ordre des chartreux au XIIIe siècle*, ed. James Hogg, Alain Girard, and Daniel Le Blévec (Salzburg: Institut für Anglistik und Amerikanistik, Universität Salzburg, 2006), 127–35; Sara Ritchey, *Holy Matter: Changing Perceptions of the Material World in Late Medieval Christianity* (Ithaca: Cornell University Press, 2014), 159–64; Halary, "Quand l'unique change de langue"; and most recently Sergi Sancho Fibla, *Escribir y meditar. La obra de Marguerite d'Oingt, cartuja del siglo XIII* (Madrid: Siruela, 2018), and Victoria Cirlot, "Escrito en el corazó. Los casos de Angela de Folingo, Marguerite Porete

y Marguerite d'Oingt," in *Voces de mujeres en la Edad Media*, ed. Corral Díaz, 249–66.
40 Noticed by Caroline Walker Bynum, *Holy Feast and Holy Fast: The Religious Significance of Food to Medieval Women* (Berkeley: University of California Press, 1987), 130.
41 See in particular the miracles related in chapter 9.
42 Grundmann, *Religious Movements*, chapter 5.
43 Edited and translated in Field, *Writings of Agnes of Harcourt*.
44 On Louis's canonization, see M. Cecilia Gaposchkin, *The Making of Saint Louis: Kingship Sanctity, and Crusade in the Later Middle Ages* (Ithaca: Cornell University Press, 2008).
45 New analysis in Field, *Courting Sanctity*, chapter 4.
46 The inventory of 1305 is printed in *Histoire de la Ville et de tout le diocèse de Paris par l'abbé Lebeuf ... nouvelle édition annotée et continuée jusqu'à nos jours par Hippolyte Cocheris* (Paris: Durand, 1870), 4:263.
47 Marco Guida, *Una leggenda in cerca d'autore: la Vita di santa Chiara d'Assisi. Studio delle fonti e sinossi intertestuale* (Brussels: Société des Bolladistes, 2010). See also Jacques Dalarun, "Du procès de canonisation à la *Légende* latine de Claire d'Assisi," *Memini: Travaux et documents* 24 (2018), https://journals.openedition.org/memini/1090.
48 Martine Pagan, "Les légendes françaises de Claire d'Assise (XIIIe–XVIe siècle): I. Inventaire et classement des manuscrits," *Études franciscaines*, n.s. 7, no. 1 (2014): 5–35.
49 Martine Pagan, "Les légendes françaises de Claire d'Assise (XIIIe–XVIe siècle): II. Édition du plus ancien manuscrit de la version longue (BnF, fr. 2096)," *Études franciscaines*, n.s. 7, no. 2 (2014): 221–72. See also Pagan, "De la *Légende* latine aux *Vies* françaises de Claire d'Assise," *Memini: Travaux et documents* 24 (2018), https://journals.openedition.org/memini/1106.
50 To be more precise, Martine Pagan argues that a first translation (the now lost exemplar) was made at Longchamp and copied into both the BnF manuscript (B) and the AN manuscript (A). The translator (or translating team) then made corrections to B, which were used to correct A.
51 The manuscript and its version of the *Vie de sainte Clare* first received significant study in François Berriot, "Les manuscrits de l'abbaye de Longchamp aux Archives de France et la Vie de sainte Claire inédite (début XIVe s.)," *Archivum franciscanum historicum* 79 (1986): 329–58. Greater precision has now been provided in Fabien Guilloux, "*La regle et la vie des Sereurs meneurs encloses*: Une traduction en langue romane de la régle d'Isabelle de France (ca. 1315–1325)," *Archivum franciscanum historicum* 106 (2013): 5–39. Guilloux had already established that the copy and translation of the rule (fols. 1–46) and the French *Vie de Claire* (fols. 82–114) made up the original contents of the manuscript and existed

prior to 1325 (other sections of the manuscript were added in 1337–9). Guilloux, however, noted that the manuscript does not appear in the abbey's inventory of 1305, and hence suggested a date of 1305–25 for the oldest section, which includes the *Vie de sainte Claire*. But the inventory of 1305 is not nearly as detailed as that of 1325 and demonstrably does not include every book held at Longchamp. For instance, at least four books owned by Isabelle of France, and thus without doubt found at Longchamp from the time of her death in 1270, are not inventoried until 1325 (earlier unpublished inventories of 1287 and 1294 are even less detailed). Thus, one might cautiously assert that this volume's absence from the 1305 inventory does not preclude the early dating proposed by Martine Pagan.

52 Medieval inventories of Longchamp's libraries consistently signal a "twin" of AN LL 1601. Both manuscripts began with Latin and French copies of the Rule of the *Sorores minores inclusae*. But whereas AN LL 1601 followed with the *Vie de sainte Claire*, the now lost "twin" had the "Vie madame Isabel, nostre sainte mere." Since LL 1601 has now been re-dated to the reign of Agnes of Harcourt, it seems highly likely that the lost twin was produced at such an early date as well.

53 See Field, *Writings of Agnes of Harcourt*, 64–7.

54 Nicole Bériou, "Sainte Claire: Sermons dans l'espace français," in *Religion et communication: Un autre regard sur la prédication au Moyen Âge* (Geneva: Droz, 2018), 489–531.

55 Otto Gecser, "Lives of St. Elizabeth: Their Rewriting and Diffusion in the Thirteenth Century," *Analecta Bollandiana* 129 (2009): 49–107, at 52–5.

56 Jacques Monfrin, ed., *Joinville, Vie de saint Louis* (Paris: Garnier, 1995), par. 96.

57 Gecser, "Lives of St. Elizabeth," 69–71.

58 Gecser, "Lives of St. Elizabeth," 73–4.

59 Gecser, "Lives of St. Elizabeth," 97–8. An English translation is found in Brigitte Cazelles, *The Lady as Saint: A Collection of French Hagiographic Romances of the Thirteenth Century* (Philadelphia: University of Pennsylvania Press, 1991), 152–69.

60 See the brief note in Gecser, "Lives of St. Elizabeth," 98n206. Excerpts from two of the poems are translated in Cazelles, *Lady as Saint*, 169–71.

61 Levente Seláf, "Párhuzamos életrajzok: Szent Erzsébet és Isabelle de France legendái," in *Árpád-házi Szent Erzsébet kultusza a 13–16. Századdan*, ed. Dávid Falvay (Budapest: Magyarok Nagyasszonya Ferences Rendtartomány, 2009), 141–50 (with French résumé). I thank the author for kindly summarizing his findings for me in 2009 and for further updating me on the status of his forthcoming critical edition of the text.

62 The *Jonas* database housed by the IRHT lists twelve manuscripts, of which the earliest appear to be BnF ms. fr. 13496, fols. 155rb–172vb (incomplete),

and Bibliothèque Mazarine ms. 1716, fols. 296–311, both from the late thirteenth century. See Anne-Françoise Leurquin and Marie-Laure Savoye, notice for "Vie de sainte Elisabeth de Hongrie, anonyme" in the database Jonas-IRHT/CNRS, http://jonas.irht.cnrs.fr/oeuvre/2150.

63 For now, see his preparatory article, "Le Modèle absolu de la princesse charitable. La première légende vernaculaire de sainte Élisabeth de Hongrie et sa réception," *Le Moyen Âge* 124 (2018): 371–96. Extracts of the text can also be consulted in the modern French translation in André Vauchez and Armelle Le Huërou, eds., *Élisabeth de Hongrie: documents et sources historiques* (Paris: Éditions Franciscaines, 2017), 391–6.

64 The book is labelled "La Vie de sainte Isabelle et de sainte Antoine abbé en un livre en français," but the "sainte Isabelle" in question here cannot be Isabelle of France (always called "madame" in these inventories); the names Elisabeth/Isabel/Isabelle/Yzabeau were considered interchangeable at the time. The inventories are AN L 1027, nos. 5 and 9. This point was established by Jacques Dalarun in *Une princesse mineure*, 276n1.

65 The description by Pierre Perrier c. 1699 is discussed in Dalarun et al., *Une princesse mineure*, at 276n1. For the text, see Sean L. Field, "Pierre Perrier's 1699 *Vie de sainte Isabelle de France*: Precious Evidence from an Unpublished Preface," *Franciscan Studies* 73 (2015): 215–47.

66 Prof. Seláf kindly indicated to me in personal correspondence that his ongoing work suggests a *terminus post quem* of 1243, and that the French prose *Vie* preceded (and was used by) Rutebeuf's rhyming life.

67 This point is amplified in Field, "Agnes of Harcourt as Intellectual."

68 Giovanni Boccali, ed., *Legenda latina sanctae Clarae virginis assisiensis* (Santa Maria degli Angeli: Edizioni Porziuncola, 2001).

69 Pagan, "Les légendes françaises de Claire d'Assise (XIIIe–XVIe siècle): II. Édition du plus ancien manuscrit de la version longue (BnF, fr. 2096)."

70 Field, *Writings of Agnes of Harcourt*.

71 Albert Huyskens, *Der sog. Libellus de dictis quatuor ancillarum s. Elisabeth confectus* (Kempten und München: Verlag der Jos. Kösel'schen Buchhandlung, 1911), 9, 1.

8 "More Useful in the Salvation of Others": Beguines, *Religio*, and the *Cura Mulierum* at the Early Sorbonne

TANYA STABLER MILLER

Sometime in the early 1270s, the secular master and founder of the Sorbonne, Robert of Sorbon (d. 1274), preached a sermon at the royal beguinage of Paris.[1] The sermon took as its theme Matthew 13:44: "The kingdom of heaven is like a treasure hidden in a field, which a man having found, hid it, and for joy thereof goes, and sells all that he has, and buys that field."[2] Expanding this theme, Robert asserted that the royal beguinage, a conspicuous feature of the urban landscape by the 1270s, represented the field in which God hid his treasure.[3] In this association between the beguinage and the field referenced in Matthew, Robert suggested that the term referred to both a residence for beguines – the location of his sermon – and a "beguine" way of life distinguished by its sociability, visibility, and position *outside* the regular orders. Rather than living lives of contemplation and solitude, beguines laboured tirelessly to effect the conversion of others, whether they lived in the world or "in religion."[4] Yet, although the beguinage was "planted with the seed of the Word of God and cultivated by contrition and confession," few believed that God would hide His treasure in such an obvious, seemingly unworthy, place.[5] As for the beguine status itself, it was not contingent upon entry into a formal institution; while not everyone could be a monk or a canon, anyone could (and should) be like the beguines.[6] Despite, or perhaps because of, this accessibility, the beguine life unfairly attracted disdain. The beguinage's lack of an abbot and approved rule – the markers of the religious *ordo* – exposed the women to "the dew of divine grace" and the "snow and hail of heavenly admonitions," but it also drew "the reproaches of neighbours."[7] Rather than downplay the beguines' unregulated life or attempt to recast the beguines as traditional nuns, Robert emphasized the women's praiseworthy, yet unfairly maligned, public-facing piety, which he credited with bringing much-needed (although often unappreciated) spiritual support to their neighbours.[8]

The Paris beguinage, founded by Robert's friend King Louis IX between 1254 and 1264, regularly hosted university masters, including several of Robert's students.[9] Far from eschewing the pastoral care of women, Robert believed that women were "more inclined to good than men" and could be useful models of piety for the broader laity and particularly for his own students, whom the Sorbonne aimed to prepare for pastoral service in the parishes.[10] Indeed, Robert preached his sermon comparing the beguinage to an open field at the feast of the relics of St. Stephen, a saint who, as Robert reminded his audience, had been particularly dedicated to the pastoral care of "holy and religious women."[11] In this sermon and others, Robert proclaimed his dedication to the *cura mulierum*, a commitment that he advocated for his students in sermons, collations, and pastoral manuals.[12] Secular clerics trained at the Sorbonne evidently absorbed and valued Robert's teachings regarding beguines. Godfrey of Fontaines, known for his later support of Marguerite Porete, attended and copied several of Robert's sermons, including the sermon comparing the beguinage to a field, into his pastoral manuscripts.[13] Sermon collections and preaching notes compiled by Robert's students, moreover, reflect a deep conviction that the attainment of pastoral objectives depended on the fervent support of beguines.[14]

Robert's observations about the beguine life offer an opportunity to revisit Herbert Grundmann's influential arguments about the contours and trajectories of the "women's religious movement" as well as the prominent place of beguines within that movement. Breaking from traditional approaches to medieval religious history, which tended to examine individual orders or "heresies," Grundmann identified the common impulses – poverty and preaching – behind the various religious communities (some labelled as heretical and some as orthodox) that emerged in the twelfth and thirteenth centuries. Beguine scholarship owes much to Grundmann's groundbreaking synthesis. Prior to the publication of *Religious Movements in the Middle Ages*, beguines and their communities were generally treated as primarily local phenomena, with most publications devoted to the histories of individual beguinages and little indication of the beguines' place within a broader context of religious enthusiasm and reform. For Grundmann, the beguines offered a particularly salient example of the vibrancy of the women's religious movement and – in light of the beguines' condemnation at the Council of Vienne (1311–12) – proof of his central argument that "all religious movements of the Middle Ages achieved realization either in religious orders or in heretical sects."[15]

The beguines' emergence and descent, according to Grundmann's narrative, was primarily the result of a failure of pastoral care. Official legislation and narratives of male opposition to the *cura mulierum* had important explanatory power for Grundmann. Drawing on prescriptive legislation and papal pronouncements, Grundmann argued that the female members of the religious movement were too numerous for existing religious orders to accommodate. Consequently, women only won access to a recognized religious order under "special circumstances" and after great resistance from male members and even greater persistence from women.[16] After the religious orders, old and new, refused or limited the incorporation of nuns, women who wished to pursue lives of chastity and prayer were left to form their own associations, eventually joining beguine communities.[17] According to this framework, beguines existed out of grudging accommodation of failed nuns who "never represented a planned form of religious life … the result of the women's religious movement insofar as it did not find reception into the new orders."[18] For Grundmann, the lack of guidance and protection from the male religious orders effectively left beguines "subject to the temptation of heretical obsession."[19]

Recent scholarship has nuanced and expanded these arguments in productive ways. Pushing beyond the rhetoric of orders and affiliations, historians of women's religious orders have offered important correctives to the narrative of male opposition to female incorporation. Returning to the archives, historians have exposed a significant contradiction between official positions and local attitudes, shedding new light on women's religious communities and their socio-spiritual significance on the ground.[20] Turning to beguines, scholars have begun, over the last two decades in particular, to evaluate these communities on their own terms as a particular but regionally variable phenomenon defined largely by a visible commitment to prayer and active service in the world.[21] Local studies have demonstrated, moreover, that beguine communities developed pastoral relationships with monastic and mendicant orders, as well as local parish clergy, often with little apparent difficulty or controversy.[22] Nevertheless, the beguines' status "athwart" the canonical categories of "religious" and "secular," particularly in light of the anti-beguine decrees issued at the Council of Vienne, continues to obscure important clerical support for the beguines' "in-betweenness" and the integral role they played in local religious life, health care, as well as the broader pastoral mission of the thirteenth-century church.[23]

Robert of Sorbon's favourable observations about beguine communities, formed over the course of a long career focused on education and pastoral care, reflect Robert's rejection of his contemporaries' privileging of monastic models. His response sheds invaluable light on diverse interpretations of the *vita apostolica* and approaches to pastoral care within a context of religious reform and renewal in medieval Paris. Focused primarily on the emergence of new religious orders and sects, Grundmann frequently presented the secular clergy as fundamentally hostile to piety "outside the cloister" and as particularly opposed to local beguine communities.[24] Yet, the pastoral care of beguines was an integral part of the Sorbonne's early mission of training theology students to go back out to the parishes to minister effectively to the laity.[25] Indeed, Robert's sermons and pastoral writings, which survive in hundreds of copies and inspired several student-authored versions, urged pastoral engagement with beguines, while emphasizing rather than concealing the beguines' "in-between" status. Against the backdrop of current debates over the university-trained master's roles and responsibilities towards the broader laity, Robert praised the beguines' earnest, public-facing pursuit of *religio* in the broad sense, asserted the secular clergy's pastoral and professional importance, and rejected the notion that a truly religious life could only be realized within a religious order.

The *Mulieres Religiosae* and the Pastoral Revolution

Born around 1200 in the Ardennes, Robert of Sorbon witnessed firsthand some of the most important institutional milestones at the University of Paris. His career coincided with the Great Dispersion (1229–31), *Parens Scientiarum* (1231), and the Secular-Mendicant conflict (1252–7). He was a student of Guiard of Laon (d. 1248), a colleague of William of Saint-Amour (d. 1272), teacher of Godfrey of Fontaines (d. c. 1309), and close friend of King Louis IX (d. 1270).[26] Inspired by the pastoral revolution of the early thirteenth century, Robert sought ways to implement the goals of Lateran IV, use the resources of the parishes to put learned men into leadership positions in the church, and ultimately bring effective pastoral care to those parishes.[27] These concerns animated the preaching of university reformers throughout the 1230s, when Robert was a student pursuing his degree in theology in Paris. As several scholars have noted, this generation of university clerics – the *parens scientiarum* generation – played a pivotal role in the institutional development of the University of Paris.[28] Less frequently acknowledged, however, are the close relationships secular clerics of the *parens scientiarum* generation forged with lay religious women. Hagiographic evidence, in particular, exposes extensive religious networks spanning the region from Paris to the Low Countries.[29]

Hundreds of sermons and collations delivered to and copied by Robert's students reflect his deep preoccupation with the interrelated issues of the clergy's morality and the spiritual guidance of the laity. In many of these sermons, Robert referenced beguines as important to these goals.[30] Praising the beguines' assertive efforts to bring their neighbours to confess and hear sermons, in spite of the hostility these efforts sometimes provoked, Robert presented these women not only as exemplars of moral behaviour but also as important partners in the clergy's efforts to convert the laity. Much like James of Vitry (d. 1240) before him, Robert recognized that the clergy alone could not implement the goals of Lateran IV.[31] Barred from preaching themselves, lay religious women could serve as effective, but pliable, exemplars of piety capable of validating the clergy's teachings and vindicating its broader goals.[32]

Pastoral concerns and the spiritual care of women were an important part of Robert's training at the University of Paris, where he studied under the secular theologian Guiard of Laon.[33] Guiard's career, while attracting relatively little attention from medieval scholars, was representative of the atmosphere of pastoral engagement at the University of Paris in the early thirteenth century. After an exceptionally lengthy regency in Paris (twelve years) and a brief stint as chancellor (in 1236), Guiard became Bishop of Cambrai, where he promoted pastoral reform, preached widely, and endorsed the beguine movement in his diocese.[34] Robert, most likely due to his mentor's influence, became canon of Cambrai in 1238.

Guiard's diocese was at the centre of a region particularly associated with the "women's religious movement" to which Grundmann drew attention. As a university master, Guiard sought out women who had gained reputations as *mulieres religiosae*. He inquired after the health of the holy laywoman Margaret of Ypres (1216–1227) when he heard she was ill and miraculously conversed with the Cistercian nun Lutgard of Aywières (1182–1246). The latter was considered miraculous because, as Thomas of Cantimpré relates, Guiard "was as completely ignorant of the Flemish language as Lutgarde was of French."[35] Along with several prominent Paris-trained theologians, including Hugh of Saint-Cher, Jacques Pantaleon, and Philip the Chancellor, Guiard participated in the evaluation of Juliana of Mont-Cornillon's (1193–1258) liturgy for her proposed Corpus Christi feast.[36] Throughout Juliana's struggles to gain approval for the feast, Guiard, known for his influential contributions to Eucharistic theology, was a steadfast supporter.[37]

As a master in Paris, Guiard preached to and about women's religious communities in both Paris and Cambrai.[38] As bishop, he was instrumental in the development of beguine communities in his bishopric. Early in his episcopate, he confirmed the foundation of the beguinages of Valenciennes, Vilvoorde, and Cambrai.[39] The Cambrai beguinage was located in Cantimpré, a southwest suburb of the city. It was the oldest beguinage of Northern France, having been recognized in 1233. In 1238, one of Guiard's first acts as bishop was to approve the community and their brand new hospital, confirming the enclosure and its possessions and forbidding any harm to the women.[40] Guiard also appointed the mistress and charged the abbey of Cantimpré with the responsibility of providing pastoral care to the women, who "burn with desire for the spiritual food of the altar."[41] As Robert later related in a sermon to university clerics in Paris, when Bishop Guiard died, the beguines of Cambrai processed barefoot – in spite of the cold – to the parish church of St. Sauveur to ask God to give them a bishop as good to them as Guiard had been.[42]

When Robert took up his position as canon of Cambrai in 1238, he must have been familiar with the stories of these holy women, which circulated throughout the region in sermons, exempla, and spiritual treatises.[43] Moreover, like his mentor Guiard, Robert embraced the idea of women as useful partners to the clergy. During his many years as canon, Robert frequented the beguinage of Cantimpré and later shared his observations about the community in sermons and collations at the Sorbonne. For Robert, the beguines of Cantimpré offered a wealth of pastoral lessons. In a collation given to his students sometime in the early 1260s on the passage *Si linguis hominum loquar* (1 Corinthians 13:1: "Though I speak with the tongues of men and of angels, and have not charity, I am become as sounding brass, or a tinkling cymbal"), Robert expounded on several definitions of *caritas* by various church fathers, humorously comparing these learned opinions with that of the people of Paris, who think that "Caritas" refers to a pig by that name belonging to Saint-Antoine.[44] Ultimately, Robert settled on the definition supplied by the mistress of the beguinage at Cantimpré, recalling a "certain master" (*quidam magister*) in the city of Cambrai who preached a sermon before the mistress of the beguinage (*magistra beguinarum*). Preaching before the mistress, the master in Robert's story – and this master may have been Robert himself – asserted that the man in whom *caritas* (or love) was rightly ordered could not help but conduct himself in a worthy manner. To this, the beguine mistress interjected, "But where, Lord, does it say in sacred scripture that caritas is disordered? For if caritas is defective and deviates from righteousness, then it is not caritas."[45] Indeed, the mistress's arguments about rightly ordered *caritas* is the driving theme of the lesson and a favourite refrain in Robert's sermons about beguines.

In a sermon preached sometime in the mid-1260s, Robert began with a familiar synodal theme: the secular clergy's duty to remain present in the parish. Reflecting contemporary concerns about absenteeism and debates about the pastoral responsibilities of the university-trained theologian, Robert launched into an elaborate comparison of the university master and the simple parish priest, asserting that the latter did more good in the parishes by virtue of being present. Significantly, Robert followed this comparison with the argument that women could be even *more* useful in the salvation of others than either the learned master or the simple priest, through their good deeds, good examples, and good words. By way of illustration, Robert told his audience about a beguine who travelled to Paris from Cambrai to acquire a copy of William Peraldus's Summa of Vices and Virtues.[46] The beguine brought the summa to a diocesan synod, where parish clergy gathered to receive instruction from the bishop. There, she tirelessly asked each priest if he might have some time before celebrating Mass to make a copy of the summa. The choice of text, like the venue in which the beguine made her case, highlights the pastoral orientation of the beguine's work. Peraldus's summa was the latest penitential compendium of vices and virtues, and it was fast becoming one of the most popular pastoral resources in France.[47] That the beguine chose it and brought it to a synod – a gathering that aimed to correct and instruct the clergy of the diocese – suggests that Robert thought the idea of a beguine supporting local efforts to enact pastoral reform would resonate with his audience. The beguine represents a link between Paris – where she acquired the summa – and the parishes. Moreover, she was effective, since it was through her efforts that the summa circulated throughout the region.

Pastoral Care and the Early Sorbonne

The sermon about the beguine from Cambrai touched on one of the central problems of pastoral care, namely its inadequacy. Drawing on the Gospel of John 10:11–16 ("I am the good shepherd. The good shepherd gives his life for the sheep"), a standard theme in synodal sermons, Robert reminded his audience that the good shepherd is the pastor who is present in his church.[48] Robert himself was obliged to finance his studies in Paris with his canonry in Cambrai, a practice to which he personally objected.[49] Church councils and papal privileges throughout the early thirteenth century sought to give promising young men the opportunity to study in cathedral schools and especially universities, with the monetary support of an ecclesiastical benefice.[50] Yet, the practice of utilizing the funds from a benefice in another region to pursue study in Paris, while widely recognized as a necessity, left the secular clergy open to charges of absenteeism and pluralism. These criticisms came particularly from their mendicant rivals, with whom the secular clergy became embroiled in a bitter conflict over university positions and privileges in the mid-1250s.[51]

Although the secular clergy initially welcomed the Dominicans (1217) and Franciscans (1219), over time the mendicants demonstrated a consistent unwillingness to join with their fellow masters to protect the university's interests.[52] The secular clergy viewed themselves as the founders of the University of Paris and the true successors to Christ's apostles. Yet, the mendicant orders challenged this narrative by claiming to fulfil the apostolic ideal more authentically than the secular clergy.[53] Although benefitting from university protections and privileges, the mendicants frequently invoked older monastic discourses critical of the university, which accused secular clerics of being worldly, ambitious, career-minded, and indifferent to the moral formation of their students. Finally, as preaching orders, the mendicants had developed an effective system for training scholars, soon outcompeting secular clerics in the race for resources, students, faculty positions, and alms of the laity.[54] By 1254, when King Louis IX returned from the crusade, the conflict remained unresolved.

Officially a canon at Cambrai, Robert retained ties in Paris, taking up administrative tasks on behalf of Louis IX and eventually becoming a "clerk of the king."[55] While we do not know when Robert became close to Louis IX, he came to exert a profound influence on the king's religious sensibilities.[56] Spiritually, Louis wanted nothing less than to "convert the world," an aspiration he shared with Robert of Sorbon.[57] Louis's pious foundations and patronage *before* embarking on the crusade are in line with traditional royal expressions of piety; after 1254, he supported communities that exemplified the conversionary impulses that shaped the remainder of his reign.[58] Between 1254 and 1261, Louis established no fewer than eight mendicant houses in the city, gave generously to the Filles-Dieu, a house for reformed prostitutes, and founded the beguinage on the city's Right Bank for women living religious lives in the world.[59]

Louis also played a significant role in the foundation of the Sorbonne. The king initiated the first property transactions on the rue Coupe-Gueule in 1254, buying up property from laypeople and ceding it to Robert to create an institution for housing and training secular clerics studying theology.[60] Prior to the Sorbonne, there was no accommodation – materially, socially, or intellectually – for secular clerics seeking to pursue theological study, which was a long course of study intensified by economic worry and emotional stress. Moreover, even as reform-minded masters sought to develop a self-image or collective identity as preachers and scholars, there existed no standard means of professionalizing secular clerics or supporting them financially.

Robert's experiences as a student and later a master form an important backdrop for his signature project. Having completed his studies around 1249, Robert continued to serve as canon in Cambrai – rather than teach in Paris – until 1257, when he became canon of Notre Dame. In the intervening years, Robert travelled between Cambrai and Paris, building a network of clerical and secular supporters in both cities and preaching sermons to parishioners, students, and, significantly, communities of religious women. Between 1254 and 1258, Robert engaged this network, piecing together with stunning energy and efficiency adjacent properties on the rue Coupe-Gueule on Paris's Left Bank – for what would eventually become the Sorbonne.[61] Indeed, the Sorbonne was an effort to resolve the inherent tensions between the need to finance theological training through parish income and the need to be resident in one's own parish to provide pastoral care. Virtuous living and responsibility for the reception of one's teaching, as well as the stability and continuation of Robert's pastoral objectives, depended on the creation of institutions. Building on a familiar concept – the hospice for poor clerics – Robert drew on his interactions with canons and beguine communities in Cambrai and later in Paris to create an institution that would build community among its members in addition to having stability and permanence.[62]

Religio and *Ordo* in the Sermons of Robert of Sorbon

Robert's aim for his college was to promote the interrelated virtues of collegiality, morality, and effective preaching, which he enforced through the college's statutes and reinforced via sermons and collations given at the college. These sermons, which exist mainly in *reportationes* made by Robert's students, point to the explicit connections their teacher made between the intellectual and moral formation of the secular clergy and collaboration with lay religious women. In the lesson Robert delivered to the college's very first members on varied learned and popular understandings of *caritas*, Robert explicitly linked beguines to the religious lives of his students, noting that without love, religious orders are of little worth. Harkening back to his days in Cambrai, Robert not only presented the beguine *magistra* as a worthy and constructive interlocutor, as we have seen, he also advocated a form of religious community outside of the religious orders, an alternative conception of religious community that was central to his vision for a new college for secular clerics and his hopes for the reform of Christendom more broadly.

A perceptive critic of his time, Robert rejected the drive to draw stark distinctions between secular and regular, between orders and lay communities, which had the negative consequence of condemning the faithful while praising the proud and hypocritical. In his sermons to students, Robert was particularly keen to defend the adoption of a religious life outside the regular orders, asserting that such a life had a clear scriptural foundation. Drawing on Corinthians 13:4 ("Love is patient, love is kind"), Robert articulated a powerful rejection of the notion that virtue was to be found only in the religious orders. Indeed, superior discipline and virtue is found in the *ordo caritatis*, which follows two rules. The first rule is patience (*Caritas patiens est*), a virtue rare even among monks, who could hardly endure the corrections of their superiors.[63] Referencing the apostles who, like "good students" (*boni scolares*), patiently bore the derision of others for their zeal in preaching the Word of God, Robert encouraged his students to honour those who insulted them, for their persecutors were their teachers in patience (*magister in patientia*).[64]

Robert's exposition on the virtue of patience is illustrative of his efforts to lay out a scriptural foundation for the secular clergy at a time of intense rivalry with the mendicant orders, who, in the eyes of Robert's secular colleague William of Saint-Amour, represented an existential threat to the secular clergy. While William famously drew upon Scripture in his *Tractatus de periculis* to level an apocalyptic attack on the mendicant orders' right to exist, Robert preached sermons that provided a scriptural foundation for the pursuit of *religio* in the world.[65] In stark contrast to William's insistence on priestly office and church hierarchy, which he believed undercut the friars' claims to preaching authority, Robert emphasized behaviour over formal entry into an approved order.[66]

Significantly, Robert's advocacy for an *ordo caritatis* led him once again back to beguines. In a lengthy discussion of the second rule (*caritas est benigna*, or "love is kind," which Robert rendered *caritas begina est*), Robert alluded to the criticisms that lay religious women and secular clerics alike faced when they adopted a visibly religious life without entering a recognized religious order.[67] Just as the beguines persisted in their efforts to bring others to lives of virtue, so too must the secular clergy. Indeed, both had a responsibility to bring others to God and to expand the ranks. In his sermons on the *ordo caritatis*, Robert implicitly questioned the value of the cloistered life with such observations as "a burning coal left alone will soon extinguish," noting that when placed among dead coals, it spreads its fire to others.[68] Secular clerics must, like the beguines, ignore those who wish to extinguish the fire of virtue through ridicule and work to convert others.[69]

One of the many criticisms of beguines was that their way of life was merely a short-lived trend, as evidenced by the apparent unfamiliarity of the label itself, which medieval observers perceived as evidence of its novelty and thus doubtful orthodoxy.[70] In his influential *vita* of Mary of Oignies, for example, James of Vitry alluded to the "new names" that the *mulieres religiosae* were called by those sceptical of the ostentatiously pious behaviour exhibited by these women.[71] Robert addressed these anxieties about novelty and the resultant name-calling, declaring that the beguine life was, in fact, nothing new.[72] In the sermon Robert preached at the beguinage of Paris, he reminded his audience of the spiritual merits of humiliating names while conveying his long history of warm relations with beguine communities by relating an exemplum he had heard from his mentor, Guiard of Cambrai, who "did much to promote the beguine life."[73] In Guiard's exemplum, merchants hide expensive cloth beneath coarse, cheap coverings, just as Christ hides his treasure (the beguines) by giving them a contemptuous name (the much-mocked label "beguine").[74]

The label *beguina*, so Robert was fond of claiming, derived from the Latin *bene igne* or a well-kindled fire that transforms other materials into itself. In the same way, beguines, through the fire of their holy example, turn others into beguines.[75] On the heels of this praise of the beguine, Robert neatly linked morality to preaching and pastoral care – and thus back to the secular clergy – by asserting tha preachers ought to make their hearts pure so that, like the disciples, they might be worthy of receiving the fire of the Holy Spirit.[76] According to Robert, the two things that make the heart pure – listening to sermons and going to confession – are the very activities that distinguish beguines from all others. The beguines' hearts, Robert claimed, are purer, and consequently they are more worthy to receive the fire of the Holy Spirit.[77]

Given Grundmann's characterization of men like Robert's colleague William of Saint-Amour as representative of an "older hierarchical order" that opposed "all new forms of religious life," Robert's praise of piety outside of religious orders is significant.[78] Indeed, Robert's sermons expressed a rather incisive critique of how the adoption of a monastic rule smoothed over individual failings, providing a certain smug comfort for its members. Drawing on the secular critiques of the monastic life, but with a characteristically light touch, Robert noted that too many passed over the Order of Love as inferior to papally recognized orders. In the sermon Robert preached at the beguinage in the early 1270s, he pointedly observed that no matter how debauched a life a man might have led previously, as soon as he enters a religious order he is universally admired for his adoption of the regular life. Those who consistently led lives of virtue in the world, without a dramatic life-turn, were objects of ridicule.[79] Yet, in Robert's view, the ideals of his age – specifically, social admiration for the dramatic conversion and contempt for the consistent, steady striving of the pastorally minded secular cleric – were misguided. Anyone with passing familiarity with the Gospels ought to understand that those who endured criticism were more authentically religious than those who received honour and praise for their entry into the regular orders.[80] Thus, Robert subtly criticized the religious orders' claims to superiority, asserting that it was best to judge others by the way they behaved in the world and the impact they had on their fellow Christians.

In several sermons, Robert made clear allusions to the apparent preference for the religious orders, a preference that troubled the secular clergy. While the public hated the "good seculars" and called them contemptuous names such as "beguin, papalard, and hypocrite," they universally honoured the Dominicans, Franciscans, and Cistercians.[81] Yet, Robert assured his audience that these victims of ridicule were blessed since it was through social humiliation and vilification that God tests those who love him. According to Robert, the good secular clerics suffered two types of persecution: mockery when people saw them suffer hardships and then slander.[82] In emphasizing slander, Robert referred to what he viewed as the tendency among the religious orders to lump the good seculars with the bad, a tendency with which beguines were also painfully familiar. Using the plight of religious laywomen to pursue a political point, Robert lamented that the slander against the good seculars ultimately hurt their chances to advance to high ecclesiastical offices. Specifically, Robert accused the unnamed detractors – perhaps the friars to whom the seculars were losing offices and students – of deliberately impeding the success of good seculars out of fear that they might surpass them in rank and learning.[83]

However honourable the secular clergy might have been, Robert recognized that institutions protected both individual virtue and corporate reputation, while offering important material and practical support. Moreover, they promised permanence. Although Robert, as we have seen, insisted that one might be "religious" without a rule and disciplined without a superior, he also knew that his community, like that of the beguines, needed order, statutes, and institutional permanence. The secular-mendicant conflict raised the stakes for Robert and his secular colleagues. Friars such as Thomas Aquinas, for instance, claimed that permanent vows were the essence of *religio* even as he and his fellow friars preached and lived active lives outside the cloister, an argument aimed at undercutting the secular clergy's claims to be the true heirs of the apostles.[84] Without overtly criticizing the friars, Robert encouraged his students and secular colleagues to think more broadly about what it meant to live as religious in the world. In this effort, Robert could draw on the writings of pastoral theologians before him (such as Peter the Chanter and James of Vitry) while pointing to the living examples of the beguines of Paris, whose founder – Robert's friend King Louis IX – also famously lived a religious life outside the cloister.

The Sorbonne and the *Cura beguinarum*

In Paris, Robert cultivated ties with the beguinage of Paris and possibly secured from its mistress permission for his students to attend sermons preached in the beguinage chapel. Robert's students copied these sermons into their personal manuscripts, later donating them to the library of the Sorbonne.[85] As these efforts to preserve Robert's teachings suggest, Robert's views on beguines were not lost on his students, many of whom were tied to dioceses with large populations of lay religious women. Significantly, this orientation was built into the college from its very inception. Robert's earlier career in Cambrai positioned him within a network that included canons from Amiens, Liège, and of course Cambrai. Reaching out to these clerics as he made the first steps to establish his college, Robert gathered a cadre of benefactors who oriented the college towards these northern regions. The secular master and canon of Amiens, Gerard of Abbeville, was an important early benefactor of the college, donating his substantial personal library (more than 300 books) to the college upon his death in 1272. In 1264, Gauthier Carne, a secular cleric from Amiens, donated 300 pounds with the stipulation that the money be used for bourses to fund scholars from Amiens.[86] Likewise, in 1266, the archdeacon of Tournai, Nicholas of Tournai, gave 500 pounds for the support of five students chosen from Tournai.[87] After Nicholas's death, the right to name the five students went to his successors as bishop of Tournai, ensuring enduring links between the Sorbonne and this region. Michel de Waringhien, bishop of Tournai until his death in 1291, further tightened this bond with an annuity for the support of students from his diocese. In 1271, Jean de Rua, canon of Amiens, likewise left to the Sorbonne an annuity to fund scholarships for two masters, presumably from Amiens.[88] These early donations ensured that approximately half – if not more – of the students studying at the Sorbonne hailed from Picardy and the Franco-Flemish borderland cities to the north, leaving an indelible mark on the college.

This orientation, practically speaking, meant that many Sorbonne scholars would later take up positions in regions where they would find themselves providing pastoral care to beguine communities, a fact that might explain the clear emphasis on beguines and the beguine life in sermon collections once housed in the medieval library of the Sorbonne.[89] Clerics affiliated with the Sorbonne donated dozens of manuscripts to the college, many of which feature sermons and devotional literature to and about beguines. For instance, Arnoul Bescochier, a Sorbonne scholar from Amiens, preserved Robert's sermons and incorporated them into his own sermons. In a sermon he preached at the beguinage of Paris in 1273, Arnoul echoed Robert's assertions that the term "beguine" was derived from the Latin word *"benigna"* (or kind).[90] The beguines, according to Arnoul, were those who took the misfortunes of others upon themselves by virtue of compassion while sharing the good with others by virtue of *caritas*.[91]

A more concrete example of pastoral relationships between the Sorbonne and laywomen's religious communities is the career of Bernard Pailly, a student of the Sorbonne in the late thirteenth century. Bernard was markedly devoted to the spiritual care of women. After his training at the Sorbonne, Bernard served as parish priest at the church of Saint-Eustache, located on the western edge of Paris's Right Bank. The church was affiliated with a small hospital, over which Bernard presided as governor. The extant tax registers of Philip the Fair (spanning the years 1292–1313) show that the streets surrounding Bernard's church were a magnet for lay religious women.[92]

These beguine households may have developed organically as a consequence of the hospital, or there might have been some connection with Bernard's position as parish priest. Whatever the connection, the two streets that converged at the entrance of the church of Saint-Eustache were dominated by small households of lay religious women. These women, at least for a time, received pastoral care from Sorbonne scholars. Bernard's successor at Saint-Eustache, Jean de Vallibus, was eventually elected provisor of the Sorbonne, serving from 1304 until 1315.[93]

Bernard Pailly's connections with the Sorbonne and Paris's lay religious communities most likely recommended him to the wealthy draper Stephen Haudry and his wife Jeanne. Naming Bernard as an executor of their estates, Stephen and Jeanne Haudry also named Bernard as the governor of their new community of *bonnes femmes*, or as they were more popularly known, the Haudriettes.[94] Although a considerably smaller community, the hospital of the Haudriettes was modelled on the beguinage of Paris. Its residents wore humble garb, prayed

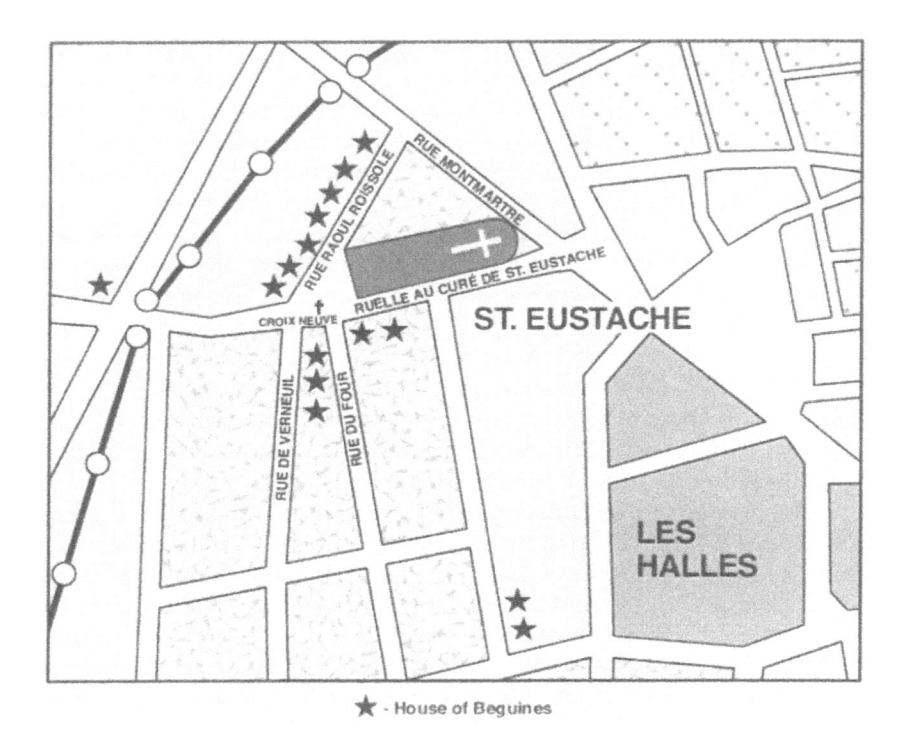

Figure 8.1. Parish of Saint-Eustache, Paris, France, ca. 1250 (Tanya Stabler Miller)

together, and supported themselves on their own labour or income. As governor, Bernard tirelessly acquired annuities and properties to support the house and its residents. In addition to leaving several manuscripts to the Sorbonne upon his death, Bernard, along with his brother William (who, significantly, went by the nickname "le beguin"), gave a large endowment to the community, enabling it to expand from thirty to thirty-two women.[95]

The career of Raoul of Chateauroux (d. 1286) is another striking example of a Sorbonne student initiating pastoral relationships with beguine communities. Raoul was a frequent presence at the city's beguinage during the 1272–3 liturgical year when he embarked on a scholarly and pastoral mission to copy and assemble a collection of sermons preached in parish churches all over Paris. In fact, Raoul's collection shows that he made a concerted effort to go to the beguinage as frequently as possible, making his way from the Sorbonne to the beguinage almost on a weekly basis.[96] Raoul also obtained sermons from the mistress of the beguinage herself, incorporating six selections from her teachings into his sermon collection.[97]

It is worth considering in this context why Raoul chose these excerpts from the mistress and how he obtained them. Raoul's collection was compiled from *reportationes* and other pastoral sources. As a frequent visitor to the beguinage chapel, Raoul might have heard the mistress deliver these sermons. If so, notes from the entire sermon may have existed at one time, as is the case in a few other excerpts in Raoul's sermon collections. Another possibility is that Raoul obtained a copy from another source, perhaps the mistress herself. In any case, Raoul's inclusion of sermons preached by a beguine alongside the writings of Parisian masters, preachers, and church fathers stands as compelling evidence of the esteem in which she – and her teachings – were held.[98]

The themes under which Raoul placed these excerpts have significant connections with Robert's thought as well as the broader pedagogical and pastoral mission of the Sorbonne, suggesting that Raoul chose the excerpts with care. The first reference to the *magistra beginarum* appears under the theme of *Amor*. As Barbara Newman and others have pointed out, beguines were thought to be experts on the subject as well as receptive listeners to teachings that drew on courtly love themes.[99] In fact, much of the material collected under the rubric *Amor* had some connection with beguines and vernacular spirituality.[100] The collection of authoritative material on *Amor* begins with an early version of an Old French rhyme known as the *Amour* verses, a popular and widely circulated poem on the Passion.[101] The mistress's contribution, also a love poem, names the "four ways that the Love of God is acquired."[102] The mistress's poem is then followed by a citation from none other than Bishop Guiard of Laon on reciprocal love between God and the soul, and an excerpt from Sorbonne scholar Arnoul Bescochier on the four ways love is "proved."[103] Thus the *Distinctiones* in the Sorbonne manuscript suggest that interactions with lay religious women, similarly described in hagiographical texts and in Robert's sermons, were theologically and pastorally fruitful.

Throughout the late thirteenth century, the Sorbonne's commitment and connection to the pastoral care of women was part of a broader reform program initiated by the college's founder and woven into the community's core mission to produce effective preachers. Rather than a burden to be avoided or grudgingly accepted, the pastoral care of women was an integral part of the Sorbonne's early mission of training theology students to go back out to the parishes to minister effectively to the laity. Indeed, Robert infused his teachings with appeals to his students to make the pastoral care of beguines a priority. They listened. As one of Robert's students later wrote in his preaching notes, "no one is a good preacher or confessor unless he supports the beguinage."[104]

An examination of the Sorbonne founder's writings to and about beguines demonstrates that the pastoral impulses often attributed to the "new" orders, particularly the mendicants, were shared by their secular rivals. Robert's sermons and pastoral writings, which exist in multiple copies and were stored in the medieval library of the Sorbonne, engaged with current debates over teaching authority, pastoral care, and the secular clergy's roles and responsibilities in the instruction of the broader laity, revealing that the boundaries between the university and the public were in fact always quite permeable. Yet, Robert's participation in the religious movements of his time is obscured by the Sorbonne's own foundation narrative, which ironically neglects the pastoral priorities of its actual founder and the vibrant socio-spiritual networks of which he was a part. Recognizing their common spiritual impulses and priorities, Robert ascribed monastic ideals to beguines and secular clerics, thereby calling into question the special status of the regulars while defending the earnest pursuit of *religio* in the sense of a life turn. The connections the early Sorbonnists made with lay religious women shed important light, then, on the extent to which university scholars took seriously their pastoral obligations as well as the process by which the Sorbonne coalesced as an institution. Finally, these relationships provide compelling evidence for one of the most important and salient points in Grundmann's synthesis: the important role women played in medieval religious culture.

NOTES

1 On the beguinage of Paris, see Tanya Stabler Miller, *The Beguines of Medieval Paris: Gender, Patronage, and Spiritual Authority* (Philadelphia: University of Pennsylvania Press, 2014). On the founding of the Sorbonne, see Palémon Glorieux, *Aux origines de la Sorbonne*, vol. 1, *Robert de Sorbon, l'homme, le collège, les documents* (Paris: J. Vrin, 1965–6), and more recently Denis Gabriel, *La 'Maison des pauvres maîtres' de Robert de Sorbon: Les débuts de la Sorbonne (1254–1274)* (Paris: Classiques Garnier, 2014).

2 Nicole Bériou has edited this sermon, which was copied by the secular cleric and theologian Godfrey of Fontaines into one of his pastoral manuscripts (BnF Lat. 16507.) See Nicole Bériou, "Robert de Sorbon: Le prud'homme et le béguin," *Comptes-rendus de l'Académie des inscriptions et belles-lettres* (1994): Appendix I, 486–95. For Robert's own copy of the sermon (BnF Lat. 16471, fols. 99va–105ra), see Bériou, "Robert de Sorbon,"

Appendix II, 496–508. All translations, unless otherwise indicated, are my own.

3 Situated against the walls of Philip Augustus on the city's Right Bank in the bustling parish of Saint-Paul, the court beguinage housed perhaps 400 women. Miller, *The Beguines of Medieval Paris*, 14–15.

4 "Et specialiter uidetur iste thesaurus esse absconditus in beguinagio, quia inter alios ipsi et ipse habent feruens desiderium ad Deum et feruentiores sunt in conuersione peccatorum quam ceteri, unde plus laborant ad salutem et conuersionem peccatorum quam alii, ubicumque fuerunt illi beguini vel beguine, siue in seculo siue in religione." BnF Lat. 16507, fol. 322b, ed. Bériou, "Le prud'homme," 490.

5 "Sed campus Christi de quo facit mentionem euuangelium colitur per contritionem et confessionem, seminatur autem semine uerbi diuini." BnF Lat. 16507, fol. 322a, ed. Bériou, "Le prud'homme," 489.

6 In Robert's version, he asserts "In agro enim communiter et ex omni parte et de facili sine obstaculo patet introitus, quia quilibet in quocumque statu sit potest esse beguinus, immo nullus recipitur in beguinagio qui alios ad hoc non attrahit pro posse suo, sed non quilibet potest esse monachus, presbiter uel canonicus." BnF Lat. 16471, fol. 99vb ed. Bériou, "Le prud'homme," 496–7.

7 In the margins of his personal copy of a sermon in which he likens the beguinage to a field in which God has hidden the treasure of the Kingdom of Heaven, Robert glossed the term *beguine*, noting "ager est sub celo sine medio et sine regimine et defensione, alioquin non reciperet rorem uel pluuiam diuine gratie nec niuem et grandinem celestium amonitionum uel obiurgationum proximorum, et sic est de beguinagio." BnF Lat. 16471 fol. 100ra, ed. Bériou, "Le prud'homme," 497.

8 "Sed qui sunt in beguinagio ponuntur in publiquo ut succurrant aliis spiritualiter." BnF Lat. 16507 fols. 322a–322b. ed. Bériou, "Le prud'homme," 490.

9 On preaching at the Paris beguinage, see Nicole Bériou, "La prédication au béguinage de Paris pendant l'année liturgique 1272–1273," *Recherches augustiniennes* 13 (1978): 105–229, and Miller, *The Beguines of Medieval Paris*, 81–102.

10 "Vnde videntur in hoc proniores quam viri ad bonum." Bruges, Bibliotheek Grootseminarie, 447b, ff. 64va–vb, quoted in F.N.M. Dieckstra, "Robert de Sorbon on Men, Women and Marriage. The Testimony of his De Matrimonio and Other Works," in *People and Texts: Relationships in Medieval Literature*, ed. Thea Summerfield, Keith Busby, and Erik Kooper (Leiden: Brill, 2007), 73.

11 "Mulieres sancte et religiose" BnF Lat. 16507, fol. 322b, ed. Bériou, "Le prud'homme," 488.

12 Sermons and collations delivered at the Sorbonne demonstrate that the college was not just a residence for secular clerics. Like the mendicant *studia*, it functioned as a place of learning. See Claire Angotti, "Presence d'un enseignement au sein du college de Sorbonne: collationes, disputationes, lectiones (XIII–XV siecle) Bilan et hypotheses," in *Le système d'enseignement occidental (xie–xve siècle)* Cahiers de Recherches Médiévales 18, ed. T. Kouamé (Paris: Honoré Champion Éditeur 2009), 89–111.

13 See note 2 above. Another Sorbonne student – Jean of Essômes – also possessed a copy. BnF Lat. 16496, fols. 48v–50v. On the manuscripts Jean of Essômes donated to the Sorbonne, see Madeleine Mabille, "Les manuscits de Jean d'Essômes conservés à la Bibliothèque Nationale de Paris," in *Bibliothèque de l'École des Chartes* 130 (1972): 231–4.

14 One of Robert's students, the secular theologian Pierre de Limoges, donated 120 of his manuscripts to the Sorbonne upon his death in 1306. One was a pastoral miscellany containing sermons and exempla of Jacques de Vitry and other materials for preachers, including three folios of preaching notes titled "De benignis." The notes, in addition to explaining the importance of beguines to the secular clergy's pastoral mission, are interspersed with quotations from Robert's best-known pastoral treatises, including *Cum repetes* and *De tribus dietis*. BnF Lat. 15972, fols. 174r–176v. On Robert's pastoral treatises, see Glorieux, *Aux origines de la Sorbonne*. On the redactions and paraphrases made by Robert's students of their master's work, see. Frans N. M. Diekstra, "'Die drie dachvaerden' and Robert de Sorbon's 'De tribus dietis': An Edition of the Middle Dutch Text together with its Latin Source," in *Mediaevistik* 12 (1999): 257–330, at 259.

15 Herbert Grundmann, *Religious Movements in the Middle Ages* (Notre Dame, IN: University of Notre Dame Press, 1995), 1.

16 "[O]nly special circumstances made it possible for religious women's communities to win recognition as autonomous convents and win access to an order." Grundmann, *Religious Movements*, 139.

17 This pattern of rejection is, for Grundmann, the context for the beguine movement: "When the women's houses of the Premonstratensians and the Cistercians were no longer able or willing to absorb into their own ranks an ever-increasing women's religious movement, and women could no longer endure the secular clergy's blind, hateful treatment of evangelical piety practiced outside the cloister as if it were a heretical menace, the beguines emerged as a new form of religious life, beseeching the curia for protection." See Grundmann, *Religious Movements*, 80.

18 Grundmann, *Religious Movements*, 139

19 Grundmann, *Religious Movements*, 134.

20 Anne E. Lester, *Creating Cistercian Nuns: The Women's Religious Movement and its Reform in Thirteenth-Century Champagne* (Ithaca: Cornell University

Press, 2011), 9–11; Constance H. Berman, "Were There Twelfth-Century Cistercian Nuns?" *Church History* 68 (1999): 824–64; and more recently, Constance H. Berman, *The White Nuns: Cistercian Abbeys for Women in Medieval France* (Philadelphia: University of Pennsylvania Press, 2018). Several recent studies on medieval nuns and devout laywomen's communities have noted that evidence for institutional affiliation or incorporation is often misleading or even "fictitious." See Maiju Lehmijoki-Gardner, "Writing Religious Rules as an Interactive Process: Dominican Penitent Women and the Making of Their 'Regula,'" *Speculum* 79 (2004): 660–87, and Alison More, *Fictive Orders and Feminine Religious Identities, 1200–1600* (Oxford: Oxford University Press, 2018). Indeed, as Sherri Franks Johnson has shown, the focus on female incorporation or affiliation is not productive for understanding women's religious communities. See Sherri Franks Johnson, *Monastic Women and Religious Orders in Late Medieval Bologna* (Cambridge: Cambridge University Press, 2014).

21 Walter Simons, *Beguine Communities in the Medieval Low Countries, 1200–1565* (Philadelphia: University of Pennsylvania Press, 2001); Jennifer K. Deane, "Beguines Reconsidered: Historiographical Problems and New Directions," *Monastic Matrix* (2008), Commentaria 3461, http://monasticmatrix.org/commentaria/article.php?textId=3461. See also the essays in Letha Böhringer, Jennifer Kolpacoff Deane, and Hildo van Engen, eds., *Labels and Libels: Naming Beguines in Northern Medieval Europe* (Turnhout: Brepols, 2014); for the early modern period, see the essays in Alison Weber, ed., *Devout Laywomen in the Early Modern World* (London: Routledge, 2016).

22 Jennifer K. Deane, "*Geistliche Schwestern*: The Pastoral Care of Lay Religious Women in Wurzburg," in *Partners in Spirit: Women, Men and Religious Life in Germany, 1100–1500*, ed. Fiona Griffith and Julie Hotchin (Turnhout: Brepols, 2013), 237–70; Miller, *The Beguines of Medieval Paris*.

23 Jennifer K. Deane, "From Case Studies to Comparative Models: Würzburg Beguines and the Vienne Decrees," in *Labels and Libels: Naming Beguines in Northern Medieval Europe*, ed. Letha Böhringer, Jennifer Kolpacoff Deane, and Hildo van Engen (Turnhout: Brepols, 2014), 53–82. On beguines and health care work, see Sara Ritchey, *Acts of Care: Recovering Women in Late Medieval Health* (Ithaca: Cornell University Press, 2021).

24 Grundmann, *Religious Movements*, 80.

25 Curiously, Robert of Sorbon features in Grundmann's account of what he perceives as an abrupt shift in medieval attitudes towards beguines that occurred sometime in the mid-1250s. Pairing Robert's praise of beguines with those of James of Vitry (whose positive assessment of the beguine life actually dated two generations before Robert's), Grundmann claimed that the beguines then quite "suddenly ... began to appear to

contemporaries in a different light." Grundmann's spokesperson for this abrupt change, William of Saint-Amour, was, however, a contemporary and colleague of Robert's, and their assessments of beguines were expressed around the same time. More curiously, Grundmann, while acknowledging that William's main target was the mendicant orders, takes William's accusations at face value, asserting that William's "accusations indicate changes in the beguines themselves, changes which were moving contemporaries less prejudiced than the Parisian theologian to condemn beguines." Grundmann, *Religious Movements*, 141.

26 Although there have been a number of valuable studies of Robert's life and career, they are mainly focused on his signature project, the Sorbonne. See, in particular, the studies cited in note 1 above. William Chester Jordan discusses Robert's influence on Louis IX in *Men at the Center: Redemptive Governance under Louis IX* (Central European University Press, 2012), 1–36.

27 On the pastoral reformers at the University of Paris, see John W. Baldwin, *Masters, Princes, and Merchants: The Social Views of Peter the Chanter and His Circle* (Princeton, NJ: Princeton University Press, 1970); Nicole Bériou, *L'avènement des maitres de la Parole: La prédication a Paris au XIIIe siècle* (Paris: Institut d'etudes augustiniennes, 1998), I:1–10; Stephen C. Ferruolo, *The Origins of the University: The Schools of Paris and Their Critics, 1100–1215* (Stanford: Stanford University Press,1985).

28 On the *Parens scientiarum* generation, see Spencer Young, *Scholarly Community at the Early University of Paris: Theologians, Education and Society, 1215–1248* (Cambridge: Cambridge University Press, 2014).

29 Walter Simons, *Cities of Ladies: Beguine Communities in the Medieval Low Countries, 1200–1565* (Philadelphia: University of Pennsylvania Press, 2001), esp. chap. 1, and Anneke B. Mulder-Bakker, *Lives of the Anchoresses: The Rise of the Urban Recluse in Medieval Europe* (Philadelphia: University of Pennsylvania Press, 2005). While not the focus of either study, both note ties between Paris-trained theologians and the holy women of the southern Low Countries.

30 Miller, *The Beguines of Medieval Paris*, esp. chap. 4.

31 Jessalynn Bird, "The Religious's Role in a Post-Fourth-Lateran World: James of Vitry's *Sermones ad Status* and *Historia Occidentalis*," in *Medieval Monastic Preaching*, ed. Carolyn Muessig (Leiden: Brill, 1998), 209–29.

32 On the ways in which women could serve as useful allies in the church's efforts to stamp out heresy and promote the sacramental system articulated in the Fourth Lateran Council, see Dyan Elliott, *Proving Woman: Female Spirituality and Inquisitional Culture in the Later Middle Ages* (Princeton: Princeton University Press, 2004); Jo Ann McNamara, "Rhetoric of Orthodoxy: Clerical Authority and Female Innovation in the Struggle with Heresy," in *Maps of Flesh and Light: The Religious Experience of Medieval Women Mystics*, ed. Ulrike Wiethaus (Syracuse:

Syracuse University Press, 1993); André Vauchez, "Prosélytisme et action antihérétique en milieu féminin au XIIIe siècle: la Vie de Marie d'Oignies (d. 1213) par James of Vitry," *Problèmes d'Histoire du Christianisme* 17 (1987): 95–110; Kasper Elm has also noted instances in which secular and regular clerics sought to deploy devout laypeople as an auxiliary army in their efforts to influence the laity. See Kaspar Elm, "*Vita regularis sine regula.* Bedeutung, Rechtsstellung und Selbstverständnis des Mittelalterlichen und Frühneuzeitlichen Semireligiosentums," in *Häresie und Vorzeitige Reformation im Spätmittelalter*, ed. František Šmahel (Munich: Oldenbourg Verlag, 1998), 239–73.

33 On Guiard's life and career, see P.C. Boeren, *La vie et les oeuvres de Guiard de Laon, 1170 env-1248* (The Hague: M. Nijhoff, 1956).

34 On Guiard's support for beguine communities in his diocese, see Boeren, *La vie et les oeuvres de Guiard de Laon*, 81–7. On Guiard's career in Paris, see Young, *Scholarly Community at the University of Paris*, 85–6.

35 Barbara Newman, ed., *Thomas of Cantimpré: The Collected Saints Lives—Abbot John of Cantimpré, Christina the Astonishing, Margaret of Ypres, and Lutgard of Aywières*, trans. Margot H. King and Barbara Newman (Turnhout: Brepols, 2008), 175 and 176 (Life of Margaret of Ypres) and 268 (Life of Lutgard of Aywières).

36 See Mulder-Bakker, *Lives of the Anchoresses*, 90; and Barbara R. Walters, Vincent Corrigan, and Peter T. Ricketts, eds., *The Feast of Corpus Christi* (University Park: Pennsylvania State University Press, 2006), 7–10.

37 For Guiard's sermons on the Eucharist (*On the Twelve Fruits of the Sacrament*), see Boeren, *La vie et les oeuvres de Guiard de Laon*, 320–32. On Guiard's Eucharistic theology and the women's religious movement in the southern Low Countries, see Wybren Scheepsma, *The Limbourg Sermons: Preaching in the Medieval Low Countries at the Turn of the Fourteenth Century*, trans. David F. Johnson (Leiden: Brill, 2008), and, more recently, Sara Ritchey, "Saints' Lives as Efficacious Texts: Cistercian Monks, Religious Women, and Curative Reading, c. 1250–1330," *Speculum* 92 (2017): 1101–43.

38 Guiard frequently preached at Saint-Antoine-des-Champs, the Cistercian convent outside Paris. P. C. Boeren, *La vie et les oeuvres de Guiard de Laon*, 40–4.

39 See note 34 above.

40 Archives Départementales du Nord (henceforth ADN), 3 G 538, fol. 51–2.

41 ADN 161 H 1 fols. 10–11.

42 BnF Lat. 15955, fol. 68va. Significantly, this manuscript contains 39 sermons preached by Guiard, including an abbreviated version of the Twelve Fruits of the Eucharist (shortened to eight fruits, see fol. 135v–136r).

43 Suzan Folkerts, "The Manuscript Transmission of the *Vita Mariae Oigniacensis* in the Later Middle Ages," in Anneke B. Mulder-Bakker, ed., *Mary of Oignies: Mother of Salvation* (Turnhout: Brepols, 2006), 221–41.

44 "Multi sunt qui nesciunt quid est caritas, sed credunt, quando audiunt loqui de ea, quod sit porcellus Sancti Antonii, qui appellatur Charitatz." BnF Lat. 15971, fol. 72ra.

45 "In villa de Cambrai predicabat quidam magister coram magistram beginaram, dicens quod si homo haberet rectam caritatem, omnia bona faceret. Et ipsa dicit: 'Domine, ubi invenisti vos in divina pagina caritatem claudam? Quia, si clauda est et deviat a rectitudine, iam non est caritas." BnF Lat. 15971, fol. 72v.

46 "Exemplum de begina quae venit Parisius emere Summam de viciis et virtutibus; quae cum moraretur in quadam civitate ad quam sepe veniebant presbiteri subditi illi civitati, accommodebat eis per quaternos huiusmodi Summam, primo querendo si erant ociosi, quando missam celebraverant, ita quod per totam regionem illam multiplicavit eam." BnF Lat. 15955, fol. 307va–307vb.

47 Siegfried Wenzel, "The Continuing Life of William Peraldus's Summa vitiorum," in *Ad litteram: Authoritative Texts and Their Medieval Readers*, ed. Mark D. Jordan and Kent Emery Jr. (Notre Dame, IN: University of Notre Dame Press, 1992), 135–63.

48 "Pastor debet esse presens in ecclesia sue et personaliter residere." BnF Lat. 15955, fol. 307va.

49 As Robert succinctly put it in another one of his many sermons on the topic: "The students whose studies in Paris were financed by benefices elsewhere were like physicians who took their pay, but then left the patient, in order to come to the university to learn how to practice medicine in the first place." BnF Lat. 15971, fol. 198.

50 Frank Pegues, "Ecclesiastical Provisions for the Support of Students in the Thirteenth Century," *Church History* 26 (1957): 307–18.

51 On this conflict, see Michel-Marie Dufeil, *Guillaume de Saint-Amour et la polémique universitaire parisienne, 1250–1259* (Paris: J. Picard, 1972), and "Le roi Louis dans la querelle des mendiants et des séculiers," *Septième centenaire de la mort de Saint Louis: Actes des colloques de Royaument et de Paris (21–27 mai 1970)* (Paris: Les Belles Lettres, 1976), 281–9.

52 In 1229, the mendicant orders refused to take part in a strike called in response to violent attacks on the university's members. Hastings Rashdall, *The Universities of Europe in the Middle Ages*, ed. F. M. Powicke and A. B. Emden, 2nd ed., 3 vols. (Oxford: Oxford University Press, 1936), 1:372–7. In the spring of 1253, the mendicants again refused to participate in another university strike in response to a brutal assault on four students, one of whom was killed. Dufeil, *Guillaume de Saint-Amour*, 5.

53 Decima L. Douie, *The Conflict Between the Seculars and the Mendicants at the University of Paris in the Thirteenth Century* (London: Blackfriars, 1954), and Penn R. Szittya, *The Antifraternal Tradition in Medieval Literature* (Princeton,

NJ: Princeton University Press, 1986), 44–6. See also Yves M.-J. Congar, "Aspects ecclésiologiques de la querelle entre mendiants et séculiers dans la seconde moitié du xiiie siècle et le début du xive siècle," *Archives d'histoire doctrinale et littéraire du Moyen Âge* 28 (1961): 35–151.

54 David D'Avray, *Preaching of the Friars: Sermons Diffused from Paris before 1300* (Oxford: Oxford University Press, 1985), 50.

55 Glorieux, *Aux origines de la Sorbonne*, vol. II, *Le Cartulaire de la Sorbonne* (Paris: J. Vrin, 1965–6), no. 167.

56 Miller, *The Beguines of Medieval Paris*, 22–5. See also, Jordan, *Men at the Center*, 11–36.

57 William Chester Jordan, *Apple of His Eye: Converts from Islam in the Reign of Louis IX* (Princeton, NJ: Princeton University Press, 2019), 1. In addition to (attempting to) ban prostitution, gambling, blaspheming, and dueling, Louis put increasing pressure on Jews to convert and even brought Muslim converts to France to ensure the success of their significant life turn.

58 Meredith Cohen, *The Sainte-Chapelle and the Construction of Sacral Monarchy* (Cambridge: Cambridge University Press, 2014).

59 On the Filles-Dieu, see Keiko Nowacka, "Persecution, Marginalization, or Tolerance: Prostitutes in Thirteenth-Century Parisian Society," in *Difference and Identity in Francia and Medieval France*, ed. Meredith Cohen and Justine Firnhaber-Baker (Farnham, UK: Ashgate, 2010), 175–96. For a comprehensive overview of Louis's religious foundations in Paris, see Cohen, *Sainte-Chapelle*, esp. 171–94.

60 Glorieux, *Le Cartulaire de la Sorbonne*, esp. nos. 167 and 231.

61 For a useful analysis of these property transactions, see Denis Gabriel, *La 'Maison des pauvres maîtres' de Robert de Sorbon: Les débuts de la Sorbonne (1254–1274)* (Paris: Classiques Garnier, 2014).

62 While there existed residences for arts students – such as the Dix-huit, Saint-Thomas-du-Louvre, Bons-Enfants de Saint-Honoré, and Bons-Enfants de Saint-Victor – the Sorbonne was the first college to provide accommodation to graduate students pursuing doctorates in theology. On the colleges for arts students, see Astrik L. Gabriel, "Motivation of the Founders of Medieval Colleges," in *Garlandia: Studies in the History of the Medieval University* (Notre Dame, IN: University of Notre Dame Press, 1969), 211–23. As a secular canon, Robert was familiar with efforts to "regularize" the secular clergy. On this point, see Caroline Walker Bynum, *Docere Verbo et Exemplo: An Aspect of Twelfth-Century Spirituality* (Missoula, MT: Scholars Press, 1979), 50–4, and Bird, "The Religious's Role in a Post-Fourth-Lateran World," 220.

63 "Scias ergo quod primus punctus est quod caritas patiens est vt innuit apostolus quam non habent multi. Etiam claustrales remurmurantes correctioni abbatis uel superioris sui. Tales qui sic impacienter sustinent

correctionem non sunt in ordine prefate caritatis." BnF Lat. 16507, fol. 237ra.

64 "Hoc non faciebant sancti apostoli. Erant enim boni scolares immo de contumeliis illatis sibi gaudebant." BnF Lat. 16507, fol. 237rb. For a thorough summary of Robert's sermons urging his students to endure, and even embrace, ridicule for the sake of moral improvement (including his sermons mentioning beguines), see Frans N. M. Diekstra, "The Pursuit of Virtue and the Fear of Derision: Robert de Sorbon (1201–1274) on Beguinage and False Shame," *Mediaevistik* 22 (2009): 117–240.

65 On William's antifraternal attacks, see Szittya, *The Antifraternal Tradition*, chapter 1.

66 See Tanya Stabler Miller "'Love Is Beguine': Labelling Lay Religiosity in Thirteenth-Century Paris," in *Labels and Libels: Naming Beguines in Northern Medieval Europe*, ed. Letha Böhringer, Jennifer K. Deane, and Hildo van Engen (Turnhout: Brepols, 2014), 135–50.

67 "Secundus caritatis punctus est quod caritas est benigna siue beguina." BnF Lat. 16507, fol. 236vb.

68 "Carbo enim mortuus inter multos uiuos cito accenditur uiuus autem solus relictus cito moritur. Carbo etiam bene accensus multos mortuos carbones reaccendit et uiuificat." BnF Lat. 16507, fol. 236vb.

69 "Sic peccator unus inter mutos bonos cito conuertitur et etiam unus solus bonus ut prelatus uel socius uel beghina bonis exortationibus uel operibus multos peccatores aliquando conuertit et tepidos in amore Dei accendit." BnF Lat. 16507, fol. 236vb.

70 Letha Böhringer, Jennifer K. Deane, and Hildo van Engen, eds., *Labels and Libels: Naming Beguines in Northern Medieval Europe* (Turnhout: Brepols, 2014).

71 James of Vitry, *The Life of Mary of Oignies*, trans. Margot King, in *Mary of Oignies: Mother of Salvation*, ed. Anneke Mulder-Bakker (Turnhout: Brepols, 2006), 43.

72 "[B]eguina cum tamen quidam dicant quod beguinagium nichil sit et quod novitates sunt. Falsum dicunt. Caritas enim benigna est siue beguina, et omnes qui sunt in ordine caritatis…. Unde beguinagium non est nomen novum." BnF Lat. 16507, fol. 237rb.

73 "Episcopus Guiardi, qui multum sustinebat beguinagium, ponebat tale exemplum." BnF Lat. 16507, fol. 423ra, ed. Bériou, "Le prud'homme," 492.

74 Bériou, "Le prud'homme," 492–3.

75 "Item caritas benigna est id est bene ignita. Ignis combustibile in suam naturam convertit. Sic beguinus alios exemplo sui beguinos facit pro posse suo." BnF Lat. 16507, fol. 237vb.

76 "Unde Spiritus sanctus in linguis igneis apparuit cuius rationem reddit Gregorius: quia spiritus sanctus quos replet eloquentes et ardentes facit." BnF Lat. 16507, fol. 237vb.

77 "Inuenit corda discipulorum receptacula munda. Duo autem faciunt cor mundum que duo sunt in veris beguinis scilicet auditus uerbi Dei.... Item confessio facit cor mundum.... Et tales qui libenter audiunt uerba Dei et frequentant confessionem uocantur beguini. Et ideo corda habent mundiora, sic digniores sunt igne sancti spiritus." BnF Lat. 16507, fols. 237vb–238ra.

78 Grundmann, *Religious Movements*, 141.

79 "Vnde quantumcumque fuerit homo honoratus si intret beguinagium et fiat beguinus, uilipenditur plus ceteris. Non sic autem est in aliis ordinibus, immo conuerso quantumcumque homo fuerit peruersus et diffamatus, si intret religionem dicetur quod est probus homo et multum honorabitur, et ista patent ad sensum vnicuique. Nunc autem magni sapientes huius mundi bene uident quod homo sit sancte uite et quod honoretur, sed quod sit sancte uite et probus homo et quod uilipendatur et illudatur nequaquam possunt uidere." BnF Lat. 16507, fol. 423ra., ed. Bériou, "Le prud'homme," 491. One wonders if Robert was thinking here of the dramatic conversion performance of John of St. Giles, who in 1230 paused in the midst of preaching a sermon on the virtues of evangelical poverty to request a Dominican habit. John's dramatic entry into the Dominican Order was not only noteworthy in its staging but also in its timing and long-term effects for the University of Paris.

80 "Inter omnes ordines seu religiones plus despicitur beguinagium uel uilipenditur; nunc autem sic est quod homo sancte uite siue probus homo est honorandus non despiciendus, etiam eius religio est honoranda, et quia illi et ille qui sunt in beguinagio sunt sancte et honeste ut uidetur, et desiderant suam salutem et aliorum ut videtur, ideo beguinagium est honorandum et omnes qui sunt in illo. Et tamen,ut iam prius dictum est, plus ceteris uilipenduntur." BnF Lat. 16507, fol. 423ra, ed. Bériou, "Le prud'homme," 491.

81 "Nullum certe nomen bonum et odiosum est tantum aut eiectum sicut nomen bonorum secularium. Non enim eiectum est nomen Predicatorum aut Minorum aut Cisterciencium sed ualde honorabile solum autem nomen secularium bonorum eiectum; alii beghino, alii papelardos, alii ypocritas eos uocant et ideo promissione Domini uidento beati." BnF Lat. 16507, fol. 286vb.

82 BnF Lat. 16507, fol. 287ra.

83 "Opere secuntur bonos seculares impediendo eorum promotionem in ecclesiis prebendis uel dignitatibus." BnF Lat. 16507, fol. 287ra.

84 John Van Engen, "Friar Johannes Nyder on Laypeople Living as Religious in the World," in *Vita Religiosa im Mittelatter: Festschrift für Kaspar Elm zum 70. Geburtstag*, ed. Franz J. Felten, Nikolas Jaspert, and Stephanie Haarländer (Berlin: Duncker and Humbolt, 1999), 583–615.

85 Miller, *The Beguines of Medieval Paris*, 81–4.
86 Gabriel, *La 'Maison des pauvres maîtres,'* 191–2.
87 Ibid., 192.
88 Ibid., 193.
89 See Miller, *The Beguines of Medieval Paris*, 81–102.
90 "Unde ego nescirem proprius vocare beguinam quam unctam. Begina enim idem est quod begnigna et begnigna idem est quod uncta." BnF Lat. 16482, fol. 119vb.
91 "[U]t quando una sancta anima est ita bene uncta gratia Spiritus sancti que dicitur pietas, habet unum affectionem ad auxiliandum et subveniendum indigentiam omnium indigentium si posset. Appropriat enim sibi mala aliena per compassionem, et sua bona communicat aliis per caritatem." BnF Lat. 16482, fol. 119vb.
92 I established the existence of this cluster by tracing individual households of beguines through the seven extant tax rolls, three of which remain unpublished. The invaluable database available at the Institut de Recherche et d'Histoire des Textes (IRHT), while essential for tracking occupations and personal identifiers, cannot show clusters by location, necessitating a close analysis of the manuscripts themselves. See Miller, *The Beguines of Medieval Paris*, chap. 3.
93 Glorieux, *Aux origines de la Sorbonne*, vol. 2, 253.
94 Michael Connally, "Les 'Bonnes Femmes' de Paris: Des communautes religieuses dans une societe urbaine du bas Moyen Age" (doctoral thesis, University of Lyon II, 2003). Connally did not mention the earlier part of Bernard Pailly's career at the Sorbonne. Indeed, I did not make the connection myself until after publishing *The Beguines of Medieval Paris*.
95 Connally, "Les 'Bonnes Femmes' de Paris," chap. 3, http://theses.univ-lyon2.fr/documents/lyon2/2003/connaly_m#p=0&a=top.
96 Utilizing the invaluable appendices in Beriou, *L'avènement des maitres de la Parole: La predication a Paris au XIIIe siecle* (Paris: Institut d'etudes augustiniennes, 1998), it is possible to establish the frequency of Raoul's visits to the Paris beguinage.
97 BnF Lat. 16482. On this manuscript, see Beriou, *L'avènement des maitres de la Parole*.
98 Nicole Bériou was the first to note the significance of this inclusion, observing that the excerpts themselves are artefacts of the mistress's teachings. They are more than this, however. As part of a distinctions collection, the beguines' teachings became a *citable* authority intended for incorporation into the sermons of university clerics.
99 Barbara Newman, *Medieval Crossover: Reading the Secular Against the Sacred* (Notre Dame, IN: University of Notre Dame Press, 2013), 122–44.
100 Miller, *The Beguines of Medieval Paris*, 121–2.

101 On this poem, see Sylvia Huot, "Popular Piety and Devotional Literature: An Old French Rhyme About the Passion and Its Textual History," *Romania* 115 (1997): 451–94.
102 "Quatuor modis accusatur amor dei. Deus enim amando accusatur, in amando custoditur, et servat illos qui ipsum amant, et sufficit eis qui eum amant. Len aquert deu en amant, si l'en gadde un en se ke l'en eyme, et si garde sun amant, et suffit a cheus ke leyment." BnF Lat. 16482, fol. 3vb.
103 BnF Lat. 16482, fol. 3vb.
104 "Notam que nullus est bonum predicator vel confessor nisi velit sustinere beginagium," BnF Lat. 15972, fol. 174r.

9 Between Charity and Controversy: The Grey Sisters, Liminality, and the Religious Life

ALISON MORE

Throughout Christian history, women have been called to religious life outside of traditional institutional structures. As their forms of life were shaped by local needs and conventions, there was little uniformity among these movements. Most scholarship regards them as newer versions of established orders, but this is only part of the story. These women moved beyond traditional categories and created new socially shaped forms of devotion. Churchmen responsible for their *cura* had no rubric under which these women could be discussed. Consequently, an inconsistent program of labels with no real meaning came into existence. Women who occupied this liminal space were known by such names as beguines, tertiaries, penitents, *monache di casa*, and any number of other variations.[1] None of these terms had a clear legal definition, and all were applied arbitrarily. Both medieval canonists and modern scholars have made repeated attempts to establish clear parameters for these forms of quasi-religious life.[2] Although these women never achieved canonical status and there was never clarity on the names by which they were known, a number of order-like federations were created. Many of these, however, have been forgotten. It would seem that the complexities of piecing together a history from fragments means that the stories of certain quasi-religious groups remain untold. The discussion that follows is an attempt to recover the tale of one such federation of women known as the Grey Sisters.

At first glance, the details of their story seem unremarkable. Named for their grey habit, these women are associated with Northern France, the Low Countries, and, through historical revisionism, the New World. They are generally discussed as part of the Franciscan third order and often thought to have a particular focus on health care.[3] Closer inspection of these women and the context from which they emerged, however, shows that the term "grey" describes more than the indeterminate colour of their habits. Unravelling the layers of history and historiography reveals the many grey areas in the history of these sisters. As we will see, they not only stood between the religious and secular spheres but also between order and, if not heresy, at least controversial heterodoxy. Despite their complex identity, the Grey Sisters were a distinct and largely successful federation of active religious women before fading into obscurity.

In the World, but Not of It

The foundation of the Grey Sisters can be traced to the 1413 bull *Personas vacantes*.[4] Yet, this was not the creation of a new way of life but, rather, a new attempt at approving one that already existed. For centuries, men and women throughout Europe had pursued a vocation of active service in the secular world. Hagiography and sermon *exempla* recount dozens of examples of holy men and women who served the poor and suffering while remaining part of the secular world: Marie of Oignies, Juette of Huy, and Lutgard of Aywières served lepers in Liège; Margaret of Cortona ran a small hospital in Umbria; Elizabeth of Hungary served the poor and infirm in the German regions.[5] Health care was provided by many women who lived as religious in the world, but it was by no means the only expression of active devotion. While women who lived this vocation were clearly recognized as having something other than a lay status, they were not recognized as religious by canon law.[6] Instead, women who sought a vocation of service within the secular world began to arouse the concern of certain canonists. Individual churchmen, such as Guibert of Tournai, complained that he "did not know what to call such women: ordinary women or nuns as they neither lived in the world nor out of it."[7] Pious laywomen were accused of spreading mistranslations of Scripture, teaching, or even preaching in public, and criticized for regular contact with secular men.

In the early thirteenth century, communities of women engaged in service and active charity were relatively informal. In his *Dossier de l'ordre de la pénitence*, Gilles Gérard Meersseman includes regulatory documents from a number of penitential groups that lived vocations of active charity.[8] Unlike religious rules, the regulatory material in these documents neither provided canonical legitimacy nor formal affiliation with a particular order. Instead, they regulated matters such as clothing, the ownership of property, and liturgical obligations.[9] Canon law regarded those that followed these regulations as members of the laity, despite the obviously devotional aspects of their existence: that is, they were not "religious" in the legal sense of the word, despite living lives dedicated to the Lord. Regulatory documents became more prescriptive from the mid-thirteenth century onward. In particular, they often sought to counteract the penitents' extra-regular status by demanding they form ties with religious orders.[10] At the same time, local bishops in Northern Europe often placed communities of pious lay or quasi-religious women under the *cura* of Cistercians or secular clerics.[11]

In 1289, the Franciscan pope Nicholas IV issued the bull *Supra montem*, which contained the first papally approved rule for penitents throughout the church.[12] By consciously blurring the lines between pious lay communities and religious orders, *Supra montem* took the process of regularization to an entirely new level. It proved to be both an effective regulatory document and a source of confusion to later historians. *Supra montem* stated that Francis of Assisi had founded a "third" order that allowed men and women to adopt a religious status while living in the secular world. In effect, this was an attempt to create the illusion that tertiaries were members of a religious "tertiary" order – a status that was not recognized in canon law.[13] More importantly, adopting the rule in *Supra montem* allowed the claim that tertiary communities had been founded prior to the 1215 prohibition on religious rules, which was restated at the Second Council of Lyon in 1274.[14] While Nicholas's rule did not create a canonical order, invocation of Francis as the founder of an order of penitents shaped later perceptions of those that followed this rule. Adhering to the canonical minutiae does not seem to have been important to women. Instead, their communities seemed open to a variety of models of holiness and had no desire to be confined to a single order. The rule in *Supra montem* proved invaluable to churchmen charged with the *cura mulierum*. For their purposes, the rule functioned as a hallmark of orthodoxy that would later prove useful as an instrument of regularization.

In 1298, Boniface VIII (r. 1294–1303) issued the decretal *Periculoso*, which demanded that all canonically recognized religious women be enclosed.[15] As a result, certain canonists concluded that unenclosed women, such as beguines, penitents, and tertiaries, were not recognized as "religious" in any legal sense. As many quasi-religious groups took vows and wore distinct habits, however, it was difficult to insist that their members were entirely lay. Moreover, a vocation of service necessitated remaining in the world and was incompatible with enclosure. The canonical arguments surrounding this issue have resulted in a trail of contradictory regulatory material. The 1289 rule provided a partial solution: Women who professed this rule followed a pontifically approved way of life and could arguably be accepted as officially religious. Consequently, they were less vulnerable to accusations of misconduct or heterodoxy because of their unenclosed status.[16]

The conveniences of adopting the 1289 rule only increased in the fourteenth century. In 1311, the Council of Vienne addressed the topic of religious women. The conciliar decree *Ad nostrum* condemned several errors attributed to beguines and referred to them as "pernicious women" who were involved in "detestable practices."[17] A second decree from Vienne, *Cum de quibusdam*, appears to be a direct contradiction to *Ad nostrum*. It absolved pious women "who live honourably in hospices," stating that they were allowed to "follow the Lord who inspired them."[18] However, the council did not establish guidelines for distinguishing the "pious women" from their unruly and potentially heretical sisters.[19] As a result, liminal women who were neither lay nor religious found themselves the subject of continuing canonical consternation. Later canonists argued about whether women who followed vocations of active charity could be regarded as religious in a legal or technical sense.[20] Due to the difficulties of establishing an orthodox female religious identity, those responsible for the *cura* of beguines encouraged them to adopt hallmarks of orthodoxy (particularly enclosure and religious rules) in the early fourteenth century. It is no surprise that both the 1289 rule and the Rule of St. Augustine became increasingly popular at this time. These served as clear identity markers for two distinct groups. Neither group constituted a canonical order, but both were used to claim legitimacy for later order-like units.

The boundaries and (re)configurations of quasi-religious groups were constantly changing. Problems of clarifying the precise meaning of Vienne's condemnation and the role quasi-religious women could play in (and between) the church and society were debated throughout the fourteenth century. The difficulties caused by contradictory prescriptive and canonical documents were compounded by the fact that those in positions of ecclesiastical authority were often unaware of the precise status of women in their dioceses.[21] Instead of nuanced understandings of the women's – often complex – canonical position, they relied on external signs as indicators of the communities' orthodoxy.

In addition to a problematic canonical status, the active devotion of these women could also be controversial. This was particularly evident in relation to caring for the sick. As Adam Davis has pointed out, many hospital communities were founded in the twelfth and thirteenth centuries as part of an emerging culture of charity.[22] Functioning as centres of health care, poor relief, and hospices, hospitals that emerged at this time were both diverse and intrinsically linked to the local communities. In addition to larger houses of charity, the designation "hospital" encompassed smaller and informal communities that were founded to care for the poor and infirm.[23] While not all quasi-religious communities chose this as their active vocation, scholars such as Anne E. Lester, Elma Brenner, and Lucy Barnhouse have drawn attention to numerous hospitals, hospices, and houses of charity attached to quasi-religious movements.[24]

For the most part, hospital communities functioned as autonomous institutions. The Fourth Lateran Council of 1215 had given no more than a passing mention to hospital communities and those who served the suffering. There appears to have been little attempt at uniformity in either their establishment or administration. After the Council of Vienne (1311–12), there was a concerted effort to reaffirm the charitable and religious obligations of hospital communities and to bring them under the jurisdiction of local bishops.[25] However, the Council did little to regularize the life of women who worked in these institutions. In addition to the controversy inspired by their irregular status, there were particular dangers inherent in serving the sick. Along with the intimacy of the setting (often a bedchamber), nursing sisters had physical contact with the male patients they bathed or whose wounds they tended. While a medieval hospital or leprosarium was hardly conducive to romance, the physical closeness raised some concerns over the women's modesty. At the same time, there were controversies over whether hospital service was a form of religious life or a profession that should bring material rewards.[26] Jacques de Vitry, the popular preacher and later bishop of Acre, had a particular interest in the poor and in charitable institutions. While he acknowledged that many hospitals where "the fervour of charity, the unction of piety, the decor of honesty [and] the severity of discipline had not departed," there were others that justified collecting alms by "giving a little to the poor and infirm while using the rest for personal gain."[27]

Reform, Schism, and Regularization

From the later fourteenth century onward, the Observant movement, a comprehensive program of reform, swept through religious orders across Europe. Members of this movement were aware of the many difficulties and controversies in religious life and sought to restore order to Christianity.[28] Observant reformers from all orders spread their ideals through preaching and texts offering religious instruction. Many took their responsibility to religious women very seriously, and female communities – particularly communities of women known as tertiaries – were subject to the Observant program of reform. Observant reformers used tools such as references to "order" in chronicles and tools such as the 1289 Rule or the Rule of St. Augustine to create an order-like framework. As a result, the irregular and extra-regular identities of quasi-religious women were replaced by more canonically recognizable forms of life.[29] Unlike early penitential communities, "tertiary" groups attached to the Observance were increasingly both regulated and monasticized and soon came to constitute virtual (if non-canonical) new orders.

Given their goals of uniformity and order, it is perhaps surprising to find numerous differences in Observant emphasis – both between and among orders. Among the Franciscans, an examination of the liturgical texts or libraries of quasi-religious women shows that Observants in Northern Europe placed considerable emphasis on establishing a regulated identity associated with a religious order.[30] After professing or adopting the so-called Franciscan rule of 1289, houses often acquired a number of texts emphasizing the lives or deeds of saints associated with the Franciscan family or containing the writings of prominent Franciscan theologians. In this way, houses of unenclosed and unaffiliated penitents throughout the Low Countries were recast as Franciscan tertiaries.

Observant reform became an important influence in establishing a uniform Franciscan third order. Clinging to the myth of a potential return to an age of order in the church, Observant Reformers endeavoured to write anything problematic out of official histories. With tertiaries, they embraced the myth that Francis of Assisi (d. 1226) had founded three distinct orders in a Franciscan family. The fact that there was never a clear "third" or penitential order did not deter them in the least. Observants wrote a history of a tertiary order, supported by a significant contingent of saints, authorities, and important communities. Nevertheless, even within the Observant unity there were points of discord. For instance, Southern Observants placed emphasis on enclosure. Among Southern federations (such as the communities surrounding Montegiove), this came to function as a hallmark of orthodoxy. In the North, particularly in the Low Countries, this seems to have been less of an issue. Northern federations or order-like units (including the Chapters of Utrecht and Zepperen) had different criteria. These groups followed the 1289 Rule but had links with the *Devotio moderna*.[31] The order-like federations were to provide a model for some of the later groups, some of which had a measure of canonical legitimacy.

The irregularities the Observants had sought to remedy only became worse. In the later fourteenth century, the church experienced a crisis in the structure of authority that created further uncertainty and chaos. In 1378, Pope Gregory XI died. A conclave that took place in April that same year elected Bartolomeo Prignano as the archbishop of Bari to the papal throne. He chose the name Urban VI. The choice of Prignano was controversial, and certain factions maintained that the "election" had taken place under duress. In September 1378, a separate conclave in Fondi deposed Urban and elected Robert of Geneva as pope. Robert took up residence in the papal palaces at Avignon, where he reigned under the name Clement VII. From 1378 to 1407, there were separate papal curia in Rome and Avignon.[32] In 1407, an attempt by the Council of Pisa to resolve the question of multiple popes had the unintended consequence of proclaiming yet a third contender, Alexander V. In 1410, Alexander was succeeded by John XXIII, who reigned until the schism was resolved by the Council of Constance and the election of Martin V in 1415. The question of allegiance to a particular pope was often decided by either geography or political alliances. Of the three men claiming to be pope, the Pisan Alexander and John had the widest base of support throughout Europe.[33]

Despite some consensus on John's authority, what few historical sources exist do not paint a flattering portrait of his character, let alone his orthodoxy. Born to a noble family from Naples, John (or Baldassare Cossa, as he was then known) was rumoured to have earned a small fortune through piracy. His later studies in canon law at the University of Bologna were portrayed more as an attempt to secure his social standing than a sincere desire to serve the church. He quickly earned a reputation for earning money through unscrupulous practices and indulging his voracious appetite for sexual misadventure;[34] yet, it would appear that the accounts of his degeneracy were somewhat exaggerated. After his "election" in 1410, Cossa, or John XXIII, took a decisive role in solving troublesome canonical difficulties.[35] Among his other decisions, John took lasting steps towards regulating penitent women.[36]

In 1413, he issued the bull *Personas vacantes*, which provided some semblance of canonical legitimacy to a group that became known as the Grey Sisters. As a condition of his blessing, John required that the sisters profess the so-called Franciscan Rule of 1289, as well as binding and perpetual vows of obedience, poverty, and chastity. The rule did not insist that they observe the practice of enclosure.[37] At the same time, *Personas vacantes* regulated community life. Unlike the 1289 Rule, it set definite guidelines for the appointment of officials and made public profession mandatory. The same bull also set out a detailed quasi-monastic *cursus* in which the tertiaries were obliged to observe the Hours of the Virgin. These sisters were also required to distinguish themselves from their lay counterparts by wearing a scapular and the grey tunic, which resulted in them becoming known as the "Grey Sisters."

Rather than creating new foundations, this bull provided certain tertiaries with official recognition and protection from the usual criticisms that had been levelled at such groups since the thirteenth century. The tertiaries in question were from Bergue-Saint-Winoc, Dixmude, Furnis, Nieuport, Poperinghe, and Ypres.[38] Professing the 1289 Rule did not constitute membership in any canonical group, yet its Franciscan associations were already clear. It was enough to ensure that the Grey Sisters were perceived as members of the Franciscan third order. There was, however, no Franciscan connection. Indeed, the links between the Grey Sisters and the friars are, if anything, even more precarious than those set out by *Supra montem*. John's statutes make it clear that members of "his" third order were to have their own general chapters and to remain independent of any established order. This federation was predominantly located in the diocese of Cambrai, where John's papacy was recognized. Given that John was seen as an anti-pope or pretender to the papal throne in much of Europe, it could be expected that the already ambiguous status of the Grey Sisters would be subject to further scrutiny. Nevertheless, his solution would later have broader and unarguably orthodox appeal. In 1430, the post-schismatic Martin V confirmed *Personas vacantes* and added the communities of Dunkirk, Hondschoodt, and Saint-Omer to the communities included in the network of Grey Sisters. His successor, Eugenius IV, added the communities of Doornik, Liège, and Cambrai in 1436.[39] Although the regularizing efforts did not result in a singular cohesive order, the results were significant. Those responsible for the sisters generally shared both a commitment to regularizing the active life and a desire for regularity. As a result, the Grey Sisters came to constitute a federation of communities with a relatively consistent way of life. In this regard, it was not unlike the Chapter of Zepperen or the Chapter of Utrecht, which formed small groups within the larger grouping of communities associated with the Franciscan third order.[40]

Even among this first small network of houses, there were very different forms of life. They were united only by a shared papal privilege confirming their right to live lives of active service. Some women known as Grey Sisters lived in convents and observed the Divine Office; others practiced some degree of mendicancy. One feature that remained fairly consistent was that the sisters were involved in caring for the sick, either in their own homes or in convent hospitals. Given that the approval of the Grey Sisters was intended to offer a comprehensive solution for a multifaceted problem, some contrast between internal divisions and official ideals is only to be expected. The designation of Grey Sisters not only outlasted the schism but also expanded throughout the fifteenth century. Dixmude, one of the original houses of the Grey Sisters, boasted a charitable Table of the Holy Spirit and later became home to the hospital of St. Jan. The houses of Bernay and Douai were founded as hospitals. Other communities focused on running almshouses or other forms of service in the community. In 1440, the community of Grey Sisters in St. Catherine in the town of St. Omer obtained separate regulation and papal approval for their form of life.[41]

The creation of hospital communities took on a new dimension in the mid-fifteenth century with the creation of three new federations of Grey Sisters who had care of the sick at the heart of their charism. As with other aspects of Observant influence, the houses of Grey Sisters in the Observant milieu became subject to increasing regularization and specialization. Instead of the diverse forms of charity sanctioned by John XXIII's original bull, the sisters were increasingly encouraged towards the ministry of caring for the sick. In 1430, Philip the Good married Isabella of Portugal, the daughter of John of Portugal and Philippa of Lancaster. Though far from a mainstream figure, Isabella soon became influential in the finances, politics, and spiritual life of her new realm. Instead of simply the quiet piety often praised by chroniclers, it seems that Isabella was also an advocate of the new active devotion that concentrated on care for the poor and suffering.[42] Isabella was an ardent supporter of the Grey Sisters, and she founded houses in Merville, Lille, Aire, Ghent, Valenciennes, Béthune, Bruges, and Mons.[43] Each of these foundations enjoyed significant political and financial support. Unlike earlier communities of Grey Sisters, whose charism included care of the sick among other forms of charity and service, Isabella's foundations had this as their primary ministry.

In 1458, Pius II approved a new federation of Grey Sisters that worked primarily in hospitals.[44] The motherhouse of this federation was the hospital of Notre Dame du Soleil, founded at St. Omer. Originally founded near Hautpont, this community was revitalized through a donation from William of St. Audegone and became the *Filles du soleil de l'ordre de saint François*. This new community was placed under the spiritual care of the Observant Franciscans, and, like Isabella's foundations, existed primarily to serve the infirm.[45] Other charitable dimensions of their ministry certainly existed and are attested to by their popular appellation, *Soeurs de la soupe*, a name conferred on them for their work feeding the poor and needy.[46]

In 1474, Sixtus IV created a third distinct federation of Grey Sisters, which encompassed communities in St. Omer, Abbeville, Montreiul, and Hesdin.[47] This new federation was also under Observant care but was overseen by brothers of the French Observance. As well as the three distinct federations of Grey Sisters, there were a number of irregular, unaffiliated, or tertiary houses throughout Northern Europe. In 1465, Paul II expanded the network to include an additional eight communities in Northern France. In 1487, Innocent VIII confirmed the incorporation of the community of Scottish hospital sisters at St. Martha into the federation. St. Martha's was first given official status as religious on the grounds that the women who lived there already followed the vocation of the "Franciscan Grey Sisters."[48] Unsurprisingly, given the shared mission of serving the sick, there was some overlap between the communities, and changes in *cura* and affiliation were not uncommon.

The Observants responsible for their *cura* took pains to ensure that their way of life was recognized as orthodox. In 1483, Jean Crohin, general of the Cismontaine Observant Franciscans, and the *visitator* Jacques Stoëtlin, wrote a series of statutes for the "Soeurs grises hospitalières."[49] These statutes make it clear that they were written to regulate a federation of sisters whose primary vocation was to care for the suffering. The rule itself not only made provisions for women who cared for the sick inside smaller hospital communities or hospices within the convent, but also for those who were required to enter the homes of the suffering if there were other "honest women" present.[50] To protect their souls (and reputation) they were required to journey to these homes in pairs or groups. To prevent over-familiarity with particular patients, there were limits on the amount of time the sisters could spend in any one house.

In addition to their conduct while carrying out their ministry, the 1483 rule governed other parts of their life. While the Grey Sisters could leave their communities for the purpose of their charitable mission, their way of life was recognizably monastic. The sisters were to observe periods of silence during meals, take part in a chapter of faults, wear official habits, and participate in the prayer life of the community. They were also to receive regular visits from Observant Provincials to ensure the purity of their intentions and their fidelity to both their religious vocation and commitment to service. The same statutes were later revised and confirmed in 1528 by Jean de la Haye.[51] Similar developments were occurring in communities of hospital sisters under Observant influence elsewhere in Europe. A case in point is the communities of Franciscan Beatas from Durango, which later became known as a house of Clares.[52] Like the French communities, these sisters had close ties with the Observant Franciscans who encouraged them to adopt a system of regularization.[53] The unifying desires of the Franciscan Observants were ultimately unsuccessful. While they had secured status for communities and small federations of Grey Sisters, they did not create a canonical order. Like the earlier beguines and other quasi-religious women, individual houses of Grey Sisters had different methods of foundation, different patrons, and different vows. Despite the difficulties in considering the Grey Sisters as a group, it is essential to draw attention to the legacy of their founding bull, the 1413 *Personas vacantes*. From this time onward, women's work in the secular community was perceived as having official canonical recognition.

Sixteenth-Century Developments

Despite having Observant and even pontifical support for active charity, women who lived active vocations continued to be canonically problematic. Controversies over the precise way female communities fit into the ecclesiastical landscape continued into the sixteenth century. In 1517, the eleventh session of the Fifth Lateran Council acknowledged members of the third order as part of the church and affirmed their right to live as they chose. At the same time, the Council was adamant that there was a discernible difference between quasi-religious movements that conformed to the religious life and those that remained part of the laity. Councillors decreed that the "monastic" tertiaries should be granted the same rights as religious ones, but other pious lay associations had no legal claim to this status.[54] Those present at the council were not opposed to the existence or devotional practices of tertiaries but simply questioned the rights of unenclosed and unofficial groups to receive the privileges attached to being a canonically recognized religious order. The (often) contradictory legislation applied to tertiaries in the fifteenth century meant that the process of determining which groups were "official" was far from obvious. Groups such as the Grey Sisters, who were given multiple identities, were seldom mentioned in canonical decisions designed to establish an overarching framework.

The sixteenth century saw numerous attempts at regularization, most of which echo and attempt to correct many of the purely canonical problems with status addressed by earlier canonists. In 1521, Leo X introduced another rule for the "Franciscan" third order. Close examination of the rule and its contents suggests that Leo's attempt was to resolve ongoing issues such as authority, vows, and enclosure. Unfortunately, the rule was neither accepted by the diverse Franciscan milieu nor embraced by canonists. The same is true for Alanus Insulanus's tripartite rule for the three branches of the third order. It was adopted as a solution in what is now Spain and Portugal, creating even more divisions within the so-called third order. Within new (and relatively small) networks, the issues connected with irregularity had been internally resolved. In most of the church, however, there were still variations both between federations and between houses. Questions that had followed women who lived lives of active devotion persisted. Like their earlier sisters, extra-regular and irregular women, including the Grey Sisters, still found ways to contribute to both church and society. Following a familiar pattern, these women underwent a process of assimilation to dominant models, in which their unique societal contribution received less attention than their claims to orthodoxy.

Despite the best efforts of high-ranking churchmen, non-enclosed groups continued to be controversial. In 1563, the twenty-fifth session of the Council of Trent confirmed that religious women (*moniales*) were to be enclosed.[55] While the council seemed to agree that enclosure was necessary for *moniales*, there were a number of dissenting voices regarding whether this should also apply to non-monastic groups, such as penitents and tertiaries.[56] At the same time, officials from major religious orders, including the Franciscans, Dominicans, Augustinians, and Carmelites, argued that it was improper to expect tertiaries to observe something they had not promised when entering religious life.[57] In 1566, the newly elected Pius V put an end to the ambiguity through his bull *Circa pastoralis*. The bull was explicit in its claim that the need for enclosure applied to *all* communities of women – whether the vows were expressed tacitly or explicitly, whatever name they went by, and regardless of what their own rules said about enclosure.[58]

In 1568, Pius V recognized that this was necessary and permitted one official exception to *Circa pastoralis*. In his *Ea est officii nostri*, Pius distinguished the *moniales tertii ordinis* (who were to be enclosed) from *sorores tertii ordinis* (who were free to continue lives of active service).[59] Pius confirmed that these *sorores* were permitted to continue in their way of life provided that they accepted spiritual care and direction from the Observant friars. Friars who were responsible for groups that claimed an association with the 1413 bull *Personas vacantes* argued that this applied to the women under their care.[60] In a canonical peculiarity, the same legislation was now being used to support the existence of numerous completely separate groups. Needless to say, this was far from conducive to the long-sought universal rubric for those who lived between the religious and secular worlds. Instead of solidifying the institutional existence of each group involved, the canonical emphasis was on creating status for recognizable categories of religious ways of life rather than small federations. Consequently, defending the canonical status of the third order took precedence over defending the status of the Grey Sisters, who have been subsequently relegated to a historical footnote.

Another difficulty was that communities of women who practiced active charity began to distance themselves from the official religious life and cultivate identities as communities of pious laywomen. The women who pursued this option belonged to groups later seen as secular institutes.[61] Although often praised as a new type of religious community, the secular piety lived in these houses resembled the active devotion of Grey Sisters and other extra-regular religious women. While some belonged to nursing orders, either the Franciscan Grey Sisters or the Augustinian Black Sisters, other groups formed were made up of pious laywomen who wished to carry out this type of service. The (often Jesuit) protectors of these latter groups frequently invoked the 1413 exemption in *Personas vacantes* as an indication that their way of life had canonical acceptance and recognition. Again, the resulting orders and quasi-orders were far from uniform. Instead of systematic regularization, *Personas vacantes* had provided nothing more than means of legitimizing irregular and extra-regular ways of life.

Conclusions

There is no indication that the women known as the Grey Sisters made any changes to their way of life in response to the new legislation for tertiaries. Nevertheless, the fact that the legislation surrounding active women and tertiaries continued to evolve indicates that their existence was not a universal solution to the problem of extra-regular religious life. While there was no clear advantage to the continued imprecision and multiple grey areas associated with women who lived between canonical states, there was also no clear solution to the problems they raised. Controversies associated with their way of life, and what precisely constituted "service" or "charity," meant that they also existed between order and heresy. There had always been men and women who longed to dedicate themselves to Christian service while remaining part of the secular world. From approximately the early thirteenth century onward, these new forms of life became prominent enough to merit canonical attention. This attention was not aimed at creating a "third" way but at regulating it. Those charged with this task often attempted to impose a singular model, and their efforts were doomed to fail from the very beginning.

The convoluted and often contradictory canonical trail surrounding the Grey Sisters is inconsistent with the popular image of them simply being tertiaries who worked in health care. Here, we must consider issues of how history is written. It should be noted that the dominant voices in the debate over the status of the Grey Sisters were male clerics and not the sisters themselves. While the same is true for the histories of women in many religious orders, the fact that the existence of the Grey Sisters was an institutional solution to an ongoing problem changes the discussion slightly. The Grey Sisters came to represent an ideal for the Observants and other churchmen who recognized the need for an active vocation. Consequently, the historical trail that follows this group is more focused on controversy and resolution than on preserving a legacy. Scholars who are intent on recovering their voices must read between the lines and reconcile ideal pious depictions with canonical criticisms. The difficulties inherent in this process often results, as with the Grey Sisters, in historical obscurity.

The Grey Sisters represented one of the more successful attempts to regulate women who lived betwixt and between official states. While they have largely disappeared into obscurity, their legacy has persisted into the modern world. It is, perhaps, interesting to draw attention to the Grey Sisters of Charity in particular. Founded in Montreal by the widowed Marguerite d'Youville in 1737, the Grey Sisters fought for the rights of the poor and cared for the infirm. Like the earlier beguines or Grey Sisters, Marguerite's sisters broke with social convention and lived a ministry of charity. Although they did not claim any direct lineage from the beguines or fifteenth-century Grey Sisters, the statutes of Marguerite's community justify their somewhat unorthodox ministry with a reference to the 1413 *Personas vacantes*.[62] Again, the spirit of active charity and devotion that was both shaped by and in response to the social world continued to be a part of their communities. When discussing these "new" movements in the New World, Elizabeth Rapley remarked that "nuns were being made where no nuns were supposed to exist."[63] In a technical sense, this is certainly true – only because the status of women carrying out active ministry had been in question for so long.

NOTES

1 On problems of terminology for quasi-religious women, see the essays in Letha Böhringer, Jennifer Kolpacoff Deane, and Hildo van Engen, eds, *Labels and Libels: Naming Beguines in Northern Medieval Europe* (Turnhout: Brepols, 2014).
2 On the canonical difficulties associated with these women, see Elizabeth Makowski, *"A Pernicious Sort of Woman": Quasi-Religious Women in the Later Middle Ages* (Washington, DC: Catholic University of America Press, 2005).
3 The basic history of these women is set out in Raffaele Pazzelli, *St. Francis and the Third Order* (Chicago: Franciscan Herald Press, 1989),

128–37. The archival material is surveyed in the careful work of Marc Carnier, *De Communauteiten van Teriarissen van Sint-Franciscus* (Brussels: Algemeen Rijksarcheif, 2002). However, a study of its implications remains to be written. As Craig Harline has pointed out, tracing their origins is "notoriously complicated." See Craig Harline, "Actives and Contemplatives: The Female Religious of the Low Countries before and after Trent," *The Catholic Historical Review* 81 (1995): 541–67, at 546. The regulations followed by the Grey Sisters have been cited as influencing a modern group, also known as the Grey Sisters, founded by Marguerite d'Youville. See John Watts, *A Canticle of Love: The Story of the Franciscan Sisters of the Immaculate Conception* (Edinburgh: John Donald, 2006), 24.

4 John XXIII, "Personas vacantes," in *Annales Minorum*, ed. Luke Wadding (Rome: Typis Rochi Bernabò, 1761), 9: no. 535; 18: 653–4.

5 For a discussion of miraculous healing, see Sara Ritchey, "Affective Medicine: Later Medieval Healing Communities and the Feminization of Health Care Practices in the Thirteenth-Century Low Countries," *The Journal of Medieval Religious Cultures* 40 (2014): 113–43.

6 For a detailed discussion, see Anne E. Lester, "Cares Beyond the Walls: Cistercian Nuns and the Care of Lepers in Twelfth- and Thirteenth-Century Northern France," in *Religious and Laity in Western Europe 1000–1400: Interaction, Negotiation, and Power*, ed. Emilia Jamroziak and Janet Burton (Turnhout: Brepols, 2006), 197–224.

7 "Et apud nos mulieres aliae, de quibus nescimus, utrum debeamus eas vel saeculares vel moniales appelare, partim enim utuntur ritu saeculari, partim etiam regulari." Guibert of Tournai, "*Collectio de scandalis ecclesiae*," in Aubertus Stroick, ed., *Archivum Franciscanum Historicum* 24 (1931): 33–62, at 58.

8 "Propositum des humiliés," in G. G. Meersseman, *Dossier de l'ordre de la pénitence au XIIIe siècle* (Fribourg: Editions Universitaires, 1961; 2nd ed., 1982), 276–82; "Premier propositum des pauvres Lombards," in ibid., 284–6; "Propositum des pénitents dirigés par les pauvres catholiques," in ibid., 286–8; "Deuxième propositum des pauvres Lombards," in ibid., 288–9.

9 See Isabelle Cochelin, "Règle," and "Statuts," in *Histoire et Dictionnaire du monachisme en Orient et en Occident, des origines au XXIe siècle*, ed. Daniel-Odon Hurel (Paris: Éditions du CNRS, forthcoming).

10 In 1246, the Liégeois bishop, Robert of Thourotte, approved a non-canonical rule for beguines in his diocese. While this rule is found in the archives of a number of beguine communities, it is generally supplemented by statutes written by the local priest or bishop. In 1247, Innocent IV mandated that the penitents in Lombardy and Florence be placed under the supervision of Franciscan confessors. See, Meersseman, *Dossier*, 57–9.

11 See Simone Roisin, *L'hagiographie Cistercienne dans le diocèse de Liège au XIIIe siècle* (Louvain: Bibliothèque de l'Université, 1947).
12 Meersseman, *Dossier*, 75. See Alison More, "Institutionalizing Penitential Life in Later Medieval and Early Modern Europe: Third Orders, Rules and Canonical Legitimacy," *Church History: Studies in Christianity and Culture* 83 (2014): 296–322.
13 On the third order, see Hildo van Engen, *De derde orde van Sint Franciscus in het middeleeuwse bisdom Utrecht* (Hilversum: Verloren, 2006). See Maiju Lehmijoki-Gardner has pointed out that an identical situation existed for the early penitents who were connected to the order of preachers but not canonically a part of the Dominican order before 1405. See Maiju Lehmijoki-Gardner, "Writing Religious Rules as an Interactive Process: Dominican Penitent Women and the Making of Their 'Regula,'" *Speculum* 79 (2004): 660–87.
14 In 1274, the Second Council of Lyons observed the ineffectiveness of the 1215 decree and noted that many religious groups founded between 1215 and 1274 had caused problems for the universal church. For this reason, it not only renewed the prohibition of 1215 but also attempted to suppress all orders that had been founded without papal approval in the intervening years. See Norman Tanner, ed., *Decrees of the Ecumenical Councils*, 2 vols. (London: Sheed and Ward, 1990), 1: 326.
15 Elizabeth Makowski, *Canon Law and Cloistered Women: Periculoso and its Commentators, 1298–1545* (Washington, DC: The Catholic University of America, 1997), 65–6.
16 See Alison More, *Fictive Orders and Feminine Religious Identities, 1200–1650* (Oxford: Oxford University Press, 2018), 37–9.
17 Elizabeth Makowski raises questions about the precise dating and authorship of this bull. See Makowski, "A Pernicious Sort of Woman," 23–50, esp. 24–5.
18 Tanner, *Decrees of the Ecumenical Councils*, 1: 374.
19 For a discussion see, Jacqueline Tarrant, "The Clementine Decrees on the Beguines: Conciliar and Papal Versions," *Archivum Historiae Pontificae* 12 (1974): 300–8.
20 More, *Fictive Orders*, 63–86.
21 For example, a fifteenth-century community of extra-regular women in Groningen was referred to as "beguines of the third order rule of St Francis." See Folkert J. Bakker, *Bedelorden en begijnen in de stad Groningen tot 1594* (Maastrich: Van Gorcum, 1988), 160. Mariengaarde in Monnickenendam, which had adopted the rule in 1403, and the community of Maria of Nazareth, which was described as "sisters of the order of penitence of St. Francis" ("*zusteren in der oirde van penitencien sente Franciscus*") were founded with the 1289 Rule, although they did not have

any affiliation with the Franciscan order. See Sabrina Corbellini, "Een oude spiegel voor nieuwe maagden," *Ons geestelijk erf* 80 (2009): 171–98, at 182.

22 Adam J. Davis, *The Medieval Economy of Salvation: Charity, Commerce, and the Rise of the Hospital* (Ithaca: Cornell University Press, 2019), 1–32.

23 For further discussion, see Davis, *The Medieval Economy*, and James William Brodman, *Charity and Religion in Medieval Europe* (Washington, DC: Catholic University of America Press, 2009).

24 Lester, "Cares Beyond the Walls," 197–224; Elma Brenner, *Leprosy and Charity in Medieval Rouen* (London: The Boydell Press, 2015); Lucy Barnhouse, *Houses of God, Places for the Sick: Hospitals in Communities of the Late Medieval Rhineland* (forthcoming).

25 Brodman, *Charity and Religion*, 83–8.

26 While the work carried out by each foundation had a distinctly religious character, many were secular foundations with no official connections to any religious order. The more "religious" houses were often run by communities that included a priest, who was responsible for sacramental care of the community as well as a number of men and women who had made some form of vows (whether formal or informal) and were dedicated to improving their worlds. In some areas of Europe, particularly in France, there was a definite push to ensure that hospitals were both closely regulated and placed under religious authority, and that they were served by both religious men and women. The papal legate, Cardinal Robert of Courson, convened six regional synods of bishops in France between 1213 and 1215. See Brodman, *Charity and Religion*.

27 Jacques de Vitry, *The Historia occidentalis of Jacques de Vitry*, ed. J. F. Hinnesbusch (Freiburg: The University Press, 1972), cap. 29, 148–9.

28 Bert Roest, "Observant Reform in Religious Orders," in *Christianity in Western Europe c. 1100–c. 1500*, ed. Miri Rubin and Walter Simons (Cambridge: Cambridge University Press, 2009), 446–57. For a discussion of particular aspects, see the essays in James D. Mixson and Bert Roest, eds., *Observant Reform in the Later Middle Ages and Beyond* (Leiden: Brill, 2015).

29 See Sylvie Duval, *"Comme des Anges sur Terre" Les Moniales Dominicaines et les débuts de la réforme Observante, 1385–1461* (Rome: École Française de Rome, 2015); Alison More, "Dynamics of Regulation, Innovation, and Invention," in Mixson and Roest, *Observant Reform in the Late Middle Ages and Beyond*, 85–110.

30 Alison More, "Religious Order and Textual Identity: The Case of Franciscan Tertiary Women," in *Nuns' Literacies: The Antwerp Dialogue* (Leiden: Brill, 2017), 69–79.

31 On the two Chapters see, van Engen, *De derde orde*.

32 See Hélène Millet, *L'Église du Grande Schisme 1378–1417* (Paris: Picard, 2009). As well as regularizing tertiary houses, John was influential in

combating the heresies of John Wyclif and Jan Hus. He even seems to have been willing to resolve the schism itself, although evidence suggests this was true only if it was resolved in his favour.

33 For a discussion, see Philip Daileader, "Local Experiences of the Great Western Schism," in *A Companion to the Great Western Schism, 1378–1417*, ed. Joëlle Rollo-Koster and Tom Izbicki (Leiden: Brill, 2009), 89–121. The Pisan popes were recognized by England, France (excluding some principalities in the South), most of the Empire (although not by Emperor Rupert himself), and by nine important Germanic archbishops. See Howard Kaminsky, "The Great Schism," in *The New Cambridge Medieval History*, ed. Michael Jones (Cambridge: Cambridge University Press, 2000), 696.

34 Eustace J. Kitts, *Pope John the Twenty-Third and Master John Hus of Bohemia* (London: Constable, 1910), 1–14. For an overview of studies on John XXIII, see Hélène Millet, "John XXIII (c. 1360–1419)," in *Encyclopedia of the Middle Ages*, ed. André Vauchez et al. (London and Chicago: James Clark & Co., 2001), 1: 771. See Millet, *L'Église du Grande Schisme*, 113–15.

35 In particular, he took a decisive stand on Jan Hus and played an active role in the papal penitentiary dealing with matters of penance, marriage, and the validity of sacraments. See Kitts, *John the Twenty-Third*, 52–74.

36 In addition to differences in the perception of papal privilege between regions, there were often differences of opinion within a single house. See Daniel Bornstein, "Introduction" to Bartolomeo Riccoboni, *Life and Death in a Venetian Convent*, trans. Daniel Bornstein (Chicago: University of Chicago Press, 2000), 1–24.

37 It is important to note that the tertiaries were not simply to profess allegiance to their legitimate superiors but explicitly "*Domino Iohanni Papae & suis successoribus canonicae intrantibus.*" John XXIII, "Personas vacantes," 654.

38 John XXIII, "Personas vacantes," 9: no. 535; 18: 653–4.

39 Martin confirmed *Personas vacantes* in *Ex apostolicas sedis providentia* (*Bullarium Franciscanum*, VII, n. 1891, 736). Eugenius added his approval with *Ad apostolicae dignitatis apicem* (*Bullarium Franciscanum*, n.s. 1: n. 264, 121).

40 Unlike the Grey Sisters, these Chapters are seldom discussed outside of studies on the Third Order. See van Engen, *De derde orde*, 339–49; Gabriele Andreozzi, ed., *Il Terzo ordine regolare di San Francesco nella sua storia e nelle sue lege* (Rome: Editrice Franciscanum, 1993–94), 2: 503–62.

41 Eugenius IX, *Dum sedulae mentis*, in *Annales Minorum*, 9: 115.

42 P. de Oudegherst, *Les chroniques et annales de Flandres* (Antwerp, 1571), 2:692. See Monique Sommé, *Isabelle de Portugal, duchesse de Bourgogne: Une femme au pouvoir au XVe siècle* (Lille: Presses Universitaires du Septentrion, 1998), 451–78.

43 Sommé, *Isabelle de Portugal*, 468–74. See Bertrans Schnerb, "Piété et culture d'une noble dame au milieu du XVe siècle: l'example de Marguerite de Bécourt, dame de Santes," in *Au Cloitre et dans le Monde*, ed. Patrick Henriet and Anne-Marie Legras (Paris: Presses de l'Université Paris-Sorbonne, 2000).
44 *Bullarium Franciscanum*, n.s. 1: 530, no. 1055.
45 *Bullarium Franciscanum*, n.s. 2: 292, no. 552.
46 Pierre Moracchini, "La Mise sous Clôture des Sœurs Grises de la Province Franciscaine de France Parisienne, au XVIIe siècle," in *Les religieuses dans le cloître et dans le monde*. Actes du Deuxième Colloque du C.E.R.C.O.R., Poitiers, 29 Septembre–2 Octobre 1988 (Saint-Étienne: Publications de l'université de Saint-Étienne, 1994), 635–65.
47 Henri Lemaître, "Une bulle inédite de Sixte IV (1474) en faveur des soeurs de la celle," *Revue d'histoire franciscaine* 4 (1927): 361–4.
48 For a detailed analysis of this community, see Alison More, "Tertiaries and the Scottish Observance: St Martha's Hospital in Aberdour and the Institutionalisation of the Third Order," *Scottish Historical Review* (2015): 121–39.
49 Henri Lemaitre, "Statuts des Religieuses du Tiers-ordre franciscain dites sœurs grises hospitalières (1483)," *Archivium Franciscanum Historicum* 4 (1911): 713–31.
50 Ibid., 727.
51 M. Goyens, *De oorspronkelijke statuten der grauzusters van Vlaanderen in 1483 opgesteld* (Ghent, 1884).
52 As with the appellation "Grey Sister" or "Tertiary," the term "Clares" is often used as shorthand for women who had some connection to the Franciscan friars, whether as monasticized tertiaries, *moniales*, or penitents. For the problems associated with this term, see Roest, *Order and Disorder*.
53 Ignacio Omaechevarria, "Religiosas docentes, hospitalarias y misioneras a fines de la edad media," *Revista Española de Derecho Canónico* 9 (1954): 989–1003.
54 "To avoid the cheapening of ecclesiastical censures, and sentences of interdict being regarded as of little importance, members of the said third orders are in no way to be admitted to hear divine services in the churches of their orders during a period of interdict. But those living in an official group, or dwelling with enclosure, and women who are leading a life of virginity, celibacy, or chaste widowhood under an expressed vow and with a habit ought to enjoy the privileges of the order of which they are tertiaries." Translated in Tanner, *Decrees of the Ecumenical Councils*, 2: 648. This session took place in 1516, and was presided over by Leo X. The council itself lasted from 1512 to 1517. See Alison More, "Institutionalization of Disorder: The Franciscan Third Order and

Canonical Change in the Sixteenth Century," *Franciscan Studies* 71 (2013): 147–62.

55 Specifically, the Council restated and reaffirmed the decree *Periculoso*, passed by Boniface VIII in 1298. See Tanner, *Decrees of the Ecumenical Councils*, 2: 777–8. For a discussion of *Periculoso*, see James Brundage and Elizabeth Makowski, "Enclosure of Nuns: The Decretal *Periculoso* and its Commentators," *Journal of Medieval History* 20 (1994): 143–55.

56 Raymond Creytens includes several examples of bishops and religious leaders who argued that tertiary groups should be permitted to live in "open monasteries," as they had either never observed enclosure or had lived under simple (rather than solemn) vows. See Raymond Creytens, "La Riforma del Monasteri Femminile dopo i Decreti Tridentini," in *Il Concilio de Trento e la Riforma Tridentina*, ed. Jedin Hubert et al. (Rome: Herder, 1963), 49–57.

57 From the Augustinians: "Procurator ordinis D. Augustini. – Nullus potest cogi ad id quod est consilii. Clausura non est de substantialibus trium votorum, exemplum Religiosorum quibus non est indicta clausura. - Nullus debet obligari ad plura et arctiora quam regula ordinaverit, et beatus Augustinus in Epist. 109 non precipit. clausuram etc. - Aliquae moniales habent privilegium Pauli III ut possint vivere in observantia absque clausura. Ergo ex vi decreti non precipitur omnibus clausura etc. – Videretur expedire ut non exirent. Sed censet non licere eas cogere." From the Franciscans: "Procurator ordinis Sit Francisci. – Quod constitutio Bonifatii non fuit ab omnibus approbata. Ideo illae tantum moniales quae profitentur clausuram cogantur etc., aliae vero non; quia subditi extra promissum non debent cogi, ut ait B. Bernardus. Hortentur tamen omnes etc." Cited in Creytens, "La riforma," 57–8.

58 "Universas et singulas moniales, tacite vel expresse Religionem professae, etiam si conversae aut quocumque alio nomine appellentur, etiam si ex institutis vel fundationibus earum Regulae ad clausuram non teneantur, nec unquam in earum monasteriis seu domibus, etiam ab immemorabili tempore, ea servata non fuerit, sub perpetua in suis monasteriis seu domibus debere de coetero permanere clausura, iuxta formam dictae Constitutionis Bonifacii Papae VIII praedecessoris nostri, quae incipit: Periculoso, in sacro concilio Tridentino approbatam, et innovamus in omnibus et per omnia, ac illam districte observare mandamus." In *Bullarium diplomatum et privilegiorum sanctorum romanorum Pontificum Taurensis*, 25 vols. (Augustae Taurinorum: Seb. Franco, et al., 1862), 7: 447–50. See Creytens, "La Riforma," 62–77.

59 *Annales Minorum*, 20: 568–70.

60 These were somewhat exceptional by observant standards. See Philippe Annaert, "Vie Religieuse Féminine et Société dans les Pays-Bas Catholiques. La Réforme des Tertiaires Franciscaines aux XVI–XVIII

Siècles," in *Liber Amicorum Raphaël de Smedt*, ed. Jacques Paviot (Leuven: Peeters, 2001), 3: 305–30 (at 307).
61 Marie Amélie Le Bourgeois, *Les Ursulines d'Anne de Xainctonge (1606)* (Saint-Étienne: Éditions Universitaires, 2003), 114–38; Elizabeth Rapley, *The Dévotes: Women and Church in Seventeenth-Century France* (Montreal and Buffalo: McGill/Queens University Press, 1990). See Susan E. Dinan, *Women and Poor Relief in Seventeenth-Century France: The Early History of the Daughters of Charity* (Aldershot: Ashgate, 2006), 17–22.
62 See Watts, *A Canticle of Love*, 24.
63 Rapley, *Dévots*, 112.

10 Women, Power, and Religious Dissent: Why Women Never Became Heresiarchs

JANINE LARMON PETERSON

On 17 August 1300, a woman named Maifreda da Pirovano told an inquisitor of Milan, Guido da Cocconato, what she had stated to others: a woman named Guglielma of Milan (d. 1281) had been the Holy Spirit incarnate; Maifreda had distributed consecrated hosts in an imitative form of Mass over which she had presided on multiple occasions; and devotees had kissed her hand and feet in anticipation of her becoming the pope after Guglielma's future Second Coming.[1] The inquisitors condemned Maifreda as a relapsed heretic, executing her and burning her body along with the exhumed bones of Guglielma.[2] Maifreda clearly functioned as a leader of what inquisitors deemed a heretical sect, rather than merely believing or following doctrinal error.[3] She "preached" (*praedicat*) to others, and assumed both doctrinal and sacerdotal roles among her co-believers in Guglielma's divinity.[4] She justified the beliefs of the group in front of others when a member questioned the validity of Guglielma as the Holy Spirit.[5] As a result, according to canon law, Maifreda was a heresiarch: a teacher and defender of doctrinal error, not just someone who held unorthodox views.[6] Yet medieval inquisitors categorized Maifreda as a relapsed heretic instead of a heresiarch. A similar identification was made for the object of her devotion, the deceased Guglielma, as well as for other female teachers and preachers of perceived heretical views in the later Middle Ages, such as Margherita of Trent and Marguerite Porete.

There was no distinct line between orthodoxy and heterodoxy during this period, even within the church hierarchy. There are many examples of contested sanctity, in which local clerics sided with citizens in venerating someone who was viewed by inquisitors or popes as heretical.[7] Nevertheless, it is notable that inquisitors and other church authorities seemed to exclusively apply the term "heresiarch" to men in the later Middle Ages, such as Dolcino of Novara, Gerardo Segarelli, Guido

Lacha, and Meco del Sacco, among others. The standard historiographical explanation for this phenomenon is that male clerics saw women as gullible and duplicitous, but too intellectually and emotionally weak to attract followers and command others unless it was through the use of deception, sorcery, magic, or witchcraft. Even feminist literature on late medieval spirituality and heretical movements, as discussed below, generally follows this explanatory trend. While this misogynistic view certainly existed during the period, by accepting it at face value historians tend to overlook women who appropriated spiritual authority and leadership roles outside of the strictures of the institutional church.

Herbert Grundmann's seminal monograph, *Religious Movement in the Middle Ages*, brought attention to and amplified the agency of women who participated in late medieval spiritual movements, including those the papacy considered heretical.[8] This essay builds on his insights to examine cases that could expand how modern historians consider female religious authority and explain why medieval inquisitors did not generally label women as "heresiarchs." I argue that spiritual laywomen did have leadership roles in perceived heretical groups regardless of the nomenclature used at the time. More broadly, they achieved political roles through associated activities, even within spaces traditionally identified as private or domestic. Yet, popes and inquisitors almost exclusively used the appellation "heresiarch" for enemies who threatened the church's territorial political power, and that group did not include women. There was therefore a gendered understanding of female leadership roles, but one that is more nuanced than generally accepted and demands deeper interrogation of surface-level definitions and assumptions regarding both late medieval women and late medieval clerics. The evidence reveals that there was a disjunction between the canon law definitions of heretic and heresiarch, and the inquisitorial implementation of those laws, due to papal and institutional concerns of the late thirteenth and early fourteenth centuries. This context explains why there were no so-called female heresiarchs, and offers an opportunity to reassess laywomen's roles in religious leadership outside of the traditional institutional frameworks of public versus private power.

Gendering Heresy

Prevailing religious and medical views helped to form a gendered paradigm about religious authority within the medieval clerical elite. In 1 Corinthians, St. Paul asserted, "[L]et women keep silence in the churches: for it is not permitted them to speak, but to be subject ... for it is a shame for a woman to speak in the church."[9] His statement, which barred women from preaching, is one among many that was (and is) used to justify the prohibition on women becoming members of the secular clergy. Women certainly held positions of spiritual authority in the medieval church. They were abbesses of convents or double monasteries, founded religious orders, and became venerated and canonized saints.[10] Some even attained political authority through mystical visions that allowed them to counsel or chastise popes, such as Birgitta of Sweden or Catherine of Siena.[11] The Roman Church, however, largely denied power to religious laywomen who operated outside of the institutional church structure, did not have noble or royal connections, and/or lacked the support of a male cleric who also usually served as her confessor.[12]

Medieval theologians like Jean Gerson and scholars like Nicole Oresme considered women less capable of "discerning spirits," or the truth and falsity of visions, due to the consequent lack of theological training and, often, literacy.[13] Thus, female religious roles were limited to serving as models of appropriate behaviour, teaching, and morally exhorting others. The church needed women as spiritual teachers, as the new order of St. Ursula used to their advantage during the Protestant Reformation.[14] While teaching was theoretically acceptable, the clerical elite increasingly controlled teaching about points of doctrine as the Middle Ages progressed.[15] Tanya Stabler Miller has demonstrated that secular clerics, such as Robert of Sorbon (d. 1274), viewed thirteenth-century female beguines in Paris as "disseminators of the fruits of their interactions with preachers," but by the Council of Vienne (1311–12) the church condemned female teaching among the beguines in *Cum de quibusdam* due to its similarity to public preaching.[16] *Cum de quibusdam* became codified into the Clementine Constitutions with Pope Clement V's revision and was part of the last group of decrees added to the *Corpus Iuris Canonici*, the medieval compilation of canon law.[17] By the late Middle Ages, Dominican and, later, Franciscan inquisitors used rumours of unlicensed female lay teaching that touched on doctrinal points as a justification for an inquisitorial inquiry, such as the one that occurred with Guglielma's devotees in Milan.

Late medieval clerical authorities considered heresy "the denial of a formally proclaimed truth of revelation, but applied [it] also to the stance of any Christian who out of contumacy refused to submit to the guidance of the Church."[18] The creation of the inquisitorial office in the early thirteenth century demonstrates that clerics assessed the perceived spread of heresy, which could affect the broader population, as a serious threat.[19] It is within this context that the division between being a heretic versus a heresiarch emerged. A single heretic could be misled or considered what was called at the time "of simple mind." Consequently, they could perhaps be brought back into the Christian fold if they learned from their error and repented. Those who did not repent, or were sentenced for heresy a second time, could be executed.[20] In contrast, canon law defined a heresiarch as a "teacher of [doctrinal] error" who not only errs oneself but also "defends the error of others."[21] A person who provided hospitality or a willing ear to those who articulated erroneous doctrine, or saw merit in their points, was a heretic; a person who supported that erroneous doctrine publicly and persuaded others to believe in it was a heresiarch. The distinction made was between a believer and a leader.

Concepts of gender and sexuality affected how inquisitors characterized heretics and heresy. Scriptural passages included descriptions of women as *mulierculae*, "silly little women," and examples that cemented the idea of female inferiority and lack of discernment.[22] Church fathers, such as St. Jerome in his treatise *Adversus Jovinianum*, ascribed both simplicity and duplicity to female nature: Women were not only easily deceived but also devious enough to intentionally deceive others.[23] The authority given first to Galenic, then to Aristotelian, medical theory complemented the prevailing scriptural interpretation of women as inferior to men. In the Galenic/Hippocratic/Aristotelian humoral system, women were thought to embody rampant sexuality because of their physiology.[24] Based on these traditions, theologians and educated clerics thought women were prone to seduce men into error, both through their words and their bodies.[25] Scholars such as Dyan Elliott and Nancy Caciola have persuasively argued that over the course of the Middle Ages clerics increasingly viewed female spirituality as suspect in its very nature, due in part to concerns about women's perceived heightened gullibility and sexuality.[26] R.I. Moore recounted one description of two women, supposed followers of the suspected heretic Diotesalvo, in Florence around 1200: "Milita of Monte-Meato and Julieta of Florence ... [were] both daughters of iniquity. They adopted the semblance of religion, so that by appearing eager to hear the holy offices they seemed to be sheep though in reality they were wolves. The bishop was deceived by their religious disguise ... these snakes in the grass drew many men and women into the labyrinth of their heresy under the pretext of piety."[27] In this account, the women's duplicity threatened the souls of Florentines and the religious authority of the unsuspecting bishop.

By the thirteenth century, clerical authors connected religious dissent and female sexuality, with the latter seen as a problem for maintaining spiritual constancy. Building on church fathers such as Tertullian and

Eusebius, the new literature compared women who dared to "preach" with Jezebel, who personified polluting female sexuality.[28] Like Eve, Jezebel allegedly deceitfully misled her male companion, her husband King Ahab. These religious views, combined with medical theories about sex difference, linked female preaching with heresy and rampant sexuality. Moneta of Cremona's anti-heretical tract, for instance, identified all heretics with Jezebel, thus linking heresy, women, preaching, and impurity.[29] Inquisitors and theologians in manuals and treatises also ascribed sexual deviance to unmonitored lay religious groups, such as the *pauperes Christi*, as well as to other movements like the so-called Free Spirits (*spiritus libertatis*) or Cathars.[30] The connection between women as simple, devious, and sexually voracious predators famously reached a descriptive height in the *Malleus Malleficarum* (1483), which laid the foundation for women to be categorized as witches for the next two centuries.[31]

It is no surprise that gendered views of heresy and heretics came to have greater import in the late Middle Ages. As Herbert Grundmann, André Vauchez, and Robert Bartlett have shown, this was a period during which both female and male spirituality flourished.[32] This lay religiosity coincided with what was perceived as a rise in heresy, another potential outlet for women to express views on doctrine and influence others.[33] Clergy were particularly concerned about beliefs that contained purported anti-clerical and anti-sacerdotal elements that denied the efficacy of the sacraments, thus negating the need for male priests and potentially opening avenues for female lay spiritual authority. Unregulated religious movements lacked official oversight, and could further blur the lines between women instructing others on behaviour and women preaching about or interpreting doctrine. Thus, in theory, heterodox sects presented a greater opportunity for laywomen to attain positions of spiritual leadership. Some earlier scholarship used examples such as female participation in Bible study within the Lollards of England, or the ostensible female preaching in heresies such as the Cathars or Waldensians, to argue this point, but there is little evidence to substantiate the assumption that unorthodox groups provided a broader scope for women to obtain religious authority. The evidence does demonstrate, however, that clerics believed women were participating in larger numbers in heretical movements. For example, Richard Abels and Ellen Harrison determined that 45 per cent of deponents whom inquisitors questioned in Languedoc in 1245–6 identified women as "heretical [Cathar] ministers" (called the *perfecti*).[34] The gendered nature of heresy provided a ready-made framework for women to be labelled heresiarchs. In practice, however, this was not the case.

Defining Heresiarchs: Case Studies

Clerical authors, popes, and inquisitors rarely distinguished between heretics and heresiarchs in accordance with canon law, as discussed above, in the later Middle Ages. While there was a medieval canonical definition of a heresiarch, it was mostly sixteenth-century clerics active during the Reformation who were concerned with tracing and cataloguing individuals who they believed deserved the title, such as Bernard of Luxembourg or Luis de Paramo.[35] Medieval popes and inquisitors seemed reluctant to label anyone a heresiarch, perhaps because doing so would implicitly acknowledge a challenge to the authority of the pope or institutional church. Inquisitors or popes used this term primarily to label men regarded as political enemies of the pope, not for anyone who posed a spiritual threat to the institutional church or Christian souls. The following brief examples look at a few instances from Italy and France in the thirteenth and fourteenth centuries to demonstrate that late medieval popes and inquisitors ascribed heterodox leadership to perceived territorial and political enemies, which was a role they did not envision women occupying.

A compelling case for a female heresiarch, for example, might be made for Maifreda da Pirovano, the subject of the opening vignette, who was a relation of the Visconti lords in Milan, the devotee of Guglielma of Milan, and a leader of a sect deemed heterodox in 1300. The Guglielmites have garnered scholarly attention after Barbara Newman's pioneering studies of the group, and Marina Benedetti's edition of surviving documents from the inquisitorial process.[36] A woman named Guglielma (d. 1281), perhaps of royal Bohemian lineage, moved to Milan around 1260 and gained a reputation as a pious woman. By all accounts, Guglielma herself appears to be an unlikely heresiarch. She lived humbly and in relative obscurity, spending her time counselling others on how to live in accordance with Christian morals. She had a reputation for performing healing miracles, although evidence for this gift is limited. Her piety attracted the admiration of a number of Milanese citizens and members of the Cistercian abbey of Chiaravalle, where the monks erected an altar over her tomb and conducted celebrations on the day of her body's translation. Besides this modest cult, Guglielma had a circle of intimate followers who became ardent devotees of her divinity. These so-called Guglielmites believed she was not just holy, but that she was also the Holy Spirit incarnate. Maifreda and a man named Andrea Saramita emerged as leaders and disseminators of these beliefs.[37] In 1300 inquisitors examined over seventy-two Guglielmite devotees, including Maifreda. The result was that inquisitors condemned Guglielma posthumously as a heretic, exhumed and burned her body, and destroyed her altar at Chiaravalle and all images of her in other churches and religious establishments in Milan. They sentenced Maifreda, Andrea, and another follower as relapsed heretics and executed them, while other sectarians paid fines and/or had to wear penitential yellow crosses.

Andrea and Maifreda were co-conspirators who spearheaded the creation of the group's beliefs after Guglielma's death. According to Andrea's testimony before the Milanese inquisitors Guido da Cocconato and Rainerio da Pirovano on 13 August 1300, Andrea maintained "that he heard this from the said Guglielma, that she was born on Pentecost and the said Andrea, speaking onetime or another with sister Maifreda about the said Guglielma, stated that between them [i.e., Andrea and Maifreda] they believed and it appeared to them that it ought to be so: that just as the Archangel Gabriel announced to blessed Mary the incarnation of Christ, so it seemed to them that the Archangel Raphael announced to Lady Constance the Queen of Bohemia [i.e., Guglielma's mother] the incarnation of the said Guglielma."[38] The most significant aspect of this testimony is that Andrea and Maifreda developed these beliefs together. These two admirers of Guglielma interpreted her birth on Pentecost as a sign, one that led them to construct other ideas about how Jesus's birth and death prefigured that of Guglielma, such as both having an Annunciation. Based on this unorthodox doctrinal foundation, the circle of devotees who came to be known as the Guglielmites believed that Guglielma was God. As part of the Trinity, she suffered in the same flesh as Christ during the Passion and came back to earth as the Holy Spirit. They alleged that Guglielma/the Holy Spirit chose to return in female form because otherwise she would have died just like Christ, and the world would have been destroyed.[39] Although theologically this idea is problematic, it was the basis for the group's vision of spiritual reform. Believers thought that, as the Holy Spirit, Guglielma's purpose in returning to earth was to establish a renewed church. Since the Holy Spirit incarnated in female form, the Guglielmites thought the pope of the new age would be a woman. This church would be established after the Second Coming of Guglielma, at which time all the Jews, Saracens, and those "outside the Church" (presumably heretics, excommunicates, and apostates) would be saved, through voluntary conversion.[40]

While Andrea and Maifreda both held important roles within the group, it was Maifreda who would be at the centre of the renewed church that believers thought would be established after Guglielma's Second Coming. The idea that Guglielma – a woman – was divine provided a unique opportunity for another woman, Maifreda, to attain the top position among the sectarians. Maifreda's authority went far beyond teaching others of Guglielma's supposed divinity. For members of the Guglielmites, Maifreda was not just the future pope. She was the physical extension of Guglielma's will and her "rock" upon which a revitalized church would be built. She was the female parallel to St. Peter to whom God, in the incarnation of Guglielma, entrusted the renewed Christian church of Guglielmite belief, as two female devotees asserted to inquisitors.[41] By the time of the inquiry in 1300, Maifreda had pastoral, doctrinal, apostolic, and even sacerdotal responsibilities. She healed other followers by dispensing the miracle-working water that had washed Guglielma's remains and preached to devotees about Guglielmite beliefs, Guglielma's miracles, and the Gospels and the Epistles.[42] As already noted, she ensured "orthodoxy" among followers by rebuking sectarians who doubted Guglielma's divinity, and blessed and distributed hosts at gatherings and feasts where wine was also present, including during a special celebration on Easter of 1300.[43] The similarity between the Guglielmite ceremonies and the giving of the Eucharist is striking; Maifreda essentially presided over an alternate form of the Catholic Mass. Through the unique views of the Guglielmites, Maifreda attained a status and authority within the sect that was only allowed to men in the Roman Church and that her male co-leader, Andrea Saramita, did not achieve.

The record is ambiguous about Guglielma's own role in promulgating ideas about her divinity since it is based on individual memories of what she said two decades before the inquisitorial process. Some witnesses claimed she chastised believers; others testified she had once been cited for heresy. Ultimately, medieval inquisitors condemned Maifreda, Andrea, and Guglielma (posthumously) all as heretics, not as heresiarchs. Later authors portrayed Guglielma in different ways as a deviant heresiarch presiding over "pagan orgies" of her followers, as in Gabrio de Zamorei's *Sermo de fide* (c. 1371–5), or as a pious and suffering daughter of a king of England who escaped from burning at the stake to live out her life as a nun, as in the *Life* written by Antonio Bonfadini (c. 1425) and adapted into a play by Antonia Pulci (c. 1490).[44] Yet, the contemporary evidence suggests that if inquisitors were to call anyone a heresiarch it would have been Maifreda, the woman who took on particularly male religious roles, publicly preached unorthodox ideas, and defended heretical beliefs to others. Maifreda's leadership role, however, was not acknowledged in the Middle Ages and was erased from Guglielmite existence by the time Bernardino Corio wrote his history of Milan in 1519, in which he cast Andrea as the protagonist of the heresy.[45] By canon law definition, Maifreda qualified as a heresiarch for putting the salvation of Christians at stake and challenging the pope's religious authority. The fact that the term was never used to refer to Maifreda strongly suggests that it was applied in only very rare instances in the thirteenth and fourteenth centuries.

One of the instances in which "heresiarch" was used during this time – but not for a female leader – occurred in the case of the Apostolic Brethren (sometimes referred to as Apostles or Dolcinists).[46] Margherita of Trent, or Margherita Boninsegna (d. 1307), has been called the "spiritual sister" of Dolcino of Novara, the recognized leader of the movement, in a relationship paralleling that of Maifreda da Pirovano and Andrea Saramita of the Guglielmites.[47] This lay movement emerged circa 1260 around a man named Gerard Segarelli. Under Segarelli a fluid group of people desired to live the *vita apostolica*. They came under investigation when several male members were accused of sexual impropriety. After Segarelli was burned as a relapsed heretic in 1300, Dolcino took control of the movement. His views were much more apocalyptic and political. In 1303 Dolcino wrote an epistle in which he claimed that sometime after 1304 Frederick III of Sicily would destroy the cardinals and the pope. The Apostles would then unite with the "spirituals," be graced by the Holy Ghost, and establish a renewed church.[48] In response to the treatise, Pope Boniface VIII called a crusade against the Apostolic Brethren. Dolcino, with perhaps 1,400 followers, including Margherita of Trent and another close associate, Longino Cattaneo, fled to the hills above Vercelli, where they fought Boniface's crusaders with the support of local anti-papal lords. The fourth crusade called against Dolcino and his followers was victorious in 1307, and the bishop of Vercelli took Dolcino, Margherita, and Longino into custody. All three were tortured and executed. Margherita and Longino were burned, and Dolcino was publicly torn apart with hot pincers.[49]

In this case, both medieval clerics, such as the Bolognese inquisitor Guido of Vicenza, and early modern authors, such as Bernard of Luxembourg, labelled Dolcino a heresiarch.[50] Although details about Margherita's role within the Apostolic Brethren are unknown, her formal execution without any evidence of being relapsed implies that the inquisitors recognized her as a leader. Yet, she was not called a heresiarch by any contemporaries who discussed the group, such as Salimbene de Adam or Bernard Gui, and early modern authors erased her from their accounts, similar to their treatment of Maifreda da Pirovano.[51] Margherita was executed for being a heretic, although she was a co-leader of a group that, in the church's view, jeopardized the spiritual welfare of Christians enough to prompt Pope Boniface VIII to call four crusades against them. The example of Margherita and Dolcino demonstrates that clerical authorities used "heresiarch" sparingly and, when they did, applied the term to those who were perceived to have enough power to challenge the pope's political authority. Dolcino was the one who mobilized lay lords into an anti-papal force and promoted the destruction of the papacy in his epistle. As a result, he was the one categorized as a heresiarch.

Maifreda and Margherita deserved the term "heresiarch," based on the official canon law definition. Both of them, however, had male co-leaders of the spiritual world view they avowed, which might have mitigated the recognition of their roles within the patriarchal system of late medieval Christian society. Marguerite Porete (d. 1310) is an example of a woman who was singularly in control of her beliefs and how she disseminated them. The details of her life and the accusations against her have been vexed with errors and assumptions, which Sean L. Field has masterfully addressed in his book about her trial.[52] Marguerite was the author of a treatise addressing how to achieve the pinnacle of divine love. The text was discovered and attributed to her in 1946 and is published today under the title *The Mirror of Simple Souls*.[53] Marguerite's ideology of achieving union with God by destroying the self's desire and will prompted Parisian university masters, canon lawyers, and inquisitors to examine the treatise. During the first half of the fourteenth century there was a new concern about ideas that could be viewed as undermining free will, as seen in the inquisitorial trials of astrologers Peter of Abano (d. 1316) and Cecco of Ascoli (d. 1327), both of whom were accused of sorcery and sentenced for heresy for this reason. Although Marguerite's text did not claim that free will is diminished through the process of "annihilating" the soul that she advocated, the way in which she described it was enough to raise theological questions. In addition, unlike most of the other female vernacular literature during this period, Marguerite did not present her book as authorized by God through mystical visions and legitimized by a confessor, abbess, or other institutional religious authority.[54] The scope of Marguerite's influence in her community is unknown, but there is enough evidence from other inquisitorial trials, such as the first process against Meco del Sacco (d. c. 1344), to indicate that the mere fact that her ideas were in writing and could be copied and distributed, or orally repeated from a single reading of the text, was cause for grave concern. There is evidence that Marguerite herself attempted to circulate her text (including to a bishop) even after the Bishop of Cambrai cited her, burned her treatise, and warned her to cease holding or disseminating her views. Marguerite also had at least one supporter, Guiard of Cressonessart, who seemed willing to circulate her ideas and who was imprisoned along with Marguerite by the inquisitor William of Paris. Her potential following within the beguin/beguine community of Paris – or the potential for a following, considering her insistent articulation of her views – could have been enough for William of Paris to condemn Marguerite as a heresiarch. Instead, she was executed as a relapsed heretic.[55] The anonymous continuation of Guillaume de Nangis's chronicle provocatively called her a *"pseudomulier* (false woman),*"* suggesting that her activities went beyond that of the social and religious station in which women should remain. Like the other case studies so far, even so no medieval authors designated her a heresiarch.[56] Marguerite's case once again illustrates that there was reluctance in the medieval period to use the term unless the pope's political power was threatened.[57]

One final example of a woman whom inquisitors could have termed a heresiarch, and in this case actually did, is Na Prous Boneta (d. 1328). Na Prous was influenced by the ideas of the radical Franciscan leader Peter John Olivi (d. 1298). In 1325 Na Prous confessed to having visions in which God came to her and told her, "[Y]ou shall be the *donatrix* of the Holy Spirit."[58] She asserted that her spirit and that of the dead Olivi were "one and the same" and that God now ruled the church through them in spirit, as he had through the flesh of Christ and the Virgin Mary.[59] Na Prous believed that the pope, John XXII, was the Antichrist. Under her watch humankind would again be redeemed, in an apocalyptic world view reminiscent of the Guglielmites.[60] Akin to Maifreda da Pirovano of that group, Na Prous promoted her alleged special position as the vehicle for the Holy Spirit's return to earth. She told inquisitors that after her first vision she wanted her "other women companions and people to know what had happened."[61] Her sister and female servant were acolytes who believed her vision that God told her that she was "the herald of the advent of the Holy Spirit."[62] Na Prous's inner circle of believers was seemingly limited, but her scope was broad: She espoused her visions to male beguins, a notary, and other townspeople. Louisa Burnham has argued that Na Prous also exercised spiritual influence in her community, enough to persuade incarcerated beguins not to confess to inquisitors.[63]

Unlike the examples already discussed, the inquisitor in this case, Henry de Chamayo, twice formally identified Na Prous as a heresiarch. While not disputing Burnham's assessment of Na Prous's visionary role in the beguin community in which she lived, the actual language of Chamayo's sentence demonstrates a conflation between the canonical definitions of heretic and heresiarch. The pertinent passage states, "We pronounce, judge, and declare through and with this decree [that] you, Na Prous, [are] impenitent and, in the stubbornness of your contumacy, [are] a heretic and heresiarch … we release you, as a impenitent and obstinate heretic and heresiarch, to the secular justice."[64] The terms "heretic" and "heresiarch" are repeatedly qualified by adjectives that emphasize the fact that she refused to repent. Contumacy seems the salient characteristic that defined Henry of Chamayo's understanding of both terms, with no canonical distinction between the labels. Yet, Burnham has persuasively argued that Chamayo used the term "heresiarch" carefully. If the surviving copies are accurate, he applied "heresiarch" to those who were specifically linked to Peter John Olivi and apocalyptic thought within the Languedocian beguin community, such as the former friar Raymond Johannis, but not to those who held other unorthodox beliefs, such as the layman Limosus Nigri, although Nigri himself admitted he tried to preach his beliefs to others.[65] This distinction, and the historical context, is crucial for understanding the anomaly of Na Prous being categorized as a female heresiarch. Chamayo was stationed in the heart of an area with a large beguin community, which had wide-ranging familial and horizontal networks, shortly after John XXII condemned their ideas and determined that they should be prosecuted as heretics.[66] The inquisitor's single-minded focus, as a papal agent, was to stop the spread of Olivi's posthumous influence once his ideas were declared heretical. For Chamayo, any of the beguins, including Na Prous Boneta, was a threat to the pope's political power due to their beliefs.

Maifreda, Margherita of Trent, Marguerite Porete, Na Prous Boneta, and perhaps Guglielma of Milan all disseminated ideas that inquisitors considered heterodox among groups of people who looked to them for leadership. However, inquisitors, popes, and other clerical authorities only applied "heresiarch" to one of these women, Na Prous Boneta, and the records suggest that the reason was both localized in space and time and specific to a particular inquisitor. Although views regarding heresy were gendered and women were considered inferior in medieval society, two points complicate the view that religious authorities did not label women as heresiarchs just because they were women and, therefore, considered simple or weak. Contemporary popes or inquisitors in the later Middle Ages rarely used the term "heresiarch" at all. When they did, it was applied to those who challenged the political, rather than the religious, power of the papacy. For example, the term *heresiarchus* was never applied to Gerardo Segarelli (mentioned above), who started a large-scale lay movement that spread from central Italy to southern Germany, or to Maifreda da Pirovano, who claimed she would take over the papal seat. The pope used the label, however, for Segarelli's successor, Dolcino of Novara, who mobilized an army of disaffected lords against the pope, yet not for his co-leaders, such as Margherita of Trent. The scholar Marsiglio of Padua (d. 1342) merited the term because of his book *Defensor Pacis*, in which he claimed that the pope only had authority by what Rousseau might have later termed the "general will" of the Christian laity.[67] Inquisitors refrained from the appellation in the condemnation of Marguerite Porete (d. 1310), who also wrote a treatise that was thought to contain dangerous views, and who was similarly obstinate in her alleged heretical beliefs. The difference in these examples is that Marguerite focused on one's personal relationship to God, rather than the wider authority of the pope and the institutional church.

The easiest explanation for the dearth of female heresiarchs in the later Middle Ages is that, within the patriarchal structure of the church, popes and inquisitors did not view women – intellectually or charismatically – as capable leaders. While this might have been true, the evidence shows that this answer alone is simplistic. There was a disjunction between the theory and practice of canon law definitions that depended on context. Thirteenth- and fourteenth-century popes and papal agents saw challenges to their territorial ambitions as the greatest threat. Thus, men like Matteo and Galeazzo Visconti, or Rainaldo and Obizzo III d'Este, became the subjects of inquiries for heresy and/or sorcery on very little (if any) evidence.[68] All the individuals mentioned in this essay lived during the pontificate of two popes: Boniface VIII and John XXII. Both faced intense criticism from both clerical and lay members of society, and they experienced challenges to their political power as lay lords of the Papal States. Popes did not hesitate to use inquisitors as a weapon against their political enemies. It was when religious leaders, such as Dolcino, fuelled political uprisings that religious authorities used the term heresiarch. Women, no matter how publicly notorious they might have been, generally did not have access to the type of political capital to pose a substantive threat to popes or the idea of the papal monarchy. This does not mean that women in movements categorized as heretical did not attain spiritual and political power. These case studies demonstrate that examining laywomen's roles and experiences in groups identified with religious dissent outside of the confines of standard nomenclature provides broader avenues for investigating women's spiritual authority in the late Middle Ages. One of the avenues to interrogate is the prevalent, but arguably too simple, categories used to describe power: ones that equate public with political power and private with domestic space.

The Politics of Public versus Private

From even the small number of examples discussed in this essay, women clearly had important spiritual roles in both larger heterodox sects and domestic circles. Their influence on the latter manifested itself in public, and had political repercussions. Women in groups considered "heretical" are therefore part of, rather than in opposition to, "orthodox" women who found other outlets for their spirituality in the later Middle Ages, such as mysticism, beguinages, or institutional orders.

Early studies of women in heretical movements focused on how these groups provided opportunities for women to gain public authority. Scholars like Peter Biller and Shulamith Shahar complicated that view. They argued that so-called heterodox women had authority over their own religious experience and that of others, just as in orthodox Christianity, but this power was exercised in the private realm, or the domestic sphere.[69] Common examples cited were Waldensian women living in female communities, or Cathar women engaging in domestic proselytization to their husbands and sons. These arguments upheld the framework of "orthodox" and "heterodox," which has now come under deep scrutiny. These examples show, however, that women's activities in smaller communities or more private venues gave them power and agency. In contrast, some scholars have argued that the church perceived any form of female spirituality to be transgressive, particularly in the later Middle Ages.[70] Influential thirteenth- and fourteenth-century mystics needed male collaborators to shield them, which tipped the scales so that church officials viewed them as lauded visionaries rather than suspected heretics.[71] This focus equates spiritual power with political authority in a public setting. While this understanding was present in the Middle Ages, the case studies already discussed show that this distinction was not consistently applied. The case of Maifreda da Pirovano is a clear example. She held both public and political authority through her sacerdotal rites at the Benedictine convent of Chiaravalle and other religious institutions.

Recent scholarship argues that the assumption about public and private power being in opposition is untenable when speaking of gender and medieval religion.[72] In the introduction to an edited volume on domestic devotions, Maya Corry, Marco Faini, and Alessia Meneghin contend that domestic space was fluid yet central to spiritual life, noting that "rituals that took place in the church, confraternal hall or street had domestic aspects and meanings ... [and] domestic devotions were enmeshed with institutional forms of piety."[73] This public aspect of private devotions is seen regularly in the *vitae* of late medieval holy laywomen, many of whom created "healing communities," to use Sara Ritchey's term.[74] Women's roles in heretical movements can be viewed similarly from outside these standard binaries. Na Prous Boneta's recalling her visions to household members, Maifreda's performing rituals in religious establishments, and Margherita of Trent's participating in the creation of a spiritual collective identity while hiding from crusaders were all public actions. Even the private deeds of purported heterodox laywomen, such as not going to church and harbouring or breaking bread with suspected heretics, were public. Observers saw, noted, and interpreted these actions, as did institutional authorities, since any of them could prompt inquisitors to question an individual for heresy.[75]

So-called domestic influence, therefore, was not relegated to the domestic sphere, nor was it apolitical. For instance, a Bolognese woman named Maria told a friar in 1304 that she had invited members of Dolcino's group into her house and given them bread. She declared that she did not regret it because "you see that inquisitors and the brothers have persecuted those who are of the number of the Apostles [i.e., Dolcino's Apostolic Brethren]; they are certainly evil because these Apostles are good men."[76] This was a domestic act of a woman giving food in her own home to men she knew.[77] With the simple act of inviting them in and giving them bread, however, she challenged the authority of the inquisitors and, by extension, the pope since the inquisitors were his agents. A private comment about the character of heretics in comparison to local clergy became a political act just by its verbal articulation. A man named Cursius Nero Bonelle, for instance, asserted to a friend in 1301 that "the Roman Church is a church of malignant men, and that whatever the priests and their prelates and the brother preachers and the brother minors do and have done is for the extraction and extortion of money from simple men of the world who are called Christians and for keeping them under their feet, by telling them good words and seducing them into giving them money, and that all the works of the prelates and brother preachers and minors and other religious were a pretense and deceptive."[78] Remarks like these demonstrate the fluidity between what was considered private/domestic, and public/political, in the later Middle Ages when viewed through a non-institutional lens.

Women actively participated in this political dialogue through their words and actions in their homes, villages, and other meeting places. While Maifreda da Pirovano obviously had a remarkable amount of authority for a woman due to Guglielmite ideology, other female followers had important roles in the sect. The Humiliate house of Biassono and its residents seem to have been deeply involved. After Guglielma's translation to Chiaravalle in 1282, Biassono erected a shrine within their house upon which rested a vial that contained the water and wine with which Guglielma's body had been washed. They also painted a depiction of Guglielma and Jesus freeing captives, presumably Jews and Saracens, from prison.[79] Based on the surviving notarial books, about forty-four of the seventy-two Guglielmites questioned were female (not including ten monks of Chiaravalle). Some were Humiliate and some were lay wives and mothers of men also implicated in the heresy. At times it was clearly the wife or mother who brought the husband into the circle of devotees and had an authoritative role in their participation.[80] Similarly, women in the Apostolic Brethren sought young, unattached girls and placed them to live with older women who would teach them their beliefs, as attested in an inquisitorial register of Bologna from 1291–1310.[81]

In conclusion, there were no medieval female heresiarchs because there was a divide between the meaning of "heresiarch" in theory and its use in practice during the later Middle Ages. Although canonists created a definition, popes and inquisitors applied it in a very limited scope to laypeople they saw as a viable threat to papal sovereignty and, in particular, the pope's terrestrial power. Those perceived enemies were usually men, and sometimes men without strong ties to what could be considered heterodox religious movements. If modern scholars used medieval definitions, then perhaps Maifreda and Margherita would have the same legacy as Dolcino of Novara. However, even medieval popes and inquisitors themselves did not adhere to the categories of heretic and heresiarch, and neither should modern scholars. The limitations of these terms obscure the many roles women played in religious movements and the influence they had on others and on church policy and institutions. Whether in a religious establishment or at home, whether wealthy or poor, women clearly held spiritual power in terms of conceiving and disseminating both orthodox and allegedly heterodox beliefs. They promoted and monitored their beliefs among others in a way that was public and politicized within the context of the intertwined nature of late medieval religion and politics. Women, both orthodox and presumed heterodox, had power, authority, and leadership in a variety of ways that were public and political in their homes, village meeting places, and spiritual establishments. Male authorities indeed could have thought of women as more transgressive and tried to limit those expressions of authority. By and large they did not do so by utilizing the term "heresiarch" unless that person posed a challenge to the terrestrial and political authority of the person in St. Peter's seat.

NOTES

1 Marina Benedetti, ed., *Milano 1300: I processi inquisitoriali contro le devote e i devoti di santa Guglielma* (Milan: Libri Scheiwiller, 1999), 124. Parts of this essay were presented at the 122nd Annual Meeting of the American Historical Association in Washington, DC, and the Annual Meeting of the New York State Association of European Historians at LeMoyne College, Syracuse, New York. I am indebted to attendees as well as the editors and reviewers for their feedback.

2 A letter from Pope John XXII to the Archbishop of Milan in 1322 provides evidence for Maifreda's fate (Luisa Muraro, *Guglielma e Maifreda: Storia di un'eresia femminista* [Milan: La Tartaruga, 1985], 91). On the practice of burning bodies, including for relapsed heretics, see Romedio Schmitz-Esser, "The Cursed and the Holy Body: Burning Corpses in the Middle Ages," *Journal of Medieval and Early Modern Studies* 45 (2015): 131–57; and Michael D. Barbezat, *Burning Bodies: Communities, Eschatology, and the Punishment of Heresy in the Middle Ages* (Ithaca: Cornell University Press, 2018), esp. 109–26.

3 While the unorthodox nature of Guglielmite belief within an organized group of followers definitely existed in late thirteenth-century Milan, there is a valid and important critique about the actual existence of organized heresy and the labels that are used to identify those groups, such as Cathars, especially in the twelfth and early thirteenth century. For an overview of this debate, see Deborah Shulevitz, "Historiography of Heresy: The Debate over 'Catharism' in Medieval Languedoc," *History Compass* 17 (2019): 1–11. All the Anglicized names used to refer to groups of believers are the terms in which members addressed themselves and each other in the sources, with the exception of the Guglielmites, which is the standard term used in modern scholarship.

4 Benedetti, *Milano 1300*, 66, 80, 84, 92, 106, 110, 114, 118, 120, 230.

5 Benedetti, *Milano 1300*, 224–6.

6 See discussion in section 1, below.

7 Many examples are discussed in my earlier publications, particularly Janine Larmon Peterson, *Suspect Saints and Holy Heretics: Disputed Sanctity and Communal Identity in Late Medieval Italy* (Ithaca: Cornell University Press, 2019). Throughout this essay I use the term "heresy" or "sect" with the understanding that it does not connote objective truth but, rather, refers to the subjective realities of medieval clerics.

8 Herbert Grundmann, *Religious Movements in the Middle Ages*, trans. Steve Rowan (Notre Dame, IN: University of Notre Dame Press, 1995), esp. 75–88 and 233–5.

280   Janine Larmon Peterson

9   1 Corinthians 14:34–5. All biblical quotations are from the Douay-Rheims version of the Bible unless otherwise noted.
10 While there are too many examples to cite, just a few of the most famous in western Europe in these categories during the central to later Middle Ages include Hildegard of Bingen and the abbesses of Fontevrault, Clare of Assisi and Birgitta of Sweden, and Marie of Oignies and Angela of Foligno.
11 *The Revelations of St. Birgitta of Sweden*, trans. Denis Searby, 2 vols. (New York: Oxford University Press, 2006), 1: 41, and discussion in Unn Falkeid, "The Political Discourse of Birgitta of Sweden," in *A Companion to Birgitta of Sweden and Her Legacy in the Later Middle Ages*, ed. Maria H. Oen (Leiden: Brill, 2019), 80–102; Catherine of Siena, *Letters of St. Catherine of Siena*, 2 vols., ed. Suzanne Noffke (Tempe: ACRMS, 2000–1), especially her letters to Pope Gregory XI and other religious and secular authorities during 1375–6 (2: 189–259), and discussion in Blake Beattie, "Catherine of Siena and the Papacy," in *A Companion to Catherine of Siena*, ed. Carolyn Muessig, George Ferzoco, and Beverly Mayne Kienzle (Leiden: Brill, 2012), 73–98.
12 See John Coakley, *Women, Men, and Spiritual Power: Female Saints and Their Male Collaborators* (New York: Columbia University Press, 2006) and the essays in Catherine M. Mooney, ed., *Gendered Voices: Medieval Saints and Their Interpreters* (Philadelphia: University of Pennsylvania Press, 1999).
13 Nancy Caciola, *Discerning Spirits: Divine and Demonic Possession in the Middle Ages* (Ithaca: Cornell University Press, 2003), 1–30; Dyan Elliott, "Seeing Double: John Gerson, the Discernment of Spirits, and Joan of Arc," *The American Historical Review* 107 (2002): 26–54; Nicole Oresme, "Tractatus de configurationibus qualitatum et motuum," in *Nicole Oresme and the Medieval Geometry of Qualities and Motions*, ed. Marshall Clagett (Madison: University of Wisconsin Press, 1968), 342–5. Ermine de Reims is one mystic who negotiated the process of discerning "counterfeit" saints in her visions of saints and demons without institutional censure; see Renate Blumenfeld-Kosinski, *The Strange Case of Ermine de Reims: A Medieval Woman Between Demons and Saints* (Philadelphia: University of Pennsylvania Press, 2015).
14 Querciolo Mazzonis, *Spirituality, Gender, and the Self in Renaissance Italy. Angela Merici and the Company of St. Ursula (1474–1540)* (Washington, DC: The Catholic University of America Press, 2007), 52–94.
15 Alcuin Blamires, "Women and Preaching in Medieval Orthodoxy, Heresy, and Saints' Lives," *Viator* 26 (1995): 135–52; Bert Roest, "Female Preaching in the Late Medieval Franciscan Tradition," *Franciscan Studies* 62 (2004): 119–54; and Claire M. Waters, *Angels and Earthly Creatures: Preaching, Performance, and Gender in the Later Middle Ages* (Philadelphia: University of Pennsylvania Press, 2004), 121–42.

16 Tanya Stabler Miller, *The Beguines of Medieval Paris: Gender, Patronage, and Spiritual Authority* (Philadelphia: University of Pennsylvania Press, 2014), 82; see also 84–3, 100–2, and 154–5.
17 Elizabeth Makowski, *"A Pernicious Sort of Woman": Quasi Religious Women and Canon Lawyers in the Later Middle Ages* (Washington, DC: Catholic University of America Press, 2005), 23–50.
18 James Heft, *John XXII and Papal Teaching Authority*, Texts and Studies in Religion 27 (Lewiston, NY: E. Mellen Press, 1986 [1977]), 110.
19 Malcolm D. Lambert, *Medieval Heresy: Popular Movements from the Gregorian Reform to the Reformation* (Cambridge, MA: Harvard University Press, 2002 [1977]), 115.
20 Henry Charles Lea, *A History of the Inquisition of the Middle Ages*, 3 vols. (New York: Cosimo Classics, 2005 [1888]), 1:536–42.
21 Emil Friedberg, ed., *Corpus iuris canonici*, 2 vols. (Leipzig: Bernhard Tauchnitz, 1881), 1:999 C.24 q. 3c. 32. All translations are my own unless otherwise noted.
22 2 Timothy 3:6 (Vulgate edition). Other books, such as Genesis 1:26–27, 2:21–24, and 3:1–24, supported this interpretation.
23 St. Jerome, *Adversus Jovinianum*, in *St Jerome: Letters and Select Works*, Nicene and Post-Nicene Fathers, Second Series, vol. 6, ed. Henry Wace and Philip Schaff (Peabody, MA: Hendrickson, 1995), 346–414.
24 Joan Cadden, *Meanings of Sex Difference in the Middle Ages: Medicine, Science, and Culture* (New York: Cambridge University Press, 1995); Monica H. Green, "Female Sexuality in the Medieval West," *Trends in History* 4 (1990): 127–58; and Joyce E. Salisbury, "Gendered Sexuality," in *Handbook of Medieval Sexuality*, ed. Vern L. Bullough and James A. Brundage (New York: Garland Publishing, 2000), 81–102.
25 Anthropologists call this systemic social structure of gender the "Delilah complex," or the belief that women ultimately betray men, a construction that is the result of fears around the subaltern female potentially overturning the social structure whose foundation is their very subordination; see Mary C. Douglas, *Purity and Danger: An Analysis of Concepts of Pollution and Taboo* (New York: Routledge, 2002 [1966]), 154. R.I. Moore utilized this methodology in his assessment of the low status accorded to medieval women; see R.I. Moore, *The Formation of a Persecuting Society: Power and Deviance in Western Europe 950–1250* (Cambridge, MA: Blackwell Publishing, 1990 [1987]), 100–1.
26 Dyan Elliott, *Proving Woman: Female Spirituality and Inquisitional Culture in the Later Middle Ages* (Princeton, NJ: Princeton University Press, 2004) and *The Bride of Christ Goes to Hell: Metaphor and Embodiment in the Lives of Pious Women, 200–1500* (Philadelphia: University of Pennsylvania Press, 2012); Caciola, *Discerning Spirits*.

27 Quoted in R.I. Moore, *The War on Heresy* (Cambridge, MA: Harvard University Press, 2012), 239.
28 These ideas were disseminated in intellectual treatises; recent scholarship has problematized the issue of whether these theoretical ideas affected the relationship on the ground between clerics and women, especially with women in religious communities or orders. See Jennifer C. Edwards, *Superior Women: Medieval Female Authority in Poitiers' Abbey of Sainte-Croix* (Oxford: Oxford University Press, 2019), esp. 136–200; Lezlie Knox, *Creating Clare of Assisi: Female Franciscan Identities in Later Medieval Italy* (Leiden: Brill, 2008), esp. 57–122; Anne E. Lester, *Creating Cistercian Nuns: The Women's Religious Movement and Its Reform in Thirteenth-Century Champagne* (Ithaca: Cornell University Press, 2011 [2017]), esp. 78–116; Catherine M. Mooney, *Clare of Assisi and the Thirteenth-Century Church: Religious Women, Rules, and Resistance* (Philadelphia: University of Pennsylvania Press, 2016), esp. 54–88; and Beverly Mayne Kienzle, "The Prostitute-Preacher. Patterns of Polemic Against Medieval Waldensian Women Preachers," in *Women Preachers and Prophets through Two Millennia of Christianity*, ed. Beverly Mayne Kienzle and Pamela J. Walker (Berkeley: University of California Press, 1998), 99–113.
29 Moneta of Cremona, *Adversos Catharos et Valdenses libri quinque*, ed. Thomas A. Ricchini (Ridgewood, NJ: Gregg Press, 1964), 443.
30 For primary sources regarding sexual deviance in the *pauperes Christi*, see Salimbene de Adam, *The Chronicle of Salimbene de Adam*, ed. and trans. Joseph L. Baird, Guiseppe Baglivi, and John Robert Kane (Binghamton: SUNY Press, 1986), 251; for the Free Spirit, see the list of beliefs in Rome, Biblioteca Casanatense, ms. 1730, fo. 39r; for an example of purportedly dualist beliefs that one cannot commit sin "from the waist down" connected to Cathars, see Antoine Dondaine, "La Hiérarchie cathare en Italie, II: Le 'Tractatus de hereticis' d'Anselme d'Alexandrie, O.P.," *Archivum fratrum praedicatorum* 20 (1950): 308–10. The "Free Spirits" alluded to here are those of central and southern Italy and probably related to the *fraticelli*. The existence of an organized, pan-European group of Free Spirits remains largely debunked after Robert Lerner's criticism; see Robert E. Lerner, *The Heresy of the Free Spirit in the Later Middle Ages* (Notre Dame, IN: University of Notre Dame Press, 1972).
31 Henricus Institoris and Jacobus Sprenger, *Malleus Maleficarum*, trans. P. G. Maxwell-Stuart (New York: Manchester University Press, 2007), especially Part I, questions 6, 9, and 15 and Part II, question 1, chapter 1.
32 Grundmann, *Religious Movements*, esp. 69–74; André Vauchez, *Sainthood in the Later Middle Ages*, trans. Jean Birrell (Cambridge: Cambridge University Press, 1997), esp. 145–246; Robert Bartlett, *Why Can the Dead Do Such Great Things? Saints and Worshippers from the Martyrs to the Reformation*

(Princeton, NJ: Princeton University Press, 2013), 57–84. For specifically Italy, see Franco Dal Pino, *Il Laicato italiano tra eresia e proposta pauperistico-evangelica nei secoli XII–XIII* (Padua: Università di Padova, 1984).

33 Whether there was actually an emergence of heretical beliefs or this perception was invented by an elite seeking to expand their authority, as R.I. Moore argued, is hotly contested. Essays by John H. Arnold and Mark Gregory Pegg reflect the varied concerns in the debate. See Moore, *Formation of a Persecuting Society*; John H. Arnold, "The Cathar Middle Ages as a Methodological and Historiographical Problem," 53–78, and Mark Gregory Pegg, "The Paradigm of Catharism; or, the Historian's Illusion," in *Cathars in Question*, ed. Antonio Sennis (Woodbridge: York Medieval Press, 2016), 21–52.

34 Richard Abels and Ellen Harrison, "The Participation of Women in Languedocian Catharism," *Mediaeval Studies* 41 (1979): 225.

35 Bernard of Luxembourg, *Catalogus haereticorum* (Cologne: Eucharius Cervicornus, 1522); Luis de Paramo, *De origine et progressu officii sanctae inquisitionis* (Madrid: Ex Typographia Regia, 1598).

36 The inquisitorial process is published in Benedetti, *Milano 1300*, from which the following overview derives. The most substantial studies on the group are Marina Benedetti, *Io non sono Dio: Guglielma di Milano e i Figli dello Spirito santo* (Milan: Edizioni Biblioteca Francescana, 1998) and Barbara Newman's essays: "WomanSpirit, WomanPope," in Newman, *From Virile Woman to WomanChrist* (Philadelphia: University of Pennsylvania Press, 1995), 182–223; "The Heretic Saint: Guglielma of Bohemia, Milan, and Brunate," *Church History* 74 (2005): 1–38; and "Agnes of Prague and Guglielma of Milan," in *Medieval Holy Women in the Christian Tradition*, ed. Rosalynn Voaden and Alastair Minnis (Turnhout: Brepols, 2010), 557–79.

37 Janine Larmon Peterson, "Social Roles, Gender Inversion, and the Heretical Sect: The Case of the Guglielmites," *Viator* 35 (2004): 203–19.

38 Benedetti, *Milano 1300*, 172.

39 Benedetti, *Milano 1300*, 214.

40 The idea of converting non-Christians was prevalent in the thirteenth century, although the methods used or envisioned varied: through an apocalyptic view of spiritual renewal, as with the Guglielmites; through forced conversions; or through praise and favours to attract converts. All of these techniques are placed within an argument of a thirteenth-century preoccupation with moral reform in William Chester Jordan's recent book *The Apple of His Eye: Converts from Islam in the Reign of Louis IX* (Princeton, NJ: Princeton University Press, 2019), esp. 1–20.

41 Benedetti, *Milano 1300*, 118.

42 The latter were "new" versions of the biblical books written by members of the group themselves (Benedetti, *Milano 1300*, 100).

284   Janine Larmon Peterson

43   Benedetti, *Milano 1300*, 72, 106, 110, 156, 164, 216.
44   Zamorei cited in Stephen Wessley, "The Thirteenth-Century Guglielmites: Salvation Through Women," in *Medieval Women*, Studies in Church History 14, ed. Derek Baker (Oxford: Basil Blackwell, 1978), 290; Antonio Bonfadini, *Vite di S. Guglielma regina d'Ungheria e di S. Eufrasia vergine romana*, ed. G. Ferraro (Bologna: Gaetano Romagnoli, 1878); Antonia Pulci, "The Play of Saint Guglielma," trans. James Wyatt Cook, in *Florentine Drama for Convent and Festival: Seven Sacred Plays* (Chicago: University of Chicago Press, 1996), 103–33.
45   Bernardino Corio, *L'historia di Milano* (Venice: Giorgio de'Cavalli, 1565), 367–8; modern edition as *Storia di Milano*, 2 vols., ed. Anna Morisi Guerra (Turin: Unione tipografico, 1978), 1:563–4.
46   Dolcino's followers noted that they themselves and others referred to the group as "Apostles" (*consueverant appellari apostoli*) or "those of Heaven" (*celorum*). See Lorenzo Paolini and Raniero Orioli, eds., *Acta S. Officii Bononie ab anno 1291 usque ad annum 1310*, 3 vols., Fonti per la storia d'Italia, 106 (Rome: Istituto storico italiano per il Medio Evo, 1982–4), 1: no. 77, p. 111 and 2: no. 679, p. 461, respectively. For the history of the movement, see Brian Carniello, "Gerard Segarelli as the Anti-Francis: Mendicant Rivalry and Heresy in Medieval Italy, 1260–1300," *Journal of Ecclesiastical History* 57 (2006): 226–51; and Jerry B. Pierce, *Poverty, Heresy, and the Apocalypse:The Order of Apostles and Social Change in Medieval Italy, 1260–1307* (New York: Continuum, 2012).
47   Heinrich Brueck, *History of the Catholic Church*, 2 vols. (New York: Benziger Brothers, 1884), 2:261. See Marina Benedetti, "Margherita da Trento," in *Dizionario Biografico degli Italiani*, vol. 70 (Rome: Istituto dell'Enciclopedia Italiana Treccani, 2007), 159–60.
48   The "spirituals" Dolcino mentioned probably refer to the Joachimite notion of the "spiritual men" who would guide the church in its last age, rather than Spiritual Franciscans. On the former, see Marjorie Reeves, *Joachim of Fiore and the Prophetic Future* (New York: Sutton Publishing, 1999 [1977]), 1–22; on the latter, including the dating of when the term "Spiritual Franciscans" became prevalent, see David Burr, *The Spiritual Franciscans: From Protest to Persecution in the Century After Saint Francis* (University Park: Pennsylvania State University Press, 2001), esp. vii–x, 317–18, and 344–6.
49   Salimbene, *Chronicle*, 117–19.
50   Paolini and Orioli, *Acta S. Officii*, 2: no. 579 and no. 893; Bernard of Luxembourg, *Catalogus haereticorum*, f. 20v.
51   Salimbene, *Chronicle*, 117–19; and Bernard Gui, *Additus ad Historia fratris Dulcini di anonimo sincrono e De secta illorum qui se dicunt esse de ordine Apostolorum di Bernardo Gui*, ed. A. Segarizzi, *Rerum Italicarum Scriptores* 9:5 (Città di Castello: Tipi della casa editrice S. Lapi, 1907), 449–53.

52 Sean L. Field, *The Beguine, the Angel, and the Inquisitor: The Trials of Marguerite Porete and Guiard of Cressonessart* (Notre Dame, IN: University of Notre Dame Press, 2012), on which the following overview is based (see 1–6 for the issues within her historiography).
53 Marguerite Porete, *The Mirror of Simple Souls*, trans. Edmund Colledge, J. C. Marler, and Judith Grant (Notre Dame, IN: University of Notre Dame Press, 1999).
54 Field, *The Beguine*, 9–10.
55 Lea, *History of the Inquisition*, 2: 577–8.
56 Paul Verdeyen, ed., "Le Procès d'inquisition contre Marguerite Porete et Guiard de Cressonessart (1309–1310)," *Revue d'histoire ecclésiastique* 81 (1986): 88–9. Although Marguerite Porete's sentence was first published in 1888, some modern historians, such as Ernest W. O'Donnell, erroneously called her a heresiarch; O'Donnell, *The Beguines and Beghards in Medieval Culture* (New Brunswick, NJ: Rutgers University Press, 1954), 490.
57 See Sean L. Field's assessment of Marguerite as compared to her contemporaries who challenged secular authorities (Field, *The Beguine, the Angel, and the Inquisitor*, 18).
58 "The Confession of Na Prous Boneta," in *Medieval Women's Visionary Literature*, ed. and trans. Elizabeth Petroff (New York: Oxford University Press, 1986), 286.
59 Petroff, "Confession of Na Prous Boneta," 288.
60 David Burr, "Na Prous Boneta and Olivi," *Collectanea franciscana* 67 (1997): 482.
61 Petroff, "Confession of Na Prous Boneta," 284.
62 Petroff, "Confession of Na Prous Boneta," 285.
63 Louisa A. Burnham, "The Visionary Authority of Na Prous Boneta," in *Pierre de Jean Olivi (1248–1298)*, ed. Alain Boureau and Sylvain Piron (Paris: Vrin, 1999), 319–39. The beguins of southern France, where Na Prous lived, were of the sect called Cathars, rather than the northern French beguins/beguines, who were a lay group who lived in voluntary communal poverty. On the Cathars, see Malcolm Lambert, *The Cathars: Dualist Heretics in Languedoc in the High Middle Ages* (New York: Routledge, 2013 [2000]); for a critique of the scholarship on the Cathars, see Mark Gregory Pegg, *A Most Holy War: The Albigensian Crusade and the Battle for Christendom* (New York: Oxford University Press, 2008).
64 "The Sentence of Na Prous Boneta," in Lea, *History of the Inquisition*, 3: 654.
65 Burnham, "Visionary Authority," 320.
66 On the beguins of southern France, see Louisa A. Burnham, *So Great a Light, So Great a Smoke: The Beguin Heretics of Languedoc* (Ithaca: Cornell University Press, 2008); and Alan Friedlander, *The Hammer of the Inquisitors: Brother Bernard Délicieux and the Struggle Against the Inquisition in*

Fourteenth-Century France (Boston: Brill, 2000). The classic text describing the communal networks in Languedoc is Emmanuel Le Roy Ladurie, *Montaillou: The Promised Land of Error*, trans. Barbara Bray (New York: G. Braziller, 1978).

67 John XXII used the term *heresiarchus* in his excommunication of Marsiglio on 9 April 1327 [Heinrich Denzinger, *Enchiridion symbolorum: definitionum et declarationum de rebus fidei et morum* (Freiburg: Herder, 1908)], 495.

68 Robert Michel, ed., "Les process de Matteo et de Galeazzo Visconti," *Mélanges d'archéologie et d'histoire* 19 (1909): 269–327; F. Bock, ed., "Der Este-Prozess von 1321," *Archivum Fratrum Praedicatorum* 7 (1937): 41–95.

69 Peter Biller, "The Preaching of the Waldensian Sisters," *Heresis* 30 (1999): 137–68 and "Cathars and Material Women," in Peter Biller and A. J. Minnis, eds., *Medieval Theology and the Natural Body* (Woodbridge: York Medieval Press, 1997), 61–107; Shulamith Shahar, *Women in a Medieval Heretical Sect: Agnes and Huguette the Waldensians*, trans. Yael Lotan (Rochester: Boydell, 2001). See Anne Brenon, "The Voice of the Good Women: An Essay on the Pastoral and Sacerdotal Role of Women in the Cathar Church," in *Women Preachers*, ed. Kienzle and Walker, 114–33.

70 Makowski, *"A Pernicious Sort of Woman,"* along with the scholars mentioned previously.

71 John Coakley, "Gender and the Authority of Friars: The Significance of Holy Women for Thirteenth-Century Franciscans and Dominicans," *Church History* 60 (1991): 445–60, and Coakley, *Women, Men and Spiritual Power*.

72 See, for example, Alison More, "Institutionalizing Penitential Life in Later Medieval and Early Modern Europe: Third Orders, Rules, and Canonical Legitimacy," *Church History* 83 (2014): 297–323; and Jennifer Kolpacoff Deane, "Pious Domesticities," in *The Oxford Handbook of Women and Gender in Medieval Europe*, ed. Judith Bennett and Ruth Mazo Karras (New York: Oxford University Press, 2013), 262–78.

73 Maya Corry, Marco Faini, and Alessia Meneghin, "Introduction," in *Domestic Devotions in Early Modern Italy*, ed. Corry, Faini, and Meneghin (Leiden: Brill, 2018), 3.

74 Sara Ritchey, "Affective Medicine: Later Medieval Healing Communities and the Feminization of Health Care Practices in the Thirteenth-Century Low Countries," *Journal of Medieval Religious Cultures* 40 (2014): 113–43.

75 James B. Given, *Inquisition and Medieval Society: Power, Discipline, and Resistance in Languedoc* (Ithaca: Cornell University Press, 1997), 91–140.

76 Paolini and Orioli, *Acta S. Officii*, 2: 487, no. 702.

77 On the issue of hospitality, see Jennifer Kolpacoff Deane, "Hospitality and Home in the Middle Ages," in *A Cultural History of the Home*, vol. 2, ed. Katherine L. French (London: Bloomsbury, 2020).

78 Paolini and Orioli, *Acta S. Officii*, 1: 127–8, no. 89.
79 Benedetti, *Milano 1300*, 180 and 80, respectively.
80 Benedetti, *Milano 1300*, 58, 64, 78, 80, 176.
81 Paolini and Orioli, *Acta S. Officii*, esp. testimony in vol. 2.

11 Navigating Saintly Circles: Margherita Colonna and the Women's Religious Movement in Rome

LEZLIE KNOX

In late December 1280, a pious young noblewoman lay dying. Margherita Colonna spent her final days in prayer surrounded by members of her powerful family and the women who lived with her in the informal religious community she had established in Mount Praenestino, a mountain hamlet in the Colonna patrimony to the east of Rome. Two remarkable *vitae* preserve accounts of this time.[1] Now bound together in a single manuscript, these unique texts document her family's extraordinary and ultimately unsuccessful efforts to achieve Margherita's canonization.[2] Together they present a portrait of an unpretentious woman dedicated to charity and the service of others, who both experienced mystical visions and was featured in those of others close to her and her family.

The author of the first text was her eldest brother, Senator Giovanni Colonna, who began writing about his sister shortly after her death.[3] Franciscan friars from communities supported by the family aided his efforts by collecting evidence of her miracles. The senator even hosted an event at the Church of San Pietro in Mount Praenestino, where Margherita had been buried, so that these witnesses might come together and testify publicly, thereby drawing greater attention to her saintly charisma.[4] Marginal notes now incorporated into the text by a later copyist indicate that he intended to ask a subsequent editor to add other stories about his sister's visions and subsequent miracles. The text suggests that Giovanni stopped adding to it around 1285, when the Colonna family translated Margherita's tomb from Mount Praenestino to the Church of San Silvestro in Capite located in the heart of their neighbourhood in Rome. It seems quite likely that the senator expected that this new shrine would become a pilgrimage site and generate more examples of Margherita's holiness to include in the *vita*. This church now also became the new home of Margherita's small community where the women professed their first monastic vows, thereafter becoming enclosed Franciscan nuns (*Sorores Minores Inclusae*).[5] Their institutional identity was unique among female convents in the Italian peninsula during the later thirteenth century, as most convents affiliated with the Franciscan Order were part of the Order of Saint Clare, who professed the 1263 rule approved by Pope Urban IV.[6] It is not clear why the Colonna chose this rule for San Silvestro in Capite, although it did serve to highlight the distinctness of the community and emphasize their affiliation with the Franciscan friars.

This relocation also appears to have inspired another brother, Cardinal Giacomo Colonna, to seek additional evidence for his sister's saintliness. He commissioned one of Margherita's companions, Stephania, to compose another text, which she worked on for the next three years. We know about Stephania only from her self-identification in the text's dedicatory letter and references to her own personal experiences, but she too may have been a Colonna relative, given the familiarity with the family that emerges in her account. Her text complemented Giovanni Colonna's earlier one by adding stories about Margherita's religious vocation, additional visions, and miracles, as well as details about the sisters' life on Mount Praenestino. Unfortunately, Stephania's account lacks information about the community after their founder's death, suggesting that some sections have been lost. In fact, her text, which survives in a different hand from that of the earlier *vita* compiled by Giovanni Colonna, ends abruptly in the middle of a word. Awkward passages where quotations from other documents were not fully integrated into Stephania's prose indicate that later editing was intended for her text as well.[7]

In sum, these two *vitae* can be read as preliminary materials meant to contribute to a canonization inquest concerning Margherita Colonna. To attract additional attention, San Silvestro in Capite was intended to serve as a focal point for her cult in Rome where visitors might pray at her tomb, which may have served as a shrine with a space for displaying a head reliquary.[8] Indeed, the Colonna family may have expected her canonization process to move forward in short order, especially with the election of their ally, Cardinal Jerome Masci, to the papal throne as Pope Nicholas IV (1288–91).[9]

Yet, Margherita's saintly cult never achieved much momentum outside the Colonna family itself.[10] Most scholars with reason have attributed the campaign's failure to the family's notorious conflict with Pope Boniface VIII (1294–1303).[11] Antagonism between the two parties reached a climax in 1298, when the pope declared a crusade against the Colonna cardinals, Margherita's brother Giacomo, and their nephew Pietro and authorized the destruction of their family properties in Rome and the surrounding countryside.[12] The Colonna cardinals eventually fled to Avignon, where their attention turned away from Margherita and towards other holy women and men.[13]

These events, as well as the enmity between the Colonna and the pope's Caetani family, well deserve their place as significant markers of elite power strategies and struggles in thirteenth-century Rome.[14] This essay, however, reconsiders and contextualizes Margherita's unlikely canonization and argues that its failure was due not only to political machinations but also to Rome's particular spiritual economy at the close of the thirteenth century. Indeed, even as pious memory identified Margherita Colonna as a Franciscan holy woman, she is better understood as an exemplar of the lay piety that had long flourished in the city. Her status as an independent religious woman dedicated to charity represents an important expression of Herbert Grundmann's scholarly "discovery," the medieval women's religious movement.[15] By examining Margherita's spiritual identity based on evidence from her life – her lived experience and her hagiographical *vitae* – and comparing her with contemporaries, we have evidence for the continued utility of Grundmann's term for thinking about expressions of lay female spirituality in medieval Rome. It signals the women's agency in shaping their religious experiences outside the institutional confines of the religious orders and ecclesiastical hierarchy.

The Women's Religious Movement in Medieval Italy

The study of female religious experience in later medieval Italy owes a clear debt to Grundmann's pioneering study. His influence is represented not only in the widespread recognition of the phrase *il movimento religioso femminile* but also by the notable attention scholars have devoted to the intersections between apostolic poverty as a spiritual ideal, female communities, and the Franciscan Order, especially after his updated 1961 edition was translated into Italian in 1974.[16] Although Grundmann had emphasized the spontaneous origins of the movement and credited the ecclesiastical hierarchy with uniting some communities under the aegis of the new mendicant orders, the study of women and the Franciscan movement has dominated the study of religious women in the Italian peninsula.[17] More recently, detailed regional studies have challenged this view and document instead the complex landscape of female religious life throughout the Italian peninsula. Luigi Pellegrini's useful synthesis of this research identifies three interconnected points that characterize thirteenth-century Italy and that offer a useful orientation for considering opportunities for Margherita Colonna and her contemporaries.[18]

First, while the curial model of regularizing female houses by enclosing them and incorporating them into the Franciscan Order defined the experience of some foundations in central and northern Italy (who were identified as the Order of Saint Clare after 1263), there were always those who sought other degrees of affiliation with the Friars Minors as well as various independent groups and individuals. Second, this point obviously means that we cannot collapse female religious experience into one single spiritual affiliation, be it Franciscan or otherwise. For example, Catherine Mooney has confirmed the limited influence of Clare of Assisi's vision of female Franciscanism focused on apostolic poverty, while Sherri Franks Johnson has demonstrated how older forms of monastic life maintained their appeal even with the success of the mendicant orders.[19] Finally, these differences produced significant regional variations. Central and northern Italy witnessed expansive spiritual creativity with religious communities, ranging from formal monastic institutions to informal ones of varying endurance. Towns often supported devotional cults focused on holy laywomen, such as those concerning Rose of Viterbo (d. 1251) and Margaret of Cortona (d. 1297), who were both associated with the Franciscan movement, as well as others who were not, including Fina of San Gimignano (d. 1253), Zita of Lucca (d. 1272), and Giovanna of Signa (d. 1307).[20] In contrast, southern Italy, which was less urbanized, lacked such exemplars of female charismatic authority and generally had fewer religious houses.[21] The Abruzzo, the geographical region to the east of Rome's Lazio, represented a sort of transitional area between these northern and southern models. Female communities there tended to be more traditionally monastic, holding fixed endowments and benefiting from ecclesiastical patronage, even as their foundresses' spiritual charisma emphasized charity to others.[22]

At first glance, thirteenth-century Rome appears too exceptional to fit into this religious topography.[23] The city's status as the spiritual centre of Latin Christendom was enhanced by the presence of the reforming papacy and its curial pomp. It was home to more than 400 churches and numerous religious sites connected to the early Christian period that attracted pilgrims and produced relics.[24] Yet, Rome was also home to a vibrant local religious culture defined by its parishes, collegiate chapels, confraternities, and hospitals, as well as male and female monastic foundations.[25] Remarkably, the religious identity of the Roman commune has received less attention than many other Italian urban centres. This is due in part to the city's symbiotic relationship with the papacy, as well as the limited surviving evidence. Few detailed chronicles or extensive notarial records survive from before the mid-fourteenth century.[26] But the existing evidence does show that religious women – including nuns, semi-religious women, recluses, and the devout laity who moved around the city – were all a critical part of the city's spiritual landscape. In fact, thirteenth-century Rome complicates one of Grundmann's most influential ideas about the medieval women's religious movement: the ultimate success of the papal agenda to institutionalize, regularize, and enclose religious women within convents incorporated into the new religious orders. Indeed, quite strikingly, such a project of institutionalization did not occur in a systematic way within the city of Rome, where medieval sources reveal that a more complex and flexible model of female religious life persisted into the later Middle Ages.

Roman Convents and the Orders

At the start of the thirteenth century, Rome had only eight female monastic communities. Each was independent and fairly small, with surviving records identifying fewer than ten nuns in most houses.[27] By the early fourteenth century, this number had doubled, with the early fourteenth-century Catalogue of Turin listing 18 convents housing 470 nuns.[28] This growth reflected the involvement of the papal curia and a deeper interest in the new religious orders. However, a brief consideration of the establishment of convents connected to the Dominican, Franciscan, and Cistercian Orders also raises important questions about the relationship between religious reform and the spiritual identities of Roman nuns.

Pope Innocent III had first directed his attention to the city's convents in 1204, when he forbade them from selling their property without curial approval. Innocent was also concerned with male houses divesting themselves of their properties, and more generally with the lack of central governance for communities following the Rule of Benedict, but here he couched his censure as part of his particular concern for the nuns (*cura nobis specialis*).[29] Four years later he proposed establishing a sort of super-convent (*coenobium universale*) that would bring together professed nuns and other religious women from around the city into a single foundation at San Sisto on the city's outskirts. In contrast to contemporary norms of openness and communal charitable engagement, which defined most existing communities, Innocent's proposed convent would be strictly enclosed, even though he valued the visibility of Rome's nuns on some occasions. When he promoted intercessional processions to support crusading efforts, the pope called for nuns to lead the women's processions.[30] Although Innocent died before renovations on San Sisto were completed, his successor, Pope Honorius III, continued to support the project. The latter commissioned Saint Dominic to place San Sisto under the care of the Friars Preacher – that is, the Dominicans – in 1221. Their project ultimately was successful. The convent housed up to seventy nuns by the end of the century, and its constitutions came to be adopted by other Dominican convents.[31] However, in looking at Dominic's efforts, we see tensions over this new form of life.

Sister Cecilia was a seventeen-year-old nun at the convent of Santa Maria in Tempuli when Dominic first sought to persuade the city's nuns to move to the new convent at San Sisto. Nearly a half century later, she dictated her memories of that time to a fellow nun.[32] Cecilia explained that most convents refused to consider Dominic's proposal, but from Santa Maria in Tempuli all but one sister agreed, provided they could bring along their well-known icon of the Virgin. Yet, when they arrived at San Sisto, the nuns were shocked to find that they were now expected to remain within the cloister and that visits from their families would be restricted. Their relatives similarly complained, as did some Romans whose access to the popular icon was now restricted. Dominic was able to convince the women to remain and to renew their oath of obedience to him. However, he took away their keys and assigned lay brothers to provide for the community and ensure the nuns remained strictly enclosed. Recalling this event fifty years later, Cecilia suggested that the nuns were attracted to Dominic's spiritual charisma and the opportunity to be associated with the Friars Preacher, which led them to adopt a new rule and accept strict enclosure. However, their ultimate compliance should not obscure their initial reluctance, which may well be the best surviving example of resistance from smaller communities of religious women in the city who also wanted to maintain their own traditions. Indeed, it is striking how few Roman convents were connected to the main religious orders in thirteenth-century Italy.

By 1233 there was also a convent affiliated with the Friars Minor, San Cosimato in Trastevere (also known as Saints Cosmas and Damian). It would remain the only Franciscan convent in the city until the Colonna established San Silvestro in Capite in Rome in 1285. San Cosimato's origins appear more obscure compared to San Sisto's. Surviving charters and bulls do not clarify whether the relationship between the community and the Franciscan Order resulted from the efforts of the papal legate Cardinal Hugolino (the future Pope Gregory IX) to regularize communities, or if an existing community of sisters identified independently with the Franciscan movement's spiritual ideals.[33] The latter was possible as Francis had spent time in Trastevere, where he likely stayed at the home of a pious laywoman, Jacoba de' Settesoldi.[34] Claudia Bolgia has suggested that memories of the saint's visits to that neighbourhood would have remained present in the late thirteenth century as younger people heard stories from their parents and grandparents.[35] If this is the case, it suggests that some community members desired a connection to the Franciscan Order or Francis's own spiritual charisma. As with other Franciscan convents, that relationship was perhaps more one of pastoral care than literal adherence to spiritual ideas like apostolic poverty, as the community did not seem to protest material endowments or identify with Clare's foundation in Assisi at San Damiano.[36] Indeed, financial security – especially for female communities – supported their growth and allowed for stronger patronage connections. By the early fourteenth century, the Catalogue of Turin listed thirty nuns at San Cosimato and two Friars Minor responsible for their pastoral care.[37]

In the mid-1250s, a Cistercian convent existed at San Pancrazio, replacing a Benedictine monastery.[38] Papal bulls suggest these nuns were originally a community of *repentite* who lived behind the Church of Santa Maria Sopra Minerva and had adopted the Cistercian habit and customs. Their reasons for doing so have not survived in the historical records, and in fact their motivations may have come from outside the community. Joan Barclay Lloyd suggests that Cardinal John of San Lorenzo in Lucrina, both a member of the Cistercian Order and founder of other Cistercian convents, might have been the initiator of this shift.[39] Although penitents, often referred to as *bizzoke* or *zoccoli* in addition to *repentite*, were common throughout the city, as discussed below, they do not seem to have attracted as much attention from curial reformers as was the case in central and northern Italy. Rome notably had no communities of tertiaries before the later fourteenth century.[40] Like the two mendicant-affiliated communities, San Pancrazio similarly had endowments that supported approximately thirty-five nuns. Thus, we might ask what made these convents affiliated with the new orders different from the reformed female houses following the Rule of Benedict that also existed in the city?[41] These convents, whether Franciscan, Dominican, or Cisterian, were all strictly enclosed, and surviving evidence does not indicate whether they had distinct spiritual profiles in terms of the sisters' communal lives. Moreover, their foundations do not seem to have been a part of their order's larger devotional strategies for defining their place in Rome. Rather, the mendicant orders established their identities through their friars' churches.

Finally, when considering the women's religious movement in Rome, it appears that a fully cloistered life was less appealing for Romans compared to other possibilities. Baronial families, including the Colonna, tended to seek marriage alliances for their daughters rather than place them in convents.[42] Indeed, compared to elsewhere in medieval Europe, Rome's urban aristocracy also did not patronize religious houses as part of their dynastic strategies, at least until the fourteenth century, when there are more examples of connections between charity, spiritual charisma, and power.[43] In earlier centuries, service as cardinals (and popes) had provided a reliable income that could be used to increase both their aristocratic families' territorial holdings and religious influence.[44] This situation thus allowed other options for religious life beyond the purview of the religious orders to develop prominence. For some Roman women, it was an appealing option.

Independent Religious Women in Rome

Although challenging to identify in the source base, independent religious women living outside of formal monastic communities played a critical role in defining Rome's spiritual landscape. Pilgrims who came to Rome during the early thirteenth century would have made offerings to recluses who lived in cells near churches and along city walls.[45] We lack precise information about their numbers, as well as details of their individual lives and social backgrounds, but intriguing references to these women and their persistence in Rome have survived. For example, Sister Cecilia described how Dominic healed two recluses who lived along the pilgrimage route between the Lateran and the Church of Santa Croce. Sister Bona lived alone in a tower cell attached to the Lateran Gate, cared for by a woman known as Jacobina. Having heard about her reputation for piety, Dominic visited her regularly to hear her confession and offer her Communion. During one of these visits, he cured her from an infestation of worms.[46] The other recluse, Sister Lucia, lived behind the Church of Santa Anastasia. Her weakened arm was cured by the saint when he blessed her with the sign of the cross. This particular miracle story is interesting, as it notes that not only was Dominic accompanied by a large group of friars, but Cecilia shared that she herself had also visited Sister Lucia many times before she entered the convent.[47]

Francis of Assisi also became acquainted with a recluse named Prassede, who lived in a tower cell in Trastevere and whom he later healed in a posthumous miracle. Francis's prolific biographer, Thomas of Celano, described how one night she fell from her rooftop terrace, resulting in serious injuries. Prassede dislocated her shoulder and broke her leg and foot in multiple places. Unable to move and in great pain, she prayed to

Francis, suggesting that their personal relationship made her as deserving as those who had never met him yet were cured by his intervention. She then fell asleep (or passed out from pain) and experienced a vision of Francis, who was able to cure her completely. Thomas first wrote about Prassede's miracle in the mid-1230s, but when he returned to her story in the 1250s, he either knew more details or was interested in embellishing the miracle story to more clearly associate her with the Franciscan Order.[48] The later version elevated her anonymous clerical advisors to the cardinalate and claimed that Francis was so moved by her piety that he received her religious vow and provided her with a Franciscan habit and cord.[49] Thomas also now described her as "among the best known religious women in the City and in Roman circles." He recognized the contemporary appeal of recluses and their persistence in the city when he added a note that she had refused the advice and ultimately the order of her clerical advisors to have other "religious women" (*alicuius religiosae feminae*) support her.[50] Prassede was extraordinary due to her relationship with Francis, but she also was one of many. The Catalogue of Turin claimed there was a total of 260 recluses or enclosed women in the city (*summa omnium reculsarum sive incarceratarum urbis*) as a reminder, the contemporary population of nuns was 470).[51]

Although their presence is less obvious in the surviving sources, Rome was also home to pious laywomen who remained in their homes but were members of confraternities, founders of hospitals, and patrons of other religious sites. Indeed, their own homes could serve as devotional sites. Thomas of Celano confirmed how Roman noblewomen often dedicated a space in their homes for prayer, which they would decorate with an image of their preferred saintly advocate. One woman had a small devotional image of Francis but was frustrated that the artist had not represented the stigmata. Then, once while she gazed at it in prayer, the wounds appeared. Amazed, the woman called her daughter to confirm that it was not a trick of her mind or confusion that the painting had originally shown Francis with the stigmata. Although the daughter assured her mother, later she wondered again if she had forgotten their original presence. This doubt led to a second miracle: the wounds disappeared from the painting, thereby confirming their divine placement.[52] This story returns us to Margherita Colonna and a consideration of smaller independent and fleeting penitential groups.

Giovanni Colonna's *vita* provided intriguing information about a woman known as Lady Altrude of the Poor, who had lived with his sister for a period.[53] No known contemporary evidence survives about her outside his text, although she was clearly well known in Rome. She presumably came from an elite family, as she was known as Lady and had the means to support herself. Giovanni Colonna also described her as an elderly woman, having committed herself to living in chastity and prayer since childhood. Altrude began her days hearing Mass at Santa Maria in Aracoeli, the main residence of the Friars Minor in Rome, and then visited different altars and shrines around the city accompanied by a female companion. This example shows how freedom of movement and the ability to visit key religious sites in the city remained an important component of the Roman religious experience. Perhaps she and Margherita met in one of these churches. When the latter joined her household, Margherita did not accompany them but rather stayed home to clean and cook. Presumably Altrude also gave alms to the poor as well, as highlighted by the epithet in contrast with the honorific title *Domina*. We cannot know, of course, how many women there were like Altrude in thirteenth-century Rome, but her example suggests that there were spaces outside monastic institutions for religious women to pursue their pious and charitable activities and to do so with other women in attendance, creating networks of open lay religious communities and associations that rarely appear in the written record.

Margherita Colonna's Piety and the Women's Religious Movement

Giovanni Colonna was not an early supporter of his sister's religious vocation. In fact, his *vita* begins with his admission that he and Giacomo often had been at cross purposes when it came to their guardianship of Margherita after the death of their parents. As head of the family, Giovanni arranged for Margherita to marry a Roman noble, although she firmly and repeatedly rejected his plan.[54] By contrast, both the senator's and Stephania's accounts indicate that Giacomo was Margherita's primary supporter within the family, encouraging her determination to remain a virgin and ultimately helping her establish her small community on Mount Praenestino. However, there appeared to have been an alternate plan in which Margherita became a nun at the convent of Santa Chiara in Assisi. Giovanni Colonna acknowledged that the Franciscan Minister General had approved her entry but cryptically stated that illness prevented her from doing so.[55] Based on the type of community she ultimately established, it may be that Margherita (with Giacomo's support) was not interested in the more conventional path of enclosed religious life that her older brother might have considered most appropriate. Although the details of the siblings' debates do not emerge in chronological sequence, they do reveal a fundamental tension between the appeal of more traditional monastic institutions and

Margherita's insistence on living an independent life of pious service outside the confines of a convent's enclosure.

Margherita is often identified as a Franciscan holy woman, although she only entered into the order's hagiographic tradition with Mariano of Florence's 1519 history of the Order of Saint Clare, which incorrectly remembered her as an enclosed nun. Her Franciscan identity deserves attention. After persuading her eldest brother that she had no intention to marry, the siblings at first considered establishing a new convent for her in Rome. This never occurred – Giovanni referred at different times to obstacles and shame that they did not carry out this plan – but never explained these circumstances. Given the discussion above, it is curious that San Cosimato, the Franciscan convent in Trastevere, was never mentioned in the *vitae* as an option. That may reflect just how far it was from the Colonna's neighbourhoods in Rome (that is, from their sphere of influence) as well as Margherita's own desires. He also stated that Margherita wanted to construct a new building, rather than adapt an existing one, although this desire was not for her own purposes but, rather, for her subsequent followers.[56] He suggested that their failure to establish this foundation led to Margherita's great desire to enter Santa Chiara in Assisi, which the Franciscan Minister General gave her permission to do, as noted above.[57] However, it seems more likely that this initiative to become an enclosed nun, and specifically to join the Franciscan Order of Saint Clare, was prompted by her brothers. The Colonna family were strong supporters of the Franciscan Order and active patrons of friaries throughout their patrimony. Cardinal Giacomo included friars in his household, and we have already seen how Senator Giovanni called on other friars to collect stories about his sister's miracles.[58] Whether illness actually prevented Margherita from entering the convent in Assisi, both *vitae* actually make clear that she herself was not interested in the cloister. While Giovanni explained how she wore the habit of the sisters in Assisi, Stephania associated Margherita's dress directly with Clare of Assisi.[59] In other words, her spiritual identification was with the earliest followers of Francis.

Margherita also expressed this commitment through caring for the poor. Once she and Giacomo had obtained her dowry, they set aside plans to fund a monastery and instead directed the money towards charitable purposes. Margherita provided clothing, food, and medicine to those in need. She also offered alms to Roman churches and shrines, lodging for pilgrims, and support for poor women who wanted to enter religious institutions. She even made loans (without expecting repayment) or provided anonymous funding for those who had fallen on hard times.[60]

Between 1273 and 1277, Margherita travelled between Giovanni's house in Rome and three different locations: Mount Praenestino, a Marian shrine at Vulturella, and Lady Altrude's house in Rome. In each case, she lived with a small community of pious women. With them, she fasted regularly, devoted herself to prayer, and even wore a hair shirt under her clothing, all clear signs of piety without any particular religious affiliation. Moreover, she dedicated herself to helping others, a charitable ideal that she infused into the religious community she founded. Ultimately, Giovanni appeared to have understood that her model was Francis of Assisi himself: "[S]he took up from [Francis] the cross which he bore and preached. For, just as he left everything behind, she did [too], she make herself poor, and what she had begun did not fall from her heart. And she, the very least of the *minores*, served the poor of Christ and the servants of Christ just as he had."[61]

Conclusion

That Margherita Colonna never became a saint was not due to a failure of her charismatic authority or a collapse of dynastic ambitions. Rather, her life and devotional model illustrate the fluidity of medieval women's spiritual lives, as well as the ways in which their forms of life often existed outside the parameters of religious institutions. In this particular case, she represents a form of active piety typical of Roman urban religiosity. We know about her spiritual ideals as well as her interests in supporting a community of pious women due to her family's circumstances, which first produced and then preserved these remarkable *vitae*. The later history of the institutions associated with her followers has helped to identify her as an example of the female movement connected to Francis of Assisi and the religious orders that developed in his wake. However, a careful reading of these texts shows the ways in which Margherita's piety existed both within and outside these institutional settings. Grundmann's legacy is to remind us to look for the organic and flexible arrangements that existed in practice, often at the women's direction, even as normative documents sought to regularize these examples.

NOTES

1 Livarius Oliger, ed., *B. Margherita Colonna († 1280): Le due vite scritte dal fratello Giovanni Colonna senatore di Roma e da Stefania monaca di S. Silvestro in Capite* (Rome: Facultas Theologica Pontificii Athenaei Seminarii Romani, 1935). My discussion of these texts and Margherita herself builds on the

300   Lezlie Knox

translation and commentary project I undertook with Larry F. Field and Sean L. Field: *Visions of Sainthood in Medieval Rome: The Lives of Margherita Colonna by Giovanni Colonna and Stefania* (Notre Dame, IN: University of Notre Dame Press, 2017), hereafter cited as *Visions*.

2   The manuscript is now in Rome's Biblioteca Casanatense, catalogued as ms. 104. For a full description of the manuscript, see Field, Knox, and Field, *Visions*, 205–6.

3   Giovanni Colonna's personal involvement in drafting his sister's *vita* was unusual. Certainly, other elite families sought to promote their holy relatives as saints, and increasingly Europe's ruling families claimed that sainthood was passed through their bloodlines (the concept of *beata stirps*). But even when promoting the cults of various holy women became central to their own claims of royal authority, as Sean Field has recently demonstrated for the Capetians, few close relatives actively collected miracles or wrote down their own memories, as in the example of Margherita Colonna, where her two brothers and perhaps a niece were active hagiographers. See Sean L. Field, *Courting Sanctity: Holy Women and the Capetians* (Ithaca: Cornell University Press, 2019), as well as earlier studies, such as Gábor Klaniczay, *Holy Rulers and Blessed Princesses: Dynastic Cults in Medieval Central Europe* (Cambridge: Cambridge University Press, 2002).

4   Field, Knox, and Field, *Visions*, 141, refers to this event as well as the friars' efforts to collect miracles.

5   For the sixteenth-century account of Margherita's translation, see Field, Knox, and Field, *Visions*, 202–4. See also 144–54 for the bull transferring the sisters and approving their profession of the rule of the *Sorores Minores*.

6   This document followed earlier papal legislation that allowed for pastoral relationships with the Friars Minor but also allowed for financial endowments unlike the *formula vitae* composed by Clare of Assisi, which was adopted by only a handful of communities. A useful introduction to the complex institutional and legislative history for women affiliated with the Franciscan Order in Italy is Maria Pia Alberzoni, *Clare of Assisi and the Poor Sisters in the Thirteenth Century* (St. Bonaventure: Franciscan Institute Publications, 2004), especially the last two chapters, which centre the discussion away from Clare of Assisi's San Damiano as an institution model. For a discussion of the rule for the *Sorores Minores Inclusae*, composed by Isabelle of France and a team of Franciscan friars for the convent she established near Paris, see Sean L. Field, *Isabelle of France: Capetian Sanctity and Franciscan Identity in the Thirteenth Century* (Notre Dame, IN: University of Notre Dame Press, 2006), especially chap. 3 and 4.

7   Giovanni Colonna's *vita* runs from pages 1 to 26, while Stephania's is 27–38. We concluded that the two *vitae* likely were copied at San Silvestro

in Capite during the first decades of the fourteenth century, based on the distinct handwriting and parchment of each *vita*. They were bound together by at least the late fifteenth century. See Field, Knox, and Field, *Visions*, 205–7, for a fuller discussion.

8 A fourteenth-century registry recorded a head reliquary, although its location (or, rather, that of the sixteenth-century reliquary which succeeded it) is not currently known. Subsequent restorations also mean that we do not know the original location of Margherita's tomb. Stephania referred to two Colonna nieces who were inspired to profess vows and join the community after praying at their aunt's tomb. See Field, Knox, and Field, *Visions*, 177–8.

9 Field, Knox, and Field, *Visions*, 48–51, addresses reasons why his support did not materialize. Previously, Masci had been Minister General of the Franciscan Order (1274–9) and then bishop of Palestrina (elected 1281) in the heart of the Colonna territory.

10 Their campaign for Margherita's canonization was recognized by contemporaries, including at least one who considered the family's efforts unseemly until a miracle persuaded otherwise. See examples of their efforts to collect miracle stories in Field, Knox, and Field, *Visions*, 134–53 and 183.

11 For example, Giulia Barone, "Le due vite di Margherita Colonna," in *Esperienza religiosa e scritture femminili tra medioevo ed età moderna*, ed. Marilena Modica (Acrireale: Bonnano, 1992), 25–32; Robert Brentano, *Rome Before Avignon: A Social History of Thirteenth-Century Rome* (Los Angeles: University of California Press, 1990), 174–83.

12 The *Cronaca Romana* by the Vicenzan procurator Guidotto Spiapasto has a succinct account that nonetheless captures the drama of these events: "Item eodem anno [1297] mense maii die jovis in festo asencionis domini X kall. ipse dominus bonifacius papa in sancto petro de urbe denunciavit coram populo cardinalium et prelatorum dominum jacobum et dominum petrum de colompna cardinales excomminicatos scismaticos hereticos et patarenos et ipsis privavit capello rubeo officio cardinalatus et omnibus dignitatibus clericalibus prebendis et beneficiis suis que habebant ab ecclesia romana et publicavit etiam omnia ipsorum bono ecclesie romane. Item fecit de omnibus filiis domini Johannis de columpna et eorum sequacibus usque ad quartam generacionem et omnes domos ipsorum de urbe fecit dirrui et devastari." See D. D. Bortolan, ed., "Cronaca Romana dall'anno 1288 al 1301," *Archivio Veneto* 33 (1887): 425–33, quotation from 430.

13 See Field, Knox, and Field, *Visions*, 54–8, for their relationships with Angela of Foligno, Clare of Montefalco, and Spiritual Franciscans, such as Angelo Clareno. Emily Graham has considered the family's later strategies, especially Pietro Colonna's foundation of a new Franciscan

convent in Rome, which also diverted attention from San Silvestro in Capite. See Graham, "Memorializing Identity: The Foundation and Reform of San Lorenzo in Panisperna," *Franciscan Studies* 75 (2017): 467–95.

14 Most studies of medieval Italy mention this event. For example, a recent survey begins its chapter on the Roman nobility with their conflict. See Jean-Claude Maire Vigueur, *The Forgotten Story: Rome in the Communal Period*, trans. David Fairservice (Rome: Viella, 2016), 167–9 (originally published in French in 2010).

15 The phrase is Robert Lerner's from his introduction to the English translation, in Herbert Grundmann, *Religious Movements in the Middle Ages* (Notre Dame, IN: University of Notre Dame Press, 1995), xx.

16 See Herbert Grundmann, *Movimenti religiosi nel Medioevo: ricerche sui nessi storici tra l'eresia, gli ordini mendicanti e il movimento religioso femminile nel XII e XIII secolo e sulle origini storiche della mistica tedesca* (Bologna: Il Mulino, 1974). Two conferences held shortly afterward reflect the translation's influence and in turn helped shape research agendas for the next two decades. See *Movimento religioso femminile e francescanesimo nel secolo XIII. Atti del VII convegno internazionale. Assisi, 11–13 ottobre 1979* (Assisi: Società Internazionale di Studi Francescani, 1980) and Roberto Rusconi, ed., *Il Movimento religioso femminile in Umbria nei secoli XIII–XI. Atti del Convegno internazionale di studio nell'ambito delle celebrazioni per l'VIII centenario della nascita di S. Francesco d'Assisi. Città di Castello, 27–28–29 ottobre 1982.* (Florence: La Nuova Italia Editrice, 1984).

17 Grundmann's choice of the term "movement" reflects the organic nature of religious inspiration during the High Middle Ages outside institutions. Chapters 4 ("The Origin of the Women's Religious Movement") and 5 ("The Incorporation of the Women's Religious Movement into the Mendicant Orders") remain critical for thinking about their institutionalization; see especially his summation on 134. Part of the dominance of the Franciscan tradition results from excellent Italian research centres which hold regular conferences, such as Scuola Superiore di Studi Medievali Francescani, sponsored by the Pontificio Ateneo Antoniaum, and the Società Internazionale di Studi Francescani that is part of the Centro Italiano di Studi sull'alto Medioevo.

18 Luigi Pellegrini, "Female Religious Experience and Society in Thirteenth-Century Italy," in *Monks and Nuns, Saints and Outcasts: Religion in Medieval Society. Essays in Honor of Lester K. Little*, ed. Sharon Farmer and Barbara H. Rosenwein (Ithaca: Cornell University Press, 2000), 97–122. Continuity in these trends, including Grundmann's influence, is also manifest in the extensive bibliography reflecting smaller conferences and theses drawn on by Bert Roest for his discussion of the institutional development of female Franciscanism in Italy. See Bert Roest, *Order and Disorder: The Poor Clares between Foundation and Reform* (Leiden: Brill, 2013), esp. 80–5.

19 Catherine M. Mooney, *Clare of Assisi and the Thirteenth-Century Church* (Philadelphia: University of Pennsylvania Press, 2016). Johnson's work also challenges another idea derived from Grundmann's focus, namely that conflict over pastoral care typically defined relations between religious men and women. See Sherri Franks Johnson, *Monastic Women and Religious Orders in Late Medieval Bologna* (Cambridge: Cambridge University Press, 2014).

20 An important new study of these figures is Mary Harvey Doyno, *The Lay Saint: Charity and Charismatic Authority in Medieval Italy, 1150–1350* (Ithaca: Cornell University Press, 2019). She argues that the success of these cults increasingly depended on their hagiographers' ability to mitigate the women's lay status by emphasizing connections to the religious orders, such as the Franciscans. Their independence, reflected in their visionary charisma as well as life outside a cloister, could threaten religious authorities. As part of an elite family with close connections to the Franciscan Order, Margherita's cult had the potential to succeed.

21 E. Ann Matter's bibliographic essay on Italian religious women reflects this difference, and all her examples come from northern Italy, "Italian Holy Women: A Survey," in *Medieval Holy Women in the Christian Tradition, c. 1100–c. 1500*, ed. Alastair Minnis and Rosalynn Voaden (Turnhout: Brepols, 2010), 529–55.

22 Pellegrini, "Female Religious," 114–19.

23 James A. Palmer offers a pithy orientation to current studies of thirteenth- and fourteenth-century Rome in "Medieval and Renaissance Rome: Mending the Divide," *History Compass* 15 (2017), https://doi.org/10.1111/hic3.12424.

24 This number – more properly 414 – comes from the "Catalogue of Turin," an inventory of the city's religious institutions created by Roman clergy between 1312 and 1330. See "Il Catalogo di Torino" in *Codice Topografico della città di Roma*, ed. R. Valentini and G. Zucchetti (Rome: Fonti per la Storia di Italia, 1980), 3:291–318. Its usefulness, as well as its limits, as a source for Roman religious culture is evident throughout the essays published in the same journal in 2009. See *Vita religiosa a Roma* (secoli XIII–XV) Estratto da *Archivio della Società Romana di Storia Patria* 132 (2009).

25 A new collaborative project has begun to explore the connections between the city's inhabitants and its monastic institutions. See Giulia Barone and Umberto Longo, eds., *Roma religiosa. Monasteri e città (secoli VI–XVI)*, in *Reti Medievali Rivista* 19 (2018): 263–543.

26 The principal study of Italian communal religion does *not* consider Rome, which reflects those source limitations. See Augustine P. Thompson, *Cities of God: The Religion of the Italian Communes, 1125–1325* (University Park: Pennsylvania State University Press, 2005). See Palmer's discussion for studies that do look at elements of this local culture in closer detail.

27 A pioneering study of women's religious life in Rome is Brenda Bolton, "Daughters of Rome: All One in Christ Jesus," *Studies in Church History* 27 (1992): 101–15.
28 For challenges related to the Catalogue, as well as difficulties establishing an accurate census of Roman convents, see Alfonso Marini, "Monasteri femminili a Roma nei secoli XIII–XV," *Archivio della Società Romana di Storia Patria* 132 (2009): 81–108.
29 See Bolton, "Daughters of Rome," 107 for a discussion of this letter. For the broader European context of his efforts, see Anne E. Lester, *Creating Cistercian Nuns* (Ithaca: Cornell University Press, 2011), esp. 88–92.
30 Innocent III first issued an encyclical calling for a major procession in 1212 in support of the crusade against the Almohads in Iberia. That procession's success – the Christian armies won a notable victory at Las Navas de Tolosa – led in 1215 to *Quia Maior* calling for monthly repetitions in support of the Fifth Crusade, albeit with separate processions for the women where possible. These documents are translated in Jessalynn Bird, Edward Peters, and James M. Powell, eds., *Crusade and Christendom: Annotated Documents* (Philadelphia: University of Pennsylvania Press, 2013), 82–4 and 108–9.
31 For a more detailed discussion, with references to earlier scholarship, see Guido Cariboni, "Domenico e la vita religiosa femminile. Tra realtà e finzione istituzionale," in *Domenico di Caleruega e la nascita dell'ordine dei frati Predicatori. XLI Convegno storico internazionale del Centro italiano di studi sul Basso Medioevo – Accademia Tudertina (Todi dal 10 al 12 ottobre 2004)* (Spoleto: Centro Italiano di Studi Sull'Alto Medioevo, 2005), 327–60.
32 Angelus Walz, "Die 'Miracula Beati Dominici' der Schwester Cäcilia: Einleitung und Text," *Miscellanea Pio Paschini – Lateranum* ns 2 (Rome, 1948): 293–326. For a sensitive reading of Cecilia's perspective, see Anne L. Clark, "Under Whose Care? The Madonna of San Sisto and Women's Monastic Life in Twelfth- and Thirteenth-Century Rome," in Teodolinda Barolini, ed., *Medieval Constructions in Gender and Identity: Essays in Honor of Joan M. Ferrante* (Tempe: Arizona Center for Medieval and Renaissance Studies, 2005), 29–42. Rather than presuming that an affiliation with the Dominicans was always desired, she brings out the sense of loss felt by many in the community.
33 The convent's chronicle by Sister Caterina Osimo dates from the late Middle Ages and gives little attention to the community's origins. See K.J.P. Lowe, *Nuns' Chronicles and Convent Culture in Renaissance and Counter-Reformation Italy* (Cambridge: Cambridge University Press, 2003), 61–71, as an introduction.
34 Thomas of Celano's biographies of Francis as well as other contemporary Franciscan sources refer to the close friendship between this Roman noblewoman and Francis. While these accounts focus mainly on how she was divinely inspired to travel to Assisi to attend his deathbed (bringing

linens for burial and Francis's favourite almond cookies), they also reveal a long-standing friendship and mutual support. See, for example, the version in the *Assisi Compilation*, in Regis J. Armstrong, J. A. Wayne Hellmann, and William J. Short, eds., *Francis of Assisi: Early Documents* 3 vols. (New York: New City Press, 2000), 2: 121–3.

35 Claudia Bolgia, *Reclaiming the Roman Capitol: Santa Maria in Aracoeli from the Altar of Augustus to the Franciscans, c. 500–1450* (New York: Routledge, 2017), 108–9. She also discusses a devotional painting and fresco that demonstrate local interest in Francis.

36 I have discussed the desire for connection with the Friars Minor, in *Creating Clare of Assisi: Female Franciscan Identities in Later Medieval Italy* (Leiden: Brill, 2008), 87–122. It is worth reemphasizing here that few thirteenth-century Italian convents were connected to San Damiano or Clare's spiritual ideals.

37 Compare the bull *Quotiens a Nobis*, in *Bullarium Franciscanum*, 1: 249–52 (1238).

38 Joan E. Barclay Lloyd, "The Church and Monastery of S. Pancrazio, Rome," in *Pope, Church and City: Essays in Honour of Brenda M. Bolton*, ed. Frances Andrews et al. (Leiden: Brill, 2004), 245–66.

39 Lloyd, "The Church and Monastery of S. Pancrazio, Rome," 256–7.

40 Marini, "Monasteri femminili a Roma," 96–7; for the literature on Rome's tertiaries, see also the comments of Anna Esposito, "Il Mondo della religiosità femminile Romana," in the same volume, 149–72.

41 Giulia Barone, "Chierici, monaci, e frati," in *Roma medieval*, ed. André Vauchez (Rome: Edizioni Laterza, 2006), 211.

42 Vigueur, *The Forgotten Story*, 188, drawing on the extensive prosopographical studies of Sandro Carrocci, *Baroni de Roma. Dominazioni signorili e lignaggi aristocratici nel duecento e nel primo trecento* (Rome: École Française de Rome, 1993).

43 Carla Keyvanian discussed the development of such strategies in *Hospitals and Urbanism in Rome, 1200–1500* (Leiden: Brill, 2015).

44 This strategy for increasing political and religious influence was recognized by chroniclers at least since Giovanni Villani in the fourteenth century. For this reference and a broad discussion, see Vigueur, *The Forgotten Story*, esp. 175–96.

45 Katherine Brophy Dubois, "Stranger and Sojourners: Pilgrims, Penance and Urban Geography in Late-Medieval Rome" (unpublished PhD diss., University of Michigan, 2001).

46 Walz, "Miracula Beati Dominici," 322–3. I have characterized this space as a sort of anchoritic cell due to the description of their visits occurring across a window, which allowed them to see each other and pass through items such as the consecrated Host and even one of the worms that had infested her chest.

47 Walz, "Miracula Beati Dominici," 323: "quam etiam soror Cecilia, antequam in monasterio esset pluries viderat." Although her reference is not precise, Cecilia may be referring to the period before or while she was living in the community at Santa Maria in Tibertina, i.e., before becoming an enclosed nun at San Sisto.

48 The earliest version occurs in his abridgement of his first life (c. 1232–7). See Jacques Dalarun, *The Rediscovered Life of St. Francis of Assisi by Thomas of Celano*, trans. Timothy J. Johnson (St. Bonaventure, NY: Franciscan Institute Publications, 2016). He then expanded it in his *Treatise on Miracles* (1250–2); see the translation in no. 181 in Armstrong, et al., *Francis of Assisi: Early Documents*, 2: 462–3. Knowledge of the story would have increased after it was included in Bonaventure's *Major Legend*.

49 As the editors note, receiving vows from women was explicitly contrary to Francis's earliest regulations for the Friars Minor (see Earlier Rule 12:4), 462 n.a.

50 "Praxedis, religiosarum famosissima in Urbe ac orbe Romano" is the description from the *Treastise on Miracles*, which continues with her refusal to have others live with her because of her religious vow.

51 This comparison is noted in Esposito, "Il Mondo," 168. "Il Catalogo," 318.

52 Thomas reported that he himself had met this pious woman, *Treatise on Miracles*, 405–6.

53 Field, Knox, and Field, *Visions*, 106–10. The Latin text describes her thus: "Unde a pauperibus accepit cognomen et nominabatur domina Altruda pauperum, upsa etiam Christi pauper." See Oliger, 152.

54 Field, Knox, and Field, *Visions*, 66–73. The second chapter presents a sort of overview of Giovanni's plans for Margherita in contrast to Giacomo's encouragement. In other sections, he referred to Margherita's rejection of her trousseau and rebuffing of two Dominicans who were sent by her potential mother-in-law to encourage her to change her mind (Field, Knox, and Field, *Visions*, 73, 87). Stephania also mentioned the proposed marriage (Field, Knox, and Field, *Visions*, 160–1).

55 Field, Knox, and Field, *Visions*, 99–101.

56 Field, Knox, and Field, *Visions*, 92, 100.

57 The text does not mention the date directly, although we can reconstruct it to 1274, or about two years after she refused the proposed marriage, by references to other events. See Field, Knox, and Field, *Visions*, 72 and 109, including our discussion of the identity of the Minister General.

58 Field, Knox, and Field, *Visions*, 132–8 describes friars who accompanied Giacomo to Margherita's deathbed and participated in the vigil after her death.

59 Compare Field, Knox, and Field, *Visions*, 89 and 168.

60 Field, Knox, and Field, *Visions*, 93–4.

61 Field, Knox, and Field, *Visions*, 91.

12 The "Clever Girls" of Prague: Beguines, Preachers, and Late Medieval Bohemian Religion[1]

JANA GROLLOVÁ

In the late thirteenth-century Czech narrative "On the Bad Years after the Death of King Otakar," the anonymous author lists a wide range of people across various social categories, classes, and positions of power in medieval Prague.[2] From secular lords and elite clergy to citizens and children, he sketches the city's social topography for posterity at a pivotal historical moment.[3] Beguines are included in this list, following "married women" and preceding "widows" and "virgins," evidently acknowledged as members of respected, local semi-religious communities.[4] As in western Europe, beguine communities were gatherings of pious single women; independent of formal religious vows, they generally lived together in donated houses, prayed for the souls of donors, and performed charitable acts, such as making clerical cloth or teaching girls.[5] Recent work on medieval lay religious women in the west (especially France, the Low Countries, and Germany) has focused on shifting beguines from marginal status to the centre of analysis. Such new scholarship illuminates the close ties between beguines and their broader socio-spiritual settings: elastic relationships with priests, mendicants, educated laymen, families, local institutions, reform movements, and so on.[6]

This essay explores the rich historical context of fourteenth- and fifteenth-century Prague centred on beguine communities and activities, which was both comparable to patterns elsewhere yet had some distinct contextual differences. Although Czech beguines developed and sustained vital relationships with priests, mendicants, and educated laymen, as did lay religious women elsewhere in Europe, this web of relationships was specifically mediated by devotional texts and sermons. In turn, the active involvement of many beguines in the Bohemian reformation and revolution enabled anti-Hussite critics to turn that interconnectedness against them in their own literary productions.

In satirical and exhortatory texts, hostile writers mocked the women's textual and literate pretensions and involvement in preaching and reform, citing such behaviours as fundamentally disgraceful evidence of Hussite depravity. Within the crucible of Bohemian reformation and revolution, late medieval Prague thus offers a rich site in which to explore the vibrant realm between orders and heresy.

The Bohemian Context

As thirteenth-century eschatological expectations fuelled a new emphasis on biblical study and the active pursuit of good deeds in western Europe, so too did the new currents of devotion inspire creativity in the urban and rural territories of Bohemia. The emergence and influence of Czech beguine communities is closely connected to two broader spiritual currents of the high Middle Ages, which were also formative for lay religious expression across other regions of Christendom: the apostolic model as an inspiration for lay gatherings, and clergy's pastoral preaching to women on themes of Christian morality. The influence of the apostolic church and active lay service therein were especially important.[7] With these currents came new opportunities for laypeople, including beguines, to engage with theological education in parishes. Laywomen supported not only the establishment of new ecclesiastical institutions but also the spread of vernacular literature as its recipients and initiators of its creation.[8]

Simultaneously, a discernible shift took place in pastoral focus and practice. Expressed through the vital new conduit of preaching, themes of Christian morality were extended beyond monasteries and universities and for the first time came to shape the sphere of lay audiences. This occurred first in homiletic and subsequently in vernacular literature, and reveals changing perspectives about medieval monastic ideals.[9] In the new vernacular literature, original teachings aimed at identifying and classifying sin, or outlining pastoral relationships and process in the confessor's aids, began to focus instead on illustrative, individual examples of the *imitatio Christi* in everyday life.[10] In the context of the reformist movements and participatory strivings of laypeople, Christian morality became a didactic and catechetical tool – one popularized for the laity in preaching circles of the thirteenth century.[11]

The new ideal of lay education in which women played a prominent role was not without complications. In particular, the medieval preaching mission fundamentally cast listeners as active consumers and propagators of the preacher's interpretations.[12] Thus the desire to realize the ideal of the *vita apostolica* across medieval society opened up priests' attitudes towards women – not only in theological terms but also on an individual basis regarding the specific female Christians under their pastoral care. As scholarship over the last few decades has demonstrated, positive and spiritually mutual relationships between laypeople and clergy (especially women) sprang forth from a wide variety of spaces that spanned traditional notions of "church" and "home" – including domestic chapels, reformist gatherings, and beguine communities, Although the Czech record does not have a large number of preserved written or visual sources about beguines, it does offers a range of homiletics – postils, preaching collections, preaching manuals, and theological or moral treatises aimed at beguines – which shed light on the relationships between preachers and devout laywomen.

The interest of preachers in educating lay people, both women and men, created space for the composition of texts intended for such readers. In addition, the founding of Charles University in 1348 offered an opportunity for the lower nobility to study, without their sons claiming to be awarded a university degree or entering the clergy. Education offered lords and knights the opportunity to pursue a clerical career in the imperial court or in the administration of the households of wealthier lords. However, many of them, after returning to their estates, supported in-home education. The influence of university education was reflected in their homiletic knowledge and level of ability to apply the acquired theoretical learning in practice. Unburdened by duties of the ordinary parish agenda, they were able to study homiletic practices and biblical exegesis and to influence the literary awareness of their listeners. Their style of learning was based on the traditions of synod and monastic preaching. From the point of view of formal observance of the basic requirement of educating believers in questions of faith, the content of preaching comprised mainly the interpretation of prescribed prayers, doctrinal texts, and selected biblical passages.

In addition to moralist treatises of the late Middle Ages, preachers spread preacher's handbooks and collections of stories known as *exempla* among laymen.[13] The ways of addressing laymen were individuated, with visual material playing a large role, as did the so-called lists of sins.[14] The treatises dealing with the seven deadly sins also ranked among very popular topics in vernacular literature in the Czech Republic, not least because of the translations that spread in the Czech lands in the fourteenth century. The growing interest in vernacular literature used by laymen for practical solidarity or private piety culminated in the writing of religiously edifying literature penned in the Czech mother tongue. Beginning in the second half of the fourteenth century, moral and doctrinal treatises were translated from Latin, but these religious-educational writings were increasingly composed directly in the vernacular. This would not have been possible without the parallel process of cultivating literary Czech, which gradually became able to handle the terminologically complex theological themes. Laywomen, including beguines, had a voice in religious and political life during the Czech Reformation, and their influence is also discernible in the early days of the Hussite movement.[15]

Beguine Communities in Prague

Our knowledge of medieval beguine communities in the city of Prague stems from the work of Václav Vladivoj Tomek, a nineteenth-century historian and archivist of Prague.[16] Tomek's collection of civic records contains ample evidence pertaining to the existence of houses or congregations of beguines already in the later thirteenth century, including topographical locations which he designated with specific numbers (as indicated below).[17] These records, however, share a methodological drawback compared with those for beguine gatherings in the west – namely that they often reflect the *final* rather than *initial* phase of a beguine community, that is, its legal demise. In such cases, municipal authorities confiscated the houses after the house endowment ceased to exist and sold them to private individuals.[18] As a result, the records are heavily skewed to a later date and negative context; references to original community foundations, and subsequent decades or years of membership and habitation are scarce in the Czech environment. The documentation problem for the early history of Prague beguines is comparable to that elsewhere across Europe and remains an issue for further reflection and exploration.

Beguine communities were generally made possible by the donations or bequests of city patricians, after whom the communities were often named. In the sources they are frequently referred to as the homes of souls (*domus animarum*). In the pre-Hussite period, beguinages received significant support mainly from women originating from the highest aristocratic and bourgeois circles. The development correlates to the growth of Prague's prestige as the imperial residence city and the seat of the archbishopric and the university.[19] For example, the noble Rosenberg family, which held the leading position in the Czech political hierarchy, ranked among the great supporters of not only the new religious orders but also semi-religious and lay movements and initiatives.[20] Such foundations soon became an integral part of the medieval city, as evidenced by several references in chroniclers' reports.

In keeping with patterns in western beguine communities, the social composition of Prague beguines tended to change across the fourteenth century, with a significant increase in the numbers of women hailing from the lower social strata. As many have observed, the houses offered refuge to single women without financial means to join a formal convent, charitably supported by civic entities or burghers themselves.[21] Such women's associations centred on mutual support in leading a pious life of benefit to the broader community. Laywomen who possessed their own property also supported various other charitable activities. In 1397, Petra of Říčany bequeathed fourteen "kopa" of annual rents from houses next to the Monastery of St. Ambrose to the convent of the same monastery.[22] Beguine activity was thus closely linked to charitable activities; the material security of beguine houses allowed women to have active involvement in pastoral activities in the parish, such as caring for the sick or offering minor assistance in burghers' homes or hospitals.[23]

How did the Czech beguines live?[24] The women and girls did not take oaths, but by joining the house they accepted the prescribed regulations, the details of which varied according to localities and regions. Without constant obligations of eternal vows, the beguines consciously and voluntarily chose to limit contact with the secular life by living together in devotion to God and in specialized houses set up for this purpose (*domus beginarum* or also *animarum, domus elemosinariae*).[25] Most of the houses were modest wooden structures, donated by private benefactors, and endowed – given so-called eternal salaries – with funds largely used for the women's common meals.[26] Generally the communities consisted of fewer than ten women, an exception being the exclusive endowment in Hradčany, where sources refer to twelve household members.

Income from the foundation obligated the women to pray for the soul of the founder, or possibly his family, which is why the houses are in the vicinity of churches and private chapels. The extraordinary freedom towards parish administration in Prague was enjoyed by the specific communities of women around Milíč of Kroměříž's Jerusalem and Jan Hus's Bethlehem Chapel, as will be discussed below, but most of the beguinages were managed by priests of the settlements in which they were established. With the exception of a single house, the Prague beguinages were under the administration of priests in the parish in which they were located, and the endowment of these houses was therefore under the protection of spiritual law just like any other *fabrica ecclesiae*.

Each house was administered by a procurator (*procuratrix*) or master (*magistra*). The terminology to describe these relationships was flexible. We know of the internal arrangement of the congregation of beguines only from the example of the Olbram beguines and beguines in Templar, as they came to be known. The superior of the Olbram beguines was called a procurator; beguines in Templar preferred the title "mistress."[27] The internal management of the houses was based on a limited number of places that were subject to the endowments made at the time of foundation. As in religious communities, members of the founder's families and their heirs or successors were given preference in the case of a vacant place. In exchange for this preference, they were guaranteed the protective power of the family. The houses were often founded by pious women for their female housekeepers, but other women could join. Although the sources are not uniform in their description, the beguines were dressed in simple, dark-coloured robes, typically grey. Common life also assumed respect for several strict rules governing beguines (especially the prohibition against unsanctioned wandering); breaking these rules could also mean exclusion from of the house, if not excommunication.

Like their counterparts across Christendom, beguine life crossed the boundaries between several culturally important categories – namely those of wife, mother, and nun. Czech beguines simultaneously were and were not viewed by contemporaries as nuns; they could spend a day in the house but also work in the city; they could live in the community headquarters or alone in a house; they could stay in the community and freely leave the house at any time. Some lived on a share of family property, while others survived on donations or work, including activities related to textile production. In some houses, beguines wore identical garb, similar to a habit, while others' uniforms consisted merely of simple and humble clothing. With their minimal daily needs and dedicated modesty, these women provided affordable and cheap labour in urban households. They spun, wove, sewed, and laundered; they also provided temporary assistance with chores when someone fell ill.[28] Among the deeds of practical mercy provided by beguines, the records also indicate teaching girls, nursing the sick in various settings, and caring for the dying and deceased. In sum, beguine communities offered a solution to pressing social needs while also providing for poor, unmarried and widowed, aged, or abandoned women.

Although the breadth of these services gained them popularity in the urban environment, the complex socio-spiritual position of Czech beguines also drew an undercurrent of negative responses. Criticism is most visibly reflected on the semantic or rhetorical level when naming the women in these communities.[29] In Bohemian sources, the term "beguine" carried connotations of heresy and moral ambivalence, as it did across western Europe. Satirical songs also poked fun at beguines, sometimes cheerfully and sometimes with a tone of more hostile mockery, for their presumptive hypocrisy and lasciviousness. Yet, the specific Czech moniker of "clever girls" (*chytré horákyně*) is an intriguing and unusual appellation for lay religious women, suggesting a specific association between lay religious women and intellectual or literary endeavours – whether in reality or simply in popular perception.

Early Beguine Topography (Thirteenth and Fourteenth Centuries)

The preserved Czech sources explicitly mention beguines for the first time in 1279 in the list of participants in a ceremonial mass at the Strahov Monastery in Prague, which the Bishop Tobiáš of Bechyně (d. 1296) conducted immediately after his election. Although the phenomenon also emerged beyond the city, the largest number of churches/houses were in Prague. In this period the number of beguine houses located in the historic four Prague city boroughs (Old and New Town situated on the right bank of the Vltava River, and Lesser Town and Hradčany on the left bank) peaked.[30] The community called *Jeruzalém* (Jerusalem) founded by Milíč of Kroměříž (Milicius de Chremsir, d. 1374) features characteristics of beguines, though the women there were never designated as such in Milíč's *Životopis* (*Biography*).[31] The community reportedly provided protection to former prostitutes whose residences and income had disappeared with the closure of the Old Town's notorious red-light district. The women's acceptance into the community depended on their voluntary repentance and "return" to faith and thereby salvation. The *Životopis* highlights the repentant women's interiority and passion for prayer, confession, and their ecstatic reception of the Eucharist.

Sources allow us to map the location of beguine houses or similar lay communities, mainly in Prague's Old Town. In his *History of the City of Prague* (*Dějiny města Prahy*), the nineteenth-century historian Václav Vladivoj Tomek identified more than twenty such gatherings, only one of which was in the elite neighbourhood of Hradčany, near the imperial court at Prague Castle.[32] That community was more exclusive, consisting of women from the upper social strata.[33] By far the largest concentration of beguine houses was in the Old Town, which also corresponds to the growing population concentration in this area. Within the Old Prague urban setting, they were clustered near parish churches or convents, especially those of mendicant orders with the Churches of St. James the Greater and St. Francis.

The earliest appearance of beguine houses is difficult to ascertain today due to the gradual urbanization that occurred over the course of the nineteenth and twentieth centuries. The later construction, however, did provide an opportunity for archaeological excavation, which allowed future researchers to reconstruct the area and map medieval developments – for example, the existence of the Church of St. Benedict under what is now a department store near the city walls. In this area was the first such *domus animarum* (no. 684), situated on today's Rybná Street in the right corner of the street opposite the city walls; the first report of the house as most likely inhabited by beguines dates to 1407.[34]

Walking down the busy commercial street in the direction of the Old Town Square, visitors today can still pass a house leading to a side street that connects this main street with the surroundings of the Church of St. James the Greater, where a Minorite convent stood. Several houses of beguines mentioned in sources from the beginning of the fifteenth century were located in the passageway to the street.[35] What is interesting about the site is, first, its proximity to the former Templar court and, second, a new neighbour who appeared in the second decade of the fifteenth century. A representative of the burgher Zmrzlík family became the women's new neighbour, an individual who would rise rapidly up the social ladder at the court of King Wenceslas I of Luxembourg (1361–1419) until he was eventually promoted to knighthood with the epithet of Svojšín. Representatives of this family became famous not only as zealous reformers and later part of the radical Hussite movement but also as important patrons of vernacular literature and translations of the Bible into Czech – a topic to which we will return shortly.

Another beguine community resided in a house east of the Templars (no. 669). They were named after their founders, the Bolek family, and are first mentioned in sources in 1406.[36] References to these women disappear following the seizure of the house as a mortuary and its sale to a private person.[37] Another house on the north side of the cluster of houses (no. 670) was inhabited by the beguines of Kadanský.[38] The date of its founding is unknown, but they survived through the early fifteenth century only to disappear over the course of the Hussite period.[39] The cluster of houses in this area also includes beguines who inhabited the corner house on Templar street, through which the said passage from Celetná to Templová Street (no. 589) led; in fact, the house still bears the same name, "Templar."[40] Beguines certainly occupied the house from the early fifteenth century, although the community was probably originally founded significantly earlier, in the second half of the fourteenth century.[41] Unlike the previous houses, the "Templar" community survived the Hussite Wars.[42]

In 1467, devout women were granted a new endowment in the legacy of Catherine of Nyněchov, a member of what was most likely a yeoman family. The bequest granted them six scores of groschen for an annual rent or stipend from her inheritance in Lochkov behind Chuchle, "with yards, villages, meadows, half of forests, groves, streams, ponds, vineyards, willows, and all will" ("*s dwory kmecími, s dědinami, lukami, polovicí lesů, hájů, potoků, rybníků, vinic, vrbin i se vší zwolí*"). As the donor, Catherine herself appointed Samuel of Hrádek and Valečov as the endowment's administrator and director; Samuel would then appoint an executor to fill the role after his own death.[43] Near the beguines described in the alley behind Templar (no. 648), other beguines are also mentioned around the year 1403, but their endowment was anonymous and disappears from the record during the Hussite movement, when the house was seized by the municipality and sold to a private person.[44] Finally, the house of Posenpach beguines (no. 684) was located near the Church of St. James the Greater and butcher shops where Old Town burghers bought their meat. They were first mentioned in 1407, and the community was documented as extant in 1476, after the Hussite Wars.[45]

A third area of the city containing beguine communities was that of the so-called Convent of St. Agnes, near the city walls on the right bank of the Vltava River. The complex of convent buildings was first formed by the Convent of Poor Sisters of St. Claire founded by St. Agnes of Bohemia together with the adjacent hospital. Later, the Minorite convent with the Church of St. Francis was added, thereby creating a double-convent complex. This location is the sole indicator in the Czech environment of a link between beguines and the medieval textile sector, since drapery frames (*curia tentoriarum, ramhof*) were located near the site and one of the beguine community founders was a cloth dealer.

Many of these women were likely tertiaries as well, that amorphous category referring to some kind of an association (formal or otherwise) with the Franciscan Third Order.[46] In the area of the Church of St. Francis, we can identify the house of Freiberger beguines (later also known as Hopfners) among the beguinages. Around 1360, the Prague burgher Henzl Freiberger gave the beguines his house (no. 858) located on the street behind the old coal market by the monastery garden. After his death, his widow (Klára Hopfnerová) administered the endowment and changed the community's name to Hopfner (record from 1398).[47] Soon thereafter, however, it suffered a fate similar to other beguinages – disappearing during the Hussite period, when the house was sold back into private possession.[48] Beguinages near the Church of St. Francis also included a house (no. 792) inhabited by beguines since 1363; located on the street leading from the old coal market to the Church of St. Francis. The house's residents were known as the "Geunher" beguines. In contrast to those described above, this community survived the Hussite movement.[49]

The identification of male lay communities is even more ambiguous. Czech sources only hint at their identity as so-called hermits. In 1384, Prague Archbishop Johann von Jenstein (1350–1400) bought a house in Opatovice in the New Town of Prague (no. 155). Unfortunately, there are no records of their further activities or any other mention of their customs. The sources only state that during the life of Johann von Jenstein the house belonged to his assets, but hermits continued living in the house after his death.[50] As mentioned before, the greatest number of reports concerning the arrangement and management of the house have been preserved from the Olbram beguines (no. 932) on Kostečná Street (from Old Town Square, the first street to the right from Pařížská leads to the Church of St. Salvator).[51] One of the oldest beguinages in Prague, it was founded by a member of the Olbran family with a Chapel of All Saints and a permanent chaplain. The chapel originally had a special endowment in the village of Zelenec near Horní Počernice, from which the beguines regularly received 1,200 Czech groschen every year.[52] Space was provided for six beguines, who were to attend worship at the Chapel of All Saints. In terms of spiritual administration, they were subject to the chaplain, who was called a provost or director (*praepositus et director*).[53] In this case, we even know the names of chaplains and stewards at the Chapel of All Saints.[54] Unfortunately, the turbulent events in Prague during the Hussite period ended the activities of this community; like other ecclesiastical properties, the house became a municipal holding and was thereafter sold to a private owner.[55]

Fifteenth-Century Beguines, Families, and Bohemian Reform

After the founding of Bethlehem Chapel (1391), beguines who had previously aligned themselves with mendicants, and in some cases had drawn similar suspicion concerning their orthodoxy, gradually became acquainted with the new reform direction of preaching. This move of beguines towards representatives of the reform movement could also be one of the reasons for the increasing private initiative of pious laywomen and burgher interest in establishing new beguinages after 1400.[56] As the fame and familiarity of Jan Hus's preaching and his pastoral work spread between 1400 and 1414, his targeted preaching to women in the beguine milieu, as well as his new view towards the role and importance of preaching in religious life, inspired his listeners to take an active approach to faith and adopt a change in behaviour and morality.

According to contemporary reports, all of Prague attended Hus's sermons; like Milíč of Kroměříž, Hus leveraged his contacts with wealthy burghers – from securing alms for the poor to having lunch with elite university masters.[57] In addition to politically influential patrons and supporters, a group of women also formed around Hus, who, following the example of Saint Clare of Assisi (1194–1253), lived near Bethlehem in a semi-religious community of devout virgins and widows who devoted themselves to charity while caring for the sick and performing other merciful deeds. Though the sources do not label them specifically as "beguines," they retained both private possessions and the independence and mobility by which the form of life was recognizable. Hus wrote *Dcerka* (Daughter) to encourage them in that choice: Writing in the Czech vernacular, he promoted their communities as a manifestation of lay spirituality and the desire to deepen the religious life. In this context, vernacular songs, too, became part of Hus's oeuvre for the women.[58] Among Hus's other supporters (and later protectors) was Anna of Frimburk, wife of the supreme mint master of Petr Zmrzlík of Svojšín, who ordered the Czech translation of the Bible. Some of these women, such as Anna of Mochov, provided Hus refuge in their castles during his exile from Prague. Perhaps the most significant of his female defenders was Anna Zajicova of Hazmburk; she was not only the archbishop's sister but also was married to the royal councillor John of Milheim, patron of Bethlehem Chapel and Hus's contact, mediator, and negotiator between the court and the church.

During the decades of the late fourteenth and fifteenth centuries, the era of Bohemian reform and Hussite revolution, marked association is visible between leading families, reformist preaching, and beguine communities. One exceptional example is the community founded by the elite Rosenberg family in Prague's Old Town.[59] First mentioned in 1416, the beguinage of the Lords of Rosenberg, as it was known, was located near Bethlehem Chapel, which Hus's preaching had made famous between 1402 and 1413.[60] The renowned Jerusalem community founded by Milíč was also situated not far from this house. Evidence suggests that here, as was often the case with beguine communities in Central Europe, the community was older than its first documented mention would indicate. Tomek posits a foundation date around 1400. The Rosenberg beguinage was probably located in today's Konviktská Street (no. 262/9), but the medieval plot stretched back towards Betlémská Street (no. 262/10). Oldřich of Rosenberg himself (d. 1390) was active in the new local circles of reform, and he communicated regularly with the Prague preacher Milíč of Kroměříž. Indeed, the dissolution of Jerusalem after Milíč's death likely prompted the Rosenberg beguinage to provide refuge to the suddenly homeless penitents.[61] The community is mentioned again in 1488, referred to as "At the Three Black Stars" (*U tří černých hvězd*).

Another prominent family who supported beguines and founded houses for them in Prague was the Štuka family. By 1365, beguines had acquired from them a small house for communal life (no. 624) on Týnská Street, located behind the Church of the Virgin Mary before Týn on the Old Town Square.[62] The community survived the Hussite movement and was still referenced in the civic record as late as 1488.[63] After 1400, the number of new beguinage foundations again grew quite rapidly, creating a second wave in the Old Town. These newer communities included a group of women first mentioned in 1406 as living in Konrad Fogl's house (no. 802), near the Church of St. Francis.[64] In 1410, sources mention another new congregation of beguines, this time in the house of Jan Weilburk (no. 803). This house was also located in the vicinity of the King's Court, near the present-day Powder Tower and Art Nouveau Municipal House. The King's Court neighbourhood also offered refuge to the beguines of Frána Brněnský, mentioned for the first time in 1410.[65] Another house (no. 665) near the city fortifications of the Old Town fell into the area of the defunct Church of St. Benedict.[66] The same location was also home to the Fledl beguines, who first appear in sources in 1404. The rooms they occupied were located in the back of house no. 673 on Rybná Street, a part of which is unfortunately – like the church – also located today under the Kotva department store.[67] In 1415, we hear for the first time about the Pillung beguines (no. 674), also known as the Nindertheimer beguines, located near the so-called King's Court at the Powder Tower.[68]

On the opposite side of Old Town, sources mention new foundations of two beguinages behind the blacksmith's house, forming a corner with Liliova Street (no. 184, no. 185), which stood on the plots between Anenská Street and Karlova Street.[69] The location is not too far from the Dominican monastery at the Church of St. Klement (today Klementinum), which completed the Dominican convent with the Church of St. Anna situated on the other side of this location facing the Vltava River. Sources designate the beguinages in this locality as those of Klára Silberzeigerová and are mentioned for the first time in 1414. The last new beguinage from the beginning of the fifteenth century is another a house near Milíč's Jerusalem (number 293 in Tomek's map), which was inhabited by beguines of unknown affiliation.

Czech beguines were often actively involved in the legal purchase and administration of a community. Since 1401, one Anežka (or Agnes) of Štítný was first the owner of half of a house next to Bethlehem Chapel (no. 254).[70] Two of Anežka's friends, the sisters Ludmila and Catherine of Pasovaře, lived in the house with her. In 1402, Agnes bought the other half of the house; although the later form of possessing the house together with Catherine of Pasovaře is not documented in the sources, records indicate that in 1407 Catherine of Pasovaře returned her portion of the house back to Agnes of Štítný, who sold it again. The last sources to mention Agnes date to 1409, when she apparently still lived in the house. Later that year, the house was assigned to another woman, the noblewoman Střezka of Čejkovice, who in turn transferred part of her ownership in 1409 to the virgin sisters Bětka, Anežka, Zdenka, and Ofka. Twenty years later, by 1429, a "Bětka" resided in the house, though it is uncertain whether she is the same sister. The next owners of the house after the sisters were again beguines – a Bonuška, followed by the virgin Mary of Ostrý.[71] Other women lived in a house opposite Bethlehem Chapel in today's Konviktská Street, on a corner next to a narrow street leading to the current Bartolomějská Street (no. 291). Purchased in 1410 by the virgin Petra of Říčany, the house and community were clearly active in Hus's network. Petra's name appears in the circle of his friends, and he apparently held her virtuous life in high regard. She offered refuge in her house to other devout virgins, and they lived together in the house until 1418.

Beguine communities near Bethlehem Chapel are also documented in the period after the Hussite Wars. In 1449 and again in 1473, a certain Eliška is mentioned, a beguine who possessed a wooden (or plank hollow) house near the chapel (no. 253) and next to the former house of Agnes of Štítný. As an endowment, the house was passed on to other "virgins" until the beginning of the sixteenth century. In addition, there were three beguine gatherings next to each other (no. 293) on the land of Milíč's Jerusalem. Two women referred to as "virgins," Catherine and Zdena, lived in one of them between 1429 and 1433; in the second, during the same period, another virgin, Kateřina (1429) lived there, followed by the virgin Markéta (1433). The third house was inhabited by beguines and called a "house of requiem." Due to the lack of an endowment, the house was abandoned; it was subsequently taken over by a woman named Anna, who was granted that authority upon the recommendation of the Utraquist lay administrator Václav Koranda Jr. (1425–1519). In 1524, another Anna requested that the town council appoint a married couple (Martin and Barbara Domaválený) as community guardians, responsible for inhabiting it with suitable persons, virgins, or widows dedicated to serving the Lord.[72] Yet, even as beguines in Prague explored affinities for lay theological learning and Bohemian reform, Czech beguine life could also be ecumenical. As was the case in early modern German beguine communities, particularly to the north, Czech beguines were not always associated with novel reform and devotional practices. For example, the daughter of the Archbishop of Prague Albert of Uničov (Sigismundus Albicus de Uniczow, 1358–1427), Catherine, became a beguine. Her guardian was Master Christ of Prachatice himself (Christianus de Prachaticz, 1370–1439).[73]

In 1473, Dorota "Mydlářka," the wealthy widow of Old Town burgher Jakub Mydlář, bequeathed a house in today's Bethlehem Street (between 268 and 269) to her female domestic staff – namely a cook and two virgin housekeepers – to live there together "in love and unity and awe of God." She provided material security and livelihood to the women through the payment of pensions from two of her other houses and rent from one shop.[74] In turn, the recipients were to remember her and pray for her and her husband's soul. Dorota's foundation was organized and managed internally in a manner consistent with patterns across the continent. As determined in her will, two neighbours and two female burghers would appoint guardians of the house. In turn, the guardians would appoint and supervise a housekeeper, the gathering's superior member who was responsible for day-to-day management of the community. The guardians were directed to heed counsel provided by Master Václav Betlémský (probably meaning Master Václav of Drachov, 1395–1461, preacher at Bethlehem Chapel) regarding the election of a superior. Dorota Mydlářka evidently had affection for the beguine way of life, as she provided an endowment to Catherine and Dora in the house next to Bethlehem (no. 254); their neighbour, Virgin Elisabeth (at no. 253); and the beguines "in the house of Mrs. Zdena," which is probably the beguine of that name mentioned at Milíč's Jerusalem. Similarly, in 1482, Bětka of Prague bequeathed her inheritance at Královice to the "honest maid [the housekeeper Maruška] and women" living in the house.[75]

Most striking in terms of the intertwining of Czech lay devotional enthusiasm and female institutional initiatives is the women's house in Hradčany. The community was founded by the devout widow Kateřina Kapléřová of Sulevice for twelve beguines, virgins, or widows, "who would leave the futility of this world and devote themselves to the service of God."[76] For this purpose, she bequeathed them her own house in Hradčanské Square (no. 185) and the village of Wesce, probably close to Čáslav.[77] Over time, it has become a custom in written sources of Czech provenance to designate these women as beguines. Although such women led a devotional life in the house similar to the manner of other beguines, the difference remained that they possessed their own income and thus did not have to rely upon charitable endowments for security.[78]

In her will, Kateřina Kapléřová commanded that the endowment be administered by the vicars of the Archbishopric of Prague after her death. Noting that in preaching lies the path to salvation, she also provided support for a second preacher in the Metropolitan Church of St. Vitus, who was to be provided an annual salary of 600 groschen to preach in Czech every holiday except Sunday in Advent and to fast three times a week. The exclusive position of the beguines in Hradčany and their interconnection with an emphasis on preaching and lay theological education soon drew followers to Prague.[79] A number of affluent widows were among those who moved from the countryside to the city, purchasing houses in which other pious women were then sheltered. Together, they lived communally in the houses and inspired ever more followers in turn – many of whom engaged in reading inspirational religious literature in the vernacular.[80]

Lay Theology and Prague Beguines

As groups of spiritually likeminded laypeople crystallized around the shared longing to unite the soul with Christ, some chose expression through enthusiastic visions or frequent reception of the Eucharist; others developed scripturally based devotional practice. This environment created such demand for biblical translations that it prompted a new, more consistent effort to summarize older partial translations into one whole textual unit. Indeed, the emerging interest in language studies and manuscript comparison inspired scriptural study which, in turn, generated new textual knowledge. Late medieval preachers' interest in the education of laymen created a space in which to disseminate and reinforce lessons in Christian morality through literature in national languages – especially sermons.[81] Sermons bore a twofold significance in late medieval Prague: On the one hand, they served as didactic tools for attaining individual and communal moral discipline; on the other hand, they made difficult and sometimes abstract theological teachings accessible to the general public. As the impetus for spiritual education shifted from the monastery to the university to the public square, that process of accessibility is visible in the choice of topics and their reworking, first in Latin homiletics and later in vernacular literature. From the original teaching concerned with identifying sins, classifying them, outlining relationships, and making practical use of confessional aids, vernacular literature moved towards an illustrative example and an individual pattern of active imitation of the Christian ideal in everyday life. These models and ways of thinking came to influence and respond to the needs and interests of laywomen as well.

Tomáš of Štítný: Writings and Beguine Readers

Of the many Czech authors contemplating spirituality and reform in the fourteenth century, Tomáš of Štítný is the only known reformer who systematically devoted himself to vernacular religious educational literature for the needs of laymen. In accordance with the standard method, he worked from the biblical text outward. Štítný believed that by moving through the Scripture, the Christian acquires knowledge; in preaching, he can deepen and refresh it; and through the example of saints, he acquires a model for living in generosity and serving God. Morally oriented allegorical sermons put into the mouths of God, Christ, and the saints brought to life model lessons and principles. His writings and collections of translations written in Czech were widely read in beguine circles, although the author did not designate them solely for this purpose.[82] Štítný dedicated, or intentionally wrote, several texts to his daughter, a beguine named Agnes. Inspired by the words of Milíč of Kroměříž and the new emphasis on individual responsibility for education and life in the Christian faith, he perceived the need to pass his knowledge and attitudes on to his children, but he also recognized the need to communicate to them in a language and idiom they understood. Equally important was his effort to constantly educate himself. His revised texts and the new editions of his anthologies, dealing with the same themes again and again, reveal an extension of his own horizon of learning through continual reading of his favourite works.

In the early 1390s, he began writing *Řeči nedělní a sváteční*, which drew inspiration from the postils of that period and not only formed the basis for preaching but also emerged as a literary unit to be read to a wider audience.[83] This text served as a basis for devotional meditation for those who, due to illness or any other reason, must renounce Sunday Mass. The sermons consisted of abstracts of the church fathers' homilies (notably Augustine, Gregory the Great, Bernard of Clairvaux, the Venerable Bede, and others).[84] As a tutor, Tomáš of Štítný was well aware of the need for an illustrative example to show that the celebrated ideals and declared claims of the Christian life that could be read in the Bible were also feasible in the simple life of a Christian full of daily struggles. He, like other Czech writers, used expressive mystical and visionary texts to teach spiritual lessons to lay believers.

For this same reason, Štítný dedicated many texts to his beguine daughter, Agnes, including the Book of Christian Teachings from the so-called Opatovice Anthology. The manuscript is held in the Library of the National Museum and dates to the beginning of the fifteenth century. This new and final elaboration of the Book of the Doctrine of the Christian can be dated to around 1401–2. The comprehensive anthology consists of tracts divided into two parts. The first part deals with sins, while the second focuses on virtues. Of the sixty-three total preserved sermons, twenty focus on saints, including Lucy, Háta (Agáta/Agnes), Dorota, and Barbora.[85] Although Tomáš of Štítný asked how best to respect and honour the saints, he never discusses the miracles attributed to saints within the hagiographic tradition. He reminds us that the saints are God's friends, so as helpers and supporters in the daily needs of the believers, they should be respected by the church in general and be loved by Christians. Illustrative examples of these saints serve as a gift from God to a sinful man, and it is, therefore, laudatory for the church to show devotion to their memory. By their example, preachers can remind people of the idea that not everyone will receive all the gifts, but each individual can serve God according to his own powers and abilities. Thus, the great variety of saints, each honoured for different qualities, offer a needed variety of Christian exemplary behaviour.

For Štítný, the significance of each saint was rooted in a specific biblical statement, one either directly attributed to the saint or linked to the memory of the saint and read during Mass on the saint's feast day. A saint was above all an example to follow in action: Saints revealed to the general public that one may fulfil the demands placed upon them if they humbly ask God in prayer for help. Preaching thus reinforced Štítný's efforts for quiet, objective instruction which first led to the forms for raising a family but later was extended to the whole community of the house and its staff, and more broadly to a readership circle of Štítný's acquaintances.

Štítný's major work, however, was a translation of *Revelationes* by the Catholic mystic Bridget of Sweden (1303–73) into Czech, a volume he wrote for and dedicated to his daughter, Agnes.[86] Bridget's work demonstrates the relationship between a priest and a pious woman, offering signs of mutual influence between the confessional and pious layman and women, whose interests meet in an emphasis on preparing and nurturing the education of informed preachers and spiritual shepherds. The interpretation is based on the principle of typological series; each forms a closed part of the content, which allows the reader to use each part individually or relate it to others. Thus, for Agnes, he transformed *Revelationes* into a compendium of ethical interpretations that could serve as a preaching guide. The application to preaching practice is also indicated by a number of copies of *Revelationes* with numerous additions and interpretations, of which the oldest preserved manuscript in which these appendices appear comes from Prague University circles and dates back to 1386.[87] The popularity and spread of the work among laymen is reflected in the rapidly reproduced translations of *Revelationes* into other languages (Swedish, Italian, English, Polish, German, etc.) from the end of the 1380s. Thanks to the exceptional position of Prague University and the mobility of its students and masters in Central Europe, Prague became the centre for the distribution of Bridget's *Revelationes*.[88]

Štítný used one of the manuscripts created in the Prague editorial network for his own translation. According to Pavlína Rychterová, the manuscript from the Library of the Prague Metropolitan Chapter C 87 was a small probable volume.[89] Štítný received a copy under circumstances unknown today, but he paid sufficient attention to it and returned to the work repeatedly in the spirit of his traditional method. Two versions of the text have been preserved, which designate Bridget as a saint in the preface and which dates the preface of the Czech translation to the time of her canonization, i.e., 1391. Štítný's translation contains only about a quarter of the original work, and the recipients for whom the translation was intended also influenced the selection of texts. The first version is preceded by Štítný's preface, which implies that the translation was made for his daughter, Agnes. For her needs, he found it important to translate completely the first two books of *Revelationes*, and he further selected sections from the third, fourth, seventh, and eighth books. He divided this text into chapters to correspond with the original and to respect the internal layout. The text was subsequently shortened for the needs of the second edition, intended as it was for a wider circle of lay readers.

In striking contrast to many of his theologically minded contemporaries, Tomáš of Štítný was remarkable for his relative moderation. His work contains no dogmatic radicalism. He defends the ability of man to find truth on his own, and his criticisms are shrewd and sometimes unexpected as he seeks and chooses what he finds good or instructive from many different sources. Dialogue, in which ideas and attitudes are refined, represents a valuable process in his search for truth. For example, even as he felt compelled to take a stance on moral decline among the clergy and monks in his day, his response was nonetheless original in its moral and educational, rather than doctrinal, emphasis. In his criticism of moral decline, he adopted a critical stance towards everyone involved, assigning degrees of responsibility for decadence and sin. For example, a layman who sits in a tavern next to a priest and gets drunk with him bears the same blame for his neighbour's misdemeanour as the priest himself.

Tomáš of Štítný's work thus offers a unique source for researching the attitudes of laypeople towards contemporary events, and for tracing changes in the concept of piety, morality, and critiques of the clergy. With the concept of Christians' individual responsibility for their life, he introduced the challenge of Christian upbringing into discussions of the family setting. Thus, his work also provided a model for the application of theoretical Catholic morality to the practical, daily life of a Christian. The writings discussed here are just a fragment of the larger corpus of similarly oriented literature that spread as religiously educated literature written in the vernacular. Although moral and doctrinal tracts written in Latin were prevalent, vernacular translations increased from the second half of the fourteenth century. Their increasing number documents the growing interest in this literature among the laity, both men and women.[90] Out of Štítný's five children, only Anežka or Agnes (d. 1414) survived him, and after his death she bought a house near Bethlehem Chapel, where she lived a pious life in the company of like-minded women.[91] Agnes's move to the city and her exemplary life in the beguine community further contributed to the spread of Štítný's writings in Prague.[92]

Beguines, Female Lay Piety, and the Hussite Wars

The same dynamic quality discussed above underpins the history of Prague beguines during the reform movement and the Hussite Wars.[93] The education of Hussite women, or rather their literacy, also sparked amazement and respect among their opponents. The interest in the reading of religious literature within lay circles brought the Czech Reform movement closer to the beguines, as evidenced by the Czech satirical poem *Bekyně*.[94] Preachers received strong support from women mainly on the question of frequently receiving the Eucharist and later taking the Eucharist in both forms, the bread and the wine.[95] In the case of the radical Hussite movement, which denied the real transformation of Christ's body in the Mass, we encounter women who courageously marched to the town hall to complain about the "heretical" interpretation of the sacrament, as witnessed by the chronicle of Vavřinec of Březová (1370–1437).[96] The religious response was at times ambivalent regarding the deep interest of the beguines in religious literature and was later criticized by their own ranks of Hussite or later Utraquist preachers (Jan Rokycana, 1396–1471, or Pavel Žídek, Paulus de Praga, 1413–1471).[97]

Czech sources also testify to the beguines' interest in church music and describe them as great promoters of vernacular liturgical singing, as described in a letter from Štěpán of Dolany (Stephanus Dolanensis, d. 1421), abbot to Carthusian Prior Vallis Josaphat in Dolany near Olomouc.[98] Nuns also became famous for liturgical singing – especially those who accepted the Hussite movement, even as they remained true to their religious vows. Originally hailing from various Prague convents, Prague's nuns were gathered into a single community at the Convent of St. Anna in the Old Town once the war broke out. Headed by Eliška, daughter of the Hussite governor in Domažlice, Jan Řitka of Bezdědice (d. 1446), the monastery became a seat of the radical Hussite movement.

Over time, beguine communities tended to radicalize under Hussite influence. Nonetheless, only a small minority went as far as supporting Tábor's teaching and the most radical form of the Hussite movement.[99] Just as attitudes towards reform varied by and within families at all strata of medieval Czech society, so too did beguines adhere to a range of positions – sometimes shaped by their family identity. For example, the aforementioned beguine Regina Chotková, a keen supporter of the Hussite preachers, was also the granddaughter of Bernard Chotek, an outspoken and stubborn critic of Hus and his followers. Likewise, Catherine, the illegitimate daughter of the Archbishop of Prague, Albík of Uničov, who was forced to leave the country after the outbreak of the Hussite Wars, was a beguine under the spiritual protection of Master Christian of Prachatice, a friend and follower of Jan Hus. Such differences of affiliation during this period suggest that women made choices for themselves about whom to support or with whom to ally themselves when it came to religious interpretation and community.

By promoting Bible reading and the interpretation of texts in the vernacular, the Hussite movement played an important role in changing the attitude of laymen and women to preaching. On the basis of Hus's writings, sermons declared the active duty of every person to preach, without limitation to the spiritual state, including laymen and women.[100] For example, vernacular sources provide a glimpse of this practice through the experience of a housemaid named Kačka. In the records before 1378, Kačka was described as having contemplated – that is, thought about and commented upon – the sermon given earlier at church when she returned home along with (land)ladies and other ministers. The testimony of this record documents women's practices of contemplating religious topics in close private circles, a probable step towards theological discussion among women.[101] However, the articles of 1417 explicitly state that neither a layman nor a woman should be admitted to the church to preach there.[102] The practice was specifically mentioned in a critical letter from the anti-Hussite Štěpán of Dolany, in which he refers to a woman who preached in Prague before 1417.[103] Women were actively involved in events unfolding on the streets of Prague; for example, when three young men were executed, women (possibly beguines) cared for the bodies, which they covered with sheets and publicly mourned.[104]

The hostile anti-Hussite songs entitled "Hussite Verses" (*Verše na husity*) further suggest how radical reformers had popularized preaching and the gradual laicization of theological education.[105] A treatise by Andreas de Broda (d. 1427) on the origins of the Hussites mentions their practice of hiring salaried laymen and women as prophets of the truth, i.e., preachers.[106] The active participation of Hussite women in meetings and quarrels of political parties is documented by a satiric piece on beguines and Pavel Žídek.[107] The actions of women were also sharply criticized by Jan of Příbram (d. 1448), who critiqued them for the unreasonable nature of a crowd that is blind and deaf to reasoning and unprepared for discussion. Příbram's description of moderates meeting with Tábor radicals likens women's behaviour to mass insanity – in the case of disagreement, they were only able to chant mass, and thereby they outshouted everyone and drowned out any criticisms.[108]

The relationships and activities of Prague beguines within their many communities provide a rare opportunity to see a fuller, more organic picture of how laywomen's piety and influence could grow within a late medieval booming urban centre – not only within the context of literacy and vernacular preaching but also as outgrowths of regionally specific theological, reform, and political developments generally studied in isolation from "beguine" history. Textual relationships via vernacular preaching and composition demonstrate that in Prague, as elsewhere, there was significant clerical support for lay religious women and enthusiasm for their literary activities – indeed, the overlap of blood kinship, spiritual kinship, and textual production clearly played a role, one that merits further exploration. Yet, although the precise circumstances of fourteenth- and fifteenth-century Prague were in some ways distinct from those of the better-known urban histories of Germany, France, England, and the Low Countries, beguines in Prague also found themselves in a comparable situation to their sisters in the west: Facing resistance to as well as support for their religious participation, and having their literacy turned against them as a weapon of critique, beguines were eternally positioned as between orders and heresy.

NOTES

1 This study is a part of the research supported by the Czech Science Foundation within the project GA ČR 18-20335S: *Bekyně a kazatelé. Mezi mravním ideálem, homiletikou a pastorační praxí v českých zemích 14.–16. století* (Beguines and Preachers. Between the Moral Ideal, Homiletics and Pastoral Care in the Czech Lands in the period of the 14th–16th Century).

2 "O zlých letech po smrti krále Otakara" in *Fontes rerum Bohemicarum. Cosmae chronicon Boemorum cum continuatoribus*, ed. Cosmas and Josef Emler, 6 vols. (Prague: Nákladem Musea království Českého, 1874), 2: 435; Václav Vladivoj Tomek, *Dějepis města Prahy*, 12 vols. (W Praze: W Kommissi u F. Riwnáce, 1855–1901), 3: 233.

3 "clericorum, nobilium baronum, militum, civium, laycorum, rurensium, mulierum maritatarum, begynarum, viduarum, infantum, iuvenum et virginum...."

4 Cosmas and Josef Emler, ed., *Fontes rerum Bohemicarum. Cosmae chronicon Boemorum cum continuatoribus* (Prague: Nákladem Musea království Českého, 1874), 2: 339–40: "Quanta autem confluentia ad primae missae celebrationem clericorum, nobilium baronum, militum, civium, laycorum, rurensium, mulierum maritatarum, begynarum, viduarum, infantum, iuvenum et virginum congregata fuerit, si eadem multitudo armis vestita fuisset, confoederata omnium voluntate in unam, Pragensis civitas durante sponsionis voluntate inexpugnabilis per multa temporum momenta inconvulsa permaneret." With regard to Czech beguines, see Marguerite Porete, *Zrcadlo prostých duší* (Prague: Malvern, 2013), 319; see epilogue to the Czech translation in Martin C. Putna, *Mysticism from the house with a garden* (Mystika z domku se zahrádkou): *From the Cultural History of the Beguine Movement* (Prague: Malvern, 2013), 305–21.

5 František Ekert and Jiří Reinsberg, *Posvátná místa král. hl. města Prahy: dějiny a popsání chrámů, kaplí, posvátných soch, klášterů a jiných pomníků katolické víry a nábožnosti v hlavním městě království Českého*, 2 vols. (Prague: Volvox Globator, 1996), 2: 377–9, 425; Ekert and Reinsberg, *Posvátná místa král. hl. města Prahy*, 2: 378.

6 See, for example, Alison More, *Fictive Orders and Feminine Religious Identities, 1200–1600* (Oxford: Oxford University Press, 2018); Tanya Stabler Miller, *The Beguines of Medieval Paris: Gender, Patronage, and Spiritual Authority* (Philadelphia: University of Pennsylvania Press, 2014); Letha Böhringer, Jennifer Kolpacoff Deane, and Hildo van Engen, eds., *Labels and Libels: Naming Lay Religious Women in Northern Medieval Europe* (Turnhout: Brepols, 2014); and Fiona Griffiths and Julie Hotchin, eds., *Partners in Spirit: Women, Men, and Religious Life in Germany (1100–1500)* (Turnhout: Brepols, 2014).

7 See the article by Neslihan Şenocak in this volume.
8 From Latin *vernacularis*, domestic. In medieval literature, the term refers to literature written in a language other than Latin. See Robert Allan Houston, *Literacy in Early Modern Europe: Culture and Education 1500–1800* (London Longman, 1988); Dorothea Kullman, *The Church and Vernacular Literature in Medieval France* (Toronto: Pontifical Institute of Medieval Studies, 2009); Jan Lehár, *Česká literatura od počátků k dnešku* (Prague: Lidové Noviny, 2008) – see also therein the references to the older literature.
9 Jana Grollová, *Memento mori. Obraz života a smrti v písemné tradici středověkého kazatelství* (Ostrava: Ostravská univerzita, Filozofická fakulta, 2017), 294–318.
10 Lawrence J. Johnson, *Worship in the Early Church: An Anthology of Historical Sources* (Collegeville: MN: Liturgical Press, 2009).
11 Sarah Hamilton, *The Practice of Penance 900–1050* (Woodbridge: Boydell, 2001).
12 On this theme, see Herbert Grundmann's classic essay "Women and Literature in the Middle Ages: A Contribution on the Origins of Vernacular Writing," in *Herbert Grundmann (1902–1970): Essays on Heresy, Literacy, and Inquisition*, trans. Steven Rowan, ed. Jennifer Kolpacoff Deane (Woodbridge: York Medieval Press, 2019). See also Sean L. Field's essay in this volume; and Sean L. Field, *Isabelle of France: Capetian Sanctity and Franciscan Identity in the Thirteenth Century* (Notre Dame, IN: University of Notre Dame Press, 2006).
13 Medieval morality collectively denotes a set of Christian ethical teachings. Despite its diverse origins, in medieval perceptions it found a comprehensive interpretation projected onto the united ideal of Christian religious life in its various patterns of early, high, and late medieval society. The peak in homiletics was reached between the thirteenth and fourteenth century. Collections of exempla were created, for example, as *Gesta Romanorum*; on the translation to old Czech, called Roman Stories (*Příběhy římské*), see František Šimek, ed., *Příběhy římské. Staročeská Gesta Romanorum* (Prague: Odeon, 1967).
14 Otto Zöckler, "Das Lehrstück von den sieben Hauptsünden. Beiträge zur Dogmen- und zur Sittengeschichte, in besonders der vorreformatorischen Zeit," in *Biblische und kirchenhistorische Studien* 3, ed. Otto Zöckler (Munich: C.H. Beck, 1893); Richard Newhauser, ed., *The Seven Deadly Sins. From Communities to Individuals* (Leiden: Brill, 2007), 1–20; Jana Grollová and Daniela Rywiková, *Militia est vita hominis. Sedm smrtelných hříchů a sedm skutků milosrdenství v literárních a vizuálních pramenech českého středověku* (České Budějovice and Ostrava: Veduta, 2013), 241–59, which offers an overview of the bibliography on the topic; Iohannes Cassianus, "Collationes," in *Corpus Scriptorum Ecclesiasticorum Latinorum 13*, X, ed. Michael Petschenig and Gotfried E. Kreuz (Cologne: Verlag der Österreichischen Akademie der Wissenschaften, 2004), http://www.csel

.eu; J.P. Migne, *Patrologiae cursus completus. Series Graeca*, 161 vols. (Paris: Imprimerie Catholique, 1857–1880), vol. 40.

15 The Czech Reformation is a concept referring to the reformist stream of the late Middle Ages and early modern period formed in the territory of the Czech Kingdom. It was not a monolithic and unchanging flow but was split into many directions, from conservative to radical emancipated groups, though pluralistic views shared common doctrinal elements (accepting in both kinds/Utraquism, emphasizing God's Word preached in plain language, emphasizing the immediate relationship between man and God, and opposition to secular flamboyance and Church wealth). In terms of time, the concept of the Czech Reformation may include the period of the Hussite movement and the resulting Utraquist Church in the Czech lands and the Unity of the Brethren. Despite the influence of the German and Swiss Reformation on the Czech environment, they did not merge with the Czech Reformation. The defeat of the Czech Estates at the Battle of White Mountain against the Habsburgs and the associated end of religious freedom and the re-Catholicization of the Czech Lands, confirmed by the Peace of Westphalia of 1648, marked the end of the Czech Reformation as a separate reform stream. The work of Czech historians forms a basic overview and references to literature: Jiří Kejř, *Z počátků české reformace* (Brno: L. Marek, 2006); František Šmahel, *Husitská revoluce*. 2 vols. *Kořeny české reformace* (Prague: Karolinum, 1996).

16 Tomek, *Dějepis města Prahy*, 3: 233.

17 Tomek, *Dějepis města Prahy*, 9: 163.

18 Tomek, *Dějepis města Prahy*, 9: 163.

19 Rostislav Nový, "Ženské řeholní a laické komunity v předhusitské Praze," in *Žena v dějinách Prahy*, ed. Jiří Pešek and Václav Ledvinka (Prague: Scriptorium, 1996), 41–6; Tomek, *Dějepis města Prahy*, 3: 233.

20 Towards the end of the fourteenth century, the complex of the Český Krumlov double monastery was probably expanded to include a house of beguines, donated by Anna, the widow of Jindřich of Lipá, which was situated at the eastern wall of the Minorite monastery. Viz Johann Matthäus Klimesch, ed., *Urkunden- und Regestenbuch des ehemaligen Klarissinenklosters in Krumau* (Prague: Verein für Geschichte der Deutschen in Böhmen, 1904), 67–9; Helena Soukupová "Klášter minoritů a klarisek v Českém Krumlově," *Průzkumy památek* 2 (1999): 69–86, at 73.

21 Régine Pernoud, *Žena v době katedrál* (Prague: Vyšehrad, 2002), 40. From the French original: Régine Pernoud, *La Femme au temps des cathédrales* (Paris: Stock, 1980).

22 Tomek, *Dějepis města Prahy*, 3: 106.

23 The beguines' tradition of service in hospitals under the patronage and endowment of private individuals can be demonstrated in later

periods. For example, in the hospital of the Štuka family, located near the Church of St. Ambrose, mention of a mistress and sisters of the same hospital is preserved from 1436; the conditions of their cohabitation were very similar to the ways of beguines. Tomek, *Dějepis města Prahy*, 9: 184; see also Václav Vladivoj Tomek, *Základy starého místopisu Pražského* 6 vols. (W Praze: Nákl. Králowské, 1865–1875 [1870]), 2: 234.

24 Anna Císařová-Kolářová, *Žena v hnutí husitském* (Prague: Sokolice, 1915), 108–39.
25 Tomek, *Dějepis města Prahy*, 3: 232–4.
26 Tomek, *Dějepis města Prahy*, 3: 233.
27 Tomek, *Dějepis města Prahy*, 3: 234.
28 Lily Braun, *Ženská otázka, její dějinný vývoj a její hospodářská stránka* (Prague: Samostatnost, 1902), 40. From the German original: Lily Braun, *Die Frauenfrage ihre geschichtliche Entwicklung und wirtschaftliche Seite* (Leipzig: Verlag von S. Hirzel, 1901).
29 See the satirical-polemic song from the beginning of the Hussite movement, *Slyšte ještě bratřie milí*, mocking beguines as "stuttering." Comp. Bohuslav Havránek, Josef Hrabák, and Jiří Daňhelka, eds., *Výbor z české literatury doby husitské* (Prague: Nakladatelství Československé akademie věd, 1963–4), 257.
30 Tomek, *Dějepis města Prahy*, vols. 3 and 9; Václav Vladivoj Tomek, *Základy starého místopisu Pražského. Vol. 1, Staré město Pražské* (Prague: Nákladem král. České společnosti nauk, 1866).
31 Josef Truhlář, ed., "Život Milíče z Kroměříže/Vita venerabilis presbyteri Milicii, praelati ecclesiae Pragensis," in *Fontes rerum bohemicarum. Vitae sanctorum et aliorum quorundam pietate insigniím* (Prague: Nákladem Musea Království Českého, 1873), 1: 401–30.
32 Tomek, *Dějepis města Prahy*, 1: 128–9, 232–3, 439–40.
33 Ekert and Reinsberg, *Posvátná místa král. hl. města Prahy*, 2: 377–9.
34 Tomek, *Dějepis města Prahy*, 2: 149.
35 Tomek, *Dějepis města Prahy*, 2: 152.
36 Tomek, *Dějepis města Prahy*, 2: 151; Ekert and Reinsberg, *Posvátná místa král. hl. města Prahy*, 2: 377–9, 425.
37 Tomek, *Dějepis města Prahy*, 9: 163.
38 Tomek, *Dějepis města Prahy*, 2: 152.
39 Tomek, *Dějepis města Prahy*, 2: 151; Ekert and Reinsberg, *Posvátná místa král. hl. města Prahy*, 2: 377–9; Tomek, *Dějepis města Prahy*, 9: 163.
40 There was a courtyard belonging to the Prague group of Templars. See Templarius Bohemicus, *Praha templářská = Praga templariorum* (Beroun: Machart, 2014); Ekert and Reinsberg, *Posvátná místa král. hl. města Prahy*, 2: 425–6.

41 Tomek, *Dějepis města Prahy*, 2: 150; Ekert and Reinsberg, *Posvátná místa král. hl. města Prahy*, 2: 377–9, 425; Tomek, *Dějepis města Prahy*, 3: 233.
42 Tomek, *Dějepis města Prahy*, 9: 163–4.
43 Tomek, *Dějepis města Prahy*, 9: 163–4.
44 Ekert and Reinsberg, *Posvátná místa král. hl. města Prahy*, 2: 377–9; Tomek, *Dějepis města Prahy*, 3: 163.
45 Located in the part of the city known as ulice Masná (mezi Ungeltem a Kotvou); Ekert and Reinsberg, *Posvátná místa král. hl. města Prahy*, 2: 377–9; Tomek, *Dějepis města Prahy*, 9: 163–4.
46 Alison More, *Fictive Orders and Feminine Religious Identities, 1200–1600*, (Oxford: Oxford University Press, 2018).
47 Tomek, *Dějepis města Prahy*, 2: 209–10.
48 Tomek, *Dějepis města Prahy*, 9: 163.
49 Tomek, *Dějepis města Prahy*, 3: 163.
50 Tomek, *Dějepis města Prahy*, 3: 234.
51 Ekert and Reinsberg, *Posvátná místa král. hl. města Prahy*, 2: 377–9; Tomek, *Dějepis města Prahy*, 3: 128–38, 232–4, 439–40.
52 Tomek, *Dějepis města Prahy*, 3: 233.
53 Tomek, *Dějepis města Prahy*, 3: 234.
54 Mikuláš (d. 1364), Křišťan Ekartův z Prachatic (1373), František (1373), Jordán (†1375), Vavřinec Menhartův z Prahy (1380), Matěj (od roku 1380), Jan z Prahy (1402–12), Matěj (1418), mistr Bořek Bořitův z Prahy (od roku 1418).
55 Tomek, *Dějepis města Prahy*, 2: 202.
56 Tomek, *Dějepis města Prahy*, 3: 438–9.
57 The emphasis on preaching to this day is evidenced by fourteen collections in approximately ninety manuscripts, divided according to the type of preaching into synodal and academic, the most famous in terms of content and form, preaching modified in book form by the so-called postils, and last but not least, reference to the delivered speeches written by Hus listeners, the so-called Bethlehem preaching. See Anna Císařová-Kolářová, *Posluchačky v kapli Betlemské* (Prague: Kalich, 1947), 13; see Eva Kamínková, *Husova betlémská kázání a jejich dvě recense* (Prague: SPN, 1963).
58 Jan Hus, *Dcerka: o poznání cesty pravé k spasení*, ed. František Žilka (Prague: Kalich, 1995); Císařová-Kolářová, *Žena v hnutí husitském*, 25; Jan Hus, *Listy Husovy* ed. Bohumil Mareš, (Prague: A. Hajn, 1911).
59 Members of this noble family held posts in the highest provincial authorities and numbered among the most powerful aristocratic families in the Czech Lands. They often donated significant sums of money to Church institutions, and they frequently took an active part in charitable activities.

60 Tomek, *Dějepis města Prahy*, 2: 180.
61 Zikmund Winter, *Kulturní obraz českých měst: život veřejný v XV. a XVI. věku.* (Prague: Nákladem Matice České, 1890–2), 2: 115; Zikmund Winter, *Život církevní v Čechách: kulturně-historický obraz z XV. a XVI. století* (Prague: Česká akademie císaře Františka Josefa pro vědy, slovesnost a umění, 1895–6), s. 714.
62 Tomek, *Dějepis města Prahy*, 2: 146.
63 Tomek, *Dějepis města Prahy*, 9: 163.
64 Tomek, *Dějepis města Prahy*, 3: 163.
65 Tomek, *Dějepis města Prahy*, 2: 152.
66 Ekert and Reinsberg, *Posvátná místa král. hl. města Prahy*, 2: 377–9.
67 Tomek, *Dějepis města Prahy*, 2: 149; Ekert and Reinsberg, *Posvátná místa král. hl. města Prahy*, 2: 377–9.
68 Tomek, *Dějepis města Prahy*, 2: 151.
69 Tomek, *Dějepis města Prahy*, 2: 186.
70 The other half of the house belonged to a member of a noble family, probably the virgin Kunec of Vartenberk.
71 Tomek, *Dějepis města Prahy*, 3: 438–9.
72 Tomek, *Dějepis města Prahy*, 9: 165.
73 Tomek, *Dějepis města Prahy*, 9: 165.
74 Tomek, *Dějepis města Prahy*, 9: 166.
75 Tomek, *Dějepis města Prahy*, 9: 163–4; as to the title, see Tomek, *Dějepis města Prahy*, 8: 110.
76 Tomek, *Dějepis města Prahy*, 3: 439.
77 Tomek, *Dějepis města Prahy*, 3: 439–40.
78 Tomek, *Dějepis města Prahy*, 3: 438–9.
79 Tomek, *Dějepis města Prahy*, 3: 440.
80 Tomek, *Dějepis města Prahy*, 9: 164.
81 Šimek, *Příběhy římské*.
82 Pavlína Rychterová, "Žena a manželství v díle Tomáše ze Štítného," *Mediaevalia historica bohemica* 6 (1999), 95–109; Pavlína Rychterová, "Kirchenkritische Visionen der hl. Birgitta von Schweden und ihre Übersetzung von Thomas von Štitny," in *Pater familias. Sborník příspěvků k životnímu jubileu prof. Dr. Ivana Hlaváčka*, ed. Jan Hrdina, Eva Doležalová, and Jan Kahuda (Prague: Scriptorium, 2002), 357–79; Pavlína Rychterová, "Viklefice a její předchůdkyně," in *Člověk českého středověku*, ed. František Šmahel and Martin Nodl (Prague: Argo, 2002), 220–47; Pavlína Rychterová, "Konzepte der religiosen Erziehung der Laien im spatmittelalterlichen Böhmen. Einige Überlegungen zur Debatte über die sog. böhmische Devotio moderna," in *Kirchliche Reformimpulse des 14./15. Jahrhunderts in Ostmitteleuropa*, ed. Winfried Eberhard and Franz Machilek (Cologne: Böhlau, 2006), 219–37.

334 Jana Grollová

83 Josef Straka, *Spisy Tomáše ze Štítného. Řeči nedělní a sváteční* (Prague: Česká akademie věd a umění, 1929).
84 Detailed analysis of text and its Latin template is missing.
85 The work has been preserved in an incomplete, so-called Klementinum description, National Library of the Czech Republic, sign. XVII C 15, from which another copy was made in around 1500, the so-called Strahov, which is a part of the collections of the monastery library in Strahov (Strahov D G III 13). According to church terminology, we have preserved the preaching *sermones de tempore* (from Advent to Saturday night) and *de sanctis partis hiemalis* (from St. Andrew to Saint Ambrose).
86 Brigita of Sweden, *Vidění svaté Brigity Švédské v překladu Tomáše ze Štítného*, ed. Pavlína Rychterová (Prague: Filosofia, 2009).
87 In the text, this is also denoted as *additiones* and *declarationes*; A critical edition offers a comprehensive analysis of manuscripts, including their description, sorting, and comparison. Rychterová, *Vidění svaté Brigity Švédské*, n35.
88 Rychterová, *Vidění svaté Brigity Švédské*, 17–25.
89 Of the fourteen copies, eleven would be considered direct models of the Štítný translation, of which only four manuscripts correspond to individual errors with the Štítný translation, namely: Prague, Prague Metropolitan Chapter Library, signature C 87; Prague, National Library of the Czech Republic, VIII D 26; Kraków, Biblioteka Jagiellońska, DD III 74; and Warszawa, Biblioteka narodowa, ms. 17067.
90 Bohuslav Havránek and Josef Hrabák, *Výbor z České literatury od poČátků podobu Husovu* (Prague: Nakladatelství Československé akademie věd, 1957), 650.
91 Rychterová, *Vidění svaté Brigity Švédské*, 29; Císařová-Kolářová, *PosluchaČky v kapli Betlemské*.
92 Císařová-Kolářová, *Žena v hnutí husitském*, 108–39.
93 Císařová-Kolářová, *Žena v hnutí husitském*, 108–39.
94 *Sitzungsberichte Wiener Akademie* 39, tom. 4 (1862): 671.
95 Císařová-Kolářová, *Žena v hnutí husitském*, 108–39.
96 "Chronicon Laurentii de Brzezowa," in *Fontes rerum Bohemicarum. Tom V.*, ed. Jan Gebauer (Prague: Nákladem Nadání Františka Palackého, 1893), 400–2.
97 Jaroslav Goll, "Rokycanova Postilla," *Časopis Musea království Českého* 53 (1879): 205; Pavel Žídek, *Správovna* (Prague: Tobolka, 1908), 61.
98 Zdeněk Nejedlý, *PoČátky husitského zpěvu* (Prague: Jubilejní fond Král. České spoleČnosti nauk: RivnáČ, 1907), 40.
99 "Chronicon Laurentii de Brzezowa," 466.
100 Nejedlý, *PoČátky husitského zpěvu*, 125.

101 In this period, the word "sermon" underwent a shift in Old Czech texts, which used the same word to indicate *contemplate*, i.e., to discuss the topic in private.
102 František Palacký, ed., *Archiv Český VI. Paběrky písemností rozličných z r. 1401–1420* (Prague: W kommissí knihkupce Fridricha Tempského, 1872), 38.
103 Stephani Prioris Cartus, "Epistola ad Hussitas," in Bernardus Pez, ed., *Thesaurus anecdotorum novissimus*, 6 vols. (Augsburg Augustae Vindelicorum Graecii, 1721–29), vol. 4 (1723); Zdeněk Nejedlý, *Dějiny husitského zpěvu. 3. Jan Hus*. (Prague: Nakladatelství Československé akademie věd, 1955), 125.
104 Císařová-Kolářová, *Žena v hnutí husitském*, 30–1; viz Jan Hus, *Betlemské poselství* (Prague: Jan Laichter, 1947), 1.
105 Václav Nebeský, "Verše na Husity z rukopisu musejního," *Časopis Českého museum* 26 (1852): 140.
106 Andreas de Broda, *Traktát mistra Ondřeje z Brodu o původu husitů: Visones Ioannis, archiepiscopi Pragensis, et earundem explicationes (alias Tractatus de origine Hussitarum)*, ed. Jaroslav Kadlec (Tábor: Muzeum husitského revolučního hnutí, 1980), 1–35.
107 Jan Příbram, *Život kněží táborských*, signatura III D 28, fol. 137, Národní knihovna České republiky, Praha.
108 "Chronicon Laurentii de Brzezowa," 452.

Contributors

Letha Böhringer (PhD Universität Bonn, 1987) is a lecturer in the Historisches Institut at the Universität zu Köln and archivist at the Rheinisches Bildarchiv Köln. Her research focuses on the intersection of urban and religious history, with a particular emphasis on lay religious women's communities and institutions in the later Middle Ages. Dr. Böhringer is the co-editor of *Labels and Libels: Naming Beguines in Northern Medieval Europe* (Brepols, 2014); other publications include "Kreuzzugsprediger, Domscholaster und fromme Frauen. Beobachtungen zum klerikalen Umfeld der ersten Kölner Beginen," *Rheinische Viertelsjahrblätter* 72 (2008), and "Beginen und Schwestern in der Sorge für Kranke, Sterbende und Verstorbene. Eine Problemskizze," in *Organisierte Barmherzigkeit. Armenfürsorge und Hospitalwesen in Mittelalter und Früher Neuzeit*, ed. Artur Dirmeier (Regensburg, 2010).

Jennifer Kolpacoff Deane (PhD Northwestern University, 2000) is professor of history at the University of Minnesota Morris. Her research focuses on late medieval religious and gender history, particularly in German-speaking lands, and the intersections of communities, domestic space, hospitality, and devotion. She is the author of *A History of Medieval Heresy & Inquisition* (Rowman & Littlefield, 2011), co-editor of *Labels & Libels: Naming Beguines in Northern Medieval Europe* (Brepols, 2014), and editor of *Herbert Grundmann (1902–1970): Essays on Heresy, Inquisition, and Literacy* (York Medieval Press, 2019). She is currently completing a monograph on beguine communities in later medieval Germany.

Sean L. Field (PhD Northwestern University, 2002) is professor of history at the University of Vermont. His current research centres on the intersection of sanctity, heresy, political power, and religious institutions at and around the French royal court. Recent books include *Courting Sanctity: Holy Women and the Capetains* (Cornell, 2019); *Isabelle de France, soeur de Saint Louis. Une princesse mineure*, with Jacques Dalarun, Jean-Baptiste Lebigue, and Anne-Françoise Leurquin-Labie (Les Éditions franciscaines, 2015); *Marguerite Porete et le Miroir des simples âmes: Perspectives historiques, philosophiques, et littéraires*, edited with Robert E. Lerner and Sylvain Piron (Vrin, 2013); and *The Beguine, the Angel, and the Inquisitor: The Trial of Marguerite Porete and Guiard of Cressonessart* (Notre Dame, 2012).

Jana Grollová (PhD University of Ostrava, 2001) is a researcher and collaborator at VIVARIUM - Centre for Research in Medieval Society and Culture (Faculty of Arts) in the Czech Republic. Her research focuses on the medieval religious life, Christian morality, and gender history, particularly in the Czech lands during the Czech reform and the Hussite movement. She is the author of *Militia est vita hominis: Sedm smrtelných hříchů a sedm skutků milosrdenství v literárních a vizuálních pramenech českého středověku* (*Seven Deadly Sins and Seven Acts of Mercy in the Literary and Visual Sources of the Czech Middle Ages*) (Veduta, 2013); and *Memento mori středověkých reformních postil: Obraz života a smrti v písemné tradici českého středověkého kazatelství* (*Memento Mori Medieval Reformist Postil: The Image of Life and Death in the Written Tradition of Czech Medieval Preaching*) (Veduta, 2017). She is currently completing a monograph titled *Beguines and Preacher: Between the Moral Ideal, Homiletics and Pastoral Care in the Czech Lands in the 14th–16th Centuries*.

Lezlie Knox (PhD University of Notre Dame, 1999) is associate professor and chair of the Department of History at Marquette University. Her research has focused on the Franciscan Order in later medieval Italy, and she is currently working on one of the order's prolific chroniclers, Mariano of Florence. She has published widely on the female branch of the Order, including *Creating Clare of Assisi: Female Franciscan Identities in Later Medieval Italy* (Brill, 2008), as well as the collaborative projects *Visions of Sainthood in Medieval Rome: The Lives of Margherita Colonna by Giovanni Colonna and Stefania* with Larry F. Field and Sean L. Field (Notre Dame, 2017), and *Franciscan Women: Female Identities and Religious Culture, Medieval and Beyond*, edited with David Couturier (Franciscan Institute Publications, 2020).

Anne E. Lester (PhD Princeton University, 2003) is the John W. Baldwin and Jenny Jochen associate professor of medieval history at Johns Hopkins University. Her research focuses on the social and religious history of Europe during the High Middle Ages (1000–1400). She is the author of *Creating Cistercian Nuns: The Women's Religious Movement and*

Its Reform in Thirteenth-Century Champagne (Cornell, 2011) and co-editor of *Cities, Texts, and Social Networks* (Ashgate, 2010); *Center and Periphery: Studies on Power in the Medieval World in Honor of William Chester Jordan* (Brill, 2013), *Crusades and Memory: Rethinking Past and Present* (Routledge, 2015). Her current research focuses on medieval materiality, gender history, and social change during the period of the Crusades, and will appear as a book titled *Fragments of Devotion: Relics and Remembrance in the Aftermath of the Fourth Crusade*.

Alison More is assistant professor of medieval studies and the inaugural Comper Professor in Medieval Studies at the University of St. Michael's College at the University of Toronto. Her research investigates the intersections between social and religious culture in Northern Europe from 1250 to 1450. She is primarily interested in women's experiences, as well as alternative interpretations of absences and inconsistencies in the historical record. Her publications include *Fictive Orders and Feminine Religious Identities, 1200–1600* (Oxford, 2018); *Representing Medieval Genders and Sexualities*, edited with Elizabeth L'Estrange (Routledge, 2011); and several articles and chapters. She is co-investigator for *The Other Sister*, a project on non-cloistered religious women in medieval and early modern Europe.

Amanda Power (PhD University of Cambridge, 2002) is associate professor of history at the University of Oxford. Her research focuses on religion, power, and intellectual life in medieval Europe. She has been involved in developing the field of global medieval history, and new approaches to historical study that speak to the concerns of the mounting climate and environmental crisis. Her publications include "Globalising Cosmographies" with Caroline Pennock, *Past & Present*, 238, supplement 13 (2018), and *Roger Bacon and the Defence of Christendom* (Cambridge, 2012). She is writing a monograph, *Medieval Histories of the Anthropocene*, which explores the construction of public rationalities that dislocated humans from local ecosystems.

Janine Larmon Peterson (PhD Indiana University, 2006) is professor of history at Marist College and coordinator of medieval and renaissance studies. She is the Medieval Europe editor for the *Database of Religious History*. Her research focuses on challenges to the authority of the institutional church, particularly with regard to heresy and saints' cults, in late medieval Italy. She is currently researching the intersection of gender and the supernatural world in the Mediterranean basin. Dr. Peterson's publications include *Suspect Saints and Holy Heretics: Disputed Sanctity and Communal Identity in Late Medieval Italy* (Cornell, 2019) and articles in *Past & Present, Traditio, Viator*, and *Scriptorium*.

Neslihan Şenocak (PhD Bilkent University, Ankara, Turkey, 2002) is associate professor of history at Columbia University. She specializes in medieval religious and social history. Her research and teaching focus on popular religion, political theology, criminal justice, and medieval Italian communes. Dr. Şenocak's publications include *The Poor and the Perfect: The Rise of Learning in the Franciscan Order 1209–1310* (Ithaca, 2012) and the upcoming co-edited volumes *Teacher as Shepherd: Theology and Care of Souls at the Time of Lateran IV* with Clare Monagle (Brepols, 2022) and *Italy and Christianity, 1050–1300* with Agostino Paravicini Bagliani (Cornell, 2023). She is currently finishing a monograph on the care of souls in medieval Italy.

Tanya Stabler Miller (PhD University of California-Santa Barbara, 2007) is associate professor of history at Loyola University, Chicago. Her research focuses on lay religion, gender, and urban culture, with special emphasis on northern France. She is the author of *The Beguines of Medieval Paris: Gender, Patronage, and Spiritual Authority* (University of Pennsylvania Press, 2014), which explores the intersections between gender, spirituality, political power, and urban life in medieval Paris. Dr. Miller has also published essays on lay religion and heresy; medieval universities and masculinity; and medieval conceptions of gender.

Sita Steckel (PhD Ludwig-Maximilians Universität München, 2006) is associate professor of history at Westfälische Wilhelms-Universität Münster. Her current research focuses on controversies between religious groups within the Latin church, particularly the secular clergy, monastic, and mendicant orders during the high and later Middle Ages, including questions of gender and constructions of masculinity. Dr. Steckel is the author of *Kulturen des Lehrens im Früh- und Hochmittelalter. Autorität, Wissenskonzepte und Netzwerke von Gelehrten* (Böhlau Verlag, 2011) and numerous publications on late medieval religious movements. Recently, she co-edited the volume *Choosing My Religion: Religious Options and Alternatives in Medieval and Early Modern Christianity* with Matthias Pohlig (Mohr Siebeck, 2021).

Bibliography

Manuscripts

France

3 G 538, 161 H 1. Archives Départementales du Nord [ADN], Lille.
Carton J, 821, nos. 1–4, Acount-Inventory, Eudes de Nevers, 1266. Archives nationales, Paris.
Sermons and treatises, Bishop Guiard of Cambrai and Robert of Sorbon. Bibliothèque nationale de France [BnF] Lat.15955. Bibliothèque nationale de France, Paris.
Sermon collection with sermons of Robert of Sorbon. BnF Lat. 15971. Bibliothèque nationale de France, Paris.
Pastoral miscellany with treatises from Robert of Sorbon. BnF Lat. 15972. Bibliothèque nationale de France, Paris.
Sermons of Robert of Sorbon. BnF Lat. 16471. Bibliothèque nationale de France, Paris.
Sermons of Arnoul Bescochier, et al. BnF Lat. 16482. Bibliothèque nationale de France, Paris.
Sermons of Robert of Sorbon. BnF Lat. 16496. Bibliothèque nationale de France, Paris.
Sermons of Robert of Sorbon. BnF Lat. 16507. Bibliothèque nationale de France, Paris.
Chansonnier, dit. Chansonnier Cangé, fourth quarter of thirteenth century. BnF, Fr. 846, Paris.
Thibaut de Navarre, *Foire et Chant*, c. 1280. BnF. Fr. 12581, Paris.

Italy

ms. 104. Biblioteca Casanatense, Rome.

Primary Sources

Anselm of Havelberg. *Anticimenon: On the Unity of the Faith and the Controversies with the Greeks*. Translated by Ambrose Criste and Carol Neel. Cistercian Studies Series 232. Collegeville, PA: Cistercian Publications, 2010.

Armstrong, Regis J., J.A. Wayne Hellmann, and William J. Short, eds. *Francis of Assisi: Early Documents*. 3 vols. New York: New City Press, 1999.

Becket, Marie-France, Jean-François Godet, and Thaddée Matura, eds. and trans. *Claire d'Assise: Écrits*. Paris: Cerf, 1985.

Benedetti, Marina, ed. *Milano 1300: I processi inquisitoriali contro le devote e i devoti di santa Guglielma*. Milan: Libri Scheiwiller, 1999.

Bernard of Clairvaux. *Opera Omnia*, edited by J. Leclercq and H. Rochais. 8 vols. Rome: Editiones Cistercienses, 1957–77.

Bernard of Luxembourg. *Catalogus haereticorum*. Cologne: Eucharius Cervicornus, 1522.

Bird, Jessalynn, Edward Peters, and James M. Powell, eds. *Crusade and Christendom: Annotated Documents*. Philadelphia: University of Pennsylvania Press, 2013.

Blumenfeld-Kosinski, Renate, trans. *The Writings of Margaret of Oingt: Medieval Prioress and Mystic*. Newburyport, MA: Focus, 1990.

Boccali, Giovanni, ed. *Legenda latina sanctae Clarae virginis assisiensis*. Santa Maria degli Angeli: Edizioni Porziuncola, 2001.

Bullarium diplomatum et privilegiorum sanctorum romanorum Pontificum Taurensis. 25 vols. Augustae Taurinorum, Italy: Seb. Franco, et al., 1862.

Bock, Franz, ed. "Der Este-Prozess von 1321." *Archivum Fratrum Praedicatorum* 7 (1937): 41–95.

Bonfadini, Antonio. *Vite di S. Guglielma regina d'Ungheria e di S. Eufrasia vergine romana*. Edited by G. Ferraro. Bologna: Gaetano Romagnoli, 1878.

Bortolan, D. D., ed. "Cronaca Romana dall'anno 1288 al 1301." *Archivio Veneto* 33 (1887): 425–33.

Caesarius of Heisterbach. "Vita Engelberti." In *Die Wundergeschichten: Einleitung, Exempla und Auszüge aus den Predigten des Caesarius von Heisterbach*, edited by Alfons Hilka, c. 7, 245–6. Publikationen der Gesellschaft für Rheinische Geschichtskunde 1. Vol. 3. Bonn: Hanstein, 1933–7.

"Il Catalogo di Torino." In *Codice Topografico della città di Roma*, edited by R. Valentini and G. Zucchetti, 291–318. Vol. 3. Rome: Fonti per la Storia di Italia, 1980.

Catherine of Siena. *Letters of St. Catherine of Siena*. Edited by Suzanne Noffke. 2 vols. Tempe: ACRMS, 2000–1.

Cazelles, Brigitte. *The Lady as Saint: A Collection of French Hagiographic Romances of the Thirteenth Century*. Philadelphia: University of Pennsylvania Press, 1991.

Chazaud, Alphonse-Martial, ed. "Inventaire et comptes de la succession d'Eudes, Comte de Nevers (Acre 1266)." *Mémoires de la Société nationale des antiquaries de France* 32 (1870): 164–206.
Colledge, Edmund, J.C. Marler, and Judith Grant, trans. and intro. *Margaret Porete, The Mirror of Simple Souls*. Notre Dame, IN: University of Notre Dame Press, 1999.
"The Confession of Na Prous Boneta." In *Medieval Women's Visionary Literature*, edited and translated by Elizabeth Petroff, 284–90. New York: Oxford University Press, 1986.
Corio, Bernardino. *Storia di Milano*. Edited by Anna Morisi Guerra. 2 vols. Turin: Unione tipografico, 1978.
Courtois, Gaston. *The States of Perfection According to the Teaching of the Church: Papal Documents from Leo XIII to Pius XII*. Translated by John A. O'Flynn. Dublin: M.H. Gill and Son, 1961.
Dalarun, Jacques, Sean L. Field, Jean-Baptiste Lebigue, and Anne-Françoise Leurquin-Labie, eds. and trans. *Isabelle de France, sœur de Saint Louis. Une princesse mineure*. Paris: Éditions franciscaines, 2014.
Dalarun, Jacques, ed. *The Rediscovered Life of St. Francis of Assisi by Thomas of Celano*. Translated by Timothy J. Johnson. St. Bonaventure, NY: Franciscan Institute Publications, 2016.
De Broda, Andreas, and Jaroslav Kadlec, eds. *Traktát mistra Ondřeje z Brodu o původu husitů "Visones Ioannis, archiepiscopi Pragensis, et earundem explicationes (alias Tractatus de origine Hussitarum)."* Tábor, Muzeum husitského revolučního hnutí, 1980.
Denifle, Heinrich, and Emile Chatelain, eds. *Chartularium Universitatis Parisiensis*. 4 vols. Paris: Delalain, 1889–97.
Dondaine, Antoine. "La Hiérarchie cathare en Italie, II: Le 'Tractatus de hereticis' d'Anselme d'Alexandrie, O.P." *Archivum fratrum praedicatorum* 20 (1950): 234–324.
Duraffour, Antonin, Pierre Gardette, and Paulette Durdilly, eds. *Les œuvres de Marguerite d'Oingt*. Paris: Société d'Édition Les Belles Lettres, 1965.
Ekbert of Schönau [Eckbertus Schonaugiensis]. "Sermones." In *Patrologia Latina*, edited by J.P. Migne. Vol. 195, Cols. 11–102. Paris: Migne, 1855.
Esser, Cajetan, ed. *Opuscula sancti patris Francisci Assisiensis*. Grottaferrata: Collegii S. Bonaventurae Ad Claras Aquas, 1978.
Field, Larry F., Lezlie S. Knox, and Sean L. Field., ed. and trans. *Visions of Sainthood in Medieval Rome: The Lives of Margherita Colonna by Giovanni Colonna and Stefania*. Notre Dame, IN: University of Notre Dame Press, 2017.
Field, Sean L., intro. and trans. *The Rules of Isabelle of France: An English Translation with Introductory Study*. Additional documents translated by Larry F. Field. St. Bonaventure, NY: Franciscan Institute Publications, 2014.

– ed. and trans. *The Writings of Agnes of Harcourt: The Life of Isabelle of France and the Letter on Louis IX and Longchamp.* Notre Dame, IN: University of Notre Dame Press, 2003.

Flamare, H. de. "La Charte de départ pour la Terre-Sainte de Gaucher de Châtillon, baron de Donzy." *Bulletin de la Société Nivernaise* 13 (1886–9): 174–82.

Florennes, Gerard of. "Acta Synodi Atrebatensis." In *Patrologia Latina*, edited by J.P. Migne, 1269–1312. Vol. 142. Paris: Migne, 1853.

Friedberg, Emil, ed. *Corpus iuris canonici.* 2 vols. Leipzig: Bernhard Tauchnitz, 1881.

Garay, Kathleen, and Madeleine Jeay, trans. *The Life of St. Douceline, a Beguine of Provence.* Cambridge: D.S. Brewer, 2001.

Gallia christiana in provincias ecclesiasticas distributa. 16 vols. Paris: V. Palme, 1715–1865.

Gebauer, Jan, ed. *Fontes rerum Bohemicarum.* Tom V. Prague: Nákladem Nadání Františka Palackého, 1893.

Guarnieri, Romana, and Paul Verdeyen, eds. *Marguerite Porete, Le mirouer des simples ames/Margaretae Porete Specvlvm simplicivm animarum.* CCCM 69. Turnhout: Brepols, 1986.

Gui, Bernard. *Additus ad Historia fratris Dulcini di anonimo sincrono e De secta illorum qui se dicunt esse de ordine Apostolorum di Bernardo Gui.* Edited by A. Segarizzi, 449–53. *Rerum Italicarum Scriptores* 9:5. Città di Castello: Tipi della casa editrice S. Lapi, 1907.

Guibert of Tournai. "*Collectio de scandalis ecclesia.*" Edited by Aubertus Stroick. *Archivum Franciscanum Historicum* 24 (1931): 33–62.

Havránek, Bohuslav, Josef Hrabák, and Jiří Daňhelka, eds. *Výbor z České literatury doby husitské.* Prague: Nakladatelství Československé akademie věd, 1963–4.

Hildebert of Le Mans. "Hildeberti Cenomannensis Epistolae." In *Patrologia Latina*, edited by J.P. Migne, cols. 151–311. Vol. 171. Paris: Migne, 1854.

Hildegard of Bingen. *Epistolarivm. Pars prima, I–XC.* Edited by Lieven van Acker. CCCM 91. Turnhout: Brepols, 1991.

Huillard-Breholles, Jean Louis Alphonse, and A. Lecoy de la Marche. *Titres de la maison ducale de Bourbon.* 2 vols. Paris: H. Plon, 1867–74.

Hus, Jan. *Betlemské poselství.* Prague: Jan Laichter, 1947.

Hus, Jan, and Bohumil Mareš, eds. *Listy Husovy.* Prague: A. Hajn, 1911.

Hus, Jan, and František Žilka, eds. *Dcerka: o poznání cesty pravé k spasení.* Prague: Kalich, 1995.

Huygens, R.B.C., ed. *Lettres de Jacques de Vitry, 1160/1170–1240.* Leiden: Brill, 1960.

Huyskens, Albert. *Der sog. Libellus de dictis quatuor ancillarum s. Elisabeth confectus.* Kempten und Munich: Verlag der Jos. Kösel'schen Buchhandlung, 1911.

Humbert de Silva Candida. "Adversus Simoniacos Libri Tres." In *MGH Libelli De Lite 1*, edited by Friedrich Thaner. Hannover: Hahnsche Buchhandlung, 1891.

Institorus, Henricus, and Jacobus Sprenger. *Malleus Maleficarum*. Translated by P.G. Maxwell-Stuart. New York: Manchester University Press, 2007.

Jacques de Vitry. *The Historia occidentalis of Jacques de Vitry*. Edited by J.F. Hinnesbusch. Freibroug: The University Press, 1972.

John of Salisbury. *Policraticus, Of the Frivolities of Courtiers and the Footprints of Philosophers*. Translated by Cary J. Nederman. Cambridge Texts in the History of Political Thought. Cambridge: Cambridge University Press, 1990.

John XXIII. "Personas vacantes." In *Annales Minorum*, edited by Luke Wadding, IX, no. 535; XVIII, 653–4. Rome: Typis Rochi Bernabò, 1761.

Landulphus. "Landulfi (iunioris) Historia Mediolanensis." In *MGH SS 8*, edited by L.C. Bethmann and W. Wattenbach, 36–102. Hanover: Hahnsche Buchhandlung, 1848.

Lebeuf, Abbé Jean. *Histoire de la Ville et de tout le diocèse de Paris par l'abbé Lebeuf . . . nouvelle édition annotée et continuée jusqu'à nos jours par Hippolyte Cocheris*. Vol. 4. Paris: Durand, 1870.

– *Mémoires concernant l'histoire civile et ecclésiastique d'Auxerre et de son ancient diocese*. New edition by Ambroise Challe and Mathieu Maximilien Quantin. 4 vols. Auxerre, France: Perriquet, 1848–55.

Le Ordre de Bel-Eyse, in *The Political Songs of England, from the Reign of John to that of Edward II*, edited by Thomas Wright, 137–48. London: Camden Society, 1839.

Longchamps, Nigel de. *Speculum stultorum*. Edited by John H. Mozley and Robert R. Raymo. University of California English Studies 18. Berkeley: University of California Press, 1960.

Lorris, Guillaume de, and Jean de Meun. *The Romance of the Rose*. Translated by Charles Dahlberg. Princeton, NJ: Princeton University Press, 1971.

Marolles, Abbé de. *Inventaire des titres de Nevers*. Nevers: Paulin Fay, 1873.

Martene, Edmond, and Ursin Durand, eds. *Dialogus inter cluniacensem et cistercensem, testo in Thesaurus novus anecdotorum tomus quintus*. Paris: Lutetiae Parisiorum, 1717.

–, eds. *Thesaurus novus anecdotorum*. 5 vols. Paris: Sumptibus F. Delaulne, 1717.

Meerseman, G.G., ed. *Dossier de l'ordre de la pénitence au XIIIe siècle*. Fribourg: Editions Universitaires, 1961; second edition, 1982.

Michel, Robert, ed. "Les process de Matteo et de Galeazzo Visconti." *Mélanges d'archéologie et d'histoire* 19 (1909): 269–327.

Migne, J.P. et al., eds. *Patralogiae cursus completes . . . series Latina* [PL]. 221 vols. Paris: Garnier et Migne, 1844–1974.

Moneta of Cremona. *Adversos Catharos et Valdenses libri quinque*. Edited by Thomas A. Ricchini. Ridgewood, NJ: Gregg Press, 1964.

Monfrin, Jacques, ed. *Joinville, Vie de saint Louis*. Paris: Garnier, 1995.
Naumburg, Walram of. "Liber de unitate ecclesiae conservanda." In *Scriptores rerum germanicarum in usum scolarum*, edited by W. Schwenkenbecher, 173–284. Hanover: Hahnsche Buchhandlung, 1883.
Nebeský, Václav. "Verše na Husity z rukopisu musejního." *Časopis Českého museum* 26 (1852).
Nejedlý, Zdeněk. *PoČátky husitského zpěvu*. Prague: Jubilejní fond Král. České spoleČnosti nauk: ŘivnáČ, 1907.
– *Dějiny husitského zpěvu. 3. Jan Hus*. Prague: Nakladatelství Československé akademie věd, 1955.
Oliger, Livarius, ed. *B. Margherita Colonna († 1280): Le due vite scritte dal fratello Giovanni Colonna senatore di Roma e da Stefania monaca di S. Silvestro in Capite*. Rome: Facultas Theologica Pontificii Athenaei Seminarii Romani, 1935.
Orderic Vitalis. *The Ecclesiastical History of Orderic Vitalis*. Edited by Marjorie Chibnall. 6 vols. Oxford Medieval Texts. Oxford: Clarendon Press, 2004.
Oresme, Nicole. "Tractatus de configurationibus qualitatum et motuum." In *Nicole Oresme and the Medieval Geometry of Qualities and Motions*, edited by Marshall Clagett, 342–5. Madison: University of Wisconsin Press, 1968.
Orr, John, ed. *Les œuvres de Guiot de Provins, poète lyrique et satirique*. Publications de l'Université de Manchester. Série française 1. Manchester: Manchester University Press, 1915.
Palacký, František, ed. *Archiv Český VI. Paběrky písemností rozliČných z r. 1401–1420*. Prague: W kommissí knihkupce Fridricha Tempského, 1872.
Paolini, Lorenzo, and Raniero Orioli, eds. *Acta S. Officii Bononie ab anno 1291 usque ad annum 1310*. 3 vols. Fonti per la storia d'Italia, 106. Rome: Istituto storico italiano per il Medio Evo, 1982–4.
Paramo, Luis de. *De origine et progressu officii sanctae inquisitionis*. Madrid: Ex Typographia Regia, 1598.
Peter the Venerable. *The Letters of Peter the Venerable*. Edited by Giles Constable. 2 vols. Cambridge, MA: Harvard University Press, 1967.
Petschenig, Michael, and Gotfried E. Kreuz, eds. *Corpus Scriptorum Ecclesiasticorum Latinorum 13, X*. Vienna: Verlag der Österreichischen Akademie der Wissenschaften, 2004.
Pez, Bernardus, ed. *Thesaurus anecdotorum novissimus*. Tom. 4. Augsburg, 1723.
Philippon, E. *Œuvres de Marguerite d'Oyngt, prieure de Poleteins*. Lyon: N. Scheuring, 1877.
Porete, Marguerite. *The Mirror of Simple Souls*. Translated by Edmund Colledge, J.C. Marler, and Judith Grant. Notre Dame, IN: University of Notre Dame Press, 1999.
Pressutti, Petrus, ed. *Regesta Honorii Papae III*. 2 vols. Hildesheim: G. Olms, reprinted 1978.

Pulci, Antonia. "The Play of Saint Guglielma." In *Florentine Drama for Convent and Festival: Seven Sacred Plays*. Translated by James Wyatt Cook, 103–33. Chicago: University of Chicago Press, 1996.

Quantin, Maximilien, ed. *Cartulaire générale de l'Yonne*. 2 vols. Auxerre: Perriquet, 1854–60.

–, ed. *Recueil de pièces pour faire suite au cartulaire générale de l'Yonne*. Auxerre: Siège de la société; Paris: Durand and Pédone-Lauriel, 1873.

Regino de Prüm. "Percunctandum de confratriis et fraternitatum societatibus qualiter in paroechia agantur." In *De ecclesiasticis disciplinis et religione christiana*, in *Patralogiae Latina* [PL], edited by J. P. Migne. Vol. 132, Lb. 2, cap. v, col. 287A. Paris: Garnier and Migne, 1844–1974.

Richard of Saint Victor. "In Apocalypsin Johannis." In *Patrologia Latina*, edited by J.P. Migne. Vol. 196. Cols. 683–886. Paris: Garnier, 1880.

Richter, Aemilius Ludwig, and Aemilius Friedberg, eds. *Corpus juris canonici, 2: Decretalium collectiones*. Leipzig: Tauchnitz, 1879; reprint, Graz: Akademische Druck-und Verlagsanstalt, 1959.

Rutebeuf. *Œuvres complètes de Rutebeuf*. Edited by Edmond Faral and Julia Bastin. 2 vols. Paris: Éditions A. et J. Picard, 1959.

Rychterová, Pavlína, ed. *Vidění svaté Brigity Švédské v překladu Tomáše ze Štítného*. Prague: Filosofia, 2009.

Saint Jerome. *Adversus Jovinianum*. In *St Jerome: Letters and Select Works*, edited by Henry Wace and Phillip Schaff, 346–414. Nicene and Post-Nicene Fathers, Second Series. Volume 6. Peabody, MA: Hendrickson, 1995.

Salimbene de Adam. *The Chronicle of Salimbene de Adam*. Edited and translated by Joseph L. Baird, Guiseppe Baglivi, and John Robert Kane. Binghamton: SUNY Press, 1986.

Sbaraglia, Giovanni, ed. *Bullarium Franciscanum sive Romanorum Pontificum*. Rome, 1780. Reprint ed., Porziuncola, 1983.

Searby, Denis, trans. *The Revelations of St. Birgitta of Sweden*. 2 vols. New York: Oxford University Press, 2006.

Sigebert of Gembloux. "Apologia." In MGH *Libelli De Lite* 2, edited by E. Sackur, 436–48. Hannover: Hahnsche Buchhandlung, 1892.

"The Sentence of Marguerite Porete." In *A History of the Inquisition of the Middle Ages*, edited by Henry Charles Lea, 577–8. Vol. 2. New York: Cosimo Classics, 1888, rpt. 2005.

"The Sentence of Na Prous Boneta." In *A History of the Inquisition of the Middle Ages*, edited by Henry Charles Lea, 654. Vol. 3. New York: Cosimo Classics, 1888, rpt [2005].

Šimek, František, ed. *Příběhy římské. StaroČeská Gesta Romanorum*. Prague: Odeon, 1967.

Tanner, Norman, ed. and trans. *Decrees of the Ecumenical Councils*. 2 vols. London: Sheed and Ward, 1990.
Tobin, Frank, trans. *Mechthild of Magdeburg, The Flowing Light of the Godhead*. New York: Paulist Press, 1998.
Tomek, Václav Vladivoj. *Základy starého místopisu Pražského*. Vol. 1., *Staré město Pražské*. Prague: Nákladem král. České spoleČnosti nauk, 1866.
– "*O zlých letech po smrti krále Otakara.*" In *Fontes rerum Bohemicarum*, edited by Cosmas and Josef Emler. 2 vols., *Cosmae chronicon Boemorum cum continuatoribus*. Prague: Nákladem Musea království Českého, 1874.
– *Dějepis města Prahy*. 12 vols. W Praze: W kommissí u F. Riwnáce, 1855–1901.
"Tractatus de Investitura Episcoporum." In *MGH Libelli de lite* 2, edited by E. Bernheim, 495–504. Hannover: Hahnsche Buchhandlung 1892.
Truhlář, Josef, ed. "Život MilíČe z Kroměříže/ Vita venerabilis presbyteri Milicii, praelati ecclesiae Pragensis." In *Fontes rerum bohemicarum. Tom. I, Vitae sanctorum et aliorum quorundam pietate insigniím*. Prague: Nákladem Musea Království Českého, 1873.
Vauchez, André, and Armelle Le Huërou, eds. *Élisabeth de Hongrie: documents et sources historiques*. Paris: Éditions Franciscaines, 2017.
Verdeyen, Paul. "Le Procès d'inquisition contre Marguerite Porete et Guiard de Cressonessart (1309–1310)." *Revue d'Histoire Ecclésiastique* 81 (1986): 47–94.
Walter Map. *De Nugis Curialium – Courtiers' Trifles*. Edited by M.R. James, Christopher Nugent Lawrence Brooke, and R.A.B. Mynors. Oxford Medieval Texts. Oxford: Clarendon Press, 1983.
Walz, Angelus, ed. "Die 'Miracula Beati Dominici' der Schwester Cäcilia: Einleitung und Text." In *Miscellanea Pio Paschini—Lateranum*, 293–326. Rome: Facultas Theologica Pontificii Athenaei Lateranensis, 1948.
William of Saint-Amour. *The Opuscula of William of Saint-Amour: The Minor Works of 1255–1256*. Edited by Andrew Traver. Beiträge zur Geschichte der Philosophie und Theologie des Mittelalters N.F. 63 Münster: Aschendorff, 2003.
– *De periculis novissimorum temporum*. Edited and translated by Guy Geltner. Dallas Medieval Texts and Translations 8. Paris/Leuven/Dudley, MA: Peeters, 2008.

Secondary Sources

Abels, Richard, and Ellen Harrison. "The Participation of Women in Languedocian Catharism." *Mediaeval Studies* 41 (1979): 215–51.
Accrocca, Felice. *Francesco e la Santa Chiesa Romana: La scelta del Vangelo e la codificazione difficile di un ideale*. Assisi: Cittadella Editrice, 2015.

Adair-Toteff, Christopher. "Max Weber's Charismatic Prophets." *History of the Human Sciences* 27, (2014): 3–20.
– *Max Weber's Sociology of Religion*. Tübingen: Mohr Siebeck, 2016.
Agamben, Giorgio. *The Highest Poverty: Monastic Rules and Form-of-Life.* Translated by Adam Kotsko. Palo Alto, CA: Stanford University Press, 2013.
Aigner, Petra. "Poetry and Networking in High Medieval France (ca. 1100): Baudri de Bourgueil and His Scholarly Contacts." In *Networks of Learning: Perspectives on Scholars in Byzantine East and Latin West, c. 1000–1200*, edited by Sita Steckel, Niels Gaul, and Michael Grünbart, 33–56. Byzantinistische Studien und Texte 6. Münster: LIT, 2014.
Alberzoni, Maria Pia. *Clare of Assisi and the Poor Sisters in the Thirteenth Century*. St. Bonaventure, NY: Franciscan Institute Publications, 2004.
Alexiu, Andra. "Magistra Magistrorum: Hildegard of Bingen as a Polemicist Against False Teaching." *Medieval Worlds* 7 (2018): 170–89.
Allirot, Anne-Hélène. *Filles de roy de France: Princesses royales, mémoire de saint Louis et conscience dynastique (de 1270 à la fin du XIVe siècle)*. Turnhout: Brepols, 2010.
Alphandéry, Paul. "Quelques documents médiévaux relatifs à des états psychasthétiques." *Journal de psychologie normale et pathologique* 25 (1929): 763–87.
Alphandéry, Paul, and Alphonse Dupront. *La Chrétienté et l'idée de Croisade*. Vol. 1, *Les premières croisades*. Paris: A. Michel, 1954. Vol. 2, *Recommencements nécessaires (XII–XIII siècles)*. Paris: A. Michel, 1959.
Ames, Christine Caldwell. "Does Inquisition Belong to Religious History?" *The American Historical Review* 110, no. 1 (2005): 11–37.
– "Medieval Religious, Religions, Religion." *History Compass* 10 (2012): 334–52.
– *Righteous Persecution: Inquisition, Dominicans, and Christianity in the Middle Ages*. Philadelphia: University of Pennsylvania Press, 2008.
Amory, Frederic. "Whited Sepulchres: The Semantic History of Hypocrisy to the High Middle Ages." *Recherches de Théologie Ancienne et Médiévale* 53 (1986): 5–39.
Anderson, Margaret. "The Limits of Secularization: On the Problem of the Catholic Revival in Nineteenth-Century Germany." *Historical Journal* 38 (1995): 647–70.
Andreozzi, Gabriele, ed. *Il Terzo ordine regolare di San Francesco nella sua storia e nelle sue lege*. 2 vols. Rome: Editrice Franciscanum, 1993–4.
Angotti, Claire. "Presence d'un enseignement au sein du college de Sorbonne: *collationes, disputationes, lectiones* (xiiie–xve siècle). Bilan et hypotheses." *Cahiers de Recherches Médiévales* 18 (2009): 89–111.
Annaert, Philippe. "Vie Religieuse Féminine et Société dans les Pays-Bas Catholiques. La Réforme des Tertiaires Franciscaines aux XVI–XVIII

Siècles." In *Liber Amicorum Raphaël de Smedt*, edited by Jacques Paviot, 305–30. Leuven: Peeters, 2001.

Appelbaum, Patricia. *St. Francis of America: How a Thirteenth-Century Friar Became America's Most Popular Saint*. Chapel Hill: University of North Carolina Press, 2015.

Arnold, John H. "AHR Reappraisal: Persecution and Power in Medieval Europe." *The American Historical Review* 123, no. 1 (2018): 165–74.

– "The Cathar Middle Ages as a Methodological and Historiographical Problem." In *Cathars in Question*, edited by Antonio Sennis, 53–78. Woodbridge: York Medieval Press, 2016.

Asad, Talal. *Genealogies of Religion: Discipline and Reasons of Power in Christianity and Islam*. Baltimore: Johns Hopkins University Press, 1993.

Aurell, Martin. *The Lettered Knight: Knowledge and Aristocratic Behavior in the Twelfth and Thirteenth Centuries*. Budapest: Central European University Press, 2017.

– *Une famille de la noblesse provençale au moyen âge: les Porcelet*. Avignon: Archives du Sud, 1986.

Bailey, Michael D. "Was Magic a Religious Movement?" In *The Sacred and the Sinister: Studies in Medieval Religion and Magic*, edited by David J. Collins, 143–62. University Park: Pennsylvania State University Press, 2019.

Bakker, Folkert J. *Bedelorden en begijnen in de stad Groningen tot 1594*. Maastrich: Van Gorcum, 1988.

Balard, Michel. "L'historiographie des croisades au XXe siècle (France, Allemagne et Italie)." *Revue Historique* 302 (2000): 973–99.

– "Postface." In Alphandéry and Dupront, *La Chrétienté et l'idée de Croisade*, 573–85. Reprint, Paris: Bibliothéque de l'Évolution de l'Humanité, 1995.

Baldwin, John W. *Masters, Princes and Merchants: The Social Views of Peter the Chanter and His Circle*. Princeton, NJ: Princeton University Press, 1970.

Barbezat, Michael D. *Burning Bodies: Communities, Eschatology, and the Punishment of Heresy in the Middle Ages*. Ithaca: Cornell University Press, 2018.

Barnard, Alan, and Jonathan Spencer, eds. *Routledge Encyclopedia of Social and Cultural Anthropology*. 2nd ed. London: Routledge, 2010.

Barnhouse, Lucy. *Houses of God, Places for the Sick: Hospitals in Communities of the Late Medieval Rhineland* (forthcoming).

Barone, Giulia. "Chierici, monaci, e frati." In *Roma medievale*, edited by André Vauchez and Giulia Barone, 187–212. Rome: Edizioni Laterza, 2006.

– "Le due vite di Margherita Colonna." In *Esperienza religiosa e scritture femminili tra medioevo ed età moderna*, edited by Marilena Modica, 25–32. Acrireale: Bonnano, 1992.

Barone, Giulia, and Umberto Longo, eds. *Roma religiosa: Monasteri e città (secoli VI–XVI)*. *Reti Medievali Rivista* 19 (2018): 263–543.

Bartlett, Robert. *Why Can the Dead Do Such Great Things? Saints and Worshippers from the Martyrs to the Reformation*. Princeton, NJ: Princeton University Press, 2013.

Beach, Alison I., and Isabelle Cochelin, eds. *Cambridge History of Western Monasticism*. 2 vols. Cambridge: Cambridge University Press, 2020.

Beattie, Blake. "Catherine of Siena and the Papacy." In *A Companion to Catherine of Siena*, edited by Carolyn Muessig, George Ferzoco, and Beverly Mayne Kienzle, 73–98. Leiden: Brill, 2012.

Bell, Daniel N. "*De grisis monachis*: A Goliardic Invective against the Cistercians in London, B.L. Cotton Vespasian A.XIX." *Studia Monastica* 41 (1999): 243–59.

Benedetti, Marina. "Frati Minori e inquisizione. Alcuni casi nell'Italia medieval." *Dossiê Temático: 'Franciscanos e franciscanismos: origens e difusão.'* *Territórios & Fronteiras* 9, no. 1 (2016): 84–96.

– *Io non sono Dio: Guglielma di Milano e i Figli dello Spirito santo*. Milan: Edizioni Biblioteca Francescana, 1998.

– "Margherita da Trento." In *Dizionario Biografico degli Italiani*, 159–160. Vol. 70. Rome: Istituto dell'Enciclopedia Italiana Treccani, 2007.

Berenson, Edward. *Populist Religion and Left-wing Politics in France, 1830–1852*. Princeton, NJ: Princeton University Press, 1984.

Berger, Peter L. *The Many Altars of Modernity: Toward a Paradigm for Religion in a Pluralist Age*. Boston: De Gruyter, 2014.

Bériou, Nicole. "La prédication au béguinage de Paris pendant l'année liturgique 1272–1273." *Recherches augustiniennes* 13 (1978): 105–229.

– *L'avènement des maîtres de la Parole. La prédication à Paris au xiiie siècle*. 2 vols. Paris: *Institut d'études augustiniennes*, 1998.

– "Robert de Sorbon: Le prud'homme et le béguin." *Comptes-rendus de l'Académie des inscriptions et belles-lettres* (1994): 469–508.

– "Sainte Claire: Sermons dans l'espace français." In *Réligion et Communication: Un autre régard sur la prédication au Môyen Age*, 489–531. Geneva: Droz, 2018.

Berman, Constance Hoffman. "Archives from Houses of Cistercian Nuns and Their Evidence for Powerful Thirteenth-Century Secular Women." *Medieval Feminist Forum: A Journal of Gender and Sexuality* 51 (2016): 132–44.

– *The Cistercian Evolution: The Invention of a Religious Order in Twelfth-Century Europe*. Philadelphia: University of Pennsylvania Press, 2000.

– "Were There Twelfth-Century Cistercian Nuns?" *Church History* 68 (1999): 824–64.

– *The White Nuns: Cistercian Abbeys for Women in Medieval France*. Philadelphia: University of Pennsylvania Press, 2018.

Berriot, François. "Les manuscrits de l'abbaye de Longchamp aux Archives de France et la Vie de sainte Claire inédite (début XIVe s.)." *Archivum franciscanum historicum* 79 (1986): 329–58.

Betto, Bianca. *Le nove congregazioni del clero di Venezia (sec. XI–XV). Ricerche storiche, matricole e documenti vari*. Padua, Italy: Editrice Antenore, 1984.

Biller, Peter. "Cathars and Material Women." In *Medieval Theology and the Natural Body*, edited by Peter Biller and A.J. Minnis, 61–107. Woodbridge: York Medieval Press, 1997.

– "The Preaching of the Waldensian Sisters." *Heresis* 30 (1999): 137–68.

– "Words and the Medieval Notion of Religion." *Journal of Ecclesiastical History* 36 (1985): 351–69.

Bird, Jessalynn. "Crusade and Reform: The Sermons of Bibliothèque Nationale, MS nouv. acq. lat. 999." In *The Fifth Crusade in Context: The Crusading Movement in the Early Thirteenth Century*, edited by E.J. Mylod, Guy Perry, Thomas W. Smith, and Jan Vandeburie, 92–113. Abingdon: Routledge, 2017.

– "The Religious's Role in a Post-Fourth-Lateran World: James of Vitry's *Sermones as Status* and *Historia Occidentalis*." In *Medieval Monastic Preaching*, edited by Carolyn Muessig, 209–29. Leiden: Brill, 1998.

Bitter, Stephan. "Umdeutung des Christentums. Der baltische Theologe Erich Seeberg im Nationalsozialismus." In *Deutschbalten, Weimarer Republik und Drittes Reich 1*, edited by Michael Garleff, 267–96. 2nd ed. Cologne, Weimar, Vienna: Böhlau, 2008.

Black, Christopher F. *Italian Confraternities in the Sixteenth Century*. Cambridge: Cambridge University Press, 1989.

Blake, E.O. "The Formation of the 'Crusade Idea.'" *Journal of Ecclesiastical History* 21 (1970): 11–31.

Blamires, Alcuin. "Women and Preaching in Medieval Orthodoxy, Heresy, and Saints' Lives." *Viator* 26 (1995): 135–52.

Bloch, Monica. "A Message Carved in Stone: The Triforium Sculpture of Nevers Cathedral." In *Pictoral Languages and Their Meanings: Liber Amicorum in Honor of Nurith Kenaan-Kadar*, edited by Christine B. Verzar and Gil Fishhof, 63–9. Tel Aviv: Tel Aviv University Press, 2006.

Blumenfeld-Kosinski, Renate. "Holy Women in France: A Survey." In *Medieval Holy Women in the Christian Tradition, c. 1100–c. 1500*, edited by Alastair Minnis and Rosalynn Voaden, 241–65. Turnhout: Brepols, 2010.

– *The Strange Case of Ermine de Reims: A Medieval Woman Between Demons and Saints*. Philadelphia: University of Pennsylvania Press, 2015.

Boase, T.S.R. "Recent Developments in Crusading Historiography." *History* 22 (1937): 110–25.

Boeren, P.C. *La vie et les oeuvres de Guiard de Laon, 1170 env–1248*. The Hague, Netherlands: M. Nijhoff, 1956.

Boff, Leonardo. *Saint Francis: A Model for Human Liberation*. Translated by John W. Diercksmeir. London: SCM Press, 1985.

Böhringer, Letha, Jennifer Kolpacoff Deane, and Hildo van Engen, eds. *Labels and Libels: Naming Lay Religious Women in Northern Medieval Europe*. Turnhout: Brepols, 2014.

Bolgia, Claudia. *Reclaiming the Roman Capitol: Santa Maria in Aracoeli from the Altar of Augustus to the Franciscans, c. 500–1450*. New York: Routledge, 2017.

Bolton, Brenda. "Daughters of Rome: All One in Christ Jesus." *Studies in Church History* 27 (1992): 117–30.

Boni, Andrea. "L'obbedienza ecclesiale di S. Francesco al papa e ai vescovi." *Antonianum* 57 (1982): 113–55.

Bornstein, Daniel. "Introduction." In Bartolomeo Riccoboni, *Life and Death in a Venetian Convent*. Translated by Daniel Bornstein, 1–24. Chicago: University of Chicago Press, 2000.

Borst, Arno. "Herbert Grundmann (1902–1970)." *Deutsches Archiv für Erforschung des Mittelalters* 26 (1970): 327–53. Reprinted in Herbert Grundmann, *Ausgewählte Aufsätze* 1, 1–25. MGH Schriften 25, 1. Stuttgart: Anton Hiersemann, 1976.

Borutta, Manuel. *Antikatholizismus. Deutschland und Italien im Zeitalter der europäischen Kulturkämpfe*. Göttingen: Vandenhoeck and Ruprecht, 2011.

Bouchard, Constance Brittan. *Sword, Miter, and Cloister: Nobility and the Church in Burgundy, 980–1198*. Ithaca: Cornell University Press, 1987.

– "Three Counties, One Lineage, and Eight Heiresses: Nevers, Auxerre, and Tonnerre, Eleventh to the Thirteenth Centuries." *Medieval Prosopography* 31 (2016): 25–46.

Brandes, Wolfram, Felicitas Schmieder, and Rebekka Voss, eds. *Peoples of the Apocalypse: Eschatological Beliefs and Political Scenarios*. Millennium-Studien/Millennium Studies 63. Berlin: De Gruyter, 2016.

Brasher, Sally Mayall. *Women of the Humiliati: A Lay Religious Order in Medieval Civic Life*. New York: Routledge, 2003.

Braun, Lily. *Die Frauenfrage ihre geschichtliche Entwicklung und wirtschaftliche Seite*. Leipzig: Verlag von S. Hirzel, 1901.

Brauner, Christina, and Sita Steckel. "Wie die Heiden – wie die Papisten. Religiöse Polemik und Vergleiche vom Hochmittelalter bis zur Konfessionalisierung." In *Juden, Christen und Muslime im Zeitalter der Reformation/Jews, Christians and Muslims in the Reformation Era*, edited by Matthias Pohlig, 41–91. Schriften des Vereins für Reformationsgeschichte 219. Gütersloh: Gütersloher Verlagshaus, 2020.

Bredero, Adriaan H. *Bernard of Clairvaux: Between Cult and History*. Translated by Reinder Bruinsma. Edinburgh: T&T Clark, 1996.

– *Cluny et Cîteaux au douzième siècle: l'histoire d'une controverse monastique*. Amsterdam: APA-Holland University Press, 1985.

Breitenstein, Mirko, Julia Burkhardt, Stefan Burkhardt, and Jens Röhrkasten, eds. *Rules and Observance: Devising Forms of Communal Life*. Berlin: LIT Verlag, 2014.

Brenner, Elma. *Leprosy and Charity in Medieval Rouen*. Woodbridge: Boydell, 2015.

Brenon, Anne. "The Voice of the Good Women: An Essay on the Pastoral and Sacerdotal Role of Women in the Cathar Church." In *Women Preachers and Prophets through Two Millennia of Christianity*, edited by Beverly Mayne Kienzle and Pamela J. Walker, 114–33. Berkeley: University of California Press, 1998.

Brentano, Robert. *Rome Before Avignon: A Social History of Thirteenth-Century Rome*. Los Angeles: University of California Press, 1990.

Breuck, Heinrich. *History of the Catholic Church*. 2 vols. New York: Benziger Brothers, 1884.

Brodman, James William. *Charity and Religion in Medieval Europe*. Washington, DC: Catholic University of America Press, 2009.

Brooke, Rosalind B. *The Image of St. Francis: Responses to Sainthood in the Thirteenth Century*. Cambridge: Cambridge University Press, 2006.

– *Scripta Leonis, Rufini et Angeli sociorum S. Francisci*. Oxford: Clarendon Press, 1970.

Brundage, James, and Elizabeth Makowski. "Enclosure of Nuns: The Decretal *Periculoso* and its Commentators." *Journal of Medieval History* 20 (1994): 143–55.

Brunn, Uwe. *Des contestataires aux 'Cathares': Discours de réforme et propagande antihérétique dans les pays du Rhin et de la Meuse avant l'Inquisition*. Paris: Institut d'études augustiniennes, 2006.

Buc, Philippe. *The Dangers of Ritual: Between Early Medieval Texts and Social Scientific Theory*. Princeton, NJ: Princeton University Press, 2001.

Buffon, Guiseppe. "Le début du renouveau conciliaire France dans le milieu Franciscain (1943–1979)." *Revue d'Histoire Ecclésiastique* 105, no. 3 (2010): 689–732.

– *Sulle tracce di una storia omessa: Storiografia moderna e contemporanea dell'Ordine francescano*. Grottaferrata, Italy: Frati Editori di Quaracchi, 2011.

Bull, Marcus. *Knightly Piety and the Lay Response to the First Crusade: The Limousin and Gascony, c.970–1130*. Oxford: Clarendon Press, 1998.

– "The Roots of Lay Enthusiasm for the First Crusade." *History* 78 (1993): 353–72.

Bund, Konrad. "Die Prophetin, ein Dichter und die Niederlassung der Bettelorden in Köln." *Mittellateinisches Jahrbuch* 23 (1988): 171–260.

Burnham, Louisa A. *So Great a Light, So Great a Smoke: The Beguin Heretics of Languedoc*. Ithaca: Cornell University Press, 2008.

– "The Visionary Authority of Na Prous Boneta." In *Pierre de Jean Olivi (1248–1298)*, edited by Alain Boureau and Sylvain Piron, 319–39. Paris: Vrin, 1999.

Burr, David. *The Spiritual Franciscans: From Protest to Persecution in the Century After Saint Francis*. University Park, PA: Pennsylvania State University Press, 2001.

Burton, Janet, and Julie Kerr. *The Cistercians in the Middle Ages*. Woodbridge: Boydell, 2011.
Bynum, Caroline Walker. *Docere Verbo et Exemplo: An Aspect of Twelfth-Century Spirituality*. Missoula, MT: Scholars Press, 1979.
– *Fragmentation and Redemption: Essays on Gender and the Human Body in Medieval Religion*. New York: Zone, 1994.
– *Holy Feast and Holy Fast: The Religious Significance of Food to Medieval Women*. Berkeley: University of California Press, 1987.
– "More Popes Than Piety? Approaches to Religion in the *New Cambridge Medieval History*." *The Catholic Historical Review* 93 (2006): 268–72.
Caciola, Nancy. *Discerning Spirits: Divine and Demonic Possession in the Middle Ages*. Ithaca: Cornell University Press, 2003.
Cadden, Joan. *Meanings of Sex Difference in the Middle Ages: Medicine, Science, and Culture*. New York: Cambridge University Press, 1995.
Carbonell, Charles-Olivier. "De Ernest Renan à Paul Sabatier: naissance d'une historiographie scientifique de saint François en France (1864–1893)." In *L'immagine di Francesco nella storiografia dall'Umanesimo all'Ottocento*, 225–49. Assisi: Università di Perugia, 1983.
Carniello, Brian. "Gerard Segarelli as the Anti-Francis: Mendicant Rivalry and Heresy in Medieval Italy, 1260–1300." *Journal of Ecclesiastical History* 57 (2006): 226–51.
Carnier, Marc. *De Communauteiten van Teriarissen van Sint-Franciscus*. Brussels: Algemeen Rijksarcheif, 2002.
Carrocci, Sandro. *Baroni de Roma: Dominazioni signorili e lignaggi aristocratici nel duecento e nel primo trecento*. Rome: École Française de Rome, 1993.
Carron, Delphine. "Intus Nero Foris Cato. Une sémiologie de l'hypocrisie." In *Intus et foris: Une catégorie de la pensée médiévale?*, edited by Manuel Guay, Marie-Pascale Halary, and Patrick Moran, 171–83. Paris: Presses de l'Université Paris-Sorbonne, 2013.
Castora, Joseph Charles. "The 'Speculum Ecclesiae' of Giraldus Cambrensis and the Cistercians of Southern England and Wales." 3 vols. PhD diss., New York University, 1990.
Chenu, Marie-Dominique. *La théologie au douzième siècle*. Paris: Vrin, 1957.
– "Les signes des temps." *Nouvelle revue théologique* 87, no. 1 (1965): 29–39.
– *Nature, Man and Society in the Twelfth Century*. Translated by Lester K. Little. Chicago: University of Chicago Press, 1968.
– *Une école de théologie: le Saulchoir*. Paris: Les éditions du cerf, 1985.
Cirlot, Victoria. "Escrito en el corazó. Los casos de Angela de Folingo, Marguerite Porete y Marguerite d'Oingt." In *Voces de mujeres en la Edad Media*, edited by Corral Díaz, 249–66. Berlin: De Gruyter, 2018.
Císařová-Kolářová, Anna. *Posluchačky v kapli Betlemské*. Prague: Kalich, 1947.
– *Žena v hnutí husitském*. Prague: Sokolice, 1915.

Clark, Anne L. "Under Whose Care? The Madonna of San Sisto and Women's Monastic Life in Twelfth- and Thirteenth-Century Rome." In *Medieval Constructions in Gender and Identity: Essays in Honor of Joan M. Ferrante*, edited by Teodolinda Barolini, 29–42. Tempe: Arizona Center for Medieval and Renaissance Studies, 2005.

Clark, Christopher M., and Kaiser Wolfram, eds. *Culture Wars: Secular-Catholic Conflict in Nineteenth-Century Europe*. Cambridge: Cambridge University Press, 2003.

Coakley, John. "Gender and the Authority of Friars: The Significance of Holy Women for Thirteenth-Century Franciscans and Dominicans." *Church History* 60 (1991): 445–60.

— *Women, Men, and Spiritual Power: Female Saints and Their Male Collaborators*. New York: Columbia University Press, 2006.

Cochelin, Isabelle. "'Règle' and 'Statuts.'" In *Histoire et Dictionnaire du monachisme en Orient et en Occident, des origines au XXIe siècle*, edited by Daniel-Odon Hurel. Paris: éditions du CNRS, forthcoming.

Coffey, Mary Finbarr. "The Complexities and Difficulties of a Return *ad fontes*." In *A Future Full of Hope?*, edited by Gemma Simmonds, 38–51. Dublin: The Columba Press, 2012.

Cohen, Jeremy. *The Friars and the Jews: The Evolution of Medieval Anti-Judaism*. Ithaca: Cornell University Press, 1982.

Cohen, Meredith. *The Sainte-Chapelle and the Construction of Sacral Monarchy*. Cambridge: Cambridge University Press, 2014.

Cole, Penny J. *Preaching the Crusades to the Holy Land, 1095–1270*. Cambridge, MA: The Medieval Academy of America, 1991.

Collet, Olivier. "Littérature, histoire, pouvoir et mécénat: La cour de Flandre au XIIIe siècle." *Médiévales* 19 (2000): 87–110.

Congar, Yves-Marie. "Aspects ecclésiologiques de la querelle entre mendiants et séculiers dans la seconde moitié du xiiie siècle et le début du xive siècle." *Archives d'histoire doctrinale et littéraire du Moyen Âge* 28 (1961): 9–45.

Connally, Michael. "Les 'Bonnes Femmes' de Paris: Des communautes religieuses dans une societe urbaine du bas Moyen Age." PhD diss., University of Lyon II, 2003.

Constable, Giles. *Crusaders and Crusading in the Twelfth Century*. Farnham: Ashgate, 2008.

— "The Diversity of Religious Life and Acceptance of Social Pluralism in the Twelfth Century." In *Culture and Spirituality in Medieval Europe*, 29–47. Variorum Collected Studies Series 541. Aldershot: Variorum, 1996 [orig. 1985].

— "The Financing of the Crusades." In *Outremer: Studies in the History of the Crusading Kingdom of Jerusalem Presented to Joshua Prawer*, edited by

Benjamin Kedar, Hans Eberhard Mayer, and Raymond C. Smail, 64–88. Jerusalem: Yad Izhak Ben-Zvi, 1982.
– "The Historiography of the Crusades." In *The Crusades from the Perspective of Byzantium and the Muslim World*, edited by Angeliki E. Laiou and Roy Parviz Mottahedeh, 1–22. Washington, DC: Dumbarton Oaks, 2001.
– "Medieval Charters as a Source for the History of the Crusaders." In *Crusade and Settlement*, edited by Peter W. Edbury, 73–89. Cardiff: University College Cardiff Press, 1985.
– *The Reformation of the Twelfth Century*. Cambridge: Cambridge University Press, 1996.
– "The Second Crusade as Seen by Contemporaries." *Traditio* 9 (1953): 213–79.
Corbellini, Sabrina, and Sita Steckel. "The Religious Field during the Long Fifteenth Century. Framing Religious Change beyond Traditional Paradigms." *Church History and Religious Culture* 99 (2019): 303–29.
– "Een oude spiegel voor nieuwe maagden." *Ons geestelijk erf* 80 (2009): 171–98.
Corbet, Patrick. "Entre Aliénor d'Aquitaine et Blanche de Castille. Les princesses au pouvoir dans la France de l'Est." In *Mächtige Frauen? Königinnen und Fürstinnen im europäischen Mittelalter (11–14. Jahrhundert)*, edited by Claudia Zey, Sophie Caflisch, and Philippe Goridis, 225–47. Vorträge und Forschungen, 81. Ostfildern, Germany: Jan Thorbecke, 2015.
Corral Díaz, Esther, ed. *Voces de mujeres en la Edad Media: Entre Realidad y Ficción*. Berlin: De Gruyter, 2019.
Corry, Maya, Marco Faini, and Alessia Meneghin. "Introduction." In *Domestic Devotions in Early Modern Italy*, edited by Maya Corry, Marco Faini, and Alessia Meneghin, 1–24. Leiden: Brill, 2018.
Creytens, Raymond. "La Riforma del Monasteri Femminile dopo i Decreti Tridentini." In *Il Concilio de Trento e la Riforma Tridentina*, edited by Jedin Hubert et al., 49–57. Rome: Herder, 1963.
Cusato, Michael F. "An Unexplored Influence on the '*Epistola ad fideles*' of Francis of Assisi: The '*Epsitola universis Christi fidelibus*' of Joachim of Fiore." *Franciscan Studies* 61 (2003): 253–78.
Czock, Miriam. "Zwischen Heiligkeit und Häresie. Rhetorik und Verwendung von Bildern in Briefen zu Tanchelm, Heinrich und an Robert von Arbrissel." In *Sakralität und Devianz: Konstruktionen – Normen – Praxis*, edited by Klaus Herbers and Larissa Düchting, 253–74. Beiträge zur Hagiographie 16. Stuttgart: Franz Steiner Verlag, 2015.
Daileader, Philip. "Local Experiences of the Great Western Schism." In *A Companion to the Great Western Schism, 1378–1417*, edited by Joëlle Rollo-Koster and Tom Izbicki, 89–121. Leiden: Brill, 2009.

Dal Pino, Franco. *Il Laicato italiano tra eresia e proposta pauperistico-evangelica nei secoli XII–XIII*. Padua: Università di Padova, 1984.

Dalarun, Jacques. "Du procès de canonisation à la *Légende* latine de Claire d'Assisi." *Memini: Travaux et documents* 24 (2018). https://journals.openedition.org/memini/1090.

– *Francis of Assisi and Power*. Translated by A. Bartol. New York: Bonaventure Institute, 2007.

– *François d'Assisi en questions*. Paris: CNRS, 2016.

– *L'impossible sainteté: La vie retrouvée de Robert d'Abrissel (v. 1045–1116)*. Paris: Cerf, 1985. Reprinted in 2007.

– *The Misadventure of Francis of Assisi: Towards a Historical Use of the Franciscan Legends*. Translated by Edward Hagman. New York: Franciscan Institute Publications, 2002.

D'Arcens, Louise. *Comic Medievalism: Laughing at the Middle Ages*. Woodbridge: Boydell, 2014.

Dascal, Marcelo. "On the Uses of Argumentative Reason in Religious Polemics." In *Religious Polemics in Context. Papers presented to the second international Conference of the Leiden Institute for the Study of Religions (LISOR), held at Leiden, 27–28 April 2000*, edited by Theo L. Hettema and Arie van der Kooij, 3–20. Studies in Theology and Religion 11. Assen, Netherlands: Van Gorcum, 2004.

Davis, Adam J. *The Medieval Economy of Salvation: Charity, Commerce, and the Rise of the Hospital*. Ithaca: Cornell University Press, 2019.

D'Avray, David. *The Preaching of the Friars: Sermons Diffused from Paris before 1300*. New York: Oxford University Press, 1985.

Day, Kirsty. "Constructing Dynastic Franciscan Identities in Bohemia and the Polish Duchies." PhD diss., University of Leeds, August 2015.

– "Hagiography as Institutional Biography: Medieval and Modern Uses of the Thirteenth-Century *Vitae* of Clare of Assisi." In *Writing the Lives of People and Things, AD 500–1700: A Multi-disciplinary Future for Biography*, edited by Robert F.W. Smith and Gemma L. Watson, 261–80. Farnham: Ashgate, 2016.

de Oudegherst, P. *Les chroniques et annales de Flandres*. Antwerp, 1571.

Deane, Jennifer Kolpacoff. "Beguines Reconsidered: Historiographical Problems and New Directions." *Monastic Matrix* (2008). Commentaria 3461. http://monasticmatrix.org/commentaria/article.php?textId=3461.

– "From Case Studies to Comparative Models: Würzburg Beguines and the Vienne Decrees." In *Labels and Libels: Naming Beguines in Northern Medieval Europe*, edited by Letha Böhringer, Jennifer Kolpacoff Deane, and Hildo van Engen, 53–82. Turnhout: Brepols, 2014.

– "*Geistliche Schwestern:* The Pastoral Care of Lay Religious Women in Wurzburg." In *Partners in Spirit: Women, Men and Religious Life in Germany,*

1100–1500, edited by Fiona Griffith and Julie Hotchin, 237–70. Turnhout: Brepols, 2013.
– "Hospitality and Home in the Middle Ages." In *A Cultural History of the Home*, edited by Katherine French. London: Bloomsbury, 2020.
– "Pious Domesticities." In *The Oxford Handbook of Women and Gender in Medieval Europe*, edited by Judith Bennett and Ruth Mazo Karras, 262–78. New York: Oxford University Press, 2013.
–, ed. *Herbert Grundmann: Essays on Heresy, Inquisition, and Literacy*. Translated by Steven Rowan. Woodbridge: York Medieval Press, 2019.
Demacopoulos, George E. *The Invention of Peter: Apostolic Discourse and Papal Authority in Late Antiquity*. Philadelphia: University of Pennsylvania Press, 2013.
Denkinger, Tiberius. "Die Bettelorden in der französischen didaktischen Literatur des 13. Jahrhunderts, besonders bei Rutebeuf und im Roman de la Rose." *Franziskanische Studien* 2 (1915): 63–109, 286–313.
Dessaux, Nicolas, ed. *Jeanne de Constantinople Comtesse de Flandre et de Hainaut*. Paris: Somogy, 2009.
Diekstra, Frans N.M. "'Die drie dachvaerden' and Robert de Sorbon's 'De tribus dietis': An Edition of the Middle Dutch Text together with its Latin Source." *Mediaevistik* 12 (1999): 257–330.
– "The Pursuit of Virtue and the Fear of Derision: Robert de Sorbon (1201–1274) on Beguinage and False Shame." *Mediaevistik* 22 (2009): 117–240.
– "Robert de Sorbon on Men, Women and Marriage. The Testimony of His *De Matrimonio* and Other Works." In *People and Texts: Relationships in Medieval Literature*, edited by Thea Summerfield, Keith Busby, and Erik Kooper, 67–85. Amsterdam and New York: Rodopi, 2007.
Diem, Albrecht. "The Gender of the Religious: Wo/Men and the Invention of Monasticism." In *The Oxford Handbook of Women and Gender in Medieval Europe*, edited by Judith M. Bennett and Ruth M. Karras, 432–46. Oxford University Press, 2013.
Dinan, Susan E. *Women and Poor Relief in Seventeenth-Century France: The Early History of the Daughters of Charity*. Aldershot: Ashgate, 2006.
Dirksen, Aloys Herman. *The New Testament Concept of Metanoia*. Washington, DC: The Catholic University of America, 1932.
Döring, Pia C., ed. *Verstellungskünste. Religiöse und politische Hypokrisie in Literatur und bildender Kunst* (in preparation for 2021).
Douglas, Mary C. *Purity and Danger: An Analysis of Concepts of Pollution and Taboo*. New York: Routledge, 2002 [1966].
Douie, Decima L. *The Conflict between the Seculars and the Mendicants at the University of Paris in the Thirteenth Century*. London: Blackfriars, 1954.
Doyno, Mary Harvey. *The Lay Saint: Charity and Charismatic Authority in Medieval Italy, 1150–1350*. Ithaca: Cornell University Press, 2019.

Driedger, Michael, and Johannes C. Wolfart. "Reframing the History of New Religious Movements." *Nova Religio: The Journal of Alternative and Emergent Religions* 21 (2018): 5–12.

Dronke, Peter. *The Medieval Poet and His World*. Rome: Edizione di Storia e Letteratura, 1984.

Duara, Prasenjit. *The Crisis of Global Modernity: Asian Traditions and a Sustainable Future*. Cambridge: Cambridge University Press, 2015.

Dubois, Katherine Brophy. "Stranger and Sojourners: Pilgrims, Penance and Urban Geography in Late-medieval Rome." PhD diss., University of Michigan, 2001.

Dufeil, Michel-Marie. *Guillaume de Saint-Amour et la polémique universitaire parisienne, 1250–1259*. Paris: A. et J. Picard, 1972.

– "Le roi Louis dans la querelle des mendiants et des séculiers." In *Septième centenaire de la mort de Saint Louis: Actes des colloques de Royaument et de Paris (21–27 mai 1970)*, 281–9. Paris: Les Belles Lettres, 1976.

Dufournet, Jean. *Rutebeuf et les frères mendiants: Poèmes satiriques*. Paris: H. Champion, 1991.

Duval, André. "Le message du monde." In *Vatican II commence: approches francophones*, edited by É. Fouilloux, 105–18. Leuven: Bibliotheek van de Faculteit der Godgeleerdheid, 1993.

Duval, Sylvie. *'Comme des Anges sur Terre' Les Moniales Dominicaines et les débuts de la réforme Observante, 1385–1461*. Rome: École Française de Rome, 2015.

– "Pour une relecture de la vie religieuse féminine chrétienne en Occident à la fin du Moyen Age." *Mélanges de l'École française de Rome* 128, no. 2 (2016). https://mefrim.revues.org/2579.

Dykema, Peter A., and Heiko A. Oberman, eds. *Anticlericalism in Late Medieval and Early Modern Europe*. Studies in Medieval and Reformation Thought 51. Leiden: Brill, 1993.

Edwards, Jennifer C. *Superior Women: Medieval Female Authority in Poitiers' Abbey of Sainte-Croix*. Oxford: Oxford University Press, 2019.

Eisenbichler, Konrad. *Crossing the Boundaries: Christian Piety and the Arts in Italian Medieval and Renaissance Confraternities*. Kalamazoo, MI: Medieval Institute Publications, 1991.

– "Italian Scholarship on Pre-Modern Confraternities in Italy." *Renaissance Quarterly* 50 (1997): 567–80.

Ekert, František, and Jiří Reinsberg. *Posvátná místa král. hl. města Prahy: dějiny a popsání chrámů, kaplí, posvátných soch, klášterů a jiných pomníků katolické víry a nábožnosti v hlavním městě království Českého*. Prague: Volvox Globator, 1996.

Ellerbrock, Dagmar, Lars Koch, Sabine Müller-Mall, Marina Münkler, Joachim Scharloth, Dominik Schrage, and Gerd Schwerhoff. "Invektivität – Perspektiven eines neuen Forschungsprogramms in den Kultur- und Sozialwissenschaften." *Kulturwissenschaftliche Zeitschrift* 2 (2017): 2–24.

Elliott, Dyan. *The Bride of Christ Goes to Hell: Metaphor and Embodiment in the Lives of Pious Women, 200–1500*. Philadelphia: University of Pennsylvania Press, 2012.
– *The Corrupter of Boys: Sodomy, Scandal, and the Medieval Clergy*. Philadelphia: University of Pennsylvania Press, 2020.
– *Proving Woman: Female Spirituality and Inquisitional Culture in the Later Middle Ages*. Princeton, NJ: Princeton University Press, 2004.
– "Seeing Double: John Gerson, the Discernment of Spirits, and Joan of Arc." *The American Historical Review* 107 (2002): 26–54.
Elm, Kasper. "*Vita regularis sine regula*. Bedeutung, Rechtsstellung und Selbstverständnis des Mittelalterlichen und Frühneuzeitlichen Semireligiosentums." *Häresie und Vorzeitige Reformation im Spätmittelalter*, edited by František Šmahel, 239–73. Munich: Oldenbourg Verlag, 1998.
Elmer, Ian J. "Pillars, Hypocrites and False Brothers. Paul's Polemic against Jerusalem in Galatians." In *Polemik in der frühchristlichen Literatur: Texte und Kontexte*, edited by Oda Wischmeyer and Lorenzo Scornaienchi, 123–53. Beihefte zur Zeitschrift für die neutestamentliche Wissenschaft und die Kunde der älteren Kirche 170. Berlin: De Gruyter, 2011.
Emmerson, Richard K. "The Representation of Antichrist in Hildegard of Bingen's Scivias: Image, Word, Commentary, and Visionary Experience." *Gesta* 41 (2002): 95–110.
Emmerson, Richard K., and Ronald B. Herzman. "The Apocalyptic Age of Hypocrisy: Faus Semblant and Amant in the Roman de La Rose." *Speculum* 62 (1987): 612–34.
Engels, L.J. "Adtendite a falsis prophetis (Ms. Colmar 128, ff. 152v–153v). Un texte de Pierre Abélard contre les Cisterciens retrouvé?" In *Corona gratiarum: Miscellanea historica, patristica et liturgica Eligius Dekkers OSB*, 195–228. Vol. 2. Instrumenta Patristica et Mediaevalia 11. Brepols Publishers: Turnhout, 1975.
Erdmann, Carl. *Die Entstehung des Kreuzzugsgedankens*. Forschungen zur Kirchen- und Geistesgeschichte. Vol. 6. Stuttgart: Kohlhammer Verlag, 1935.
– *The Origin of the Idea of Crusade*. Translated by Marshall W. Baldwin and Walter Goffart. Princeton, NJ: Princeton University Press, 1977.
Escher-Apsner, Monika, ed. *Mittelalterliche Bruderschaften in europäischen Städten: Funktionen, Formen, Akteure/Medieval Confraternities in European Towns: Functions, Forms, Protagonists*. Frankfurt/Main: Peter Lang, 2009.
Esposito, Anna. "Il Mondo della religiosità femminile Romana." *Archivio della Società Romana di Storia Patria* 132 (2010): 149–72.
Esser, Cajetan. *Origins of the Franciscan Order*. Translated by Aedan Daly. Chicago: Franciscan Herald Press, 1970.

Evergates, Theodore. "Aristocratic Women in the County of Champagne." In *Aristocratic Women in Medieval France*, edited by Theodore Evergates, 73–110. Philadelphia: University of Pennsylvania Press, 1999.

– *Marie of France: Countess of Champagne, 1145–1198*. Philadelphia: University of Pennsylvania Press, 2019.

Falconieri, Tommaso Carpegna. "Le congregazioni del clero secolare a Roma e la loro documentazione (secoli X–XVI)." In *Realtà archivistiche a confronto*, 23–30. Modena, Italy: Mucchi, 2011.

Falkeid, Unn. "The Political Discourse of Birgitta of Sweden." In *A Companion to Birgitta of Sweden and Her Legacy in the Later Middle Ages*, edited by Maria H. Oen, 80–102. Leiden: Brill, 2019.

Faloci-Pulignani, Michele. "Legenda trium sociorum ex Cod. Fulginatensi." *Miscellanea francescana di storia, di lettere, di arti* 7 (1898): 81–107.

Faust, Anselm. "Professoren für die NSDAP. Zum politischen Verhalten der Hochschullehrer 1932/33." In *Erziehung und Schulung im Dritten Reich 2: Hochschule, Erwachsenenbildung*, edited by Manfred Heinemann, 31–49. Veröffentlichungen der Historischen Kommission der Deutschen Gesellschaft für Erziehungswissenschaft 4,2. Stuttgart: Klett-Cotta, 1980.

Felten, Franz J., Nikolas Jaspert, and Stephanie Haarländer, eds. Vita Religiosa im Mittelalter: Festschrift für Kaspar Elm zum 70. Geburtstag. Berlin: Duncker and Humblot, 1999.

Ferruolo, Stephen C. *The Origins of the University: The Schools of Paris and Their Critics, 1100–1215*. Stanford: Stanford University Press, 1985.

Field, Sean L. "Agnes of Harcourt as Intellectual: New Evidence for the Composition and Circulation of the *Vie d'Isabelle de France*." In *Women Intellectuals and Leaders of the Middle Ages*, edited by Kathryn Kerby-Fulton, Katie Ann-Marie Bugyis, and John Van Engen, 79–95. Cambridge: D.S. Brewer, 2020.

– "Agnes of Harcourt, Felipa of Porcelet, and Marguerite of Oingt: Women Writing about Women at the End of the Thirteenth Century." *Church History* 76 (2007): 298–329.

– *The Beguine, the Angel, and the Inquisitor: The Inquisitorial Trials of Marguerite Porete and Guiard of Cressonessart*. Notre Dame, IN: University of Notre Dame Press, 2012.

– *Courting Sanctity: Holy Women and the Capetians*. Ithaca: Cornell University Press, 2019.

– "Douceline of Digne and Isabelle of France: Forming Female Franciscan Identities in Thirteenth-Century France." In *Franciscan Women: Female Identities and Religious Culture. Medieval and Beyond*, edited by Lezlie Knox and David B. Couturier, 83–98. St. Bonaventure, NY: Franciscan Institute Publications, 2020.

– *Isabelle of France: Capetian Sanctity and Franciscan Identity in the Thirteenth Century.* Notre Dame, IN: University of Notre Dame Press, 2006.
– "Maire of Saint-Pol and her Books." *English Historical Review* 513 (2010): 255–78.
– "The Master and Marguerite: Godfrey of Fontaines' Praise of the *Mirror of Simple Souls.*" *Journal of Medieval History* 35 (2009): 136–49.
– "On Being a Beguine in France, c. 1300." In *Labels and Libels: Naming Beguines in Northern Medieval Europe*, edited by Letha Böhringer, Jennifer Kolpacoff Deane, and Hildo van Engen, 117–33. Turnout: Brepols, 2014.
– "Pierre Perrier's 1699 *Vie de sainte Isabelle de France*: Precious Evidence from an Unpublished Preface." *Franciscan Studies* 73 (2015): 215–47.
Field, Sean L., Robert E. Lerner, and Sylvain Piron, eds. *Marguerite Porete et le Miroir des simples âmes: Perspectives historiques, philosophiques et littéraires.* Paris: Vrin, 2013.
– "A Return to the Evidence for Marguerite Porete's Authorship of the *Mirror of Simple Souls.*" *Journal of Medieval History* 43 (2017): 153–73.
Flood, David. *Francis of Assisi and the Franciscan Movement.* Quezon City, Philippines: FIA Contact Publications, 1989.
– *Frère François et le mouvement franciscain.* Paris: Éditions ouvrières, 1983.
– "The Grundmann Approach to Early Franciscan History." *Franziskanische Studien* 59 (1977): 311–19.
– "Read it at Chapter: Francis of Assisi and the *Scritti.*" *Franciscan Studies* 60 (2002): 341–57.
Flood, David, and Thadée Matura. *The Birth of a Movement: A Study of the First Rule of St. Francis.* Translated by Paul Schawrtz and Paul Lachance. Chicago: Franciscan Herald Press, 1971.
Flynn, Gabriel, and Paul D. Murray, eds. *Ressourcement: A Movement for Renewal in Twentieth-Century Catholic Theology.* Oxford: Oxford University Press, 2011.
Folkerts, Suzan. "The Manuscript Transmission of the *Vita Mariae Oigniacensis* in the Later Middle Ages." *Mary of Oignies: Mother of Salvation*, 221–41. Turnhout: Brepols, 2006.
Fontette, Micheline. "Religionum Diversitatem et la Suppression des Ordres Mendiants." In *1274. Année charnière mutations et continuités. Lyon–Paris 30 septembre–5 octobre 1974*, 223–9. Colloques internationaux de Centre national de la recherche scientifique 558. Lyon: Éditions du CNRS, 1977.
Forrest, Ian. *Trustworthy Men: How Inequality and Faith Made the Medieval Church.* Princeton, NJ: Princeton University Press, 2018.
Foucault, Michel. *The Archaeology of Knowledge and the Discourse on Language.* Translated by A.M. Sheridan Smith. New York: Vintage, 1982.
– *L'Archéologie du Savoir.* Paris: Gallimard, 1969.
– *Les Mots et les choses.* Paris: Gallimard, 1966.

– *The Order of Things: An Archaeology of the Human Sciences*. New York: Vintage, 1970. Reprinted 1994.
France, John. "Holy War and Holy Men: Erdmann and the Lives of the Saints." In *The Experience of Crusading*, edited by Marcus Bull and Norman Housely, 193–208. Vol. 1. Cambridge: Cambridge University Press, 2003.
Freeman, Elizabeth. *Narratives of a New Order: Cistercian Historical Writing in England, 1150–1220*. Turnhout: Brepols, 2002.
Friedlander, Alan. *The Hammer of the Inquisitors: Brother Bernard Délicieux and the Struggle Against the Inquisition in Fourteenth-Century France*. Boston: Brill, 2000.
Frugoni, Chiara. *Francesco e l'invenzione delle stimmate: una storia per parole e immagini fino a Bonaventura e Giotto*. Torino: Einaudi, 1993.
Fuhrmann, Horst. *'Sind eben alles Menschen gewesen': Gelehrtenleben im 19. und 20. Jahrhundert*. Munich: Beck, 1996.
Furniss, Emma. "The Franciscan Order in Late-Medieval and Early-Modern Western Europe: A Historiographical Survey." *Monastic Research Bulletin* 12 (2006): 1–10.
Gabriel, Astrik L. "Motivation of the Founders of Medieval Colleges." In *Garlandia: Studies in the History of the Medieval University*, 211–23. Notre Dame, IN: University of Notre Dame Press, 1969.
Gabriel, Denis. *La 'Maison des pauvres maîtres' de Robert de Sorbon: Les débuts de la Sorbonne (1254–1274)*. Paris: Classiques Garnier, 2014.
Gailus, Manfred. "Der Berliner Kirchenhistoriker Erich Seeberg als nationalsozialistischer Theologiepolitiker." In *Täter und Komplizen in Theologie und Kirchen 1933–1945*, edited by Manfred Gailus, 216–43. Göttingen: Wallstein, 2015.
– "Die kirchliche Machtergreifung der 'Glaubensbewegung Deutsche Christen' im Jahr 1933." In *Täter und Komplizen in Theologie und Kirchen 1933–1945*, edited by Manfred Gailus, 62–80. Göttingen: Wallstein, 2015.
Galvez, Marisa. *Songbook: How Lyrics Became Poetry in Medieval Europe*. Chicago: University of Chicago Press, 2012.
– *The Subject of the Crusade: Lyric, Romance, and Materials, 1150–1500*. Chicago: University of Chicago Press, 2019.
Gaposchkin, M. Cecilia. *The Making of Saint Louis: Kingship Sanctity, and Crusade in the Later Middle Ages*. Ithaca: Cornell University Press, 2008.
Gardner, Julian. *Giotto and His Publics: Three Paradigms of Patronage*. Cambridge, MA: Harvard University Press, 2011.
Gassert, Philipp, and Alan E. Steinweis, eds. *Coping with the Nazi Past: West German Debates on Nazism and Generational Conflict, 1955–1975*. Studies in German History 2. New York: Berghahn, 2006.
Gecser, Otto. "Lives of St. Elizabeth: Their Rewriting and Diffusion in the Thirteenth Century." *Analecta Bollandiana* 129 (2009): 49–107.

Geltner, Guy. "'Faux Semblants': Antifraternalism Reconsidered in Jean de Meun and Chaucer." *Studies in Philology* 101 (2004): 357–80.
– *The Making of Medieval Antifraternalism: Polemic, Violence, Deviance, and Remembrance*. Oxford: Oxford University Press, 2012.
Giancarlo, Rocca. "Per un primo censimento delle associazioni sacerdotali in Italia dal medioevo a oggi." *Rivista di storia della Chiesa in Italia* 64 (2010): 397–517.
Gil, Francesco Victor Sánchez. "La importancia de *Archivum Franciscanum Historicum* para la historiografía Franciscana moderna balance de un centenario (1908–2007)." *Archivum Franciscanum Historicum* 101 (2008): 453–89.
Gilchrist, John. "The Erdmann Thesis and the Canon Law, 1083–1141." In *Crusade and Settlement: Papers Read at the First Conference of the Society for the Study of the Crusades and the Latin East presented to R.C. Smail*, edited by Peter W. Edbury, 27–45. Cardiff: University College Cardiff Press, 1985.
Given, James B. *Inquisition and Medieval Society: Power, Discipline, and Resistance in Languedoc*. Ithaca: Cornell University Press, 1997.
Glorieux, Palémon. *Aux origines de la Sorbonne*. Vol. 1, *Robert de Sorbon, l'homme, le collège, les documents*. Paris: J. Vrin, 1965–6.
Goetz, Walter. "Aus dem Leben eines deutschen Historikers." In *Historiker in meiner Zeit. Gesammelte Aufsätze*, 1–87. Cologne and Graz: Böhlau, 1957.
Goertz, Hans-Jürgen, *Antiklerikalismus und Reformation. Sozialgeschichtliche Untersuchungen*. Göttingen: Vandenhoeck & Ruprecht, 1995.
Golding, Brian. "Gerald of Wales and the Cistercians." *Reading Medieval Studies* 21 (1995): 5–30.
Goll, Jaroslav. "Rokycanova Postilla." *Časopis Musea království Českého* 53, nos. 1–2 (1879): 59–70, 199–211.
Goyens, M. *De oorspronkelijke statuten der grauzusters van Vlaanderen in 1483 opgesteld*. Ghent, 1884.
Graham, Emily L. "Memorializing Identity: The Foundation and Reform of San Lorenzo in Panisperna." *Franciscan Studies* 75 (2017): 467–95.
Granzow, Sven, Bettina Müller-Sidibé, and Andrea Simml. "Gottvertrauen und Führerglaube." In *Skepsis und Führervertrauen im Nationalsozialismus*, edited by Götz Aly, 38–58. Frankfurt am Main: Fischer, 2006.
Green, Monica H. "Female Sexuality in the Medieval West." *Trends in History* 4 (1990): 127–58.
Greschat, Martin. "Zwischen Aufbruch und Beharrung. Die evangelische Kirche nach dem Zweiten Weltkrieg." In *Die Zeit nach 1945 als Thema kirchlicher Zeitgeschichte*, edited by Victor Conzemius, Martin Greschat, and Hermann Kocher, 99–126. Göttingen: Vandenhoeck and Ruprecht, 1988.
Griffiths, Fiona, and Julie Hotchin, eds. *Partners in Spirit: Women, Men, and Religious Life in Germany (1100–1500)*. Turnhout: Brepols, 2014.

Grollová, Jana. *Memento mori. Obraz života a smrti v písemné tradici středověkého kazatelství*. Ostrava: Ostravská univerzita, Filozofická fakulta, 2017.

Grollová, Jana, and Daniela Rywiková. *Militia est vita hominis. Sedm smrtelných hříchů a sedm skutků milosrdenství v literárních a vizuálních pramenech Českého středověku*. České Budějovice – Ostrava: Veduta, 2013.

Gross, Michael B. *The War against Catholicism. Liberalism and the Anti-Catholic Imagination in Nineteenth-Century Germany*. Ann Arbor MI: University of Michigan Press, 2004.

Grundmann, Herbert. "Dante und Joachim von Fiore: Zu Paradiso X–XII." *Deutsches Dante-Jahrbuch* 5 (1932): 210–56.

– "Dante und Meister Eckhart." *Deutsches Dante-Jahrbuch* 18 (1936): 166–88. Reprint in *Ausgewählte Aufsätze* 1, 295–312. MGH Schriften 25, 1. Stuttgart: Anton Hiersemann, 1976.

– "Das hohe Mittelalter und die deutsche Kaiserzeit." In *Die Neue Propyläen-Weltgeschichte 2: Der Aufstieg des Germanentums und die Welt des Mittelalters*, edited by Willy Andreas, 173–350. Berlin: Propyläen, 1940.

– "Die Frauen und die Literatur im Mittelalter. Ein Beitrag zur Frage nach Entstehung des Schriftums in der Volkssprache." *Archiv für Kulturgeschichte* 26 (1935; printed 1936): 129–61.

– "Federico II e Gioacchino da Fiore." In *VII Centenario della morte di Federico II Imperatore e Re di Sicilia (10–18 dicembre 1950). Atti del Convegno Internazionale di Studi Federiciani*, 82–9. Palermo: Renna, 1952.

– *Herbert Grundmann (1902–1970): Essays on Heresy, Literacy, and Inquisition*. Edited by Jennifer Kolpacoff Deane. Translated by Steven Rowan. Woodbridge: York Medieval Press, 2019

– "Ketzerverhöre des Spätmittelalters als quellenkritische Probleme." *Deutsches Archiv für Erforschung des Mittelalters* 21 (1965): 519–75.

– "Kleine Beiträge über Joachim von Fiore." *Zeitschrift für Kirchengeschichte* n.s. 11, 48 (1929): 137–65.

– "Lex et Sacramentum bei Joachim von Fiore." In *Lex und Sacramentum im Mittelalter*, edited by Paul Wilpert, 31–48. Miscellanea Mediaevalia 6. Berlin: De Gruyter, 1969.

– "Meister Eckhart." In *Die Großen Deutschen* 1, edited by Willy Andreas and Wilhelm von Scholz, 230–45. Berlin: Propyläen, 1935. Reprint in *Ausgewählte Aufsätze* 1, 278–94. MGH Schriften 25, 1. Stuttgart: Anton Hiersemann, 1976.

– *Movimenti religiosi nel Medioevo: ricerche sui nessi storici tra l'eresia, gli ordini mendicanti e il movimento religioso femminile nel XII e XIII secolo e sulle origini storiche della mistica tedesca*. Bologna: Il Mulino, 1974.

– *Neue Forschungen über Joachim von Fiore*. Münstersche Forschungen 1. Marburg: Simons, 1950.

– "Reich und Kaisertum im Mittelalter." In *Germanische Gemeinsamkeit. Vorträge gehalten an der SS-Junkerschule Tölz*, edited by Der Reichsführer-SS. SS-Hauptamt, 73–92. Germanien und Europa 1. Posen: Feldmüller, 1944.

– *Religiöse Bewegungen im Mittelalter: Anhang: Neue Beiträge zur Geschichte der religiösen Bewegungen im Mittelalter*. Hildesheim: G. Olms, 1961.
– *Religiöse Bewegungen im Mittelalter: Untersuchungen über die geschichtlichen zusammenhänge zwischen der ketzerei, den bettelorden und der religiösen frauenbewegung im 12. Und 13. Jahrhundert und über die geschichtlichen grundlagen der deutschen mystik*. Berlin: Emil Ebering, 1935.
– *Religious Movements in the Middle Ages. The Historical Links between Heresy, the Mendicant Orders, and the Women's Religious Movement in the Twelfth and Thirteenth Century, with the Historical Foundations of German Mysticism*. Translated by Steven Rowan. Introduction by Robert E. Lerner. Notre Dame, IN: University of Notre Dame Press, 1995.
– *Studien über Joachim von Floris*. Beiträge zur Kulturgeschichte des Mittlealters und der Renaissance 32. Leipzig and Berlin, 1927.
– "Women and Literature in the Middle Ages: A Contribution on the Origins of Vernacular Writing." In *Essays on Heresy, Literacy, and Inquisition*, edited by Jennifer Kolpacoff Deane, 30–55. Woodbridge: York Medieval Press, 2019.
– "Zur Biographie Joachims von Fiore und Rainers von Ponza." *Deutsches Archiv für Erforschung des Mittlelalters* 16 (1960): 437–546.
Guida, Marco. *Una leggenda in cerca d'autore: la Vita di santa Chiara d'Assisi. Studio delle fonti e sinossi intertestuale*. Brussels: Société des Bolladistes, 2010.
Guldi, Jo, and David Armitage. *The History Manifesto*. Cambridge: Cambridge University Press, 2014.
Guilloux, Fabien. "*La regle et la vie des Sereurs meneurs encloses*: Une traduction en langue romane de la régle d'Isabelle de France (ca. 1315–1325)." *Archivum franciscanum historicum* 106 (2013): 5–39.
Habermas, Rebekka. "Piety, Power, and Powerlessness: Religion and Religious Groups in Germany, 1870–1945." In *The Oxford Handbook of Modern German History*, edited by Helmut Walser Smith, 453–80. Oxford: Oxford University Press, 2011.
Hahn, Cynthia. *Passion Relics and the Medieval Imagination: Art, Architecture and Society*. Berkeley: University of California Press, 2020.
Halary, Marie-Pascale. "Quand l'unique change de langue: Littérature spirituelle et 'langue courtoise' chez Marguerite d'Oingt." In *L'Unique change de scène. Écritures spirituelles et discours amoureux (XIIe–XVIIe siècle)*, edited by Véronique Ferrer, Barbara Marczuk, and Jean-René Valette, 137–54. Paris: Classiques Garnier, 2016.
Halle, Uta. "Archäologie, Germanen und Wikinger im Nationalsozialismus." In *Germanenideologie. Einer völkischen Weltanschauung auf der Spur*, edited by Martin Langebach, 102–38. Bonn: Bundeszentrale für politische Bildung, 2020.
Hamilton, Sarah. *The Practice of Penance 900–1050*. Woodbridge: Boydell, 2001.
Hamilton, Tracy Chapman. "Queenship and Kinship in the French *Bible Moralisée*: The Example of Blanche of Castile and Vienna ÖBN 2554." In *Capetian Women*, edited by Kathleen Nolan, 177–208. New York: Palgrave, 2003.

Harline, Craig. "Actives and Contemplatives: The Female Religious of the Low Countries before and after Trent." *The Catholic Historical Review* 81 (1995): 541–67.

Haseldine, Julian. "Friendship and Rivalry: The Role of Amicitia in Twelfth-Century Monastic Relations." *Journal of Ecclesiastical History* 44 (1993): 390–414.

Haseldine, Julian. "Friendship, Intimacy and Corporate Networking in the Twelfth Century: The Politics of Friendship in the Letters of Peter the Venerable." *English Historical Review* 76 (2011): 251–80.

Hasenohr, Geneviéve. "Retour sur les caractères linguistiques du manuscrit de Chantilly et de ses ancêtres." In *Marguerite Porete et le* Miroir des simples âmes, edited by Sean L. Field, Robert E. Lerner, and Sylvain Piron, 103–26. Paris: Vrin, 2013.

Hayton, Magda. "Prophets, Prophecy, and Cistercians: A Study of the Most Popular Version of the Hildegardian Pentachronon." *Journal of Medieval Latin* 29 (2019): 123–62.

Hebblethwaite, Peter. *John XXIII: Pope of the Council*. Rev. ed. London: Harper Collins, 1994.

Heft, James. *John XXII and Papal Teaching Authority*. Texts and Studies in Religion 27. Lewiston, NY: E. Mellen Press, 1977, rpt: 1986.

Heimpel, Hermann. "Herbert Grundmann." *Historische Zeitschrift* 210 (1970): 781–6.

Henderson, John. *Piety and Charity in Late Medieval Florence*. Chicago: University of Chicago Press, 1997.

Hendrickx, Frans. "L'histoire infortune des moniales chartreuses du Dauphiné et du Sud de la France et leur vie religieuse." *Analecta cartusiana* 55 (1982): 167–80.

Heng, Geraldine. *The Invention of Race in the European Middle Ages*. Cambridge: Cambridge University Press, 2018.

Henneau, Marie-Élisabeth. "Les Isles." In *Les Cisterciens dans l'Yonne*, edited by Terryl Kinder. Pontigny, France: Les Amis de Pontigny, 1999.

Herde, Peter. "Die Auseinandersetzungen über die Wahl Herbert Grundmanns zum Präsidenten der Monumenta Germaniae Historica (1957–1959)." *Zeitschrift für bayerische Landesgeschichte* 77 (2014): 69–135.

– "Mittelalterforschung in der Bundesrepublik Deutschland 1945–1970." In *Bausteine zur deutschen und italienischen Geschichte. Festschrift zum 70. Geburtstag von Horst Enzensberger*, edited by Maria Stuiber and Michele Spadaccini, 175–218. Bamberg: University of Bamberg Press, 2014. https://opus4.kobv.de/opus4-bamberg/frontdoor/index/index/docId/25030.

Hering, Kai. "Reform, Häresie und Schisma im frühen 12. Jahrhundert. Der Wanderprediger Heinrich, gen. von Lausanne und sein historisches Umfeld." *Cistercienser Chronik* 122/123 (2016/2015): 427–56, 93–119, 477–507.

Holzapfel, Heribert. *Handbuch der Geschichte des Franziskanerordens*. Freiburg: Herdersche Verlagshandlung, 1909.

Horn, Gerd-Rainer. *The Spirit of Vatican II: Western European Progressive Catholicism in the Long Sixties.* Oxford: Oxford University Press, 2015.
– *Western European Liberation Theology: The First Wave (1924–1959).* Oxford: Oxford University Press, 2008.
Houston, Robert Allan. *Literacy in Early Modern Europe: Culture and Education 1500–1800.* London: Longman, 1988.
Hughes, Kevin L. "Bonaventure's Defence of Mendicancy." In *A Companion to Bonaventure*, edited by Jay M. Hammond, J.A. Wayne Hellmann, and Jared Goff, 509–41. Leiden: Brill, 2013.
Huot, Sylvia. "Popular Piety and Devotional Literature: An Old French Rhyme about the Passion and Its Textual History." *Romania* 115 (1997): 451–94.
– *The Romance of the Rose and Its Medieval Readers: Interpretation, Reception, Manuscript Transmission.* Cambridge Studies in Medieval Literature 16. Cambridge: Cambridge University Press, 1993.
Iammarrone, Giovanni. "The Renewal of Franciscan Religious Life since Vatican II." Translated by Edwards Hagman. *Greyfriars Review* 9 (1995): 331–55.
Iogna-Prat, Dominique. "Alphonse Dupront ou la poétisation de l'Histoire." *Revue Historique* 300, no. 4(608) (1998): 887–910.
– *Ordonner et exclure. Cluny et la société chrétienne face à l'hérésie, au judaïsme et à l'islam (1000–1150).* 2nd ed. Paris: GF Flammarion, 2004.
Jackson, Jason Baird, ed. *Material Vernaculars: Objects, Images, and Their Social Worlds.* Bloomington: Indiana University Press, 2016.
Jahner, Jennifer A. "Verse Diplomacy and the English Interdict." In *Thirteenth Century England XV: Authority and Resistance in the Age of Magna Carta*, edited by Janet Burton, Philipp Schofield, and Björn Weiler, 99–114. Woodbridge: Boydell, 2015.
Jantzen, Kyle. *Faith and Fatherland. Parish Politics in Hitler's Germany.* Minneapolis: Fortress, 2008.
Jeay, Madeleine. "La Vie de sainte Douceline par Felipa Porcelet: les mobiles d'une hagiographe du XIIIe siècle." In *Dix ans de recherché sur les femmes écrivains de l'ancien régime: Influences et confluences. Mélanges offerts à Hannah Fournier*, edited by Guy Poirier, 17–36. Québec: Les Presses de l'Université de Laval, 2008.
Jenkins, Will. "The Mysterious Silence of Mother Earth in *Laudato Si'*." *Journal of Religious Ethics* 46, no. 3 (2018): 441–62.
Johnson, Lawrence J. *Worship in the Early Church: An Anthology of Historical Sources.* Collegeville: MN: Liturgical Press, 2009.
Johnson, Sherri Franks. *Monastic Women and Religious Orders in Late Medieval Bologna.* Cambridge: Cambridge University Press, 2014.
Jordan, William Chester. *The Apple of His Eye: Converts from Islam in the Reign of Louis IX.* Princeton, NJ: Princeton University Press, 2019.
– "*Etiam Reges*, Even Kings." *Speculum* 90 (2015): 613–34.
– "Isabelle of France and Religious Devotion at the Court of Louis IX." In *Capetian Women*, edited by Kathleen Nolan, 209–23. New York: Palgrave, 2003.

– *Men at the Center: Redemptive Governance under Louis IX*. Budapest: Central European University Press, 2012.

– "The Rituals of War: Departure for Crusade in Thirteenth-Century France." In *The Book of Kings: Art, War, and the Morgan Library's Medieval Picture Bible*, edited by William Noel and Daniel Weiss, 98–105. London: The Walters Art Museum, 2002.

Kaeuper, Richard W. *Holy Warriors: The Religious Ideology of Chivalry*. Philadelphia: University of Pennsylvania Press, 2014.

Kamínková, Eva. *Husova betlémská kázání a jejich dvě recense*. Prague: SPN, 1963.

Kaminsky, Howard. "The Great Schism." In *The New Cambridge Medieval History*, edited by Michael Jones, 696. Cambridge: Cambridge University Press, 2000.

Kaplan, Grant. "The Renewal of Ecclesiastical Studies: Chenu, Tübingen, and Theological Method in *Optatam Totius*." *Theological Studies* 77 (2016): 567–92.

Kater, Michael H. *Das "Ahnenerbe" der SS 1935–1945. Ein Beitrag zur Kulturpolitik des Dritten Reiches*. Studien zur Zeitgeschichte 6. 4th ed. Munich: Oldenbourg, 2006. https://www.degruyter.com/viewbooktoc/product/228710?null.

Kaufmann, Thomas. "'Anpassung' als historiographisches Konzept und als theologiepolitisches Programm. Der Kirchenhistoriker Erich Seeberg in der Zeit der Weimarer Republik und des 'Dritten Reiches.'" In *Evangelische Kirchenhistoriker im 'Dritten Reich,'* edited by Thomas Kaufmann and Harry Oelke, 122–272. Veröffentlichungen der Wissenschaftlichen Gesellschaft für Theologie 21. Gütersloh: Kaiser, 2002.

Kedar, Benjamin Z., and Peter Herde. *A Bavarian Historian Reinvents Himself: Karl Bosl and the Third Reich*. Jerusalem: Hebrew University Magnes Press, 2011.

Kejř, Jiří. *Z počátků České reformace*. Brno, Czech Republic: L. Marek, 2006.

Kenaan-Kader, Nurith. "Pictorial and Sculptural Commemoration of Returning or Departing Crusaders." In *The Crusades and Visual Culture*, edited by Elizabeth Lapina, April Jehan Morris, Susanna A. Throop, and Laura J. Whatley, 91–104. Burlington, VT: Ashgate, 2015.

Kerby-Fulton, Kathryn. "Hildegard of Bingen and Anti-Mendicant Propaganda." *Traditio* 43 (1987): 386–99.

– *Reformist Apocalypticism and Piers Plowman*. Cambridge Studies in Medieval Literature 7. Cambridge: Cambridge University Press, 1990.

Kerby-Fulton, Kathryn, Magda Hayton, and Kenna Olsen. "Pseudo-Hildegardian Prophecy and Antimendicant Propaganda in Late Medieval England: An Edition of the Most Popular Insular Text of 'Insurgent Gentes.'" In *Prophecy, Apocalypse and the Day of Doom: Proceedings of the 2000 Harlaxton Symposium*, edited by Nigel J. Morgan, 160–94. Harlaxton Medieval Studies 12. Donington: Shaun Tyas, 2004.

Kerr, Fergus. *Twentieth-century Catholic Theologians: from Neoscholasticism to Nuptial Mysticism.* Oxford: Blackwell, 2007.
Keyvanian, Carla. *Hospitals and Urbanism in Rome, 1200–1500.* Leiden: Brill, 2015.
Kienzle, Beverly Mayne. *Cistercians, Heresy, and Crusade in Occitania, 1145–1229: Preaching in the Lord's Vineyard.* Rochester, NY: York Medieval Press/Boydell Press, 2001.
– "Preaching as Touchstone of Orthodoxy and Dissidence in the Middle Ages." *Medieval Sermon Studies* 43 (1999): 19–54.
– "The Prostitute-Preacher. Patterns of Polemic Against Medieval Waldensian Women Preachers." In *Women Preachers and Prophets through Two Millennia of Christianity,* edited by Beverly Mayne Kienzle and Pamela J. Walker, 99–113. Berkeley: University of California Press, 1998.
Kim, Grace Ji-Sun, and Hilda Koster, eds. *Planetary Solidarity: Global Women's Voices on Christian Doctrine and Climate Justice.* Minneapolis: Fortress Press, 2017.
Kitts, Eustace J. *Pope John the Twenty-Third and Master John Hus of Bohemia.* London: Constable, 1910.
Klaniczay, Gábor. *Holy Rulers and Blessed Princesses: Dynastic Cults in Medieval Central Europe.* Cambridge: Cambridge University Press, 2002.
Klimesch, Johann Matthäus, ed. *Urkunden- und Regestenbuch des ehemaligen Klarissinenklosters in Krumau.* Prague: Verein für Geschichte der Deutschen in Böhmen, 1904.
Kluge, Stephanie. "Kontinuität oder Wandel? Zur Bewertung hochmittelalterlicher Königsherrschaft durch die frühe bundesrepublikanische Mediävistik." *Frühmittelalterliche Studien* 48 (2014): 39–120.
Knight, Gillian R. *The Correspondence between Peter the Venerable and Bernard of Clairvaux: A Semantic and Structural Analysis.* Church, Faith, and Culture in the Medieval West. Aldershot: Ashgate, 2002.
Knox, Lezlie S. *Creating Clare of Assisi: Female Franciscan Identities in Later Medieval Italy.* Leiden: Brill, 2008.
Koyré, A. "Les travaux de Paul Alphandéry." *Revue de l'histoire des religions* 105 (1932): 149–57.
Krause, Kathy. "Genealogy and Codicology: The Manuscript Contexts of the *Fille du comte de Pontieu.*" *Romance Philology* 59 (2006): 323–42.
Kullman, Dorothea. *The Church and Vernacular Literature in Medieval France.* Toronto: Pontifical Institute of Medieval Studies, 2009.
Kumler, Aden. *Translating Truth: Ambitious Images and Religious Knowledge in Late Medieval France and England.* New Haven, CT: Yale University Press, 2011.
Ladner, Gerhart B. *The Idea of Reform: Its Impact on Christian Thought and Action in the Age of the Fathers.* Cambridge, MA: Harvard University Press, 1959.

Ladurie, Emmanuel Le Roy. *Montaillou: The Promised Land of Error.* Translated by Barbara Bray. New York: G. Braziller, 1978.

Lambert, Malcolm D. *Medieval Heresy: Popular Movements from the Gregorian Reform to the Reformation.* 3rd ed. Cambridge, MA: Harvard University Press, 1977, rpt. 2002.

Landini, Lawrence C. *The Causes of the Clericalization of the Order of Friars Minor 1209–1260 in the Light of Early Franciscan Sources.* Chicago: Pontificia Universitas Gregoriana, 1967.

Le Bourgeois, Marie Amélie. *Les Ursulines d'Anne de Xainctonge (1606).* Saint-Étienne: Éditions Universitaires, 2003.

Le Goff, Jacques. *Saint Francis of Assisi.* Translated by Christine Rhone. London: Routledge, 2004.

Leblanc, Olivier. "Picardie, croisades et sires de Boves." In *Questions d'histoire orient et occident du IXe au XVe siècle (Actes du colloque d'Amiens 8,9, et 10, octobre 1998 organisé par le CAHMER),* edited by Georges Jehel, 29–55. Paris: Éditions du temps, 2000.

Leclercq, Jean. *La vie parfaite: points de vue sur l'essence de l'état religieux.* Paris: Éditions Brepols, 1948.

– "Le poème de Payen Bolotin contre les faux ermites." *Revue bénédictine* 68 (1958): 52–86.

Lehár, Jan. *Česká literatura od počátků k dnešku.* Prague: Lidové Noviny, 2008.

Lehmijoki-Gardner, Maiju. "Writing Religious Rules as an Interactive Process: Dominican Penitent Women and the Making of Their 'Regula.'" *Speculum* 79 (2004): 660–87.

Lemaitre, Henri. "Statuts des Religieuses du Tiers-ordre franciscain dites sœurs grises hospitalières (1483)." *Archivium Franciscanum Historicum* 4 (1911): 713–31.

– "Une bulle inédite de Sixte IV (1474) en faveur des soeurs de la celle." *Revue d'histoire Franciscaine* 4 (1927): 361–4.

Lerner, Robert. *The Heresy of the Free Spirit in the Later Middle Ages.* Notre Dame, IN: University of Notre Dame Press, 1972.

– "Introduction to the Translation." In *Religious Movements in the Middle Ages,* by Herbert Grundmann, ix–xxix. Translated by Steven Rowan. Notre Dame, IN: University of Notre Dame Press, 1995.

– "Joachim of Fiore as a Link between St. Bernard and Innocent III on the Figural Significance of Melchisedech." *Mediaeval Studies* 42 (1980): 417–26.

Lesky, Albin. "Hypokrites." In *Studi in Onore di Ugo Enrico Paoli,* 469–76. Pubblicazioni della Università degli studi di Firenze – Facoltà di lettere e filosofia, ser. 4, 1. Firenze: F. le Monnier, 1955.

Leson, Richard. "Heraldry and Identity in the Psalter-Hours of Jean of Flanders (Manchester, John Rylands Library, MS. Lat. 117)." *Studies in Iconography* 32 (2011): 155–98.

Lespinasse, René de. *Le Nivernais et les comtes de Nevers*. 3 vols. Paris: H. Champion, 1909–14.

Lester, Anne E. "Cares beyond the Walls: Cistercian Nuns and the Care of Lepers in Twelfth- and Thirteenth-Century Northern France." In *Religious and Laity in Western Europe 1000–1400: Interaction, Negotiation, and Power*, edited by Emilia Jamroziak and Janet Burton, 197–124. Turnhout: Brepols, 2006.

– *Creating Cistercian Nuns: The Women's Religious Movement and Its Reform in Thirteenth-Century Champagne*. Ithaca: Cornell University Press, 2011.

– "From Captivity to Liberation: The Ideology and Practice of Franchise in Crusading France." *Anglo-Norman Studies: Proceedings of the Battle Conference 2017* 40 (2018): 147–63.

– "A Shared Imitation: Cistercian Convents and Crusader Families in Thirteenth-Century Champagne." *Journal of Medieval History* 35 (2009): 353–70.

– "Translation and Appropriation: Greek Relics in the Latin West in the Aftermath of the Fourth Crusade." *Translating Christianity: Studies in Church History* 53 (2017): 88–117.

Lester, Anne E., and Willian Chester Jordan. "La-Cour-Notre-Dame de Michéry: A Response to Constance Berman." *Journal of Medieval History* (1999): 43–54.

Leube, Achim, and Morten Hegewisch, eds. *Prähistorie und Nationalsozialismus. Die mittel- und osteuropäische Ur- und Frühgeschichtsforschung in den Jahren 1933–45*. Studien zur Wissenschafts- und Universalgeschichte 2. Heidelberg: Synchron, 2002.

Lévi, Sylvain, François Proché, and Charles Picard. "Paul Alphandéry." *Revue de l'histoire des religions* 105 (1932): 139–48.

Lieburg, Fred van. "In saecula saeculorum. Long-term Perspectives on Religious History." *Church History and Religious Culture* 98 (2018): 319–43.

Lietzmann, Hilda. "Bibliographie Herbert Grundmann." *Deutsches Archiv für Erforschung des Mittelalters* 26 (1970): 354–65. Reprinted in Herbert Grundmann, *Gesammelte Aufsätze 1*, 26–37. MGH Schriften 25, 1. Stuttgart: Anton Hiersemann, 1976.

Linden, Ian. *Global Catholicism: Diversity and Change since Vatican II*. London: Hurst, 2009.

Lloyd, Joan E. Barclay. "The Church and Monastery of S. Pancrazio, Rome." In *Pope, Church and City: Essays in Honour of Brenda M. Bolton*, edited by Frances Andrews, Christoph Egger, and Constance Rousseau, 245–66. Leiden: Brill, 2004.

Logan, F. Donald. *Runaway Religious in Medieval England, C.1240–1540*. Cambridge: Cambridge University Press, 2002.

Longnon, Jean. *Les compagnons de Villehardouin: Recherches sur les croisés de la quatrième croisade*. Geneva: Librairie Droz, 1978.

Losemann, Volker. "Classics in the Second World War." In *Nazi Germany and the Humanities. How German Academics Embraced Nazism*, edited by Wolfgang Bialas and Anson Rabinbach, 306–40. London: Oneworld, 2007.

Lowe, K.J.P. *Nuns' Chronicles and Convent Culture in Renaissance and Counter-Reformation Italy*. Cambridge: Cambridge University Press, 2003.

Lu, Huanan. "Le béguinage Ste-Élisabeth à Valenciennes (XIIIe-XIVe siècles)." PhD diss., École des Hautes Études en Sciences Sociales, 2021.

Lunardi, Giovanni. *L'ideale monastico nelle polemiche del secolo XII sulla vita religiosa*. Noci: Pontificium Athenaeum Anselmianum, 1970.

Mabille, Madeleine. "Les manuscits de Jean d'Essômes conservés à la Bibliothèque Nationale de Paris." *Bibliothèque de l'école des chartes* 130 (1972): 231–4.

Maier, Christoph T. *Crusade Propaganda and Ideology: Model Sermons for the Preaching of the Cross*. Cambridge: Cambridge University Press, 2000.

– *Preaching the Crusades: Mendicant Friars and the Cross in the Thirteenth Century*. Cambridge: Cambridge University Press, 1994.

– "The Roles of Women in the Crusade Movement: A Survey." *Journal of Medieval History* 30 (2004): 61–82.

Makowski, Elizabeth. *Canon Law and Cloistered Women*: Periculoso *and its Commentators, 1298–1545*. Washington, DC: The Catholic University of America Press, 1997.

– *'A Pernicious Sort of Woman': Quasi Religious Women and Canon Lawyers in the Later Middle Ages*. Washington, DC: Catholic University of America Press, 2005.

Mann, Jill. *Chaucer and Medieval Estates Satire: The Literature of Social Classes and the General Prologue to the Canterbury Tales*. Cambridge: Cambridge University Press, 1973.

Manselli, Raoul. "Il gesto come predicazione per san Francesco d'Assisi." *Collectanea Franciscana* 51 (1981): 5–16.

Marini, Alfonso. "Monasteri femminili a Roma nei secoli XIII–XV." *Archivio della Società Romana di Storia Patria* 132 (2010): 81–108.

Matter, E. Ann. "Italian Holy Women: A Survey." In *Medieval Holy Women in the Christian Tradition, c. 1100–c. 1500*, edited by Alastair Minnis and Rosalynn Voaden, 529–55. Turnhout: Brepols, 2010.

Matura, Thadée. "L'Eglise dans les écrits de François d'Assise." *Antonianum* 57 (1982): 94–112.

Mazzonis, Querciolo. *Spirituality, Gender, and the Self in Renaissance Italy. Angela Merici and the Company of St. Ursula (1474–1540)*. Washington, DC: The Catholic University of America Press, 2007.

McClure, Julia. *The Franciscan Invention of the New World*. Basingstoke: Palgrave, 2016.

McCutcheon, Russell T. *Manufacturing Religion: The Discourse on Sui Generis Religion and the Politics of Nostalgia.* New York: Oxford University Press, 1997.
McDonnell, Ernest W. "The *Vita Apostolica*: Diversity or Dissent?" *Church History* 24 (1955): 15–31.
McGinn, Bernard. *The Flowering of Mysticism: Men and Women in the New Mysticism – 1200–1350.* New York: Crossroad, 1998.
– *Visions of the End: Apocalyptic Traditions in the Middle Ages.* New York: Columbia University Press, 1979.
McNamara, Jo Ann. "Rhetoric of Orthodoxy: Clerical Authority and Female Innovation in the Struggle with Heresy." In *Maps of Flesh and Light: The Religious Experience of Medieval Women Mystics*, edited by Ulrike Wiethaus, 9–27. Syracuse, NY: Syracuse University Press, 1993.
McWebb, Christine. *Debating the 'Roman de La Rose.' A Critical Anthology.* New York: Routledge, 2007.
Meersseman, Gilles. "Disciplinati e Penitenti del Duecento." In *Il movimento dei Disciplinati nel settimo centenario dal suo inizio (Perugia, 1260): convegno internazionale: Perugia, 25–28 settembre 1960.* Spoleto: Arti grafiche Panetto & Petrelli, 1962.
Meersseman, Gilles, and G.P. Pacini. *Ordo fraternitatis: confraternite e pietà dei laici nel Medioevo.* 3 vols. Rome: Herder editrice e libreria, 1977.
Melve, Leidulf. *Inventing the Public Sphere: The Public Debate During the Investiture Contest (c. 1030–1122).* Brill's Studies in Intellectual History 154. Leiden: Brill, 2007.
Melville, Gert. "*Duo novae conversationis ordines.* Zur Wahrnehmung der frühen Mendikanten vor dem Problem institutioneller Neuartigkeit im mittelalterlichen Religiosentum." In *Die Bettelorden im Aufbau. Beiträge zu Institutionalisierungsprozessen im mittelalterlichen Religiosentum*, edited by Gert Melville and Jörg Oberste, 1–23. Vita Regularis. Ordnungen und Deutungen religiosen Lebens im Mittelalter 11. Münster: LIT, 1999.
– *The World of Medieval Monasticism: Its History and Forms of Life.* Translated by James D. Mixson. Kalamazoo, MI: Cistercian Publications, 2016.
– "Zur Semantik von *ordo* im Religiosentum der ersten Hälfte des 12. Jahrhunderts." In *Studien zum Prämonstratenserorden*, edited by Irene Crusius and Helmut Flachenecker, 201–24. Veröffentlichungen des Max-Planck-Instituts für Geschichte 25. Göttingen: Vandenhoeck & Ruprecht, 2003.
Melville, Gert, and Anne Müller, eds. *Female 'vita religiosa' Between Late Antiquity and the High Middle Ages: Structures, Developments and Spatial Contexts.* Berlin: LIT Verlag, 2011.
Merlo, Grado Giovanni. "La storiografia francescana dal dopoguerra ad oggi." *Studi Storici* 32 (1991): 287–307.

– *Nel nome di san Francesco: Storia dei frati Minori e del francescanesimo sino agli inizi del XVI secolo*. Padua: Editrici Francescane, 2012.
– *Tra eremo e città: studi su Francesco d'Assisi e sul francescanesimo medieval*. Assisi: Edizioni Porziuncola, 1991.
Miccoli, Giovanni. *Francesco d'Assisi: realtà e memoria di un'esperienza cristiana*. Torino: Einaudi, 1991.
Michaud-Quantin, Pierre. *Universitas. Expression du mouvement communautaire dans le Moyen Âge latin*. Paris: Vrin, 1970.
Michetti, Raimondo. "Francesco d'Assisi e l'essenza del cristianesimo (a proposito di alcune biografie storiche e di alcuni studi contemporanei)." In *Francesco d'Assisi fra storia, letteratura e iconografia*, edited by Franca Ela Consolino, 37–67. Soveria Mannelli: Rubbettino, 1996.
Miller, Maureen C. *The Formation of a Medieval Church: Ecclesiastical Change in Verona, 950–1150*. Ithaca: Cornell University Press, 1993.
Miller, Tanya Stabler. *The Beguines of Medieval Paris: Gender, Patronage, and Spiritual Authority*. Philadelphia: University of Pennsylvania Press, 2014.
– "'Love Is Beguine': Labeling Lay Religiosity in Thirteenth-Century Paris." In *Labels and Libels: Naming Beguines in Northern Medieval Europe*, edited by Letha Bohringer, Jennifer K. Deane, and Hildo van Engen, 135–50. Turnhout: Brepols, 2014.
Millet, Hélène. "John XXIII (c. 1360–1419)." In *Encyclopedia of the Middle Ages*, edited by André Vauchez et al., 177. Vol. 1. London-Chicago: James Clark & Co., 2001.
– *L'Église du Grande Schisme 1378–1417*. Paris: Picard, 2009.
Minnis, Alastair J. *Magister Amoris: The Roman de La Rose and Vernacular Hermeneutics*. Oxford: Oxford University Press, 2001.
Mixson, James D., ed. and trans. *Religious Life between Jerusalem, the Desert, and the World: Selected Essays by Kaspar Elm*. Studies in the History of Christian Traditions 180. Leiden: Brill, 2016.
Mixson, James D., and Bert Roest, eds. *Observant Reform in the Later Middle Ages and Beyond*. Leiden: Brill, 2015.
Mooney, Catherine M. *Clare of Assisi and the Thirteenth-Century Church: Religious Women, Rules, and Resistance*. Philadelphia: University of Pennsylvania Press, 2016.
–, ed. *Gendered Voices: Medieval Saints and Their Interpreters*. Philadelphia: University of Pennsylvania Press, 1999.
– "Imitatio Christi or Imitatio Marie? Clare of Assisi and Her Interpreters." In *Gendered Voices: Medieval Saints and Their Interpreters*, edited by Catherine M. Mooney, 52–77. Philadelphia: University of Pennsylvania Press, 1999.
– "The 'Lesser Sisters' in Jacques de Vitry's 1216 Letter." *Franciscan Studies* 69 (2011): 1–29.

Moore, R.I. *The Formation of a Persecuting Society: Power and Deviance in Western Europe 950–1250*. Cambridge, MA: Blackwell Publishing, 1987.
– *The War on Heresy*. London: Profile, 2012; Cambridge, MA: Harvard University Press, 2014.
Moorman, John. *A History of the Franciscan Order from its Origins to the year 1517*. Oxford University Press, 1968.
Moracchini, Pierre. "La Mise sous clôture des sœurs grises de la Province franciscaine de France parisienne, au XVIIe siècle." In *Les Religieuses dans le cloître et dans le monde*. Actes du Colloque du CERCOR, Poitiers, 29 septembre–2 octobre 1988, 635–65. Saint-Étienne: Publications de l'Université de Saint-Étienne, 1994.
More, Alison. "Dynamics of Regulation, Innovation, and Invention." In *A Companion to Observant Reform in the Late Middle Ages and Beyond*, edited by James Mixson and Bert Roest, 85–110. Brill's Companions to the Christian Tradition 59. Leiden: Brill, 2015.
– *Fictive Orders and Feminine Religious Identities, 1200–1600*. Oxford: Oxford University Press, 2018.
– "Institutionalization of Disorder: The Franciscan Third Order and Canonical Change in the Sixteenth Century." *Franciscan Studies* 71 (2013): 147–62.
– "Institutionalizing Penitential Life in Later Medieval and Early Modern Europe: Third Orders, Rules and Canonical Legitimacy." *Church History: Studies in Christianity and Culture* 83 (2014): 296–322.
– "Religious Order and Textual Identity: The Case of Franciscan Tertiary Women." In *Nuns' Literacies: The Antwerp Dialogue*, edited by Virginia Blanton, Veronica O'Mara, and Patricia Stoop, 60–79. Leiden: Brill, 2017.
– "Tertiaries and the Scottish Observance: St Martha's Hospital in Aberdour and the Institutionalisation of the Third Order." *Scottish Historical Review* (2015): 121–39.
Morelle, Laurent. "Le prophétisme médiéval latin dans l'oeuvre de Paul Alphandéry: À propos d'archives récemment mises au jour." *Mélanges de l'École française de Rome, Moyen Age* 102 (1990): 513–32.
Morgenstern, Ulf. "Politische Publizistik Leipziger Ordinarien in der Weimarer Republik." In *Sachsens Landesuniversität in Monarchie, Republik und Diktatur*, edited by Ulrich von Hehl, 221–37. Beiträge zur Leipziger Universitäts- und Wissenschaftsgeschichte A 3. Leipzig: Evangelische Verlangsanstalt, 2005.
Morton, Jonathan. *The* Roman de la Rose *in its Philosophical Context. Art, Nature, and Ethics*. Oxford: Oxford University Press, 2018.
Movimento religioso femminile e francescanesimo nel secolo XIII. Atti del VII convegno internazionale. Assisi, 11–13 ottobre 1979. Assisi: Società Internazionale di Studi Francescani, 1980.

Muessig, Carolyn. "Prophecy and Song: Teaching and Preaching by Medieval Women." In *Women Preachers and Prophets through Two Millennia of Christianity*, edited by Beverly Mayne Kienzle and Pamela J. Walker, 146–58. Berkeley: University of California Press, 1998.

Mulder-Bakker, Anneke B. *Lives of the Anchoresses: The Rise of the Urban Recluse in Medieval Europe*. Philadelphia: University of Pennsylvania Press, 2005.

Muraro, Luisa. *Guglielma e Maifreda: Storia di un'eresia femminista*. Milan: La Tartaruga, 1985.

Murat, Philippe. "La croisade en Nivernais: transfert de propriété et lute d'influence." In *Le concile de Clermont de 1095 et l'appel à la croisade. Actes du Colloque Universitaire International de Clermont-Ferrand (23–25 juin 1995)*, edited by Valéry Giscard d'Estaing, 295–312. Publications de l'École française de Rome, 236. Rome: École Français de Rome, 1997.

Mylod, E.J., Guy Perry, Thomas W. Smith, and Jan Vandeburie, eds. *The Fifth Crusade in Context: The Crusading Movement in the Early Thirteenth Century*. Abingdon: Routledge, 2017.

Nabert, Nathalie. "Le vie de Béatrice d'Ornacieux par Marguerite d'Oingt, une biographie à l'ombre de la croix?" In *L'ordre des chartreux au XIIIe siècle*, edited by James Hogg, Alain Girard, and Daniel Le Blévec, 127–35. Salzburg: Institut für Anglistik und Amerikanistik, Universität Salzburg, 2006.

Nagel, Anne Christine. *Im Schatten des Dritten Reichs. Mittelalterforschung in der Bundesrepublik Deutschland 1945–1970*. Formen der Erinnerung 24. Göttingen: Vandenhoeck and Ruprecht, 2005.

– "'Mit dem Herzen, dem Willen und dem Verstand dabei': Herbert Grundmann und der Nationalsozialismus." In *Nationalsozialismus in den Kulturwissenschaften 1: Fächer – Milieus – Karrieren*, edited by Hartmut Lehmann and Otto Gerhard Oexle, 593–618. Veröffentlichungen des Max-Planck-Instituts für Geschichte 200. Göttingen: Vandenhoeck and Ruprecht, 2004.

Nagy, Piroska. "Avant-propos." *Memini: Travaux et documents* 24 (2018). https://journals.openedition.org/memini/1070.

Newhauser, Richard, ed. *The Seven Deadly Sins. From Communities to Individuals*. Leiden-Boston: Brill, 2007.

Newman, Barbara. "Agnes of Prague and Guglielma of Milan." In *Medieval Holy Women in the Christian Tradition*, edited by Rosalynn Voaden and Alastair Minnis, 557–79. Turnhout: Brepols, 2010.

– *From Virile Woman to WomanChrist*. Philadelphia: University of Pennsylvania Press, 1995.

– "The Heretic Saint: Guglielma of Bohemia, Milan, and Brunate." *Church History* 74 (2005): 1–38.

– *Medieval Crossover: Reading the Secular against the Sacred*. Notre Dame, IN: University of Notre Dame Press, 2013.
Nichols, Stephen G. "Urgent Voices: The Vengeance of Images in Medieval Poetry." In *France and the Holy Land: Frankish Culture at the End of the Crusades*, edited by Daniel H. Weiss and Lisa Mahoney, 22–42. Baltimore: Johns Hopkins University Press, 2004.
Nolzen, Armin. "Nationalsozialismus und Christentum. Konfessionsgeschichtliche Befunde zur NSDAP." In *Zerstrittene 'Volksgemeinschaft.' Glaube, Konfession und Religion im Nationalsozialismus*, edited by Armin Nolzen and Manfred Gailus, 151–79. Göttingen: Vandenhoeck and Ruprecht, 2011.
Nowacka, Keiko. "Persecution, Marginalization, or Tolerance: Prostitutes in Thirteenth-Century Parisian Society." In *Difference and Identity in Francia and Medieval France*, edited by Meredith Cohen and Justine Firnhaber-Baker, 175–96. Farnham, UK: Ashgate, 2010.
O'Donnell, Ernest W. *The Beguines and Beghards in Medieval Culture*. New Brunswick: Rutgers University Press, 1954.
Omaechevarria, Ignacio. "Religiosas docentes, hospitalarias y misioneras a fines de la edad media." *Revista Española de Derecho Canónico* 9 (1954): 989–1003.
O'Malley, John W. *What Happened at Vatican II?* Cambridge, MA: Harvard University Press, 2010.
O'Meara, Thomas F., and Paul Philibert. *Scanning the Signs of the Times: French Dominicans in the Twentieth Century*. Adelaide, Australia: ATF Press, 2013.
Onnasch, Martin. *Um kirchliche Macht und geistliche Vollmacht. Ein Beitrag zur Geschichte des Kirchenkampfes in der Kirchenprovinz Sachsen 1932–1945*. Greifswalder theologische Forschungen 20. Frankfurt/Main: Lang, 2010.
O'Sullivan, Daniel. "Thibaut de Champagne and Lyric Authoritas in ms Paris, BnF fr. 12615." *Textual Cultures* 8 (2013): 31–49.
Paciocco, Roberto. "Una conscienza tra scelta di vita e fama di santità. Francesco d'Assisi frater e sanctus." *Hagiographica* 1 (1994): 207–26.
Pagan, Martine. "De la *Légende* latine aux *Vies* françaises de Claire d'Assise." *Memini: Travaux et documents* 24 (2018). https://journals.openedition.org/memini/1106.
– "Les légendes françaises de Claire d'Assise (XIIIe–XVIe siècle): I. Inventaire et classement des manuscrits." *Études franciscaines*, n.s. 7, no. 1 (2014): 5–35.
– "Les légendes françaises de Claire d'Assise (XIIIe–XVIe siècle): II. Édition du plus ancien manuscrit de la version longue (BnF, fr. 2096)." *Études franciscaines* n.s. 7, no. 2 (2014): 221–72.

Palmer, James A. "Medieval and Renaissance Rome: Mending the Divide." *History Compass* 15 (2017). https://doi.org/10.1111/hic3.12424.

Paolazzi, Carlo. "Novità nel testo critico degli *Scripta* di Francesco d'Assisi, in rapporto all'edizione Esser." *Archivum Franciscanum Historicum* 102 (2009): 353–90.

Parker, Robyn."Creating the 'Hermit-Preachers': Narrative, Textual Construction, and Community in Twelfth- and Thirteenth-Century Northern France." PhD diss., University of Sheffield, 2014.

Paterson, Linda, with Luca Barbieri, Ruth Harvey, and Anna Radaelli. *Singing the Crusades: French and Occitan Lyric Responses to the Crusading Movement, 1127–1336*. Cambridge: D.S. Brewer, 2018.

Patschovsky, Alexander. "Studi su Gioacchino da Fiore' di Herbert Grundmann." *Florensia* 3–4 (1989–90): 113–19.

Paul, Nicholas L. "In Search of the Marshal's Lost Crusade: The Persistence of Memory, the Problems of History and the Painful Birth of Crusading Romance." *Journal of Medieval History* 40 (2015): 292–310.

– "Possession: Sacred Crusading Treasure in the Material Vernacular." *Material Religion* 14 (2018): 520–32.

– *To Follow in Their Footsteps: The Crusades and Family Memory in the High Middle Ages*. Ithaca: Cornell University Press, 2012.

Pazzelli, Raffaele. *St. Francis and the Third Order*. Chicago: Franciscan Herald Press, 1989.

Peano, Pierre. "Ministres provinciaux de Provence et Spirituels." *Cahiers de Fanjeaux* 10 (1975): 41–65.

Pegg, Mark Gregory. *The Corruption of Angels: The Great Inquisition of 1245–1246*. Princeton, NJ: Princeton University Press, 2001.

– "The Paradigm of Catharism; or, the Historian's Illusion." In *Cathars in Question*, edited by Antonio Sennis, 21–52. Woodbridge: York Medieval Press, 2016.

Pegues, Frank. "Ecclesiastical Provisions for the Support of Students in the Thirteenth Century." *Church History* 26 (1957): 307–18.

Pellegrini, Luigi. "Female Religious Experience and Society in Thirteenth-Century Italy." In *Monks and Nuns, Saints and Outcasts: Religion in Medieval Society. Essays in Honor of Lester K. Little*, edited by Sharon Farmer and Barbara H. Rosenwein, 97–122. Ithaca: Cornell University Press, 2000.

Pernoud, Régine. *La Femme au temps des cathedrals*. Paris: Stock, 1980.

Perroy, Edouard. *Les families nobles du Forez au XIIIe siècle*. Saint-Étienne: Centre d'Études Foréziennes, 1976–7.

Pešek, Jiří, and Václav Ledvinka, eds., *Žena v dějinách Prahy*. Prague: Scriptorium, 1996.

Peterson, Janine Larmon. "Social Roles, Gender Inversion, and the Heretical Sect: The Case of the Guglielmites." *Viator* 35 (2004): 203–19.

Petry, R.C. *Francis of Assisi: Apostle of Poverty*. Durham, NC: Duke University Press, 1941.

Phillips, Jonathan. *Defenders of the Holy Land: Relations between the Latin East and the West, 1119–1187*. Oxford: Clarendon Press, 1996.

Piepenbrink, Johannes. "Das Seminar für Mittlere Geschichte des Historischen Instituts 1933–1945." In *Sachsens Landesuniversität in Monarchie, Republik und Diktatur*, edited by Ulrich von Hehl, 363–83. Beiträge zur Leipziger Universitäts- und Wissenschaftsgeschichte A 3. Leipzig: Evangelische Verlangsanstalt, 2005.

Pierce, Jerry B. *Poverty, Heresy, and the Apocalypse: The Order of Apostles and Social Change in Medieval Italy, 1260–1307*. New York: Continuum, 2012.

Pietsch, Andreas, and Sita Steckel. "New Religious Movements before Modernity? Considerations from a Historical Perspective." *Nova Religio: The Journal of Alternative and Emergent Religions* 21 (2018): 13–37.

Pippenger, Randall. "Crusading as a Family: A Study of the County of Champagne, 1179–1226." PhD diss., Princeton University, 2018.

Piron, Sylvain. "Marguerite, entre les béguines et les maîtres." In *Marguerite Porete et le* Miroir des simples âmes, edited by Sean L. Field, Robert E. Lerner, and Sylvain Piron, 69–101. Paris: Vrin, 2013.

– "Marguerite in Champagne." *Journal of Medieval Religious Cultures* 43 (2017): 135–56.

Pitt, Alan. "The Cultural Impact of Science in France: Ernest Renan and the *Vie de Jésus*." *Historial Journal* 43 (2000): 79–101.

Pohlig, Matthias, and Sita Steckel, eds. *Über Religion entscheiden. Religiöse Optionen und Alternativen im mittelalterlichen und frühneuzeitlichen Christentum/Choosing my Religion: Religious Options and Alternatives in Late Medieval and Early Modern Christianity*. Göttingen: Vandenhoeck & Ruprecht, 2021.

Potworowski, Christophe F. *Contemplation and Incarnation: The Theology of Marie-Dominique Chenu*. Montreal: McGill-Queen's Press, 2001.

Powell, James. *Anatomy of a Crusade: 1213–1221*. Philadelphia: University of Pennsylvania, 1986.

Power, Amanda. "The Problem of Obedience Among the English Friars." In *Rules and Observance: Devising Forms of Communal Life*, edited by Mirko Breitenstein, Julia Burkhardt; Stefan Burkhardt, and Jens Röhrkasten, 129–67. Berlin: LIT Verlag, 2014.

– *Roger Bacon and the Defense of Christendom*. Cambridge: Cambridge University Press, 2012.

– "The Uncertainties of Reformers: Collective Anxieties and Strategic Discourses." In *Thirteenth Century England XVI*, edited by Andrew Spencer and Carl Watkins. London: Boydell and Brewer, 2017.

Priest, Robert D. "The 'Great Doctrine of Transcendent Disdain': History, Politics and the Self in Renan's Life of Jesus." *History of European Ideas* 40 (2014): 761–76.

Prudlo, Donald S., ed. *The Origin, Development, and Refinement of Medieval Religious Mendicancies*. Leiden: Brill, 2011.

Puckett, Jaye. "'Reconmenciez novele estoire': The Troubadours and the Rhetoric of the Later Crusades." *MLN* 116 (2001): 844–89.

Purkis, William. *Crusading Spirituality in the Holy Land*. Woodbridge: Boydell, 2008.

Putna, Martin C. *Mysticism from the house with a garden* [Mystika z domku se zahrádkou]. From *The Cultural History of the Beguine Movement* (Prague: Malvern, 2013).

Quantin, Maximillen. *Répertoire archéologique de département de l'Yonne*. Paris: Imprimierie Impériale, 1868.

Ramey, Lynn Tarte. "Jean Bodel's Jeu de Saint Nicolas: A Call for non-Violent Crusade." *French Forum* 27 (2002): 1–12.

Rapley, Elizabeth. *The Dévotes: Women and Church in Seventeenth-Century France*. Montreal: McGill/Queens University Press, 1990.

Rashdall, Hastings. *The Universities of Europe in the Middle Ages*. Edited by F.M. Powicke and A.B. Emden. Oxford: Oxford University Press, 1936.

Reeves, Marjorie. *The Influence of Prophecy in the Later Middle Ages: A Study in Joachimism*. Oxford: Oxford University Press, 1969.

– *Joachim of Fiore and the Prophetic Future*. New York: Sutton Publishing, 1977 rpt, 1999.

Repgen, Konrad. "Die Erfahrung des Dritten Reiches und das Selbstverständnis der deutschen Katholiken nach 1945." In *Die Zeit nach 1945 als Thema kirchlicher Zeitgeschichte*, edited by Victor Conzemius and Hermann Kocher, 127–79. Göttingen: Vandenhoeck and Ruprecht, 1988.

Renan, Ernest. *New Studies of Religious History*. New York: Scribner and Welford, 1887.

– *Vie de Jésus*. 2nd ed. Paris: Michel Lévy, 1863.

Richard, Nathalie. *La Vie de Jésus de Renan, la fabrique d'un best-seller*. Rennes: Presses universitaires de Rennes, 2015.

Riechert, Karen. "Der Umgang der katholischen Kirche mit historischer und juristischer Schuld anlässlich der Nürnberger Kriegsverbrecherprozesse." In *Siegerin in Trümmern. Die Rolle der katholischen Kirche in der deutschen Nachkriegsgesellschaft*, edited by Joachim Köhler and Damian van Melis, 18–41. Stuttgart, Berlin, and Cologne: Kohlhammer, 1998.

Rigon, Antonio. *Clero e città. 'Fratalea cappellanorum', parroci, cura d'anime in Padova dal XII al XV secolo*. Padua: Istituto per la storia ecclesiastica padovana, 1988.

Riley-Smith, Jonathan. "The Crown of France and Acre, 1254–1291." In *France and the Holy Land: Frankish Culture at the End of the Crusades*, edited by Daniel

H. Weiss and Lisa Mahoney, 45–62. Baltimore: Johns Hopkins University Press, 2004.
– *The First Crusaders, 1095–1131*. Cambridge: Cambridge University Press, 1997.
– "Towards an Understanding of the Crusade as an Institution." In *Urbs Capta: The Fourth Crusade and Its Consequences/La IVe Croisade et ses consequences*, edited by Angeliki Laiou, 71–88. Réalités byzantines 10. Paris: Lethielleux, 2005.
Rist, Rebecca. *The Papacy and Crusading in Europe, 1198–1245*. London: Continuum, 2009.
– *Popes and Jews, 1095–1291*. Oxford: Oxford University Press, 2016.
Ritchey, Sara. *Acts of Care: Recovering Women in Late Medieval Health*. Ithaca: Cornell University Press, 2021.
– "Affective Medicine: Later Medieval Healing Communities and the Feminization of Health Care Practices in the Thirteenth-Century Low Countries." *Journal of Medieval Religious Cultures* 40 (2014): 113–43.
– *Holy Matter: Changing Perceptions of the Material World in Late Medieval Christianity*. Ithaca: Cornell University Press, 2014.
– "Saints' Lives as Efficacious Texts: Cistercian Monks, Religious Women, and Curative Reading, c. 1250–1330." *Speculum* 92 (2017): 1101–43.
Robinson, Ian S. *Authority and Resistance in the Investiture Contest: The Polemical Literature of the Late Eleventh Century*. Manchester: Manchester University Press, 1978.
Roest, Bert. "Female Preaching in the Late Medieval Franciscan Tradition." *Franciscan Studies* 62 (2004): 119–54.
– "The Franciscan School System: Re-assessing the Early Evidence (ca. 1220–1260)." In *Franciscan Organisation in the Mendicant Context: Formal and Informal Structures of the Friars' Lives and Ministry in the Middle Ages*, edited by Michael Robson and Jens Röhrkasten, 269–96. Berlin: LIT Verlag, 2010.
– "Franciscan Studies and the Repercussions of the Digital Revolution: A Proposal." *Franciscan Studies* 74 (2016): 375–84.
– "Observant Reform in Religious Orders." In *Christianity in Western Europe c. 1100–c. 1500*, edited by Miri Rubin and Walter Simons, 446–57. Cambridge: Cambridge University Press, 2009.
– *Order and Disorder: The Poor Clares between Foundation and Reform*. Leiden: Brill, 2013.
Roisin, Simone. *L'hagiographie cistercienne dans le diocèse de Liège au XIIIe siècle*. Louvain: Bibliothèque de l'Université, 1947.
Roncière, Charles M. de La. *Religion paysanne et religion urbaine en toscane (c. 1280–c. 1450)*. Aldershot: Variorum, 1994.
Rosser, G. *The Art of Solidarity in the Middle Ages: Guilds in England, 1250–1550*. Oxford: Oxford University Press, 2015.

Rouse, Richard, and Mary Rouse. "French Literature and the Counts of Saint-Pol, ca. 1178–1377." *Viator* 41 (2010): 101–40. Reprinted in *Bound Fast with Letters: Medieval Writers, Readers and Texts*, 308–56. Notre Dame, IN: University of Notre Dame Press, 2013.

Ruff, Mark Edward. *The Battle for the Catholic Past in Germany, 1945–1980*. Cambridge: Cambridge University Press, 2017.

– "Katholische Kirche und Entnazifizierung." In *Die katholische Kirche im Dritten Reich. Eine Einführung*, edited by Mark Edward Ruff and Christoph Kösters Freiburg, 142–53. Basel and Vienna: Herder, 2011.

Rusconi, Roberto, ed. *Il Movimento religioso femminile in Umbria nei secoli XIII–XI. Atti del Convegno internazionale di studio nell'ambito delle celebrazioni per l'VIII centenario della nascita di S. Francesco d'Assisi. Città di Castello, 27–28–29 ottobre 1982*. Florence: La Nuova Italia Editrice, 1984.

Ryan, Michael A. "Antichrist in the Middle Ages: Plus ça change . . ." *History Compass* 7 (2009): 1581–92.

Sabatier, Paul. *Modernism: The Jowett Lectures, 1908*. New York: Charles Scribner's Sons, 1908.

– *Vie de s. François d'Assise*. Paris: Fischbacher, 1894.

Sackville, Lucy J., *Heresy and Heretics in the Thirteenth Century: The Textual Representations*. Heresy and Inquisition in the Middle Ages 1. Woodbridge: York Medieval Press, 2011.

Salisbury, Joyce E. "Gendered Sexuality." In *Handbook of Medieval Sexuality*, edited by Vern L. Bullough and James A. Brundage, 81–102. New York: Garland, 2000.

Sánchez Herrero, José, ed. *CXIX Reglas de Hermandades y Cofradía andaluzas. Siglos XIV, XV y XVI*. Huelva: Universidad de Huelva, 2002.

Sancho Fibla, Sergi. *Escribir y meditar. La obra de Marguerite d'Oingt, cartuja del siglo XIII*. Madrid: Siruela, 2018.

– "Li vida de Doucelina de Dinha, de Felipa Porcelleta. Imaginería, práticas devocionales y legitimacion de la vida beguina en el Mediterráneo." In *Voces de mujeres en la Edad Media*, edited by Esther Corral Díaz, 296–308. Berlin: De Gruyter, 2018.

Sauerländer, Willibald. *Von Sens bis Strassburg: Ein Beitrag zur kunstgeschichtlichen Stellung der Strassburger Querhausskulpturen*. Berlin: W. de Gruyter, 1966.

Scase, Wendy. *Piers Plowman and the New Anticlericalism*. Cambridge Studies in Medieval Literature 4. Cambridge: Cambridge University Press, 1989.

Scheepsma, Wybren. *The Limburg Sermons: Preaching in the Medieval Low Countries at the Turn of the Fourteenth Century*. Leuven: Brill, 2008.

Schenk, Jochen. *Templar Families: Landowning Families and the Order of the Temple in France, c. 1120–1307*. Cambridge: Cambridge University Press, 2012.

Schmidt, Hans-Joachim. "Sinngebung von Vergangenheit und Zukunft – Vorstellungen zum Antichrist im hohen Mittelalter." In *Der Antichrist*.

Historische und systematische Zugänge, edited by Mariano Delgado and Volker Leppin, 137–71. Studien zur christlichen Religions- und Kulturgeschichte 14. Stuttgart: Kohlhammer, 2011.

Schmitt, Jean-Claude. "Une histoire religieuse du Moyen Age est-elle possible? (Jalons pour une anthropologie du christianisme medieval)." In *Il mestiere di storico del Medioevo*, edited by F. Lepori and F. Santi, 73–83. Spoleto: Centro italiano di studi sull'alto Medioevo, 1994.

Schmitz-Esser, Romedio. "The Cursed and the Holy Body: Burning Corpses in the Middle Ages." *Journal of Medieval and Early Modern Studies* 45 (2015): 131–57.

Schnerb, Bertrans. "Piété et culture d'une noble dame au milieu du XVe siècle: l'example de Marguerite de Bécourt, dame de Santes." In *Au Cloitre et dans le Monde*, edited by Patrick Henriet and Anne-Marie Legras, 235–45. Paris: Presses de l'Université Paris-Sorbonne, 2000.

Schreiner, Klaus. "Gab es im Mittelalter und in der Frühen Neuzeit Antiklerikalismus?" *Zeitschrift für Historische Forschung* 21 (1994): 513–21.

Schultz, Daniel J. "Histories of the Present: Interpreting the Poverty of St. Francis." In *World of St. Francis of Assisi: Essays in Honor of William R. Cook*, edited by Bradley Franco and Beth Mulvaney, 176–92. Leiden: Brill, 2015.

Schulze, Winfried. *Deutsche Geschichtswissenschaft nach 1945*. HZ Beihefte 10. München: Oldenbourg, 1989.

Schulze, Winfried, and Otto Gerhard Oexle, eds. *Deutsche Historiker im Nationalsozialismus*. Frankfurt am Main: Fischer, 1999.

Schürer, Markus. "Innovation und Variabilität als Instrumente göttlicher Pädagogik: Anselm von Havelberg und seine Position in den Diskursen um die Legitimät religiöser Lebensformen." *Mittellateinisches Jahrbuch: internationale Zeitschrift für Mediävistik* 42 (2007): 373–96.

Seeberg, Erich. *Meister Eckhart*. Philosophie und Geschichte 50. Tübingen: Mohr, 1934.

Seláf, Levente. "Le Modèle absolu de la princesse charitable. La première légende vernaculaire de sainte Élisabeth de Hongrie et sa réception." *Le Moyen Âge* 124 (2018): 371–96.

– "Párhuzamos életrajzok: Szent Erzsébet és Isabelle de France legendái." In *Árpád-házi Szent Erzsébet kultusza a 13–16. Században*, edited by Dávid Falvay, 141–50. Budapest: Magyarok Nagyasszonya Ferences Rendtartomány, 2009.

Şenocak, Neslihan. "The Making of Franciscan Poverty." *Revue Mabillon*, n.s. 24 (2013): 5–26.

– *The Poor and the Perfect: The Rise of Learning in the Franciscan Order, 1209–1310*. Ithaca: Cornell University Press, 2012.

– "Twelfth-Century Italian Confraternities as Institutions of Pastoral Care." *Journal of Medieval History* 42 (2016): 202–25.

Shahar, Shulamith. *Women in a Medieval Heretical Sect: Agnes and Huguette the Waldensians*. Translated by Yael Lotan. Rochester, NY: Boydell, 2001.

Shulevitz, Deborah. "Historiography of Heresy: The Debate over 'Catharism' in Medieval Languedoc." *History Compass* 17 (2019): 1–11.

Siberry, Elizabeth. "The Crusading Counts of Nevers." *Nottingham Medieval Studies* 34 (1990): 64–70.

Simons, Walter. *Beguine Communities in the Medieval Low Countries, 1200–1565*. Philadelphia: University of Pennsylvania Press, 2001.

Sinex, Margaret. "Echoic Irony in Walter Map's Satire against the Cistercians." *Comparative Literature* 54 (2002): 275–90.

Šmahel, František. *Husitská revoluce. 2. Kořeny České reformace*. Prague: Karolinum, 1996.

Smith, Caroline. *Crusading in the Age of Joinville*. Aldershot: Ashgate, 2006.

Somerset, Fiona. "'Mark Him Wel for He Is on of Þo': Training the 'Lewed' Gaze to Discern Hypocrisy." *ELH* 68 (2001): 315–34.

Sommé, Monique. *Isabelle de Portugal, duchesse de Bourgogne: Une femme au pouvoir au XVe siècle*. Lille: Presses Universitaires du Septentrion, 1998.

Soukupová, Helena. "Klášter minoritů a klarisek v Českém Krumlově." *Průzkumy památek* 2 (1999): 73.

Spiegel, Gabrielle M. *Romancing the Past: The Rise of Vernacular Prose Historiography in Thirteenth-Century France*. Berkeley: University of California Press, 1993.

Stacpoole, Alberic. "The Making of a Monastic Historian – II." *Ampleforth Journal* 58 (1975): 19–38.

Stanger, Mary D. "Literary Patronage at the Medieval Court of Flanders." *French Studies* 11 (1957): 214–29.

Steckel, Sita. "Historicizing the Religious Field. Adapting Theories of the Religious Field for the Study of Medieval and Early Modern Europe." *Church History and Religious Culture* 99 (2019): 331–70.

– *Kulturen des Lehrens im Früh- und Hochmittelalter: Autorität, Wissenskonzepte und Netzwerke von Gelehrten*. Norm und Struktur 39. Cologne: Böhlau, 2011.

– "Narratives of Resistance: Arguments against the Mendicants in the Works of Matthew Paris and William of Saint-Amour." In *Thirteenth Century England XV. Authority and Resistance in the Age of Magna Charta*, edited by Janet Burton, Phillipp Schofield, and Björn Weiler, 157–77. Woodbridge: Boydell, 2015.

– "Rhetorische Spaltungen. Zur Dynamik von Invektivität im Inneren des hoch- und spätmittelalterlichen lateinischen Christentums." *Saeculum* 70 (2020): 39–74.

– "*Une querelle des theologiens*? 'Polemics' In the historiography of the secular-mendicant controversy." In *Les régimes de polémicité au Moyen Âge*, edited by Bénédicte Sère, 83–97. Rennes: Presses universitaires de Rennes, 2019.

– "Verging on the Polemical: Towards an Interdisciplinary Approach to Medieval Religious Polemic." *Medieval Worlds* 7 (2018): 2–60.
Stinson, Timothy L. "Illumination and Interpretation: The Depiction and Reception of Faus Semblant in Roman de La Rose Manuscripts." *Speculum* 87 (2012): 469–98.
Straka, Josef. *Spisy Tomáše ze Štítného. Řeči nedělní a sváteční*. Prague: Česká akademie věd a umění, 1929.
Strozier, Charles B., and Boyd, Katharine A. "The Apocalyptic." In *The Fundamentalist Mindset: Psychological Perspectives on Religion, Violence, and History*, edited by Charles B. Strozier, David M. Terman, James W. Jones, and Katherine A. Boyd, 29–37. New York: Oxford University Press, 2010.
Symes, Carol. "Popular Literacies and the First Historians of the First Crusade." *Past and Present* 235 (2017): 37–67.
Szerszynski, Bronislaw. "Praise Be to You, Earth-Beings." *Environmental Humanities* 8 (2016): 291–7.
Szittya, Penn R. *The Antifraternal Tradition in Medieval Literature*. Princeton, NJ: Princeton University Press, 1986.
Tarrant, Jacqueline. "The Clementine Decrees on the Beguines: Conciliar and Papal Versions." *Archivum Historiae Pontificae* 12 (1974): 300–8.
Taylor, Frederick. *Exorcising Hitler. The Occupation and Denazification of Germany*. New York: Bloomsbury, 2011.
Tent, James F. *Mission on the Rhine. Reeducation and Denazification in American-Occupied Germany*. Chicago: University of Chicago Press, 1982.
Terpstra, Nicholas. *Lay Confraternities and Civic Religion in Renaissance Bologna*. Cambridge: Cambridge University Press, 1995.
Terry, Wendy, and Robert Stauffer, eds. *A Companion to Marguerite Porete and the Mirror of Simple Souls*. Leiden: Brill, 2017.
Thomas, Peter D. *The Gramscian Moment: Philosophy, Hegemony and Marxism*. Leiden: Brill, 2009.
Thompson, Augustine. *Cities of God: The Religion of the Italian Communes, 1125–1325*. University Park: Pennsylvania State University Press, 2005.
– *Francis of Assisi: A New Biography*. Ithaca: Cornell University Press, 2012.
Thorpe, Lewis. "Walter Map and Gerald of Wales." *Medium Ævum* 47 (1978): 6–21.
Tietz, M. "Guiot de Provins." In *Lexikon des Mittelalters*, col. 1787. Vol. 4. Munich: Metzler, 1989.
Todeschini, Giacomo. *Franciscan Wealth: From Voluntary Poverty to Market Society*. Translated by Donatella Melucci. New York: Saint Bonaventure University, 2009.
Traver, Andrew G. "The Forging of an Intellectual Defense of Mendicancy in the Medieval University." In *The Origin, Development, and Refinement of Medieval Religious Mendicancies*, edited by Donald Prudlo, 157–96. Brill's Companions to the Christian Tradition 24. Leiden: Brill, 2011.

- "Rewriting History? The Parisian Secular Masters' Apologia of 1254." *History of Universities* 15 (1999): 9–45.
Trotter, D.A. *Medieval French Literature and the Crusades, 1100–1300*. Geneva: Librairie Droz, 1988.
Tyerman, Christopher. "Erdmann, Runciman and the End of Tradition?" In *The Debate on the Crusades*, edited by Christopher Tyerman, 182–215. Manchester: University of Manchester Press, 2011.
van Engen, Hildo. *De derde orde van Sint Franciscus in het middeleeuwse bisdom Utrecht*. Hilversum, Netherlands: Verloren, 2006.
Van Engen, John. "The Christian Middle Ages as an Historiographical Problem." *The American Historical Review* 91 (1986): 519–52.
– "Friar Johannes Nyder on Laypeople Living as Religious in the World." In *Vita Religiosa m Mittelatter: Festschrift für Kaspar Elm zum 70. Geburtstag*, edited by Franz J. Felten, Nikolas Jaspert and Stephanie Haarländer, 582–615. Berlin: Duncker & Humblot, 1999.
– "The Future of Medieval Church History." *Church History* 71 (2002), 492–522.
– "Marguerite (Porete) of Hainaut and the Medieval Low Countries." In *Marguerite Porete et le* Miroir des simples âmes, edited by Sean L. Field, Robert E. Lerner, and Sylvain Piron, 25–68. Paris: Vrin, 2013.
– "Multiple Options: The World of the Fifteenth-Century Church." *Church History* 77 (2008): 257–84.
– "Recovering the Multiple Worlds of the Medieval Church: Thoughtful Lives, Inspired Critics, and Changing Narratives." *The Catholic Historical Review* 104 (2018): 589–613.
– *Sisters and Brothers of the Common Life: The Devotio Moderna and the World of the Later Middle Ages*. The Middle Ages Series. Philadelphia: University of Pennsylvania Press, 2008.
Van Tricht, Filip. *The Latin* Renovatio *of Byzantium: The Empire of Constantinople (1204–1228)*. Leiden: Brill, 2011.
– "Robert of Courtenay (1221–1227): An Idiot on the Throne of Constantinople?" *Speculum* 88 (2013): 996–1034.
Vanderputten, Steven. *Dark Age Nunneries: The Ambiguous Identity of Female Monasticism, 800–1050*. Ithaca: Cornell University Press, 2018.
– *Medieval Monasticisms: Forms and Expressions of the Monastic Life in the Latin West*. Oldenbourg Grundriss der Geschichte. Vol. 47. Berlin: de Gruyter, 2020.
Vauchez, André. *Francis of Assisi: The Life and Afterlife of a Medieval Saint*. Translated by Michael F. Cusato. New Haven, CT: Yale University Press, 2012.
– *François d'Assisi: Entre histoire et mémoire*. Paris: Fayard, 2009.
– "François d'Assise rendu à l'histoire: l'œuvre de Giovanni Miccoli." *Etudes franciscaines*, n.s. 1 (2008): fasc. 1–2, 7–19.

– *The Laity in the Middle Ages*. Translated by Daniel E. Bornstein. Notre Dame, IN: University of Notre Dame Press, 1983.
– "Prosélytisme et action anti-hérétique en milieu féminin au XIIIe siècle: la Vie de Marie d'Oignies (+ 1213) par Jacques de Vitry." *Problèmes d'Histoire du Christianisme* 17 (1987): 95–110.
– *Sainthood in the Later Middle Ages*. Translated by Jean Birrell. Cambridge: Cambridge University Press, 1997.
Verger, Jacques. "*Coacta ac periculosa societas*. La difficile intégration des réguliers à l'Université de Paris au XIIIe siècle." In *Vivre en société au Moyen Âge: Occident chrétien VIe–XVe siècle*, edited by Claude Carozzi, Daniel Le Blévec, and Huguette Taviani-Carozzi, 261–80. Aix-en-Provence: Presses universitaires de Provence, 2008.
Vigueur, Jean-Claude Maire. *The Forgotten Story: Rome in the Communal Period*. Translated by David Fairservice. Rome: Viella, 2016.
Vincent, C. *Des chrités bien ordonnées: les confréries normandes de la fin du XIIIe siècle au début du XVIe siècle*. Paris: École normale supérieure, 1988.
– *Les confréries médiévales dans le Royaume de France: XIII–XVe siècle*. Bibliothèque Albin Michel Histoire. Paris: A. Michel, 1994.
Vitolo, Giovanni. *Istituzioni ecclesiastiche e vita religiosa dei laici nel Mezzogiorno medievale: il codice della Confraternita di S. Maria di Montefusco (sec. XII)*. Rome: Herder, 1982.
Voigt, Jörg. "Margarete Porete als Vertreterin eines freigeistig-häretischen Beginentums? Das Verhältnis zwischen den Bischöfen von Cambrai und den Beginen nach dem Häresieprozess gegen Margarete Porete († 1310)." *Meister Eckhart Jahrbuch* ('Meister Eckhart und die Freiheit') 12 (2018): 31–54.
Vollmann-Profe, Gisela, ed. *Ludus de Antichristo*. Litterae – Göppinger Beiträge zur Textgeschichte 82. 2 vols. Lauterburg: Kümmerle, 1981.
Vondung, Klaus. *Magie und Manipulation. Ideologischer Kult und politische Religion des Nationalsozialismus*. Göttingen: Vandenhoeck and Ruprecht, 1971.
Wakefield, Walter L., and Austin P. Evans. *Heresies of the High Middle Ages. Selected Sources Translated and Annotated*. Records of Western Civilization. New York: Columbia University Press, 1991.
Walsham, Alexandra. "Migrations of the Holy: Explaining Religious Change in Medieval and Early Modern Europe." *Journal of Medieval and Early Modern Studies* 44 (2014): 241–80.
Waters, Claire M. *Angels and Earthly Creatures: Preaching, Performance, and Gender in the Later Middle Ages*. Philadelphia: University of Pennsylvania Press, 2004.
– *Translating Clergie: Status, Education, and Salvation in Thirteenth-Century Vernacular Texts*. Philadelphia: University of Pennsylvania Press, 2016.

Watson, Nicholas. "Whited Sepulchres: Towards a History of Hypocrisy, 1100–1400." Paper Presentation, 2010.

Watts, John. *A Canticle of Love: The Story of the Franciscan Sisters of the Immaculate Conception.* Edinburgh: John Donald, 2006.

Weber, Alison. *Devout Laywomen in the Early Modern World.* London: Routledge, 2016.

Weber, Max. "Objectivity in Social Science and Social Policy." In *The Methodology of the Social Sciences,* edited and translated by E.A. Shils and H.A. Finch, 50–112. New York: Free Press, 1949.

Wehrli-Johns, Martina. "Voraussetzungen und Perspektiven mittelalterlicher Laienfrömmigkeit seit Innozenz III. Eine Auseinandersetzung mit Herbert Grundmanns 'Religiösen Bewegungen.'" *Mitteilungen des Instituts für Österreichische Geschichtsforschung* 104 (1996): 286–309.

Weiß, Marian. "Mittellateinische Goliardendichtung und ihr historischer Kontext: Komik im Kosmos der Kathedralschulen Nordfrankreichs." PhD diss., Justus-Liebig-Universität Gießen, 2018.

Weltecke, Dorothea. "Space, Entanglement and Decentralisation: On How to Narrate the Transcultural History of Christianity (550 to 1350 CE)." In *Locating Religions: Contact, Diversity, and Translocality,* edited by Reinhold Glei and Nikolas Jaspert, 315–44. Leiden: Brill, 2017.

– "Über Religion vor der 'Religion': Konzeptionen vor der Entstehung des neuzeitlichen Begriffs." In *Religion als Prozess: Kulturwissenschaftliche Wege der Religionsforschung,* edited by Thomas G. Kirsch, Rudolf Schlögl, and Dorothea Weltecke, 13–34. Paderborn: Ferdinand Schöningh, 2015.

Wenzel, Siegfried. "The Continuing Life of William Peraldus's 'Summa vitiorum.'" In *Ad Litteram: Authoritative Texts and Their Medieval Readers,* edited by Mark D. Jordan and Kent Emery Jr., 135–63. Notre Dame, IN: University of Notre Dame Press, 1992.

Werner, Karl Ferdinand. *Das NS-Geschichtsbild und die deutsche Geschichtswissenschaft.* Stuttgart: Kohlhammer, 1967.

Wesjohann, Achim. *Mendikantische Gründungserzählungen im 13. und 14. Jahrhundert: Mythen als Element institutioneller Eigengeschichtsschreibung der mittelalterlichen Franziskaner, Dominikaner und Augustiner-Eremiten.* Berlin: LIT Verlag, 2012.

Wessley, Stephen. "The Thirteenth-Century Guglielmites: Salvation Through Women." In *Medieval Women,* edited by Derek Baker, 289–304. Studies in Church History 14. Oxford: Basil Blackwell, 1978.

Whalen, Brett E. "Joachim of Fiore and the Division of Christendom." *Viator* 34 (2003): 89–108.

– "Joachim of Fiore, Apocalyptic Conversion, and the 'Persecuting Society.'" *History Compass* 8 (2010): 682–91.

Winter, Zikmund. *Kulturní obraz Českých měst: život veřejný v XV. a XVI. věku.* Prague: Nákladem MaticeČeské, 1890–2.

– *Život církevní v Čechách: kulturně-historický obraz z XV. a XVI. století.* Prague: Česká akademie císaře Františka Josefa pro vědy, slovesnost a umění, 1895–6.

Wogan-Browne, Jocelyn, Nicholas Watson, Andrew Taylor, and Ruth Evans, eds. *The Idea of the Vernacular: An Anthology of Middle English Literary Theory, 1280–1520.* Exeter: University of Exeter Press, 1999.

Wolf, Kenneth Baxter. *The Poverty of Riches: St Francis of Assisi Reconsidered.* Oxford: Oxford University Press, 2003.

Yee, Ethan L. "The Burden of Forgiveness: Franciscans' Impact on Penitential Practices in the Thirteenth Century." PhD diss., Columbia University, 2019.

Young, Spencer. *Scholarly Community at the Early University of Paris: Theologians, Education and Society, 1215–1248.* Cambridge: Cambridge University Press, 2014.

Zacchi, Gilberto, ed. *Realtà archivistiche a confronto: le associazioni dei parroci.* Atti del Convegno di Ravenna (24 September 2010). Modena: Mucchi Editore, 2011.

Zhang, Xue Jiao. "How St. Francis Influenced Pope Francis' *Laudato Si'*." *Cross Currents* 66 (2016): 42–56.

Zöckler, Otto. "Das Lehrstück von den sieben Hauptsünden. Beiträge zur Dogmen- und zur Sittengeschichte, insbesonders der vorreformatorischen Zeit." In *Biblische und kirchenhistorische Studien 3*, edited by Otto Zöckler. Munich: C.H. Beck, 1893.

Index

Abbeville, 250
Abelard, Peter, 95
Adtendite a falsis prophetis (anonymous, Abelard), 95–6
Abbeys, 134–5, 151, 193, 196, 219, 268
Abbots, 6, 86, 91–3, 175, 214, 326
Abels, Richard, 267
Abruzzo, 291
Acre, 152, 246
Ad nostrum (conciliar decree), 245
Agnes (beguine, daughter of Tomáš of Štítný), 322–5
Agnes of Bohemia/Agnes of Prague, Saint, 52, 315
Agnes of Harcourt, 12, 190–1, 193–204; 'Letter on Louis IX and Longchamp', 196; *Life of Isabelle of France*, 190–1, 193–4, 196–204
Agnes of Nevers, 150
Aire, 250
Alanus Insulanus, 252
Albert of Uničov /Sigismundus Albicus de Uniczow, Archbishop, 320
Albigensian Crusade, 134
Albík of Uničov, Archbishop, 326
Alexander IV, Pope, 102, 194
Alexander V, Pisan Pope, 248
allegory, 10, 79–80, 84, 322

alms, 3, 132, 134, 150, 152, 221, 246, 250, 297–8, 317
Alphandéry, Paul, 11, 130–2, 139
altar, 9, 29, 86, 151, 219, 268–9, 297
Amaury of Montfort, 137
Americas, xiv, 48
Amice of Joigny, 137
Amiens, 226–7
Andreas, Willy, 34
Anna of Frimburk, 317
Anna of Mochov, 317
Anselm of Havelberg (Premonstratensian canon), 98–9, 104–5; *Anticimenon*, 98
anthropology, 6, 133
Antichrist, 80, 85, 88–9, 91, 101, 103, 109, 111, 273
anti-clericalism, 82, 84, 108–10, 171, 267
anti-fraternalism, 82, 84, 103
antisemitism, 27
Apocalypse (four horsemen), 80–9, 95, 98
Apocalypticism, 15, 89, 223, 271, 273–4
apostles, 45–6, 55, 62, 64, 102–4, 172–3, 176–80, 221, 223, 226
apostleship, 171–2

Apostolic Brethren (religious movement), 271, 277–8
apostolic ideal. See *Vita apostolica*
apostolic life. See *Vita apostolica*
apostolic succession, 58, 178, 270, 278
Apulia, 137
Aquinas, Thomas, Saint, 175, 225
Aracoeli, 297
Arbrissel, Robert, 170
Archiv für Kulturgeschichte, 27
Ardennes, 217
Art Nouveau Municipal House, Prague, 318
asceticism, 88, 91–2, 94, 106, 108
Assisi, 54, 60, 197, 294, 298
Augsburg Settlement, 23
Augsburger Religionsfrieden. See Augsburg Settlement
Augsburg Diet, 26
Augustine of Hippo, Saint, 322; Rule of St. Augustine, 136, 245, 247
Augustinian Order, 105, 253
authenticity (monastic), 93
authenticity (religious), 10, 46, 52, 53, 80, 103, 108–9
Auxerre, 127, 135–7, 150–1
Avignon, 248, 290

Baltic, 30
Balkans, 131
baptism, xv, 9, 29
Barbora, Saint, 323
Barnhouse, Lucy, 246
Bartlett, Robert, 267
Battle of Hattin, 142
Bayerische Akademie der Wissenschaften, 26
Beatas, 251
Beatrice of Ornacieux, 190, 193–6, 201
Becket, Thomas (chapel), 135
Bede, the venerable, 322

Beguinages, 215, 276; Cambrai, 218–19; Paris, 214, 221, 224, 226–30; Prague, 310–11, 315–18; Valenciennes, 191, 218; Vilvoorde, 218
beguines, 4, 12, 14, 80, 83, 144, 192, 194, 307; and canon law, 244, 252, 255, 265; and the Czech Reformation, 307, 310, 325–7; and heterodoxy, 191, 195, 216, 224, 245, 273–4, 276, 312, 316, 327; and mysticism, 144, 191; and pastoral care/reform, 214–20, 222–4, 227–30, 308–9, 311–12, 322; of Prague, 307, 310, 312–21; and secular-mendicant conflict, 225, 230; in sermons, 214–15, 218–20, 225–7, 229; and the 'women's religious movement', 190, 215–16, 242, 327
Bekennende Kirche. See Confessing Church
Bekyně (satirical poem), 325
Benedetti, Marina, 268
Benedictine Order, xiv, 91, 93–4, 99, 175, 189, 276, 294; houses, 172; Rule of Saint Benedict, 93, 292, 294
Benson, Robert, xiv
Benz, Ernst, 31
bequests, 134, 135, 150, 310, 314
Bergue-Saint-Winoc, 249
Berlin, 25
Bernard of Clairvaux, 86, 87, 89–93, 95, 322; *Ad Robertum*, 93; *Apologia*, 93; Parables, 89; Sentences, 86; *Sermo 66*, 90
Bernard of Luxembourg, 268, 271
Bernay, 250
Bescochier, Arnoul, 227, 229
Bethlehem (chapel, Prague), 311, 316–17, 319–20, 325
Bětka of Prague, 320
Betlémský, Václav (Václav of Drachov), 320

Béthune, 142, 144, 250
Biassono (Humiliate house), 277
Bibliothèque nationale de France (BnF), 145–8, 197–8, 203–4
Biller, Peter, xix–x, 276
Birgitta/Bridget of Sweden, 265, 323–4; *Revelationes*, 323–4
bishops, 6, 86, 88, 101, 104–5, 134, 175, 218–20, 226, 229, 244, 246, 266, 271–2, 313
(von) Bismarck, Otto, xiii, 23
Black Sisters (Augustinian nursing order), 254
Blanche of Castile, 199
Bohemia, 14, 268–9, 308, 312, 315, 319; Bohemian Reformation, 307–8, 310, 317; Bohemian Revolution, 307–8, 317
Bolek family, 314
Bolgia, Claudia, 294
Bonaventure, Saint (Franciscan minister general), 194
Bonelle, Cursius Nero, 277
Bonfadini, Antonio, 270
Bonhoeffer, Dietrich, 28
Boniface VIII, Pope, 244, 271, 275, 289
Book of Revelations, 89
Book of the Doctrine of the Christian, 323
Bornkamm, Heinrich, 32
Borst, Arno, xvi, 25–6
Boves, 138
Brenner, Elma, 246
breviary, 152
Brindisi, 137, 150
de Broda, Andreas, 327
Bruges, 250
Buddhism, 110
Bull, Marcus, 133
burghers, 129, 136, 311, 315, 317, 320
Burgundy, 127
Burnham, Louisa, xix, 273–4
Burschenschaften, 24

buttresses (architecture), 127
Bynum, Caroline Walker, xiv, xx

Caciola, Nancy, 266
Caesarius of Heisterbach (Cistercian), 101
Caetani family, 290
Cambrai, 88, 218–22, 224, 226, 249, 272
canonization, 14, 196–7, 199, 204, 265, 288–90, 324
canon law, 13, 17, 104, 181, 243–4, 248, 263–6, 268, 271–2, 275
canons, 7, 81, 94, 98–9, 105, 135; 140, 172, 176, 178, 214, 218–22, 226; Notre-Dame de Tonnerre (house), 135
Canossa, xiii
Cantimpré, 218–19
Capetians, 47, 193–4, 196, 199
capitalism, 59
Capite, 288–9, 293
Carcassonne (siege), 134
cardinals, 50, 86, 105, 134, 271, 289–90, 293–6, 298
Caritas, 177, 219, 222–3, 227
Carmelite Order, 253
Carne, Gauthier, 226
Carthusian Order, 97, 99, 105, 190, 192, 195–6, 326
Čáslav, 320
Castellaneta (Apulia), 137
Catalogue of Turin, 292, 294, 296
Cathars (Albigensians), 88, 91–2, 95, 267, 276
cathedral chapter, 173, 176–8; Sens, 151
cathedral schools, 220
Catherine (beguine, daughter of Albert of Uničov), 320
Catherine of Nyněchov, 314
Catherine of Pasovaře, 319

Catherine of Siena, Saint, 265
Catholicism, 23–4, 27, 29, 46, 55–60, 62, 83
Cattanio, Longino, 271
Cecco of Ascoli, 272
Champagne (county), 136, 139; fairs, 146
Chansonniers, 140, 144–5, 152
Chapel of All Saints, Prague, 316
charisma, 4, 6, 9–10, 45–6, 48, 53, 92, 143, 193, 275, 288, 291, 293–5, 299
charity, 134–5, 137–8
Charles of Anjou, 196
Charles University, 309
Chartres, 94, 136
chastity, 91, 216, 248, 297
Châteauneuf-sur-Allier, 136
Chemnitz, 26
Chenu, Marie Dominique, xiv, 54, 56–8, 63
Chiaravalle, 268–9, 276–8
China, 48
Chotek, Bernard, 326
Chotková, Regina, 326
churches: Châteauneuf, 134; Cluny (*see* Cluny); Saint-Eustache, 227–8; San Pietro, 288; Santa Anastasia, 295; Santa Croce, 295; Santa Maria Sopra Minerva, 294; St-Adrien, 127; St-Aignan, 134; St. Anna, 318; St. Benedict, 314, 318; St-Étienne of Bourges, 134; St. Francis, 313, 315, 318; St. James the Greater, 313–15; St. Klement, 318; St. Sauveur, 219; St. Vitus, 321
Church Fathers, 181, 219, 229, 266, 322; texts, 85, 90
Christendom, xi–xii, xvii, 88, 182, 222, 291, 308, 312
Christmas, 181
Chuchle, 315

Cistercian houses: Bardelles, 134; Bellary, 134, 136; Bourras, 134; Celles, 135; Fontenay, 151; Jully, 134; La Charité, 134; L'Épeau, 134–5; Le Réconfort, 137, 151; Les Isles, 135, 151; Lézinnes, 151; Parthenon, 134; Pontigny, 134–5; Pronttmorigny, 134; Quincy, 134; Regny, 134; Rougement, 134; Saint-Loup de Noe, 151
Cistercian Order, 192, 218, 225, 244, 268, 292, 294; austerity, 93–4; customs, 93–4, 97, 172
Clare of Assisi, Saint, 51, 197, 199–200, 291, 298, 317; Clarissans, 52; Order of Saint Clare, 52, 289, 291, 298; Poor Clares, 52
Clement V, Pope, 265
Clement VII, Pope, 248
Clementine Constitutions, 265
clergy (secular), xi, 12, 80–1, 99, 102, 107–8, 176–8, 180–1, 183, 189, 193, 216–25, 230, 265, 267, 277, 307–9, 324–5
cloister, 3, 79–80, 99, 100, 217, 223, 225–6, 293–4, 298
Cluny, 64, 93; customs, 4, 93, 97, 105, 106
da Cocconato, Guido, 263, 269
Cologne, 91–2, 101, 103
colonialism, 132–3
Colonna, Giacomo, 289, 297–8
Colonna, Giovanni, 288–9, 296–9
Colonna, Margherita, 13, 288–91, 296–9
Colonna, Pietro, 289
communion, 144, 181–2, 195, 218, 270, 295, 313, 321, 325
Confessing Church, xvi, 28–9
confession, 181–2, 214, 224, 295, 313, 321, 323; public, 176

confraternities, 9, 11, 17, 170–1, 173–7, 179, 181, 183; Confraternity of Twelve Apostles, 176–8; Disciplinati; 183; Imola, 179; Laudesi, 183
Conon de Béthune, 142, 144
Constable, Giles, xiv, xx, 82, 93, 133; *Reformation of the Twelfth Century*, 82
Constantinople, 135, 150
conversion, 3, 16–17, 179, 181, 214, 221, 225, 269
Conze, Werner, 25
Corbigny, 136
Corpus Iuris Canonici, 265
Corry, Maya, 276
Cosne (chapel), 134
Council of Constance, 248
Council of Lyon (second), 244
Council of Pisa, 248
Council of Vienne, 215–16, 245–6, 265
Courson, Robert (Cardinal), 134
Courtly Love, 79, 229
Crohin, Jean, 251
cross (crusader), 127, 134, 137, 139, 141, 152
Cross (True Cross, relic), 142, 150–2
crusades, 11, 129, 134, 144, 146, 149, 151, 221, 292; art, 127; devotion (*see* devotion); historiography, 130–3, 140–2 (Barons, 138; First, 131–2, 138; Second, 138; Third, 138; Fourth, 138, 143, 152; Fifth, 129, 134, 138; Seventh, 152); preaching, 49, 130, 139; vow, 134–5, 138, 152–3
Cura mulierum, 215–16
Cusanus, Nicolaus, 30, 32

Dalarun, Jacques, xx, 200, 202
Damian, Peter, 171, 175
Damietta, 133, 135

Da Pirovano, Maifreda, 13, 263, 268–74, 276–8
Da Pirovano, Rainerio, 269
Decize (chapel), 134
Declaration of Barmen, 29
Denazification, 27, 30
Deutsches Archiv für Erforschung des Mittelalters, 27
Deutsche Christen. *See* German Christians
Devotio Moderna, xvii, xviii, 183, 247
devotion: collective, 170, 182, 184; Crusade, 129, 138; Marian, 106; and reform, 176, 250, 320; vernacular, 144, 151–2, 321–2; women, 139, 199, 242–3, 245, 253–5, 263, 276, 291, 296, 307
Diotesalvo (suspected heretic), 266
dissent, and politics, 266–7
Divine Office, 182, 249
Divine Providence, 60
Dixmude, 249–50
Dolany, 326–7
Dolcinists. *See* Apostolic Brethren
Dolcino of Novara, 263, 271–2, 275, 277–8
Domaválený, Barbara, 319
Domaválený, Martin, 319
Domažlice, 326
Dominic, Saint, 46, 293, 295
Dominican Order, 79, 101–2, 137, 140, 144, 151, 190, 192, 221, 225, 253, 265, 292–4, 318; Friars Preacher, 79, 101–2, 140, 144, 293; tertiaries, 175
Doornik, 249
Dorota, Saint, 323
Dorota 'Mydlářka', 320
Douai, 250
Douceline of Digne, 190, 193–5, 201
Druye (chapel), 134

Dunkirk, 249
Dupront, Alphonse, 132
Durango, 251

Easter, 181
Ecclesia (personification), 106
Ecclesia dei, 55, 57
École des hautes études, 131
Education, 12, 23, 29, 49, 88, 104, 106, 108–9, 140, 175, 182, 189, 216, 266, 307–10, 321–5, 327
Egypt, 134
Ekbert of Schönau (Benedictine abbot), 91
Eliška (abbess, daughter of Jan Řitka of Bezděcice), 326
Elizabeth of Hungary, 130, 199–200, 203, 243
Elliott, Dyan, 266
Elm, Kaspar, xvii
emotions, 131
enclosure, 219, 244–5, 247–8, 252–3, 293–8
endowment, 11, 134–6, 143, 149, 150–1
England, xiii–xiv, 96, 267, 270, 327
Entnazifizierung. *See* Denazification
Erdman, Carl, 11, 130–2
eschatology, 80, 85, 87–90, 94–6, 101–2, 104, 130, 308
d'Este, Obizzo III, 275
d'Este, Rainaldo, 275
Eucharist. *See* communion
Eudes of Burgundy, 152
Eudes of Rosny, 198
Eugenius IV, Pope, 249
Eusebius, 267
Eve (Old Testament figure), 267
Everwin of Steinfeld (Premonstratensian), 90

Exempla, 219, 224, 243, 309
Eymeux, 195–6

Faini, Marco, 276
fasting, 182
Felipa of Porcelet, 12, 190, 193–6, 201; *Life of Douceline of Digne*, 190, 193–4
feminism, xv, 15, 264
feudalism, xi, xii
Field, Sean L., 12, 272
Filles-Dieu (house for reformed prostitutes and penitents), 221
Fina of San Gimignano, 291
First World War, xv, 131
Flanders, 150
Fleury, 177
Florence, 266, 298
Fogl, Konrad, 318
Fondi, 248
France, 26, 88–9, 143, 153, 190–1, 193, 195–7, 199, 201, 204–5, 219–20, 228, 242, 251, 268, 307, 327
franchisement, 139, 135–7, 149, 153
Franciscan Order, 48, 55, 101, 110, 130, 171, 180, 182, 192, 225, 244, 288; criticism of, 102; 'Franciscan Question', 46, 60; Friars Minor, 45, 50, 52, 106, 291, 293–4, 297; hagiography, 10, 48, 199–201, 247, 298; and heterodoxy, 100–1, 273; historiography, 10, 46–51, 53–5, 60–3, 182; Joachites, 101; Observant Franciscans, 247, 250–1; Order of Penance, 170, 173, 180; persecution of religious minorities, 49, 265; 'Spiritual' Franciscans, 194; tertiaries, 13, 182, 242, 244, 246–9, 251–4, 294, 315; and women religious/semi-religious, 51, 140, 190, 193–5, 198, 200–1, 247, 249, 251, 254, 289–94, 296–8

Francis of Assisi, Saint, 194–5, 197, 244, 294–6, 298–9; and crusade, 130; and historiography, 45–55, 58–65; and vernacular, 3, 7, 8, 10, 15, 19
Frederick III (of Sicily), 271
'Free Spirit' (religious movement), 192, 267
Freiberger, Henzl, 315
French (heretics). *See* Cathars
French (literature), 105, 140, 229
French Revolution, xi, xii, xv, 175
friars, xiv, 4, 79–80, 82–4, 101–4, 106, 108, 151, 170, 191, 196, 198, 200–1, 223, 225–6, 249, 253, 274, 277, 288–9, 294–5, 298; Friars Minor (*see* Franciscan Order); Friars Preacher (*see* Dominican Order)
Freud, Sigmund, 131
Fulk of Neuilly, 131
Furnis, 249

Gabriel (Archangel), 269
Galvez, Marisa, 139, 141–2, 144, 146, 153
Gaucher of St-Pol, 152
Gaudium et Spes (constitution, Vatican II), 56
Gautier of Joigny, 137
Gebhardt Handbuch der deutschen Geschichte, 27
Genoa, 134
Gerard of Abbeville, 226
Gerard I of Cambrai (Bishop), 88
German (Language). *See* vernacular
German Christians, 28–9
Germany, 8, 12, 23–5, 27–9, 32, 34, 91, 100, 190, 195, 274, 307, 327
Gerson, Jean, 265
Ghent, 250
Gibbon, Edward, xii
Giotto, 45, 50, 64

Giovanna of Signa, 291
Giraldus Cambrensis, 95
Glaubensbewegung Deutsche Christen. *See* Movement German Christians
Godfrey of Fontaines, 192, 215, 217
Goetz, Walter, xv, 26–8, 30
Gospel, 19, 54, 56–7, 61, 178–9, 182, 220, 225, 270
Grandmontensians, 105
Great Depression, 26, 34
Great Dispersion, 217
Greece, 134
Gregory IX, Pope/Cardinal Hugolino, 182, 293; *Memoriale Propositi*, 182
Gregory XI, Pope, 247
Gregory the Great, Pope, 247, 322
Grey Sisters, 12–13, 242–3, 248–55
Grundmann, Herbert: biography, xv, 26–30; church membership, 27–30, 33–5; concept of 'religious movements', 8, 11, 16, 23, 34, 46, 53–4, 57, 81, 129–30, 133, 139, 153, 170–1, 179; historiography, 5–19, 23–5, 30, 46–7, 51, 53–4, 57–8, 62–3, 79, 81, 83–5, 92, 100–1, 105, 107–8, 110–11, 129–33, 140–1, 153, 170–4, 179, 181–2; and National Socialism, 25–7, 30, 33; scholarship, 30–4; on women, 12–13, 51, 133, 140, 170, 189–93, 195, 198, 201, 215–18, 230, 264, 290, 292, 299
Guglielma of Milan, 263, 265, 268–70, 274, 277–8
Guglielmites, 268–71, 273, 278
Gui, Bernard, 271
Guiard of Cambrai, 224
Guiard of Cressonart, 272
Guiard of Laon, 217–18, 229
Guibert of Tournai, 198, 243

Guida, Marco, 197
Guido of Vicenza, 271
guilds, 9, 173–4
Guillaume de Loris, 79
Guillaume de Nangis, 273
Guiot de Dijon, 144
Guiot de Provins, 105, 107
Guy III (Count of Chatillon), 150
Guy IV (Count of Forez), 135–7
Guy IV, Châtelain de Coucy, 142
Guy V (Count of Forez), 150–1, 153
Guy of Châtillon (Count of St-Pol), 135

Habilitationsschrift, 26
habit (fraternal), 50, 79
habit (monastic), 13, 88, 93–4, 105, 172
Hadewijch, 191
hagiography, 10, 46–8, 55, 130, 194, 196–7, 199–201, 217, 229, 243, 290, 298, 323
Harrison, Ellen, 267
Haskins, Charles Homer, xiv
Háta (Agáta/Agnes), Saint, 323
Haudriettes, 227
Haudry, Jeanne, 227
Haudry, Stephen, 227
Hautpont, 250
Hazmburk, 317
Heidelberg Akademie der Wissenschaften, 30
Heimpel, Hermann, 25–6, 31
Henry IV (German king), 87
Henry of Avranches, 101; *Prophetia Hyldegardis de falsis fratribus*, 101–2
Henry of Chamayo, 273–4
Henry of Lausanne, 88
heresiarch, definition of, 13, 263–4, 266–8, 271–4, 278
heresy, xvi–xvii, xix, 4–7, 9, 13–14, 16–18, 23–4, 53, 57–8, 62–3, 81, 83–5, 89–91, 96, 104, 108–9, 111, 130–1, 153, 265–6, 271–2, 275; definition of, 265; and gender, 243, 264, 266–7, 270, 274, 277–8, 312; and order, 254, 308, 327; and sexuality, 266–7
Hervé of Donzy, 129, 133–5
Hesdin, 250
heterodoxy, 13, 46, 49, 88, 100, 108–9, 243–5, 263, 267–8, 274, 276–8
Hildebert of Le Mans (Bishop), 88
Hildegard of Bingen, xv, 91, 101–4
Historische Kommission, 26, 32, 34
Hitler, Adolph, 26, 29, 33
Holy Land, 130–1, 137, 150
Holy Roman Empire, 23
Holy Spirit, 57, 135, 224, 250, 263, 268–9, 273
Hondschoodt, 249
Honorius III, Pope, 134, 293
Hopfnerová, Klára, 315
Horní Počernice, 316
hospice, 19
Hospitallers, 97, 105
hospitals, 138, 151–2, 219, 227, 243, 245–6, 249–51, 291, 296, 311, 315
hostels, 19
Houn d'Oisy, 144
household, 139–42, 144, 149, 151–2, 227, 277, 297–8, 309, 311–12
Hugh IV of St-Pol, 150
Hugh de Berzé, 143
Hugh of Amplepuis, 192
Hugh of Digne, 194
Hugh of Saint-Cher, 218
Humbert of Silva Candida (Cardinal), 86
Humiliati, 174, 181, 277–8
humility, 15, 45, 93–4, 195
Hus, Jan, 14, 311, 316, 326
Hussites, 14, 310, 314–17; criticism of, 307–8, 327; Hussite Wars, 314–15, 319, 325–6; Utraquism, 14, 319, 329

'Hussite Verses' ('*Verše na husity*'), 327
Hyères, 194

Iberia, 16
Imitatio Christi, 144, 308
India, 48
Innocent III, Pope, xvi, 53–4, 142, 182, 292
Innocent VIII, Pope, 251
Inquisitors, 63, 263–75, 277–8
International Congress on Medieval Studies, 8
Investiture Contest (Controversy), 81, 86, 89
Isabella of Portugal, 250
Isabelle, daughter of Louis IX, 199
Isabelle of France, 190–1, 193–4, 196–204
Islam, 16, 49, 110–11, 142, 152
Italian (cities), 47, 88
Italian (language). *See* vernacular
Italian (literature), 144
Italy, 26, 51, 175–7, 179, 190, 268, 274, 290–1, 293–4

Jacobina (companion of Sister Bona), 295
Jakemés *(trouvere)*, 149
Jakemés *(Roman du Castelain de Couci et de la dame de Fayel)*, 149
James of Vitry (Jacques de Vitry), 52, 218, 214, 226, 246
Jan of Příbram, 327
Jan Řitka of Bezdědice, 326
Jaucelin (Provincial Minister for Provence), 194
Jean de la Haye, 251
Jean de Joinville, 199
Jean de Meun, 79–80
Jean de Rua, 226
Jean de Vallibus, 227
Jean II of Nesle, 152

Jeanne of Flanders (Countess), 150
Jenstein, Johann von, 316
Jerome, Saint, 266; *Adversus Jovinianum*, 266
Jerusalem (Fall of), 141–2
Jerusalem (semi-religious community, Prague), 131, 311, 313, 317–20
Jesuit Order, 254
Jesus Christ, 45–6, 52, 54, 56, 59–60, 64, 87–9, 91, 141, 144, 173, 176–9, 183, 192, 221, 224, 269, 273, 278, 299, 321–2, 325
Jews and Judaism, 16, 24, 30, 33, 49, 64, 87, 96, 108, 110–11, 151, 269, 278
Jezebel (biblical figure), 267
Joachim of Fiore, xv–xvi, 26, 130
John of Milheim, 317
John of Parma, 194
John of Portugal, 250
John of Salisbury, 97, 98, 99; *Policraticus*, 97
John of San Lorenzo, 294
Johnson, Sherri Franks, 291
John XXII, Pope, 273–5
John XXIII/Baldassare Cossa, Pope, 60, 248, 250
Judeo-Arabic, 16
Juette of Huy, 243
Juliana of Mont-Cornillon, 218
Julieta of Florence, 266

Kačka (housemaid and follower of Jan Hus), 326
Kapléřová, Kateřina, 320–1
Kirchenkampf, 29
Klibansky, Raymond, 30, 31, 32
knights, 134–5, 150–2
knights hospitaller. *See* hospitallers
Knowles, Dom David, xiv
Königsberg, 26, 27

402   Index

Koranda, Václav Jr., 319
Královice, 320
Kulturkampf, 23–4, 58

Lacha, Guido, 263
Lady Altrude of the Poor, 296–7, 299
laity, 54, 57, 64, 82, 108–9, 130–1, 140, 173, 176, 178, 183, 189, 193, 215, 217–18, 221, 229–30, 243, 252, 275, 292, 308, 325
La Marche, 136
Lamprecht, Karl, 26, 34
Landeskirchen, 29
Landulf of St. Paul, 88, 89
Landulf of St. Paul (*Historia Mediolanensis*), 88
Languedoc, 267, 274,
Late Antiquity, 81, 89
Lateran Gate, Rome, 295
Lateran Palace, Rome, 295
Lateran IV/Fourth Lateran Council, 1215, 181–2, 217–18, 246
Lateran V/Fifth Lateran Council, 1517, 252
Latin, 3, 189, 192–3, 197–203, 224, 227, 309, 321, 325; authoritative language, 11, 12, 16, 140, 143, 144; Christianity, 84, 108, 111; literature, 3, 30, 91, 95; and the vernacular, 3, 17, 63, 107, 109, 139, 152; -West, 45, 47–9, 51
Latin Church. *See* Latin Christianity
Leblanc, Olivier, 138
Leclercq, Jean, xiii–xiv, 172
Lehrstuhl, 27
Leipzig, 27
Leo, IX, Pope, 252
Leo XIII, Pope; *Auspicato concessum*, 60
Lepers (*domus dei*), 15, 243. *See also* Leper Houses
Lepers (Houses), 138, 151

Lerner, Robert, 23, 26, 34
Les Écoliers (Bons-Énfants), 151
Lester, Anne E., 11, 246
Levant, 16
Library of the National Museum, Prague, 323
Library of the Prague Metropolitan, 324
Ligny, 135
Liège, 226, 243, 249
Lille, 250
linguistic turn, 15
liturgy, 131, 176, 178
Lloyd, Joan Barclay, 294
Lochkov, 315
Lollards, 267
Longchamp (female Franciscan house), 193–8, 200–1
Longue durée, 110
lordship, 129, 136–7, 149, 152
Lorris, 136
Louis IX, King of France, 138, 152, 193, 196, 198–9, 201, 215, 217, 221, 226
Low Countries, 217, 242, 247, 307, 327
Lucrina, 295
Lucy, Saint, 323
Ludmila of Pasovaře, 319
Luis de Paramo, 268
Lutgard of Aywières, 218, 243
Lyon, 192, 244

magic, 18, 264
Mahaut of Courtenay (Countess of Nevers, Auxerre, Tonnerre), 11, 127, 129, 133–8, 141, 149–53
Maier, Christoph, 133
Mailly-le-Château, 127, 136
Makowski, Elizabeth, xvii
Malleus Maleficarum, 267
manuscripts, 27, 30, 32–4, 106, 141, 145–6, 149, 177–8, 197–8, 215, 226–9, 288, 321, 323–4

Map, Walter, 95–6; *Discipulus episcopi Golie de grisis monachis*, 96
Margaret of Cortona, 243, 291
Margaret of Ypres, 218
Margherita of Trent/Margherita Boninsegna, 263, 271, 274–5, 277
Marguerite d'Youville, 255
Marguerite of Flanders (Countess), 150
Marguerite of Oingt, 12, 190–6, 201; *Life of Beatrice of Ornacieux*, 190, 192–3; *Mirror*, 190, 192, 195, 201; *Page of Meditations*, 192
Mariano of Florence, 298
Marie d'Oignies/Mary of Oignies, 130, 224
Marseille, 194
Marsiglio of Padua, 275; *Defensor Pacis*, 275
Martin V, Pope, 248–9
Mary (devotion to). *See* devotion, Marian
Mary Magdalene (Penitent house), 136
Mary (mother of Christ), 52, 182, 269, 273, 293
marriage, 88, 134–5, 139
Mass, 99, 144, 151, 176, 180, 183, 220, 263, 270, 297, 313, 322–3, 325, 327; memorial, 134–5, 151
Master Christian of Prachatice (Christianus de Prachaticz), 320, 326
Maundy Thursday, 177
Mayer, Theodor, 25
Mechthild of Magdeburg, 190–2, 195, 201; *Flowing Light of the Godhead*, 190–1
Meco del Sacco, 264, 272
Mediterranean, 16, 51, 137
Meersseman, Gilles Gérard, 175, 177, 181–2, 243
Meiner, Felix, 30, 31
Meister Eckhart, 30–3, 191; *Opera omnia*, 30

Mendicant Orders. *See* Dominican Order; Franciscan Order; Friars
Meneghin, Alessia, 276
Merville, 250
methodology, 4, 6–8, 13, 15, 47–8, 62, 310
Michel de Waringhien, 226
Milan, 89, 263, 265, 268–70, 274
Milíč of Kroměříž/Milicius de Chremsir, 311, 313, 317–20, 322; *Životopis*, Biography, 313
Milita of Monte-Meato, 266
Miller, Tanya Stabler, xix, 12, 265
miracles, 64, 152, 196, 202–4, 218, 268, 270, 288–9, 295–6, 298, 323
missal, 152
Mixson, James, xvii, xvix
modernism, 59–60
Monache di casa, 242
Monceaux (castle), 137
Moneta of Cremona, 267
monks, xiii–xiv, 52, 54, 79, 82–4, 86, 91–9, 102–3, 105, 109, 135–6, 151, 172, 176, 181, 214, 223, 268, 278, 324
Mons, 250
Montbrison, 136
Montegiove, 247
Montreal, 255
Montreiul, 250
Monumenta Germaniae Historica (MGH), 24, 27
Mooney, Catherine, 291
Moore, R.I., xix, 266
Mount Praenestino (Hamlet), 288–9, 297, 299
Movement German Christians, 29
Munich, 27
Münster, 27
Mydlář, Jakub, 320
mysticism, 18, 30, 34, 130, 132, 140, 190–1, 193, 195, 276

Nagel, Anne Christine, 26
Naples, 248
Na Prous Boneta, 273–4, 277
National Academy (Paris, Rome, Brussels, Vienna), 27
National Socialism, 10, 23, 25–30, 33–5, 131–2
Nationalsozialistsch Dozentenbund (National Socialist Association of University Lecturers), 32–3
Naumann, Friedrich, 26
Nazism. *See* National Socialism
New World, 242, 255
Newman, Barbara, 229, 268
Nicholas IV/Jerome Masci, Pope, 244, 289
Nicholas of Tournai, 226
Niemöller, Martin, 28
Nieuport, 249
Nigel de Longchamps (English Benedictine), 99; Burnellus the Ass, 99; *Speculum stultorum*, 99
Nigri, Limosus, 274
nobility, 86, 127, 132, 139–40, 144, 180, 183, 193–4, 205, 248, 265, 288, 296–7, 309–10, 319
Norbert of Xanten, 171
Normandy, 94, 193
North Africa, 16, 48
Notgemeinschaft, 30, 31
Notre Dame de Paris, 222
Notre Dame du Soleil (hospital), 250
NSDAP. *See* National Socialism
nuns, xiv, 12, 82–3, 89, 109, 135, 151, 189, 192–3, 195–8, 200, 214, 216, 218, 243, 255, 270, 289, 292–4, 296–8, 312, 326

Oakley, Francis, xiii
obedience, 45, 49, 53, 60, 64, 248, 293
observant reform movement, 246–7, 250–3, 255
Olbram family, 312, 316
Old French. *See* French (literature)
Oldřich of Rosenberg, 317
Olivi, Peter John, 273–4
Olomouc, 326
"On the Bad Years after the Death of King Otakar", 307
Opatovice Anthology, 323
Ordericus Vitalis, 94
Ordo Caritatis, 223
Oresme, Nicole, 265
orthodoxy, 6, 23, 25, 53, 62, 100, 170, 215, 224, 244–5, 247–9, 251, 253, 263, 270, 276, 278, 316

Pagan, Martine, 197, 202
Paganus Bolotinus, 94–7, 102, 104–5
Pailly, Bernard, 227
Pailly, William, 228
Pantaleon, Jacques, 218
papacy, xii, 7–8, 23, 53, 57, 62, 102–3, 130–1, 141, 183, 249, 64, 272, 274, 291
papal authority, and politics, xiii, 172, 247–8, 268, 271–2, 275
papal bulls, 11, 293–4; *Circa pastoralis*, 253; *Ea est officii nostri*, 253; *Parens Scientiarum*, 217; *Personas vacantes*, 243, 248–9, 252–5; *Supra montem*, 244, 249
Paris, 9, 17, 27, 103, 107, 176–7, 179–80, 191, 193, 195, 197–8, 214–15, 217–22, 224, 226–8, 265, 273; Ile-de-France, 136; Ile-de-la-Cité, 198
parishes, xvii, xviii, 8–9, 14, 17, 176, 215–17, 220, 222, 228–9, 291, 308–9, 311
Parménie, 195
Passion (of Christ), 144, 229, 269

pastoral care, 9, 48, 97, 101–2, 104, 179, 215–20, 222, 224, 227–30, 270, 294, 308–9, 311, 316
patronage, 9, 13, 129, 136–7, 141, 143, 145, 149–50, 152, 175, 193–4, 196, 221, 252, 291, 294–6, 298, 314, 317
Patschovsky, Alexander, 33
Paul (apostle), 88, 90, 102, 104
Paul II, Pope, 251
Paul, Nicholas, 133
Pauperes Christi, 267
peasants, 9, 127, 134, 183
Pellegrini, Luigi, 290
penitents, 8, 135, 139, 142, 153, 172, 181–3, 242–4, 247–8, 253, 294, 296, 318
Pentecost, 181
Peraldus, William, 220
Perfecti, 267
Periculoso (decretal), 244
persecution, 4, 33, 49, 55, 64, 104
Peter, Saint. *See* Apostolic succession
Peter of Abano, 272
Peter of Courtenay, 135, 136, 150
Peter the Chanter, 226
Peter the Venerable (Abbot of Cluny), 92, 93; Letter 28, 93
Petra of Říčany, 311, 319
Pfarrernotbund (Emergency Covenant of Pastors), 29–30
Pharisees, 85, 87, 93, 95, 102
Philip the Chancellor, 218
Philip the Fair, 227
Philip the Good, 250
Philippa of Lancaster, 250
Phillips, Jonathan, 133
philosophy, xiii, 30; moral, 97
Picardy, 136, 226
piety, 4, 6, 81, 87, 149, 151, 153, 182, 185, 214–15, 217–18, 221, 224, 246, 250, 254, 266, 276, 286, 290, 295–7, 299, 309, 325, 327

pilgrimage, 60, 130–1, 144, 183, 288, 291, 295, 298
Pius II, Pope, 250
Pius V, Pope, 253
Pius X, Pope, 60
Pius XI, Pope, 60
Poperinghe, 2493
Porète, Marguerite, 12, 191–3, 195–6, 201, 215, 263, 272–5; *Mirror of Simple Souls*, 191–2, 195–6, 201, 272
Portugal, 250, 252
postils, 309, 322
poverty, 11–12, 15, 45, 61, 130–1, 170–3, 179–83, 215, 248, 290–1, 294
Powder Tower, Prague, 318
Prague, 9, 14, 17, 307–8, 310–11, 313, 315–21, 324–7; Hradčany, 311, 313, 320–1; Lesser Town, 313; New Town, 313, 316; Old Town, 313–18, 320, 326
Prague Castle, 313
Prague University, 310, 317, 324
Prassede (recluse), 295–6
prayer, 15, 132, 135, 178, 180, 183, 189, 216, 251, 288, 296–7, 299, 309, 313, 323
preaching, 132, 189, 221, 322–3; heresy, 104, 131, 263, 270, 274; itinerant, 11, 12, 170, 171, 172, 173, 179, 180–3, 225; public, 13–15, 49, 103, 228, 321; universities, 48, 217, 222–3, 229; and *Vita apostolica* (*see* itinerant preaching); and women, 190, 214–15, 218–19, 222, 224, 226–7, 229–30, 243, 246, 265, 267, 299, 308–9, 316–17, 325–7
Premonstratensians, 81, 90, 98, 105
Pre-Raphaelites, xiii
priests, 7, 9, 90, 105, 177–8, 180–1, 220, 223, 227, 267, 277, 307–8, 311, 323–5
prioresses, 190, 192–5

Protestantism, xiii, xv, xvi, 9, 23–4, 29–30, 33, 171, 265
Protestant (Church), 25–6, 28; congregations, 29
Protestant Reformation, xii, 59, 82–3, 108, 110, 265, 268
Provence, 190, 194–5
Prussia, xiii, 23–4, 26, 29, 131
Prussian Königsberg University, 33
Pseudo-Turpin, 149–50; *Chronique*, 149–50; *Grail Cycle*, 149; *Life of William Marshall*, 149
Pulci, Antonia, 270

racism, 27, 29
Raoul of Chateauroux, 228
Raphael (Archangel), 269
Rapley, Elizabeth, 255
Raymond Johannis, 274
Recluses (*convertite, bizzoche*), 292, 295–6
Red Army, 26–7
Reffke, Ernst, 32
reform, 3, 6–7, 10, 12, 14–16, 19, 58–60, 81–4, 86–8, 91–2, 108–11, 129–30, 132, 138, 141, 176, 215, 217–18, 220–2, 229, 246–7, 269, 291–2, 294, 307–9, 314, 316–17, 320, 322, 325–7; Gregorian, 86–7, 93, 176; monastic, 83, 92, 97, 108, 172; Vatican II, 56–7, 60, 61–2, 64
Regino of Prüm (Benedictine abbot of Prüm), 175
Reichskonkordat, 29
Reichsstelle zur Förderung des deutschen Schrifttums, 31
Reichswehr, 27
relics (Passion), 144, 215, 291
Religio, 97, 217, 223, 225, 230
Religious Orders: Friars Minor (*see* Franciscan Order); Friars Preachers (*see* Dominican Order); and historiography, xiii, xvii, 3–7, 9–10, 17–18, 23, 34, 215–17, 292; hospital (*see* Hospitallers); mendicant orders (*see* Friars); military (*see* Templars)
Renaissance, 82, 108–10, 175
Renaissance (twelfth century), 16
Renan, Ernst, 59
rhetoric, 60, 84–93, 96, 100–4, 131, 133
Rhineland, 89
Risk, Rebecca, 133
Ritchey, Sara, 277
ritual, 18, 27, 139, 149, 276–7
Robert of Sorbon, 12, 214–30, 265
Rokycana, Jan, 325
Roman de la Rose, 79–80, 82, 85, 96–8, 100, 104–7; Faus Semblant, 79–81, 97–8, 106; Amant, 79
Roman de la terre d'Outremer, 152
Roman des Loherains, 152
Rome, 14, 27, 248, 288–99
Rose of Viterbo, 291
Rosenberg family, 310, 317
Roubaud, beguine order, 194–5
Rupert of Deutz, 171, 175
Rutebeuf (poet), 106–7, 199; *Dits*, 106; *Ordres de Paris*, 107
Rychterová, Pavlína, 324

Sabatier, Paul, 59, 60
sacramentary, 177
sacrifice, 64, 137, 141–4, 149
Saint-Denis, 196
Saint-Omer, 249
Saints, 192, 197, 200, 247, 265, 322–3
Salimbene de Adam, 271
salvation, 11, 49–50, 137, 179, 183, 271, 313, 321
Samuel of Hrádek and Valečov, 315
San Cosimato, convent of, 293–4, 298

sanctity, 11, 46, 48, 86, 88, 96, 152, 196, 263
San Damiano, convent of, 52, 197, 294
San Pancrazio, 294
San Silvestro, church/convent of, 288–9, 293
San Sisto, convent of, 292–3
Santa Chiara, convent of, 297–8
Santa Maria in Tempuli, convent of, 293
Saracens, 108, 269, 278. *See also* Islam
Saramita, Andrea, 268, 270–1
Satan, 96, 104
satire, 10, 99, 105, 312, 318, 325
Saxony, 26, 28–9
Schadewaldt, Wolfgang, 31
Schieder, Theodor, 25
serfs, 127, 129, 136, 153
sculpture, 127, 129
Second Coming, and gender, 263, 269–70
Second World War, 34, 54, 131–2
secular: and the religious, 13, 61, 64, 85–6, 89, 95, 105–6, 179, 181, 183, 192, 215–26, 230, 243–4, 252–4, 265, 311; rulership, 48, 64, 274, 307
secularism, 61
Secular-Mendicant conflict, 81, 89, 102, 106–8, 217, 221, 223, 225
Seeberg, Erich, 30–4
Segarelli, Gerardo, 263, 271, 274–5
Seláf, Levente, 199, 203
semi-religious/quasi-religious, xvii, 195, 242, 244–7, 252, 292, 307, 310, 317
sermons, 29–30, 90–1, 95, 100, 103, 138, 140, 142, 179–80, 182, 189–90, 196, 198, 214–15, 217–20, 222–30, 243, 307, 317, 321–3, 326
de'Settesoldi, Jacoba, 294
Shahar, Shulamith, 276
Silberzeigerová, Klára, 318
sin, 139, 181, 308, 324

Sister and Brothers of the Common Life, 183
Sister Cecilia (nun at convent of Santa Maria), 293, 295
Sisters Minor, 193
Sixtus IV, Pope, 250
Smith, Caroline, 133
Slavic (language). *See* vernacular
socialism, 33, 59, 60
Sorbonne, college, 12, 214–15, 217, 219, 221, 226–30
Spain, 252
speculative theology, 30
spiritual authority, 13, 46, 85–7, 99, 104, 106, 142, 172, 195; and gender, 264–5, 267, 270, 275, 277–8; and politics, 276; and private space, 277; and public space, 276–7
spirituality: apostolic (see *Vita apostolica*); historiography, 18, 47, 62, 130, 133, 264, 266–7, 276, 290; sociology, 8
St.-Adrien, 127
St.-Aignan, 135
St. Anna, convent of, 326
St. Agnes, convent of, 315
St. Ambrose, monastery of, 311
Štěpán of Dolany (Stephanus Dolanensis), 326–7
Stephania, author of Margherita Colonna's second vita, 289, 297–8
Stephen, Saint, 215
St.-Hilaire (chapel), 134
stigmata, 45, 296
Stirnemann, Patricia, 197
St. Jan, hospital of, 250
St. Martha, hospital of, 251
Stoëtlin, Jacques, 251
St.-Pol, 136
Strahov Monastery, Prague, 313
Střezka of Čejkovice, 319

Štuka family, 318
St. Ursula, order of, 265
Sulevice, 320
Svojšín, 314, 317
Syria, 134, 142, 153

Tábor, 326–7
Taoism, 110
Templar, Prague, 312, 314–15
Templars, 16, 97, 99, 105, 151
Tempuli, 293
Tertullian, 266
Thibaut IV (Count of champagne), 137, 144, 146, 149, 150
Thomas of Cantimpré, 218
Thomas of Celano, 197–8, 202, 295–6
Thomism, xiii
Tierney, Brian, xiii
Tobiáš of Bechyně, 313
Tomáš of Štítný, 322–5; *Řeči nedělní a sváteční*, 322
Tomek, Václav Vladivoj, 310, 313, 317–18; *History of the City of Prague/Dějiny města Prahy*, 313
Tonnerre, 135–6, 150–1
Trastevere, 293–5, 298
Trouvères, 144

ultramontanism, 58
Umbria, 9, 243
University of Berlin, 30–1, 34
University of Bologna, 248
University of Göttingen, 27
University of Heidelberg, 30
University of Leipzig, 25–7, 31, 33–4
University of Munich, 25, 27
University of Paris, 10, 12, 80–1, 100–2, 106, 198, 215, 217–21, 230, 272
Urban IV, Pope, 194, 289

Urban VI/Bartolomeo Prignano, Pope, 248
usury, 138
Utrecht, 9, 247, 249

Valenciennes, 191, 218, 250
Vallis Josaphat, 326
Van Engen, John, 4, 132
Vatican II. *See* reform
Vauchez, André, 267
Vavřinec of Březová, 325
Vercelli, 271
Vermanton, 136
vernacular: culture, 129, 139–41, 149; historiography, 15, 17–18, 133, 139; language (Catalan, 144; Czech, 14, 307, 309–10, 313–14, 317, 321–5; Flemish, 218, 226; French, 3, 8, 12, 144, 190, 193, 195–203, 229; German, 17, 144, 324; Greek, 17; Italian, 3, 15, 17, 290, 324; Judeo-Arabic, 1; Occitan, 144; Picard, 144; Polish, 324; Slavic, 17; Swedish, 324); and Latinity, 16; literature, 3, 10–12, 14, 16, 63, 105–9, 139, 140–5, 149–50, 152–3, 189–97, 199–201, 272, 308–10, 314, 317, 321–2, 325–6; preaching, 3, 14
Villers, 192
Vilvoorde, 218
Vincent of Beauvais, 199; *Speculum Historiale*, 199
Visconti, Galeazzo, 275
Visconti, Matteo, 275
visionaries and visionary literature, 131, 192, 194–5, 265, 272–3, 276–7, 288–9, 296, 321–2
Vita apostolica, 9–10, 12, 15, 45–50, 53–5, 57, 61, 63–4, 82, 130, 132, 170–81, 183, 221, 271, 308, 290–1, 294

Vita religiosa, 85, 99
Vltava River, 313, 315, 318
voluntary poverty. *See* poverty
Vulturella, 299

Waldensians, 174, 181, 267, 276
wealth, xviii, 48, 97, 227, 278, 309, 317, 320
Weber, Max, 46, 48, 58
Weilburk, Jan, 318
Weimar, 33
Wenceslas I of Luxembourg, 314
Werner, Karl Ferdinand, 35
Wesce (village), 320
Westphalia, 27
Wickham, Christopher, xiv
William of Paris, 273
William of Saint-Amour, 102–4, 106–7, 217, 223–4; *Ad abolendam*, 104; *Cum ex iniuncto*, 104; *Tractatus de Periculis*, 223; *Vergentis in senium*, 104

William of St. Audegone, 250
witchcraft, 264
Women's Religious Movement, xvi–xvii, 62, 130, 140, 170, 189–93, 201, 215–16, 218, 230, 264, 275–8, 290, 292, 294, 297
World War I. *See* First World War
World War II. *See* Second World War

Yolande of Hainaut, 150
Ypres, 218, 249

Zajicova, Anna, 317
de Zamorei, Gabrio, 270; *Sermo de fide*, 270
Zelenec (village), 316
Zepperen, 247, 249
Žídek, Pavel (Paulus de Praga), 325, 327
Zita of Lucca, 291
Zmrzlík family, 314
Zmrzlík, Petr, 317